FAMILY, SLAVERY, *and* LOVE *in the* EARLY AMERICAN REPUBLIC

FAMILY, SLAVERY, *and* LOVE *in the* EARLY AMERICAN REPUBLIC

The Essays of Jan Ellen Lewis

Edited by BARRY BIENSTOCK,

ANNETTE GORDON-REED, *and* PETER S. ONUF

Published by the

OMOHUNDRO INSTITUTE OF

EARLY AMERICAN HISTORY AND CULTURE,

Williamsburg, Virginia,

and the

UNIVERSITY OF NORTH CAROLINA PRESS,

Chapel Hill

The Omohundro Institute of Early American History and Culture (OI) is sponsored by William & Mary. On November 15, 1996, the OI adopted the present name in honor of a bequest from Malvern H. Omohundro, Jr., and Elizabeth Omohundro

Manufactured in the United States of America

Cover illustration: *The Plantation,* circa 1825. American, oil on wood. Gift of Edgar William and Bernice Chrysler Garbisch, 1963. Courtesy Met Collection API

Library of Congress Cataloging-in-Publication Data
Names: Lewis, Jan, 1949–2018, author. | Bienstock, Barry, editor. | Gordon-Reed, Annette, editor. | Onuf, Peter S., editor. | Omohundro Institute of Early American History & Culture, issuing body.
Title: Family, slavery, and love in the early American republic : the essays of Jan Ellen Lewis / edited by Barry Bienstock, Annette Gordon-Reed, and Peter S. Onuf.
Description: Williamsburg, Virginia : The Omohundro Institute of Early American History and Culture ; Chapel Hill : The University of North Carolina Press, Chapel Hill, [2021] | Includes bibliographical references and index.
Identifiers: LCCN 2021021845 | ISBN 9781469665634 (cloth) | ISBN 9781469665641 (ebook)
Subjects: LCSH: Lewis, Jan, 1949–2018. | United States—History—1783–1865. | United States—Politics and government—1783–1865. | United States—Social life and customs—1783–1865. | LCGFT: Essays.
Classification: LCC E301 .L57 2021 | DDC 973.07202—dc23
LC record available at https://lccn.loc.gov/2021021845

The University of North Carolina Press has been a member of the Green Press Initiative since 2003.

To Beatrice and Ida

Grandma Jan's Last Gift

CONTENTS

Family, Slavery, and Love in the

EARLY AMERICAN REPUBLIC

FIGURE 1

Portrait of the Ege-Galt Family. Attributed to William Hodgson. Circa 1801–1803. Oil on canvas. Accession no. 1976.100.1, A and B. Image no. K1978-DW-99. Courtesy, The Colonial Williamsburg Foundation, Williamsburg, Va. Gift of Mrs. V. Lee Kirby

JAN ELLEN LEWIS
Historian and Writer

ANNETTE GORDON-REED & PETER S. ONUF

Historians must be modest, living with the reality that they—human as they are—stumble blindly through the dense fog of their own confusing times. How could they possibly offer a clear, comprehensive, and truthful perspective on an increasingly distant past? But a historian with a natural gift for words and a historical imagination that reaches to the ever-changing limits of what it is possible to know can shine a light, sometimes dim and flickering, in both directions, on the present as well as the past. Jan Ellen Lewis was a great historian. She had a genius for reading her subjects between and beyond the lines. Her deft spotting of the ironies and paradoxes of their lives, their failures and hypocrisies—their strengths and weaknesses—provided openings to the greater historical understanding she so generously shared with her readers. A beautiful and nimble writer, Lewis used her first-rate intelligence to analyze and interpret her subjects' words, translating the past for the present and making lost worlds intelligible. If "the past is a foreign country," as the English novelist L. P. Hartley famously observed, Jan Lewis was a gifted interlocutor who spoke the language with native fluency. Her scholarly journeys through the history of the early American Republic illuminate its distinctive geography.[1]

Lewis's gifts were grounded in a deeply humane engagement with and recognition of her subjects' humanity, even when they so conspicuously failed to acknowledge the claims of enslaved, displaced, or marginalized contemporaries. Although she understood that writing history is necessarily a moral enterprise, she resisted the temptation to moralize. Instead, she sought to present as clear-eyed a view of her subjects and their circum-

Annette Gordon-Reed is Carl M. Loeb University Professor at Harvard Law School, and Peter S. Onuf is Thomas Jefferson Foundation Professor of History, Emeritus at the University of Virginia and Senior Fellow at Monticello's Robert H. Smith International Center for Jefferson Studies.

1. L. P. Hartley, *The Go-Between* (1953; rpt. New York, 2002), 17.

stances as possible, acutely conscious of our own moral limits and failures as well as of the past's enduring presence in our own world.

The essays in this volume show Lewis at the height of her powers as a writer and a historian. Although she can be identified with an array of methodologies and interpretative approaches reflected in the organization of this volume, she always insisted on the holism of her enterprise: she was a historian of the period she studied, not a specialist in the history of gender, or emotions, or political culture and practice, or the Constitution. She wrote with great erudition and insight on each of these areas, but her goal was always to make connections across specializations and so illuminate the lived experience of her late-eighteenth and early-nineteenth-century subjects, not to promote the interpretative pretensions of any particular historiographical school. The methodologies she deployed were justified by the results they yielded, enabling her to mine a wide array of print and manuscript sources for fugitive insights and unexpected connections. She listened carefully and sympathetically to her subjects, weaving fragmentary evidence into the stories they told—or sometimes, more revealingly, could not or would not tell—about themselves. Being so close to the matters at hand, immersed in the confusion of an evanescent moment, her subjects could not possibly grasp or question the complexity of their own circumstances. But the archive of literary fragments Lewis so assiduously assembled—despite and because of its self-serving and self-revealing biases and omissions—offers a rich vein of intimate, unrefined, and timely material for her to construct the best possible, most inclusive, and truest story she could tell about another people, Virginians or Americans, in their time and place, as they recede into an ever more distant past.

Lewis's treatment of her most famous subject, Thomas Jefferson, and his relations with his family, best exemplifies her approach. Jefferson and his enlightened contemporaries sought to distinguish and classify everything. As an Enlightened thinker in the "republic of letters," Jefferson wanted to create a world of clear distinctions: between private and public, home and world, republican friends and reactionary, aristocratic foes. Lewis's holistic approach to history and to Jefferson as an historical figure stands in stark contrast to his reductive and misleading distinctions and dichotomies. Jefferson's neat formulations had the effect of diminishing the complexity of life at Monticello and Virginia society in general and therefore of enabling him to imagine—and struggle to promote—their progressive improvement and reformation. The author of the Declaration of Independence had a philosopher's gift for articulating lofty and inspiring abstract principles and a revolutionary's impatience with obdurate facts on the ground. Lewis could sympathize with his (and our) aspirations, but she would not overlook the tensions and contradictions that characterized Jefferson's own life and, most tellingly, of acknowledged and unacknowledged family members and enslaved people in his plantation household.

Uncovering truths, illuminating circumstances, and unravelling complexities are all central to Lewis's work and allowed her to make such remarkable and influential contributions to the emerging history of the early American Republic. How we understand our national history has changed significantly from the time Lewis launched her distinguished career with *The Pursuit of Happiness: Family and Values in Jefferson's Virginia,* published in 1983. As hard as it may be to imagine now, with the myriad books and articles being published about it today, the history of the early American Republic was a moribund field when Lewis entered the historical profession. In fact, the concept of the "early American Republic" as a defined area of study barely existed. But the Society for the Historians of the Early American Republic (SHEAR), founded in 1977, would soon provide a congenial home for an increasingly diverse community of scholars with a widening range of interests and methodologies; the society's journal, *The Journal of the Early Republic,* launched in 1980, showcased the best new scholarship in the emerging field. Historians of the early Republic staked their collective claim to relevance on the rich variety of fresh approaches to interpreting the founding, broadly construed. If few practitioners thought of themselves as political historians, their broader commitment to the study of the period breathed new life into our understanding of the period's politics.

Lewis's career paralleled the belated emergence of the early Republic as a distinct field and a reconception and reperiodization of the national narrative. Trained as a colonial historian under Kenneth Lockridge, a leading figure in the new social history, she could not know that she would play a key role in carving out a new field of study. According to the then-conventional account, the Revolution and the creation of "a more perfect union" under the federal Constitution marked a continuation and culmination of colonial history. The implicit assumption was that nation making and constitution writing emerged out of prior Anglo-American experience. The American Revolution was not very revolutionary after all, most scholars agreed, particularly in comparison to the more profound transformations unleashed by the French and Russian Revolutions and the subsequent upheavals they inspired. Practically speaking, provincial Anglo-Americans were already liberal and democratic, and it was only much later in the age of Jackson that American democracy would be transformed with the ascendancy of popular party politics on a national scale. Students of the antebellum period, as the descriptor suggests, looked forward to the rupture of the Union, a bloody Civil War, and the rise to a powerful, recognizably modern nation state. In retrospect, the American Revolution could be seen as yet another civil war in which, for better or worse, the imperial union was defeated by liberty-loving (and tax-averse) secessionists.

At first Lewis and her generation of historians of early America turned away from high politics and what was derisively known as "the presidential synthesis," focusing on more fundamental, less epiphenomenal questions of social structure, class formation, family and gender relations, and the dark history of race and slavery. But they found themselves coming back to the political and constitutional history of the founding. Not surprisingly, their founding was much more complicated than the mythic founding they had rejected. In the 1980s, young historians were enjoined to "brin[g] the state back in," to resituate the old political narrative in the new contexts that social, cultural, legal, and economic historians had brought to the fore—recognizing that the organization and exercise of power in republican America would have a profound and lasting impact on those very contexts.[2]

Lewis and many other colonialists who occupied new territory in the Revolutionary and post-Revolutionary years followed the lead of their subjects, declaring their independence from the Anglocentric paradigm that had dominated early American studies. Pushing back on the colonialists' long eighteenth century and promoting new ways of understanding national history looking forward *from* 1776, historians of the early Republic showed how and why revolutionary regime change mattered—for better and, in so many newly conspicuous ways, for worse. Lewis and her talented colleagues generated historiographical excitement as they deployed new methods and approaches developed in early modern Anglo-American history. Historians of the nation's formative years found that they had new things to say at a time when a newly engaged general public was eager to listen—and, on many occasions, to talk back. Responding to growing public interest in the founding era, spurred by bicentennial celebrations and sustained by the protracted debate over American exceptionalism and other flashpoints in the ongoing culture wars, Lewis and her cohort recognized the civic and moral signifi-

2. For a classic critique of the "presidential synthesis," see Thomas C. Cochran, "The 'Presidential Synthesis' in American History," *American Historical Review,* LIII (1948), 748–759. William E. Leuchtenburg called for a new approach to politics and government in Leuchtenburg, "The Pertinence of Political History: Reflections on the Significance of the State in America," *Journal of American History,* LXXIII (1986), 585–600.

cance of telling the truest possible story of the new nation's beginnings. If Americans today can recognize each other and themselves collectively as a people, it can only be by acknowledging and engaging with their shared history. It has not always been—and will never be—a triumphant story with a simple happy ending. But it is a story that defines us as a people, drawn for many sources and beautifully told by Jan Lewis; it is a complicated story that affirms the humanity of its many subjects and seeks to make them legible to us today, across the centuries.

Jan Lewis's career as reflected in the essays collected here offers an elegant—and eloquent—introduction to the history of the early American Republic. American citizens should know how all aspects of life were experienced in the new nation's formative decades when conceptions of republican citizenship were first defined. The first three sections in this volume—"Gender in the Early American Republic," "The History of Emotions," and "Constitutional and Legal History"—show her melding her early interest in gender and emotions into insightful commentaries on social life, law, race, politics, and political economy in the early American Republic. In her presidential address to SHEAR in 2016, Lewis offered her colleagues a powerful commentary and meditation on how race and gender figured (or did not figure) in the federal Constitution, and therefore in our radically imperfect and incomplete constitution as a people.

The essays in the fourth and final section, "Jefferson Studies," confirm Lewis's status as one of the most important scholars of Thomas Jefferson of her own or any generation. She focused on the third president to better understand the world that shaped him and the world that he shaped—at home and in his homeland—over the course of a long, productive, and controversial career. "The White Jeffersons," her extraordinary essay about Jefferson's life with his legal white family with his wife, Martha, and his shadow family with Martha's half sister, the enslaved Sally Hemings, is a tour de force, epitomizing her gifts as a scholar and writer.

Whether writing about the histories of gender and emotion in early American history, or about the status of women under the Constitution's Three-Fifths Clause, or about Jefferson and his family, Jan Ellen Lewis enables readers to grasp what it must have been like to be alive at the beginning of the new nation's history—and, perhaps, even to imagine how that history might unfold in the future. For her gifts and for her gifts to us, we are eternally grateful.

Gender *in the* Early American Republic

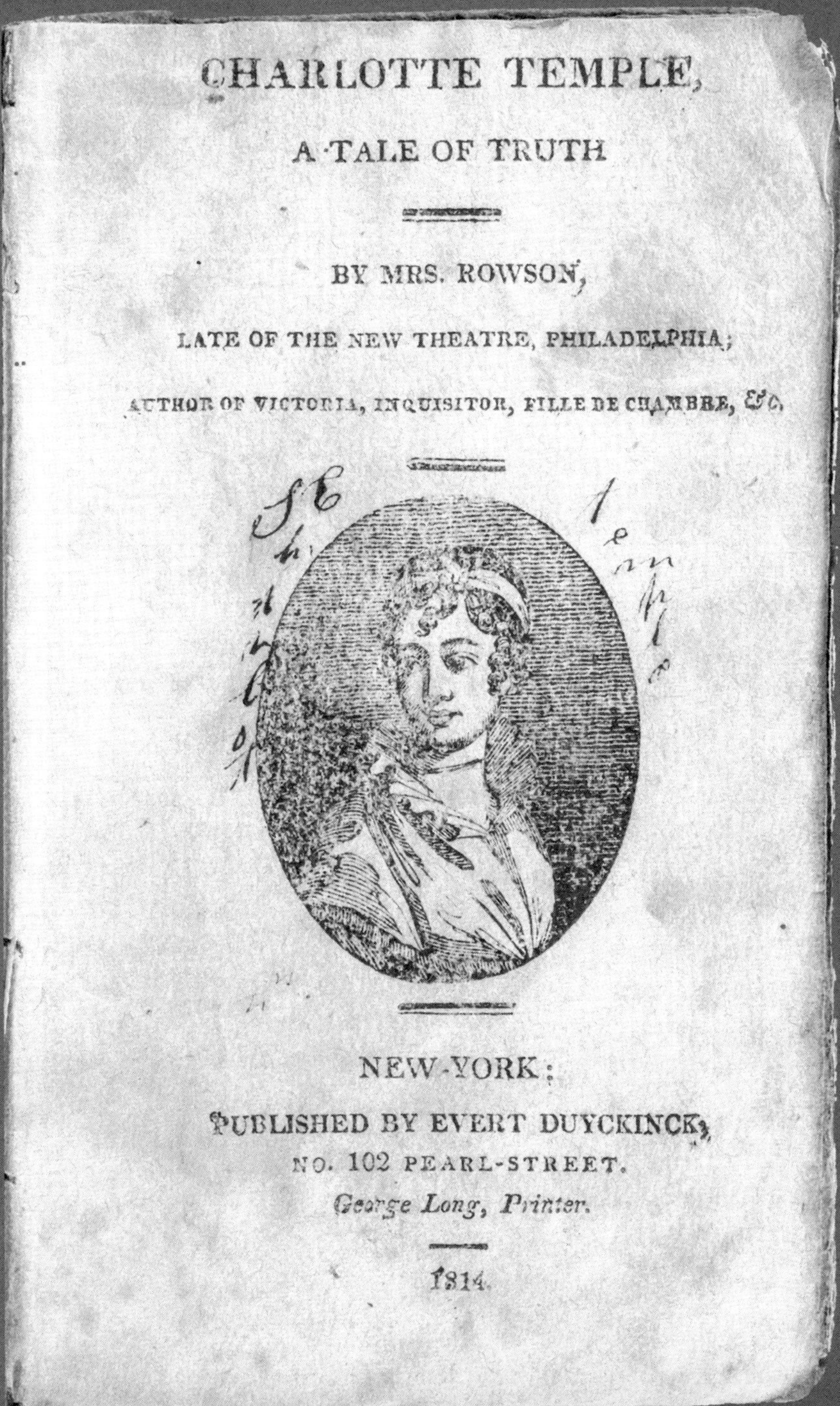

CHARLOTTE TEMPLE,

A TALE OF TRUTH

BY MRS. ROWSON,

LATE OF THE NEW THEATRE, PHILADELPHIA;

AUTHOR OF VICTORIA, INQUISITOR, FILLE DE CHAMBRE, &c.

NEW-YORK:

PUBLISHED BY EVERT DUYCKINCK,

NO. 102 PEARL-STREET.

George Long, Printer.

1814.

FIGURE 2

[Susanna Haswell] Rowson, *Charlotte Temple, A Tale of Truth* (New York, 1814), titlepage. Courtesy, American Antiquarian Society, Worcester, Mass.

GENDER IN THE EARLY REPUBLIC
The Scholarship of Jan Ellen Lewis

CAROLYN EASTMAN

When Jan Ellen Lewis undertook essays about gender, she wrote as if she were seeking to crack cultural codes. For if parsing the mysteries of the past constitutes the work of all historians, Lewis joined a rarefied group who *wrote* their essays in ways that highlight the pleasures inherent in witnessing the dramatic unpacking of one layer of meaning after another. Reading her essays on gender often delivers the same satisfaction as the dramatic conclusion of a mystery, as we watch the sleuth pull a chaos of threads together into a coherent, fulfilling, expansive explanation. As she deciphered those codes over the course of her essays, building layers of analysis and often making surprising turns along the way, she offered sweeping interpretations that crystallized our understanding of the past. Her essays vividly illuminate the critical value of using gender and cultural history to scrutinize the workings of social and political power.[1]

Lewis's essays shaped historical scholarship in two important ways. First, they exhibited how she fully modeled for others the benefits of analyzing gender rather than women per se, displaying less concern with finding evidence of women participating in history than with getting to the heart of the meanings of women's public behavior, gender roles, political engagement, and the gender dynamics of civic culture. In the mid-1980s, when some of her earliest essays appeared, the historiographic turn to gender history was still underway and its impact on the field far from clear. Some still debated whether such a turn might denude the scholarship of its feminist urgency, and even whether gender was, after all, a "useful category of historical analysis," in Joan W. Scott's 1986 phrasing. More than many of her peers, Lewis demonstrated what gender analysis could achieve and how vitally it could

Carolyn Eastman is associate professor of history at Virginia Commonwealth University.

1. The comparison to detectives and sleuths is apt, for Lewis was also an abiding fan of mysteries and thrillers.

alter the way we understand the past, as we shall see in the three essays, spanning three decades of her scholarship, that follow.[2]

Second, Lewis's scholarship is distinguished by the degree to which she also embraced the historiographic turn to cultural history already well underway during the 1980s, a turn anchored to new views of politics and social power by means of methods drawn from literary theory and cultural anthropology. She and the other scholars who took on these new methods for historical analysis sought to reimagine history's master narratives by demonstrating the fundamental significance of labor status, religious identity, gender, race, class, and ethnicity within historical structures of power, including politics. She and her cultural history peers feared that many of the best insights offered by the new social history had failed to alter those master narratives. They especially paid close analytical attention to gender, race, and class, not simply to add in previously overlooked historical actors, but to demonstrate that historians had largely failed to notice the gender, race, and class of all people in history, including elite white men. In doing so, Lewis and the rest of these scholars drew our attention to the construction and maintenance of political and cultural power.[3]

2. The transition from women's history to gender history is encapsulated in Joan W. Scott, "Gender: A Useful Category of Historical Analysis," *American Historical Review*, XCI (1986), 1053–1075; Denise Riley, *"Am I That Name?" Feminism and the Category of "Women" in History* (Minneapolis, Minn., 1988); Jane Sherron De Hart, "Women's History, Gender History, and Political History," *Public Historian*, XV, no. 4 (Autumn 1993), 77–78; Sonya O. Rose, *What Is Gender History?* (Cambridge, 2010); Bonnie G. Smith, *The Gender of History: Men, Women, and Historical Practice* (Cambridge, Mass., 1998); Scott, *Gender and the Politics of History*, rev. ed. (New York, 1999); and Judith Butler and Elizabeth Weed, eds., *The Question of Gender: Joan W. Scott's Critical Feminism* (Bloomington, Ind., 2011).

3. Scholarship on the "cultural turn" includes David Chaney, *The Cultural Turn: Scene-Setting Essays on Contemporary Cultural History* (London, 1994); James Vernon, "Who's Afraid of the 'Linguistic Turn'? The Politics of Social History and Its Discontents," *Social History*, XIX (1994), 81–97; Victoria E. Bonnell and Lynn Hunt, eds., *Beyond the Cultural Turn: New Directions in the Study of Society and Culture* (Berkeley, Calif., 1999); Peter Burke, *What Is Cultural History?* (Cambridge, Mass., 2004); Gabrielle M. Spiegel, ed., *Practicing History: New Directions in Historical Writing after the Linguistic Turn* (New York, 2005); and James W. Cook, Lawrence B. Glickman, and Michael O'Malley, eds., *The Cultural Turn in U.S. History: Past, Present, and Future* (Chicago, 2008). For the "cultural turn's" ties to feminist and gender history, see especially Kathleen Canning, "Feminist History after the Linguistic Turn: Historicizing Discourse and Experience," *Signs: Journal of Women in Culture and Society*, XIX (1994), 368–404; and Toby L. Ditz, "The New Men's History and the Peculiar Absence of Gendered Power: Some Remedies from Early American Gender History," *Gender and History*, XVI (2004), 1–35. For historians discussing the return of a master narrative and the problem of integrating all the various "parts" described by social historians, see Thomas Bender, "Wholes and Parts: The Need for Synthesis in American

There is no better place to start to unpack this quality of reasoning early in Lewis's career than with her essay "The Republican Wife: Virtue and Seduction in the Early Republic" (1987), certainly one of her most significant pieces of scholarship. On its surface, this essay announces its dedication to Linda K. Kerber's concept of "republican motherhood" enshrined in *Women of the Republic: Intellect and Ideology in Revolutionary America* (1980), already a field-defining book by the time Lewis began working on this article. During the Revolutionary era, Kerber had famously explained, some white women created new patriotic meanings for the work they undertook within families and in society. Although prevented by law from enjoying many benefits of citizenship, including voting and propertyownership, these women nevertheless integrated patriotic political values into domestic life, female education, and particularly their roles as mothers. Thus investing their work with political significance, these women in turn justified the increasing political importance of women in American society. Kerber maintained that the effects of this enhanced politicization were ultimately mixed; the popular language of republican motherhood did not bring about votes for women, alter the coverture restrictions on married women, or meaningfully change the lives of women politicized during this era. Yet she nevertheless insisted that it helped to justify women's engagement in civic culture. When she began work on "The Republican Wife," Lewis joined a small army of historians who found Kerber's insights a major intervention in the field of women's history and sought to add to the conversation.[4]

History," *Journal of American History,* LXXIII (1986), 120–136; and Lawrence Stone, "The Revival of Narrative: Reflections on a New Old History," *Past and Present,* no. 85 (November 1979), 3–24.

4. Jan Lewis, "The Republican Wife: Virtue and Seduction in the Early Republic," in this volume; Linda K. Kerber, *Women of the Republic: Intellect and Ideology in Revolutionary America* (Williamsburg, Va., and Chapel Hill, N.C., 1980). See also Kerber's "The Republican Mother: Women and the Enlightenment—An American Perspective," *American Quarterly,* XXVIII (1976), 187–205. Though it did not coin a term as memorable as "republican motherhood," Mary Beth Norton's *Liberty's Daughters: The Revolutionary Experience of American Women, 1750–1800* (Boston, 1980) appeared during the same year and offered similar findings, predominantly using social and cultural history methods. The scholarship that followed in Kerber's and Norton's wake is vast. See, for example, Ruth H. Bloch, "The Gendered Meanings of Virtue in Revolutionary America," *Signs: Journal of Women in Culture and Society,* XIII (1987), 37–58; Bloch, *Gender and Morality in Anglo-American Culture* (Berkeley, Calif., 2003); Carolyn Eastman, "The Female Cicero: Young Women's Oratory and Gendered Public Participation in the Early American Republic," *Gender and History,* XIX (2007), 260–283; Joan M. Jensen, "Not Only Ours but Others: The Quaker Teaching Daughters of the Mid-Atlantic, 1790–1850," *History of Education Quarterly,* XXIV (1984), 3–19; Mary Kelley, *Private Woman, Public Stage: Literary Domesticity*

But to characterize Lewis's "Republican Wife" as merely *building on* Kerber's findings or *joining* a conversation about their implications misses the essay's interpretive punch. Lewis argued that it was not motherhood but marriage that clarified the conundrums of republicanism—thus importantly reworking Kerber's argument. To do so, she used similar sources from the early Republic, including the mutually influential strands of biblical teaching, popular literary and prescriptive writing, and political thought. But she ultimately rejected motherhood as the central locus of women's importance to the American Republic, arguing persuasively that only during the antebellum era did the association of womanhood with motherhood become preeminent. In contrast, she demonstrated, women's roles as wives and "republicanism itself" could only fully be understood "in the context of the other." As she built her case, she demonstrated a knack for reading seemingly disparate sources with unusual insight and juxtaposing them with larger political and religious narratives. The sum total is a model of historical scholarship, to the point that it becomes difficult to read Kerber's *Women of the Republic* without pairing it with Lewis's "Republican Wife."[5]

Why republican wifehood rather than motherhood? Lewis's argument proceeds with relentless logical force. Whereas Kerber had ultimately concluded that republican motherhood had ambivalent effects on the lives of women during the early Republic, Lewis found embedded in the literature on republican marriage far more troubling, whiplash-inducing contradictions that ultimately asked women to adopt impossibly weighty and clashing responsibilities. For even as these writers held up the role of wives as paramount, granting wifehood profound social and political significance, they also placed the burden of sustaining marital bonds on the backs of women, requiring them to sacrifice the promises of republicanism. Some of these

in Nineteenth-Century America (New York, 1984); Catherine E. Kelly, *In the New England Fashion: Reshaping Women's Lives in the Nineteenth Century* (Ithaca, N.Y., 1999); Cynthia A. Kierner, *Beyond the Household: Women's Place in the Early South, 1700–1835* (Ithaca, N.Y., 1998); Margaret A. Nash, "'Cultivating the Powers of Human Beings': Gendered Perspectives on Curricula and Pedagogy in Academies of the New Republic," *History of Education Quarterly*, XLI (2001), 239–250; Nash, "Rethinking Republican Motherhood: Benjamin Rush and the Young Ladies' Academy of Philadelphia," *Journal of the Early Republic*, XVII (1997), 171–191; Marion Rust, "'Into the House of an Entire Stranger': Why Sentimental Doesn't Equal Domestic in Early American Fiction," *Early American Literature*, XXXVII (2002), 281–309; and Rosemarie Zagarri, "Morals, Manners, and the Republican Mother," *American Quarterly*, XLIV (1992), 192–215.

5. Lewis, "Republican Wife," in this volume. Lewis expands on this insight in her wonderful essay "Mother's Love: The Construction of an Emotion in Nineteenth-Century America," also included in this volume.

texts offered utopian visions of essential equality within marriage. They insisted that the Republic required harmonious marriages between mutually altruistic marital partners. Multiplied exponentially, the preponderance of such harmonious marriages would, in turn, keep the Republic afloat. More often, however, early republican writing was preoccupied with the problem of *disharmony* in marriage. What should couples do to maintain domestic tranquility when conflicts arose? Why, women "should simply yield to those of superior wisdom." The drive for social harmony both within the home and in the nation writ large thus upstaged equality and even necessitated women's capitulation to their husbands. If Lewis had initially convinced us to be impressed by so much talk of egalitarianism in marriage, this reversal is stunning.[6]

Delving further into sources that described troubled marriages, Lewis found an even darker set of problems with repercussions for the American Republic. Novels like Susanna Haswell Rowson's *Sarah* and *Charlotte Temple* as well as Hannah Foster's *The Coquette* portrayed women struggling heroically with immoral men, only to lose the battle. Scholars have usually read those books and the wider seduction literature they helped to popularize as anchored to a reformation of the gender system—cautionary tales designed to prescribe chastity as a prerequisite to female respectability. But Lewis insisted on seeing them as *political* tracts used by authors to explore to the fullest extent a key theme in republican thinking: whether virtue was enough to overcome the problem of corruption. Optimists wanted to believe that virtuous men and women could keep one another on the path of righteousness, just as virtuous citizens sustained the Republic. Female novelists like Rowson and Foster played out a different story.[7]

By the time Lewis developed her essay "Politics and the Ambivalence of the Private Sphere: Women in Early Washington, D.C." (1999), she yet again advanced our understanding of gender in the early Republic while anchoring her analysis to cultural theory (and especially the work of Jürgen Habermas), demonstrating how productive the mix of those two approaches could

6. Lewis, "Republican Wife," in this volume.

7. Ibid. On readings of seduction literature, see, among others, Cathy N. Davidson, *Revolution and the Word: The Rise of the Novel in America* (New York, 1986); Rodney Hessinger, *Seduced, Abandoned, and Reborn: Visions of Youth in Middle-Class America, 1780–1850* (Philadelphia, Pa., 2005); Mark E. Kann, *Taming Passion for the Public Good: Policing Sex in the Early Republic* (New York, 2013); Marion Rust, *Prodigal Daughters: Susanna Rowson's Early American Women* (Williamsburg, Va., and Chapel Hill, N.C., 2012); and Michael Zuckerman, "The Paradox of American Adolescence," *Journal of the History of Children and Youth*, IV (2011), 11–25.

be. At a moment in the 1990s that witnessed formidable backlash against the uses of theory in history, Lewis achieved a rare feat, not just by bringing these two bodies of theory into dialogue, but showing the historiographical payoff of doing so. "Politics and the Ambivalence of the Private Sphere" is a profound achievement and an essay of terrific persuasive power.[8]

Lewis's attention to the mutual development of both masculinity and femininity—and the analytical approach to that development—reflected a major shift in gender analysis taking place in the scholarship of the mid- to late-1990s. Inspired by Judith Butler's *Gender Trouble* and other theoretical works, she sought to understand how people *performed* gender in the past. Butler went further than Joan Scott and other gender theorists of the 1980s in insisting that gender was, in essence, theatrical: individuals developed their own self-presentations by engaging with, improvising on, and rehearsing a variety of cultural scripts about how gender could be performed. Those ephemeral self-presentations shifted depending on their audience or context, and sometimes took place in public places and for public effect, as it did for the male members of Congress and their female auditors whom Lewis scrutinized in this essay.[9]

What made this essay doubly influential was Lewis's engagement with scholarship that scrutinized gender and the public sphere during the 1990s. Habermas, whose groundbreaking work on the bourgeois public sphere had drawn the attention of many historians, had demonstrated relatively little concern about women's participation in public (or with gender at all). In his wake, feminist theorists had offered influential readings of women's public

8. Jan Lewis, "Politics and the Ambivalence of the Private Sphere: Women in Early Washington, D.C.," in this volume; Jürgen Habermas, *The Structural Transformation of the Public Sphere: An Inquiry into a Category of Bourgeois Society,* trans. Thomas Burger (Cambridge, Mass., 1989).

9. Judith Butler, *Gender Trouble: Feminism and the Subversion of Identity* (New York, 1990). See also Butler, "Performative Acts and Gender Constitution: An Essay in Phenomenology and Feminist Theory," *Theatre Journal,* XL (1988), 519–531; and Butler, *Bodies That Matter: On the Discursive Limits of "Sex"* (New York, 1993). For historical treatments, see, for example, Kathleen M. Brown, *Good Wives, Nasty Wenches, and Anxious Patriarchs: Gender, Race, and Power in Colonial Virginia* (Williamsburg, Va., and Chapel Hill, N.C., 1996); Sandra M. Gustafson, *Eloquence Is Power: Oratory and Performance in Early America* (Williamsburg, Va., and Chapel Hill, N.C., 2000), esp. chaps. 1 and 6; Jane Kamensky, *Governing the Tongue: The Politics of Speech in Early New England* (New York, 1997); Susan Kattwinkel, "Women on Southern Stages, 1800–1865: Performance, Gender, and Identity in the Golden Age of American Theater," *Journal of Southern History,* LXXXIV (2018), 150–151; Renée M. Sentilles, *Performing Menken: Adah Isaacs Menken and the Birth of American Celebrity* (Cambridge, 2003); and Timothy Sweet, "Masculinity and Self-Performance in the *Life of Black Hawk,*" *American Literature,* LXV (1993), 475–499.

engagement, beginning a process of reconsidering the gendered connotations of *public* and *private.* Some historians had found women in public but had focused their attention on later eras—the ways that women's public roles had grown more active and political primarily over the course of the antebellum years and toward the turn of the twentieth century. In the earliest part of the nineteenth century, their research had suggested, women largely served as props for the new political order. Lewis's findings in "Politics and the Ambivalence of the Private Sphere" could not have been more strikingly different. To reach those conclusions, she selected a distinctive site of analysis: legislators' congressional debates in the Capitol building before audiences that included considerable numbers of women deeply engaged in this drama of national development.[10]

She started by tracking those women attendees, noting that few historians had discussed women much at all when writing about the early history of Washington, D. C.—but she revealed right away that her focus encompassed much more than women's mere presence. Women "helped constitute the public," she explained, using constitutional language. "Their presence ratified and legitimated the proceedings of the new national government,

10. Habermas, *Structural Transformation of the Public Sphere.* For feminist responses to Habermas, see, among others, Lauren Berlant, *The Queen of America Goes to Washington City: Essays on Sex and Citizenship* (Durham, N.C., 1997); Dena Goodman, "Public Sphere and Private Life: Toward a Synthesis of Current Historiographical Approaches to the Old Regime," *History and Theory,* XXXI (1992), 1–20; Nancy Fraser, "Rethinking the Public Sphere: A Contribution to the Critique of Actually Existing Democracy," *Social Text,* nos. 25/26 (1990), 56–80; and Michael Warner, *Publics and Counterpublics* (Brooklyn, N.Y., 2002). On women and the public sphere in history, see Elaine S. Abelson, *When Ladies Go A-Thieving: Middle-Class Shoplifters in the Victorian Department Store* (New York, 1989); Jeanne Boydston, "Making Gender in the Early Republic: Judith Sargent Murray and the Revolution of 1800," in James Horn, Jan Ellen Lewis, and Peter S. Onuf, eds., *The Revolution of 1800: Democracy, Race, and the New Republic* (Charlottesville, Va., 2002), 240–266; Susan Branson, *Those Fiery Frenchified Dames: Women and Political Culture in Early National Philadelphia* (Philadelphia, 2001); Sarah Deutsch, *Women and the City: Gender, Space, and Power in Boston, 1870–1940* (New York, 2000); Susan Glenn, *The Female Spectacle: The Theatrical Roots of Modern Feminism* (Cambridge, Mass., 2000); Linda K. Kerber, "Separate Spheres, Female Worlds, Woman's Place: The Rhetoric of Women's History," *Journal of American History,* LXXV (1988), 9–39; Joan B. Landes, *Women and the Public Sphere in the Age of the French Revolution* (Ithaca, N.Y., 1988); Charlene M. Boyer Lewis, *Ladies and Gentlemen on Display: Planter Society at the Virginia Springs, 1790–1860* (Charlottesville, Va., 2001); Mary P. Ryan, *Women in Public: Between Banners and Ballots, 1825–1880* (Baltimore, 1990); David S. Shields and Fredrika J. Teute, "The Republican Court and the Historiography of a Women's Domain in the Public Sphere," *Journal of the Early Republic,* XXXV (2015), 169–183; and Judith R. Walkowitz, *City of Dreadful Delight: Narratives of Sexual Danger in Late-Victorian London* (Chicago, 1992).

and they did so both as citizens and as women, that is, as part of the general public, undifferentiated by sex." She followed with a discussion of why it mattered that women were there, and how it mattered. That women filled the galleries—and more—meant that they became integral to the very idea of a public for whom those legislators spoke.[11]

Delving into a description of what these oratorical displays looked like from the perspective of their female attendees, she described a moment during the Webster-Hayne debate in 1830 when the galleries overflowed with eager auditors, such that the senators grandly gave up their own seats to women and then used the women's presence as an opportunity to enhance their authoritative positions as orators. Lewis wrote, "The woman who occupied the senator's chair, while he stood by her side declaiming, served as a prop to his oration, as did the women who displaced the other senators from their seats, as did the women who sat in the galleries and heard Daniel Webster proclaim, 'Liberty *and* Union, now and forever, one and inseparable.'" Understanding the embodied contexts of speeches like Webster's reveals an entirely different side to the words they spoke—words that, when we read them on the page, might convey an image of a man speaking only to other men. Lewis flipped the script, showing that we cannot understand the effectiveness of their delivery without understanding the significance of the women in the room and their perceived importance to the public. Women's presence in the Senate chamber altered the delivery, the argument, and the meaning of the words spoken.[12]

Having shown us the extent of women's attendance and their presence even on the Senate floor, her essay then makes one final turn to examine men's gendered performances. We have long known that members of Congress carefully crafted their oratorical personae to maximize their eloquent power. But Lewis found another shade of complexity: the extent to which these men sought to convey to themselves and their female audiences not just rational brilliance but emotional sensitivity. "The perfect speech was part act of God, part mesmerism; it robbed listeners of their speech and put tears in their eyes," she explained. Men as well as women gave their highest praise to the speakers most capable of reducing their auditors to tears. This was a different performance of male oratorical power than the one we might expect if we had only read those words on a page. These sensitive dramati-

11. Lewis, "Politics and the Ambivalence of the Private Sphere," in this volume; Catherine Allgor, *Parlor Politics: In Which the Ladies of Washington Help Build a City and a Government* (Charlottesville, Va., 2000), appeared a year later.

12. Lewis, "Politics and the Ambivalence," in this volume.

zations of masculine power had the effect of justifying distinctions between public and private, male and female, even as they seemed to transcend those distinctions.[13]

In the last twenty years of her research and writing, Lewis displayed a growing concern with and a gift for scrutinizing gender within the realm of political and constitutional thought, as we shall see in more detail later in this volume. Her 2011 essay, "Rethinking Women's Suffrage in New Jersey, 1776–1807," illuminates her facility with these subjects. But going further, this article reveals a capacity to join in an active scholarly conversation about a subject, yet still offer an original, far-reaching conclusion that went beyond that provided by previous scholars. In this case, she tackled the thirty-some years in New Jersey's history when single and widowed women, as well as free blacks and nonnaturalized immigrants, had the right to vote if they possessed sufficient property to clear the state's property restriction and paid state taxes. It was the only state in the early United States that granted this right.[14]

Other scholars had trod similar ground before, trying to make sense of this case. The earliest efforts suggested that perhaps legislators had made a mistake in allowing women to vote, but subsequent historians demonstrated that, indeed, the legislators apparently made those choices with full understanding of the implications. Some focused their gaze on the establishment of this right to vote, characterizing this as an instance of state legislators following "their revolutionary beliefs to their logical, if unexpected and untraditional, conclusion," as Rosemarie Zagarri wrote. Other scholars scrutinized the ultimate decision to close down access to the vote starting in 1807, speculating that the rising success and power of the Republicans led them to restrict the franchise (on the presumption that women and free African Americans preferred voting for Federalists). For the most part, this literature characterized New Jersey's thirty-year embrace of the franchise for propertied, unmarried women as an odd outlier in the early Republic: "The New Jersey Exception," in Zagarri's phrasing.[15]

13. Ibid.

14. Jan Ellen Lewis, "Rethinking Women's Suffrage in New Jersey, 1776–1807," in this volume.

15. Rosemarie Zagarri, *Revolutionary Backlash: Women and Politics in the Early American Republic* (Philadelphia, 2007), 30–37; Delight Wing Dodyk, "Woman Suffrage," in Maxine N. Lurie and Marc Mappen, eds., *Encyclopedia of New Jersey* (New Brunswick, N.J., 2004), 881–882; Irwin N. Gertzog, "Female Suffrage in New Jersey," "Women, Politics, and the Constitution," special issue, *Women and Politics,* X, (1990), 47–58; Judith Apter Klinghoffer and Lois Elkis, "'The Petticoat Electors': Women's Suffrage in New Jersey, 1776–

Lewis advanced a different argument. She suggested, in fact, that the story of women's voting in New Jersey reflected something fundamental, rather than marginal or exceptional, about American history. Both the initial decision to give women the vote as well as the ultimate debate that led to shutting off that right, she argued, placed this "at the center of American history," for the story in New Jersey exemplified a broader pattern of a community seeking to "define its membership." To restrict those boundaries during the early Republic, some claimed that the presence of women and African Americans at the polls had led to voter fraud; others sought to change citizenship rules for recent immigrants. Similar efforts to limit the boundaries of citizenship continued throughout the nation and across time. As Lewis demonstrated, Americans hotly debated the question of who deserved the franchise as well as the rights of citizenship—and they would continue to debate it over the ensuing decades.[16]

New Jersey solved its alleged problem of voter fraud in a distinctive way—and that solution, too, placed this case "at the center of American history." "Difficulties in determining the status of women and blacks were resolved by withdrawing the right to vote of all women and all black people," Lewis wrote in her lucid, and devastating, manner. At the same time, "difficulties in determining the wealth of white men were resolved by making all taxpaying men eligible to vote." This seeming reversal of earlier Revolutionary ideals might not appear so radical were it not for the final insight she provided. The framers of these new guidelines elected to view these changes as a restatement of "the true sense and meaning of the constitution . . . according to the intent of the framers thereof," as the revised New Jersey law now read. Characterizing radical withdrawals of right as the original intent of the framers, she suggested, has as long a history as the reversals themselves.[17]

From examining the republican preoccupation with marriage as a means of establishing a firm basis for the new Republic, to the performance of masculinity and femininity in the halls of Congress, and finally the shifting negotiations of female citizenship and the body politic, these essays reveal how

---

1807," *Journal of the Early Republic,* XII (1992), 159–193. Lewis cites other scholars who have joined to discuss this period in New Jersey's history.

16. Lewis, "Rethinking Women's Suffrage," in this volume.

17. Ibid; "Supplement to the Act Entitled 'An Act to Regulate the Election of Members of the Legislative Council and General Assembly,'" chap. II, in *Acts of the Thirty-Second General Assembly of the State of New-Jersey* (1807), 14, quoted ibid.

much Lewis taught us about gender during the early Republic. By attending closely to the possibilities posed by the scholarship of her peers, Jan Ellen Lewis's writings shaped the study of early American gender and politics. Moreover, as we shall see throughout this volume, she made it impossible for us to disentangle her concerns with gender from her examinations of the history of emotions, the law and constitutional thought, and Jefferson studies.

But the historiographical payoff she provided is only one part of the pleasure of reading Lewis's writings. One cannot help seeing the delight she took in unpacking the meanings of important cultural texts, scrutinizing the logic that undergirded them, and providing big, satisfying conclusions to help us understand the past. In the end, Lewis's crowning achievement was to offer groundbreaking insights that crack the cultural codes of the past, and to do so in essays of masterful style that underscore the manifest rewards of uncovering those insights.

The Republican Wife

Virtue and Seduction in the Early Republic

When the American colonists commenced rebellion against the British government and assumed the separate and equal station to which they believed the laws of God and nature both entitled them, they found in marriage—"that SOCIAL UNION, which the beneficent Creator instituted for the happiness of Man"—a metaphor for their ideal of social and political relationships. In the republic envisioned by American writers, citizens were to be bound together, not by patriarchy's duty or liberalism's self-interest, but by affection, and it was marriage, they believed, more than any other institution, that trained citizens in this virtue. "L," writing in the *Royal American Magazine* in 1774, explained why this "social union is so essential to human happiness." The married man, he wrote, "by giving pleasure . . . receives it back again with increase. By this endearing intercourse of friendship and communication of pleasure, the tender feelings and soft passions of the soul are awakened with all the ardour of love and benevolence. . . . In this happy state, man feels a growing attachment to human nature, and love to his country." Marriage was the very pattern from which the cloth of republican society was to be cut.[1]

Revolutionary-era writers held up the loving partnership of man and wife in opposition to patriarchal dominion as the republican model for social and political relationships. The essays, stories, poems, and novels that estab-

This essay was originally published as Jan Lewis, "The Republican Wife: Virtue and Seduction in the Early Republic," *William and Mary Quarterly*, 3d Ser., XLIV (1987), 689–721.

1. "Thoughts on Matrimony," *Royal American Magazine* . . . (Boston), January 1774, 9. Historians have explored the anti-patriarchal dimensions of the Revolution. See Jay Fliegelman, *Prodigals and Pilgrims: The American Revolution against Patriarchal Authority, 1750–1800* (Cambridge, 1982); Edwin G. Burrows and Michael Wallace, "The American Revolution: The Ideology and Psychology of National Liberation," in Donald Fleming and Bernard Bailyn, eds., *Perspectives in American History*, VI (Cambridge, Mass., 1972), 167–306; Winthrop D. Jordan, "Familial Politics: Thomas Paine and the Killing of the King, 1776," *Journal of American History*, LX (1973), 294–308; and Melvin Yazawa, *From Colonies to Commonwealth: Familial Ideology and the Beginnings of the American Republic* (Baltimore, 1985). Fliegelman has noted that the Revolutionary generation found in the "affectionate union" of marriage an alternative to the patriarchal model of political relationships (Fliegelman, *Prodigals and Pilgrims*, chap. 5).

lished this model created in republican marriage an ideal that drew upon recent social trends and infused them with political meaning; in so doing, their authors created for women an important new political role, not so much as mothers, as Linda K. Kerber has suggested, but, rather, as wives. As an indispensable half of the conjugal union that served as the ideal for political as well as familial relationships, the Republican Wife exemplified the strengths and weaknesses of the Revolutionary era's notion of woman's role and, indeed, of republicanism itself; neither can be understood fully except in the context of the other.[2]

Because historians have begun to question whether American political discourse in the period 1775–1815 can be understood in terms of republicanism alone, it is important to note that the adjective *republican* will be used here much as Americans of the period used it—to signify not only classical republicanism but also that fusion of civic humanism and evangelical ardor achieved by Americans on the eve of the Revolution. The key to republicanism is virtue, the self-sacrificial and disinterested quality that was prized in both sacred and secular traditions.[3] The premium that republican thought

2. Linda Kerber coined the term "Republican Motherhood" to describe the peculiar political mission assigned to American women in the Revolutionary era. In an influential article and book, she used it to characterize the indirect political role that women were to play by "raising sons and disciplining husbands to be virtuous citizens of the republic" (Kerber, "The Republican Mother: Women and the Enlightenment—An American Perspective," *American Quarterly,* XXVIII [1976], 187–205 [quotation, 203]; and Kerber, *Women of the Republic: Intellect and Ideology in Revolutionary America* [Williamsburg, Va., and Chapel Hill, N.C., 1980]). Although Kerber focused upon the domestic rather than the maternal character of woman's political participation, her term has taken on a life of its own and is often assumed to say more about motherhood than Kerber herself ever claimed. (See, for example, Mary Beth Norton, "The Evolution of White Women's Experience in Early America," *American Historical Review,* LXXXIX [1984], 616–619; Jane Rendall, *The Origins of Modern Feminism: Women in Britain, France, and the United States, 1780–1860* [New York, 1984], esp. chap. 2; and Mary P. Ryan, *Womanhood in America: From Colonial Times to the Present,* 3d ed. [New York, 1983], 102–104.) Indeed, as Ruth H. Bloch first suggested, comparatively little attention was paid in the period 1785–1815 to the republican dimensions of motherhood in relation to women's other roles (Bloch, "American Feminine Ideals in Transition: The Rise of the Moral Mother, 1785–1815," *Feminist Studies,* IV, no. 2 [June 1978], 125–126, n. 67). Kerber later argued that "republican motherhood was a conceptualization which grafted the language of liberal individualism onto the inherited discourse of civic humanism," which could not, in and of itself, "effectively describe an active role for women in the republic" (Kerber, "The Republican Ideology of the Revolutionary Generation," *American Quarterly,* XXXVII [1985], 484, 486, 488). The argument here is that American republicanism offered women a role as wives. It was left to liberalism, as Kerber suggests, to extol the political dimensions of motherhood.

3. See, especially, Gordon S. Wood, *The Creation of the American Republic, 1776–1787* (Williamsburg, Va., and Chapel Hill, N.C., 1969); his analysis of the meaning of republican-

placed upon disinterestedness has obscured the revolutionary nature of its views about women. To be sure, republican theorists were unwilling to think of women, or any other group, as having different and perhaps antagonistic interests; hence, they did not address women as a distinct class. Republicanism assumed, however, that America's dawning glory would cast its beneficent rays upon the whole of society, a new and different society in which women would be required to play a new and unprecedented role.[4]

If we would understand the role designed for women in the early national era, we must look to that body of Anglo-American literature that addressed political issues indirectly and found a wide and appreciative audience among the rapidly expanding reading public. Jay Fliegelman has shown that when we read those popular literary, pedagogical, and didactic works for their political meaning, we gain a new perspective on both the development of political thought in the eighteenth century and the intimate connections between family and polity in contemporary thought. Much of the commentary about woman's nature and her proper role can be found in novels and in the fiction and essays of the period's growing number of popular magazines.[5]

---

ism informs this essay. For a discussion of the meaning of virtue to contemporary Americans, see Ruth H. Bloch, "The Gendered Meanings of Virtue in Revolutionary America," *Signs: Journal of Women in Culture and Society,* XIII (1987), 37–58. A useful review of the literature of republicanism is provided by Robert E. Shalhope, "Republicanism and Early American Historiography," *William and Mary Quarterly,* 3d Ser., XXXIX (1982), 334–356. Although republicanism can be described as a wholly secular ideology, and the exact contributions of religious thought and feeling to it are certainly debated, its religious dimension must be recognized; as a popular ideology—that is, as one that was expressed in fiction and magazines by writers who reflected more than they shaped its key beliefs—republicanism was an amalgam of secular and sacred elements. Perhaps its ability to tap so many in-some-ways-contradictory roots explains republicanism's broad and enduring appeal.

4. For republican hostility to "interest," see Wood, *Creation of the American Republic,* esp. 53–65. For the history of women in the era of the Revolution, see Gerda Lerner, "The Lady and the Mill Girl: Changes in the Status of Women in the Age of Jackson," in Lerner, *The Majority Finds Its Past: Placing Women in History* (New York, 1979), 15–30; Joan Hoff Wilson, "The Illusion of Change: Women and the American Revolution," in Alfred F. Young, ed., *The American Revolution: Explorations in the History of American Radicalism* (DeKalb, Ill., 1976), 383–445; Mary Beth Norton, *Liberty's Daughters: The Revolutionary Experience of American Women, 1750–1800* (Boston, 1980); and Kerber, *Women of the Republic.* For a review of this literature, see Norton, "Evolution of White Women's Experience," *American Historical Review,* LXXXIX (1984), 593–619.

5. Fliegelman, *Prodigals and Pilgrims.* For the growth of literacy, see Kenneth A. Lockridge, *Literacy in Colonial New England: An Enquiry into the Social Context of Literacy in the Early Modern West* (New York, 1974). For the tastes of the American reading public, see David Lundberg and Henry F. May, "The Enlightened Reader in America," *American Quarterly,* XXVIII (1976), 262–293; Garry Wills, *Inventing America: Jefferson's Declaration of Independence* (Garden City, N.Y., 1978), esp. pt. 4; and Herbert Ross Brown, *The Sentimental*

Americans drew no clear distinctions between that which was fiction and that which was not, between works addressed to men and works addressed to women, or even between British literature and original American creations; nor should we. Moreover, what concerns us here is the meaning that American men and women could derive from popular literature. The moral message in what might seem a diverse body of works was remarkably consistent. Magazine editors, for example, aimed both to instruct and to entertain, devoting their periodicals to "knowledge and entertainment," "entertaining knowledge," and "amusement and instruction." They and their readers could find knowledge entertaining and a properly written piece of fiction instructive.[6] Fiction served to illustrate the workings of character. In the moral world of the eighteenth century, character was all, and the study of character was an important aspect of moral philosophy, itself a branch of post-Newtonian natural science. Here art and science might fuse.[7]

Similarly, although some periodicals seem to have been addressed primarily to men and others to women, most welcomed both sexes as readers and authors and printed articles that presumably were of interest to women as well as men.[8] No magazines intended exclusively for women were published in America until early in the nineteenth century. The themes of courtship, marriage, and seduction figured to a greater or lesser extent in a wide range of early national publications, not only the *Boston Weekly Magazine* but also, for example, Paine's *Pennsylvania Magazine* and Webster's *American Magazine.* The topic of marriage was not reserved to women or their magazines, for it was an issue of public, indeed political, import.[9]

Finally, we must note that much of what was read in America had been written in Britain. Popular British novels were brought out in American editions, and American editors, unable to fill their periodicals with origi-

---

Novel in America, 1789–1860 (Durham, N.C., 1940), esp. chap. 1. The relevance of literature to an understanding of women's history has been explored by Mary Sumner Benson, *Women in Eighteenth-Century America: A Study of Opinion and Social Usage* (1935; rpt. Port Washington, N.Y., 1966); and Janet Wilson James, *Changing Ideas about Women in the United States, 1776–1825* (New York, 1981).

6. *General Magazine, and Impartial Review, of Knowledge and Entertainment* (Baltimore), 1798; *Lady's Magazine; and Repository of Entertaining Knowledge* (Philadelphia), 1792; *New-York Weekly Museum, or Polite Repository of Amusement and Instruction,* 1814.

7. See Gordon S. Wood, "Conspiracy and the Paranoid Style: Causality and Deceit in the Eighteenth Century," *William and Mary Quarterly,* 3d Ser., XXXIX (1982), esp. 414.

8. See, for example, letter in *American Magazine . . .* (New York), December 1787, 3, welcoming *"fair readers"* as both subscribers and correspondents.

9. Frank Luther Mott, *A History of American Magazines, 1741–1850,* I (Cambridge, Mass., 1958), 139.

nal works, borrowed freely from each other and from their British counterparts.[10] Yet what matters is not only the origin and intent of such works but also the lessons Americans might have derived from them. Bernard Bailyn has shown the special meaning British political writings had for Americans immersed in an imperial crisis. So also with the popular literature of marriage.[11]

A British work might be edited for the American audience in ways that made it more applicable to the American situation. In *Clarissa,* the novel of the patriarchal family par excellence, the heroine is, as Fliegelman has put it, "purely a victim caught between two tyrannies," that of the father and that of the seducer. Although Richardson held the disobedient daughter partly responsible for her sad fate, eighteenth-century American editions of the book removed that assessment of the heroine from both the subtitle and the introduction, making Clarissa instead the innocent victim of male arrogance, imperiousness, and design. Yet *Clarissa* was more than a seduction story; it was a political parable with particular lessons for Americans, as a fearful John Adams recognized when he observed that "Democracy is Lovelace, and the people are Clarissa."[12]

Americans who aimed for the separate station of a viable republic would have to learn better than Clarissa how to resist the tyrannies and seductions that republican theorists were certain they faced. Because eighteenth-century thought placed the family and the state on one continuum, that of "society," and did not yet—as the nineteenth century would—erect a barrier between the private sphere of the family and the public one of the world, it could dramatize issues of authority in terms of relationships between members of a family. Accordingly, the young woman's quest for a suitable husband and her attempt to navigate between the eighteenth-century's Scylla of overweening power and its Charybdis of seductive liberty was the nation's plot as well.[13]

10. For the popularity of British works in America, see Fliegelman, *Prodigals and Pilgrims,* chap. 2. For the reprinting of British articles in American magazines, see Mott, *History of American Magazines,* I, 14–15.

11. In particular, see Bernard Bailyn, *The Ideological Origins of the American Revolution* (Cambridge, Mass., 1967); and Bailyn, *The Origins of American Politics* (New York, 1968).

12. Fliegelman, *Prodigals and Pilgrims,* 83–88 ("purely," 87); John Adams to William Cunningham, Jr., Mar. 15, 1804, in *Correspondence between the Hon. John Adams, Late President of the United States, and the Late Wm. Cunningham, Esq. . . .* (Boston, 1823), 19, also cited ibid., 237 ("Democracy"). Fliegelman's observation refers to abridgments only.

13. See Note 1, above; and Richard Sennett, *The Fall of Public Man* (New York, 1977).

Americans, successfully completing a revolution against one sort of tyranny, were bound to conclude that their young men and women could also achieve independence. The anti-patriarchalism of Revolutionary ideology dictated that tyranny presented the most immediate and obvious threat to American happiness and patriarchal domination the chief obstacle to happy and virtuous marriage. According to the republican view, patriarchs such as "The Inexorable Father," who was "unfeeling as adamant, hard of heart as the nether mill stone," threatened always to block the happiness of their children; in this case, the father refused to let his daughter marry a promising young physician who was too honest to enrich himself by overcharging his patients.[14]

So resonant was this anti-patriarchal theme that well after the Revolution American magazines published articles excoriating "parents, who are daily offering up the honour and happiness of their children at the shrine of interest and ambition," much as the British government had sacrificed its American colonies.[15] Instead, "marriages would be contracted from motives of affection, rather than of interest." Fortunately, such unions were possible in "happy America," where partible inheritance—"provided our conduct does not render us unworthy"—formed "the basis of equality and the incitement to industry and caution." If America's sons and daughters were educated to "virtue and good morality," they would choose to marry for love rather than interest. Being capable of exercising sound judgment, children were not obligated to obey the injunctions of narrow-minded or rapacious parents.[16]

14. "The Inexorable Father," *Massachusetts Magazine . . .* (Boston), October 1791, 619–620. See similarly "The Unfeeling Father," ibid., May 1792, 286; and "The Precipitate Lover; A Moral Tale," *Gentleman and Lady's Town and Country Magazine* (Boston), October 1784, 227–232.

15. "Essay on Parental Care and Filial Duty," *New-York Magazine . . .*, January 1794, 49. This article might well have originated in Britain, for it speaks of "rich and noble parents." See also "On the Treatment of the Fair Sex," *Lady's Magazine and Musical Repository* [New York], April 1801, 214: "It has been remarked, that the public affairs of most nations have been conducted with more or less elegance, dexterity, and success, as they respectively restrain or give freedom to their women." Such articles had as their object proving (or bringing about) American superiority, of which the status of women was deemed a fit measure. See also Wood, *Creation of the American Republic,* 46–48, 97–107.

16. "Improvements Suggested in Female Education," *New-York Magazine,* August 1797, 407; "Lindor to Caroline; Containing the Story of Philander and Honoria," *Massachusetts Magazine,* May 1792, 312, 313. See also "On Marriage," *Gentlemen and Ladies Town and Country Magazine . . .* (Boston), March 1789, 85–86; "On Parental Authority," *Lady's Maga-*

The rhetoric of marriage bears the same relationship to the prevailing customs as does republican ideology to the events it sought to shape and define: in each case, the terms of analysis explained long-range trends by turning them into dramas enacted by villains and heroes—or, more commonly, heroines. Historians of the family have shown that parental control of marriage declined over the course of the eighteenth century, while children's autonomy increased.[17] That trend had its roots in the Reformation; Protestantism, with its insistence that "mutual comfort" was one of marriage's primary purposes, had licensed the consensual, affectionate union.[18] Although American Puritan ministers still retained for parents, by virtue of their supposedly superior wisdom, a key role in selecting their children's mates, they nonetheless recognized that "marriage is one of the weightiest actions of a person's life, and as the Yoke fellow is suitable or unsuitable, so that Condition is like to be very comfortable or uncomfortable." Nor did wealth establish a potential spouse's suitability. As Cotton Mather rhymed it, "The Wretch that is alone to *Mammon* Wed, / May chance to find a *Satan* in the Bed." Interest alone, whether personal or dynastic, had never been an acceptable basis for marriage in the colonies; what changed were, on the one hand, determinations of who was best qualified, the parents or the children, to recognize merit in a potential spouse and, on the other, perceptions of how likely the affections of marriage were, in and of themselves, to assure lasting happiness. During the eighteenth century, parents grew less willing

---

zine; and Repository of Entertaining Knowledge, October 1792, 239; and "The Censor; Number VII," *Christian's, Scholar's, and Farmer's Magazine . . .* (Elizabethtown, N.J.), April–May 1790, 45–46.

17. See Daniel Scott Smith, "Parental Power and Marriage Patterns: An Analysis of Historical Trends in Hingham, Massachusetts," *Journal of Marriage and Family,* XXXV (1973), 419–428; Robert A. Gross, *The Minutemen and Their World* (New York, 1976), 98–102; Daniel Blake Smith, *Inside the Great House: Planter Family Life in Eighteenth-Century Chesapeake Society* (Ithaca, N.Y., 1980), chap. 4; and Jan Lewis, *The Pursuit of Happiness: Family and Values in Jefferson's Virginia* (New York, 1983), 187–203. See also Randolph Trumbach, *The Rise of the Egalitarian Family: Aristocratic Kinship and Domestic Relations in Eighteenth-Century England* (New York, 1978), chap. 2; and Lawrence Stone, *The Family, Sex, and Marriage in England, 1500–1800* (New York, 1977), chaps. 7, 8.

18. See Stone, *Family, Sex, and Marriage,* 135–142; Steven Ozment, *When Fathers Ruled: Family Life in Reformation Europe* (Cambridge, Mass., 1983), chap. 1; Laurel Thatcher Ulrich, *Good Wives: Image and Reality in the Lives of Women in Northern New England, 1650–1750* (New York, 1982), chap. 6; John Demos, *A Little Commonwealth: Family Life in Plymouth Colony* (New York, 1970), 82–99, 150–170; and Edmund S. Morgan, *The Puritan Family: Religion and Domestic Relations in SeventeenthCentury New England,* new ed. (New York, 1966), chap. 2. See also Jean-Louis Flandrin, *Families in Former Times: Kinship, Household, and Sexuality,* trans. Richard Southern (Cambridge, 1979), 145–173.

or able to exert the full range of pressures at their command to shape their children's destinies; the balance tipped in favor of the younger generation's discretion.[19]

Rhetoric that implicitly likened late-eighteenth-century parents to designing court ministers, bent upon subjecting their dependents, grossly exaggerated the control that parents retained over their children's marriages and overstated the power parents had held a century earlier. Nonetheless, the rhetoric of marriage, much like that of politics, served both to expose underlying fears and to legitimate and encourage patterns that had already come to prevail.

Republican theorists endeavored to show how, in a post-patriarchal world, citizens could govern themselves, how they could form a society bound by love rather than fear. Because they deemed marriage the school of affection, authors who wrote about the institution were addressing one of their age's most pressing questions: how to make citizens fit for a republic. For example, if the choice of a mate were, or should be, the individual's, he or she must know how to select wisely. And if the parents no longer did, or should, have control, substitute parents could still give advice, which they did at great length in numerous tracts and essays. Parents did not abdicate; rather, they refashioned themselves into friendly paternalists who exerted influence in their families by more subtle, psychological means and in the wider world by words of friendly counsel.[20] The author of "A Father's Advice to His Daughters" recommended that his own daughters and those of other men "place confidence in those who have shown affection for you in your early days, when you were incapable of making them any return." Yet even those dethroned patriarchs who posed as kind advisors believed they best served young men and women by enabling them to judiciously choose their own partners.[21]

What sort of man made the ideal husband? He was republican virtue in-

19. Benj[amin] Wadsworth, *The Well-Ordered Family* . . . (Boston, 1712), 42; [Cotton Mather], *Eureka; or, A Vertuous Woman Found* . . . (Boston, 1704), 3.

20. See Lewis, *Pursuit of Happiness,* 175–187; Jane Turner Censer, *North Carolina Planters and Their Children, 1800–1860* (Baton Rouge, La., 1984), esp. 60–64, 68–70; and Fliegelman, *Prodigals and Pilgrims,* 259–266.

21. "A Father's Advice to His Daughters," *Christian's, Scholar's, and Farmer's Magazine,* February–March 1790, 697. This article is an extract from *A Father's Legacy to His Daughters* by Dr. John Gregory of Edinburgh. Originally appearing in England in 1774, it proved one of the most popular books published in this era in America, where it went through at least fifteen editions and sold more than twenty thousand copies. See Benson, *Women in Eighteenth-Century America,* 59–60; and Fliegelman, *Prodigals and Pilgrims,* 39.

carnate, moderation personified. He was "careful without avarice, [manifesting] a kind of unconcernedness without negligence," "devout without superstition, and pious without melancholy." He should be well educated but not "a pedant." A woman should look for "virtuous conduct, good temper, discretion, regularity and industry" and a "mild and even" disposition. Unlike her European sisters, who supposedly married to raise their status, the American maid aimed at—and hoped to maintain—a happy medium, a domestic version of that steadily improving yet never-changing society that Gordon S. Wood has identified as the ideal society of republican dreams. The happily married woman would find that her husband "would be always the same, and always pleasing."[22]

The good husband was like the good citizen; he wed "not by interest but by choice," and "he treats his wife with delicacy as a woman, with tenderness as a friend." He "ever studied the happiness of the woman he loved more than his own." In fact, the ideal husband resembled more than a little the popular portrait of the Revolutionary War officer, which is precisely the occupation Royall Tyler chose for the hero of his play *The Contrast.* To ensure that the officer / suitor's character could not be mistaken, Tyler dubbed him "Colonel Manly" and gave him such quintessentially republican opinions as that ancient Greece declined because "the common good was lost in the pursuit of private interest" and that "the man who . . . can plant thorns in the bosom of an innocent, unsuspecting girl is more detestable than a common robber, in the same proportion as private violence is more despicable than open force, and money of less value than happiness." The qualities that made a man honorable in public life, then, distinguished him as a potential husband as well.[23]

Men, likewise, were supposed to select republicans as their life partners. As the author of "On the Choice of a Wife" put it, "Virtue, Wisdom, presence of mind, patience, vigour, capacity, application, are not *sexual* qualities; they belong to mankind—to all who have duties to perform and evils to endure." Echoing standard Protestant assumptions, Americans and the British writers they chose to republish argued that the most important con-

22. "The Maid's Husband," *Baltimore Weekly Magazine,* May 20, 1801, 297 ("careful," "would be"); "On the Choice of a Husband," *Columbian Magazine* (Philadelphia), February 1788, 65–67 ("pedant," 67, "mild," 66); "On the Choice of a Wife," *Gentlemen and Ladies Town and Country Magazine,* April 1789, 147 ("virtuous"); Wood, *Creation of the American Republic,* 70–75.

23. "Character of a Good Husband," *Massachusetts Magazine,* March 1789, 177, "The Suspicious Lover: A Moral Tale," September 1796, 495; Royall Tyler, *The Contrast: A Comedy in Five Acts* (1790) (Boston, 1920), 80, 82.

siderations in the selection of a wife were her "qualifications as a *companion* and as a *helper*."[24] The choice was difficult, for women were not equally qualified. Suitors should be wary of frivolity and mere physical beauty or what the author of "The Intrinsic Merits of Women" called "the fashionable follies of the age." It was not that all women were suspect but that only certain types—great beauties, heiresses, and coquettes—were likely to be dangerous. Thus "the husbands of beauties are the most miserable of husbands. . . . Vexed by the vanity, exhausted by the extravagance, tortured by the inconstancy . . . life, instead of a blessing, becomes to them a purgatory." The republican gloss is equally evident in the simple reminder that "riches . . . will never alone afford happiness to their possessors."[25]

Men and women both were advised to seek for their mates what we can recognize as embodiments of republican ideology. They were warned at even greater length to avoid certain notorious types, those associated with the despicable aspects of European court life: flatterers, deceivers, flirts, fops, coxcombs, coquettes, and all persons lacking in honor and virtue. Writers devoted so much effort to delineating the characteristics of the coxcomb and coquette that one cannot help suspecting that the type, rather than presenting a bona fide threat to naive American beaux and belles, served as a distillation, much like the tyrannical ruler or the designing minister, of what the age most feared. Flirts and fops, coxcombs and coquettes romp through the pages of republican literature with abandon. Their names are code words that signify luxury, vice, and deceit; their presence in a story points almost without exception to an unhappy ending. They promise ruin not only for themselves and their victims but also for the infant nation, for they practice habits that were commonly believed to spell the death of republics. So reasoned the author of "The Philosophy of Coquetry": "So long as the sensualities and pride of one sex shall delight in luxurious habits and ostentatious living; so long as the vanities of the other shall be gratified by splendid personal decorations, costly refinements, and glittering equipages—or, more philosophically speaking, so long as we shall be enslaved in a refined state of society, by numerous and factitious wants, we shall look in vain

24. "On the Choice of a Wife," *Lady's Magazine and Musical Repository,* March 1802, 165, 168, printed also in *Boston Weekly Magazine,* Dec. 29, 1804, 37. The articles are selections from *Letters from a Father to His Son* (1794) by John Aiken, an English physician, quoted in James, *Changing Ideas,* 143–144.

25. "The Intrinsic Merits of Women," *Christian's, Scholar's, and Farmer's Magazine,* December 1789–January 1790, 627, 628; "On the Choice of a Wife," *Universal Asylum, and Columbian Magazine* (Philadelphia), March 1792, 176–177. See also "The Choice of a Wife," *Christian's, Scholar's, and Farmer's Magazine,* August–September 1790, 351–353.

for disinterested alliances, and an union of the sexes resulting from mental attachment."[26]

Reform began with the individual; a republican society required virtuous men and women. That belief permeates the purportedly "True Story" of "Eugenia—Or the Coquette." The girl of the title has parents who are "dissipated and luxurious; they looked forward to immense wealth. . . . Pride, pomp, and luxury dazzled their eyes." Indeed, "without a particle of principle, [Eugenia's] father countenanced British depredation, at a time when the hirelings of tyranny were not sparing in the arts of devastation." In this republican vision, a nation could be no better than the individuals who constituted it. A sad fate for the nation is averted when Eugenia, who has inherited her parents' vices, jilts the decent young man who had courted her, freeing him to marry "a woman, who boasts only those real charms, . . . which constitute the perfect wife. . . . As she never experienced the deceit of a fop, so he congratulates himself, that he has escaped from the smiles of a coquette." Significantly, Eugenia herself is almost incidental to the story. It is her parents, stand-ins for a corrupt British government, and their ability to thwart a truly affectionate union that are most feared. In such a view, to fall for a coquette is to surrender republican virtue, and to flirt is to commit an act of treason.[27]

When courtship and marriage are infused with political meaning, women inevitably and inescapably become political beings. Make no mistake: these first formulations of a feminine political role were not fundamentally feminist. They were not devised by women in particular, nor was their aim primarily to enhance the position of women. The dynamic, rather, was republican and anti-patriarchal: it juxtaposed the virtuous, independent child and the oppressive, corrupting parent, and it found in the union of two virtuous individuals the true end of society and the fit paradigm for political life. Such a conceptualization of the relationship between family and polity represents more a subtle shift than a clean break from earlier models. When Puritans designated the family "a little commonwealth," they meant it to be "a schoole wherein the first principles and grounds of government and subjection are

26. "The Philosophy of Coquetry," *New-York Magazine,* November 1796, 583. The classic example, of course, is Hannah Foster's *The Coquette; or, The History of Eliza Wharton . . .* (Boston, 1797).

27. "Eugenia—Or the Coquette—A True Story," *Universal Asylum, and Columbian Magazine,* November 1792, 334–335. See also "The Flirt, a Moral Tale," ibid., June 1791, 389–391, "A Vindication of the Fair Sex, against the Charge of Preferring Coxcombs to Men of Worth and Genius," July 1792, 28–30; and "The Ladies New Catechism," *Baltimore Weekly Magazine,* May 20, 1801, 303.

learned: whereby men are fitted to greater matters in Church or commonwealth." In such a family, the relationship between parent and child was most important.[28]

When anti-patriarchalists in the eighteenth century substituted marriage for parenthood as the fundamental familial relationship, they did not, however, question the assumption that the family was society in miniature. Society still appeared as the family writ large, with the same sorts of relationships deemed appropriate for both the as-yet-undifferentiated spheres of home and world. Yet in shifting interest from the parent-child nexus to the husband-wife bond, eighteenth-century authors necessarily raised women to a new moral and political stature. When the key relationship in a society is that between father and son or ruler and subject, women may conveniently be ignored; when the most important relationship is between conjugal equals, and when the family is still seen as the correlative of the larger society, then women can no longer be overlooked. If the affectionate union between a man and his wife, freely entered into, without tyrannical interference, is the model for all the relationships in the society and the polity, then the wife, as an indispensable half of the marital union, is a political creature.

To the extent that the success of the republican endeavor rested upon the character of citizens, republicanism demanded virtue of women, not because it numbered them as citizens but because it recognized how intimately women, in consensual unions, were connected to men. A virtuous man required a virtuous mate. Moreover, republicanism called upon every means at its disposal to assure male virtue. That obsession with virtue, deriving its force from the fusion of Protestant and republican notions of character, persisted long after the Revolution had been won and the Constitution ratified. Well into the nineteenth century, Americans linked the fate of their nation to the virtues of its people.[29] Even if, as several historians have suggested, certain thinkers, before the end of the eighteenth century, had embraced liberalism and its premise of the self-interested individual, popular writers and, presumably, their audience had not.[30] One writer put it emphatically:

28. William Gouge, *Of Domesticall Duties* . . . (London, 1622), 18, quoted in Demos, *Little Commonwealth*, xix.

29. See Perry Miller, "From the Covenant to the Revival," in James Ward Smith and A. Leland Jamison, eds., *Religion in American Life: The Shaping of American Religion* (Princeton, N.J., 1961), 322–368. For the legacy of republicanism, see Drew R. McCoy, *The Elusive Republic: Political Economy in Jeffersonian America* (Williamsburg, Va., and Chapel Hill, N.C., 1980).

30. See, for example, Joyce Appleby, "Commercial Farming and the 'Agrarian Myth' in the Early Republic," *Journal of American History*, LXVIII (1982), 833–849; Appleby, "What

"Private vices are *not* public benefits." That rejection of Bernard Mandeville infused much of the early national literature, and that conceptualization of society—which continued to see the family as the microcosm of the wider world and to insist that "public good must grow out of private virtue"—held out a significant role for women.[31]

"A woman of virtue and prudence is a public good—a public benefactor." She has the power to make "public decency . . . a fashion—and public virtue the only example." And how was woman to accomplish that great end? By her influence over the manners of men. "Nothing short of a general reformation of manners would take place, were the ladies to use their power in discouraging our licentious manners." Such a role might seem trivial did Americans not consider "the general reformation of manners" one of the young nation's most important goals and did they not think women fully capable of contributing to it. Women might begin by reforming themselves, for "there is not a more certain test of national depravity, than that which presents itself in the degeneracy of female manners."[32]

Male manners, however, were of more concern, and, in changing them, women were to play their most important role. So argued men, such as the essayist who held that women who were the beneficiaries of a "virtuous and refined education" might contribute "no less to public good than to private happiness. A gentleman, who at present must degrade himself into a fop or a coxcomb in order to please the ladies, would soon find that their favour could not be gained but by exerting every manly talent in public and private life." That same view could be expressed by a woman—for example, Miss C. Hutchings, who assured her fellow boarding-school graduates of the influence of "female manners on society in general": "Were all Women rational, unaffected and virtuous, coxcombs, flatterers and libertines would no longer exist." Such arguments rested on several important new assumptions. First,

---

Is Still American in the Political Philosophy of Thomas Jefferson?" *William and Mary Quarterly*, 3d Ser., XXXIX (1982), 287–309; John Patrick Diggins, *The Lost Soul of American Politics: Virtue, Self-Interest, and the Foundations of Liberalism* (New York, 1984); and Isaac Kramnick, "Republican Revisionism Revisited," *American Historical Review*, LXXXVII (1982), 629–664.

31. "Mr. Editor," *Gentlemen and Ladies Town and Country Magazine*, July 1789, 311; "Literary Review; No. IV; The Boarding School; By a Lady of Massachusetts," *Columbian Phenix, or Boston Review*, May 1800, 278. See also "The Reflector; No. V," *Lady's Monitor* (New York), Dec. 5, 1801, 124–125.

32. "Scheme for Increasing the Power of the Fair Sex," *Lady's Magazine; and Repository of Entertaining Knowledge*, June 1792, 22–24, reprinted in *Baltimore Weekly Magazine*, Apr. 1, 1801, 241–242; "The Reflector; No. IX," *Lady's Monitor*, Jan. 2, 1802, 156.

although the concern with "manners" betokened an upper-class emphasis upon gentility, the insistence that women were—or could be—a moral force transformed manners into mores, into the moral foundation of the society. Thus "it is . . . to the virtues of the fair . . . that society must be indebted for its moral, as well as its natural preservation." Second, women were to play their moral role, not by denying their sexuality by becoming "passionless," but by using it to tempt men to be good.[33]

This conceptualization of female influence seems to have intrigued men and women in the decades just after the Revolution. Magazines printed and reprinted numbers of articles with similar titles and sentiments: "Female Influence," "Scheme for Increasing the Power of the Fair Sex," "The Influence of the Female Sex on the Enjoyments of Social Life," "The Power of Beauty, and the Influence the Fair Sex Might Have in Reforming the Manners of the World." These, with a host of similar articles, argued that the potential for beneficial female influence was almost unlimited.[34]

The height of a woman's influence was reached during the period of "love and courtship," which, "it is universally allowed, invest a lady with more authority than in any other situation [that] falls to the lot of human beings." A young man who addressed his classmates at Columbia College's commencement elaborated: "She can mould the taste, the manners, and the conduct of her admirers, according to her pleasure." Moreover, "she can, even to a great degree, change their tempers and dispositions, and superinduce habits entirely new." It was not in childhood that a man was most malleable; rather,

33. "The Influence of the Female Sex on the Enjoyments of Social Life," *Christian's, Scholar's, and Farmer's Magazine,* October-November 1789, 497, reprinted in *Universal Asylum, and Columbian Magazine,* March 1790, 153–154; "Influence of the Female Character on Society in General," *Boston Weekly Magazine,* Oct. 30, 1802, 3; "Reflector; No. IX," *Lady's Monitor,* Jan. 2, 1802, 156; Nancy F. Cott, "Passionlessness: An Interpretation of Victorian Sexual Ideology, 1790-1850," *Signs,* IV (1978), 219–236. On the changing conceptualization of woman's nature, see Ruth H. Bloch, "Untangling the Roots of Modern Sex Roles: A Survey of Four Centuries of Change," *Signs,* IV (1978), 237–252; Bloch, "American Feminine Ideals in Transition," *Feminist Studies,* IV, no. 2 (June 1978), 101–126; Catherine M. Scholten, *Childbearing in American Society, 1650–1850* (New York, 1985); and Cott, "Passionlessness," *Signs,* IV (1978), 219–236.

34. "Female Influence . . . ," *New-York Magazine,* May 1795, 297–305; "Scheme for Increasing the Power of the Fair Sex," *Lady's Magazine; and Repository of Entertaining Knowledge,* June 1792, 22–24, reprinted in *Baltimore Weekly Magazine,* Apr. 1, 1801, 241–242; "The Influence of the Female Sex on the Enjoyments of Social Life," *Christian's, Scholar's, and Farmer's Magazine,* October-November 1789, 496–497, reprinted in *Universal Asylum, and Columbian Magazine,* March 1790, 153–154; "The Power of Beauty, and the Influence the Fair Sex Might Have in Reforming the Manners of the World," *Boston Weekly Magazine,* Mar. 3, 1804, 73–74.

it was when, grown to maturity, he sought the favors of a young lady that he was most susceptible to influence. "By the judicious management of this noble passion [love], a passion with which the truly accomplished of the fair sex never fail of inspiring the men, what almost miraculous reformation may be brought about?"[35]

Once she had seduced him into virtue, the married woman's task was to preserve her husband in the exalted state to which her influence had raised him. "It rests with her, not only to confirm those virtuous habits which he has already acquired, but also to excite his perseverance in the paths of rectitude." The boldness of this formulation is stunning. What earlier Americans perceived as Eve's most dangerous characteristic, her seductiveness, is here transformed into her capacity for virtue. Woman was to lead man into rectitude, to lure him to the exercise of manly virtue. What miraculous reformations became possible when the attraction between the sexes, which for millennia had been considered the cause of the fall of mankind, could be transformed into the bedrock of the nation! Women indeed had great power—nothing less than the ability, as one magazine implored, "to make our young men, not in empty words, but in deed and in truth, republicans."[36]

That was why so much importance was attached to the education of women. Passion could and must be tempered by reason. If Eve's daughters could deserve, as one young woman put it, to be "extolled for the beauties of their minds instead of their persons, . . . then would mankind enjoy that happiness which was first intended for the happy pair in Paradise." Were women properly educated, "then will the halcyon days dawn, and human nature appear in its highest beauty and perfection." Few topics excited more interest in the early national period than education, for it seemed to hold the key to making "our women virtuous and respectable; our men brave, honest, and honorable—and the *American* People in general, *an* EXAMPLE *of* HONOUR *and* VIRTUE *to the rest of the world.*"[37] Writers were not always clear or cer-

35. "Female Influence," *New-York Magazine,* May 1795, 299, 300. See similarly Benjamin Rush, *Thoughts upon Female Education, Accommodated to the Present State of Society, Manners, and Government in the United States of America* (Boston, 1787), in Frederick Rudolph, ed., *Essays on Education in the Early Republic* (Cambridge, Mass., 1965), 25–40. See also Rush's *A Plan for the Establishment of Public Schools and the Diffusion of Knowledge in Pennsylvania . . .* (Philadelphia, 1786), ibid., 21–22.

36. "Female Influence," *New-York Magazine,* May 1795, 300; "Female Economy," *Ladies' Literary Cabinet* (New York), July 8, 1820, 67. See also "Woman," *New-York Weekly Museum,* Aug. 27, 1814, 132.

37. "On Female Education," *New-York Magazine,* September 1794, 570; "On Female Education," *Royal American Magazine,* January 1774, 10; "The Gossip—No. XXVII," *Bos-*

tain about whether the American people were naturally virtuous or whether, instead, they merely had unusual potential to be so; hence the extremes of millennial hope and overwhelming fear, as men and women envisioned both the prospect of paradise on earth and the potential for disastrous failure.[38]

Unless we recognize how grandiose American expectations could be and how terrifying was the possibility that they might not be realized, we cannot fully appreciate how central female education was to the republican agenda. Although it is true that some reformers advocated educating women so that they, in turn, could teach their children, the more important consideration, always, was to make women into fit companions for republican men and, especially, reliable guarantors of masculine virtue.[39] As one man put it, "Would the females keep in view the influence they possess on our education, they would not fail to perceive an attention to their own as nearly connected with the welfare of mankind. . . . Do they admire and respect the man of sense, and treat with contempt the coxcomb and the fop, [a young man] will, to recommend himself to their esteem, form himself to usefulness and virtue." No one argued that women were naturally more virtuous or pure than men; rather, they had the capacity to overcome weakness and become good.[40]

Nor, certainly, were all women natural republicans; the books and magazines of the age are populated with as many coquettes and flirts as coxcombs and fops. Human nature was malleable, and, if it could be bent toward good, to make a republican, it might also be warped toward evil, creating a coxcomb or coquette. Obviously, those who believed in the malleability of character rejected Calvinistic assumptions about innate depravity, and nowhere is their departure from the older orthodoxy more clear than in their expecta-

---

ton Weekly Magazine, May 28, 1803, 125. For the importance that republicans attached to education, see Lawrence A. Cremin, *American Education: The National Experience, 1783–1876* (New York, 1980), 103–147. See also the essays in Rudolph, ed., *Essays on Education.*

38. Wood, *Creation of the American Republic,* chap. 3; Miller, "Covenant to Revival," in Smith and Jamison, eds., *Religion in American Life,* 322–368; Charles Royster, *A Revolutionary People at War: The Continental Army and American Character, 1775–1783* (Williamsburg, Va., and Chapel Hill, N.C., 1979). See also "Education," *American Magazine,* December 1787, 22–26.

39. For example, "Review of the Cultivation of Female Intellect in the United States," *Literary and Evangelical Magazine* (Richmond, Va.), May 1827, 244, "Review of the Cultivation of Female Intellect in the United States—Continued," June 1827, 292; "Female Influence," *New-York Magazine,* May 1795, 300. See also Linda K. Kerber, "Daughters of Columbia: Educating Women for the Republic, 1787–1805," in Stanley Elkins and Eric McKitrick, eds., *The Hofstadter Aegis: A Memorial* (New York, 1974), 36–59.

40. "On Love," *General Magazine, and Impartial Review,* June 1798, 22.

tions of feminine virtue. Thus one essayist advised women of the enormous power they had at their disposal: "As *Milton* says, *The world lies all before them,* and it is theirs to mould it into what shape they please."[41]

That paraphrase and application of the penultimate lines of *Paradise Lost* are a good deal more sanguine than the original. So optimistic a reading of Milton, with its suggestion that the world was Eve's to make, even into a new paradise, drew upon millennial hopes that had become an integral part of American culture.[42] To be sure, such expectations did not always express a literal belief in the imminence of Christ's thousand-year reign, and they were often dampened by a lurking fear that they might not be realized. Still, the Revolution unloosed a flood of optimism—so much that some Americans could begin to think of themselves as new men, veritable American Adams, given the opportunity to make the world and themselves anew. As Paine put it, America "has it in her choice to do, and to live as happy as she pleases. The world is in her hands." This persistent strain in American thought is well known to students of American culture.[43] Yet there could be no Adam without an Eve; in the garden, as described in Genesis and by Milton, Adam had a companion who sinned first. Without Eve, Adam presumably would have remained in Paradise; that reminder of woman's unhappy role in effecting human destiny had never been far from the minds of Puritan ministers such as Cotton Mather. To the extent that the Fall was the most compelling of all biblical episodes for Puritans, woman played a central, and unenviable, role in the central drama of mankind. Milton's version of the Fall achieved wide popularity in America at the end of the eighteenth century, and not just among the heirs of the Puritans; his Eve, although more sympathetic than the stock Puritan version, still bore primary responsibility for the great calamity.[44]

41. "The Power of Beauty, and the Influence the Fair Sex Might Have in Reforming the Manners of the World," *Boston Weekly Magazine,* Mar. 3, 1804, 74; Fliegelman, *Prodigals and Pilgrims,* 15.

42. See Ruth H. Bloch, *Visionary Republic: Millennial Themes in American Thought, 1756–1800* (New York, 1985).

43. "The Last Crisis, No. XV," in Howard Fast, ed., *The Selected Work of Tom Paine and Citizen Tom Paine* (New York, 1946), 84. See, in particular, R. W. B. Lewis, *The American Adam: Innocence, Tragedy, and Tradition in the Nineteenth Century* (Chicago, 1955); and D. H. Lawrence, *Studies in Classic American Literature* (New York, 1923).

44. See, for example, Cotton Mather, *Ornaments for the Daughters of Zion; or, The Character and Happiness of a Vertuous Woman . . .* (Cambridge, Mass., 1692), 1. See also Scholten, *Childbearing in American Society,* 12. George F. Sensabaugh details the spread of Milton's works in America. Although his picture of connubial bliss was occasionally referred to in American publications before the Revolution, it was the final quarter of the century and

To move to a more helpful view of human potential, it was necessary first to come to terms with the Fall. Several avenues were available. One was to shift the focus of religion from Fall to Redemption; that path was taken, particularly in the nineteenth century, as American Protestantism became more Christocentric. Another option was for Adam, in effect, to go his own way, without Eve, remaking the world as an all-male paradise; classic American literature, written by men, followed that route in the nineteenth century. But Americans of the late eighteenth century, steeped as they were in orthodox readings of the Bible, and reminded of them by Milton, could not remake Adam and give the story of the Fall a happier ending without first remaking the woman who had been first to sin. And that is precisely what they did.[45]

Some revamped Eve clearly and consciously, offering new exegeses of Genesis, as did the author of "The Nobility of Woman Kind," who reasoned that "the man gave us death; not the woman. The woman did amiss ignorantly and from deception: But the man knew, that he did amiss." Judith Sargent Murray, writing in the *Massachusetts Magazine* under the pen name "Constantia," offered an even more positive assessment of Eve's brief residence in Eden. Eve's motive in eating the forbidden fruit, Murray suggested, was admirable; she hungered for knowledge. Even though Adam could see that his mate had grown no wiser, he nonetheless tasted the fruit himself. His motive? "A bare pusillanimous attachment to a woman! . . . Thus it should seem, that all the arts of the grand deceiver . . . were requisite to mislead our general mother, while the father of mankind forfeited his own, and relinquished the happines[s] of posterity, merely in compliance with the blandishments of a female." Thus could common assumptions about feminine moral weakness and masculine intellectual strength be turned cleverly on their heads.[46]

---

especially its last decades that brought "American acceptance of Milton's authority on a national scale" (Sensabaugh, *Milton in Early America* [Princeton, N.J., 1964], esp. 98, 110 [quotation]).

45. For the shift in religious focus from Fall to Redemption, see H. Richard Niebuhr, *The Kingdom of God in America* (New York, 1937), chaps. 3 and 4; and Ann Douglas, *The Feminization of American Culture* (New York, 1977), chap. 4. See also Fliegelman's brilliant analysis of "The Familial Politics of the Fortunate Fall," in Fliegelman, *Prodigals and Pilgrims,* chap. 3. For the remaking of the world into an all-male paradise in nineteenth-century literature, see Leslie A. Fiedler, *Love and Death in the American Novel* (New York, 1960); and Lawrence, *Studies in Classic American Literature.*

46. "The Nobility of Woman Kind," *Royal American Magazine,* March 1775, 100; "On the Equality of the Sexes," *Massachusetts Magazine,* April 1790, 223–225. See also "On Women," *Boston Weekly Magazine,* July 21, 1804, 153: "If our first parents were at all to be blamed, Adam was by far the most culpable."

Still, most writers who wished to revise popular evaluations of Eve did not take so assertively feminist a tack as to reinterpret the story of the Fall. For one reason, they might be refuted by traditional readings that kept a culpable sensuality, both feminine and masculine, at the center of the story.[47] Instead, those who were inclined to paint the first mother in more flattering hues tended to focus not so much upon her unhappy departure from Eden as upon her more pleasing qualities when she was still there. Here Americans took their cue from Milton, and, in the years just after the Revolution, his Eve "began to emerge as a pattern of womanly perfection."[48] Sometimes an author quoted Milton directly, as did Dr. John Gregory, an Edinburgh physician whose *A Father's Legacy to His Daughters* (1774) was popular in America: "Milton had my idea, when he says of Eve '*Grace was in all her steps, / Heaven in her eye, / In every gesture dignity and love.*'" Samuel Low, author of the play *The Politician Out-Witted,* must have assumed that his audience would recognize his source when he quoted the same lines, without attribution, to describe his heroine.[49]

Often Milton's influence was indirect but unmistakable; his "fair Angelic *Eve,*" created "for softness . . . and sweet attractive Grace," served as a model for the ideal woman who would display "softness and delicacy of manners, unaffecting beauty, unassuming worth, modesty happily blended with good-humour." The Miltonic influence is also clear in a poem entitled "Female Character," published in 1792:

Queen of every gentle passion,
Tender sympathy and love;
Perfect work of heav'nly fashion,
Miniature of charms above.
Love and grace in rich profusion,
Soft'ning man's ferocious soul;
All creation's fair conclusion,
Form'd to beautify the whole.

47. For example, "The Passenger—No. XXXI," *Boston Weekly Magazine,* Sept. 15, 1804, 185; and "On the Forbidden Fruit," *Massachusetts Magazine,* October 1791, 617–618.

48. Sensabaugh, *Milton,* 115.

49. [John] Gregory, *A Father's Legacy to His Daughters,* new ed. (London, 1774), 46, also quoted variously without attribution in "A Father's Advice to His Daughters," *Christian's, Scholar's, and Farmer's Magazine,* June–July 1789, 191 (quotation); and [Samuel Lowe], *The Politician Out-Witted . . .* (New York, 1789), in Montrose J. Moses, ed., *Representative Plays by American Dramatists . . . ,* [I], *1765–1819* (New York, 1918), 372.

Woman is the last of God's works, created, not, as the pre-Miltonic tradition had it, to bring about man's fall, but rather to remind him, after that event, of the paradise they had once shared and hoped still to regain.[50]

Jay Fliegelman has noted that Milton's description of Eve played an important role in "the secularization and feminization of 'grace'" in the eighteenth century, as the word took on an aesthetic meaning.[51] By the same token, woman, "Heav'ns last best gift," promised salvation; she, like Christ, pointed the way toward redemption. Yet it is redemption with a difference, for when sacred history is rewritten in such a way—as American popular writers would have it—that woman is gracious and man has not yet sinned, then we can imagine the time before the Fall when the world was Paradise and our first parents:

> In naked Majestie seemd Lords of all,
> And worthie seemd, for in thir looks Divine
> The image of thir glorious Maker shone . . .

It was to this image of prelapsarian godliness that Americans, in the era just after the American Revolution, responded.[52]

The Republican Wife, then, was Eve, and republican marriage represented Paradise, a veritable "heaven on earth." Taking their model from Milton's hymn to wedded love in Book IV of *Paradise Lost,* American publications described marriage in unabashedly Edenic terms. "The house of the married man is his paradise. . . . In the existence of a married man there is no termination[;] when death overtakes him he is only translated from one heaven to another."[53] Marriage is "the highest state of human felicity, and resembles that of the beneficent beings above." For this reason, the choice of a marriage partner was so important. A correspondent to the *Christian's,*

50. *Paradise Lost,* bk. 5, line 74, bk. 4, line 298; "On Masculine Manners in the Fair Sex," *Boston Weekly Magazine,* May 5, 1804, 109; "Female Character," *New-York Magazine,* May 1792, 315; Diane Kelsey McColley, *Milton's Eve* (Urbana, Ill., 1983).

51. Fliegelman, *Prodigals and Pilgrims,* 130. See also "On the Difference between Grace and Beauty; An Allegory," *Royal American Magazine,* February 1775, 43–45.

52. *Paradise Lost,* bk. 5, line 19, bk. 4, lines 290–293.

53. "On Matrimonial Felicity," *Gentleman and Lady's Town and Country Magazine,* September 1784, 194; "The Felicity of Matrimony," *Gentlemen and Ladies Town and Country Magazine,* August 1789, 375–376, reprinted in "Sketch of a Married Man," *New-York Magazine,* September 1797, 474. For direct references to Milton, see "On Love," *Lady's Magazine; and Repository of Entertaining Knowledge,* June 1792, 34–35; and Sensabaugh, *Milton,* notes on 42, 111–113, 195–200.

Scholar's, and Farmer's Magazine put it simply: "The Choice of a Wife" was one "on which not only [mankind's] present welfare, but even their everlasting felicity may depend."[54]

The Edenic vision of marriage, then, served to bridge the anti-patriarchalism of the eighteenth century and the domesticity of the nineteenth. If the patriarchal model of familial relationships was suited to a hierarchically organized society, and, if, as Nancy F. Cott has suggested, domesticity went hand in hand with mid-nineteenth-century democratic liberalism, the Edenic vision fit just as nicely with the canons of republicanism.[55] Like republicanism itself, Edenic republican marriage presented itself as egalitarian. Republican characterizations of marriage echoed with the words *equal, mutual,* and *reciprocal,* and marriage was described as a friendship between equals. An essay "Addressed to the Ladies," for example, urged "every young married woman to seek the friend of her heart in the husband of her affection. There, and there only, is that true equality, both of rank and fortune, strengthened by mutual interests, and cemented by mutual pledges, to be found. . . . There, and there only, will she be sure to meet with reciprocal confidence, unfeigned attachment, and tender solicitude, to sooth her every care." No word better summarizes republican notions of marriage than *friendship.* "Marriage is, or should be, the most perfect state of friendship. Mutual interest produces mutual assistance." Another writer defined the good marriage in almost the same words as "the highest instance of human friendship." "Love" was "nothing more than friendship raised to its highest pitch."[56]

Marriage, quite simply, was friendship exalted. Its pleasures derived from "mutual return of *conjugal love.* . . . When two minds are . . . engaged by the ties of reciprocal sincerity, each alternately receives and communicates

54. "Letter from Eliza," *Pennsylvania Magazine* . . . (Philadelphia), April 1776, 168, 169; "The Choice of a Wife," *Christian's, Scholar's, and Farmer's Magazine,* August–September 1790, 351–353. See similarly "On Matrimonal Felicity," *Gentleman and Lady's Town and Country Magazine,* September 1784, 193–194.

55. Nancy F. Cott, *The Bonds of Womanhood: "Woman's Sphere" in New England, 1780–1835* (New Haven, Conn., 1977), 65.

56. "On Friendship," *Christian's, Scholar's, and Farmer's Magazine,* June–July 1790, 225–226; "Praise of Marriage," *Boston Weekly Magazine,* Apr. 7, 1804, 93; "On Marriage," *Baltimore General Magazine, and Impartial Review,* July 1798, 42; "Reflections on Marriage Unions," *New-York Magazine,* October 1790, 561. See also "The Gossip—No. XXXII," *Boston Weekly Magazine,* July 9, 1803, 149; "Conjugal Love," *Massachusetts Magazine,* February 1792, 102, and "Philo; No. XIV," November 1790, 664: "Friendship is the reciprocal attachment of two persons of the same sex. *Love* of two persons of different sexes."

a transport that is inconceivable to all, but those that are in this situation." Marriage was intended, another writer concluded, "to be the basis and the cement of those numberless tender sympathies, mutual endearments and interchanges of love between the married parties themselves, which make up not the morality only, but even the chief happiness of conjugal life." Marriage was moral because it fused "virtuous love and friendship; the one supplying it with a constant rapture, and the other regulating it by the rules of reason." True marriage was quite unlike "those unnatural and disproportionable matches that are daily made upon worldly views, where interest, or lust are the only motives." True marriage was proportionate; put another way, it was symmetrical. The mutuality and reciprocity that republicans so prized were inconceivable in an asymmetrical union—the "slavery" of so-called barbaric cultures, in which women were thoroughly subordinated to men.[57]

That republican marriage was symmetrical does not mean that it was fully egalitarian; rather, men and women were opposite sides of the same coin or, as a popular fable had it, two halves of a being that had once been sundered. Neither could be whole until it found its other half.[58] Nor could the halves

57. "Conjugal Love," *Massachusetts Magazine,* February 1792, 102 ("mutual," "virtuous," "those unnatural"); "On the Pleasures Arising from an Union between the Sexes," *Columbian Magazine: or, Monthly Miscellany* [Philadelphia], January 1787, 244 ("basis"); "The Influence of the Female Sex on the Enjoyments of Social Life," *Universal Asylum, and Columbian Magazine,* March 1790, 153–154 ("slavery," 153). For the assertion that the subordination or "slavery" of women was characteristic of barbaric cultures, see, for example, "On the Treatment of the Fair Sex," *Lady's Magazine and Musical Repository,* April 1801, 214–215; "An Occasional Letter on the Female Sex," *Pennsylvania Magazine,* August 1775, 362–364; "Domestic Life of the Arabs," *Baltimore General Magazine, and Impartial Review,* July 1798, 54–57; and "The Influence of the Female Sex on the Enjoyments of Social Life," *Universal Asylum, and Columbian Magazine,* March 1790, 153–154: "Matrimony, among savages, having no object but propagation and slavery, is a very humbling state for the female sex" (153). On the other hand, the position of women in societies characterized by commerce, large cities, and an advanced, complex civilization was not necessarily more enviable. See, for example, "Marriage Ceremonies of Different Countries Compared," *Columbian Magazine,* June 1787, 491, 497: "The trade of fortune-hunting . . . seem[s] to be confined to the old crowded cities, while the tedious preliminaries of European contracts of fortunes, etc. are scarcely understood by the inhabitants of America" (497). Americans saw their society—and its women—poised somewhere between barbarity and excessive economic and cultural development with its attendant corruptions. See McCoy, *Elusive Republic,* chap. 1. See also "Education," *American Magazine,* December 1787, 22–26. To be sure, the cyclical view of the rise and fall of civilizations, which McCoy illuminates, and the linear Christian eschatology are inconsistent; nonetheless, both sorts of cultural analysis appeared side by side in the era's magazines. Perhaps the pessimistic cyclical paradigm only made the more hopeful Christian one more appealing.

58. "On Marriage," *Baltimore General Magazine, and Impartial Review,* July 1798, 43.

be fully moral when separate, for Eve's love and Adam's reason were equally necessary to the prelapsarian vision. As heirs to the Enlightenment, American republicans sought the happy medium between—or, more precisely, a fusion of—passion and intellect, head and heart. Eighteenth-century moral philosophy, as it was popularized in American magazines, taught both that passion must be regulated by reason and that "no real felicity can exist independent of susceptibility and affection, and the heart of him who is cold to the soothing voice of friendship, dead to the melting strains of love, and senseless to the plaintive pleadings of distress, is a mansion only calculated for demoniac spirits, or a cheerless dwelling for disgust and spleen." Adam and Eve, reason and love, are each indispensable, and the symmetrical marriage brings them together.[59]

By checking passion and socializing reason, the conjugal union made mankind truly virtuous; marriage was the model for society. The single life, according to John Witherspoon, writing as "Epaminondas" in the *Pennsylvania Magazine* on the eve of the Revolution, "narrows the mind, and closes the heart." He asserted unequivocally the "absolute necessity of marriage for the service of the state." The pure love of marriage formed the basis for "social virtue," for, "while other passions concentrate man in himself, love makes him live in another, subdues selfishness, and reveals to him the pleasure of ministring to the object of his love." In marriage, "the lover becomes a husband, a parent, a citizen." The "marriage institution," then, "is the first to produce moral order," for "marriage has ever been considered by every wise state as the sinew of its strength and the foundation of its true greatness." Marriage formed the basis of all other relationships, both in the family, because it led to parenthood, and in the society, because it schooled men in the disinterested benevolence that was supposed by republican ideologues to constitute virtue.[60] In sum, as an essayist in the *Key* put it, "Nothing is so

59. "On the Duties Which We Owe to Society," *Lady's Magazine and Musical Repository*, January 1801, 16 (quotation). For calls for passion to be governed by reason, see, for example, "God Gave Us Passions, and at the Same Time Gave Us Reason," *Boston Weekly Magazine*, Sept. 24, 1803, 193; and "On the Government of the Passions," *Massachusetts Magazine*, March 1789, 179–180. See also Wills, *Inventing America*.

60. "Reflections on Marriage," *Pennsylvania Magazine*, September 1775, 409, 411, 413, later published as "Letters on Marriage," in *The Works of the Rev. John Witherspoon . . .*, 2d ed., 4 vols. (Philadelphia, 1802), IV, 161–183; "On Love," *New-York Magazine*, June 1791, 311; "A Second Vindication of the Rights of Woman," *Ladies' Monitor*, Aug. 15, 1801, 12; "The Reflector; No. I," *Lady's Monitor*, Nov. 7, 1801, 92. See also "On Matrimonal Felicity," *Gentleman and Lady's Town and Country Magazine*, September 1784, 193–194; "On Love," *Lady's Magazine; and Repository of Entertaining Knowledge*, June 1792, 34–37; "Fashionable

honorable as MARRIAGE nothing so comfortable both to the body and the mind. . . . It is marriage alone that knits and binds all the sinews of society together, and makes the life of man honorable to himself, useful to others, and grateful to the God of nature. . . . Is there any thing on earth nearer heaven?" Lest that promise of heaven on earth be insufficient to persuade his readers, the writer continued: "*That* MAN *who resolves to live without* WOMAN, *or that* WOMAN *who resolves to live without* MAN, *are [sic]* ENEMIES TO THE COMMUNITY *in which they dwell,* INJURIOUS TO THEMSELVES, DESTRUCTIVE TO THE WORLD, APOSTATES TO NATURE, *and* REBELS AGAINST HEAVEN AND EARTH." The man or woman who proposed to live alone, then, was heretic and traitor both.[61]

Like republicanism, the doctrine of symmetrical marriage subordinated individual interest to the greater good of the whole. Accordingly, marriages based upon interest were to be loathed; true marriage was the model for disinterested benevolence. Unlike the canon of domesticity, in which "women's self-renunciation was called upon to remedy men's self-alienation," idealized republican marriage required men and women both to display virtue.[62] Male and female were two halves of one whole whose name was concord; the ideal marriage was a scene of prelapsarian harmony. As the author of "On the Necesity of Domestic Concord" noted, "peace" was more important even than "plenty." In order for "harmony" and "concord" to prevail, husband and wife were to be of one mind; they could not disagree.[63] To prevent a conflict-filled marriage, one must choose one's mate wisely; probably no consideration was more important than "a similarity of sentiments and disposition," for where there is "an union of souls, and a consistent harmony of mental

Miscellany," *Baltimore Weekly Magazine,* July 12, 1800, 91–92; and "On Marriage," *Baltimore General Magazine, and Impartial Review,* July 1798, 41–45.

61. "From the Genius of Liberty," *Key* (Fredericktown, Md.), Apr. 14, 1798, 105-106. Numerous articles attacked bachelors while pitying spinsters. See, for example, "Geographical Description of Bachelor's Island," *Universal Asylum, and Columbian Magazine,* April 1790, 213–214; and "The Bachelor's Will," *Massachusetts Magazine,* July 1791, 410–411.

62. Cott, *Bonds of Womanhood,* 71. The model of self-denying femininity was the mother; the idealization of motherhood, hence, was more characteristic of nineteenth-century domesticity than of late-eighteenth-century republicanism.

63. "On the Necesity of Domestic Concord," *Key,* Apr. 7, 1798, 98; "Remarks on Family Government," *Massachusetts Magazine,* June 1791, [3]52–353; "Fashionable Miscellany," *Baltimore Weekly Magazine,* July 12, 1800, 92, "The Germe of Fancy; No. V: A Panegyric on the Delights of Matrimony," October 1793, 610–612. See also "From a Mother to Her Daughter, Just on the Point of Marriage," *Boston Weekly Magazine,* May 5, 1804, 109–110; and "Conduct of St. Augustin's Mother, Monica," *Christian's, Scholar's, and Farmer's Magazine,* October–November 1790, 429–430.

ideas . . . discord will keep at an awful distance, and an universal sympathy, productive of an ineffable bliss, will ever attend them. . . . O happiness divine! source of concordant minds!" An essayist in *New York Magazine* expressed the same idea more matter-of-factly: "There cannot be too near an equality, too exact a harmony, betwixt a married couple." Indeed, "the idea of power on either side, should be totally banished."[64]

Conjugal affection, then, was not coercive. Nor did it admit of any "selfish or sensual all[o]y." Marriage was the Republic in miniature; it was chaste, disinterested, and free from the exercise of arbitrary power. And, like republican citizens, husband and wife were most likely to find happiness when, as Witherspoon suggested, they shared the same rank, the same education, and the same habits of life.[65]

It is tempting to suppose that the ideology of the republican marriage was simply the rhetorical manifestation of the newly affectionate conjugal union and that both rhetoric and reality represented positive and progressive change.[66] Yet we must remember that republicanism, like Janus, looked to the past as well as to the future; it focused more upon the welfare of the society than the well-being of the individual. Thus it had an implicitly anti-individualistic dimension, one that was exposed whenever conflict arose.[67] We can see that tendency in the ideal of marital concord, which could be—and was—used to legitimate both coverture and the exclusion of women from direct participation in politics. Indeed, the rhetoric of harmony seems

64. "A Short Sermon on Marriage," *Baltimore Weekly Magazine,* Apr. 8, 1801, 249, printed earlier in *Lady's Magazine; and Repository of Entertaining Knowledge,* August 1792, 108–110; and "On Marriage," *New-York Magazine,* December 1796, 656–657.

65. "The Ladies Friend; No. II: On Conjugal Affection," *Lady's Magazine; and Repository of Entertaining Knowledge,* September 1792, 176: "I consider a parity of understanding and temper to be as necessary towards forming an happy marriage, as an equality of years, rank, and fortune." See also "Letters," in *Works of the Rev. John Witherspoon,* IV, 169.

66. See, for example, Smith, *Inside the Great House,* chap. 4; Trumbach, *Rise of the Egalitarian Family,* chap. 2; Stone, *Family, Sex, and Marriage,* chap. 8; Smith, "Parental Power and Marriage Patterns," *Journal of Marriage and Family,* XXXV (1973), 419–428; and Ellen K. Rothman, *Hands and Hearts: A History of Courtship in America* (New York, 1984), chap. 1. Of course, heightened expectations of marriage might have worked against the end they sought to secure; see Lewis, *Pursuit of Happiness,* 187–204; and Cott, *Bonds of Womanhood,* 76–83.

67. Wood, *Creation of the American Republic,* esp. 70–75. Consider also J. G. A. Pocock's famous description of the American Revolution as "the last great act of the Renaissance" (Pocock, "Review: Virtue and Commerce in the Eighteenth Century," *Journal of Interdisciplinary History,* III [1972], 120).

almost a gloss upon the doctrine of marital unity—the English common law fiction that in marriage the husband and wife are one, and the husband is the one.[68] It has puzzled some historians that American Revolutionaries did not jettison coverture along with other pieces of undemocratic British baggage such as primogeniture and entail. Yet republican theorists prized harmony above all else; they created the ideal of the affectionate marriage not so much to liberate the individual as to assure concord in the family, the building block of society.[69]

Republicanism aimed to avoid conflict. Invoking the same principle that predicted that small republics would be the most harmonious, those who applied the theory to the family suggested that husband and wife should share similar dispositions, beliefs, and interests, that they should be as one. Even so, conflict might arise, and the recommendations republicans made to restore harmony in such unfortunate cases expose the limitations of the republican model for family and polity alike.[70]

The ideal, of course, was equality; no good republican would have disagreed with the egalitarian sentiments expressed by the woman who styled herself "A Matrimonial Republican." "The obedience between man and wife," she wrote, "is, or ought to be mutual." The catch was in the "ought to be," for here the weaknesses in the republican ideal show through. What, for example, was a wife with an errant husband to do? Although it was certainly true that "man has no more right to sin with impunity than woman," husbands seemed to fall more often, and it became a wife's duty to lure her mate back to rectitude with "the charm of good humour, and uncomplaining sweetness." In other words, only redoubled feminine virtue could reclaim a husband from masculine vice. "Dispute not with him, be the occasion what it will," advised one writer.[71] Better to let errors go unremarked, warned an-

68. For coverture, see Norma Basch, *In the Eyes of the Law: Women, Marriage, and Property in Nineteenth-Century New York* (Ithaca, N.Y., 1982), chaps. 1 and 2; and Basch, "Equity vs. Equality: Emerging Concepts of Women's Political Status in the Age of Jackson," *Journal of the Early Republic,* III (1983), 297–318. For the justification for excluding women from politics, see, for example, "Remarks on Female Politicians," *Lady's Monitor,* May 29, 1802, 324–325.

69. For example, Kerber, *Women of the Republic,* 119–121, 135–136.

70. Wood, *Creation of the American Republic,* 58, 356. See also "Reflections on Marriage Unions," *New-York Magazine,* October 1790, 561–562.

71. "On Matrimonial Obedience," *Lady's Magazine; and Repository of Entertaining Knowledge,* July 1792, 66, 67; "The Gossip—No. XV," *Boston Weekly Magazine,* Feb. 5, 1803, 61; "Rules and Maxims for Promoting Matrimonal Happiness," *Gentleman and Lady's Town and Country Magazine,* May 1784, 28. Although occasional articles and stories describe the failings of bad wives, most focus on deficient husbands. For a description of a bad wife, see

other, than to "strike . . . too often upon the unharmonious string." "The best way of a married woman to carry her points often, is to yield sometimes." Harmony, then, took precedence over equality; in the interest of concord, a woman would sometimes have to forbear.[72]

But why not the husband? In a truly reciprocal marriage, would not the two parties compromise? Almost all essayists who addressed the issue of conflict in marriage argued that it was the wife who had to bend. The responsibility for anchoring marriage fell disproportionately to women because they were, supposedly, more compliant than men, or, at least, they would find it "necessary, for political purposes, to consider man as the superior in authority." The symmetrical marriage thus gave way, under very little pressure, to a disproportionate one in which the wife, in order to maintain domestic tranquility, was expected to defer.[73]

"The Extravagant Wife: An American Tale," *Massachusetts Magazine,* July 1791, 425–426. For bad husbands, see "The Matron," *Gentlemen and Ladies' Town and Country Magazine,* December 1789, 581–582; "Genuine Letter from an Injured Wife to Her Husband," *Christian's, Scholar's, and Farmer's Magazine,* June–July 1789, 242–243; "The History of Adrastus and Camilla," *Lady's Monitor,* Mar. 20, 1802, 241; "A Female Character," *Lady's Magazine; and Repository of Entertaining Knowledge,* September 1792, 182; "Conjugal Prudence," *New-York Magazine,* March 1791, 127–128; and "Harriot; or, The Domestick Reconciliation," *Massachusetts Magazine,* January 1789, 3–7.

72. "Maternal Lesson: Advice to Married Ladies," *Massachusetts Magazine,* June 1793, 331–332; "A Letter to a Very Good Natured Lady Married to a Very Ill Natured Man," *Christian's, Scholar's, and Farmer's Magazine,* August–September 1789, 319–320.

73. "An Address to the Ladies," *American Magazine,* March 1788, 245 (quotation); "Woman; An Apologue," *Columbian Phenix, or Boston Review,* July 1800, 438–439. See also "Letter to a Very Good Natured Lady," *Christian's, Scholar's, and Farmer's Magazine,* August–September 1789, 319–320; "On the Happy Influence Arising from Female Society," *Massachusetts Magazine,* July 1795, 220–223; and "Female Biography," *Baltimore Weekly Magazine,* Aug. 9, 1800, 125. There was no consensus on whether those differences between men and women that led to the expectation that women would defer to male authority were innate or merely convenient. Some writers were themselves uncertain, as was "The Gentleman at Large," who concluded that women were morally equal to men; that their minds had a "nice and delicate texture," which proved that "the situation for which Heaven designed them in this world, is of a nature the most benevolent and engaging," while "the more rugged and invidious offices of life were appropriated to man, as being better suited to his firm and sturdy disposition"; and that women should "voluntarily" adopt certain responsibilities in the home ("The Gentleman at Large; No. III," *Columbian Phenix, or Boston Review,* May 1800, 266–269). Most writers, however, seem to have adopted a symmetrical, different-but-equal model of gender, which could manifest itself—as early as 1788—as a fully articulated version of "separate spheres." (See "An Address to the Ladies," *American Magazine,* March 1788, 241–246; "Rights of Woman," *Boston Weekly Magazine,* Oct. 30, 1802, 2, "Female Seminary; Mrs. Rowson's Academy, Newton; Concluding Address," Oct. 29, 1803, 2–3; and "Gentleman at Large," *Columbian Phenix, or Boston Review,* May 1800, 266–269.) But because these distinctions were grounded in a religio-cultural metaphor of the first parents,

Deference, of course, was the solution republicans offered for the problem of conflict in the polity; persons deficient in judgment or inferior in status, they believed, should simply yield to those of superior wisdom. Yet, although, as Wood has shown, Federalists offered the Constitution as a "republican remedy" for the republican vice of disharmony, no similar rearrangement was forthcoming for the family. Instead, as Americans displayed increasing acceptance of conflict in the market and the polity, they became less willing to tolerate it at home.[74]

The insistence upon feminine deference reveals fears about conflict in the society and nation, and not merely concern about unhappy marriages. Very few of the essays that enjoined women to complaisance mentioned those character flaws we might expect women to have confronted most frequently in their mates: irritability, distasteful habits, slovenliness, insensitivity, an inability to earn an adequate income, or even the arbitrary exercise of power. Rather, the single failing that drew the most censure—and also the most extravagant claims for the power of female influence—was infidelity. Stories with titles like "The Way to Reclaim Him; A Moral Tale" purported to show how supreme feminine virtue could recall an errant husband to the path of rectitude. In that story, as in such another as "Conjugal Prudence," the wronged wife won back her wayward husband by embracing, literally, his mistress and illegitimate offspring and by insisting upon an education for the children and an annuity (and, implicitly, banishment) for the mistress. Such acts of generosity never failed. The husband in the former story clasped his wife to his breast, "murmured out . . . 'Excellent woman! matchless wife!'" and promised "to remain immutably attached to her alone to the last moment of his existence." Similarly, the husband in the latter exclaimed, "'Thou heavenly woman! . . . is it *thus* thou upbraidest me for my infidelity to the most amiable woman that ever existed! O, my love, forgive!—but that's impossible! I am, I will be only yours.'"[75]

---

rather than in science, they were quite flexible, could be put to any number of uses, and were often inconsistent. For an analysis of the "paradoxes and contradictions" in late-eighteenth-century depictions of femininity, see Mary Poovey, *The Proper Lady and the Woman Writer: Ideology as Style in the Works of Mary Wollstonecraft, Mary Shelley, and Jane Austen* (Chicago, 1984), chap. 1 (quotation, 15).

74. Wood, *Creation of the American Republic,* chap. 11. Consider the premise of Carl N. Degler, *At Odds: Women and the Family in America from the Revolution to the Present* (New York, 1980); Cott, *Bonds of Womanhood,* 98–99; and Alexis de Tocqueville's classic analysis of the origins of individualism in *Democracy in America,* ed. Phillips Bradley, II (New York, 1980), 98–99.

75. "The Way to Reclaim Him; A Moral Tale," *Gentleman and Lady's Magazine, Etc.*

The authors of such stories seem to be exploring the farthest reaches of self-abasing virtue; they imagine the most extreme instances of domestic cruelty a wife might endure in order to see whether the depths of depravity may be exceeded by the heights of virtue. When the answer is yes, the resolution takes the form of a conversion, with the husband confessing his sins and the wife playing the part, in the words of another contrite fictional husband, of "my guardian angel sent by heaven to prevent my ruin."[76] Stripped of her original culpability, Eve is easily transformed into Christ's surrogate, able to work a sinner's "reformation." "Trust me," the wronged wife says. "I assure you, that search the habitable globe, you will meet with no woman more inclined to serve, love, obey, and oblige you, than your Emilia." Like Christ, the wife has to suffer, and like him, she redeems.[77]

It was, however, equally possible for women to suffer yet not redeem. That was the sad fate of the heroine of Susanna Rowson's *Sarah; or, The Exemplary Wife,* a novel in which "Virtue is represented, in all her native simplicity and beauty; and Vice . . . is exhibited in her own proper ugliness and deformity." Although "the story is far from being improbable," it is really a parable, with virtue pitted against vice.[78] Virtue is represented by Sarah, a lovely young woman who is forced by mercenary relatives to wed a reprobate, somewhat as if Clarissa had been made, against her will, to marry Lovelace. Although her husband keeps a mistress, even bringing her into the home he shares with his wife, and although he despises Sarah for her goodness, she never wavers in her patience, charity, or virtue. When her husband bankrupts himself and even her clothing is claimed by his creditors, she enters into service to support him and herself. And when she discovers his illegitimate child, "said she calmly . . . 'if the child owes its being to you, give orders that it be brought home, and I will see it is properly taken

(Boston), November 1784, 299–302; "Conjugal Prudence," *New-York Magazine,* March 1791, 127–128.

76. "Conjugal Affection," *Gentlemen and Ladies Town and Country Magazine,* February 1789, 4. The repentant husband wished "every man bless'd with a wife like thee to break his fall whenever he deviated from virtue's paths."

77. "Genuine Letter from an Injured Wife to Her Husband," *Christian's, Scholar's, and Farmer's Magazine,* June–July 1789, 242–243. See also "Harriot; or, The Domestick Reconciliation," *Massachusetts Magazine,* January 1789, 3–7; "A Female Character," *Lady's Magazine; and Repository of Entertaining Knowledge,* September 1792, 182; "Emilia," *New-York Magazine,* October 1793, 592–595; and "History of Adrastus and Camilla," *Lady's Monitor,* Mar. 20, 1802, 241.

78. The novel was serialized in 1804 as "Sincerity, a Novel: In a Series of Letters; By a Lady of Massachusetts," as announced in *Boston Weekly Magazine,* June 16, 1804, 136, but published as Susanna Rowson, *Sarah; or, The Exemplary Wife* (Boston, 1813).

care of; but let me entreat you not to add to the offence already committed against religion and morality, the unpardonable one of leaving your offspring to perish.' " Whereupon the errant husband explodes, " 'D——n—t——n. . . . Of all the plagues a man can have, a moralizing, sentimental, canting, hypocritical wife, is the worst.' " After years of such trials, Sarah dies, secure in her conviction that "even in thought she had never dishonoured her husband." Thereupon he marries his mistress.[79] Here there is no conversion; virtue will not prevail. Nevertheless, "who of common reflection but would prefer the death of Sarah, resigned as she was, and upheld by faith and hope, to all the splendors, wealth and honors that were ever heaped upon the heroine in the last pages of a novel" in which a heroine met only an earthly reward? To put it another way, Susanna Rowson expressed doubt about whether feminine virtue could prevail in a corrupt world.[80]

The doctrine of the Republican Wife suggested that a good wife could influence a susceptible man; *Sarah* raised the question whether she could reclaim, as well, a man who was confirmed in viciousness. The answer was that she could not. Here was a fundamental dilemma for the new nation: How could virtue be exacted from the vicious? Republican ideology offered a number of plausible ways to encourage the good to be more so; chief among them were education, benevolent reform, and female influence. But it faced an insurmountable obstacle when it confronted men who were beyond all hope of reformation. The problem was infidelity, not merely the faithlessness of a spouse but apostasy itself—the unpardonable sin; for it, republicanism had no cure.[81]

Republican advocacy of virtue was powerless before persons who had no conscience. How bedeviling this problem was can be seen when we examine the conventional seduction story. Tales such as *Charlotte Temple* and *The Coquette* may be considered as not very subtle warnings to young women

79. "Sincerity—A Novel: In a Series of Original Letters," *Boston Weekly Magazine,* May 19, 1804, 120, "Conclusion of Sincerity—A Novel: In a Series of Original Letters," June 30, 1804, 144.

80. Rowson, *Sarah,* iii.

81. On education, see Kerber, *Women of the Republic,* chap. 7; Norton, *Liberty's Daughters,* chap. 9; and Ann D. Gordon, "The Young Ladies Academy of Philadelphia," in Carol Ruth Berkin and Mary Beth Norton, [eds.], *Women of America: A History* (Boston, 1979), 68–91. For benevolent activities, see Suzanne Lebsock, *The Free Women of Petersburg: Status and Culture in a Southern Town, 1784–1860* (New York, 1984), chap. 7. For examples of women's benevolent organizations, see Fred J. Hood, *Reformed America: The Middle and Southern States, 1783–1837* (University, Ala., 1980), 151, 153, 167; and "Religious," *Boston Weekly Magazine,* Dec. 15, 1804, 29.

without dowries that their value lay in their virginity; if they would be sought after on the marriage market, they must keep that commodity intact. The sentimental tale of seduction has therefore been seen as an instrument of bourgeois respectability and middle-class conformity.[82] Such a view is not untrue, for surely no early-nineteenth-century girl enhanced her marriage prospects by squandering her virginity. Chastity *was* esteemed, but for republican as much as bourgeois reasons. Consider "Reflections on Chastity, or Female Honour," a brief definition printed in at least three magazines before 1800: "What Bravery is in man, Chastity is in woman. This virtue, by making them triumph over every wicked attempt to dishonour them, bestows on them, as the first reward of victory, an universal esteem."[83] Once again, we see the symmetrical expectations for men and women; in this case, chastity is the feminine version of the absolute standard of courage expected of Revolutionary War soldiers. For patriots like the Reverend Robert Cooper, cowardice was sin; he warned in 1775 that, "if . . . you would escape deep guilt before God, and lasting contempt among men, forward you must go. . . . You have, in a word, no alternative, but either to venture your lives bravely, or attempt to save them ignominiously; to run the hazard of dying like heroes, or be certain of living like cowards." Bravery, like chastity, was an absolute; it allowed not the slightest deviation nor tolerated any taint.[84]

Brave men and chaste women were expected to "triumph over every wicked attempt to dishonour them." What Charles Royster has said of this Revolutionary attachment to exacting standards of bravery applies to chastity as well: it reflected an evangelical tendency to establish dichotomies between good and evil, salvation and grace, God and Satan. To waver in one's courage was to fall from grace; similarly, to surrender one's chastity was to sin. Americans of the Revolutionary era held out an impossible standard of purity for women and men both. Yet the Continental army, as Royster has shown, would come to a more workable notion of human capability, as would the political theorists who framed the Constitution. Standards of

82. See Christopher Hill, "Clarissa Harlowe and Her Times," *Essays in Criticism*, V (1955), 330–331; Wendy Martin, "Profile: Susanna Rowson, Early American Novelist," *Women's Studies*, II (1974), 6–7; and Ian Watt, *The Rise of the Novel: Studies in Defoe, Richardson, and Fielding* (Berkeley, Calif., 1957). See also Cott, "Passionlessness," *Signs*, IV (1978), 219–236.

83. "Reflections on Chastity, or Female Honour," *Royal American Magazine*, February 1775, 61; "Reflections on Chastity, or Female Honour," *Massachusetts Magazine*, October 1791, 629–630; "Chastity, or Female Honour," *Key*, Feb. 17, 1798, 44.

84. Robert Cooper, *Courage in a Good Cause; or, The Lawful and Courageous Use of the Sword* . . . (Lancaster, Pa., 1775), 24–25, quoted in Royster, *Revolutionary People*, 225.

female virtue, however, fully as unrealistic as the expectation that no soldier would ever feel fear or no citizen advance his own interest, only became more rigid.[85]

In many ways, chastity was a fit emblem for republicanism, which, when infused with evangelical ardor, could demand absolute and undeviating virtue from its citizens. Hence we must read the era's popular literature of seduction not merely as cautionary tales addressed to young women but also as political tracts in which men and women explored the possibilities for virtue in a corrupt world. Surely it is significant that the most popular novel of the early national period—indeed, the most popular American novel of all until the publication of *Uncle Tom's Cabin*—was *Charlotte Temple,* Susanna Rowson's classic tale of seduction and abandonment.[86] In this novel, it takes not one but two designing men to seduce Charlotte from the path of virtue. The work is begun by Montraville, a Lovelace type who is drawn to the innocent young woman he ensnares but is unwilling to make a disadvantageous match; it is completed by his "friend" Belcour, whose only apparent motivation is to destroy both Charlotte and her faithless lover. Under such an assault, Charlotte's innocence stands not a chance.[87]

Like Charlotte and her forerunner Clarissa Harlowe, the heroines of the sentimental tales of seduction are all sympathetic. Eliza Wharton, *The Coquette,* seemed "to possess both the virtues and the graces"; her weaknesses were "an air of gaiety in her appearance and deportment" and a fatal naïveté. The flaws ascribed to the unfortunate heroines were traits that republicans

85. Royster, *Revolutionary People,* esp. 27–31, 47–49, 224–230. For other discussions of chastity, see "On the Loss of Chastity," *New-York Magazine,* April 1797, 209–210; "The Gossip—No. XXV," *Boston Weekly Magazine,* May 7, 1803, 113, "On Female Chastity," Nov. 24, 1804, 18; and "An Address to the Ladies," *American Magazine,* March 1788, 241–246: "Chastity really exists in the mind; and when this fountain is pure, the words and actions that flow from it will be chaste and delicate" (242). The best discussion of the origins of the ideal of chastity is Cott, "Passionlessness," *Signs,* IV (1978), 219–236. There is some debate about how fully American women abided by this ideal. (See, for example, Carl N. Degler, "What Ought to Be and What Was: Women's Sexuality in the Nineteenth Century," *American Historical Review,* LXXIX [1974], 1467–1490; and Peter Gay, *The Bourgeois Experience: Victoria to Freud,* I, *Education of the Senses* [New York, 1984].) But there is no question about the pervasiveness of the ideology.

86. [Susanna Haswell] Rowson, *Charlotte: A Tale of Truth,* 2 vols. (Philadelphia, 1794). For the popularity of *Charlotte Temple,* see Francis W. Halsey's introduction to the 1905 New York edition; and Fliegelman, *Prodigals and Pilgrims,* 261–262.

87. As Fliegelman notes, Charlotte's parents—who are cast in the affectionate, post-patriarchal mold—might, in theory, have protected her, and, in falling, she broke their hearts; but paternalism, no more than patriarchalism, represented an acceptable option for post-Revolutionary Americans (Fliegelman, *Prodigals and Pilgrims,* 261–262).

usually valued: "a heart . . . formed of sensibility"; "unsuspecting innocence"; "innocent herself, she expected to find others so"; a mind "pure and unsullied"; "innocence and simplicity"; "amiable, ingenuous and sensible." Pure, innocent, without guile, such young women are nothing less than contemporary versions of Eve; they are endowed with her attributes and given her signs. The unfortunate Amelia, for example, is "one of the fairest blossoms in the garden of society," while Almira is "as beautiful as the daughters of Paradise, and gentle as the breezes of the spring; her mind was spotless, and her manners artless." Such innocence fell once from Paradise, and it was destined to fall again and again in countless tales of seduction in the early Republic.[88]

We have seen that feminine influence had its limits; no wife could expect to triumph over a thoroughly corrupted man on this side of the grave. Likewise, feminine innocence was at the mercy of masculine vice. No matter how many times the story of the Fall was reenacted, it came out the same way, as a correspondent to the *Gentlemen and Ladies' Town and Country Magazine* was well aware: "Most angelic and ever-admir'd blossoms of earthly eminence—how few are the instances of thy pure innocence ever reaching the summit of that bliss, uninjured, for which thy Maker intended it." Why? Because of "'the wicked designs of artful men; men more ravenous than the hungry lions, which go about seeking whom they may devour.'" Thus he cautioned "the fair daughters of Eve," but could his warning against the "seducers of . . . female excellence" have any more success than God's to Adam and Eve?[89]

88. Foster, *Coquette,* 62; "Copy of a Letter from Miss—— to M——," *Pennsylvania Magazine,* March 1775, 114; "Innocence Betrayed," *Lady's Miscellany; or, The Weekly Visitor* (New York), Aug. 24, 1811, 282; "Story of Philenia," *Massachusetts Magazine,* December 1791, 729–730; "Maltilda," *Key,* Apr. 14, 1798, 107; "The Fatal Effects of Seduction . . . ," *Gentlemen and Ladies Town and Country Magazine,* June 1789, 250; "Melancholy Tale of Seduction," *Massachusetts Magazine,* April 1795, 41; "The Sorrows of Amelia . . . ," *Baltimore Weekly Magazine,* July 5, 1800, 87; "Treachery and Infidelity Punished," *Gentlemen and Ladies Town and Country Magazine,* August 1789, 340. Other seduction tales include "The Gossip—No. LIV," *Boston Weekly Magazine,* Feb. 18, 1804, 65; "Advice, to the Unguarded Fair of This Metropolis," *Gentlemen and Ladies' Town and Country Magazine,* November 1789, 547–548; "The Passenger—No. XI," *Boston Weekly Magazine,* Dec. 10, 1803, 25, and "The Gossip—No. XXV," May 7, 1803, 113. For different readings of the literature of seduction, in particular *The Coquette,* see Cathy N. Davidson, *Revolution and the Word: The Rise of the Novel in America* (New York, 1986), esp. chap. 6; and Carroll Smith-Rosenberg, "Reinterpreting Antebellum Culture" (paper presented at the annual meeting of the Organization of American Historians, 1987).

89. "Advice, to the Unguarded Fair of This Metropolis," *Gentlemen and Ladies' Town and Country Magazine,* November 1789, 547–548.

How closely the seduction story was modeled upon that of the Fall is even more apparent in a tale entitled "Treachery and Infidelity Punished." Almira, the picture of innocence and "as beautiful as the daughters of Paradise," is seduced by one Lothario: "Oh! the base dissembler—had ingratiated himself too far in her affections: with fondness she listened to his deceitful tales, and with too great avidity devoured his insinuating discourse." Like her mother Eve, Almira fell, for, like Eve, she faced the most artful of deceivers, Satan himself, barely disguised.[90]

Without question, most of the fictional seducers are satanic; they are described in terms that leave no doubt about their true nature. Seducers are "those reptiles, those anamacules [*sic*], who really come under the class of non-descripts in creation." Even when the deceiver is not a snake, he is animal like, "a lordly brute [who] fixed his cruel fangs" on one who was "gay . . . lovely . . . innocent . . . happy." The seducer "stalks through the polite world, like a satiated lion, who waits only the impulse of hunger to sacrifice another victim." The "vile seducer" is indeed subhuman, for he lacks the ability to love. Instead, he perverts affection, preying upon the credulity of the innocent; "falsehood guides [his] tongu[e], whilst an infamous baseness, under a plausible appearance of love or friendship, conceals a heart destitute of every feeling." The seducer is the enemy of love, and, much like the Devil who envied Adam and Eve their innocent bliss, he plots its destruction.[91]

Hannah Foster modeled Eliza Wharton's seducer at least as much on Satan as on Lovelace. Jealous of the minister Eliza seems to prefer and angered by her virtuous friends, Sanford sets out to trap the lovely girl who has caught his eye. The responsibility is hers, he claims: "If she will play with a lion, let her beware of his paw, I say." *Charlotte Temple*'s Belcour is cut from the same cloth, as are Sidney, in "Charles and Amelia; or The Unfortunate Lovers," and Orlando, who contrives Narcissa's fall. In each case, most of the plot is devoted to the stratagems used to "snare" the heroine's virtue. Such men, surely, are beyond the compass of normal experience. Each is attracted only to the most singularly virtuous of girls and is not satisfied until he has succeeded in ruining her. Judith Sargent Murray wrote that it was hard to "conceive of turpitude so *enormous,* as that which must excite

90. "Treachery and Infidelity Punished," ibid., August 1789, 340–341.

91. "Gossip—No. XXXV," *Boston Weekly Magazine,* July 30, 1803, 161, "The Seducer," May 18, 1805, 118; "On Seduction," *Massachusetts Magazine,* May 1792, 308–309; "General Characteristics of Modern Novels," *Boston Weekly Magazine,* Aug. 24, 1805, 174; "The Ladies Friend; Number IV: A Virtuous and Prudent Conduct Recommended," *Lady's Magazine; and Repository of Entertaining Knowledge,* November 1792, 265.

a being, *deliberately to perpetrate the murder of the peace of a fellow creature, without a single apparent motive to stimulate to a deed of such atrocity.*" But it should not have been difficult at all; loathsome as the creature was, his prototype could be found in Genesis.[92]

For this reason—that seduction tales essentially reenact the Fall, with the victim cast as Eve and the seducer as Satan himself—we should not read such tales too literally. Although they certainly reinforced emerging Victorian standards of sexuality, it is doubtful that this was the primary objective. Rather, they represent another chapter in the early nineteenth century's secularization of religion. In them, the seducer is a secularized—but nonetheless recognizable—version of Satan.[93] The real subject of the seduction stories is, not whether young girls should resist sexual temptation, but what hope innocence has in a corrupt world. The answer was grim, and mankind's—not merely Eve's—repeated fall had grave implications not only for women but for all of American society. That was the lesson of "The Seducer: Addressed to the Fair Daughters of America." Its author, typically, was incredulous that a being so depraved as the "base seducer" could exist: "To obtain his desires, he practices every art of dissimulation, and does not hesitate to violate the most solemn engagements. Falshood and perjury become familiar to him. . . . Such a one is a monster in creation. . . . Virtue is sacrificed to his lust." Yet it is not only his innocent victim who suffers; "the peace of individuals, families and societies is destroyed." "Such are more dangerous to meet," the author concludes, "than bears bereaved of their whelps. They ought like ravenous wolves to be hunted from civilized society." The satanic seducer was an enemy to society, the snake in the grass of the infant Republic.[94]

To the list of republicanism's stock villains, to the tyrannical ruler and the designing courtier, we must add several other names: those of the coxcomb,

92. Foster, *Coquette,* 82; Rowson, *Charlotte;* "Charles and Amelia; or, The Unfortunate Lovers, a Tale," *Baltimore General Magazine, and Impartial Review,* July 1798, 33–36; "The History of Narcissa," *Massachusetts Magazine,* March 1792, 179–181; [Judith Sargent Murray], *The Gleaner . . . ,* 3 vols. (Boston, 1798), II, 55. See also "Melancholy Tale of Seduction," *Massachusetts Magazine,* April 1795, 40–42; "An Admonition to Those Who Glory in Seducing the Affections of the Fair, and Then Deserting Them," *Universal Asylum, and Columbian Magazine,* November 1792, 303; and "The Essayist; Number VI: On the Power of Love," *Lady's Magazine; and Repository of Entertaining Knowledge,* November 1792, 255–256.

93. See also Wood, "Conspiracy and the Paranoid Style," *William and Mary Quarterly,* 3d Ser., XXXIX (1982), 420–421.

94. "The Seducer: Addressed to the Fair Daughters of America," *Baltimore Weekly Magazine,* Mar. 25, 1801, 233–234.

the coquette, and—most of all—the vile seducer. All threatened the consensual union that served as the metaphor of what republicans wanted their society to be. Yet if republicanism found ways to vanquish the tyrant and banish the sycophant, it was powerless when confronted by this most insinuating and devilish seducer. He put republicanism, as a system of belief, on trial—and he won. He revealed republicanism's fatal flaw; although it could imagine ways by which reasonably virtuous men and women could make each other more so and live with each other in harmony, it was utterly baffled by confirmed depravity. In some ways, republicanism represented a quarrel with Genesis. So long as republican-minded men and women could rewrite sacred history in such a way that the Fall never took place and Eve was never tempted, they could imagine themselves inhabiting an earthly paradise, living with their mates in a prelapsarian bliss. But the men and women who were the heirs of the Reformation could never fully forget the Fall; they knew that, when tempted by a deceiver of satanic proportions, humankind would fall and fall again.

The best solution they could devise for the inevitability of sin was the metaphor of republican marriage, in which like-minded and virtuous men and women would guide each other's steps along the paths of rectitude. Yet, in their fiction, they were drawn irresistibly to the seduction story, and there virtue—and the Republic—fell. Most of this discourse, naturally, was expressed in codes; because it was so metaphorical, we cannot read it literally. Clearly, it was, not merely sexual lust that republicans found so threatening, but immoderate desires of all kinds, ambition and self-interest chief among them. The vile seducer represented republicanism's inability to come to terms with power, which it tended to equate with evil.

Still, because women figured so prominently in it, we must ask what bearing the literature of republican marriage had for actual republican women. We see embedded in these works many of the themes that historians have already exposed: a growing acceptance of affection as the only proper basis of marriage, increasing respect for feminine virtue, the feminization of religion, the idealization of chastity, and, finally, a growing interest in the possibilities for feminine influence. These themes are all compressed into the person of the Republican Wife: affectionate, virtuous, chaste, and capable of enormous moral authority over her husband. The Republican Wife represented, in the ideology at least, a real and important role. Yet, even as an image, she was limited. Indeed, she led to a dead end, for her capability always depended upon masculine susceptibility. She had no more power than man allowed, and, even if republican doctrine suggested that men ought to welcome feminine influence, that doctrine held no sway over those who did not subscribe to its credo. That generalization, of course, describes the fundamental weakness in republicanism: it had no power over those who were not or did not want to be virtuous.

In that sense, republicanism served women no more poorly than it did men: all were baffled by unalloyed vice. Even though republicanism enhanced woman's status and legitimated improvements in her education as well as her entry into benevolent reform movements, it also placed implicit checks upon her power.[95] And it confronted her with the image of the seduced maid, condemned to fall repeatedly in tale after tale, seemingly incapable of learning from her experience. Women who wanted more status, influence, or power would have to look for another model. Thus the ideal of the wife would give way, by perhaps 1830, to that of the mother. Men might not be malleable, but children were, and they seemed to offer a more promising opportunity for the exercise of influence. Yet before that transition could be effected, the many elements that brought it about would have to fall into place: not merely a sentimental conception of motherhood—already widely shared by the end of the eighteenth century, as Ruth Bloch has shown—but also the removal of the father's place of work from the home, new views on the nature of childhood and child-rearing, and, perhaps most important of all, an acceptance of childhood conversion. This shifting of emphasis from woman-as-wife to that of woman-as-mother had important implications for reform, for it rested upon the assumption that women had a special role to play as mothers and that, consequently, they represented a separate interest.[96]

This transition in the conceptualization of woman's nature and her role would have parallels in other aspects of early national life. The 1820s and 1830s may represent a watershed. Not only would the Republican Wife be replaced by the Victorian mother, but, in other ways as well, the republican synthesis would dissolve, yielding to a more fragmented social vision. In politics, the semblance of an era of good feelings would give way to the second party system. Reform, also, would pass on to a new and more militant

95. See note 81, above.

96. See Bloch, "American Feminine Ideals in Transition," *Feminist Studies*, IV, no. 2 (June 1978), 100–126; Anne L. Kuhn, *The Mother's Role in Childhood Education: New England Concepts, 1830–1860* (New Haven, Conn., 1947); Mary P. Ryan, *The Empire of the Mother: American Writing about Domesticity, 1830–1860* (New York, 1982); Bernard Wishy, *The Child and the Republic: The Dawn of Modern American Child Nurture* (Philadelphia, 1968); Cott, *Bonds of Womanhood;* and Douglas, *Feminization of American Culture.*

phase, beyond benevolence; vague plans for colonization or the eventual abolition of slavery would yield to immediatism, and hopeful schemes to "civilize" the Indian tribes would be replaced by the reality of the reservation. The republic of harmony proved ephemeral; it simply could not work, for it faltered in the face of intransigent slaveholders, Indians who did not want to be white, drunkards who would not give up the bottle, and, most simply, men who would not reform. When confronted by such enormous obstacles, the Republican Wife, like the theory that begot her and like the original woman in whose image she was cast, tasted of the fruit of knowledge and, inevitably, fell.

Politics and the Ambivalence of the Private Sphere

Women in Early Washington, D.C.

When we compare the place of women in the planning, design, and construction of the District of Columbia to their actual presence in the new seat of government, we find ourselves in a conundrum. Women were nowhere, and they were everywhere. The men who planned and built Washington, D.C., had virtually nothing to say about women, and, if we read the official histories of the construction of the capital city and the buildings that lined its broad avenues, it appears as if virtually no plan or provision was made for women at all. We may infer that the capital city's planners and builders assumed that women as well as men would inhabit the houses that were supposed to be built on the lots that were offered for sale to the public. Yet, though we may in fact find the word *public* in many of the documents relating to the creation of Washington, it is in vain that we search for the word *woman*. We may thus—quickly, but rather safely—conclude that women played no part in the design of the nation's capital.[1]

When we read the history of life in the early years, however, we find women almost everywhere—at parties and balls, at the President's House on New Year's Day, at the boardinghouse mess, in the galleries of Congress and even on its floor. Clearly, this presence was not planned, although we

This essay was originally published as Jan Lewis, "Politics and the Ambivalence of the Private Sphere: Women in Early Washington, D.C.," in Donald R. Kennon, ed., *A Republic for the Ages: The United States Capitol and the Political Culture of the Early Republic* (Charlottesville, Va., 1999), 122–151.

1. See Joseph B. Varnum, Jr., *The Seat of Government of the United States . . .*, 2d ed. (Washington, D.C., 1854); *Documentary History of the Construction and Development of the United States Capitol Building and Grounds* (Washington, D.C., 1904); Wilhelmus Bogart Bryan, *A History of the National Capital: From Its Foundation through the Period of Adoption of the Organic Act*, 2 vols. (New York, 1914–1916); Bob Arnebeck, *Through a Fiery Trial: Building Washington, 1790–1800* (Lanham, Md., 1991); Kenneth R. Bowling, *Creating the Federal City, 1774–1800: Potomac Fever* (Washington, D.C., 1988); Bowling, *The Creation of Washington, D.C.: The Idea and Location of the American Capital* (Fairfax, Va., 1991); Jeanne F. Butler, "Competition 1792: Designing a Nation's Capitol," special issue, *Capitol Studies*, IV, no. 1 (1976), 15–96; "Special Bicentennial Issue, Washington, D.C., 1791–1991," *Washington History*, III, no. 1 (Spring / Summer 1991).

must concede that the presence of men—as distinguished from officeholders and government officials—had not been planned for or taken into account either. Washington was created as a seat of government, and habitation was only incidental to that primary purpose. Only occasionally do we get a glimpse of the place envisioned for the public in the Federal City, and this fragmentary evidence suggests that the city planners were uncertain about what role the public would or should play in the national government. It is this uncertainty, which was more about the role of the public in the new national government than about gender itself, that creates the conundrum about women's place in the capital city. On the one hand, there were those town lots that the public was expected to purchase, on the other, a clear intention that the nation's capital was not to be a commercial center, which would necessarily lead to faction, distraction, and a high cost of living. The public was expected to come to Washington, but it was not supposed to engage in the sorts of activities that would create interests antagonistic to, nor was it supposed to make any claim upon, the public good. Members of the public were supposed to attend the government as spectators.[2]

It was for this reason that public galleries were built in Congress. The construction of such accommodations for spectators was still something of an innovation. The first public galleries had been added to the Massachusetts House of Representatives in 1766 as part of a republican attempt to turn government into a "School of Political Learning." Half a dozen years later, Philadelphia artisans succeeded in obtaining similar galleries in their state assembly, and, by 1790, women were attending debates in the new national Congress sitting in Philadelphia.[3] That Congress would offer the public similar accommodations in Washington—for the same republican reasons—seems to have gone unquestioned. In 1805, responding to criticism from Benjamin Henry Latrobe, William Thornton, the Capitol's original archi-

2. Varnum, *Seat of Government,* 11–13. James Sterling Young believes that the infant capital more than fulfilled its founders' republican intention that the nation's capital be small and insignificant (Young, *The Washington Community, 1800–1828* [New York, 1966]). Young may, however, exaggerate these tendencies. In comparison to the small towns and rural districts from which many of the government officials and their families came, Washington would soon seem a bustling metropolis.

3. Thomas Young to—, Nov. 23, 1766, quoted in John C. Miller, *Sam Adams: Pioneer in Propaganda* (Boston, 1936), 110n, cited in Gary B. Nash, *The Urban Crucible: Social Change, Political Consciousness, and the Origins of the American Revolution* (Cambridge, Mass., 1979), 359 ("School"), 377; Bowling, *Creation of Washington, D.C.,* 190. See also J. R. Pole, *Political Representation in England and the Origins of the American Republic* (New York, 1966), 69–70, 277–278.

tect, observed that the chambers he had designed for the south wing of the building were large enough to accommodate a House that might someday need to seat five hundred representatives and provide a "gallery for the audience" that would come to see them. Two years later, Latrobe, the surveyor of public buildings, endeavoring to secure the Capitol chambers and committee rooms from the "idle and dissolute persons" who "ranged the whole building," defacing its walls with "obscenity" and destroying the furniture, recognized that "it is thought proper to admit, without discrimination, all persons who choose to go into the galleries," although he suggested regulating the vending of refreshments in the gallery lobbies. The public, then, was welcomed to the Capitol, where it might observe and be entertained by the proceedings on the House and Senate floors.[4]

And that is exactly what the public did; moreover, some portion of that public almost always seemed to be women. From the day in 1793 when the cornerstone of the Capitol was laid in front of "a brilliant crowd of spectators," women were on hand to observe the proceedings. Women, in other words, helped constitute the public. Their presence ratified and legitimated the new national government, and they did so both as citizens and as women, that is, as part of the general public, undifferentiated by sex, and as a distinct part of that whole. After the cornerstone of the Capitol had been placed, "the whole company retired to an extensive booth" to enjoy a barbecued ox "of which the company generally partook." We would have no idea that women were part of the "whole company" were it not for an act of gallantry on the part of President George Washington. The day was hot and sunny, and, when a physician offered him the only umbrella to be found, he "declined it with the remark, 'To the ladies with it doctor, I have been exposed to the sun *before* in the course of my life.'"[5]

Virtually every time we find a public gathering in early Washington, D.C., we find women. Not only were they there when the cornerstone of the Capitol was laid, but they were there on the cold and cloudy Saturday in Novem-

4. William Thornton, *To the Members of the House of Representatives of the United States* [Washington, D.C., 1805], 5; B[enjamin] Henry Latrobe, "Communication to the House of Representatives, October 27, 1807," in *Documentary History of the Construction and Development of the United States Capitol,* 129–130.

5. Varnum, *Seat of Government,* 31–33. Wilhelmus Bogart Bryan also describes the laying of the cornerstone but does not mention the presence of women (Bryan, *History of the National Capital,* 213–214). It is not always easy to find evidence of the presence of women at public occasions, not necessarily because women were not there, but either because the original sources are mute on this question or, as is often the case, subsequent historians have omitted the evidence that earlier sources provided.

ber 1800 when John Adams made his first speech to both houses of Congress. "There were a great many People[,] the Galleries were full," Anna Maria Thornton, the wife of the Capitol's designer reported. "The Ladies sat and stood below on the same floor as the Senate etc." Throughout the early national and antebellum periods, at least, women were present as spectators to the debates in Congress and even in the Supreme Court; they were present, as well, at important ceremonial occasions such as inaugurations and the president's New Year's Day open house; and the elite among them mixed and mingled with the male leadership of the new nation and emissaries from foreign governments at capital balls, levees, squeezes, and even the boardinghouse mess. Women, then, not only helped constitute Washington society—in both its senses, as the totality of human relationships and the fashionable social class—but participated in its politics.[6]

It has, of course, been almost an axiom of women's history that women were excluded from politics at this time—so much so that even those historians who have begun to challenge this premise have still assumed that national electoral and deliberative politics were such fundamentally and inherently masculine endeavors that women could not have participated in any significant way.[7] Thus Paula Baker has suggested that we need "a more inclusive definition of politics than is usually offered," one that will enable us to recognize that "men and women operated, for the most part, in distinct political subcultures." Building upon Baker, Mary P. Ryan has argued that, after 1825, women, who had been "barred from politics and government" by Revolutionary ideology, began "to enter public life on their own terms." Lori D. Ginzberg has come closest to reformulating our understanding of women's participation in politics when she noted that, "both before

6. "Diary of Mrs. William Thornton, 1800–1863," *Records of the Columbia Historical Society*, X (1907), 214.

7. Mary P. Ryan has argued that "the centralization of political power stimulated by the Revolution and institutionalized by the Federal Constitution . . . fundamentally reshaped the context of women's politics. When political decisions were made at these higher, more formal and remote levels they became largely inaccessible to women. . . . With the relocation of the national capital on the open landscape that would become Washington, D.C., the center of national politics became a male bastion, situated amid a ramshackle collection of men's boardinghouses. To put it simply, the federation of the United States created a remote public sphere that distanced women even further from public power" (Ryan, *Womanhood in America: From Colonial Times to the Present*, 3d ed. [New York, 1983], 70). In her subsequent work, Ryan has modified this position considerably. See Ryan, *Women in Public: Between Banners and Ballots, 1825–1880* (Baltimore, 1990). For one reformulation, see Joan Holf, *Law, Gender, and Injustice: A Legal History of U.S. Women* (New York, 1991), esp. chap. 1, "The Masculinity of U.S. Constitutionalism," 24–48.

and after the advent of the woman suffrage movement, women strode in and out of legislative halls—places where, in theory, females were not welcome. There they lobbied for new laws, sought appropriations for their organizations, and argued for changes in their own status." Yet, she observes, for women to enter the political arena necessarily involved them in a contradiction: whatever we may understand by the term *politics,* in antebellum America its connotations were partisan, competitive, interest based, and amoral—everything women were supposed not to be. The consensus, even among those who document women's involvement, is that women held no legitimate place in early national and antebellum politics.[8]

How was it, then, that Anna Maria Thornton and other Washington women came to be sitting in the galleries and standing on the floor of the Senate when John Adams made his speech in 1800? Mary P. Ryan has suggested that, when women appeared in post-Revolutionary public ceremonies where they were recognized as women, they served to ratify the essentially masculine character of republican politics and to legitimate women's exclusion from it. In this light, we may read Washington's proffering the umbrella to the ladies as a ceremonial inscribing his masculinity: he defines himself both by the toughness of his skin and his gallantry; that is, he defines himself in relationship to women.[9]

Women might have served as props to the new political order, underscoring its inherent masculinity. But when we look at Anna Maria Thornton's de-

8. Paula Baker, "The Domestication of Politics: Women and American Political Society, 1780–1920," *American Historical Review,* LXXXIX (1984), 622; Ryan, *Women in Public,* 172, 177; Lori D. Ginzberg, *Women and the Work of Benevolence: Morality, Politics, and Class in the Nineteenth-Century United States* (New Haven, Conn., 1990), 68–69. For more evidence of women's participation in politics, see Elizabeth Regine Varon, "'We Mean to Be Counted': White Women and Politics in Antebellum Virginia" (Ph.D. diss., Yale University, 1993). Although this essay defines politics somewhat differently than Michael McGerr does, it is informed by his assertion that, in politics, "style not only affects the perception of substance; it is substance. . . . The forms of politics arc critical measures of social freedom and equality. As the system of symbols and institutions that bind people to politics and government, style can make it easier or harder for men and women to translate their political impulses into political action" (McGerr, "Political Style and Women's Power, 1830–1930," *Journal of American History,* LXXVII [1990], 865).

9. Ryan, *Women in Public,* 24–30, 171–172. "The female body was a transitive semiotic device: it passed meaning beyond women themselves to civic values cherished by male citizens. Whether as the consort of the elite, the invocation of sensuality, or the pedestal for classic iconography, female symbols served as much to exclude as to incorporate women into the robust civic culture of 1825" (ibid., 28–29). See, similarly, Carroll Smith-Rosenberg, "Dis-Covering the Subject of the 'Great Constitutional Discussion,' 1786–1789," *Journal of American History,* LXXIX (1992), 841–873.

scription of her trip to hear the president's speech, it is difficult to read it that way. On Friday, November 21, she noted in her diary, "Heard that the President is to make his Speech tomorrow." The next day, she and her mother, accompanied by "our neighbour Miss Brown and Mr. Winstanley," took the carriage to the Capitol, while her husband and a male friend walked. The event was one that she had been anticipating; she went to Congress, as she put it, "to hear the president make his Speech." A few weeks later, on December 11, Anna Maria Thornton along with a small group of male and female friends and relations returned to Congress "to hear the Debates—we went into the Gallery and the Speaker sent a Member to invite us into the Lobby—Soon after we went down both House[s] adjourned." It stands to reason that Thornton would have wanted to attend Congress and witness its proceedings. Not only had she frequently visited the Capitol while it was being built, often accompanying female visitors to see the edifice her husband had designed, but she seems to have maintained an interest in national affairs. "Read the newspapers, worked etc," she would write in her diary at the end of a day.[10]

Applying the theories of Jürgen Habermas to eighteenth-century America, Michael Warner has described how the medium of print, in particular newspapers, helped constitute what Habermas has called the "bourgeois public sphere." Although Warner generally accepts Habermas's formulation that the public sphere took form in the eighteenth century as a "reading public," he qualifies Habermas's contention that the bourgeois public sphere was in its nature universalizing because it "anticipated in principle that all human beings belong to it." Radical as this idea might be, Warner argues, "It did not in practice allow access to the public arena for women" or to other propertyless, and consequently less literate, groups. "Because the same differentials of gender, race, and class allocated both citizenship, on one hand, and active literacy, on the other hand, freehold and discourse could coincide without necessarily entailing a liberalization of power."[11]

10. "Diary of Mrs. William Thornton," *Records of the Columbia Historical Society,* X (1907), 213, 214, 220. For visiting the Capitol, see ibid., 95, 146, 166, 192; for reading newspapers, see ibid., 93, 99, 101, 114, 133, 136, 192, 195, 218.

11. Jürgen Habermas, *The Structural Transformation of the Public Sphere: An Inquiry into a Category of Bourgeois Society,* trans. Thomas Burger (Cambridge, Mass., 1989), 56; Michael Warner, *The Letters of the Republic: Publication and the Public Sphere in Eighteenth-Century America* (Cambridge, Mass., 1990), 39, 48. Warner's discussion of Habermas is on 39. For the argument that both men and women participated in the "republic of letters" "but the underlying structural differences in their moral views [led] them to different inflections of [the] shared language" of "whig political discourse," see Frank Shuffelton, "In Differ-

Nonetheless—even though female literacy lagged behind that of men and even though women were, with few exceptions, restricted from the franchise and the ownership of property—women such as Thornton read the newspapers, discussed politics, and thereby helped constitute the bourgeois public sphere. Surely, that was what Margaret Bayard Smith, the wife of a prominent Washington newspaper editor, was doing when she told her sister-in-law in 1818 about her recent visit to Congress to hear Henry Clay and explained that, "as you will read the speech in the paper, I will not detail it, although I could repeat almost the whole of it." Similarly, Catherine Mitchill, the wife of a senator from New York, wrote her sister that she would not describe the House debate on the Embargo Act in detail: "If you read the newspapers you have seen this report at full length." Nonetheless, she included a clipping that reprinted the resolutions under debate "so that you may understand it better."[12]

In reading newspapers and discussing their contents, such women underscore the inclusive and universalizing nature of the public realm of letters. These women, to be sure, were the exception, for only the elite had the education and leisure to read newspapers and attend the debates in Congress; yet their participation in a public that was constituted by reading and writing demonstrates that gender alone was neither in principle nor in practice exclusionary. It is likewise significant that men seemed to expect that some women, at least, would share their interest in politics and would, as a matter of course, want to read about the work of Congress and discuss affairs of state. Louis McLane, a congressman from Delaware, at the beginning of

---

ent Voices: Gender in the American Republic of Letters," *Early American Literature,* XXV (1990), 289–304 (quotations, 295).

12. Margaret Bayard Smith to Anna Maria Smith, January [1818], in Gaillard Hunt, ed., *The First Forty Years of Washington Society Portrayed by Family Letters of Mrs. Samuel Harrison Smith (Margaret Bayard)* (New York, 1906), 145–146; Catherine Mitchill to Sister [Margaret Miller], Dec. 19, 1808, Papers of Catherine Mitchill, Library of Congress, Washington, D.C. On April 3, 1806, Mitchill described John Randolph for her sister, observing, "I suppose you have read his speeches in the Newspapers," and, on August 17, 1808, she commented, "The political news I expect you read in the Newspaper." For female literacy, see Kenneth A. Lockridge, *Literacy in Colonial New England: An Enquiry into the Social Context of Literacy in the Early Modern West* (New York, 1974); for the extent of the female franchise in this period, see Judith Apter Klinghoffer and Lois Elkis, "'The Petticoat Electors': Women's Suffrage in New Jersey, 1776–1807," *Journal of the Early Republic,* XII (1992), 159–193. For the limits on female propertyholding, see Marylynn Salmon, *Women and the Law of Property in Early America* (Chapel Hill, N.C., 1986); and Norma Basch, *In the Eyes of the Law: Women, Marriage, and Property in Nineteenth-Century New York* (Ithaca, N.Y., 1982).

what would be a long political career, assumed that the wife he had left at home would be following congressional business in the newspapers so that all he had to do was fill her in on what transpired behind the scenes. He thought it important, for example, to tell her that the speeches she would read in the newspaper were in fact polished and edited for the reading public: "All those who have already spoken, are now busily preparing speeches for the press, so that in a day or two you will have before you all the speeches which were, *not delivered*." Gouverneur Morris sent his European friend the princesse de la Tour et Taxis just such an edition of the debates in the Senate in which he had recently participated. "I send you, charming Princess, these things because knowing as you do what passes everywhere else, you may perhaps wish to see what we are doing in this little corner of the universe." Men sometimes even expected more interest in public affairs than women were willing to manifest. Mary Bagot, the wife of the British minister to the United States, was obviously taken aback by the behavior of the men she encountered when she and her husband stopped in an inn in Virginia: "After breakfast . . . I found myself in the common room with a dozen fellows—waggoners and heaven knows who—all of whom entered into conversation and talked politics with me." If we accept Habermas's definition of the bourgeois public sphere as "the sphere of private people com[ing] together as a public," then surely we can locate it in that room in a Virginia inn.[13]

Catherine Mitchill helped create the public realm, too, not only when she described for her husband a meteor shower in Connecticut but when he shared her account with his fellow congressmen. "Your account of the atmospheric phenomenon . . . preceded all the letters to the Connecticut delegation, and even outran the newspapers," Samuel Mitchill told his wife. "It was, therefore, the great authority on which the news was told, and has been quoted to Senators, Representatives, and other great and curious personages." Catherine Mitchill also participated in the public sphere when she lobbied successfully for a pension for a war veteran and his wife, who had come to her husband seeking assistance. "My Husband has delivered her over to me, saying that he thinks a Lady will have more influence with congressional Gentlemen than one of their own sex." Mrs. Mitchill pre-

13. Louis McLane to Kitty [McLane], [Jan. 10, 1818], Papers of Louis McLane, Library of Congress (See also his letters of Dec. 10, 1817, and Jan. 16, 1819); Gouverneur Morris to Princess de la Tour et Taxis, June 20, 1802, excerpted in Anne Cary Morris, ed., *The Diary and Letters of Gouverneur Morris,* II (New York, 1888), 425; David Hosford, ed., "Exile in Yankeeland: The Journal of Mary Bagot, 1816–1819," Oct. 21, 1817, *Records of the Columbia Historical Society,* LI (1984), 47; Habermas, *Structural Transformation,* 27.

vailed upon her "family"—the mess at the home where she and her husband boarded—eventually securing the votes of all but one, enlisted the aid of one other woman, and lobbied both houses of Congress.[14] Throughout the antebellum period (at least) women would continue to lobby Congress for projects of particular interest. That is how Cornelia Hancock found herself in January 1864 in the Senate, where Charles Sumner assured her that "the freedman's bureau will be established; says I must not be in a hurry, all things are coming round right."[15]

To say that women helped constitute the public sphere, that they petitioned Congress and even lobbied its members, however, is not to claim that they wielded power in the same way that men did; it is not even to say that they wielded power at all. The conventional assumption that women were excluded from politics is not, of course, without some basis in fact. The limits and reach of women's inclusion in politics are nicely captured by one of Senator Samuel Mitchill's digressions in a letter to his wife. He explained that his letters to her were so long because he thought about her so often. "You must remember, too," he mused, "that you are one of my constituents, and that I am in some degree responsible for you for my public conduct. In the theory of our Constitution women are calculated as political beings. They are numbered in the census of inhabitants to make up the amount of population, and the Representatives are apportioned among the people according to their numbers, reckoning the females as well as the males. Though, therefore, women do not vote, they are nevertheless represented in the national government to their full amount." Until then, when

14. Samuel Latham Mitchill to Catherine Mitchill, Dec. 30, 1807, in "Dr. Mitchill's Letters from Washington, 1801–1813," *Harper's New Monthly Magazine,* LVIII (1879), 752; Catherine Mitchill to Sister [Margaret Miller], Jan. 28, 1812, and Feb. 21, 1812, Papers of Catherine Mitchill. As Fredrika J. Teute demonstrates in her essay "Roman Matron on the Banks of Tiber Creek: Margaret Bayard Smith and the Politicization of Spheres in the Nation's Capital," in Donald R. Kennon, ed., *A Republic for the Ages: The United States Capitol and the Political Culture of the Early Republic* (Charlottesville, Va., 1999), 89–121, Margaret Bayard Smith considered lobbying President James Madison for a judgeship for her brother-in-law and, a decade later, along with several other women, successfully interceded with Secretary of State Henry Clay for a clerkship for Martha Jefferson Randolph's son-in-law. See Margaret Bayard Smith to Jane B. Kirkpatrick, July 2, 1815, and Smith to Maria Bayard Boyd, Oct. 24, 182[8?], in Margaret Bayard Smith Papers, Library of Congress.

15. Cornelia Hancock to Mother, Jan. 20, 1864, in Henrietta Stratton Jaquette, ed., *South after Gettysburg: Letters of Cornelia Hancock, 1863–1868* (1937; rpt. New York, 1956), 40–41. For other examples of women petitioning Congress, see Ginzberg, *Women and the Work of Benevolence,* chap. 3.

writing her, he had "always referred to our social and conjugal relation. I now write you in [your] sovereign and political capability."[16]

Samuel Mitchill's observations on the nature of female political capacity were only half joking; in a few sentences, he accurately captured the complex nature of female citizenship. Women were indeed political beings—but ones who could not vote. Although it is inaccurate to say that Senator Mitchill and his colleagues "found it impossible to imagine adult women as anything other than wives," the sort of representation they granted women was something more than virtual but less than actual, for how was Catherine Mitchill or any woman in her "sovereign and political capability" supposed to secure her representative's accountability? Women were accorded a limited agency; they could speak to power, but they could not exercise it.[17]

What, then, did it mean to be part of the public sphere yet not to participate in government, as either a voter or officeholder? When we examine women's engagement with national government in early Washington, we see that the public sphere and politics—if by that we mean electoral politics—were not coterminous. Perhaps it is not so much that, as Paula Baker has suggested, men and women operated in distinct political subcultures as that electoral politics represented an all-male enclave in the wider public sphere in which men and women both participated. But perhaps even this distinction is insufficiently precise: When Catherine Mitchill shepherded a bill through both houses of Congress and Cornelia Hancock buttonholed Charles Sumner on the Senate floor, can we safely claim that women played no role in what we call electoral politics?

Nevertheless, the question that should concern us is, not how much par-

16. Samuel Latham Mitchill to Catherine Mitchill, Dec. 8, 1804, in "Dr. Mitchill's Letters," *Harper's New Monthly Magazine,* LVIII (1879), 748. Mitchill continued: "This ordinary share of political influence is possessed by all women. But your situation is widely different. You formerly had a Representative in the House of Representatives to yourself, and latterly (oh, the nature of woman!) you have actually become possessed of a Senatorial vote which is half the weight of the commonwealth in the other branch of Congress. Considering you thus as one among the sovereign people, I have thought it proper from time to time to give you an account of my behavior" (ibid., 748–749).

17. Linda K. Kerber, "The Paradox of Women's Citizenship in the Early Republic: The Case of Martin vs. Massachusetts, 1805," *American Historical Review,* XLVII, no. 2 (1992), 378. See also Kerber's *Women of the Republic: Intellect and Ideology in Revolutionary America* (Williamsburg, Va., and Chapel Hill, N.C., 1980), chap. 9. For the nature of female citizenship, see Jan Lewis, "'Of Every Age, Sex, and Condition': The Representation of Women in the Constitution," *Journal of the Early Republic,* XV (1995), 359–387, also reprinted in this volume.

ticipation, but what sort. What does it tell us about the nature of American government and politics in the early national era if we know that, at a time when none could vote, some women lobbied Congress, and many more sat in the galleries for congressional debates and attended presidential inaugurations? To answer our question, we need to look closely at women's engagement with government, to see how they understood their participation in the public sphere.

Why, for example, did Catherine Mitchill attend the debates in Congress? Perhaps the answer to this question is obvious: she was interested in politics. She explained it to her sister this way: "As there are few amusements here, this is quite a fashionable place of resort for the Ladies, and when there is any interesting subject of debate before the House, this is to me, a very agreeable way of spending the morning." An engrossing debate promised women entertainment in a city that offered them little else to do than engage in an endless round of formal visits, and the prospect of seeing one of the nation's greatest orators could even attract women from outside the city's bounds. Charlestonian Caroline Gilman was delighted to arrive in Washington on the eve of one of Henry Clay's speeches: "Mr. Clay speaks tomorrow on the Land Bill. I can scarcely think of sleep when this prospect is before me."[18] Virtually every time a debate of any significance was held in Congress, women were present. Women, then, made up part of the audience for the speeches and exchanges that we have come to regard as constituting the "golden age" of Congress.[19]

This was also a golden age of theater, and the comparison between the stage and the halls of Congress was not lost upon astute observers such as Catherine Mitchill and Margaret Bayard Smith. When the House was debating the Embargo Act and Catherine Mitchill heard that the debate was likely to continue late into a Saturday night, she "swallowed" her "meal in haste, took a beau [for a respectable woman would not go to Congress unescorted], and proceeded to the Capitol. . . . I trip'd up the winding stair

18. Catherine Mitchill to Sister [Margaret Miller], Apr. 3, 1806, Papers of Catherine Mitchill; Caroline Gilman, *The Poetry of Travelling in the United States* (New York, 1838), 5. For a description of Washington society, see Barbara G. Carson, *Ambitious Appetites: Dining, Behavior, and Patterns of Consumption in Federal Washington* (Washington, D.C., 1990).

19. See Papers of Catherine Mitchill; Hunt, ed., *First Forty Years of Washington Society;* Daniel Webster to Mrs. Ticknor, Jan. 17, 1825, in George Ticknor Curtis, *Life of Daniel Webster,* 2 vols. (New York, 1870), I, 231; and Gilman, *Poetry of Travelling,* 5–11. For use of "golden age," see Robert V. Remini, *Henry Clay: Statesman for the Union* (New York, 1991), 447.

case to the gallery where the Ladies sit, and there beheld the wise of the nation in their magnificent Hall." She listened to several hours of speeches, finally leaving at ten in the evening. "I was much gratified with the novelty of the entertainment. It was as good as going to a play, but here all the characters are real instead of fictitious."[20]

Two decades later, Margaret Bayard Smith was equally captivated by the theatricality of congressional proceedings when she described the famous debates between senators Daniel Webster of Massachusetts and Robert Y. Hayne of South Carolina to her sister: "Almost everyone is thronging to the capitol to hear Mr. Webster's reply to Col. Hayne's attack on him and his party. A debate on any political principle would have had no such attraction. But personalities are irrisistible. It is a kind of moral gladiatorship, in which characters are torn to pieces, and arrows, yes, poisoned arrows, . . . are hurled by the combatants against each other." Women were witnesses to the spectacle: "The Senate chamber, is the present arena and never were the amphitheatres of Rome more crowded by the highest ranks of both sexes than the senate chamber is. Every seat, every inch of ground, even the steps, were *compactly* filled, and yet not space enough for the ladies—the Senators were obliged to relinquish their chairs of State to the fair auditors who literally sat in the Senate. One lady sat in Col. Hayne's seat, while he stood by her side speaking . . . . It was supposed yesterday that there were 300 ladies besides their attendant beaux on the floor of the Senate." It was, in fact, the presence of women that helped transform the proceedings of Congress into a form of spectacle.[21]

Although women seem to have attended congressional debates from the outset, not everyone was pleased with this situation. Margaret Bayard Smith thought that the presence of so many women was a novelty, one that she much lamented. "I cannot but regret that this dignified body would become such a scene of personality and popular resort."[22] But two decades earlier, John Randolph of Roanoke had also complained about the spectators. During a closed session, Catherine Mitchill was told by some of the members of the House, Randolph had held forth for three hours in what was "the most boisterous, indecent and inflamatory they ever witnessed. . . . He abused

20. Catherine Mitchill to Sister [Margaret Miller], Dec. 19, 1808, Papers of Catherine Mitchill.

21. Margaret Bayard Smith to Mrs. Kirkpatrick, Jan. 26, 1830, in Hunt, ed., *First Forty Years of Washington Society,* 310. The debate over tariff protection and land policy raised the momentous issue of the character of the Union.

22. Ibid., 310.

the President, the admn. and everybody, not even the Ladies escap'd; for in one part of his speech, he said, 'Give me that liberty of speach which is understood in the Gallery—not the green Gallery, filled with frippery and swindlers—I mean the upper Gallery filled with the honest people.'" In an aside, Mitchill explained that the "green Gallery" was the one usually filled by women, while the "upper Gallery" was claimed by "the rabble, black and white."[23] Randolph, considered one of the great orators of his day, felt himself constrained by the presence of women.[24]

In this context, Senator Hayne's willingness to yield his seat to a woman at a time when he knew that all ears—and eyes—were upon him suggests that, by the time he debated Daniel Webster, he and his congressional colleagues spoke in a way that women could respond to. The woman who occupied the senator's chair, while he stood by her side declaiming, served as a prop to his oration, as did the women who displaced the other senators from their seats, as did the women who sat in the galleries and heard Daniel Webster proclaim, "Liberty *and* Union, now and forever, one and inseparable!" Such oratory helped forge American nationalism in "an age when the dramatic encounters of great men in politics claimed the nation's attention and, many thought, determined its future." In the drama of American democracy, women were assigned the best seats in the house.[25]

23. Catherine Mitchill to Sister [Margaret Miller], Apr. 3, 1806, Papers of Catherine Mitchill. Consider also Richard Henry Lee's reaction to the female audience that listened in New York in 1790 to Congress discuss where to locate the nation's capital. On viewing the women in the galleries, he observed that their presence said, "As you vote, so will we smile.—A severe trial for susceptible minds—And a very unfair (if I may say that Ladies can do anything unfair) whilst the Abundant beauty of Philadelphia had not an equal opportunity of shewing its wishes" (Richard Henry Lee to [Thomas Lee Shippen], July 6, 1790, in James Curtis Ballagh, ed., *The Letters of Richard Henry Lee,* II, *1779–1794* [New York, 1914], 532, cited in Bowling, *Creation of Washington, D.C.,* 190). Although Lee seems to suggest that the wishes of these women should be considered by Congress—in other words, that Congress represents women, as it does men—his suggestion, like Randolph's, is that women interfere with the normal proceedings of Congress. His implication is that in order to win the (sexual) favors of women, men will attempt to please them, and, consequently, if men were to be confronted by an equally beautiful group of women, they would attempt to win their favor in the same way; men cannot help responding to women in a sexualized way, even when they should be debating political issues rationally. The responses of Lee and Randolph seem to be typical of an older, Revolutionary generation; a subsequent generation of politicians would come to accept women as a natural part of their political audience.

24. See, for example, Catherine Mitchill to Sister [Margaret Miller], Feb. 28, [1809], Papers of Catherine Mitchill, referring to "the greatest Orator Mr. J. Randoph"; and Louis McLane to Kitty [McLane], [Jan. 10, 1818], Papers of Louis McLane.

25. *Register of Debates in Congress . . . ,* VI (Washington, D.C., 1830), 80, quoted in Merrill D. Peterson, *The Great Triumvirate: Webster, Clay, and Calhoun* (New York, 1987),

Why did women flock to the halls of Congress, and why did senators yield them their seats? Perhaps it is sufficient to say that women found the business of their nation inherently compelling. What can one add to Catherine Mitchill's explanation to her sister of why she had been spending two or three hours a day listening to the debates: "They are now very interesting, in as much as the resolutions under discussion involve the question of war." The nation's leadership likewise assumed that women—or at least women of their class—would want to observe congressional proceedings. In 1825, Daniel Webster wrote Mrs. George Ticknor from the floor of the House while Henry Clay was addressing it on the issue of the Cumberland Road:

> The ladies are all present, inside the House, [although Webster was not certain that he recognized any of those present]. Mr. Clay speaks well. I wish you were here to hear him. The highest enjoyment, almost, which I have in life, is in hearing an able argument or speech. The development of *mind,* in those modes, is delightful. In books, we see the result of thought and of fancy. In the living speaker, we see the thought itself, as it rises in the speaker's own mind. And his countenance often indicates a *perception* before it gets upon his tongue. I have been charmed by observing this operation of minds which are truly great and vigorous; so that I sometimes am as much moved, as in reading a part of Milton and Shakespeare, by a striking and able argument, although on the dryest subject.

In describing for his female correspondent what the ladies in the gallery and he himself were observing that day, Webster was encompassing all of them in a public sphere, not simply reporting a speech.[26]

Jay Fliegelman has described a late-eighteenth-century "elocutionary revolution" in which "public speaking became reconceptualized . . . as an occasion for the public revelation of a private self. Such a private self would then be judged by private rather than public virtues: prudence, temperance, self-control, honesty, and, most problematically, sincerity." By this process of communication, the orator or political leader could forge consensus by stimulating his audience's natural sociability. The orator would

---

178. For accounts of the Webster-Hayne Debate, see Peterson, *Great Triumvirate,* 5–6, 171–179; and Charles Sellers, *The Market Revolution: Jacksonian America, 1815–1846* (New York, 1991), 314–315.

26. Catherine Mitchill to [Margaret Miller], Dec. 13, 1811, Papers of Catherine Mitchill; Webster to Ticknor, Jan. 17, 1825, in Curtis, *Life of Daniel Webster,* I, 231.

speak, not so much to the mind of his audience, but to its emotions; as he himself displayed a feeling, the audience would, as Webster put it, "see the thought itself," and it would be moved. The members of the audience would be linked to the speaker—and to each other—by ties of sympathy. Indeed, that is precisely the experience that Caroline Gilman sought when she went to Congress to observe Henry Clay "wield the lever of human sympathies."[27]

The speaker, then, was thought to embody his message, and, although, as Fliegelman notes, such an assumption made the question of an orator's sincerity both central and highly problematic, democratic doctrine made the people and their emotional response to the speaker's oratory the ultimate judge. In fact, the audience's reaction to an orator often determined his effectiveness as a political leader. When Louis McLane entered the House in 1818, he was overcome by anxiety as he contemplated making his first speech. He told his wife that, "if a new member falls off, or fails to arrest attention, he is not listened to again." A few days later, he explained that "it is not the number of speeches which [a man] makes here, but the force of what [he] says that gives a man weight and respectability in the House."[28]

As McLane waited for the right moment to embark upon his oratorical career, he observed closely his fellow congressmen, assessing the forcefulness of their public speech. One day he went to the Senate chamber to hear a speech by Harrison Gray Otis on behalf of a claim by an aged veteran of the Revolutionary War. Otis's "enunciation is excellent," McLane reported, "his manner extremely graceful, his language pure and impressive, brilliant without being tawdry, and splendid without bombast." Otis "drew a picture of the aged Hero of the revolution which drew tears from the eyes of the whole Senate." McLane began to report the "substance" of the speech, but then stopped short. "I should do injustice to Otis to attempt to follow him. His praise is in the effect produced in the Senate, which seemed to have been struck from above, and who adjourned after they recovered from the trance into which the speech had placed them, without another word." The perfect speech was part act of God, part mesmerism; it robbed its listeners of their speech and put tears in their eyes.[29]

In such accounts of effective oratory, speaking is often described as manly.

27. Jay Fliegelman, *Declaring Independence: Jefferson, Natural Language, and the Culture of Performance* (Stanford, Calif., 1993), 2, 24; Gilman, *Poetry of Travelling*, 6.

28. Louis McLane to Kitty [McLane], [Jan 10, 1818], and Jan. 15, 1818, Papers of Louis McLane.

29. Louis McLane to Kitty [McLane], Jan. 29, 1818, Papers of Louis McLane.

Louis McLane wrote approvingly of William Pinkney's argument before the Supreme Court: "His manner is exceedingly eloquent, manly and powerful. I could not [imagine?] an orator with more grace and elegance to preserve that manly power, which after all is necessary to give effect to the effort." If powerful speaking was the essence of manliness, then to be moved by such oratory could make one implicitly a woman. In March 1805, Samuel Mitchill described for his wife "one of the most affecting scenes of my life." Aaron Burr had just made his farewell address to the Senate, speaking "with so much tenderness, knowledge, and concern that it wrought upon the sympathy of the Senators in a very uncommon manner. Every gentleman was silent, not a whisper was heard." After Burr had finished and departed the Senate floor, shutting the door behind him, "the firmness and resolution of many of the Senators gave way, and they burst into tears. There was a solemn and silent weeping for perhaps five minutes. . . . My colleague, General Smith, stout and manly as he is, wept as profusely as I did. He laid his head upon his table and did not recover from his emotion for a quarter of an hour or more." Mitchill himself was no less affected, for, "though it is more than three hours since Burr went away, I have scarcely recovered my habitual calmness. Several gentlemen came up to me to talk about this extraordinary scene, but I was obliged to turn away and decline all conversation." To be moved by a speech was to be overcome by emotion, to lose one's resolution and firmness, one's very manhood; it was to become a woman.[30]

But when Samuel Mitchill wrote from the Senate floor to describe for his wife the effect of Burr's farewell speech and to tell her how he wept and how stout and manly senators lost their firmness and resolution, he was anything but ashamed. Twice he told his wife that he had never experienced anything so "affecting." This was an experience he craved. Such descriptions of the effect of political oratory suggest that the political realm, indeed, American nationalism itself, was a community of feeling in which the standard of membership was established by the responsive woman. To cry on the Senate floor might appear unmanly, but, in truth, Samuel Mitchill suggested, it was simply to respond appropriately to an affecting scene.

After her first visit to the Supreme Court, Margaret Bayard Smith worried that the presence of women was adversely shaping the nature of the arguments. She told her sister:

30. Louis McLane to Kitty [McLane], Feb. 11, 1819, Papers of Louis McLane; Samuel Latham Mitchill to Catherine Mitchill, Mar. 2, 1805, in "Dr. Mitchill's Letters from Washington," *Harper's New Monthly Magazine*, LVIII (1879), 749–750.

> Curiosity led me against my judgement to join the female crowd who throng the . . . court room. A place in which I think women have no business. The effect of female admiration and attention has been very obvious, but it is a doubt to me whether it has been beneficial, indeed I believe otherwise. A member told me he doubted not, there had been much more speaking on this account, and, another gentleman told me, that one day Mr. Pinckney had finished his argument and was just about seating himself when Mrs. Madison and a train of ladies enter'd,—he recommenced, went over the same ground, using fewer arguments but scattering more flowers. And the day I was there I am certain he thought more of the female part of his audience than of the court, and on concluding, he recognized their presence, when he said, "He would not weary the court, by going thro a long list of cases to prove his argument, as it would not only be fatiguing to them, but inimical to the laws of good taste, which *on the present occasion,* (bowing low) he wished to obey." The court was crowded while he spoke; the moment he sat down, the whole audience arose, and broke up, as if the court had adjourn'd.

It appeared to Margaret Bayard Smith that Pinkney shaped the form of his presentation to the expectations of his female audience, aspiring more to popularity than to arguing points of law.[31]

There is powerful evidence that men addressed theatrical oratory to men as much as to women. Thirty-five years after Daniel Webster argued for the integrity of his alma mater's charter as a private institution in *Dartmouth College* v. *Woodward* in 1818, Dr. Chauncey A. Goodrich remembered the audience as "consisting chiefly of legal men, the *élite* of the profession throughout the country." Justice Joseph Story, writing only eleven years after the case, noticed, however, that "a large assemblage of ladies" helped make up the audience.[32]

Webster's oration on that occasion is well known; much like his debate with Hayne, it helped establish his reputation. Goodrich remembered the effect it had upon listeners:

31. Margaret Bayard Smith to Mrs. Kirkpatrick, Mar. 13, 1814, in Hunt, ed., *First Forty Years of Washington Society,* 96–97.

32. Letter of Chauncey A. Goodrich to Rufus Choate, 1853, in Curtis, *Life of Daniel Webster,* I, 169; Bertha M. Rothe, ed., *The Daniel Webster Reader* (New York, 1956), 127–128 ("large assemblage," 128).

> Mr. Webster entered upon his argument in the calm tone of easy and dignified conversation. . . . He . . . went on for more than four hours with a statement so luminous, and a chain of reasoning so easy to be understood, and yet approaching so nearly to absolute demonstration, that he seemed to carry with him every man of his audience without the slightest effort or uneasiness on either side. . . . Now and then, for a sentence or two, his eye flashed and his voice swelled into a bolder note, as he uttered some emphatic thought; but he instantly fell back into the tone of earnest conversation which ran throughout the great body of the speech.[33]

Goodrich described the speech as "pure reason," but it went right to the heart, as much as to the mind. Justice Story had commenced listening with his pen in hand, but he never had to take a note. Story later commented, according to Goodrich, that "everything was so clear, and so easy to remember, that not a note seemed necessary." Near the end of his argument, Goodrich recalled, Webster described his alma mater in the words that have since become famous:

> "It is, sir, as I have said a small college. And yet there are those who love it—" Here the feelings which he had thus far succeeded in keeping down, broke forth. His lips quivered; his firm checks trembled with emotion; his eyes were filled with tears, his voice choked, and he seemed struggling to the utmost simply to gain that mastery over himself which might save him from an unmanly burst of feeling. I will not attempt to give you the few broken words of tenderness in which he went on to speak of his attachment to the college. The whole seemed to be mingled throughout with the recollections of father, mother, brother, and all the privations and trials through which he had made his way through life. Every one saw that it was wholly unpremeditated, a pressure on his heart, which sought relief in words and tears.[34]

Webster's argument seemed not so much a legal brief as an effusion of the heart, whose natural outpouring was words and tears. The effect of such a performance upon the justices of the Court was predictable. "The deep fur-

33. Letter of Chauncey A. Goodrich to Rufus Choate, 1853, in Curtis, *Life of Daniel Webster,* I, 169–171.
34. Ibid., I, 170.

rows" of Chief Justice John Marshall's "cheek expanded with emotion, and his eyes suffused with tears." The rest of the Court and all of the audience pressed forward "to catch each look and every movement of the speaker's face. If a painter could give us the scene on canvas—those forms and countenances, and Daniel Webster as he there stood in the midst—it would be one of the most touching pictures in the history of eloquence. . . . There was not one among the strong-minded men of that assembly, who could think it unmanly to weep, when he saw standing before him the man who had made such an argument, melted into the tenderness of a child." After Webster had completed his speech, the Court, of course, fell silent for some period of time, until everyone could recover and come "gradually back to his ordinary range of thought and feeling." Story would later say that "the whole seemed but an agonizing dream, from which the audience was slowly and almost unconsciously awakening."[35]

Mesmerist, seducer, camp-meeting preacher: the orator, as Story described the experience, "wrought" his audience up "to the highest excitement; many were dissolved in tears; many betrayed the most agitating mental struggles; many were sinking under exhausting efforts to conceal their own emotion." This was the public sphere of oratory in its golden age, when men aspired to make each other weep, so that they might themselves seek relief in words and tears. It was a realm in which the public and the private fused, as the orator became the sum total of his family experience, the embodiment of his father, mother, and brothers; it was the memory of his family that filled the orator's heart to overflowing and melted him into the tenderness of the child he had once been. Habermas has noted that in one of its manifestations, the public sphere of letters—and of oratory, we might add—brought together private persons as they communicated about their own subjectivity.

35. Ibid., I, 171; Everett Pepperrell Wheeler, *Daniel Webster: The Expounder of the Constitution* (New York, 1905), 30, quoted in Claude Moore Fuess, *Daniel Webster, I, 1782–1830* (Boston, 1930), 232n. Story's account, first published in 1905 and, according to Fuess, prepared by Story for an edition of Webster's speeches printed in 1830, is remarkably similar to Goodrich's in its description of the effect of Webster's oratory: "There was an earnestness of manner, and a depth of research, and a potency of phrase, which at once convinced you that his whole soul was in the cause. . . . And when he came to his peroration, there was in his whole air and manner, in the fiery flashings of his eye, the darkness of his contracted brow, the sudden and flying flushes of his cheeks, the quivering and scarcely manageable movements of his lips, in the deep guttural tones of his voice, in the struggle to suppress his emotions, in the almost convulsive clenchings of his hands without a seeming consciousness of the act, there was in these things what gave to his oratory an almost superhuman influence. . . . There was a painful anxiety towards the close" (Wheeler, *Daniel Webster,* 30, quoted ibid.).

If we were to substitute the words *private self* for *subjectivity,* Daniel Webster might well have accepted the formulation. For what was he doing to forward his case but presenting himself as a private person among his peers in a way that other persons could understand? In other words, Webster was demonstrating his humanity, his membership in the community of all those who think and feel. Women may not have been present when Webster argued his case, but they might as well have been, for the subjectivity Webster communicated was that of humanity, which encompassed both men and women.[36]

The Dartmouth College case, the Webster-Hayne debate, and all the other set pieces of American oratory raise the question of the relationship between the emotion prompted by these small dramas and what we traditionally have considered politics. *Dartmouth College* v. *Woodward,* after all, was about the sanctity of contract, and the Webster-Hayne debate ostensibly concerned itself with national policy regarding public lands. Merrill D. Peterson has concluded that Webster knew that "the pathetic address . . . whatever its power in the courtroom, was beneath the dignity of the law." Although we need not accept Peterson's implicit judgment that such issues possess an inherent dignity, while public weeping does not, we must ask how these components of national politics fit together. Modern accounts of these episodes often heighten the supposed contradiction between the emotive and substantive elements of politics. One of Webster's biographers tells us that those who filled the Senate chamber to hear Webster's response to Hayne on January 26, 1830, were "no doubt more interested in the clash of personalities than in profound constitutional principles," and, as if to prove his point, mentions the three hundred women who supposedly filled the audience. Another suggests that Webster's nationalism was well calculated to advance his political career, and another still, while describing vividly the reaction of Webster's audience in the Senate on the twenty-sixth (Webster later said, "I never spoke in the presence of an audience so eager and so sympathetic"), does not mention the three hundred women. Whatever distinctions we might be inclined to make between personalities and constitutional principles, Webster and his audience seemed to regard them, almost like liberty and union, as one and inseparable.[37]

36. Wheeler, *Daniel Webster,* 30, quoted in Fuess, *Daniel Webster,* I, 232n.

37. Peterson, *Great Triumvirate,* 100–101; Maurice G. Baxter, *One and Inseparable: Daniel Webster and the Union* (Cambridge, Mass., 1984), 183; Robert F. Dalzell, Jr., *Daniel Webster and the Trial of American Nationalism, 1843–1852* (New York, 1972), 26–28; To Mr. [Warren] Dutton, Mar. 8, 1830, in Fletcher Webster, ed., *The Private Correspondence of Daniel Webster,* I (Boston, 1857), 494.

The presence of so many women on the floor of Congress and the sight of Supreme Court justices melting into tears calls into question the paradigm of separate spheres. We have become accustomed to thinking that nineteenth-century Americans divided their world into separate male and female spheres; to the male sphere, they assigned politics, economics, "the dignity of the law," and to women, the home. These spatial spheres supposedly conformed to the distinctive natures of men, who were rational, and women, who were emotive. Even those historians who have most effectively critiqued this paradigm still find it a useful "metaphor for complex power relations in social and economic contexts" and suggest that "the metaphor remains resonant because it retains some superficial vitality," for "our private spaces and our public spaces are still in many important senses gendered." Yet, even as metaphor, the construct of separate male and female spheres is of limited usefulness in explaining why Daniel Webster saw women as among the most eager and sympathetic audience he ever addressed and why stout and manly congressmen filled the public halls of government with their tears.[38]

So we confront a dilemma, and some of it is the product of the way we have come to think about women and politics. On the one hand, the first generation of modern women's historians customarily deployed the trope of separate spheres, particularly for the nineteenth century. On the other, political historians have generally assumed, as Joan Wallach Scott has noted, that gender was "antithetical to the real business of politics." The presence of women in Congress or the sight of Supreme Court justices reduced to tears does not accord with our notion of the Capitol as a male realm or politics as a wholly masculine enterprise. But if Scott and other historians of gender are correct in asserting that "gender constructs politics," it may be that the women who attended Congress and the men who wept there might have performed a critical role in shaping the way the American political system operated in its formative years.[39]

When women came to the halls of government, they transformed the Capitol into a kind of Victorian parlor, that is, a semipublic place in a private home, governed by the customs of polite society. In other words, when women went to Congress or when the men who were already there behaved

38. Linda K. Kerber, "Separate Spheres, Female Worlds, Woman's Place: The Rhetoric of Women's History," *Journal of American History*, XLV (1988), 9–39 (quotations, 28, 39).

39. Joan Wallach Scott, *Gender and the Politics of History* (New York, 1988), 46.

as if they were in a parlor, Congress became more like those realms of society where the rules of gentility and politeness, rather than calculations of power or interest, prevailed. The presence of women transformed Congress into Habermas's "bourgeois public sphere."[40]

We are accustomed to thinking in terms of a contrast between public and private spheres. In Habermas's theory, however, the more significant contrast or division, historically at least, was the one between the state and the bourgeois public sphere. Habermas has theorized that what he has called this sphere was created in the seventeenth and eighteenth centuries, when private people came together as a public. When Habermas talks about persons being "private," he means simply that they were not part of the state; they did not hold office, and, as a result, they had no public authority. Habermas describes the process by which "a political consciousness developed in the public sphere of civil society, which in opposition to absolute sovereignty, articulated the concept of and demand for general and abstract laws and which ultimately came to assert itself" in the form of public opinion "as the only legitimate source of this law." As Michael Warner and Jay Fliegelman have shown, this aspect of Habermas's theory enriches our understanding of the American Revolution; although Habermas drew most of his examples from the histories of England and France, surely we can see a process like this at work in the colonies as newspaper writers and pamphleteers helped American men and women establish a conviction that public opinion, and not the king, was the source of general and abstract laws.[41]

If such assumptions could lead a people into a revolution that would proclaim the sovereignty of the people, they also had embedded within them certain contradictions that Habermas describes but whose implications he does not draw out. And it is these contradictions—what Habermas calls "the ambivalence of the private sphere"—that may help us understand the presence of women in the halls of Congress. Habermas has noted that the private sphere, the realm of society that was not the state and out of which the bourgeois public sphere emanated, really had two parts. One was the realm of work and property, and the other was the family. Although when juxtaposed against the state each of these realms appeared distinctly "private," both had distinct functions. On one side of the private sphere was

40. See Karen Halttunen, *Confidence Men and Painted Women: A Study of Middle-Class Culture in America, 1830–1870* (New Haven, Conn., 1982), 58–60.

41. Habermas, *Structural Transformation,* 54.

the realm of civil society, of exchange and labor, which would give specific meaning to the term *private property* and later the concept of private enterprise. On the other was that of the conjugal family, out of whose experiences proceeded "the ideas of freedom, love, and cultivation." Eventually, these two parts of the private sphere would come to appear distinct and separate, so that within the intimacy of the family, private persons would begin to see themselves as independent even from their own private economic activities. As Habermas puts it, they would begin to consider themselves "as persons capable of entering into 'purely human' relations with one another." Although the distinction between these two aspects of the private sphere may be clear to us, they were not clear to those persons who used the term *private* to comprise both those economic activities and human relationships that were—or they thought should have been—beyond the reach of the state.[42]

When Louis McLane went to Congress as one of his state's representatives in 1817, he told his wife it was only "to gather up the fragments of my shattered fortune." Business failures had left him near bankruptcy, and public service seemed his only available course. That winter he told his beloved Kitty that "I assure you I take much more pleasure in reading of my dear little Bob climbing the tree . . . than I do in the dull debate which is going on upon the Bankrupt Bill," and, a few days later, he asked her rhetorically, "Why should a man give up his domestick comforts and enjoyments for the empty honour of serving the Publick?" Only a great national crisis might require a man "to make some sacrifice of Private interest and comfort."[43] When McLane combined both his fortune and his family into the notion of "private interest and comfort" and contrasted it to public service, he was repeating a formulation that had been enshrined in American political and social thought. In *Common Sense,* Thomas Paine had observed that

> society is produced by our wants, and government by our wickedness; the former promotes our happiness *positively* by uniting our affections, the latter *negatively* by restraining our vices. . . .
>
> Society in every state is a blessing, but government even in its best state is but a necessary evil.

42. Ibid., 48, 55.

43. Louis McLane to Kitty [McLane], Dec. 2, 1817, Feb. 19, 1818, and Feb. 24, 1818, Papers of Louis McLane. See, similarly, Jan Lewis, *The Pursuit of Happiness: Family and Values in Jefferson's Virginia* (New York, 1983), 209–210.

The critical distinction—for Paine as well as for McLane—was between society and government; domestic pleasures and private economic activities fell on the same side of that great divide.[44]

As Habermas has noted, these two aspects of the private sphere and hence the "circles of persons who made up the two forms of [the] public" created when private persons came together were not "completely congruent." Although women "took a more active part" in the public sphere of letters—and, we should add, served as an audience for oratory—because they could not own property, they clearly were excluded from civil society, the realm of exchange and labor, which was predicated on the ownership of property. The obfuscation of the distinction between these two components of the public sphere, Habermas suggests, served a practical purpose. When private persons shifted from discussing ideas of love, freedom, and cultivation, the notions of humanity that were inculcated and nurtured in the family, to talking about themselves as propertyowners who wished to influence public policy, then they brought to those discussions of economics and politics the conviction that they were speaking in the name of humanity itself. This conviction only enhanced their effectiveness as political agents. "The fully developed bourgeois public sphere," Habermas concludes, "was based on the fictitious identity of the two roles assumed by the privatized individuals who came together to form a public: the role of propertyowners and the role of human beings pure and simple." This is what he means by "the ambivalence of the private sphere." The claims of humanity, then, could be used to sanction the political arrangements made by the owners of property. And when we remember that the very notion of humanity was nourished in the family and universalized in the realm of letters, we can see that the critical role played by women was to make it appear that the operations of power, when informed by public opinion, were both natural and humane.[45]

Women, then, appeared to bring the values of the family to bear upon the workings of power. As Caroline Gilman put it, in Washington, "the play of social feelings softens the glow of powerful intellect." When one of her particular favorites rose to speak in Congress—and uttered the words *"My constituents!"*—she felt "as if the reputation of a father or brother was at stake." Any place that women went, and any time that men seemed to act like women, or, more precisely, demonstrated their common humanity, as when

44. Thomas Paine, *Common Sense* (1776) (New York, 1976), 65.
45. Habermas, *Structural Transformation,* 56.

they wept on an affecting occasion, assured that whatever transpired took place in the name of a common humanity.[46]

Habermas identifies this conflation of propertyowners with "human beings as such" as an ideology. In fact, it is the ideology that sustained the American Republic in its formative years (and still prevails today). We can see how this ideology worked in the early national period by returning to Webster's argument in the Dartmouth College case.[47]

Although the case was about contracts, Webster did not let his case rest on the rights of private property; or, to be more precise, he defined "private" in a way that made it encompass the public good, and he redefined "public" so that it took on the attributes of selfishness and narrow self-interest that are often associated with the private sphere. He focused upon the charitable and benevolent purposes of the college, and, indeed, it was precisely at these points that his presentation became most sentimental. "Individuals have a right," Webster insisted, "to use their own property for purposes of benevolence, either towards the public, or towards other individuals. They have a right to exercise this benevolence in such lawful manner as they may choose; and when the government" rescinds the contract, "it is not law but violence." Webster defined property expansively, in implicitly Lockean terms, as that to which one had a fundamental right that the state could not impair. "That all property," he scoffed, "of which the use may be beneficial to the public, belongs therefore to the public, is quite a new doctrine." Webster insisted that public ends—such as charity and education—were far better served by private institutions than by the state. If government took responsibility for benevolence, he warned, then, "benefactors will have no certainty of effecting the object of their bounty. . . . Colleges and halls will be deserted by all better spirits and become a theatre for the contentions of politics. Party and faction will be cherished in the places consecrated to piety and learning." It was private individuals and corporations, then, that stood for the public interest, not the state, which represented only contention, faction, and the selfish strivings of political men.[48]

This is a remarkable formulation, for it insists that public benefits come from the private realm (not Mandeville's private vices, but private virtues) and that there is, really, no public other than that created by private individu-

46. Gilman, *Poetry of Travelling,* 5–6, 10.

47. Habermas, *Structural Transformation,* 88.

48. "Webster's Argument in the Dartmouth College Case," in Rothe, *Daniel Webster Reader,* 147–148, 162–163.

als; certainly, the public is not represented by the state. The purpose, then, of Webster's emotion in arguing the case was to illustrate this formulation by embodying it; his evident feeling demonstrated the benevolence of private interests.

Women, then, played a critical—if hidden—part in the ideology that sustained American politics. By embodying the private realm and bringing its virtues into the public, women legitimated politics. Women's ideological function had to be obscured, however, for, if it were acknowledged that the ranks of the property holders and humanity itself were not coterminous, then the edifice that the ideology sustained would collapse.[49] The ambivalence—and indeed, the tensions—inherent in this system derived from its simultaneous universalizing and privatizing tendencies. On the one hand, the universalist assumptions of a common humanity would seek out and attempt to destroy the anomalies it encountered, most particularly slavery, but also the civil disabilities of women. On the other hand, Morton J. Horwitz suggests, nineteenth-century American political, social, and economic thought "sought to establish a separate, 'natural' realm of non-coercive and nonpolitical transactions free from the dangers of state interference and redistribution." These were the forces that defined American politics in its formative decades. Women were at once caught in and gave form to its central ambivalence.[50]

49. See ibid., 85. See also Jan Lewis, "Motherhood and the Construction of the Male Citizen in the United States, 1750–1850," in George Levine, ed., *Constructions of the Self* (New Brunswick, N.J., 1992), 143–163.

50. Morton J. Horwitz, *The Transformation of American Law, 1870–1960: The Crisis of Legal Orthodoxy* (New York, 1992), 11.

Rethinking Women's Suffrage in New Jersey, 1776–1807

For a brief period after the American Revolution, some women were allowed to vote, in one of the thirteen new states. The New Jersey constitution of 1776 enfranchised not only men who met the property requirement but women as well. The specific language:

> All Inhabitants of this Colony, of full Age, who are worth Fifty Pounds proclamation Money, clear Estate in the same, and have resided within the County in which they claim a Vote for twelve Months immediately preceding the Election, shall be entitled to vote for Representatives in Council and Assembly; and also for all other publick Officers, that shall be elected by the People of the County at Large.

This piece of early American political, legal, and gender history was so exceptional that for many years historians wrote it off as an accident of wording. As Mary Beth Norton put it, "The constitution's phraseology probably represented a simple oversight on the part of its framers."[1]

This essay was originally published as Jan Ellen Lewis, "Rethinking Women's Suffrage in New Jersey, 1776–1807," *Rutgers Law Review,* LXIII (2011), 1017–1035. Citations to legal and public documents have been changed to conform with Omohundro Institute of Early American History and Culture house style. Jan Lewis dedicated this essay to the memory of her colleague John M. Payne, Board of Governors Distinguished Service Professor at Rutgers School of Law, Newark.

1. Constitution of New Jersey, 1776, article IV; Mary Beth Norton, *Liberty's Daughters: The Revolutionary Experience of American Women, 1750–1800* (Boston, 1980), 19. For a description of the New Jersey Constitution as "an ambiguity in the law and the indifference of the community," see Gerda Lerner, "Women Vote in New Jersey—1790–1807," in Lerner, *The Female Experience: An American Documentary* (1977; rpt. New York, 1992), 323. Thomas Fleming explained the enfranchisement of women by calling the constitution "hastily written"; see Fleming, *New Jersey: A History* (New York, 1984), 94. For an observation that "the case of New Jersey was an anomaly," see Dorothy A. Mays, *Women in Early America: Struggle, Survival, and Freedom in a New World* (Santa Barbara, Calif., 2004), 383. Richard P. McCormick said that "whether the term 'inhabitants' included women, aliens, Negroes, and slaves was unclear and was to be a source of confusion and controversy"; see

Historians have come to understand that the enfranchisement of single, propertied women was no accident or oversight but that New Jersey legislators instead intended propertied women to vote. Thus, Delight Wing Dodyk in her article on "Woman Suffrage" in the *Encyclopedia of New Jersey* matter-of-factly notes the gender-neutral provision of the state constitution, acknowledging that "women of property are known to have voted in several elections in the late eighteenth and early nineteenth centuries" until the right was rescinded in 1807. Dodyk relies upon two articles, one by Irwin N. Gertzog and the other by Judith Apter Klinghoffer and Lois Elkis. These historians, along with Rosemarie Zagarri in her book *Revolutionary Backlash: Women and Politics in the Early Republic,* have filled in much of the thirty-one-year history of women's voting in New Jersey.[2]

Although it is now widely understood among historians that New Jersey's enfranchisement of women was not an oversight, it still remains, as Zagarri puts it, "the New Jersey Exception." New Jersey is the outlier, lonely and a bit inexplicable. Yet, situated within the context of post-Revolutionary struggles to set the bounds of the political community, New Jersey's history makes more sense. Like the other states in the new nation—and the nation itself—it had to define its membership. As the history of voting rights in the United States makes clear, setting these boundaries has been an ongoing process, highly malleable and responsive to internal and external trends. The definition of political community in the decades immediately after the Revolution provides the proper context for understanding New Jersey's brief his-

McCormick, *The History of Voting in New Jersey: A Study of the Development of Election Machinery, 1664–1911* (New Brunswick, N.J., 1953), 69–70. J. R. Pole contended that the enfranchisement of women in New Jersey was the result of a "gap in the constitution," which "had been drawn up with a haste"; see Pole, "The Suffrage in New Jersey, 1790–1807," New Jersey Historical Society, *Proceedings,* LXXI (1953), 51–52. Nineteenth-century American feminists, however, were well aware that women had voted in New Jersey, which, they argued, was the intent of the 1776 constitution; they used this history to argue for the enfranchisement of women. See Elizabeth Cady Stanton, Susan B. Anthony, and Matilda Joslyn Gage, eds., *History of Woman Suffrage,* II, *1861–1876* (Rochester, N.Y., 1881), 731–732; and Charles B. Waite, "Who Were Voters in the Early History of This Country?" *Chicago Law Times,* II (1888), 397, 411. I am indebted to Professor Ann Gordon for the last reference.

2. Delight Wing Dodyk, "Woman Suffrage," in Maxine N. Lurie and Marc Mappen, eds., *Encyclopedia of New Jersey* (New Brunswick, N.J., 2004), 881–882; Irwin N. Gertzog, "Female Suffrage in New Jersey, 1790–1807," "Women, Politics and the Constitution," special issue, *Women and Politics,* X (1990), 47–48; Judith Apter Klinghoffer and Lois Elkis, "'The Petticoat Electors': Women's Suffrage in New Jersey, 1776–1807," *Journal of the Early Republic,* XII (1992), 159–193; Rosemarie Zagarri, *Revolutionary Backlash: Women and Politics in the Early American Republic* (Philadelphia, 2007). See also Alexander Keyssar, *The Right to Vote: The Contested History of Democracy in the United States* (New York, 2000), 5.

tory of women's voting. In recounting this history, I will put New Jersey at the center of American history, rather than the periphery, my way of honoring the legacy of my colleague John M. Payne.[3]

Despite earlier arguments that women somehow slipped in—that is, were not explicitly excluded or included as voters in the New Jersey constitution—because the legislators were sloppy, writing in haste, we can see that the provision setting out the qualifications for the franchise was rather carefully crafted, the product of compromise. Filled with Revolutionary ardor, some New Jerseyans had wanted suffrage extended to every taxpayer, while others were willing to extend the vote—but not quite so far. One New Jerseyan, writing as "Essex" in 1776, explicitly argued for liberalized qualifications for voting, declaring that "widows paying taxes [should] have an equal right to a vote, as men of the same property." The important point is that successive provincial congresses debated the qualifications for voters from late 1775 through the first half of 1776, altering the property requirement several times and finally deciding on a fifty-pound threshold in either possessions or cash, rather than the more restrictive landownership requirement.[4] One of the 1776 drafts of the constitution used the word "he" to identify voters, but subsequent language was gender neutral.[5] All of this, as Klinghoffer and Elkis argue, suggests strongly that the New Jersey legislators intentionally

3. Zagarri, *Revolutionary Backlash,* 30; Keyssar, *Right to Vote.* Michael Walzer notes that each political community is a "bounded world"; see Walzer, *Spheres of Justice: A Defense of Pluralism and Equality* (New York, 1983), 28–31.

4. Essex, "To the Author of Common Sense, Number IV," *New York Journal; or, The General Advertiser,* Mar. 7, 1776, [1], quoted in Marc W. Kruman, *Between Authority and Liberty: State Constitution Making in Revolutionary America* (Chapel Hill, N.C., 1997), 105 (Kruman notes that the author might have been William DeHart [191n]); McCormick, *History of Voting in New Jersey,* 66–71; Klinghoffer and Elkis, "'Petticoat Electors,'" *Journal of the Early Republic,* XII (1992), 165–167.

5. "Proceedings of Provincial Congress of New Jersey," Feb. 16, 1776, in *Minutes of the Provincial Congress and the Council of Safety of the State of New Jersey* (Trenton, N.J., 1879), 373. Other authors have cited "Journal of the Votes and Proceedings of the Provincial Congress of New Jersey . . . ," Oct. 25, 1775, ibid., 231, as evidence of "he" being used to describe voters, but this record pertains to a different proposal before the provincial congress—one from Salem County advocating that, along with Freeholders, "some householders, or reputable single men, as are possessed *bona fide* of a personal estate of the value of fifty Pounds Proclamation money, or upwards, and have been resident at least one year in the County, may be admitted to vote." See, for example, Klinghoffer and Elkis, "'Petticoat Electors,'" *Journal of the Early Republic,* XII (1992), 165. Yet this additional evidence reinforces that, however quickly the state constitution might have been drafted, for a number of months the provincial congress debated proposals to liberalize suffrage, and, in some of them, suffrage was explicitly restricted to men.

enfranchised propertyowning single women, or, at the very least, made no efforts to disenfranchise them.[6]

Moreover, the implicit inclusion of women, as well as blacks and aliens, in the term *inhabitant* is consistent with New Jersey's generally liberal construction of the franchise. Nine of the original thirteen states required voters to be freeholders, and only three established property requirements that were lower than New Jersey's. The residency requirement of one year in the county was not the most liberal at the time—some states required only six months and several had no residency requirement at all—but it was less restrictive than the citizenship requirement that would become the norm by the middle of the nineteenth century. Only four states, all in the South, restricted the vote to whites (although, by 1855, all states but five banned blacks from the polls). New Jersey's enfranchisement of women, along with that of blacks and aliens, and its low property threshold for voting marks it as one of the most liberal jurisdictions at the time, making its subsequent restriction of the franchise a useful case study for those who would want to understand the ways in which early national jurisdictions defined membership in the political community.[7]

To return to the enfranchisement of women: Had there been any ambiguity, subsequent legislatures would have had ample opportunity to clear it up. As Zagarri has noted, only five of the first state constitutions explicitly restricted the vote to men, but nowhere other than in New Jersey did women actually vote.[8] Indeed, in 1777 and 1783, legislators used the pronoun "he" in election laws, seemingly restricting the vote by gender, but perhaps we should consider the use of the male pronoun as the ambiguity.[9] Two women's names appear on a 1787 Burlington County poll list, although we do not have evidence that women voted during the confed-

6. Klinghoffer and Elkis, "'Petticoat Electors,'" *Journal of the Early Republic,* XII (1992), 166.

7. "Table A.1; Suffrage Requirements: 1776–1790," in Keyssar, *Right to Vote,* 55, 328–329.

8. Zagarri, *Revolutionary Backlash,* 31; "Table A.1; Suffrage Requirements," in Keyssar, *Right to Vote,* 328–329.

9. "An Act for Regulating the Election of the Members of the Legislative-Council and Assembly, Sheriffs and Coroners of the State of New-Jersey," chap. XXX, in *Acts of the General Assembly of the State of New-Jersey* . . . (Burlington, N.J., 1777), 54–61; "An Act for Regulating the Election of Members of the Legislative-Council and Assembly, Sheriffs and Coroners, of the State of New-Jersey, and of Delegates to Represent the Said State in the Congress of the United States," chap. XI, in *Acts of the Eighth General Assembly of the State of New-Jersey* (Trenton, N.J., 1784), 15–23.

eration period.[10] Nor have historians found any discussion of the issue.[11] In 1790, however, the vote was explicitly extended to (propertied single) women in seven counties of the state, by use of the phrase "he or she," referring to voters, and then to all propertied single women in the state in 1796, only to be rescinded (along with the vote for free blacks and aliens as well) a decade later, in 1807.[12]

It may be helpful to repeat this chronology:

- 1776 constitution uses gender neutral language
- 1777 and 1783 election laws speak of voter as "he"
- 1790 statute for seven counties refers to voter as "he or she"
- 1796 statute now uses "he or she" for voters in all New Jersey counties
- 1807 statute restricts the vote to *"free, white, male citizen[s]"*[13]

When we look at the chronology, it might give the appearance of a muddle. Nevertheless, if we retrace the history, the intent of successive legislatures

10. McCormick, *History of Voting in New Jersey,* 78n.

11. See, for example, Zagarri, *Revolutionary Backlash,* 35; and Klinghoffer and Elkis, "'Petticoat Electors,'" *Journal of the Early Republic,* XII (1992), 164–168.

12. "An Act to Regulate the Election of Members of the Legislative-Council and General Assembly, Sheriffs and Coroners, in the Counties of *Bergen, Monmouth, Burlington, Gloucester, Salem, Hunterdon and Sussex,*" chap. CCCXXII, in *Acts of the Fifteenth General Assembly of the State of New-Jersey . . .* (Burlington, N.J., 1790), 669–675; "An Act to Regulate the Election of Members of the Legislative-Council and General Assembly, Sheriffs and Coroners, in This State," chap. DCXXXIV, in *Acts of the Twenty-First General Assembly of the State of New-Jersey . . .* (Trenton, N.J., 1797), 171–178; "A Supplement to the Act Entitled 'An Act to Regulate the Election of Members of the Legislative Council and General Assembly, Sheriffs and Coroners in This State;' Passed at Trenton the Twenty-Second Day of February, One Thousand Seven Hundred and Ninety-Seven," chap. II, in *Acts of the Thirty-Second General Assembly of the State of New-Jersey . . .* (Trenton, N.J., 1807), 14–17.

13. Constitution of New Jersey, 1776, article IV; "Act for Regulating the Election of the Members of the Legislative-Council and Assembly . . . ," chap. XXX, in *Acts of the General Assembly of the State of New-Jersey* (1777), 54–61; "Act for Regulating the Election of Members of the Legislative-Council and Assembly," chap. XI, in *Acts of the Eighth General Assembly of the State of New-Jersey* (1784), 15–23; "Act to Regulate the Election of Members of the Legislative-Council and General Assembly," chap. CCCXXII, in *Acts of the Fifteenth General Assembly of the State of New-Jersey* (1790), 669–675; "Act to Regulate the Election of Members of the Legislative-Council and General Assembly," chap. DCXXXIV, in *Acts of the Twenty-First General Assembly of the State of New-Jersey* (1797), 171–178; "Supplement to the Act Entitled 'An Act to Regulate the Election of Members of the Legislative Council and General Assembly,'" chap. II, in *Acts of the Thirty-Second General Assembly of the State of New-Jersey* (1807), 14–17.

becomes more clear. New Jersey was attempting an experiment in democracy, tweaking the formula every few years. Let us start from the premise that the gender neutral language of 1776 was not a mistake or an oversight. After all, the language of the 1790 statute clearly enfranchised propertied single women, and, in so doing, built on the constitution's foundation. A few years later, when some New Jerseyans decided that the vote should be taken away from women, they pointed anxiously to the constitution, which, they believed, *did* enfranchise women. Nor am I sure that the use of the pronoun "he" in 1777 and 1783 should be read as limiting the franchise to males. Let's look closely at the 1790 statute. Paragraph 11 begins by repeating the standard constitutional qualifications of voters—"all free Inhabitants of this State of full Age, and who are worth Fifty Pounds Proclamation Money clear Estate in the same, and have resided within the County . . . for twelve Months"—and adds an innovation, that "no Person" may vote in a county other "than that in which he or she doth actually reside." So that's clear: voters may be both men and women. But paragraph 9 describes the process by which every voter should "deliver his Ballot" on which were to be the "Names of the Persons for whom he votes."[14]

How can this confusion be explained? I think perhaps by the genuine novelty of the enfranchisement of women. This was so radical, so much an innovation that the legislators could not keep their pronouns straight.[15]

Make no mistake, what New Jersey did was radical. It carried Revolutionary doctrine to its furthest—but logical—extreme. As a general proposition, let me state that the problem—or the possibility—of Revolutionary thought was that it could not easily be contained. Once Revolutionary principles were articulated, there was no controlling them. Anyone could pick them up and use them for their own purposes. Even no taxation without representation. It was, of course, among the most hallowed principles of British constitutional thought, and aggrieved colonists threw it back at Britain to protest what they considered the unfair taxation of the Sugar and Stamp Acts. There ensued a long debate about the nature of representation. But it was not too complex for women to pick up on, and, in 1778, the widow Hannah Lee Corbin, sister of the famous Virginia patriot, Richard Henry Lee, asked her brother to explain just why it was that she, a propertied widow, was not al-

14. "Act to Regulate the Election of Members of the Legislative-Council and General Assembly," chap. CCCXXII, in *Acts of the Fifteenth General Assembly of the State of New-Jersey* (1790), 669–675; Edward Raymond Turner, "Women's Suffrage in New Jersey: 1790–1807," *Smith College Studies in History,* I (1916), 165, 173–174.

15. Zagarri, *Revolutionary Backlash,* 31.

lowed to vote. He squirmed, unable to give her a good answer: "The doctrine of representation is a large subject, and it is certain that it ought to be extended as far as wisdom and policy can allow; nor do I see that either of these forbid widows having property from voting. . . ."[16]

When New Jersey enfranchised single propertied women, it effectively answered the question that Corbin would ask two years later: Why should not a widow with property vote? The underlying assumption was republican: the ownership of property in one's own name made for the independence that was thought necessary for citizens of a republic.[17] The property qualification that New Jersey set was, as we have seen, among the lowest in the new nation, and anyone who held that minimal amount in his or her own right—including blacks, aliens, and single women—was considered a member of the political community entitled to vote.[18]

Having now discussed the doctrine behind the enfranchisement of women in New Jersey, we can turn to the politics, how it played out on the ground. New Jersey politics were rough and tumble, more than a little corrupt. Much has been written about the politics of the 1790s, the trouble that Americans had in establishing both the mechanisms and culture of a functioning democratic republic. In New Jersey, women voters got caught up in the maelstrom that was democracy being born. Consider what happened in 1790. The statute of that year explicitly enfranchised women—"he or she"—but only in seven counties, most of them in the south and west. I do not believe that this meant that propertied single women necessarily could *not* vote elsewhere, but, even so, it is worth looking at what happened to get a sense of New Jersey politics. The explicit enfranchisement was one of the outcomes of the reforms instituted after the tumultuous first congressional election of 1789. The West Jersey conservatives, who were then known as the Junto

16. Richard Henry Lee to Mrs. Hannah [Lee] Corbin, Mar. 17, 1778, in Philip B. Kurland and Ralph Lerner, eds., *The Founders' Constitution,* I (Chicago, 1987), chap. 13, document 11 (on file with the DuPont Library, Stratford Hall), available at http://press-pubs.uchicago.edu/founders/documents/v1ch13s11.html; Zagarri, *Revolutionary Backlash,* 31; Gordon S. Wood, *The Radicalism of the American Revolution* (New York, 1992); Edmund S. Morgan and Helen M. Morgan, *The Stamp Act Crisis: Prologue to Revolution* (Chapel Hill, N.C., and Williamsburg, Va., 1953), 13, 15.

17. Keyssar, *Right to Vote,* 4; Gordon S. Wood, *The Creation of the American Republic, 1776–1787* (Williamsburg, Va., and Chapel Hill, N.C., 1969), 46–90.

18. Constitution of New Jersey, 1776, article IV; McCormick, *History of Voting in New Jersey,* 70. As Richard P. McCormick observes, "[Dropping the property qualification to £50] marked a fundamental departure from the concept that political rights were connected with landed property"; see McCormick, *Experiment in Independence: New Jersey in the Critical Period, 1781–1789* (New Brunswick, N.J., 1950), 80. See also Keyssar, *Right to Vote,* 14.

(and who would later become Federalists once there was a Federalist party), used every means at their disposal to elect their slate in the at-large election. They kept the polls in their region open—for months, until after the votes in the northern counties had been counted, so that they would know just how many votes they needed to prevail. They even succeeded in getting Essex County's vote thrown out.[19]

When the legislature convened the next year, it decided that some sort of reform was necessary. By a wide majority, it adopted a number of electoral reforms, the combined effect of which was to make voting easier but more orderly. Voting would now take place in townships, rather than the larger counties, but voters could vote only in the township of their residence. In fact, it was in this provision that the language clearly enfranchising women appeared: "No Person shall be entitled to vote in any other Township or Precinct, than that in which he or she doth actually reside at the Time of the Election." These reforms also limited the number of days the polls could remain open and set rules for counting votes. In addition, for the first time, voting was restricted to "free Inhabitants."[20]

These reforms applied to only seven of New Jersey's counties. Historians do not agree about why this should have been the case. Richard P. McCormick notes that the reforms passed by a significant majority and hence do not seem to have been designed to punish the Junto counties. He suggests that the seven counties essentially volunteered to adopt the reforms.[21] Irwin N. Gertzog believes that there might have been some political horse trading in the drafting of the legislation, with some of the provisions making vot-

19. Carl E. Prince, *New Jersey's Jeffersonian Republicans: The Genesis of an Early Party Machine, 1789–1817* (Williamsburg, Va., and Chapel Hill, N.C., 1967); John R. Howe, Jr., "Republican Thought and the Political Violence of the 1790s," *American Quarterly,* XIX (1967), 147; Marshall Smelser, "The Federalist Period as an Age of Passion," *American Quarterly,* X (1958), 391; Joanne B. Freeman, *Affairs of Honor: National Politics in the New Republic* (New Haven, Conn., 2001); "Table A.1; Suffrage Requirements," in Keyssar, *Right to Vote,* 328–329; McCormick, *History of Voting in New Jersey,* 91; Richard P. McCormick, "New Jersey's First Congressional Election, 1789: A Case Study in Political Skulduggery," *William and Mary Quarterly,* 3d Ser., VI (1949), 237.

20. "Act to Regulate the Election of Members of the Legislative-Council and General Assembly," chap. CCCXXII, in *Acts of the Fifteenth General Assembly of the State of New-Jersey* (1790), 669–675; McCormick, *History of Voting in New Jersey,* 91; Prince, *New Jersey's Jeffersonian Republicans,* 9; Klinghoffer and Elkis, "'Petticoat Electors,'" *Journal of the Early Republic,* XII (1992), 172.

21. McCormick, *History of Voting in New Jersey,* 91. Only three legislators voted against the reforms. See Turner, "Women's Suffrage in New Jersey," *Smith College Studies in History,* I (1916), 168.

ing more difficult and others—the establishment of polling places in each township, the explicit enfranchisement of women—designed to increase the Junto / Federalist vote. He implies that this was the first New Jersey law to explicitly enfranchise (propertied single) women.[22] However, if the 1776 New Jersey constitution had, in fact, enfranchised single propertied women, then the insertion of "he or she" into the 1790 legislation, which applied to only seven counties, should not be considered as a change or reform of the existing laws governing elections. In any event, the phrase "he or she" was repeated in the 1796 statute, which applied to all thirteen of New Jersey's counties, suggesting that New Jersey was reiterating explicitly its 1776 commitment to the enfranchisement of propertied single women—and keeping in place the enfranchisement of free blacks and aliens (if explicitly excluding for the first time slaves).[23]

Although the names of two women appeared on one poll list in 1787, until 1797, when the franchise for propertied single women was extended explicitly to the northern counties as well, there is no record that any New Jersey women voted. But, after 1797, there is abundant record of women voting in New Jersey. It is not clear why this was the case, but it seems most likely that it resulted from the growth of the first parties. New Jersey was split between Federalists and Democratic-Republicans, and many elections were hotly contested. Both parties began competing for the votes of women, or, as the critics of women's voting had it, dragging in women voters to add to their party's totals. To a certain extent, this is what's to be expected in competitive elections: each side will try to expand the electorate in order to increase its number of voters.[24]

Consider what happened in Essex County in 1797. The polls were open for two days. By the second day, when it appeared to the Federalists that they

22. Gertzog, "Female Suffrage in New Jersey," *Women and Politics,* X (1990), 51–52. See also Klinghoffer and Elkis, "'Petticoat Electors,'" *Journal of the Early Republic,* XII (1992), 172.

23. "Act to Regulate the Election of Members of the Legislative-Council and General Assembly," chap. CCCXXII, in *Acts of the Fifteenth General Assembly of the State of New-Jersey* (1790), 669–675.

24. McCormick, *History of Voting in New Jersey,* 78n, 193n; Prince, *New Jersey's Jeffersonian Republicans,* 76–78. It is impossible to tell, from the available evidence, whether the increase in women's voting was a result of the explicit enfranchisement of propertied single women in all counties in the 1797 statute or because increased "party strife" drew more voters to the polls. See Klinghoffer and Elkis, "'Petticoat Electors,'" *Journal of the Early Republic,* XII (1992), 175.

were about to be outvoted, they began, it was reported, to round up their voters, many of them supposedly indifferent:

> They sent carriages into the country to bring out the farmers. They were obliged to beg them, even to treat them, so indifferent are the people to their privileges [that is, they bought the votes with cheap drink]. . . . In spite of all their efforts . . . , they received the news that the opposing party . . . was prevailing. In this extremity they had recourse to the last expedient; it was to have the women vote. . . . They scurried around collecting them. I need not say that the number of the latter was very small.[25]

Historian Carl E. Prince believes that the actual number of women who voted in New Jersey was small, because, once the vote was withdrawn, there was no discernible impact on voting totals.[26] Yet the numbers may not be as important as the change wrought in the political culture. Customary toasts to the "Fair Sex," a staple of political rallies in the period, took on a different meaning when some of those women were potential voters, not merely ornaments to the political process. Thus, in Stony Hill, New Jersey, Republicans saluted "the fair daughters of America; those who voted in behalf of Jefferson and Burr in particular." According to one account, even Alexander Hamilton actively campaigned among women. Apparently, he and Senator Matthias Ogden had "so far ingratiated themselves in the esteem of the federal ladies of Elizabeth-Town, and in the lower part of the state, as to induce them . . . to resolve on turning out to support the federal ticket" in 1800. Both parties competed actively for women's votes.[27]

The enfranchisement of women was controversial, however. I have suggested that this enfranchisement was the logical and furthest extension of

25. Julian Ursyn Niemcewicz, *Under Their Vine and Fig Tree: Travels through America in 1797–1799, 1805 with Some Further Account of Life in New Jersey,* trans. and ed. Metchie J. E. Budka (1797–1807; rpt. Elizabeth, N.J., 1965), 22–23, cited in Klinghoffer and Elkis, "'Petticoat Electors,'" *Journal of the Early Republic,* XII (1992), 176.

26. Prince, *New Jersey's Jeffersonian Republicans,* 134.

27. Zagarri, *Revolutionary Backlash,* 85 ("Fair Sex"); "Mr. KOLLOCK, by Giving the Following a Place in Your Paper . . . ," *New-Jersey Journal* (Elizabethtown, N.J.), Mar. 24, 1801, [3], cited in Klinghoffer and Elkis, "'Petticoat Electors,'" *Journal of the Early Republic,* XII (1992), 181, "Communicated," *Centinel of Freedom* (Newark, N.J.), Dec. 16, 1800, [3], cited ibid., 170. For both parties' efforts to court women's votes, see Klinghoffer and Elkis, "'Petticoat Electors,'" *Journal of the Early Republic,* XII (1992), 176–182.

Revolutionary ideology, and, thus, female enfranchisement was debated in that context. One supporter of women's voting explained:

> Our daughters are the same relations to us as our sons; we owe them the same duties; they have the same science, and are equally competent to their attainments. The contrary idea originated in the same abuse of power, as monarchy and slavery, and owes its little remaining support to stale sophistry.[28]

Others worried, however, that the revolution would go too far (a concern that was exacerbated by the French Revolution). An 1806 Fourth of July orator in Morristown recognized that "our *constitution* requires a voter to be possessed of 50 £" (the minimum property requirement for voting). Echoing orthodox Revolutionary thought, he continued, "The prevailing *theory*, is that taxation and representation should go together." But revolutions might lead to anarchy.

> Our *practice* outstrips them both, in its liberality, and makes no invidious exceptions. It admits to the pole [*sic*] people of all sexes, colors, tongues, characters, and conditions. . . . In our unbounded generosity, we would admit to a participation of our choicest rights, the lame, and the halt, and the blind [as well as] . . . the worthless and the penniless;—as motley a groupe as the day of Pentecost or the pool of Bethesda ever witnessed.

Here was the explicit statement that the boundaries of the political community were too expansive; rights were not for all.[29]

This was a debate that had been going on for several decades, between those who welcomed the liberalizing tendencies of the Revolution and those who feared they would undermine the social order. The 1790s debate over naturalization of new citizens has particular bearing. The first Naturalization Act (1790), whose terms were rather liberal—offering citizenship to any "free white person" who had resided in the U.S. for two years, was "of good

28. "An Oration; Delivered by a Citizen of the United States, on the Fourth of July," *Genius of Liberty* (Morristown, N.J.), Aug. 7, 1800, [2], cited in Klinghoffer and Elkis, "'Petticoat Electors,'" *Journal of the Early Republic,* XII (1992), 179.

29. Henry Ford, *An Oration, Delivered in the Presbyterian Church at Morris-Town, July 4, 1806* (Morristown, N.J., 1806), 11, quoted in Zagarri, *Revolutionary Backlash,* 33.

character," and swore to uphold the Constitution—was itself the product of a debate about what it meant to be an American. Was it a matter of volition and consent, or was it a matter of character, itself the product of experience and culture? As immigration, the prospect of war with France, and partisan conflict all increased, the nation twice tightened the qualifications for naturalization, lengthening the probation period in 1795 to five years and then, in 1798, to fourteen years (the highest it has ever been). In the 1798 debate, the most conservative Federalists argued against admitting any aliens at all to full citizenship and instead advocated a two-tier system of residents, who could own property but not vote or hold office, and full citizens. Even Jeffersonians favored stricter qualifications for citizenship. They merely worried, as one put it, "that gentlemen . . . will go too far in this business."[30]

So, too, with women: Should they be eligible for full participation in the political community? How far should the principles of the Revolution be taken? One of the most well-known, and revealing, discussions on this topic was that between Abigail Adams and her husband, John. Abigail, by the way, noted with approval New Jersey's enfranchisement of women. In 1797—just a short time after the enfranchisement of women was explicitly extended to all New Jersey counties, so the news must have spread like wildfire—Abigail Adams told her sister that if the Massachusetts constitution had been as "liberal" as New Jersey's and "admitted the females" to vote, she would have certainly voted for her sister's friend.[31]

By this time, Abigail Adams had been advocating expanded women's rights for more than two decades. In a famous letter to her husband, then in Philadelphia leading the colonies to independence, she had said:

30. "An Act to Establish an Uniform Rule of Naturalization," Mar. 26, 1790, in Richard Peters, ed., *The Public Statutes at Large of the United States of America, from the Organization of the Government in 1789, to March 3, 1845 . . .* , I (Boston, 1845), 103; *The Debates and Proceedings in the Congress of the United States . . . ; Fifth Congress; Comprising the Period from May 15, 1797, to March 3, 1799, Inclusive* (Washington, D.C., 1851), 1780; Zagarri, *Revolutionary Backlash,* 33; Larry E. Tise, *The American Counterrevolution: A Retreat from Liberty, 1783–1800* (Mechanicsburg, Pa., 1998); Rogers M. Smith, "Constructing American National Identity: Strategies of the Federalists," in Doron Ben-Atar and Barbara B. Oberg, eds., *Federalists Reconsidered* (Charlottesville, Va., 1998), 19–21; Rogers M. Smith, *Civic Ideals: Conflicting Visions of Citizenship in U.S. History* (New Haven, Conn., 1997), 153–164; Jan Ellen Lewis, "Defining the Nation: 1790 to 1898," in Daniel Farber, ed., *Security v. Liberty: Conflicts between Civil Liberties and National Security in American History* (New York, 2008), 117, 120–126.

31. Abigail Adams to Mary Cranch, Nov. 15, 1797, in Stewart Mitchell, ed., *New Letters of Abigail Adams, 1788–1801* (Boston, 1947), 112, cited in Zagarri, *Revolutionary Backlash,* 33.

> I long to hear that you have declared an independancy—and by the way in the new Code of Laws which I suppose it will be necessary for you to make I desire you would Remember the Ladies, and be more generous and favourable to them than your ancestors. Do not put such unlimited power into the hands of the Husbands. Remember all Men would be tyrants if they could. If perticular care and attention is not paid to the Laidies we are determined to foment a Rebelion, and will not hold ourselves bound by any Laws in which we have no voice, or Representation.
>
> That your Sex are Naturally Tyrannical is a Truth so thoroughly established as to admit of no dispute. . . . Why then, not put it out of the power of the vicious and the Lawless to use us with cruelty and indignity with impunity.[32]

John replied two weeks later, in a jocular, flirtatious manner, refusing to engage seriously with her views. He did raise, however jokingly, the concern that everyone had become rebellious.

> As to your extraordinary Code of Laws, I cannot but laugh. We have been told that our Struggle has loosened the bands of Government every where. That Children and Apprentices were disobedient—that schools and Colledges were grown turbulent—that Indians slighted their Guardians and Negroes grew insolent to their Masters. But your Letter was the first Intimation that another Tribe more numerous and powerfull than all the rest were grown discontented.—This is rather too coarse a Compliment but you are so saucy, I wont [*sic*] blot it out.[33]

It was only in a letter a month later to James Sullivan that John Adams treated seriously the question of equality, asking how far Revolutionary principles should be extended. He began with John Locke—and agreed: "It is

32. Abigail Adams to John Adams, Mar. 31, 1776, in L. H. Butterfield, ed., *Adams Family Correspondence*, I, *December 1761–May 1776* (Cambridge, Mass., 1963), 369–370. For a somewhat different reading of this letter and Abigail's subsequent exchange with her husband, see Elaine Forman Crane, "Political Dialogue and the Spring of Abigail's Discontent," *William and Mary Quarterly*, 3d Ser., LVI (1999), 745–774. Crane has demonstrated that many of Abigail Adams's phrases were either direct quotations from or allusions to the works of contemporary or recent writers and political theorists.

33. John Adams to Abigail Adams, Apr. 14, 1776, in Butterfield, ed., *Adams Family Correspondence*, I, 382–383.

certain in Theory, that the only moral Foundation of Government is the Consent of the People." This is the starting point. "But," he asked, "to what an Extent Shall We carry this Principle?"

> Shall We Say, that every Individual of the Community, old and young, male and female, as well as rich and poor, must consent, expressly to every Act of Legislation? No, you will Say. This is impossible. How then does the Right arise in the Majority to govern the Minority, against their Will? Whence arises the Right of the Men to govern Women, without their Consent? Whence the Right of the old to bind the Young, without theirs.[34]

So where do we draw the line, Adams asked Sullivan. He answered his own question: with women, for they cannot be admitted into government

> because their Delicacy renders them unfit for Practice and Experience, in the great Business of Life, and the hardy Enterprizes of War, as well as the arduous Cares of State. Besides, their attention is So much engaged with the necessary Nurture of their Children, that Nature has made them fittest for domestic Cares.[35]

For Adams, women were the easiest case. Nature disqualified them from voting and actively giving their consent to government. And, once one group had been excluded, then the basis had been laid for excluding other groups as well, by establishing it as a principle that some could be excluded. Adams's greatest concern, incidentally, was not slaves but poor men, who frightened him. He needed a rationale for excluding them from participation in government. In fact, Adams would just as soon not talk about it. "Depend upon it, sir, it is dangerous to open So fruitfull a Source of Controversy and Altercation, as would be opened by attempting to alter the Qualifications of Voters. There will be no End of it."[36]

Yet there was New Jersey, opening up the issue. Not only had it enfranchised single, propertied women but it had also admitted to the polls free blacks and aliens.[37] And over the years, it had effectively eliminated the prop-

34. John Adams to James Sullivan, May 26, 1776, in Robert J. Taylor, ed., *Papers of John Adams,* IV, *February–August 1776* (Cambridge, Mass., 1979), 208.

35. Ibid., 210.

36. Ibid., 211; Wood, *Radicalism of the American Revolution,* 27; Keyssar, *Right to Vote,* 19.

37. For a period, even slaves might have been enfranchised. See Turner, "Women's Suf-

erty requirement for voting as well. The fifty-pound requirement could be cash, not land; moreover, it was up to the local election inspectors to determine whether a person actually voted or not. Richard P. McCormick estimates that, by the mid-1780s, as many as nine out of ten adult white men were eligible to vote.[38]

As a result, in hotly contested elections, the electorate swelled—something characteristic of modern democracies.[39] Newspapers began to report that, in some cases, women provided the decisive margin. It was said that Federalist women had provided 150 votes for Jonathan Dayton, who became a senator. Under such circumstances, expediency could trump conviction. Joseph Bloomfield had been reported as pledging "in the most positive manner that not a female should be brought on the election ground" but "was seen rallying the *petticoat electors,* and hurrying them and others to the poll."[40]

Not all of these accounts, many of which come from the partisan press, can be taken at face value. The one from a Democratic-Republican paper that in 1802 claimed that, "in some townships," women "made up almost one fourth of the total number of votes" seems dubious, while the worry of a Federalist opponent of women's voting that no fewer than ten thousand women were eligible and might be presumed to vote is sheer hysteria.[41] It does seem

---

frage in New Jersey," *Smith College Studies in History,* I (1916), 178. See also McCormick, *History of Voting in New Jersey,* 93. In the 1790 statute, McCormick notes the insertion of the word "free" for the first time: "Thus slaves were for the first time explicitly barred from voting. . . ." In 1802, one Jeffersonian alleged that Federalists had secured election "by the illegal votes of proxies, boys, beggars, foreigners, and slaves" ("True American," *True American* [Trenton, N.J.], Nov. 15, 1802, [3], quoted in Turner, "Women's Suffrage in New Jersey," *Smith College Studies in History,* I [1916], 180). For a reference alleging that Federalists obtained the vote of African American slaves, see also "The Centinel," *Centinel of Freedom,* Jan. 11, 1803, [3], cited in Turner, "Women's Suffrage in New Jersey," *Smith College Studies in History,* I (1916), 180n. These allegations that slaves voted may, however, be an expression of partisan hysteria more than fully reliable evidence.

38. McCormick, *Experiment in Independence,* 81, 90–91; McCormick, *History of Voting in New Jersey,* 77.

39. See, for example, Michael E. McGerr, *The Decline of Popular Politics: The American North, 1865–1928* (New York, 1986), 3.

40. "Political," *Centinel of Freedom,* Nov. 20, 1804, [1], cited in Klinghoffer and Elkis, "'Petticoat Electors,'" *Journal of the Early Republic,* XII (1992), 185 (Klinghoffer and Elkis misspell Dayton as Drayton).

41. "For the True American," *True American,* Oct. 25, 1802, [1], also quoted in Klinghoffer and Elkis, "'Petticoat Electors,'" *Journal of the Early Republic,* XII (1992), 183, [William Griffith], *Eumenes: Being a Collection of Papers, Written for the Purpose of Exhibiting Some of the More Prominent Errors and Omissions of the Constitution of New-Jersey . . .* (Trenton, N.J., 1799), quoted ibid., 177 (Federalist estimate of ten thousand female voters). Neale McGoldrick and Margaret Crocco say that "estimates suggest that as many as 10,000

clear, however, from several reports, that election inspectors were lax in the enforcement of the qualifications for voters. There was effectively no property qualification for voting; there were occasional reports of slaves voting; and it is not clear that female voting was restricted to unmarried propertied women only.[42] Let us look again at what Abigail Adams said—that she would have voted for a particular candidate had Massachusetts had the same law as New Jersey. But she could not have voted under New Jersey law—she was a married woman. There was clearly some slippage in the popular understanding of the law and some slippage in its enforcement as well. In 1797, one newspaper complained about the "husbands and sweethearts" who ushered their women to the polls, while, in 1802, when one election was contested, it was claimed "that married women voted." It should be noted that this evidence comes from complaints, typically from those who lost the elections. There were also claims that unpropertied black women were voting.[43]

It is a bit hard to disentangle these issues—the fact that women voted at all and the fact that unqualified women might have been voting, particularly since the issues were often conflated at the time. But, almost from the moment that women began voting in any discernible numbers after 1797, there were complaints about the practice and calls for the franchise to be rescinded. One writer insisted that permitting women to vote was "in direct

---

women in New Jersey voted in some years between 1790 and 1807." See McGoldrick and Crocco, *Reclaiming Lost Ground: The Struggle for Woman Suffrage in New Jersey* (self-pub., 1993), 2.

42. For loose enforcement of voting qualifications, see McCormick, *Experiment in Independence,* 81; and note 37, above. Turner asserted that, in 1806, "Women and girls, black and white, married and single, with and without qualifications, voted again and again. And finally men and boys disguised as women voted once more, and the farce was complete"; see Turner, "Women's Suffrage in New Jersey," *Smith College Studies in History,* I (1916), 182. It is difficult to assess the credibility of this assertion. In its form—with men dressing in drag—it conforms to the image of the world turned upside down.

43. "Communications," *Centinel of Freedom,* Oct. 18, 1797, [3], quoted in Turner, "Women's Suffrage in New Jersey," *Smith College Studies in History,* I (1916), 175n, *Votes and Proceedings of the Twenty-Seventh General Assembly of the State of New-Jersey . . .* (Trenton, N.J., 1802), Nov. 16, 1802, 73, quoted ibid. See also W[illiam] A. W[hitehead], "Female Suffrage," *National Intelligencer,* Oct. 13, 1857, quoted in *Historical Magazine,* I (1857), 360, 362 (reporting that Chief Justice [Joseph Coerten] Hornblower had told him that he could recall only one instance of a woman's voting "and that was when a husband and wife happened to differ *politically* . . . and, in order to neutralize the vote of the former, the latter resolved to exercise the elective franchise"). Slippage would continue even after the franchise had been restricted. According to one report from 1871, election officials sometimes let the occasional woman, alien, or black person vote. See Lucius Q. C. Elmer, "History of the Constitution of New Jersey, Adopted in 1776, and of the Government under It," in New Jersey Historical Society, *Proceedings,* 2d Ser., II (1871), 133, 153.

violation of the spirit and intention of the law." Yet, even when the propriety of women's voting was challenged, New Jersey continued actively to affirm that right. In 1800, the assembly turned down as redundant a recommendation to amend the constitution to make clear that propertied single women were entitled to the vote: "Our Constitution gives this right to maids or widows *black or white.*" Two years later, the assembly refused to overturn an election that was contested on the grounds "that married women voted," and, two weeks after that, it voted down a proposal "to exclude all persons from voting excepting free white males."[44]

By 1807, however, the tide had turned. The impetus was the raucous Essex County referendum in that year to determine whether the new courthouse would be built in Newark or Elizabeth. This was an intraparty squabble among Democratic-Republicans. Corruption was rampant, the likes of which, according to Carl E. Prince, had not been seen since 1789. Newark won, even though voter turnout in Elizabeth was 279 percent.[45] Some number of the extra voters were women—or men impersonating them. According to one account, written some decades later:

> Men usually honest seemed lost to all sense of honor, so completely were they carried away by the heat of the strife. Women vied with the men, and in some instances surpassed them, in illegal voting. Only a few years ago there were living in Newark two ladies, who, at the time of the election in their 'teens, voted six times each. Married women, too, indignant, perhaps, at being placed on the same political level as children and idiots, in defiance of the law, cast their ballots. Governor Pennington is said to have escorted to the poles "a strapping negress." Men and boys disguised themselves in women's attire, and crowded about the polls to assist in winning the day for Newark.[46]

44. "The Centinel," *Centinel of Freedom,* Nov. 2, 1802, [3], cited in Turner, "Women's Suffrage in New Jersey," *Smith College Studies in History,* I (1916), 174, "The Centinel," *Centinel of Freedom,* Nov. 11, 1800, [3], cited ibid., *Votes and Proceedings of the Twenty-Seventh General Assembly* (1802), Nov. 16, 1802, 73, cited ibid., 175; *Votes and Proceedings of the Twenty-Seventh General Assembly* (1802), Nov. 29, 1802, 110.

45. Pole, "Suffrage in New Jersey," New Jersey Historical Society, *Proceedings,* LXXI (1953), 55; Prince, *New Jersey's Jeffersonian Republicans,* 133–134. "Obviously," Prince concludes, "women and perhaps Negroes voted freely in this election" (ibid., 134).

46. William H. Shaw, *History of Essex and Hudson Counties, New Jersey,* I (Philadelphia, 1884), 213. A contemporary account, in the form of rhyming verse, depicted the election in similar terms: "For they call'd in bog trotters, and negroes I'm told / And young boys and girls of a dozen years old. . . ." (Pole, "Suffrage in New Jersey," New Jersey Historical

This corruption—most of which must have been committed by white men—was the last straw for those who had been opposed to New Jersey's expansive franchise. The next legislature passed a statute that effectively amended the constitution by legislation.[47] The argument was that the constitution never could have intended to enfranchise blacks, women or aliens so that a statute stating that the vote was limited to *"free, white, male, citizen[s]"* would be sufficient. By easy majorities, the new law passed. Its preamble explained the rationale:

> WHEREAS doubts have been raised, and great diversities in practice obtained throughout the state in regard to the admission of *aliens, females,* and *persons of color,* or *negroes* to vote in elections, as also in regard to the mode of ascertaining the qualifications of voters in respect to *estate;*—AND WHEREAS, it is highly necessary to the safety, quiet, good order and dignity of the state, to clear up the said doubts by an act of the representatives of the people, declaratory of the true sense and meaning of the constitution, and to ensure its just execution . . . according to the intent of the framers thereof.

Henceforth, the vote would be restricted to free white male taxpaying citizens.[48]

The statute noted doubts and uncertainties in voting practice in New Jersey but resolved them in different ways. Thus, difficulties in determining the status of women and blacks were resolved by withdrawing the right to vote of all women and all black people. Difficulties in determining the wealth of white men were resolved by making all taxpaying men eligible to vote. And

Society, *Proceedings,* LXXI [1953], 56). See also William A. Whitehead, "A Brief Statement of the Facts Connected with the Origin, Practice, and Prohibition of Female Suffrage in New Jersey," New Jersey Historical Society, *Proceedings,* 1st Ser., VIII (1858), 104; and John Lambert, *Travels through Canada, and the United States of North America, in the Years 1806, 1807, and 1808 . . . ,* 2d ed., II (London, 1814), 313–315.

47. Alexander Keyssar noted, "New Jersey seemed uniquely cavalier about altering suffrage requirements by statute rather than constitutional amendment"; see Keyssar, *Right to Vote,* 32.

48. Turner, "Women's Suffrage in New Jersey," *Smith College Studies in History,* I (1916), 183–184; "Supplement to the Act Entitled 'An Act to Regulate the Election of Members of the Legislative Council and General Assembly,'" chap. II, in *Acts of the Thirty-Second General Assembly of the State of New-Jersey* (1807), 14. The first paragraph restated the longstanding property requirement of fifty pounds, clear estate, and the second paragraph effectively redefined that requirement downward by saying that any man who paid taxes was to "be adjudged . . . to be worth fifty pounds" (Ibid., 15).

these changes were billed as progressive reform—just as was the removal of the vote from blacks in the Jim Crow era.[49]

Many historians have noted that the nineteenth-century expansion of voting rights for white men came with restrictions upon those of free blacks and, in the case of New Jersey, women and aliens as well.[50] This is also an important chapter in the history of gender and American politics: increasingly, the American voter was defined as white and male, and this change is, in fact, intrinsic to what Sean Wilentz has called "the rise of American democracy."[51]

In New Jersey, these changes were clearly part of the continuing efforts to reform the state's electoral process. The ostensible goal was to eliminate corruption. But why exclude some groups while embracing others? Several historians have suggested that the limitation of the franchise was a deal struck between Federalists and Democratic-Republicans, each side jettisoning a portion of its constituency. Women and blacks, it was believed, tended to vote Federalist, and the 1804 enactment of a gradual emancipation plan promised to increase the number of eligible black voters, while aliens voted Democratic.[52]

Yet Federalists such as William Griffith and Republicans such as John Condit both argued for the exclusion of women, with Condit adding blacks and Griffith aliens to those who were to be excluded. The agreement to limit the franchise required a rationale, as well, and this can be found in the preamble to the statute. These changes were also necessary, it was argued, for "the safety, quiet, good order and dignity of the state." Here was the language, not of rights or obligations, but of prudence and propriety.[53]

49. Michael McGerr, *A Fierce Discontent: The Rise and Fall of the Progressive Movement in America, 1870–1920* (New York, 2003), 189.

50. Jacob Katz Cogan, "The Look Within: Property, Capacity, and Suffrage in Nineteenth-Century America," *Yale Law Journal,* CVII (1997), 473; Nancy F. Cott, *The Bonds of Womanhood: "Woman's Sphere" in New England, 1780–1835* (New Haven, Conn., 1977), 98–100. Such discussions focus on the shift toward "natural," supposedly inherent qualities as the basis for citizenship, which, nevertheless, does not explain the exclusion of aliens from the polls. See also Smith, "Constructing American National Identity," in Ben-Atar and Oberg, eds., *Federalists Reconsidered,* 19–40; and Keyssar, *Right to Vote.* Keyssar, however, discusses aliens.

51. See Sean Wilentz, *The Rise of American Democracy: Jefferson to Lincoln* (New York, 2005), 186–187, 192–195 (describing the disenfranchisement of blacks, but not recognizing its connection to the expansion of the franchise for white men).

52. Gertzog, "Female Suffrage in New Jersey," *Women and Politics,* X (1990), 56; Klinghoffer and Elkis, "'Petticoat Electors,'" *Journal of the Early Republic,* XII (1992), 12, 18.

53. "Supplement to the Act Entitled 'An Act to Regulate the Election of Members of the

The comments of several of the advocates of franchise restriction suggest that they regarded it as a matter of sensibility, then, as much as fundamental principles. Condit railed against "the vote of a negro slave, herself the property of another negro slave." A Federalist bemoaned "a melancholy picture of the morals of the people . . . excites the most unpleasant sensations in the breast of every person favourably disposed to free, elective government." Another observer thought "a more wicked and corrupt scene was never exhibited in this State, or in the United States." William Griffith was similarly offended: "It is perfectly disgusting," he observed, "to witness the manner in which women are polled at our elections. Nothing can be a greater mockery of this invaluable and sacred right, than to suffer it to be exercised by persons, who do not even pretend to any judgment on the subject." Likewise, the enfranchisement of aliens necessarily had a "degrading and baneful tendency" that was a "scandalous . . . outrage upon the rights of American suffrage." The enfranchisement of women, blacks, and aliens was, on its face, such men suggested, offensive to white male citizens.[54]

Yet how could New Jersey's constitution be squared with this "mockery" of the "invaluable and sacred right" to vote? Griffith struggled with the contradiction. On the one hand, there was "the *letter* of the charter," and, on the other, "*political right* and the nature of things." Legal scholar Jacob Katz Cogan has argued that, increasingly, voters were identified by who they were, that is their presumed inherent qualities, rather than what or how much they owned, and those inherent qualities were those of the white American male citizen.[55]

And so, if New Jersey's franchise of women (and blacks and aliens) was contrary to "the nature of things," then surely it could not have been the intent of the constitution's framers to enfranchise these groups. By this logic,

Legislative Council and General Assembly,'" chap. II, in *Acts of the Thirty-Second General Assembly of the State of New-Jersey* (1807), 14; Marion Thompson Wright, "Negro Suffrage in New Jersey, 1776–1875," *Journal of Negro History,* XXXIII (1948), 168, 175 (Wright spells Condit's name as "Condict"); Turner, "Women's Suffrage in New Jersey," *Smith College Studies in History,* I (1916), 183–184; [Griffith], *Eumenes,* 33–39; Rudolph J. Pasler and Margaret C. Pasler, *The New Jersey Federalists* (Cranbury, N.J., 1975), 14.

54. "Sketch of Mr. Condit's Speech on the Election Bill, in the House of Assembly," *True American,* Nov. 23, 1807, [3], quoted in Wright, "Negro Suffrage in New Jersey," *Journal of Negro History,* XXXIII (1948), 175; "Trenton Federalist," *Trenton Federalist,* Feb. 23, 1807, [3], quoted in Turner, "Women's Suffrage in New Jersey," *Smith College Studies in History,* I (1916), 183n, "New-Jersey Journal," *New-Jersey Journal,* Feb. 17, 1807, [2], quoted ibid., 183; [Griffith], *Eumenes,* 33, 35.

55. [Griffith], *Eumenes,* 33; Cogan, "Look Within," *Yale Law Journal,* CVII (1997), 473.

the 1807 statute restricting the franchise for these groups (while expanding it for white male citizens) was not a fundamental change but instead merely a restatement "of the true sense and meaning of the constitution" designed "to ensure its just execution . . . according to the intent of the framers thereof."[56]

In ten short years, it had become unimaginable to New Jersey's legislators that their predecessors had ever intended to enfranchise any women, or any blacks or aliens, either. And so the perimeters of the Republic were pulled in, and New Jersey's brief experiment in an inclusive franchise was redefined as bad interpretation and a piece of its history reimagined as nothing more than a bad dream.

56. "Supplement to the Act Entitled 'An Act to Regulate the Election of Members of the Legislative Council and General Assembly,'" chap. II, in *Acts of the Thirty-Second General Assembly of the State of New-Jersey* (1807), 14.

The History *of* Emotions

FIGURE 3

Portrait of the Smith Family. Attributed to Captain James Smith. Circa 1807. Accession no. 2011.100.1, A and B. Image no. D2017-JBC-0411-0042. Courtesy, The Colonial Williamsburg Foundation, Williamsburg, Va. Museum Purchase

EMOTION AND THE PURSUIT OF HISTORICAL INSIGHT IN THE WORK OF JAN ELLEN LEWIS

NICOLE EUSTACE

Emotions history did not yet exist as a term when Jan Lewis published her pathbreaking first book, *The Pursuit of Happiness: Family and Values in Jefferson's Virginia,* in 1983. To read her preface to that book now is to listen to someone struggling to give name to a field she herself was in the midst of creating. "How such a change in feeling about the family—and, indeed, in feeling about feeling itself—took place is the subject of this work," she said. Lewis knew that trying to focus analysis on something so amorphous as emotion was far from the norm in the Revolutionary-era historiography of the day; she hastened to reassure her readers of the scholarly bona fides of her project, asserting, "This is a historical work; the methods are primarily those of the historian." By 1998, when she and Peter Stearns introduced the essays in *An Emotional History of the United States,* Lewis sounded far less defensive. "Do the emotions have a history?" the joint editors asked rhetorically in the very first line of their introduction. "Of course," they answered immediately. The essays reproduced in sequence here illuminate the iterative process through which Lewis arrived at this conviction.[1]

Lewis's ultimate investigations of the connections between emotion and politics likewise required her to innovate new modes of analysis, since many of the first historians to turn their attention to emotion focused on its effects on "hearth and home." The subtitle to *The Pursuit of Happiness: Family and Values in Jefferson's Virginia* reveals Lewis's initial grounding in the history of the family. She began by seeking to uncover how domestic life was

Nicole Eustace is professor of history at New York University.

1. Jan Lewis, *The Pursuit of Happiness: Family and Values in Jefferson's Virginia* (New York, 1983), xiv, xvi; Peter N. Stearns and Lewis, "Introduction," in Stearns and Lewis, eds., *An Emotional History of the United States* (New York, 1998), 1. It would be decades before formal guides to method in emotions history would be published. See, for example, Susan J. Matt and Stearns, eds., *Doing Emotions History* (Urbana, Ill., 2014).

conducted in a revolutionary age, not to demonstrate how daily life contributed to a revolution. Initially, as she explained in her 1982 essay "Domestic Tranquillity and the Management of Emotion among the Gentry of Pre-Revolutionary Virginia," she intended to examine the gentry's private life: "What values directed their behavior at home," she asked, "Of what did their emotional life consist?" Yet over the course of some two decades of writing and reflection, Lewis became ever more convinced of the inextricable links between emotional culture and political ideology, between the regulation of emotion and the ordering of civic life. By the time she came to coedit the crucial 1998 volume with Stearns, she was ready to argue in her essay, "'Those Scenes for Which Alone My Heart Was Made': Affection and Politics in the Age of Jefferson and Hamilton," that historians must "consider the place of emotion in the politics of the early national era in American history." This advance dovetailed closely with the evolution in her thinking about the history of women and gender. The more Lewis came to view the family as constitutive of politics, rather than—as early Americans themselves often claimed—a simple refuge from it, the more she was able to elucidate the political meanings of emotion.[2]

From the beginning, Lewis focused on analyzing the social import of emotions rather than treating them as purely personal; therein lay the seeds of her eventual conviction that they ought to be considered political. In "Domestic Tranquillity and the Management of Emotion among the Gentry of Pre-Revolutionary Virginia," Lewis argued that historians who claimed to see evidence that an "affectionate domestic circle . . . encouraged appreciation of the individual, expression of emotion, and exploration of feeling" were far off base. To the contrary, Lewis argued that "neither self-expression nor individuality was a goal; each might disrupt the tranquillity the gentry so prized." Lewis wanted to reveal "character, temperament, and values" among the colonial Virginia gentry, and she never mentioned politics in the essay. Yet her emphasis on the limits of eighteenth-century individualism had implications for political philosophy that she was to explore in later work.[3]

2. Lewis, *Pursuit of Happiness,* 58; Lewis, "Domestic Tranquillity and the Management of Emotion among the Gentry of Pre-Revolutionary Virginia," Lewis, "'Those Scenes for Which Alone My Heart Was Made': Affection and Politics in the Age of Jefferson and Hamilton," both in this volume.

3. Lewis, "'Those Scenes for Which Alone My Heart Was Made,'" and Lewis, "Domestic Tranquillity," both in this volume. For example, Lewis's approach contrasted with that of

In the meantime, as Lewis set out to understand the mechanism by which members of the pre-Revolutionary Virginia gentry attempted to accommodate their emotions to prevailing standards, she groped for a theoretical framework and turned repeatedly to the language of the theater. Lewis argued that the records of emotion left behind by her subjects in letters and diaries were not transparent representations of their lived experience but rather closely curated approximations of cultural ideals. As she sought an analytical model for understanding such records of emotion, Lewis spoke repeatedly of emotional performances. She sought to contrast "the public stage" with "the gentry's private life." She spoke of how the gentry "struck a posture" when needed or donned "a mask." In her most sustained comments, Lewis explained that the kind of emotional language commonly used by gentry children was "stilted because the role was scripted, and most children learned their lines." Implicitly, Lewis was drawing on the theories of the midcentury sociologist Erving Goffman, whose masterwork *The Presentation of Self in Everyday Life* (1959) advanced an influential dramaturgical model of social life.[4]

Lewis pondered the impact of such efforts at emotional control, questioning whether cultural expectations about the boundaries of acceptable expression changed the way that people experienced and interpreted their own inner feelings. "To be sure," she told readers, "restraint was partly a matter of style, but it was more than that." She found that in private as in public settings people did not reveal, even to themselves, anything more than convention allowed. In short, "the style became the substance."[5]

Lewis's ruminations on the relationship between inward feelings and outward expressions of emotion anticipated the direction emotions history would take fifteen years later when a historian of the French Revolution, William Reddy, took up the problem and posited the existence of what he called "emotives." In a June 1997 article in *Current Anthropology*, Reddy ex-

---

Lawrence Stone, who asserted in his widely influential book, *The Family, Sex, and Marriage in England, 1500–1800,* that "the central theme of this book is the extraordinary changes in attitudes towards the individual and towards emotion that occurred between 1660 and 1800." See Stone, *Family, Sex, and Marriage in England, 1500–1800* (New York, 1977), 118.

4. Lewis, "Domestic Tranquillity," in this volume. Compare with Erving Goffman, *The Presentation of Self in Everyday Life* (New York, 1959). Historian of early Virginia Rhys Isaac also wrote on "script formulas" and "roles," noting that such terms had "become so much a commonplace not only of sociological but of everyday discourse." Isaac cited Goffman directly. See Isaac, *The Transformation of Virginia, 1740–1790,* 2d ed. (Williamsburg, Va., and Chapel Hill, N.C., 2012), 351, 376n, 412n.

5. Lewis, "Domestic Tranquillity," in this volume.

plained that because emotion statements were neither purely "constative" nor entirely "performative," a new concept was needed to "capture the two-way character of emotional utterances and acts, their unique capacity to alter what they 'refer' to or what they 'represent.'" Reddy proposed the term "emotives" to denote such statements. Here we can see that Lewis's early 1980s work offers a conceptual bridge between Goffman's 1950s work on acts of performance and Reddy's late 1990s emphasis on utterances that worked in multidirectional ways to shape as well as articulate experience. Reddy ultimately argued that "emotional control is the real site of the exercise of power"; it was to power relations within the family that Lewis turned to explore the impact of the restrained emotional style favored by the pre-Revolutionary Virginia gentry.[6]

Lewis observed that members of the Virginia gentry preferred that emotions be managed: "the proper ones expressed and the others squelched." They believed that "the sweet peace of domestic tranquillity could be purchased only by chaining the individual's emotions." Against those who claimed the Virginia gentry for modernity on the basis of their supposed embrace of individualism, Lewis placed a strong body of evidence that communitarian concerns constrained free expression.[7]

Strategic decisions to participate in, or refrain from, emotional exchanges had material implications. Lewis explicitly tied the idea of emotional "management," introduced by Goffman, to forms of emotional labor. Arguing that emotional and material resources could be exchanged as equivalents among family members, she demonstrated that gifts and allowances provided by parents could be recompensed by the emotional offerings of their children. Lewis explained, "repaying, literally, a parent was one way of discharging the child's debt, but men and women whose parents were materially secure could . . . discharge their debts in other ways. . . . By sending money or a noble sentiment they were playing the part of the dutiful." In analyzing how members of the Virginia gentry attempted to resolve financial obligations by performing particular emotions, Lewis foreshadowed Arlie Russell Hochschild's landmark book, *The Managed Heart: Commercialization of Human Feeling* (1983), which appeared the following year.[8]

6. See William Reddy, "Against Constructionism: The Historical Ethnography of Emotion," *Current Anthropology*, XXXVIII (1997), 327–351, esp. 327, 331; and Lewis, *Pursuit of Happiness*, 99.

7. Lewis, "Domestic Tranquillity," in this volume.

8. Ibid. Compare with Arlie Russell Hochschild, *The Managed Heart: Commercialization of Human Feeling* (Berkeley, Calif., 1983).

Nevertheless, in spite of her early recognition that emotional regulation corresponded to financial contributions—and thus that emotion management was a true form of work—Lewis ultimately emphasized cultural factors more than economic ones in seeking to explain the "emotional style" prevalent among the Virginia gentry. In her later refinements on this point in *Pursuit of Happiness,* she argued that "although it is tempting to link new forms of family relationship in Virginia to the poor state of that region's economy"—and by the phrase "new forms of family" she meant the more emotionally expressive, inward, individualistic style common in the post-Revolutionary period—"it is more accurate to say that a troublesome economy made more palpable and pressing an alteration in family form that was considerably more widespread." Building on this claim, Lewis then turned, in her concluding section, away from economic explanations of emotional change in favor of a focus on the influence of culture, from the rise of evangelical religion to the impact of private reading, diary keeping, and letter writing within a small circle of intimates. This tension in cultural versus economic explanatory mechanisms of emotional change continued to occupy Lewis in her subsequent writing projects.[9]

When she wrote "Mother's Love: The Construction of an Emotion in Nineteenth-Century America" in 1989, Lewis focused intently on the interrelated processes of the cultural production and social construction of emotion. Interrogating nineteenth-century claims about "the irrepressible nature of a mother's love" provided Lewis with a perfect case study of how "ideology" could shape prevailing assumptions about emotion. Following Jay Fliegelman's analysis of how "revolt against patriarchy dethroned both fathers and kings," she inserted motherhood, and mother love, into political analysis—reaffirming her long-held belief that "the histories of politics and the family in this era are entwined." With the family serving as the model for the state, the domestic and the political could never be disentangled.[10]

Lewis now turned to a "very useful neologism" that had been "coined" in 1985 by the scholars Peter N. Stearns and Carol Z. Stearns, the term *emotionology*. The Stearnses used it to "denote 'the collective emotional standards of a society,'" and Lewis found in it exactly what she needed to de-

9. Lewis, "Domestic Tranquillity," in this volume; Lewis, *Pursuit of Happiness,* 175, 216.

10. Jan Lewis, "Mother's Love: The Construction of an Emotion in Nineteenth-Century America," in this volume.

scribe the political inflections of putatively private emotions. Lewis mined the burgeoning new category of secular and religious advice books aimed at mothers and found that such works defined maternal roles by mandating that mothers engage in emotional regulation: "'It is the province of the mother to cultivate the affections, to form and guard the moral habits of the child.'" We might assume that intensified interest in emotion presaged an enhanced interest in individualism. Yet Lewis recognized a key point: advice writers were calling for generalized feminine emotions they linked to virtue and "moral habits," and they placed no value in the nuances of any particular woman's emotions. "It was the feelings that a woman had in common with other women that were prized, not intense or idiosyncratic emotions," Lewis explained. Instrumentality defined the recommended approach to emotion.[11]

Other scholars tied the transformation in women's emotional and moral positioning—from heirs of the passionate sins of Eve to avatars of the self-sacrificing virtues of Christ—to the emergence of market economies and the localization of morality in the private sphere. Yet Lewis insisted that cultural factors predominated over material ones. As Lewis analyzed the expectations for emotion prevalent in the early Republic, she noted how closely religious and political imperatives for emotional regulation coincided. The sacrifice of personal feelings in the service of virtuous emotional homogeneity enacted the sort of self-discipline required to vanquish Christian sin and political corruption alike. Lewis explained, "*self-government,* of course, was a term with a resonance in both religious and political discourse; in a democratic society, which had rejected authoritarian forms of control, it became all the more necessary for individuals to learn to govern themselves." However often advice books implied that mothers' "province" of "affection" was located apart from the rest of society, confined to the home, Lewis insisted that ideals for maternal emotion always operated in the service of religiously inflected political ideologies.[12]

Lewis's empirical findings concerning the conjoined influence of religion and politics on the emotional ideals that defined maternal roles led her back into theoretical debates about the vectors of historical change. "Historians have usually linked the nineteenth century's idealization of motherhood to the early stages of industrialization and the removal of men's work from the home," she observed. "Yet, if structural changes alone could explain the exaltation of self-sacrificing motherhood, that ideal surely would have been

11. Ibid.
12. Ibid.

modified as the society and economy continued to change." The valorization of motherhood persisted, Lewis explained, because beyond any simple connection to unstable economic systems, mother love, as an ideal, "is part of our national civil religion, reflecting an American fusion of democratic and Christian thought." Without denying the influence of economic structures in historical change, Lewis argued that civic life could not be fully understood without reference to culture.[13]

Debates about the role of culture in the making of emotion continued to frame Lewis's thinking a decade later when her essay, "'Those Scenes for Which Alone My Heart Was Made': Affection and Politics in the Age of Jefferson and Hamilton," was published in *An Emotional History of the United States,* the volume she coedited with Stearns. Now Lewis focused on "affection," an emotional form much discussed by political leaders of the early Republic. She emphasized that "such expressions of affection were not . . . merely . . . natural outpourings . . . . Rather, they rested on and indeed sustained a particular social vision." Lewis remained focused on what she termed the "sociology of the emotions," tapping the newly published correspondence of Angelica Schuyler Church "to consider the place of emotion in the politics of the early national era in American history." For Lewis, the combined analysis of family, emotion, and politics remained by far the most generative intellectual nexus, and there was nothing "natural" about it.[14]

Again, Lewis addressed the problem of how to imagine the "spheres" of life in early America. Whereas women's historians in the late 1970s and early 1980s had devoted a great deal of attention to early American rhetoric advocating for women's separation into the private sphere of home and family, Lewis took the lead in challenging the reality and influence of that archetype. Specifically, she contended that "the critical distinction for the first generation of American political leaders was between government and society, including the family, rather than between home and the public sphere." Attention to the history of emotion provided Lewis with new avenues to understanding the formation of American civic life.[15]

She argued that founding men like Jefferson and Hamilton, despite their

13. Ibid.

14. Lewis, "'Those Scenes for Which Alone My Heart Was Made,'" in this volume; Stearns and Lewis, "Introduction," in Stearns and Lewis, eds., *An Emotional History,* 1–14, esp. 7.

15. Lewis, "'Those Scenes for Which Alone My Heart Was Made,'" in this volume.

other political differences, imagined a reciprocal system in which government was formed for the protection of society and, conversely, society—and the social bonds of affection men and women created within it—provided "the basis for national unity." The social and the political did remain separate spheres in this civic model, but this "emotional geography" did not divide neatly by gender into private and public realms, given that women's participation remained essential to the maintenance of society and society played a critical function in supporting the state.[16]

If Lewis's mature work on emotions history stands out for its nuanced approach to analyzing the overlay of personal and political affections, her earlier work took a similarly careful approach to analyzing intersections of emotion and race. Returning to the *Pursuit of Happiness* reveals that Lewis always depicted racial slavery as central to the emotional life of Virginia's white gentry. Lewis insisted that the so-called "happiness" of the white gentry of Revolutionary Virginia could not be understood apart from their entanglement with enslaved blacks.

Lewis rested her enduring skepticism concerning the significance of individualism in early American life on her analysis of the shaping role of slavery in the emotional lives of the Virginia planter class. She described how members of the planter class attempted to deny this basic aspect of their lives: "Again and again, independence was equated with happiness. . . . Independence was not merely a prerequisite for happiness: It was joy itself." And yet, as Lewis also noted, "There is more than a little irony in the fact that the first generation of Americans to commit themselves to the pursuit of happiness would find so much sadness instead." Lewis offered a clear explanation for this apparent emotional paradox, one that resonates today perhaps even more fully than it did in 1985: slavery. Elite Virginians' celebrations of their independence required that they engage in strenuous denials of the defining truth of their lives: "the fact that the planters were dependent upon their slaves."[17]

16. Ibid. Lewis aligned herself directly with C. Dallett Hemphill and Lucia McMahon in the introduction to the volume with Stearns; see Stearns and Lewis, "Introduction," in Stearns and Lewis, eds., *An Emotional History,* 12. See Hemphill, "Class, Gender, and the Regulation of Emotional Expression in Revolutionary-Era Conduct Literature," ibid., 33–51, McMahon, "'While Our Souls Together Blend': Narrating a Romantic Readership in the Early Republic," 66–90, esp. 68.

17. Lewis, *Pursuit of Happiness,* 108, 110, 230.

Lewis stood at the forefront of efforts to understand how sentimental culture and slavery could be complementary rather than contradictory systems of value. She broke new ground with her conclusion that, in the mouths of Jefferson and his fellows, rising sentimentality only led to claims that "slavery might be moral if planters loved their slaves." In other words, Lewis offered the key insight that slaveholders deployed sentiment in aid of slavery's rehabilitation, *not* in service of its eradication. However, Lewis's ability to analyze the interrelationship of emotional culture with the slave economy was hampered by the prevailing view of the 1980s that slavery existed before and beside, but not within, capitalism.[18]

Lewis wrote at a time when scholars largely accepted the idea of slavery as a premodern institution that existed outside the market economy. Lewis stated:

> In the South and in Virginia, the dilemma was particularly complex. . . . The attempt of fathers to create a New World landed gentry flew in the face of . . . an increasingly commercial economy. . . . In grounding their ideal of independence in plantation slavery, southerners wedded their vision to both the land and a form of labor that the modern world was finding increasingly repugnant.

To be clear, Lewis herself never entirely accepted this characterization of slavery as nothing more than a labor system that ran, at least ideally, in a premodern world isolated from commerce. To the contrary, she noted tartly that "with a depleted soil but a prolific labor force, Virginians often discovered that their most valuable commodities were human." Nevertheless, she continued to emphasize that Virginians themselves "were disinclined to consider their own slaves as a form of merchandise." In light of the vast amount of recent work on human commodification in Atlantic slavery, Lewis might refine this section if she were here to revisit these issues today.[19]

18. Ibid., 222. Compare with Garry Wills, *Inventing America: Jefferson's Declaration of Independence* (New York, 1978), 159, 282. Of course, we now recognize that Eric Eustace Williams first published *Capitalism and Slavery* (Chapel Hill, N.C., 1944) more than forty years before Lewis published. However, not until late 1984, by which point Lewis's book was already in press, was it urgently brought to the attention of scholars beyond Caribbean specialists. See Hilary Beckles, "Capitalism and Slavery: The Debate over Eric Williams," *Social and Economic Studies,* XXXIII, no. 4 (December 1984), 171–189.

19. Lewis, *Pursuit of Happiness,* 113, 142–143. See also Jennifer L. Morgan, *Laboring Women: Reproduction and Gender in New World Slavery* (Philadelphia, 2004); Stephanie E. Smallwood, *Saltwater Slavery: A Middle Passage from Africa to American Diaspora* (Cam-

Without the benefit of this important future work, Lewis was left to consider the meaning of the emotional shifts she was documenting within then-available understandings of economic history. Lewis claimed that "although sociologists and social historians have often linked the modernization of family and personality to the structural transformations associated with the industrial revolution, such analysis cannot directly explain the changes that occurred in the late eighteenth-century slaveholding, agricultural society that was Virginia." Here we can see clearly the lingering influence on Lewis's thought of the southern insistence that theirs was an agricultural not a commercial society.[20]

And yet, in spite of this, Lewis did offer tantalizing indications of how her work could be aligned with coming scholarship on slavery, capitalism, and the alienations of commodification. She declared that for southerners "idealization of the family . . . perhaps can be better understood as a response to the ambivalence created by the growth and spread not so much of industry as of commerce." For me, this is the signal sentence in the whole book. It makes clear that she did see crucial links between the South's distinctive emotional culture and its reliance on the commercial trade in human beings. In this Lewis proved herself to be, as she so often was, well ahead of her time.[21]

At the very same moment that Lewis broached that insight, scholars such as Albert O. Hirschman and Thomas L. Haskell were advancing the contrary argument that capitalism itself helped spur the rise of sensibility. In their view, long-distance markets at last overcame the innate limitations on the reach of humane feelings, broadening the span of sympathy to the farthest reaches of the globe: capitalism catalyzed humanitarianism. So long as slavery remained analytically separate from market capitalism, this line of thinking could go unchallenged. Yet today we recognize that neither slavery's avoidance of mechanization nor its lack of a free market in labor prevented it from producing staple crops for sale in a global market nor, most especially, from profiting off human commodification. So it matters greatly that

---

bridge, Mass., 2008); Lorena S. Walsh, *Motives of Honor, Pleasure and Profit: Plantation Management in the Colonial Chesapeake, 1607–1763* (Williamsburg, Va., and Chapel Hill, N.C., 2010); Jennifer L. Anderson, *Mahogany: The Costs of Luxury in Early America* (Cambridge, Mass., 2012); and Caitlin Rosenthal, *Accounting for Slavery: Masters and Management* (Cambridge, Mass., 2018).

20. Lewis, *Pursuit of Happiness,* 175, 216.

21. Ibid., 222.

Lewis showed that sentimentalism, commercialism, and American slavery all emerged together and operated in mutually reinforcing fashion.[22]

Readers of this volume not only have the opportunity to trace the development of Lewis's work on emotion, power, and politics over decades but also to imagine where we might yet go if we continue along the trajectory she set. Lewis spent decades engaged in close study of the effects of cultural constructions on the exercise of power. All that she lacked was the full recognition, widespread today, that the rise of free markets for commodities helped define the emergence of capitalism and, thus, that slave markets—and the emotional culture enabling them—were very much implicated in capitalism's rise. As we reconsider the relationship between capitalism and slavery today, she might agree that we likewise need to reassess the emotional transformations that accompanied and enabled the rise of slavery's capitalism. And, if by chance Lewis did not concur, no doubt she would say so directly and seize the moment to initiate another great round of debate.[23]

22. See Albert O. Hirschman, *The Passions and the Interests: Political Arguments for Capitalism before Its Triumph* (1977; rpt. Princeton, N.J., 2013); Thomas L. Haskell, "Capitalism and the Origins of Humanitarian Sensibility, Part 1," *American Historical Review,* XC (1985), 339–361; and Haskell, "Capitalism and the Origins of Humanitarian Sensibility, Part 2," *American Historical Review,* XC (1985), 547–566. The Haskell articles are reprinted in Thomas Bender, ed., *The Antislavery Debate: Capitalism and Abolitionism as a Problem in Historical Interpretation* (Berkeley, Calif., 1992), 107–160.

23. On the slave trade as the vanguard of free market capitalism, see Gregory E. O'Malley, *Final Passages: The Intercolonial Slave Trade of British America, 1619–1807* (Williamsburg, Va., and Chapel Hill, N.C., 2014), 28–29.

Domestic Tranquillity and the Management of Emotion among the Gentry of Pre-Revolutionary Virginia

When Frederick Jones of Virginia visited his North Carolina kin in 1757, he fell in love. He married his cousin, Jane Swann, made his home with his wife's folks, and several years later reflected that, except for his separation from his own family, "in every other circumstance of life, I have the greatest reason to be vastly happy and thankful to the wise disposer of all things and upon the whole submit and agree . . . that whatever is is right." The story is in many ways unexceptional. By the early decades of the eighteenth century, the Virginia gentry had cause for the complacency reflected in Jones's evocation of Alexander Pope. After a tumultuous first century, Virginia's planter elite had come to preside over a society that was demographically secure and socially at peace.[1]

Studies of the character, temperament, and values of the Virginia gentry have given us pictures of its members at horse races and at worship, astride their favorite mounts and in the front rows of their parish churches, always proving their prowess and displaying their persons, always on top or in front. Self-confident and extroverted, the gentry exuded self-assurance on the public stage. We know both the impression that they wanted to make on others and the importance to them of making an impression. Less clear is

This essay was originally published as Jan Lewis, "Domestic Tranquillity and the Management of Emotion among the Gentry of Pre-Revolutionary Virginia," *William and Mary Quarterly,* 3d Ser., XXXIX (1982), 135–149.

1. Frederick Jones to Thomas Jones, Feb. 10, 1765, Papers of the Jones Family, Library of Congress, Washington, D.C.; Edmund S. Morgan, *American Slavery, American Freedom: The Ordeal of Colonial Virginia* (New York, 1975), chaps. 14–18; Allan Kulikoff, "The Colonial Chesapeake: Seedbed of Antebellum Southern Culture?" *Journal of Southern History,* XLV (1979), 531–537; Carole Shammas, "English-Born and Creole Elites in Turn-of-the-Century Virginia," in Thad W. Tate and David L. Ammerman, eds., *The Chesapeake in the Seventeenth Century: Essays on Anglo-American Society* (Williamsburg, Va., and Chapel Hill, N.C., 1979), 274–296; T. H. Breen, "Horses and Gentlemen: The Cultural Significance of Gambling among the Gentry of Virginia," *William and Mary Quarterly,* 3d Ser., XXXIV (1977), 240–241.

the nature of the gentry's private life. What values directed their behavior at home? Of what did their emotional life consist?[2]

Historians have suggested that the eighteenth-century Chesapeake gentry, like their English counterparts, nurtured and cherished an intimate and harmonious household. The affectionate domestic circle embraced fathers and mothers, daughters and sons, inspiring their love for one another; it encouraged appreciation of the individual, expression of emotion, and exploration of feeling. The gentry family, it is argued, fostered love and self-expression, warmth and individuality—the lineaments, if not the flesh, of a recognizably "modern" family. The private writings of the pre-Revolutionary Virginia gentry, men and women alike, however, disclose that, for them, neither affection nor self-expression was yet an unqualified value; both were managed and restrained in the service of a higher good, domestic tranquillity.[3]

2. See esp. Rhys Isaac, "Evangelical Revolt: The Nature of the Baptists' Challenge to the Traditional Order in Virginia, 1765 to 1775," *William and Mary Quarterly*, 3d Ser., XXXI (1974), 345–368; Isaac, *The Transformation of Virginia, 1740–1790* (Williamsburg, Va., and Chapel Hill, N.C., 1982); and Breen, "Horses and Gentlemen," *William and Mary Quarterly*, XXXIV (1977), 239–257.

3. Daniel Blake Smith, *Inside the Great House: Planter Family Life in EighteenthCentury Chesapeake Society* (Ithaca, N.Y., 1980), 22, 291; Philip Greven, *The Protestant Temperament: Patterns of Child-Rearing, Religious Experience, and the Self in Early America* (New York, 1977), 265–331; Lawrence Stone, *The Family, Sex, and Marriage in England, 1500–1800* (New York, 1977), 221–269. Stone believes that there is an "almost uncanny" similarity between Smith's findings and his own, that gentry family life in England and in the Chesapeake was essentially the same (see "Original Sins," *New York Review of Books*, XXVIII [Feb. 5, 1981], 35). For a different view, see Michael Zuckerman, "William Byrd's Family," *Perspectives in American History*, XII (1979), 255–311. The discussion that follows is part of a study of the changing emotional life of the Virginia gentry from about 1700 to 1830, based on a wide reading of personal documents. Historians are now using the term *gentry* to designate those "few" families in each county who "dominated civil, ecclesiastical, and military affairs. Although the members of these families were substantially wealthier than the great majority of white planters, they were not a class in a narrow economic sense. Their cultural style as well as their financial position set them apart" (Breen, "Horses and Gentlemen," *William and Mary Quarterly*, XXXIV [1977], 240n). To a certain extent, the group was self-defining, including those who signed their names "Gentlemen," along with members of their families. Despite that his evidence comes from Virginia, Philip Greven suggests that the genteel of all colonies shared a similar temperament; he often, however, distinguishes southerners from northerners (Greven, *Protestant Temperament*, 308, 319). Daniel Blake Smith, whose reading of personal documents from the Chesapeake region is nearly exhaustive, believes that, although there might have been some regional variations, one can safely generalize about the experience for well-to-do planters, primarily Anglican, "living in the more densely settled regions of Tidewater" (Smith, *Inside the Great House*, 23). The conclusions reached in this essay, though differing from those of Greven and Smith, should be applicable to the plantation gentry of the Chesapeake and may to some extent hold for the wider South in the years before the Revolution.

Let us begin with Frederick Jones and his vast happiness. Such satisfaction was typical of the gentry, but it was at least as much a statement of faith as of fact, shaping their prayers as much as their praise. So ardently did Virginians desire peace at home that they struck a posture of complacency, as if a mask of composure might pass for the real thing. Surely that was the case with Jones, whose studied self-satisfaction hid an abiding bitterness he was unwilling to reveal.

When the young man fell in love with his cousin, the couple's parents entered into the negotiations that regularly preceded gentry marriages. The girl's mother, also Jane Swann, approvingly observed that the couple "had enough to Enable them on their first coming together to set out in the world in a way to live comfortably, and Provide for a Family," so that neither set of parents was under immediate necessity of contributing more. Although the children were free to live with them until her husband, Samuel Swann, could "set them out in the world," Mrs. Swann hoped that her Virginia cousins could help, for "young people . . . are impatiently fond of having something seperate [*sic*] of their own to improve and manage." Samuel's letter to Jones's father was more explicit. Because he had suffered from a bad harvest and a failed investment and had heavy current expenses, including the costs of educating his only other child, a son, in England, he could give his daughter no dowry. Nevertheless, at Samuel's death, Jane would receive a share equal to her brother's, "which will be sufficient to make [the couple's] circumstances Easy in the world." Swann made clear that he expected young Jones to receive an equal share with his brothers and sisters in his father's estate.[4]

Such negotiations reveal widely shared expectations about family relationships. Prospering parents felt an unquestioned obligation to "launch" their children "out into some happy subsistence in this world." So well understood was this responsibility that one planter, Henry Fitzhugh, could invoke it in cutting off trade with a London merchant who refused to extend further credit: "You must know I have [a] large family, and the chiefest of my estat[es] entailed on a few of my children so that I [am?] under a necessity of purchasing lands for th[e] others which I can now for ready money do to advantage under the present condition of our country."[5] Premarital nego-

4. Jane Swann to Elizabeth Jones, Sept. 7, 1757, Papers of the Jones Family, Samuel Swann to Thomas Jones, Sept. 8, 1757; Edmund S. Morgan, *Virginians at Home: Family Life in the Eighteenth Century* (Williamsburg, Va., 1952), 30–34.

5. William Fitzhugh to Oliver Luke, Aug. 15, 1690, in Richard Beale Davis, ed., *William*

tiations consisted in actualizing and making specific the general obligation. In a typical exchange, Fitzhugh advised Francis Thornton that he was "well pleased with your son and what you have given him. . . . I will give them three hundred and seventy five pounds currentlcy [*sic*], the one half of which I oblige myself to pay this market as soon as my Rents can be collected and disposed off [*sic*] and the other half to be paid next year, also three slaves." Children, knowing what they might receive from their parents, accepted these commitments as their due.[6]

How such expectations could shape family relations is well illustrated by Frederick Jones. He and his cousin were married in North Carolina in 1757 and, by early the next summer, were making plans to return to Virginia. The young husband wrote his father, Thomas (who, unbeknown to the son, had recently died), requesting a pole chair; his wife's pregnancy made it impossible for her to ride horseback. "Was there any such thing to be had here, my Father in Law would not allow me giving you this Trouble," Frederick explained. A chair ordered from England could not arrive in time; "besides I would choose to avoid it; indeed I think it is more than I expect from him, as he has acted so generously by me, since my Marriage as well as before." His father-in-law hoped to sell land for Virginia currency so that Frederick could buy slaves when he returned to Virginia. Frederick implored his father for the chair, asking that its value be deducted from his inheritance and promising that he would be accountable for it to his brothers and sisters. "Your complying," he suggested, "will be a particular Instance of yours and my Mother[']s Love and Affection to me, as it will be advancing so much for me toward my Share or Part, which I have no reason to expect 'till your Death to share with the rest." Young Jones asked no more than his due. Two months later, thinking that his brothers and sisters might be anxious, he explained to one brother, also Thomas, why he preferred not to ask the chair of Samuel Swann: "I should choose to avoid being under obligations of this Nature, so soon to my Father in Law, tho' his unbounded Generosity and

---

Fitzhugh and His Chesapeake World, 1676–1701 (Chapel Hill, N.C., 1963), 279; Henry Fitzhugh to John Bland, 1764, Henry Fitzhugh Papers, David M. Rubenstein Rare Book and Manuscript Library, Duke University, Durham, N.C. See also Catesby Cocke to Sister [Elizabeth] Jones, speaking of "those desirable purposes of making a decent provision for my children, and of finishing my days with as much peace as this world can afford" (September 1753, Papers of the Jones Family).

6. Henry Fitzhugh to Francis Thornton, April 1757, Henry Fitzhugh Papers. See also Richard Corbin to Messrs. Hanbury, June 18, 1760, Richard Corbin Letterbook, Richard Corbin Papers, John D. Rockefeller, Jr., Library, Special Collections, Colonial Williamsburg Foundation, Williamsburg, Va.

Goodness has already layn me under greater obligation, I doubt I shall ever be able to compensate."[7]

Frederick Jones used the language of an almost mechanical reciprocity in explaining his dilemma. As a son, he felt entitled to a share of his parents' estate. He was reluctant to accept such aid from his wife's father, knowing that he would ultimately be called on to balance the accounts in some way. The young man, however, never received the pole chair from his parents, and so he and his wife remained in North Carolina, no doubt increasing their already large debt of gratitude to Samuel Swann. The Swanns must have been delighted with the arrangement. Mrs. Swann had borne only two children and dreaded an empty house. As his daughter's family began to grow, Samuel boasted that she was "likely to make up for the deficits of her Mother." Frederick might still have preferred to live in his native Virginia. When informed of his mother's death and the plans for the disposition of her estate, he did not hide his bitterness from his brother. The estate was to be portioned among the four brothers and four sisters. "Had my father thought proper to have divided [his estate] between his four Sons," Jones complained, "it might have been the means of our spending our days happily near each other, and have afforded pretty Settlements,—but as he ordered it otherwise, it deprives us from ever hoping to have so great a blessing."[8]

Frederick's brothers and sisters established their families in Virginia, and he remained in North Carolina. A number of years later, Frederick's brother Thomas explained that he would not be able to pay the debt he owed Frederick resulting from the sale of their parents' estate. Frederick was "in much pain to be informed your Circumstances are not so easy and clear as I very sincerly [*sic*] wish they were," but he could not forgive the debt, for "the present Situation of my affairs, undoubtedly calls very pressingly for it; and it is no small disappointment and obstacle to my advancing and improving my Estate for my increasing family, as I might otherwise do." Jones had a young family; providing for them was his greatest obligation, a responsibility he had assumed the moment he married. He would demonstrate his love and

7. Frederick Jones to Thomas Jones [Sr.], June 5, 1758, Papers of the Jones Family, Frederick Jones to Thomas Jones [Jr.], July 7, 1758. For a genealogy of the Jones family, see "The Cocke Family of Virginia," *Virginia Magazine of History and Biography,* V (1897), 192–194.

8. Samuel Swann to Thomas Jones, July 7, 1758, Papers of the Jones Family, Frederick Jones to Thomas Jones, June 8, 1762. See also Frederick Jones to Thomas Jones, May 22, 1763, and Jan. 10, 1765, ibid.

affection for his children by establishing them in the world. He knew from experience that a father who defaulted would surrender his claim to companionship and affection from his offspring.[9]

Parents, then, owed their children a settlement. The obligation was both material and measurable. More striking than the formal style of Frederick's letter to his parents is that he demanded, and then intended to provide for his own children, something tangible as "a particular Instance of . . . Love and Affection." Emotions were presented formally; the manner of expression in a young man's letter to his parents was appropriate to the sentiment: the style was precise, restrained, mannered; the emotion clear, explicit, external. When Jones later spoke of his vast happiness, his thankfulness to God, and his conviction "that whatever is is right," these sentiments covered his feelings of disappointment in his parents and antagonism toward his siblings. Clearly, the manner of expression and the emotional style sought to check and control human feelings.

That the aim was restraint emerges in the correspondence of other Virginians in the pre-Revolutionary period. Several examples, once again from the Jones family but typical of the gentry, should serve to make the point. After the death of their father, Thomas Jones became guardian of his younger brother Walter. When the latter went to Edinburgh to study medicine, he came to depend on his brother as a son on a father. Anxious at not having received funds from home for more than a year, Walter reasoned that "some unexpected event has obliged you to withhold the Testimonies of that Kindness and affection, which I have always Experienced and which Love and gratitude have as constantly prompted me to deserve." This is the language of Frederick Jones: reciprocating love was the right of a dutiful and loving son, and parental affection should be demonstrated materially. How did a young man acquire such a mechanical and external notion of love? Consider that seven years earlier, when Walter in a letter had misspelled "write" as "right," his older brother had lectured him: "This is the Consequence of being thoughtless, and Passionate, which follies, I hope you will endeavour for the Future to Conquer." If such a trifle could seem so heinous, surely passion was feared. Consider also the proud letter Thomas drafted to his brother in 1770 when Walter received his medical degree: "It caused such an emotion in me that obliges me to leave the room, I can imagine you have no conception of the feeling and know not what I mean. . . . However let it

9. Frederick Jones to Thomas Jones, Jan. 23, 1770, ibid.

suffice that I love you." In the final copy, Thomas omitted that last clause; an explicit declaration of love was not appropriate.[10]

Strong emotions, even of love, were to be blunted and curbed. To be sure, this restraint was partly a matter of style, but it was more than that when the elder Thomas Jones (in fact mourning the death of his horse) proclaimed, "It is my opinion we ought not to have any immoderate concern for any thing that happens to us in this world." And the style became the substance when young men schooled in emotional restraint were able to think of family relationships as formal contracts.[11]

Several historians have viewed the eighteenth-century Virginia gentry family as particularly affectionate, shaped by that "surge of sentiment" that would distinguish so-called modern families from their more traditional European antecedents.[12] Surely, if a young man could and did demand from his family "testimonies of . . . Kindness and affection," love was one of the bases of family life; yet pre-Revolutionary gentry relationships lacked—or, more precisely, stifled—emotional intensity. Put another way, love was important, but it was not central. Both within and without the family, other ideals—such as peace and moderation—prevailed, creating the context within which emotion might safely be displayed.[13]

10. Walter Jones to Thomas Jones, Apr. 4, 1767, ibid., Thomas Jones to Walter Jones, [circa 1760], Thomas Jones to Walter Jones, Mar. 10, 1770.

11. Thomas Jones to Elizabeth Jones, Sept. 12, 1736, ibid.

12. The phrase is Edward Shorter's from *The Making of the Modern Family* (New York, 1975), 6. Shorter believes that the presence of "romantic love" in eighteenth-century New England and Virginia distinguished New World families from their more "traditional" European counterparts (65). Affection in eighteenth-century Virginia families is also discussed by Edmund S. Morgan in *Virginians at Home.* He is inclined to note the emotional similarities of eighteenth-century Virginians and modern Americans, thereby diminishing the significance of changing conventions. Both Philip Greven's *Protestant Temperament* (which little concerns itself with change and eschews "modernization theory") and Daniel Blake Smith's *Inside the Great House* describe an affectionate, intimate Chesapeake gentry family. It should be noted that, although Smith believes that, after 1750, "planter family life changed significantly," much of his evidence—especially for the presence of affection within the family—is drawn indiscriminately from both halves of the eighteenth century (21). My examination of letters and diaries from the period 1700–1830 suggests that the most significant changes took place in the decades after the Revolution. See Jan Ellen Lewis Grimmelmann, "This World and the Next: Religion, Death, Success, and Love in Jefferson's Virginia" (Ph.D. diss., University of Michigan, 1977). See also Russell Lindley Blake, "Ties of Intimacy: Social Values and Personal Relationships of Antebellum Slaveholders" (Ph.D. diss., University of Michigan, 1978).

13. For the increasing importance of love in nineteenth-century Virginia families, see Grimmelmann, "This World and the Next," chap. 5. For a discussion of the centrality of love

If parents had clear material obligations to their children, so also had children duties to their parents. They showed their love by their deportment. Even when grown, they were expected to be cheerful and obedient—in the language of the time, a "comfort" to their parents in their old age. When the planter William Fitzhugh heard that his mother had experienced misfortune, he released money to his brother in England to aid her. "I . . . do think it both our dutys . . . not to suffer one to want, who gave us our being, nor suffer her to strugle to live, who (under God) gave us life here," he explained. "Nature, duty, the Laws of God and Man . . . command . . . to give the utmost help to a distressed Parent." Fitzhugh was doing no more than adopting for himself a standard he held for others. The sentiment and language were similarly stilted when Fitzhugh hoped that a cousin's son would "as he grows in years . . . grow in grace, truly to serve his God, and then without question you his Parents will find him abound with all dutifull observance, and due Obedience." Repaying, literally, a parent was one way of discharging the child's debt, but men and women whose parents were materially secure could lighten the burdens of old age and discharge their debts in other ways. When he completed his college education, John Clopton hoped he would "cease to be so expensive" to his father. He appreciated the older man's "paternal kindness . . . for which may I ever retain a grateful Sense, study to be an Honour to your old Age by diffusing thro' the world the Fruits of that liberal Education you have been so careful to give me." The language is mannered, but, significantly, Fitzhugh and Clopton felt that by sending money or a noble sentiment they were playing the part of the dutiful son.[14]

The language was stilted because the role was scripted, and most children learned their lines. In the wider world, the gentry were bound to assert themselves, prove their prowess, leave their mark. They were trained to act with more restraint and less individuality at home: the goal was a family life that was at once simple and affectionate.[15] So long as a son or daughter was

---

in modern society, see Ernest Becker, *The Denial of Death* (New York, 1973), esp. 160–170, on "The Romantic Solution."

14. Elizabeth Ronald to Madam, May 21, 1775, Parker Family Papers, Liverpool Record Office, microfilm, John D. Rockefeller, Jr., Library, Special Collections; William Fitzhugh to Henry Fitzhugh, Apr. 22, 1686, in Davis, ed., *William Fitzhugh,* 171, William Fitzhugh to William Fitzhugh, Jan. 30, 1686/7, 198; John Clopton to William Clopton, Sept. 31 [*sic*], 1775, Clopton Family Papers, 1629–1915, David M. Rubenstein Rare Book and Manuscript Library. See also Theo[doric]k Bland to Frances Randolph, Sept. 26, 1777, Tucker-Coleman Papers, Earl Greg Swem Library, Special Collections, The College of William and Mary, Williamsburg, Va.

15. For the implications of such a conceptualization of the ideal family life, see Richard

obedient and appreciative, most parents felt amply repaid for the expense and care of rearing them. Where expectations were clear and simple, children could be confident that they had discharged their duties. An exception that helps prove the rule of reciprocity comes from the agitated domestic experiences of Landon Carter, an unusually bitter and bad-humored man, who found his children a continual disappointment. Carter contrasted their disobedience to his devotion to his own father. When his father was declining, Carter used to sleep at his head, to comfort and divert him. "I did it with both duty and pleasure," Carter boasted to his diary, "but I fancy not a child of mine but would refuse even their duty." In fact, Carter kept a diary in the hope that his offspring would one day read it and recall how they had failed him; in it, he recorded his frequent quarrels with his children, one daughter-in-law, and his son-in-law.[16]

The most serious confrontations were with his eldest son, Robert Wormeley Carter, who lived with his wife and children in his father's home. The younger Carter, a notorious gambler, was as relaxed as his father was rigid, and the great difference in temperaments made arguments inevitable. The two men could not refrain from goading one another; their disputes revealed deep tensions. During an afternoon tea, Landon remarked "in a joke" that his son probably thought they should drink tea, an expensive commodity, only once a week. As the father told the story, his son's "replye was neither ought you to use it any more than we." The father retorted, "What Sir, can't I spend my own money[?]" Robert answered, "By God You will have none to spend soon. I replyed I might owe about £1000. His [*sic*] answered . . . than [he] would not pay it. I then indeed grew outrageous and said it was a damned infamous lie etc. For which I do suppose Mr. Carter leaves the house. . . . Indeed he said abundance more and I replyed as tauntingly . . . he had been my dayly curse." When he cooled, the son told the father that,

Sennett, *The Fall of Public Man* (New York, 1977), 89–107. Although there is much in Sennett's discussion of the cosmopolitan culture of Paris and London in the eighteenth and nineteenth centuries that is not applicable to pre-Revolutionary Virginia, his work is richly suggestive.

16. Landon Carter, June 25, in Jack P. Greene, ed., *The Diary of Colonel Landon Carter of Sabine Hall, 1752–1778*, 2 vols. (Charlottesville, Va., 1965), II, 835–836, Sept. 3, 1774, 856. For Landon Carter's biography and personality, see Greene's excellent introduction to the diary, also published separately as Greene, *Landon Carter: An Inquiry into the Personal Values and Social Imperatives of the Eighteenth-Century Virginia Gentry* (Charlottesville, Va., 1965). For Carter's father, Robert "King" Carter, see Louis Morton, *Robert Carter of Nomini Hall: A Virginia Tobacco Planter of the Eighteenth Century* (Williamsburg, Va., 1941), chap. 1.

although it would be inappropriate to instruct a stranger how to spend his money, a man might take such a liberty with his father, since the son would be obliged to pay the debts the father left at death. The elder Carter concluded that "Sons are determined against the least indulgence to the Grey hour of a Parent."[17]

Landon Carter was extremely proud of the skill with which he had worked his plantation, established all his children, and, contrary to his gibe, avoided debt. He was outraged that Robert could not so manage his share as to make money rather than draw from his father. The estate he had given his son was worth three hundred pounds a year if directed properly. "I have tried every way to be better treated, but cannot even Purchase it of him; many are the Pounds that I have paid out of my Pocket for him; but nothing will do." Carter would never understand why the obedience he believed he had bought from his son was not forthcoming; after all, he had paid his own father what he owed him.[18]

Robert thought his father's demands were excessive, and with good reason; Landon was a self-styled patriarch in whose home a subservient role was difficult, especially for a son whose temperament was so different. After Landon disrupted one of Robert's card parties, removing the table and cards, the father and son argued. The father recorded, "I was told by the 40 year old man he was not a child to be controuled; but I answered 40 ought to hear reasons." A month after the outburst over the tea, ten years before the interrupted card game, Robert had determined to move from the house in order "to avoid the frequent quar[rels between?] Father and me." He changed his plans when he learned that such an action would cause his father to "take away the maids that tended my Children, and that he would not aid me but distress me." This threat made the son "bid adieu to all Satisfaction, being compelled to live with him who told me I was his daily curse; and who [imp]uted to me his Negroes running away. . . . But he is still my Father and I must [torn] bear with every thing from him; in order [to lead a?] quiet life." To protect his own children's interests, Robert resolved to remain in his father's house, to refrain from criticizing his management, to renounce all interest in "domestic affairs," and to endure insult and humiliation. All this he attempted for twelve years, until Landon died. Despite the acrimony,

17. Landon Carter, July 6, 1766, in Greene, ed., *Diary of Colonel Landon Carter,* I, 314–315. By Carter's own reckoning four years later, he was in debt "but a very trifle"; thus he was teasing his son more than a little (July 19, 1770, ibid., I, 447).

18. Landon Carter, July 19, 1770, ibid., I, 447, Aug. 12, 1774, II, 848–849.

he was constrained both by his sense of obligation to his own children and by his belief that sons ought to be obedient and domestic life quiet.[19]

The ideal was peace. Another planter, exasperated by a fifty-year-old brother who was exhausting both his funds and his patience, lectured him on the proper conduct of domestic life. "You were heartily welcome to the best accommodations my house afforded," Catesby Cocke assured his brother William, "and should always have been so, if you could have been contented." William's financial "Extravagancies," however, were more than Catesby could support. "As my only Study in life is to make my Self and every one about me easy," he explained, "your manners . . . are a bar to my peaceable Scheme." Therefore, he wrote, "compose your Self, preserve sobriety, forbear being troublesome, particularly borrowing. Stay quietly at your home, wherever you make it, and resolve to spend no faster than it comes in." When William Cocke interfered with his brother's "peaceable Scheme," he exhausted his welcome.[20]

It is a commonplace of southern history that the family was of overriding importance, that the family line took precedence over the individual. True, family obligations were taken seriously, but it is easy to oversimplify. Notions of family responsibility were neither vague nor overarching. More important was a particular vision of domestic happiness. The premium was placed, not on honor (as those who emphasize the traditional nature of southern culture would expect), nor on affection (as those impressed by its modernity believe), but on peace.[21]

As a result, Virginians of the gentry class were neither introspective nor self-critical. They masked and moderated their feelings; consequently, they did not expect or demand intimacy with others. In 1769, one man could inform a good friend of his recent marriage in these words: "Last Tuesday

19. Landon Carter, Mar. 15, 1776, ibid., II, 1002; Robert Wormeley Carter Diary, Aug. 25, 1766, typescript, John D. Rockefeller, Jr., Library, Special Collections.

20. Catesby Cocke to Sr., Mar. 11, 1752, Papers of the Jones Family, C[atesby] C[ocke] to [William Cocke], November 1752, C[atesby] C[ocke] to [William Cocke], Dec. 3, 1752.

21. A succinct statement of the case for the traditionalism (and hence the social importance or "familialism") of the supposedly "patriarchal" southern family can be found in Bertram Wyatt-Brown, "The Ideal Typology and Ante-Bellum Southern History: A Testing of a New Approach," *Societas,* V, no. 1 (Winter 1975), 1–29. See also, typically, Eugene D. Genovese, *The Political Economy of Slavery: Studies in the Economy and Society of the Slave South* (New York, 1961), 28: "The planters . . . set the tone of social life. Theirs was an aristocratic, antibourgeois spirit with values and mores emphasizing family and status, a strong code of honor, and aspirations to luxury, ease, and accomplishment. In the planters' community, paternalism provided the standard of human relationships." See similarly Anne Firor Scott, *The Southern Lady: From Pedestal to Politics, 1830–1930* (Chicago, 1970), 14–21.

Miss Kendall gave me her hand, and I am happy in having all the reason in the world to believe that her heart also gave me the preference to every other person." The language is in some measure conventional, but the convention itself is revealing, for it dissociates the heart from the hand; and, once again, behavior—here, the act of marrying—serves as a sufficient index of love. Edmund Randolph voiced the belief on which the convention was based. At the time of his wedding, he did not believe that marital happiness "depended upon an exclusive preference being given to [the husband] before all other men, and I desired nothing more than that she should sincerely persuade herself, that she could be happy with me." If he did not expect his bride to know and love him deeply, neither did he stare into her soul. Writing three-and-a-half decades after his marriage, Randolph noted that he had not at that time "reflected much upon that range of qualities which I afterwards found to be constituents of marital happiness." Virginians did not like to reflect on matters of feeling.[22]

Emotional intensity between husband and wife, as between parent and child, was avoided. Landon Carter, for example, found a Mrs. Foy "more fond of her husband Perhaps than the politeness of the day allows of." There is the suggestion that good manners or even happiness required the curbing of instinct and its expression. Margaret Parker, pregnant for the first time and distressed by her husband's sudden departure on an extended business trip, thought she could "bear the disap[p]ointment better at any time than this as I expect within these two months to stand in need of some such a comforter as you but I will not make you uneasy with complaints and will summon all my small stock of philosophy to wait with patience till that mercifull director of all things . . . Shall think fitt to bless me with meeting you again." The only acceptable way in which the young bride could reveal her anxiety was by saying that she would hide her true feelings for fear of disturbing her husband's peace: in baring her emotions, she feared she did wrong.[23]

Of all experiences, the death of loved ones might have shattered the mask of composure, yet Virginians kept their descriptions of death and their letters

22. William Ronald to James Parker, Oct. 14, 1769, Parker Family Papers; Edmund Randolph, "Mrs. Edmund Randolph," Mar. 25, 1810, Edgehill-Randolph Papers, Albert and Shirley Small Special Collections Library, University of Virginia, Charlottesville, Va. Randolph was aware that times and conventions had changed, that marriage had become—in the ideal, at least—more romantic. For changing views on marriage in the early nineteenth century, see Grimmelmann, "This World and the Next," chap. 5.

23. Landon Carter, July 27, 1774, in Greene, ed., *Diary of Carter,* II, 837, 814–815; Margaret Parker to James Parker, Apr. 31 [*sic*], 1765, Parker Family Papers.

of consolation brief, fully aware that dwelling on the subject might stimulate the emotional excess they found so threatening. For example, when Anne Blair told her sister Martha Braxton about the unexpected death of another young woman, she did not linger on the news: "Who would have thought when last we saw Miss Brown so blooming, her Fate was so near a Crisis? but hold! we'll quit this gloomy subject." The obvious lesson, that death comes without warning, would not be drawn; rather, it would be defended against. Virginians refused to dwell on even the deaths of those dearest to them. When his infant daughter died, Frederick Jones wrote to his brother Thomas, "Providence has been pleased to handle us lately very Severely. . . . Enough of that melancholy Subject."[24] The melancholy thought occurs but is stifled: men and women told each other that death was not to be discussed, grief not to be indulged. Did the gentry perhaps mourn in private, revealing to themselves more than convention let them show to the world? In fact, the style was the substance: death was no more the subject of pre-Revolutionary diaries than of letters. For example, on his tenth wedding anniversary, Robert Wormeley Carter wrote tersely: "I have now living two Sons and a Daughter my Wife has miscarried five times; brought a dead Child and lost a fine little Boy about 18 months."[25] The information noted, no more was to be said. Consider William Byrd II's reaction to the death of his ten-month-old son: "God gives and God takes away; blessed be the name of God." He compared his stoicism favorably to his wife's grief. She "was much afflicted but I submitted to His judgment better, not withstanding I was very sensible of my loss, but God's will be done." Proud of his ability to check his emotions, Byrd scrutinized his wife, finding signs of grief, evidence of weakness, up to twelve days after their son died. By the standards of the nineteenth century, eighteenth-century Virginians mourned visibly hardly at all.[26]

Such emotions were not to be explored; instead, Virginians summoned reason to control feeling. Hence, Thomas Jones informed his brother that the death of their elderly mother "could not be of any great Stock to you, it

24. Anne Blair to Martha Braxton, Aug. 21, 1769, in "Letter of Anne Blair to Martha Braxton," *William and Mary Quarterly*, 1st Ser., XVI (1908), 179; Frederick Jones to Thomas Jones, Jan. 10, 1765, Papers of the Jones Family.

25. Robert Wormeley Carter Diary, July 15, 1766. See also his entries for Feb. 22 and July 7, 1766; and "Journal of Col. James Gordon," Sept. 10, 1760, *William and Mary Quarterly*, 1st Ser., XI (1903), 202, Aug. 1, 1762, 232.

26. William Byrd II, June 3–14, 1710, in Louis B. Wright and Marion Tinling, eds., *The Secret Diary of William Byrd of Westover, 1709–1712* (Richmond, Va., 1941), 186–191. For different patterns of mourning in the early nineteenth century, see Grimmelmann, "This World and the Next," chap. 3.

being no more than you might hourly expect to hear. . . . Your Grief must have ceased as soon as your reflection took place." Similarly, when Frances Randolph's sister died leaving several young daughters, she was told by her brother, "Alas Fanny tis in vain for us to grieve at Misfortunes." That message was reiterated by her sister-in-law, who shared her grief: "But as you say . . . it is of little use to dwell . . . on Melancholy Subjects." The Virginian temperament—active and external—saw in mourning no practical benefit.[27]

As in other realms of life, the gentry strove for balance when confronted by death. The bereaved were advised to count their remaining blessings, weighing them against the loss. A young woman sorrowed when "a sweet little girl of my brother's died" but found some consolation in the reflection that "my brother and Sister Hansford will soon be blest with a pledge of their mutual affection which will in some measure compensate for the loss of their other dear little Angel." It is not that such men and women were lacking in feeling, for the characterization of a baby as a "dear little Angel" certainly betokens affection, albeit a studied affection.[28]

The complexity of feelings about love and death is illustrated by the letter of consolation William Ronald wrote to two friends, a married couple, when he learned that one of their two young sons had died. He was relieved that they had lost the infant rather than the older child: "I could not help being a good [deal] pleased at finding your loss so small in comparison to what [it might have been]. However tender the heart may be, and whatever the attachment a parent may have to his offspring, the heart can be but little affected with their loss in comparison with what we feel when deprived of those whose infant prattle and dawning reason . . . has deeply impressed their image in our breasts, and fancy long after paints to us what the little innocent would have been in their riper years had not Death untimely cut them off."[29] Once again, there is something in Virginian thought that is

27. Thomas Jones to [Frederick Jones], [circa 1762], Papers of the Jones Family; Theodorick Bland to Frances Randolph, Aug. 1, 1777, Tucker-Coleman Papers, Martha Bland to Frances Randolph, Aug. 12, 1777.

28. A. Hansford to Molly Craig, Sept. 14, 1782, Galt Family Papers, John D. Rockefeller, Jr., Library, Special Collections.

29. Ronald to Parker, Oct. 14, 1769, Parker Family Papers. For a different reading of this passage and, more broadly, eighteenth-century Virginians' attitudes about death, see Smith, *Inside the Great House*, 267–273. Daniel Blake Smith remarks on Ronald's "commiseration": "It was very difficult for a parent to accept such a loss, Ronald noted, 'when deprived of those whose infant prattle and dawning reason . . . has deeply impressed their image in our Breasts'" (ibid., 268–269). In omitting Ronald's comparison, Smith makes him seem more unqualifiedly sentimental and compassionate, more "modern," than he in fact was. See also Walter Jones to Thomas Jones: "When I heard of the Death of your youngest child I . . . re-

detached and jarring; here it is the juxtaposition of a sentimental view of infancy with a matter-of-fact stance toward infant mortality. Childhood is rhapsodized, but not the child. Lest one think that children were treasured only after they had passed through the first perilous months, consider Peter Fontaine's thoughts about the death of his grown niece. Fontaine agreed that his "brother's loss is great in being deprived of his only daughter, in the bloom of her years." He reminded his brother and sister-in-law, however, that "your two precious lives . . . are of, much more consequence towards directing and providing for the four hopeful boys under your management, who as yet are but young, and beginning to launch out into the world." As much as parents loved their children, the death of a child was not considered irreparable. Fearing grief, striving for equanimity, Virginians looked to the brighter side.[30]

Virginians seemed to grieve most when, through death, the reciprocal bonds, the mutual expectations and responsibilities, between family members were broken. Fontaine, after all, hoped that his brother and sister-in-law would live to establish their sons in the world. An orphaned girl "labour'd under many disadvantages" because of her guardians' "incapacity for doing any essential services." A child without a protector was at a great loss. Although consoled by the good life his daughter had led, Landon Carter considered her death a "Severe stroke indeed to A Man bereft of a Wife and in the decline of life because at such periods 'tis natural to look out for such Connections that may be reasonably expected to be the support of Greyhairs and such an one I had promised myself in this child in Particular."[31]

The gentry sought a family life that was composed and balanced, reciprocal and restrained. It is no coincidence that all these adjectives could be used to describe the religion to which they subscribed. True, the Anglican Church was unobtrusive, which is merely one way of saying that it voiced the

ceived some comfort, that Heaven had spared those who had already endeared themselves to me" (July 23, 1769, Papers of the Jones Family).

30. Peter Fontaine to Brother Moses, Apr. 17, 1754, in [Jacques Fontaine], *Memoirs of a Huguenot Family* . . . , [ed. and trans.] Ann Maury (New York, 1853), 343. Fontaine might also have considered young women more dispensable than young men. T. H. Breen argues that colonial Virginians coupled a "rejection of the past . . . with a deep-seated belief in man's ability to reshape his environment" ("Of Time and Nature: A Study of Persistent Values in Colonial Virginia," in Breen, *Puritans and Adventurers: Change and Persistence in Early America* [New York, 1980], 164–196 [quotation, 170]). Breen analyzes Virginians' temporal horizons, but I believe that the peculiar combination of faith and denial he finds also characterized their beliefs about emotion and human relationships.

31. S. Norton to Frances Randolph, June 27, 1777, Tucker-Coleman Papers; Landon Carter, Apr. 25, 1758, in Greene, ed., *Diary of Carter,* I, 221.

values of its parishioners. As Henry F. May has written, "A good many Virginians simply took the Church for granted as a familiar source of comfort and instruction, with words and actions appropriate to the daily rounds of life and also to its great emergencies." It held forth order, moderation, decency, and a reasoned optimism, while discouraging "too much speculation about predestination and eternal punishment." Virginians were taught that an all-wise Dispenser planned things for the best. Belief in a divine order mitigated anxiety about the unknown and despair over the uncontrollable.[32]

By and large, the gentry accepted the doctrines of the church without question, for they found reflection itself discomforting. As Landon Carter observed, "I see it is a good thing to have some business to keep our thoughts employed for the man who cannot divert the present moment falls naturally into a disponding [*sic*] way and makes even the common cares of life a very heavy weight upon himself." If anything, religion was used to ward off disturbing thoughts and feelings. Finding himself sinking into a melancholy mood, Carter took action: "I shook myself and roused into a religeous [*sic*] mood of doing all I could."[33] Religion meant self-exertion rather than self-examination. The gentry tried not to think too hard about perplexing matters; they "did not wish to have their feelings touched deeply." One's duty was to do one's best and trust in God. Religion was part of the dominant mode, external and active. It aided Virginians in their search for tranquillity.[34]

The gentry's self-assurance, geniality, and careful good manners almost obscure the fact that the appearance of ease, at home as well as abroad, depended on those manners. Ease was achieved not effortlessly, as they wished, but intentionally, as they needed. Philip Greven, in his discussion of the "genteel" temperament, has noted that the gentry used "politeness"—that is, convention—to protect themselves against "unpleasantness, discomfort, . . . and intimacy." Beneath their manners lay a fear of unpleasant thoughts and disturbing feelings. Within the family, these men and women tried to avoid unpleasantness by encouraging affection on the one hand, yet by stifling intimacy on the other. Family life was to be warm: not cold, and certainly not hot. Emotions were to be managed: the proper ones expressed and the others squelched. Neither self-expression nor individuality was a goal; each might disrupt the tranquillity the gentry so prized. The "intimate distance"

32. Henry F. May, *The Enlightenment in America* (New York, 1976), 67.

33. Landon Carter, Feb. 28, 1771, in Greene, ed., *Diary of Carter,* I, 544; Greene, *Landon Carter,* 35–36.

34. Greven, *Protestant Temperament,* 325.

(Greven's phrase) with and from those they loved could be secured only in a world in which domestic relations were regarded as simple and individuals were seen as similar in their emotional constitutions. The gentry family indeed sought a domestic life that was simple, predictable, and secure. Yet, as affection was encouraged at home, domestic life would inevitably inspire the kinds of intense emotions it was intended to restrain. "Intimate distance" is, after all, an oxymoron, and Virginians on the eve of the Revolution were repressing those very passions that the new modes of familial intimacy were creating. The sweet peace of domestic tranquillity could be purchased only by chaining the individual's emotions.[35]

35. Ibid., 265, 311. See also Sennett, *Fall of Public Man,* 94–98.

Mother's Love

The Construction of an Emotion in Nineteenth-Century America

When the Reverend John Todd told the readers of the *Mother's Magazine* in 1839 that "God planted this *deep,* this *unquenchable, irrepressible* love for her offspring, in the mother's heart," he was expressing the conventional wisdom of his day. In mid-nineteenth-century America, a woman who opened any ladies' magazine or advice book would read that a mother's love was eternal, that "no circumstance, no earthly changes can destroy the mother's love," that "to love children, is the dictate of [her] nature." Nature and God both made women to be mothers and implanted in their hearts a love that was pure and holy. This was the premise upon which the doctrine of women's separate sphere rested. Just as the philosophy and form of democratic government proceeded from Jefferson's self-evident truths, so the nineteenth-century's description of woman's nature and role derived from seemingly incontrovertible assumptions about the nature of a mother's love.[1]

Historians, of course, may question that which earlier generations took for granted, asking how it was that certain propositions came to be accepted as self-evident truths. We know that in 1776 belief in the equality of man was more of a novelty than Jefferson's self-confident statements would lead us to suppose. Likewise, the irrepressible nature of a mother's love was, in the 1830s, an idea whose time had only recently come. The writers who proclaimed these truths were, as much as Jefferson, the architects of an ideology. They described a world as they wanted it to be, and they could not imagine an America, as they wanted it to become, without a mother's love.

To compare the antebellum exponents of maternal love to Jefferson is, perhaps, not so strained a conceit as it might at first appear, for the idealization of mother's love was brewed in the same cauldron as Revolutionary political thought. Historians have recognized that the histories of politics and

This essay was originally published as Jan Lewis, "Mother's Love: The Construction of an Emotion in Nineteenth-Century America," in Andrew E. Barnes and Peter N. Stearns, eds., *Social History and Issues in Human Consciousness: Some Interdisciplinary Connections* (New York, 1989), 209–229.

1. John Todd, "Address to Mothers," *Mother's Magazine* (New York), November 1839, 249; E. L., "The Mother's Affection," *Ladies' Magazine, and Literary Gazette* (Boston), July 1833, 320; L. H. Sigourney, *Letters to Mothers* (Hartford, Conn., 1838), 47.

the family in this era are entwined. The Revolutionary brew was seasoned by a variety of ingredients—republicanism, liberalism, evangelical Protestantism, sensationalist psychology—and, just as each of these strands of thought would contribute to political thought, so, too, would they affect the conceptualization of family roles. The late-eighteenth-century's revolt against patriarchy dethroned both fathers and kings, and it said that citizens in a society, like members of a family, should be bound together by affection, rather than duty.[2]

This transformation in political and familial thought would make room for a new ideal of motherhood, one that would be flavored by all the ingredients in the Revolutionary brew. Indeed, as Ruth H. Bloch has shown, the first positive characterizations of motherhood date to this period.[3] Before the Revolution, early Americans, particularly in the Puritan colonies, were rather fearful of feminine emotion. They considered women more passionate and, hence, more dangerous than men. And even mother's love, because it was both indulgent and unqualified, was mistrusted. As Laurel Thatcher Ulrich has observed of northern New England, "Mothers represented the affectionate mode in an essentially authoritarian system of child-rearing." In a "patriarchal order," "mother love or any other form of human love could never be an unqualified good." The Revolution undermined patriarchy, and it made of affection a political virtue, the glue of civil society. In so doing, it allowed women, who were supposedly naturally affectionate, a political role.[4]

This new appreciation for affection was the contribution of sensationalist psychology, which had also facilitated a new interest in the education of young children. Eighteenth-century faculty psychologists argued that the characters of children could be shaped, that human nature was to some degree malleable. Sensationalist psychology, in both its Lockean and Scot-

2. See Jay Fliegelman, *Prodigals and Pilgrims: The American Revolution against Patriarchal Authority, 1750–1850* (Cambridge, 1982); Melvin Yazawa, *From Colonies to Commonwealth: Familial Ideology and the Beginning of the American Republic* (Baltimore, 1985); Ruth H. Bloch, "The Gendered Meanings of Virtue in Revolutionary America," *Signs: Journal of Women in Culture and Society,* XIII (1987), 37–58; Jan Lewis, "The Republican Wife: Virtue and Seduction in the Early Republic," *William and Mary Quarterly,* 3d ser., XLIV (1987), 689–721, also reprinted in this volume.

3. Ruth H. Bloch, "American Feminine Ideals in Transition: The Rise of the Moral Mother, 1785–1815," *Feminist Studies,* IV, no. 2 (1978), 100–126.

4. Laurel Thatcher Ulrich, *Good Wives: Image and Reality in the Lives of Women in Northern New England, 1650–1750* (New York, 1982), 154. See also Nancy F. Cott, "Passionlessness: An Interpretation of Victorian Sexual Ideology, 1790–1850," *Signs,* IV (1978), 219–136.

tish Common Sense forms, had been popularized in eighteenth-century America, softening Calvinist notions of innate depravity.[5] By the end of the eighteenth century, many Americans were accustomed to believing that children were born with a set of faculties, some of which—reason and affection, for example—were to be developed, and others—self-interest and the passions—needed to be controlled. To be sure, different schools placed different premiums upon certain faculties, with some trusting more to reason and others with more confidence in affection, just as they disagreed about how dangerous self-interest might be. By the nineteenth century, such distinctions almost disappeared, as the popular writers who adapted faculty psychology for the American audience used Lockean, Common Sense, and Calvinist assumptions almost indiscriminately.[6] Nineteenth-century didactic writers adapted eighteenth-century sensationalist psychology in another way: they said that moral education should be performed especially—indeed, almost exclusively—by mothers. Locke, the Common Sense philosophers, and Calvinist ministers had all assumed that fathers—or, at the very least, parents—played the crucial role in the education of the young. Why, in the nineteenth century, was this responsibility shifted to women? Much of the answer lies in the growing belief that the work of moral education had to begin even earlier, for the child's character was formed in the early years, while it was still in the mother's care.

Moreover, once evangelical Protestant denominations were prepared to accept the validity of childhood conversion, as they increasingly were by the mid-nineteenth century, mothers acquired an important new role.[7] Evan-

5. Useful discussions are provided by Fliegelman, *Prodigals and Pilgrims,* esp. 9–29; Daniel W. Howe, "The Political Psychology of *The Federalist,*" *William and Mary Quarterly,* 3d Ser., XLIV (1987), 485–509; and Garry Wills, *Inventing America: Jefferson's Declaration of Independence* (Garden City, N.Y., 1978), esp. part 4. Consider also Perry Miller, "The Rhetoric of Sensation," in his *Errand into the Wilderness* (New York, 1956), 166–183.

6. See, for example, John S. C. Abbott, *The Mother at Home; or, The Principles of Maternal Duty* (New York, 1833), 66; "Hints for Maternal Education," *Mother's Magazine,* August 1834, 113, 114; S. F. W., "Woman's Sphere," *American Ladies' Magazine* (Boston), May 1835, 264; Sarah W. Gordon, "It Should Be Love," *Mother's Assistant and Young Lady's Friend* (Boston), March 1849, 53, H. Clark, "The Ruined Son," October 1845, 74; "The Beginning," *Ladies' Magazine* (Boston), January 1829, 4; H. S. E., "On Early Domestic Education," *Mothers' Monthly Journal* (Utica, N.Y.), January 1837, 6; C. Sedgwick, "A Plea for Children," *American Ladies' Magazine,* February 1835, 95; [Virginia Cary], *Christian Parent's Assistant; or Tales, for the Moral and Religious Instruction of Youth* (Richmond, Va., 1829), x; "What Virtue Is," *Mother's Magazine,* August 1834, 115, D. M. L., "Early Habits of Industry," February 1834, 17; "Let Reason Dictate," *Mothers' Monthly Journal,* November 1837, 170–171.

7. See "The Conversion of Children," *Mother's Magazine,* November 1835, 161–164,

gelical views about youthful conversion built upon secular ones about the malleability of character, giving mothers a new responsibility. The work of redemption had to begin early, when a child was still in its mother's care; and, to the extent that evangelicals believed that the world had to be reclaimed, individual by individual, the home became the main arena for conversions. As the Reverend John Abbott put it, *"Mothers have as powerful an influence over the welfare of future generations, as all other earthly causes combined."* The redemption of the world depended upon "the power of divine truth" and "Christianity, as taught from a mother's lips. In a vast majority of cases the first six or seven years decide the character of the man." "The mothers of our race," he continued, "must be the chief instruments in its redemption." Mothers, thus, had it in their power to achieve not only the salvation of their children but also that of the entire world. Mothers occupied the key "place in the grand scheme which shall renovate the world." Mrs. Elizabeth Hall expressed the millennial hopes of evangelical maternal advisers when she told American mothers "the destiny of a redeemed world is put into your hands; and it is for you to say, whether your children shall be respectable and happy here, and prepared for a glorious immortality."[8]

Women were called by God to be mothers; their work was nothing less than His own. But it was a work that was to be performed first and foremost in the United States, giving the mothers' mission both a sacred and a secular cast. One author who advocated the conversion of the young insisted that *"the designs which God seems to have respecting this Republic, are to be accomplished by the moral renovation of the young."* Religious writers believed that American society in the early nineteenth century was approaching a crisis; they looked to mothers for the solution. "By what means," asked the *Mother's Magazine* in 1833, "can the population of this great country, increasing, as it is, with fearful rapidity, be so enlightened and reformed, that our boasted liberty shall not disintegrate into gross licentiousness?" Sarah Josepha Hale provided the answer: "If the future citizens of our republic, are to be worthy of their rich inheritance, they must be made so, principally through the virtue and intelligence of their mothers." Secular and sacred

---

December 1835, 179–181, O. M., "Remarks on 'Conversion of Children,'" February 1836, 24–25, C. A. Goodrich, "Hints on the Conversion of Children," May 1838, 97; "From the Christian Herald," *Religious Remembrancer* (Philadelphia), July 20, 1816, 187.

8. Abbott, *Mother at Home,* 152–154; L., "Be Wise to Do, as Well as Learn," *Mothers' Monthly Journal,* April 1837, 56; Elizabeth S. Hall, "A Mother's Influence," *Mother's Assistant,* February 1849, 25. See also M. H. Boynton, "Third Annual Report of the Louisville Baptist Maternal Association," *Mother's Journal, and Family Visitant* (New York), February 1846, 50.

advocates of the importance of maternal influence shared certain assumptions about the crisis "in a country where the 'people govern.'" Many would have agreed that, "*self-government* both for adults and children, seems almost the only available resource left us in the present state of society in this country." *Self-government,* of course, was a term with a resonance in both religious and political discourse; in a democratic society, which had rejected authoritarian forms of control, it became all the more necessary for individuals to learn to govern themselves, to control their sinful and antisocial impulses both.[9]

Indeed, in the minds of the authors of maternal advice literature, sin and selfishness were usually considered one and the same. Although we may distinguish between the sacred and secular elements of the motherhood paradigm, they were often fused in the popular mind. The didactic writers who idealized motherhood envisioned an American empire that was also the Kingdom of God on earth, precisely because their ideal for society drew jointly from evangelical Protestantism, late-Enlightenment political thought (both republican and liberal), and sensationalist psychology.[10] These separate strands became part of the fabric of American culture; all were woven, for example, into an essay published in the *Mother's Magazine* in 1833: "It is the province of the mother to cultivate the affections, to form and guard the moral habits of the child, for the first ten years of its life, and to all intents and purposes the character of the *man* or *woman* is substantially laid as early as that period." So argued the author of "Family Government Essential to National Prosperity." "While, therefore, the father is engaged in the bustling affairs of active life, the mother, with almost irresistible sway, is forming the characters of the future defenders of our faith, the administrators of our laws, and the guardians of our civil liberties and lives."[11] Here we see all the elements of the new paradigm: a liberal appreciation of civil liberties is grafted onto the older, republican insistence upon the importance of the character of the citizenry and a Scottish Common Sense philosophers' concern for the cultivation of the affections. And we see, also, the separation of the private sphere of the home from the "bustling"—and presumably corrupt—"affairs of active life" in the public arena. As many historians have

9. "Conversion of Children," *Mother's Magazine,* December 1835, 179–181, "Family Government Essential to National Prosperity," March 1833, 35; "The Beginning," *Ladies' Magazine,* January 1829, 3–4; D. B. L. Wade, "Letter from Mrs. Wade," *Mother's Journal, and Family Visitant,* January 1846, 13–15.

10. H. Richard Niebuhr, *The Kingdom of God in America* (New York, 1937).

11. "Family Government," *Mother's Magazine,* March 1833, 36.

noted, the responsibility for training children fell to mothers almost by default, as more fathers began to work outside the home. By the time this structural change had taken place, however, women were already assumed to be peculiarly suited to the task at hand.[12]

The intellectual basis for the separation of woman's private sphere of the home from the public sphere of the world had been laid well before the United States turned into the industrial and urban nation early-nineteenth-century critics feared it would become. Women, and consequently mothers, were assumed to be more moral than men because they were isolated from the world. As Nancy F. Cott has noted, Christian doctrine had always contrasted the virtues of heaven with the vices of the world; in the early nineteenth century, as women and men increasingly were segregated into separate spheres, and—as the masculine, public sphere of the world became ever more suspect—women and their arena profited from the comparison, and the home took on the attributes Christians had once reserved for heaven.[13] The authors of maternal advice literature accepted this assumption when they likened home to Paradise and mothers' work to that of Christ. "Our first mother found a paradise," Catharine Sedgwick wrote, and "her daughters have each the more enviable privilege and distinction of creating one at pleasure." The home was designed to redeem the world.[14]

Although a mother's work was performed at home, in private, it had enormous public importance; it was, fundamentally, of a political and religious nature, for it aimed at preparing children for entry into a particular society. And it was this logic—the needs of nineteenth-century American society, as informed by both political and religious thought—that would dictate the characteristics of the children who should be created and the qualities of the mothers who would create them.[15]

If the work of salvation was to be performed in woman's sphere, it necessarily meant that women were especially suited to the task. Much as the nineteenth century fragmented the world into a private heavenly sphere and an amoral public domain, it would also divide the set of faculties that once had

12. For evidence that would support this analysis, see W., "Woman's Sphere," *American Ladies' Magazine,* May 1835, 266.

13. See Nancy F. Cott, *The Bonds of Womanhood: "Woman's Sphere" in New England, 1780–1865* (New Haven, Conn., 1977).

14. Sedgwick, "Plea for Children," *American Ladies' Magazine,* February 1835, 94. See similarly, W., "Woman's Sphere," ibid., May 1835, 262.

15. For Mary P. Ryan's analysis of the family's function as that of *"social reproduction,"* or, the process "whereby people, rather than goods, are created," see Ryan, *Cradle of the Middle Class: The Family in Oneida County, New York, 1790–1865* (Cambridge, 1981), 15.

been thought to belong to men and women both. In the process, the rational faculties were assigned to men, and the emotional ones—which the rise of sentimentalism had endowed with a higher value—to women. This new formulation is evident in the new view of marriage that had become popular by the beginning of the nineteenth century. Man's reason now was thought necessary to check woman's emotion, while feminine affection was required to socialize masculine rationality. Thus, under the influence of faculty psychology, feminine qualities were deemed necessary to the social order, for it was women who fit men for society. In the early decades of the nineteenth century, this paradigm of republican marriage—like republican political thought itself—would collapse, but one of its fundamental assumptions—that feminine qualities served a social function—would endure, as the focus of feminine socializing was shifted from adult men to children.[16]

By 1830, the feminine social role had been redefined: women were to prepare their children, and especially their sons, for membership in society. If this society, with its separate private and public spheres was recognizably that of the nineteenth century, it still retained eighteenth-century moral philosophy's belief that social order could be maintained only by the affection that men bore for one another, the sympathies that they shared. "What," asked the *Ladies' Magazine, and Literary Gazette,* "are the good works of women which she was created to perform? She was born to perpetuate the reign of all good and gentle affections in the world, and to diffuse through all society a spirit of love, of forbearance, of happiness." Evangelicals agreed that "it is the province of the mother to cultivate the affections," and, like more secular writers, they believed that such qualities were necessary to society.[17]

Like their colonial ancestors, nineteenth-century American family advisers still thought of the family as a little commonwealth. As one magazine writer put it in 1830, "A family is society in miniature; home is its location." But now, "woman is its presiding spirit." Put another way, the family represented society as these writers wanted it to be. In the "world . . . we behold every principle of justice and of honor, and even the dictates of common honesty disregarded, and the delicacy of our moral sense is wounded; we see the general good, sacrificed to the advancement of personal interest." Only

16. See Lewis, "Republican Wife," *William and Mary Quarterly,* XLIV (1987), 689–721.

17. Sedgwick "Plea for Children," *Ladies' Magazine, and Literary Gazette,* February 1835, 93; "Family Government," *Mother's Magazine,* March 1833, 36. See similarly, "The Beginning," *Ladies' Magazine,* January 1829, 4.

in the family could we "expect pure, disinterested attachment." Only "there sympathy, honor, virtue, are assembled . . . there disinterested love, is ready to sacrifice every thing at the altar of affection." It was this love, expressed in its perfect form by mothers, that was to remake and redeem the world. "Can a more charming picture be drawn," asked the *Mother's Magazine* rhetorically, "than a family cemented together and governed by the control[l] ing influence of love? Love—flowing from the hidden spring in a mother's heart . . . flowing on deeper and wider as it goes, till neighborhood, friends, and country are refreshed by its living waters!" Mother's love was the very basis of the social order, its blood and sinew both.[18]

At a sociological level, the doctrine of maternal influence said that the feminine principle of love was necessary in order to temper the selfishness evident in an increasingly individualistic age. At a psychological level, it insisted that men, to some extent, ought to be feminized; it was the responsibility of mothers to implant in their sons, in particular, an affectionate heart. To be sure, many maternal advisers, such as Catharine Beecher, believed women responsible for the intellectual education of their children, but more often it was emphasized that "the mother holds, as it were, the hearts of her children in her hand," and it was the heart that she was intended to train.[19] She was supposed to teach her children how to love; that is, to teach them what she knew best. She was to make her children like herself. As one adviser explained it, "The control of youthful appetite and passion, is . . . best committed to those, whose nature and situation best prepare them to enforce by example what they teach by precept. . . . The plastic hand of maternal affection moulds the susceptible being after the likeness of its own loveliness." Properly trained, a mother's sons would meet adulthood with a woman's heart. Thus it was, explained one writer, that "the talents of the female are the transmitted inheritance of her sons."[20]

And by what process were children to be made like their mother? It was generally believed that "children learn more by example than by precept." A mother was to be what she wanted her children to become. A mother was

18. "Woman," *Ladies' Magazine[,] and Literary Gazette,* October 1830, 441, L. E., "Home," May 1830, 217–218; "The Happy Family," *Mother's Magazine,* May 1839, 111; John Demos, *A Little Commonwealth: Family Life in Plymouth Colony* (New York, 1970).

19. See Kathryn Kish Sklar, *Catharine Beecher: A Study in American Domesticity* (New Haven, Conn., 1973).

20. W., "Woman's Sphere," *American Ladies' Magazine,* May 1835, 264; "The Peculiar Facilities Afforded to Mothers for Training up Their Children for God," *Mother's Magazine,* May 1837, 104; "The Mother of Washington," *Ladies' Magazine, and Literary Gazette,* September 1831, 385.

supposed "not . . . to teach virtue, but to inspire it." This she would accomplish simply by being herself, experiencing her natural and irrepressible love for her children. The secret of "The Mother's Power" was "this principle of attachment [that] is as much a part of a mother's nature, as the heart and the blood parts of the human frame."[21] A mother's love would inspire her children's love in return. The mother "teaches our hearts the first lesson of love . . . around [her] our affections twine as closely and surely, as the young vine clasps itself about the branch that supports it: our love for [her] becomes so thoroughly a part and portion of ourselves, that it bids defiance to time and decay." The children of such a mother would come to "revere her as the earthly type of perfect love. . . . They cannot but desire to conform themselves to such models." From their mothers' example, children would learn how to love. They would carry this affection with them always, not merely as the memory of maternal tenderness, but as the standard for human behavior in an unredeemed world.[22]

The conventions of mother's love held that it was eternal; it was "untiring," "imperishable," "unquenchable," and "irrepressible." Such judgements carried a double meaning: the mother's love was eternal, not only because it outlived the mother herself as it was preserved in her children's memories. It was eternal in another sense, as well, for it was reincarnated in her children, who carried it with them always, as a talisman and an almost corporeal part of themselves. The *Mother's Magazine* advised that "the mother must dwell in the heart of the child, and be, as it were, the soul of its every action—enter into all its joys—feel its every sorrow." This characterization of maternal love reflected Christian doctrines of eternal life. But, if standard evangelical exhortations advised sinners to accept Christ into their hearts so that they might be born again, the paradigm of mother's love conveyed the message from Christ's point of view: you will live again. And so mothers were told that their children "will go forth with the impress of a mother's hand, deep, imperishable. Yes! you will live in your children."[23]

21. S. S. C., "The Connection between Piety and Usefulness in Mothers," *Mothers' Monthly Journal,* January 1837, 12; "Maternal Influence," *Mother's Magazine,* April 1841, 84; "The Mother's Power," *Mother's Magazine,* XII, October 1844, 314. Such language became conventional. See also Sigourney, *Letters to Mothers,* 16.

22. John A. Bolles, "The Influence of Women on Society," *Ladies' Magazine, and Literary Gazette,* June 1831, 256; Maria J. McIntosh, *Woman in America: Her Work and Her Reward* (New York, 1850), 77.

23. E. H. Chapin, "A Mother's Love," *Mother's Assistant,* July 1845, 9; Frederick, "Maternal Affection," *Casket; or, Flowers of Literature, Wit, and Sentiment* (Philadelphia), April 1827, 133–134; Todd, "Address to Mothers," *Mother's Magazine,* November 1839, 249, "Ex-

Different writers expressed the same idea in different ways, but always the message was the same: the child was the mother reborn. Mary Virginia Terhune instructed mothers to "ask your heart . . . if there is not a strange fullness of joy in watching the reproduction of your traits, physical, mental and moral, in your child?" Another writer regarded the influence of the mother on her child the same way: "Her expressions, her feelings, her passions become almost imperceptibly a part of his nature." By this process of moral and emotional replication, the identities of mother and child were merged. If the mother's love was irresistible, it meant that the mother and child were merged. She would make "impressions" that would "stamp" her children "not only *indelibly,* but *eternally.*"[24] The mother's child became, as Lydia Sigourney put it, her "twin-soul." Although most advisers alerted mothers to the *"great diversity in the natural dispositions of children,"* they never seriously considered that the child should become anything other than the mother writ large. From the mother's perspective, then, the child was self, rather than other. That is why Sigourney, in another remarkable turn of phrase, could instruct her mother to regard her baby as a "fragment of your self."[25]

We have come, then, to the kernel of the emotionology of motherhood.[26] A mother focused her love upon a susceptible infant mind. "Working, like nature . . . , she . . . sends forth from [her] heart, in pure and temperate flow, the life-giving current" and "her warm affections and quick irrepressible sympathies." The influence of eighteenth-century faculty psychology is clear; according to its doctrines, the infant would necessarily bear the imprint of his mother's love. He would mimic her affection, learning to love just as he was loved. Yet the object of this love was the mother herself; the very process of loving would obliterate the distinctions between—the separateness of—mother and child. The popular writer "Fanny Fern" under-

tracts from Reports of Maternal Associations," February 1841, 46; L., "Be Wise to Do," *Mothers' Monthly Journal,* April 1837, 56. See similarly Sedgwick, "Plea for Children," *Ladies' Magazine, and Literary Gazette,* February 1835, 97.

24. Marion Harland [Mary Virginia Hawes Terhune], "A Christmas Talk with Mothers," in *The Christmas Holly* (New York, 1867), 53; "Extract," *Mother's Magazine,* January 1840, 24; "Prospectus," *Mother's Magazine,* January 1833, 3.

25. Sigourney, *Letters to Mothers,* 25, 31; Abbott, *Mother at Home,* 39, 40. See also T. S. Arthur, *Anna Lee; or, The Maiden, the Wife, and the Mother* (rpt. London, n.d.), 186.

26. This very useful neologism has been coined by Peter N. Stearns and Carol Z. Stearns to denote "the collective emotional standards of a society." See "Emotionology: Clarifying the History of Emotions and Emotional Standards," *American Historical Review,* XC (1985), 813–836 (quotation, 813).

stood the dynamic perfectly when she described the essence of motherhood: "Another outlet for thy womanly heart; a mirror, in which thy smiles and tears shall be reflected back; a fair page, on which thou, God-commissioned, mayst write what thou wilt; a heart that will throb back to thine, love for love." Like Narcissus, looking into the mirror, the loving mother adored her own reflection.[27]

Here, in the doctrine of motherhood, we can see the creation of a powerful mythology. It offers the mother a sort of omnipotence. It denies, or offers the means for denying, the strangeness and separateness of her children, by making them part of the mother herself. In defining children as beings who are designed to embody and return their mother's love, it authorizes a profound form of self-love. And, in suggesting that the mother's love will be replicated in the child, and the child's child, for generations to come, it promises immortality. No wonder that "maternity" could become, for women, "part of our religion."[28]

Yet, if the nineteenth-century doctrine of motherhood was, in part, a religion that established rather grandiose notions about the power of a mother's love, it must be remembered that this effect was incidental. The doctrine was not designed to increase feminine power or even a sense of power, for it grew out of an ideology whose very objective was to vanquish power with love, to replace selfishness with affection and virtue. Thus, the doctrine of maternal influence was bound to take away with the same hand that which it gave. Mothers could be powerful only if they renounced power, loved only if they renounced self, immortal if they were willing to die.

Consider Catharine Sedgwick's description of an ideal mother, her friend Anne, "one of those strong characters that must do for itself the hardest work." And how did she train her children? "By the atmosphere of affection and kindness with which she surrounded herself, [rather] than by any direct bearing of authority upon them." The mother had to be what she wanted her children to become. Then, in the confines of the family circle, the "exercise of absolute power" might be "softened by perfect love." Somewhat like Christ, a mother was to be active only in "the fullest exercise of those virtues denominated *passive.*" Indeed, mothers were barely to "exercise" at all. When observing her growing children, would not a mother naturally "say, with a smile, a sigh—perchance a tear—'I felt, or thought, or longed

27. McIntosh, *Woman in America,* 25; Fanny Fern [Sarah P. Parton], *Ruth Hall and Other Writings,* ed. Joyce W. Warren (New Brunswick, N.J., 1986), 24.

28. "Maternity," *Casket,* October 1828, 472.

[to see] the same at her years.'" A mother could not act; she might feel, or think, or long; she should "surround herself" with an "atmosphere"; she could smile, sigh, and shed a tear.[29]

The mother was, as the maternal advisors liked to say, "the first book read, and the last one laid aside, in every child's library. Every look, word, tone, gesture . . . makes an impression."[30] Because everything about her could leave an indelible mark, she had to make certain that everything about her was designed to create the right impressions. It was not only what she did, but how she looked, sounded, and seemed that was important. Although advisors might tell mothers how to feed, clothe, and instruct their offspring, much of their attention was devoted to less active endeavors. An article on "How to Speak to Children" described, not the words and ideas to be conveyed, but how to achieve the right tone of voice. In this sense, the real work of childrearing was to be focused upon the woman herself, as she tried to make herself a fit model for imitation.[31]

Even a woman's appearance had to be altered to make her a good mother. T. H. Gallaudet reminded the mother of "the influence of her *countenance, voice, and general air and manners.*" Adapting eighteenth-century psychological assumptions for his own age, addressing the nineteenth century's anxieties about the discrepancies between appearance and reality, he argued that the face was the *"index and agent of the soul."* Character and countenance mirrored one another. Like a phrenologist, Gallaudet believed that the exterior of the person reflected her moral qualities. And, like a Common Sense philosopher, he believed that the moral qualities of the parent might by *"the sympathy of sentiment"* be communicated to her offspring. Therefore, it was imperative that the mother learn "to improve in all the heaven-like expressions of countenance," making herself look like Christ.[32]

29. Catharine M. Sedgwick, "Look before You Leap," *Columbian Lady's and Gentleman's Magazine* (New York), January 1846, 13; H., "Thoughts on the Education of Girls," *Mothers' Monthly Journal,* July 1837, 106; "Woman," *Ladies' Magazine and Literary Gazette,* October 1830, 445; Harland, "Christmas Talk," in *The Christmas Holly,* 53.

30. "Affecting Confession and Warning," *Mothers' Journal, and Family Visitant,* April 1846, 119. See similarly P., "Parental Consistency," *Mother's Magazine,* February 1833, 22.

31. "How to Speak to Children," *Mother's Assistant,* January 1850, 12.

32. T. H. Gallaudet, "The Mother's Face," *Mother's Magazine,* January 1838, 16, 17, April 1838, 74–75. The ideal mother exhibited a "Christ-like loveliness" (ibid., February 1838, 30). See similarly the observation "Heaven has imprinted on the mother's face something which claims kindred with the skies," in "The Mother," *Mother's Magazine,* XII, July 1844, 223. For the nineteenth century's concern for sincerity, see especially Karen Halttunen, *Confidence Men and Painted Women: A Study of Middle-Class Culture in America, 1830–1870* (New Haven, Conn., 1982); Fliegelman, *Prodigals and Pilgrims,* 240–242; and Louis J. Kern,

If children were such impressionable creatures that they could absorb their mother's character from the expression upon her face, then she would have to be enormously careful not to disclose, even inadvertently, any thought or feeling she did not want her child to acquire. Mothers were warned not to "permit the anxieties of your mind to mantle your countenance with forbidding gravity or gloom." And, because the countenance and the voice were reflections of the mother's character, it was likewise necessary for her to control her thoughts and feelings, lest they betray her and ruin her child. The mother "must always be dignified, calm, consistent with herself. . . . She must never be observed to betray a weakness, changeableness or vascillation [*sic*] of character." "The mother," the author continued, "must be at all times, agreeable, entertaining, amiable and tender."[33] Mothers were urged to suppress all negative emotions and to cultivate a placid cheerfulness. Again and again, mothers were told which feelings might be enjoyed and which were to be denied. Sigourney advised that "every irritable feeling should . . . be restrained." She asked her readers to forgive her "for repeatedly pressing on mothers, to wear the lineaments of cheerfulness." Similarly, Alphonse Perren told mothers that "an even temper is indispensable to the cheerfulness of home," while the *Mother's Magazine and Family Monitor* insisted that "a *good disposition*," one that was "kind," "considerate," and "unselfish," was "the most important requisite in domestic life."[34] All these advisors assumed that women could manipulate and control their emotions, that a mother was able "to cultivate all good dispositions and noble aspirations—to overcome and subdue all evil propensities." Emotion could be overcome by will.[35]

Although women were believed to be, in a general sense, more emotional than men, possessing "superior strength of heart," that did not mean they were to express whatever they felt.[36] Feminine emotionality was fundamen-

---

An Ordered Love: Sex Roles and Sexuality in Victorian Utopias—The Shakers, the Mormons, and the Oneida Community (Chapel Hill, N.C., 1981), 35–40.

33. "How Shall a Mother Secure the Confidence of Her Children?" *Mother's Magazine*, July 1836, 105; J. S., "For Who Hath Despised the Day of Small Things," *Mothers' Monthly Journal*, July 1837, 101.

34. Sigourney, *Letters to Mothers*, 28, 63; "Home and Its Influences, *Mother's Magazine and Family Monitor* (New York), March 1853, 80, L. L. H., "The Most Important Requisite in Domestic Life," March 1854, 88. See similarly Ralph W. Allen, "Family Government," *Mother's Assistant*, December 1849, 126.

35. "Mental and Moral Qualities Transmissible from Parents to Children," *Mother's Magazine*, February 1841, 41.

36. "Maternal Traits of Feeling," *Ladies' Magazine[,] and Literary Gazette*, August 1830,

tally passive; women might register feeling, deeply and indiscriminately, but they were not to transmit everything they might feel. The nineteenth century expected women, no less than men, to exercise self-control. Indeed, for mothers to be able to teach their sons essential lessons in self-control, they must be able to control themselves. Hence, advisers told women to "bear in mind, that, in governing, we should begin with our own hearts." A woman endowed with "warm feelings" and "quick apprehension" would have to exercise "self-control" so that she might display only a "calm good sense." Emotion was not in itself an unqualified good. Rather, mothers were enjoined to govern and, indeed, to manipulate their feelings for the benefit of their children. Thus, in a chapter entitled "The Mother's Difficulties," Abbott insisted, "We must bring our own feelings and our own actions under a system of rigid discipline, or it will be in vain for us to hope to curb the passions and restrain the conduct of those who are looking to us for instruction and example." Put another way, the natural and spontaneous outpourings of a mother's heart might interfere with the mother's true mission. Her most strenuous efforts would have to be directed at herself.[37]

Is there a contradiction here? After all, the maternal advisers certainly believed that a mother's love was natural and irrepressible, and they agreed that one of the attributes that qualified women for motherhood was their ability to sympathize with their children, to feel what they felt. Were women born to be mothers, or was it an office that was to be achieved? Were women suited as they were, or did they have to be changed? The maternal advisers did not confront this question directly, but, taken as a body, their writings offer this answer. Individual women were to strive to realize their feminine potential by deliberately cultivating that within themselves which was supposed to be the most naturally and essentially feminine. The advisors thus betrayed their suspicion of female emotionality in the full range of its possible manifestations; they idealized feeling only to the extent that it was an expression of the generalized socializing affections or sympathies that Common Sense philosophers had glorified. More particular, individualized emotion was quite another matter. It was the feelings that a woman had in common with other women that were prized, not intense or idiosyncratic emotions.

Emotion was construed instrumentally; it had certain purposes and was

---

373–374. See Carol Zisowitz Stearns and Peter N. Stearns, *Anger: The Struggle for Emotional Control in America's History* (Chicago, 1986), 49.

37. L. S. Cushman, "Report of the Philadelphia Union Maternal Association," *Mothers' Monthly Journal,* June 1837, 93; "The Satin Pelisse," *Ladies' Magazine and Literary Gazette,* December 1830, 540; Abbott, *Mother at Home,* 62, 64, 66.

to be shaped to serve those ends. Only in this context does the advice given by the *Mother's Magazine* in 1833 make sense. "P" told mothers to "*feel* for your child . . . for whatever your feelings are, he will know them; you cannot elude his eagle eye." So mothers must feel the right feelings, but they must "beware of disclosing [their] feelings, or at least, let there not be an apparent *attempt* to exhibit them, either to himself or to others. This would be most ruinous. Rather let him feel that there exists in your bosom a well-spring of feeling and anxiety, which others know nothing of, and which even he cannot fathom." P told mothers that they must craft a maternal persona, a woman who was quintessentially feeling and self-effacing. She must eradicate almost entirely all evidence of will and intention, perhaps modeling herself after P's own mother, who prayed early in the morning, before her family awoke, almost—but not quite—eluding the watchful eye of her child. She must create the illusion that she had subdued all feeling, any interest in self, and all desire to exercise power. She might reveal only the scintilla of the crafted self that escaped her extraordinary efforts at self-suppression.[38]

The mother was an actor on the stage of eternal life and death. She must see herself as her children would see her; she must observe herself playing her assigned role. "Mother, watch yourself," wrote P. "Your child watches you; his eye watches every motion; his ear is bent to catch every sound from your lips." Again P warned, "Mother, watch yourself; how can you expect your Saviour's blessing if you slight his most solemn and repeated injunction to watchfulness?" And a third time, most emphatically, "Mother! watch yourself! Should the inquiry be made about your children—Who slew all these? How could you bear to have all eyes turned on you, as their murderer!"[39]

The mother had it in her power to secure for her child eternal life, or to consign him to perdition. Because the stakes were so high, it was "a mother's imperious duty to make any and every sacrifice, to rescue her child." Maternal advisers insisted unequivocally that "a mother's duties ought to take precedence before everything else." Quite simply, a mother had "no right to seek her own pleasure more than that of her children, or her own improvement more than theirs."[40] Americans could exhort mothers to self-sacrifice because they considered unselfishness a cardinal virtue; indeed, it was just

38. P., "Parental Consistency," *Mother's Magazine,* February 1833, 23.

39. Ibid., 24.

40. A Mother, "Thoughts on Mothers' Responsibility," *Mothers' Monthly Journal,* March 1837, 41; Arthur, *Anna Lee,* 221; Sedgwick, "Plea for Children," *Ladies' Magazine, and Literary Gazette,* February 1835, 96–97.

what mothers were supposed, by precept and example, to teach.[41] Moreover, self-sacrifice was thought to bring its own sort of pleasure. So reasoned Sigourney, who observed that "the most disinterested, have the best materials for being happy. . . ." "May it not therefore be assumed," she asked, "that the subjugation of self, is happiness?" The mother's mission was to live for her child; this would bring her happiness here, and her child happiness hereafter.[42]

Curiously, the maternal advisers never predicted whether the mother herself might look forward to salvation; their interest was only in the future of the child. Indeed, mothers were reborn, not in heaven, but in their children; they sacrificed themselves in a most profound sense. Here is the way Sigourney explained the "Privileges of the Mother": "No longer will you now live for self,—no longer be noteless and unrecorded, passing away without name or memorial among the people. It can no more be reproachfully said of you, that 'you lend all your graces to the grave, and keep no copy.'" Life everlasting came to a woman only through her child. The subtext of the maternal advice literature was that women, like Christ, were the instruments of someone else's salvation.[43]

And, like Christ, they would have to die that their children might live. The maternal advice literature makes this point effectively, if indirectly. We may consider the exhortations to self-sacrifice and the suppression of feeling as a generalized expression of the belief that mothers must pay dearly for the happiness of their children. But it is in fiction, especially in short, instructive tales, that this message comes through most clearly.

Again and again, maternal advisers imagined the moment when mother and child separated. This was the test of maternal influence: Had the child learned from his mother's example? Abbott summarized the basic assumption: "When a son leaves home, and enters upon the busy world, many are the temptations which come crowding upon him. If he leaves not his mother with established principles of religion and self-control, he will most assuredly fall before these temptations." If all went as it was supposed to, the child would have internalized his mother's values, her voice, her countenance, and her prayers; they would serve as his conscience. Many men who wrote for women's magazines testified to the efficacy of maternal influence. "S," for example, described his falling away from God after he left his mother's home

41. See, for example, "Extract from a Letter," *Mother's Magazine,* April 1835, 63.

42. Sigourney, *Letters to Mothers,* 56, 193.

43. Ibid., 9.

and his later conversion, which he credited to his mother: "If my heart has ever been renewed—if my sins have been forgiven, I feel I owe it, through the mercy of God, to a *pious mother's prayers.* . . . The memory of those prayers, wherever I am, still, like a guardian angel, hovers over my heart to restrain me from evil, and cheer me onward in the way of life." Just as the maternal advice literature postulated, S carried his mother with him, in his heart; Christ's surrogate, she effected his salvation.[44]

That is the way the paradigm worked, from the perspective of the child. Many confessions—or pseudo confessions, for it is impossible to assess the veracity of these tales—told the same story.[45] Only occasionally were such tales recounted from the mother's point of view. If children, when grown, might expect to enjoy the fruits of their mothers' labors, the mothers themselves would have to trust to faith. The *American Ladies' Magazine* put it this way, beginning with the standard sentiment: "The maternal influence, in moulding these wonderful minds, is a triumph of which our sex may well be proud. . . . There is a connexion between duties performed and blessings secured, which is always certain." Then follows the caution. "The faithful mother may not see this fulfil[l]ment during her life; but she can and will feel its benignant and cheering hope." Mothers, then, should not expect fulfillment on this side of the grave. Implicit is the assumption that mothers will not see their labors rewarded; for that they will have to trust to God.[46]

It is necessary to read these stories from the mother's perspective to understand fully the nature of the mother's mission and the purpose of maternal love as they were defined by nineteenth-century maternal advisers. One tale may serve to represent them all. Fanny Fern's "A Mother's Influence" focuses upon the moment when a young man takes his leave from the parental home. Young Will Low has decided to go to sea. His father, an old-fashioned patriarch, has made his life unbearable. The son, however, will miss his mother, who is, as he tells a friend, "the only humanized portion of my heart—the only soft spot in it. She came to my bed-side last night, after

44. Abbott, *Mother at Home,* 15; S., "The Mother in Her Closet," *Mother's Magazine,* October 1840, 226.

45. The following discussion is based upon: C. D., "Maternal Influence," *Mother's Magazine,* July 1840, 160–164, H. W., "I Had a Mother," July 1838, 157–158, D. R. W., "Maternal Influence," November 1840, 254–255; Wm. H. Thayer, "The Mother's Grave," *Mother's Assistant,* April 1849, 83–84; Mary, "My Mother's Grave," *Casket,* February 1829, 87; J. S. L., "My Mother's Death," *Mother's Magazine and Family Monitor,* March 1853, 94–95; G. M. D., "The Deathless Influence of a Mother's Love," *Mother's Magazine,* XII, May 1844, 129–132.

46. "Woman's Way to Eminence," *American Ladies' Magazine,* September 1834, 388.

she thought I was asleep, gently kissed my forehead, and then knelt by my bedside. . . . I shall never be an infidel while I can remember my mother." Mrs. Low has mastered the conventions; she reveals her emotion only when she thinks she is unobserved. She tries to suppress her feelings, but the next morning her "hand trembled as she passed her boy's cup" at his last meal at home. "She did not trust herself to speak—her heart was too full." Will, of course, observes the signs of his mother's emotion, her "swollen eyelids" and "his favorite little tea-cakes that she had busied herself in preparing for him." All that she could utter was the simple prayer, " 'God keep my boy!' " This was the ritual mother's prayer, an incantation to protect her son and secure his salvation.[47]

And so Will Low went to sea, enacting a scenario that seems to have been the realization of a mother's greatest fears. In tale after tale, separated sons went to the city, or, more often, to sea—the masculine communities that appear as the antitheses of the female-dominated home. And, as in all of these tales, the son gave in to temptation. Of course he felt guilt, but, "when that angel whisper, 'God keep my boy,' palsied his daring hand," he would drink another cup "to drown again more recklessly 'that still small torturing voice.' " He was too ashamed even to write home. Finally satiated, Will returned home, on what proved to be the day of his mother's funeral. A neighbor explained that after Will left home " 'she began to droop like a willow in a storm, and lose all heart, like. Doctor's stuff didn't do any good, as long as she got no news of the boy.' " Will's sins, then, have killed his mother.[48]

Will's "conscience," however, "did its office. Long years of mad folly passed in swift review before him; and over that insensible form a vow was made, and registered in Heaven." Mrs. Low's death worked her son's conversion, and he, in turn, persuaded his father also to repent. The story ends with the two men entering church, as the older Low comments, " 'Your mother should have lived to see this day, Will.' " But, of course, she could not have. So directly is Will Low's conversion linked to the death of his mother that we cannot miss seeing the causal connection. Finally and firmly transplanted into her son's heart, Mrs. Low has served her life's function: she now *may* die. And in order to secure her husband's and especially her son's rebirth, she now *must* die. The narrative and the logic both are established by the life of Christ. Mrs. Low's death, like that of Christ, was necessary for

47. Fanny Fern [Sarah P. Parton], "A Mother's Influence," in *Fern Leaves from Fanny's Port-Folio*, 2d ser. (Auburn, N.Y., 1854), 252–256.

48. Ibid., 255–256.

her son and her husband to be reborn. She made the greatest sacrifice that a mother—and a Christian—could make; she gave her life for her child. Ultimately, a mother's influence depended upon her willingness to give herself fully and to deny herself finally. And it was only after she had gone to this extreme that she realized her destiny. A correspondent to the *Mother's Magazine* explained the effect of a mother's death this way: "Blessed are they in the earth, who possess the inestimable dowry of a pious mother's grave!—I had almost said, the example and counsel of a living mother could hardly equal in power, upon the filial heart, the silent but thrilling preaching of a departed one." There was no "almost" about it. The mother atoned for her child's sins; she forgave him still; she died that he might achieve eternal life. The mother was Christ.[49]

The paradigm of mother's love must be read as an elaborate parable that patterns the mother's nature and destiny after that of Christ. Not only the moral tales invented by Fanny Fern and the others but the entire corpus of maternal advice literature in early- to mid-nineteenth-century America was directed to achieving the conversion of the nation's children. Sometimes the message was secularized, and mothers were enjoined to prepare their children for entry into a democratic society. But, even in those cases, the design bore an evangelical imprint: citizens of the Republic were supposed to manifest the recognizably Christian traits of self-sacrifice, sinlessness, and benevolence toward their fellow man. So it is not surprising that, if mothers were designated the instruments of conversion, a mother's life story, as it was imagined by the maternal advisers, would read like a parable. Endowed with "a love, next in patience to that of a Redeemer," her career would be like that of the great Converter; to redeem, she must die. The logic of the paradigm of maternal influence could have it no other way, so closely was it patterned after the narrative of Christ's life.[50]

We see, then, theology and democracy, engaged in a dialectic that would determine the shape of nineteenth-century American culture. The paradigmatic mother was this dialectic's creature, designed to serve its ends. Historians have usually linked the nineteenth century's idealization of motherhood to the early stages of industrialization and the removal of men's work from the home. Yet, if structural changes alone could explain the exaltation

49. Ibid., 256; H. M. D., "A Mother's Grave," *Mother's Magazine,* June 1837, 138.
50. Sigourney, *Letters to Mothers,* 55.

of self-sacrificing motherhood, that ideal surely would have been modified as the society and economy continued to change; in our current, postindustrial age, it might seem an anachronism. But, because the ideal is part of our national civil religion, reflecting an American fusion of democratic and Christian thought, it persists. Even though most Americans no longer expect mothers to act as agents of conversion, they still think that maternal love can redeem.[51]

Indeed, since the early nineteenth century, Americans have increasingly looked to love for salvation; they have attached to love a transcendent importance.[52] Yet love is an emotion, a feeling that can be experienced and expressed in a variety of ways. In commenting upon an earlier version of this article, John Demos suggested that those of us who study the history of emotions should consider making a commitment to a theoretical position regarding the study of emotion. He noted that he has found psychologist Silvan Tomkins's account of affective experience particularly useful. Tomkins has "identified eight 'primary affects,'" which are "inborn and intrinsic to the species": "(1) Interest / Excitement; (2) Distress / Anguish; (3) Fear / Terror; (4) Anger / Rage; (5) Disgust / Contempt; (6) Shame / Humiliation; (7) Surprise / Startle; (8) Enjoyment / Joy." Readers of *Entertaining Satan: Witchcraft and the Culture of Early New England* have an example of how effectively a historian may use Tomkins's work to illuminate a chapter in history. But as Robert I. Levy noted in discussion, "love" nowhere appears on Tomkins' list; it would not seem to be a "primary affect."[53]

Instead, *love* is a social construction, a term that, in different times and places, takes on different meanings. Historians, then, have a role in analyzing the changing cultural meanings of *love,* of helping us to understand—to use Raymond Carver's words—"What We Talk about When We Talk about

51. See, for example, Cott, *Bonds of Womanhood;* Ryan, *Cradle of the Middle Class;* Ann Douglas, *The Feminization of American Culture* (New York, 1977); and Bloch, "American Feminine Ideals in Transition," *Feminist Studies,* IV, no. 2 (1978), 100–126.

52. See, for example, Jan Lewis, *The Pursuit of Happiness: Family and Values in Jefferson's Virginia* (New York, 1983). Consider also this observation by Robert N. Bellah et al., in *Habits of the Heart: Individualism and Commitment in American Life* (Berkeley, Calif., 1985), 291, that "many Americans are concerned to find meaning in life not primarily through self-cultivation but through intense relations with others."

53. John Putnam Demos, *Entertaining Satan: Witchcraft and the Culture of Early New England* (New York, 1982), 184, 461. For Demos's use of Tomkins, see ibid., esp. 184–194. Comments by Robert I. Levy, at first biennial conference on Social History, "Social History and Issues in Consciousness and Cognition," Carnegie Mellon University, May 10–11, 1988, noted by author.

Love."[54] When Freud said that "a mother is only brought unlimited satisfaction by her relation to her son; this is altogether the most perfect, the most free from ambivalence of all human relationships," he was talking about love in a way not very different from the antebellum maternal advisors who also believed that a mother's love was pure, unconflicted, and fundamentally self-denying.[55] Yet we must wonder about the effect of this advice literature upon the women who read it and, perhaps, took it to heart; family historians have barely begun to study the experience of mothers in the nineteenth century. As in the paradigm, living, fully dimensional mothers slip from our view. Still, we may speculate whether certain pathologies that psychologists and psychoanalysts have attributed to women—their masochism, their narcissism, their calculated presentation of self—may be the unintended result of the peculiar definition Americans have attached to the term *mother's love.*[56]

In Robert Stone's novel *Children of Light,* the protagonist responds to his lover's plea for help: "'I would die for you,' he said. It was true, he thought, but not really helpful." Nor, surely, is it very helpful for mothers to liken themselves to Christ or to see in their willingness to die for their children an appropriate test of their love.[57]

54. This is the title of Raymond Carver's collection of short stories, *What We Talk about When We Talk about Love* (New York, 1981), which includes the story of the same title.

55. Sigmund Freud, *New Introductory Lectures on Psychoanalysis,* trans. and ed. James Strachey (New York, 1965), 133.

56. See for example Nancy Schrom Dye and Daniel Blake Smith, "Mother Love and Infant Death, 1750–1920," *Journal of American History,* LXXIII (1986), 329–353; Ulrich, *Good Wives;* Lewis, *Pursuit of Happiness,* chaps. 3 and 5; and Sylvia D. Hoffert, "'A Very Peculiar Sorrow': Attitudes toward Infant Death in the Urban Northeast, 1800–1860," *American Quarterly,* XXXIX (1987), 601–616.

57. Robert Stone, *Children of Light* (New York, 1986), 231–232.

"Those Scenes for Which Alone My Heart Was Made"

Affection and Politics in the Age of Jefferson and Hamilton

It was almost summer 1793, and Thomas Jefferson was still in Philadelphia. He had told President George Washington the previous fall, before Washington's reelection, that he wanted to resign as secretary of state and return to Monticello. The conflict within Washington's cabinet, particularly with Secretary of the Treasury Alexander Hamilton, had become too intense for Jefferson to bear much longer. Washington was reluctant to let Jefferson quit, so Jefferson consented to stay "perhaps till summer, perhaps autumn." Jefferson would not return to his beloved Monticello until the beginning of the next year. In the meantime, he would become embroiled in the controversy surrounding the reckless new French minister, Citizen Edmond Genet. Although Jefferson would eventually come to repudiate Genet, who was defying the president's proclamation of neutrality in the war between France and Britain, it was not before Hamilton's allies had questioned Jefferson's patriotism.[1]

In the midst of this tumult, a letter from Jefferson's friend Angelica Schuyler Church was particularly welcome. Only a few years before, when Jefferson was serving as his nation's minister to France, Mrs. Church had been part of a circle of men and women with whom Jefferson had passed many happy hours. This group—Jefferson called it "our charming Coterie of Paris"—included Mrs. Church, Madame de Corny, the Italian-born English miniaturist Maria Cosway, and the American painter John Trumbull. Mrs. Church's letter brought to Jefferson's mind "remembrances which are very dear to it, and which often furnish a delicious resort from the dry and

This essay was originally published as Jan Lewis, "'Those Scenes for Which Alone My Heart Was Made': Affection and Politics in the Age of Jefferson and Hamilton," in Peter N. Stearns and Lewis, eds., *An Emotional History of the United States* (New York, 1998), 52–65. Letters originally cited in the Angelica Schuyler Church collection at the Albert and Shirley Small Special Collections Library, University of Virginia, Charlottesville, Va., have been changed to published sources wherever possible.

1. Thomas Jefferson, "Notes of a Conversation with George Washington," Feb. 7, 1793, in Julian P. Boyd et al., eds., *The Papers of Thomas Jefferson*, 43 vols. (Princeton, N.J., 1950–), XXV, 154.

oppressive scenes of business." Jefferson went on to complain about the trials of a life in government. "Never was any mortal more tired of these than I am. I thought to have been clear of them some months ago: but circumstances will retain me a little while longer, and then I hope to get back to those scenes for which alone my heart was made."[2]

Jefferson's great rival Hamilton was also considering resigning from the cabinet, even though he more than Jefferson had accomplished his aims. Like Jefferson, he poured his heart out to Church, the beloved sister of his wife, Eliza. In December 1793, he reported to Church on the coming political season, which promised "some volcanic exhibitions." "But how oddly are all things arranged in this sublunary scene. I am just where I do not wish to be. I know how I could be much happier; but circumstances enchain me. It is however determined that I will break the spell."[3]

Here were two of the country's most important political leaders, so influential that the nation they helped create still bears their imprint, lamenting that they would rather be somewhere else. The acquisition by the Albert and Shirley Small Special Collections Library at the University of Virginia of the Angelica Schuyler Church collection, which includes her letters from both men, affords us an opportunity to consider the place of emotion in the politics of the early national era in American history.[4] Despite their significant disagreements on matters of policy and political economy, Jefferson and Hamilton voiced similar views about politics, society, and emotion in their letters to Mrs. Church. Both described a political world that was emotionally unfulfilling. The seat of the government that the American Revolution

2. Thomas Jefferson to John Trumbull, Jan. 10, 1817, in J. Jefferson Looney, et al., ed., *The Papers of Thomas Jefferson: Retirement Series,* 15 vols. (Princeton, N.J., 2004—), X, 654; Jefferson to Angelica Schuyler Church, June 7, 1793, in Boyd et al., eds., *Papers of Thomas Jefferson,* XXVI, 215.

3. Alexander Hamilton to Angelica Church, Dec. 27, 1793, in Harold C. Syrett, ed., *The Papers of Alexander Hamilton,* 27 vols. (New York, 1961–1987), XV, 593. A year after the December 1793 letter, Hamilton told Church that he still planned to resign from Washington's cabinet. See Hamilton to Church, Dec. 8, 1794, ibid., XVII, 428. In a later letter, he gloated, "Our own Jacobins have made a violent effort against me, but a complete victory has been gained to their utter confusion" (Hamilton to Church, [June 19–20, 1796], ibid., XX, 233).

4. I am indebted to Karin Wittenborg, University Librarian, Alderman Library, University of Virginia, for making photocopies of the Angelica Schuyler Church Correspondence, 1716–1865, Accession no. 11245, Albert and Shirley Small Special Collections Library, University of Virginia, Charlottesville, Va., available to me. Much of the collection has already been published in Syrett, ed., *Papers of Alexander Hamilton;* and Boyd et al., eds., *Papers of Thomas Jefferson.* One of the letters in the collection, Jefferson's to Church's daughter Catherine, has not, however, been previously published.

had created was, for both men, as Hamilton stated, "where I do not wish to be." Instead, both claimed that they would rather be, as Jefferson put it, "liberated from the hated occupations of politics." Were they serious, we ask? Jefferson did resign from the Washington administration, but he returned in 1797 as vice president and remained in public office through 1808. Hamilton also remained in office. It is almost unimaginable that these men—brilliant thinkers and political animals if ever there were—would willingly have returned home to leave the business of government to lesser men. Yet both men, speaking for their generation of political leaders, were deeply serious. It is not so much that they could have left government behind but that they felt deep ambivalence about a life of public service. Both—Jefferson more than Hamilton, to be sure—had serious misgivings about government. Those reservations about government are part of their legacy to us. When the founding fathers gave us our government, they gave us also a set of views about it, a sense that the "occupations of politics" were to be hated rather than revered.[5]

This notion that political life was less than fulfilling, that it left some significant human needs unmet, has become part of our collective political life—and our collective emotional life as well. To some extent, the sense that politics was despicable is part of the republican legacy. Classical republican thought, as adapted by American Revolutionaries, held that the power of the state was so inherently corrupting that its offices should be filled, not by lifetime politicians, but by men who temporarily and reluctantly abandoned their private pursuits for brief periods of public service. The model was the Roman senator Cincinnatus, who left his plow when his nation called.[6]

Yet, if Americans of the Revolutionary age maintained the republican distrust of the state and its underlying suspicion of power, they also added new elements to the formulation and, in the process, changed it. First, they described in exquisite detail the emotional deprivations of a public life. Jefferson, for example, complained that political life was "a dreary scene where envy, hatred, malice, revenge, and all the worse passions of men are marshalled to make one another as miserable as possible." Second, those who were creating the world of American politics in the Revolutionary age imag-

5. Thomas Jefferson to [Angelica Schuyler] Church, Nov. 27, 1793, in Merrill D. Peterson, ed., *Thomas Jefferson: Writings: Autobiography, A Summary View of the Rights of British America, Notes on the State of Virginia, Public Papers, Addresses, Messages, and Replies, Miscellany, Letters* (New York, 1984), 1013.

6. See Garry Wills, *Cincinnatus: George Washington and the Enlightenment* (Garden City, N.Y., 1984).

ined private life as the reverse image of the despised world of politics. Although republican thought had always feared the corrupting tendencies of public life, it never detailed them as fully as later Americans would, nor did it ever elaborate the fulfillments of private life. Post-Revolutionary Americans thought differently than their ancestors about the emotions and emotional life. As precursors to the romantics, Americans of this era thought that emotions had to be demonstrated and, indeed, performed.[7] Hence, they imagined the opposite worlds of politics and private life as stage sets on which men (and women) could act out their emotional lives. For Jefferson, the political world was a "dreary scene," while private life offered "scenes for which alone" the heart was made. Finally, and as a necessary corollary, emotional life itself was valued. The performance of certain emotions—in particular, sympathy and affection—was one of the objects of life; this was the measure of humanity. Protecting this sort of life, one in which men and women realized their humanity by demonstrating their affection, was, in turn, among the chief purposes of politics. In this way, emotion was woven into the fabric of politics. The challenge for political leaders and thinkers of Jefferson and Hamilton's generation was to create a politics that protected the humane emotions without endangering them. Both used their correspondence with Church to work out this problem.[8]

Of course, both men were wrestling with a difficult dilemma, one that goes to the nature of politics itself. Neither devoted much thought to the place of women in this new political world. Yet to speak of political life as unfulfilling and to contrast it to a different and more authentic one in which men like Jefferson and Hamilton believed that they "could be much happier" reverses one of the commonplaces of modern women's and political history. For the past several decades, women's historians have pointed out that women have been excluded from the public world and confined to the private one, and they have suggested that women's exclusion from public life came because women were believed to lack the qualities necessary for

7. Thomas Jefferson to Martha Jefferson Randolph, Feb. 8, 1798, in Edwin Morris Betts and James Adam Bear, Jr., eds., *The Family Letters of Thomas Jefferson* (Columbia, Mo., 1966), 155; Jay Fliegelman, *Declaring Independence: Jefferson, Natural Language, and the Culture of Performance* (Stanford, Calif., 1993). See also Gerald N. Izenberg, *Impossible Individuality: Romanticism, Revolution, and the Origins of Modern Selfhood, 1787–1802* (Princeton, N.J., 1992).

8. Consider Thomas L. Haskell, "Capitalism and the Origins of the Humanitarian Sensibility, Part I," in Thomas Bender, ed., *The Antislavery Debate: Capitalism and Abolitionism as a Problem in Historical Interpretation* (Berkeley, Calif., 1992), 107–135, and Haskell, "Capitalism and the Origins of the Humanitarian Sensibility, Part II," 136–160.

successful political engagement. Supposedly less rational than men and incapable of the disinterested discourse that governing required, women had to be kept out of politics for the good of the commonwealth. The exclusion of women from politics and public life, then, is supposedly a necessary consequence of their greater emotion; politics, like the men who participate in it, has been deemed, or so the argument goes, a wholly rational realm. Yet, when the men who founded the American system of government complain in this very clear way about political life and long for the world inhabited by women like Church, we must question the common wisdom.

We might begin by examining in more detail what it was about politics that men like Jefferson and Hamilton found so distressing. It has long been known that American politics in the 1790s was particularly contentious, even violent, as verbal battles sometimes led to duels. The fierceness of politics in this era was the product of both intense ideological conflict and the structure of politics itself. Federalists and Democratic-Republicans disagreed fundamentally on important matters of economic and foreign policy, and both believed that the very survival of the new nation depended on their pursuing the correct course. In addition, national politics were less stable and more popular than the founding fathers had anticipated. Turnover in Congress was high, and newspapers kept the public both informed and agitated. Men who had entered political life in the much smaller arenas of colonial government were unprepared for the wider stage of national politics. They soon learned how to cultivate public opinion, but not how to channel it.[9]

I have argued elsewhere that American politics would not become stable and free from violence until men like Jefferson learned to expect less personally from public life, that is, not until political leaders found other sources for their identity. In Jefferson's case, he came to expect less gratification from politics and public life and more from his family. As a defense against politi-

9. John R. Howe, Jr., "Republican Thought and the Political Violence in the 1790s," *American Quarterly,* XIX (1967), 147–165; Marshall Smelser, "The Federalist Period as an Age of Passion," *American Quarterly,* X (1958), 391–419; Richard Buel, Jr., *Securing the Revolution: Ideology in American Politics, 1789–1815* (Ithaca, N.Y., 1972); Drew R. McCoy, *The Elusive Republic: Political Economy in Jeffersonian America* (Williamsburg, Va., and Chapel Hill, N.C., 1980); Jack N. Rakove, "The Structure of Politics at the Accession of George Washington," in Richard Beeman, Stephen Botein, and Edward C. Carter, II, eds., *Beyond Confederation: Origins of the Constitution and American National Identity* (Williamsburg, Va., and Chapel Hill, N.C., 1987), 261–294; Joanne B. Freeman, "Dueling as Politics: Reinterpreting the Burr-Hamilton Duel," *William and Mary Quarterly,* 3d Ser., LIII (1996), 289–318; Jan Lewis, "'The Blessings of Domestic Society': Thomas Jefferson's Family and the Transformation of American Politics," in Peter S. Onuf, ed., *Jeffersonian Legacies* (Charlottesville, Va., 1993), 109–146, also reprinted in this volume.

cal attacks, he chose to believe that the public never knew him the way his family did. Even on his deathbed, he brooded. "In speaking of the calumnies which his enemies had uttered against his public and private character with such unmitigated and untiring bitterness," Jefferson's grandson reported, "he said that he had not considered them as abusing him; they had never known *him.* They had created an imaginary being clothed with odious attributes, to whom they had given his name." Jefferson was too committed to the government that he helped create to stay away from it for long. To cope with its demands, Jefferson split his personality; the public might have his labor, but it could not claim his true self. This was the same distinction that he drew between "the oppressive scenes of business" and "those scenes for which alone my heart was made."[10]

Although Hamilton, like Jefferson, recoiled from the personal demands of office in 1793 and 1794, unlike Jefferson he did not retire temporarily. Nor was he able to split his self into a public persona, unknown to most of the nation, and a private self, known and loved by friends and family. Hamilton rested his identity on fame, the love and admiration of his nation. He could not imagine living without it, and so he met his death in a duel, attempting to defend his honor before the world. Jefferson, then, represented the future of American politics. To survive—literally—American political leaders would have to learn how to develop thick skins. Like Jefferson, they did it by denying the public the ability to hurt them. They learned not to rest their identities completely on the public's approval. Instead, they would look to family and friends for the love and affirmation that public life could not guarantee.[11]

To a certain extent, this is a familiar formulation. At first glance, it corresponds to the picture of separate male and female spheres that women's historians have sketched for us. From them we have learned that in the antebellum period, Americans believed that men and women were fundamentally different, that men were strong and rational and women weak and emotional, that the world beyond the home was stressful and amoral at best and that home was nurturing, restorative, and fundamentally moral. According

10. Thomas Jefferson Randolph to Henry S. Randall, n.d., in Sarah N. Randolph, *The Domestic Life of Thomas Jefferson . . .* (1871; rpt. Charlottesville, Va., 1978), 428; Lewis, "'Blessings of Domestic Society,'" in Onuf, ed., *Jeffersonian Legacies,* 109–146.

11. Lewis, "'Blessings of Domestic Society,'" in Onuf, ed., *Jeffersonian Legacies,* 109–146; Freeman, "Dueling as Politics," *William and Mary Quarterly,* 3d Ser., LIII (1996), 289–318. For the importance of fame in this era, see Wills, *Cincinnatus;* and Douglass Adair, "Fame and the Founding Fathers," in Adair, *Fame and the Founding Fathers: Essays by Douglass Adair,* ed. Trevor Colbourn (New York, 1974), 3–26.

to the doctrine of separate spheres, as historians have called it, home was the reward for struggle in the world of work: this was where men returned at the end of the day for succor and sustenance. The doctrine of separate spheres, then, served simultaneously to complement and to critique the world of work; it made it possible, by compensating men for their efforts with the rewards of home, and at the same time undermined it, by denying it moral legitimacy and ultimate significance. According to the doctrine of separate spheres, the structure of modern American life—the way work and family life were configured—rested on the belief in fundamental and natural sexual difference: men by their nature were suited for the public sphere, and women, by theirs, to repair the damage done to men in their struggles.[12]

Obviously, this formulation bears a striking resemblance to the contrast that Jefferson established between "the oppressive scenes of business" and "those scenes for which alone my heart was made." There is, however, an important difference: according to women's historians, the doctrine of separate male and female spheres developed in the antebellum period, when the early stages of industrialization and capitalist development removed men's work from the home. Jefferson and Hamilton sought refuge not from work—that is, not from participation in the market—but from politics. Both complained to Church before the economic transformation that women's historians have argued was the source for the doctrine of separate spheres. Hamilton's economic policy was designed to bring about those changes, while Jefferson's was intended to prevent or forestall them. It was not the world of work that troubled them but that of politics. Political leaders like Jefferson and Hamilton, then, delineated an emotional distinction between home and politics in advance of the economic transformations that have usually been cited as the source of that distinction.

It was, then, something about politics itself that not only made a life in government ultimately unfulfilling but also led political leaders to seek refuge in a world for which the "heart was made." The revulsion against politics was, at least in part, a perhaps natural reaction to the political violence of the 1790s. It was also grounded in political thought itself. The ideas about government developed by American political leaders in the era of the

12. See, for example, Nancy F. Cott, *The Bonds of Womanhood: "Women's Sphere" in New England, 1780–1835* (New Haven, Conn., 1977); Kathryn Kish Sklar, *Catharine Beecher: A Study in American Domesticity* (New Haven, Conn., 1973); Barbara Welter, "The Cult of True Womanhood, 1820–1860," *American Quarterly,* XVIII (1966), 151–174; and Mary P. Ryan, *Cradle of the Middle Class: The Family in Oneida County, New York, 1790–1865* (Cambridge, 1981).

American Revolution criticized politics and set up a separate sphere—one that these leaders called "society"—as superior.

Perhaps the most succinct statement of this political disparagement of politics—for such it was—was made by Thomas Paine in *Common Sense,* the influential pamphlet he wrote in 1776. It appeared in the very first sentence, and it is the premise on which Paine's call to revolution rested. "Some writers," Paine began, "have so confounded society with government, as to leave little or no distinction between them; whereas they are not only different, but have different origins." This distinction, between society and government, was precisely the one that both Jefferson and Hamilton invoked in their letters to Church. "Society," Paine continued, "is produced by our wants, and government by our wickedness; the former promotes our happiness *positively* by uniting our affections, the latter *negatively* by restraining our vices. . . ." In Paine's estimation, "Society in every state is a blessing, but government even in its best state is but a necessary evil."[13]

Government was not an end in itself. Rather, it served to protect society. But what exactly was meant by the term *society?* American Revolutionaries like Paine drew much of their thinking about government from John Locke, who in his *Two Treatises of Government* (1690) had asserted that government was a human creation, designed for mutual protection. The contrast that Locke drew most sharply, however, was between government and a so-called state of nature, rather than between government and society. Yet, in the century after Locke, the development of a robust civic culture and a thriving middle-class urban and town social life gave palpable meaning to the term *society.* In the parlance of the eighteenth century, and as developed by philosophers of the Scottish Enlightenment such as Francis Hutcheson and Thomas Reid, society included all those institutions and places where men and women came together; it occupied the space between the solitary individual and government. Society was where men and women realized their human potential. As Pennsylvanian James Wilson, one of the authors of the Constitution, explained, "We are fitted and intended for society, and . . . society is fitted and intended for us." Repeating Paine's emphasis on the term *affection,* Wilson explained that "we have all the emotions, which are necessary in order that society may be formed and maintained: we have tenderness for the fair sex: we have affection for our children, for our parents, and for our other relations: we have attachment to our friends." Society, then, was both an expression and the realization of human nature. Man—that is,

13. Thomas Paine, *Common Sense* (1776) (New York, 1976), 65.

men and women—was created for society, and that meant the expression of certain desirable emotions. As Jefferson put it, "Nature hath implanted in our breasts a love of others, a sense of duty to them, a moral instinct, in short, which prompts us irresistibly to feel and to succor their distresses. . . . The Creator would indeed have been a bungling artist, had he intended man for a social animal, without planting in him social dispositions." The purpose of government was to protect this realm, the one in which people exercised their natural affections and expressed their positive emotions. This was what Wilson meant when he said that government was "instituted for the happiness of society."[14]

It was also why men like Jefferson and Hamilton dreamed about leaving government to return to private life. Public service could never be ultimately fulfilling, for it provided no outlet for what Jefferson called the "social dispositions." When Church's daughter Catherine congratulated Jefferson on his ascendancy to the presidency in 1801, he demurred that "the post is not enviable, as it affords little exercise for social affections." These affections—the attachment that men and women felt for each other, as family members and as friends—were the glue that held society together, or, as Hamilton put it, "this great cement of society." Nurtured in the family, the bonds of affection radiated outward, Hamilton explained, as if in concentric circles, from the family to the neighborhood, thence to the community, and finally to government. The founders of the new national government knew that one of their greatest challenges was to stimulate affection for the new national government, since such attachments were strongest for objects closest to home.[15]

Affection, then, represented, not simply the warm attachment of men and women for their families or of good friends for one another, but the cement that held people together in society. Affection was, not simply a private or personal emotion, but a social one. It was also the basis for national unity, as the citizens of the nation were to be joined together as if they were members of a loving family. Urging his countrymen to ratify the Constitution in 1787, James Madison asked them not to listen to those who told them that "the people of America, knit together as they are by so many chords of affection, can no

14. James Wilson, *Lectures on Law . . .* , (1791), in Robert Green McCloskey, ed., *The Works of James Wilson,* 2 vols. (Cambridge, Mass., 1967), I, 233 ("We are fitted," "We have all the emotions"), 239 ("instituted"); Thomas Jefferson to Thomas Law, June 13, 1814, in Peterson, ed., *Thomas Jefferson: Writings,* 1337 ("Nature").

15. Thomas Jefferson to Catherine Church, Mar. 27, 1801, in Boyd et al., eds., *Papers of Thomas Jefferson,* XXXIII, 459; Alexander Hamilton, "The Federalist No. 17," in Jacob E. Cooke, ed., *The Federalist* (Middletown, Conn., 1961), 107.

longer live together as members of the same family." The family, then, was both the source and model for the nation. It inculcated the feelings of affection, and it demonstrated them in practice. Although Federalists like Hamilton hoped to make the nation worthy of affection, they never set the nation up as a substitute for or superior to the family or society, which is another way of saying that there has never been in America a powerful statist tradition. The purpose of government was to protect society, not to serve as an end in itself.[16]

Cut off from society while they served in government, Jefferson and Hamilton used their correspondence with Church to sustain the bonds of affection that, they believed, made their lives meaningful. Much of every letter that each man wrote her consisted of an invocation of their mutual affection. "I am with you always in spirit: be you with me sometimes," Jefferson wrote in 1788. He told her daughter Catherine that his family's interest in her was not a favor, "but gratifications of our own affections to an object which had every quality which might endear her to us." Such language was repeated again and again in Jefferson's letters, displacing news and opinions and becoming instead the subject of the letter. Although Hamilton was more inclined than Jefferson to discuss politics with Mrs. Church, he, too, waxed affectionate in his letters. After her visit in 1789, Hamilton asked her to "imagine" what he and his wife "felt" when they saw her off. Then, not trusting to her imagination, he told her: "We gazed, we sighed, we *wept*, and casting 'many a lingering longing look behind' returned home to give scope to our sorrows, and mingle without restraint our tears and our regrets."[17]

Such expressions of affection were not, as they sometimes appeared, merely the natural outpourings of a warm heart. Rather, they rested on and indeed sustained a particular social vision, one that assigned different emotions to separate realms. When Mrs. Church returned to her homeland from Europe, Jefferson warned her that "you will find that the agitations of Europe have reached even us, and that here, as there, they are permitted to disturb social life: that we have not yet learnt to give every thing to it's proper place, discord to our senates, love and friendship to society." He thought that her "affections," however, would "spread themselves over the whole family of the good, without enquiring by what hard names they are politically called." Affection, especially of the feminine sort, could make society

16. James Madison, "The Federalist No. 14," in Cooke, ed., *Federalist*, 88.

17. Thomas Jefferson to Angelica Schuyler Church, Aug. 17, 1788, in Boyd et al., eds., *Papers of Thomas Jefferson*, XIII, 521, Jefferson to Catherine Church, Jan. 11, 1798, XXX, 24, Jefferson to Angelica Schuyler Church, June 7, 1793, XXVI, 215; Alexander Hamilton to Angelica Church, [Nov. 8, 1789], in Syrett, ed., *Papers of Alexander Hamilton*, V, 501.

both moral and whole by rewarding the good and ignoring the arbitrary distinctions of politics. Jefferson, after all, was writing to his great adversary's beloved sister-in-law. He entertained the fantasy that her affection could repair the ruptures caused by partisan wrangling.[18]

This sociology of the emotions, which suggested that feminine emotion could not only constitute society but also repair the ruptures of politics, points to another limitation in the historians' paradigm of separate male and female spheres. It has already been suggested that this paradigm is flawed because it links the development of an ideology of sexual difference to the removal of men's work from the home by industrialization. The paradigm also misrepresents nineteenth-century thinking about the public and private realms in arguing that nineteenth-century Americans believed that women were naturally suited for the private sphere of the home and men for the public sphere of business and politics. Several modifications of this notion may be in order. First, the critical distinction for the first generation of American political leaders was between government and society, including the family, rather than between home and the public sphere. Second, this distinction was not predicated on a notion of sexual difference; that is, these were not separate male and female spheres. To be sure, government was a masculine realm. But society embraced both men and women, and, hence, it was social and political function more than ideas about gender that set the emotional geography.

What are the implications of these statements? Several historians have suggested that the liberal state created by the French and American Revolutions rested on and required the exclusion of women from government.[19] Whatever the case may be for France, American government did not necessitate the exclusion of women. Second, because the purpose of American government was to protect society, which included women, to a certain degree, the object of government was the protection of women.[20]

Yet this is not to suggest that men like Jefferson believed that men and women were identical or even fundamentally the same. Political leaders of this generation believed that sexual difference was grounded in nature. "Male and female," Paine wrote in *Common Sense,* "are the distinctions of nature."

18. Thomas Jefferson to Angelica Schuyler Church, May 24, 1797, in Boyd et al., eds., *Papers of Thomas Jefferson,* XXIX, 396–397.

19. See in particular Joan B. Landes, *Women and the Public Sphere in the Age of the French Revolution* (Ithaca, N.Y., 1988).

20. Jan Lewis, "'Of Every Age Sex and Condition': The Representation of Women in the Constitution," *Journal of the Early Republic,* XV (1995), 359–387, also reprinted in this volume.

Women were softer than men, and with a special gift for society. They enjoyed, Jefferson told Mrs. Church, "the happy privilege" of leaving "to the rougher sex, and to the newspapers, their party squabbles and reproaches." Writing to an American female correspondent, Anne Willing Bingham, from Paris in 1788, Jefferson described a "world" gone "politically mad," where "men, women, [and] children" talked about nothing but politics. "Society is spoilt by it." Jefferson hoped that America would preserve its sanity and that women would remain "contented to soothe and calm the minds of their husbands returning ruffled from political debate." Jefferson was troubled by what he saw in Paris, for he made similar comments to Church. "The tender breasts of ladies," he told her, "were not formed for political convulsion; and the French ladies miscalculate much their own happiness when they wander from the true field of influence into that of politicks."[21]

Politics, then, was emotionally draining. It dissipated the affections that were created within the family and society. It also stimulated a whole array of undesirable emotions, ones that Jefferson listed from time to time: "jealousies, . . . hatred, and . . . rancorous and malignant passions," "envy, hatred, malice, revenge, and all the worse passions of men," "cabal, intrigue and hatred," and, simply, "the bad passions of the heart." Were these, then, the bad passions of men or of the heart? Certainly, they were specific to a certain place—the political sphere, a place where women were rarely if ever found. At the same time that political thinkers in the age of Jefferson described society as a realm comfortably inhabited by men and women both, they described government as one occupied by men only. They left it for later generations to debate whether it was custom or nature that kept women out of the political realm.[22]

This sociology of the emotions, which assigned certain emotions to politics and others to society, was, I have suggested, an integral part of the political thought of the Revolutionary era. It was constructed by men like Jefferson and Hamilton and expressed in their letters to Church. Thus far we have examined emotion and politics by reading their letters to her. But what of her replies? Did she understand the relationship among these terms the way

21. Paine, *Common Sense,* 72; Jefferson to Church, May 24, 1797, in Boyd et al., eds., *Papers of Thomas Jefferson,* XXIX, 396–397; Jefferson to Anne Willing Bingham, May 11, 1788, in Peterson, ed., *Thomas Jefferson: Writings,* 922; Jefferson to Angelica Schuyler Church, Sept. 21, 1788, in Boyd et al., eds., *Papers of Thomas Jefferson,* XIII, 623.

22. Jefferson to Martha Jefferson Randolph, June 8, 1797, in Betts and Bear, eds., *Family Letters,* 146, Jefferson to Martha Jefferson Randolph, Feb. 8, 1798, 155, Jefferson to Mary Jefferson Eppes, Feb. 15, 1801, 196, Jefferson to Martha Jefferson Randolph, Jan. 16, 1801, 191.

her male correspondents did? Did she think of government and society as opposites and disparage government as they did?

She did not. If Jefferson and Hamilton's letters to her were exercises in affection that created and maintained the bonds of attachment that were supposed to sustain society, hers, by and large, were efforts at patronage politics. In 1793, she wrote Hamilton to recommend the vicomte de Noailles, Lafayette's brother-in-law, who was emigrating to America. A year later, she asked him to "extend" his "care," that is, to serve as a patron, to another of her emigre friends, the duke de Liancourt. Her letters to Jefferson were similar, asking his assistance for the vicomte de Noailles and President Washington's for the marquis de Lafayette. These were the sorts of letters that men and women of influence routinely wrote to each other in the eighteenth century, asking the intercession of one friend for another. Mrs. Church used the term *friend* again and again to make it clear that she was talking about a particular sort of relationship. For example, in her letter recommending the vicomte de Noailles to Hamilton, she noted that he was "a friend of mine," that the vicomte knew of Hamilton as "my friend," and that she herself was Hamilton's "faithful friend." The duke de Liancourt, she told Hamilton, came to America "without a friend, unless my dear Brother . . . will extend to [him] his care." The letter asking Jefferson's intercession with Washington on Lafayette's behalf was written "to solicit your friendship for a friend of yours and mine."[23]

This was the language not so much of affection as of patronage. Eighteenth-century Anglo-American and French politics was animated not by interests, as in modern politics, or even some notion of the public good, but by personal connections in which one earned and cemented loyalty by doing favors for friends. When Church described someone as a friend, she wanted to convey that he was a person to whom she felt the obligation to render assistance. Among friends, such debts of service were interchangeable, so that one of her friends would naturally feel obliged to assist another of her friends; that, after all, was the very purpose of a letter of introduction from one friend to another. When Mrs. Church told her brother-in-law that the duke de Liancourt had no friends in America unless Hamilton would "extend [him] his care," she did not mean that the duke was lacking in social acquaintances; she meant that he had no one to help him out. Women like Church with ac-

23. Angelica Church to Alexander Hamilton, Feb. 17, 1793, in Syrett, ed., *Papers of Hamilton,* XIV, 89, Church to Hamilton, Sept. 19, 1794, XVII, 251–252; Angelica Schuyler Church to Thomas Jefferson, Aug. 19, 1793, in Boyd et al., eds., *Papers of Jefferson,* XXVI, 722–723, Church to Jefferson, Feb. 17, 1793, XXV, 215.

cess to power were more than willing to pursue it to assist friends. This was the way eighteenth-century politics worked.[24]

The Revolution, however, ushered in a new sort of politics, one that raised questions about a politics driven by personal connections. Too many inept and corrupt colonial officials had obtained their positions by working the levers of patronage; too many talented colonists had been, it seemed, excluded from the halls of government. Democracy demanded equal access to power, rather than its domination by a small clique of well-connected families. As a result, political leaders in the new nation found themselves having to turn down pleas for assistance that would have been honored several decades earlier. In 1808, Jefferson explained at great length to Catherine Church Cruger, now married, why he could not intercede on behalf of her husband and provide him with the license that he wanted. "It would have been a great gratification," Jefferson wrote, "had the occasion permitted me to be useful to you" by assisting her husband. But the procedures and schedule for granting such licenses had been "duly announced" in the newspapers "some months ago," and the deadline was long passed. Moreover,

> living, as we do, in a country governed by fixed rules, nothing can be done for one which is not done for every other in an equal case. [H]owever gratifying it might be to our private feelings to indulge these by dispensations in particular cases, yet for the mass of society the doctrine of an equal measure to all is of unquestionable value, and I am sure will be approved by our good understanding and disinterested justice, as well as by mr. Cruger's.[25]

Hamilton offered a similar lesson in democratic politics to his sister-in-law when she asked him to help secure an appointment for her father, that is, Hamilton's father-in-law. "There is no proof of my affection which I would not willingly give you. How far it will be practicable to accomplish your wish respecting your father is however very uncertain. Our republican ideas stand much in the way of accumulating offices in one family. Indeed I doubt much whether your father could be prevailed upon to accept." This was a particularly unkind cut, for it suggested that men—Hamilton and Philip Schuyler—understood the practices of modern politics much better than a

24. Gordon S. Wood, *The Radicalism of the American Revolution* (New York, 1992).

25. Thomas Jefferson to Catherine Church Cruger, Dec. 15, 1808, Founders Online, https://founders.archives.gov/documents/Jefferson/99-01-02-9320.

woman like Church. Moreover, by removing patronage from the obligations of friendship, Jefferson and Hamilton were redefining the term. *Friendship* was divested of its instrumental, political dimension; now it entailed only sociability and affection. Women like Church were being stripped of the only significant political power they had held, the ability to call friends—in the older meaning of the term—and kinsmen to account. All that they could now command was a return of their affection.[26]

Democratic politics redefined, or, to be more precise, gave a new political meaning to female emotion. Affection was to be encouraged, but it had to be kept in its rightful place. As Jefferson had told Church, Americans had to learn to put every emotion in its "proper place; discord to our senates, love and friendship to society." By rejecting women's claims on their patronage for male friends and relations, Jefferson and Hamilton were helping to teach Americans that lesson. If it strayed too far—or in too intense a form—from its natural realm, female emotion could undermine democratic politics. Jefferson complained to Bingham that in Paris, women spent too much time away from home, consumed by "the empty bustle of Paris." In America, however, "the intervals of leisure are filled by the society of real friends, whose affections are not thinned to cob-web, by being spread over a thousand objects." Affection, then, could be endangered if it were spread too thin.[27]

And, according to Hamilton, it could also create trouble if it were concentrated too highly. In the *Federalist* Number 6, he worried about conflicts among nations that had "their origin intirely in private passions." In elaborating this concern, he made it clear that such private passions all too easily might involve women. He noted that the "celebrated Pericles" had destroyed a city "in compliance with the resentments of a prostitute" and that "the influence which the bigottry of one female, the petulancies of another, and the cabals of a third, had in the co[n]temporary policy, ferments and pacifications of a considerable part of Europe are topics that have been too often descanted upon not to be generally known." He was referring to Madame de Maintenon, who secretly married Louis XIV of France and persuaded him to persecute the Huguenots; the duchess of Marlborough, an advisor to England's Queen

26. Alexander Hamilton to Angelica Church, Jan. 31, 1791, in Syrett, ed., *Papers of Hamilton,* VII, 608. See similarly Hamilton's exchange with Catherine Greene, the widow of Revolutionary War general Nathanael Greene: Greene to Hamilton, [May 30, 1790], in Syrett, ed., *Papers of Hamilton,* VI, 448–450, Greene to Hamilton, July 26, 1791, VII, 457–458, Hamilton to Greene, Mar. 8, 1791, VIII, 165–166.

27. Thomas Jefferson to Anne Willing Bingham, Feb. 7, 1787, in Peterson, ed., *Thomas Jefferson: Writings,* 887–888.

Anne, who was involved in numerous intrigues; and Madame de Pompadour, the mistress of Louis XV and another notorious intriguer, who even played a role in selecting ministers and setting policy. Almost nowhere in the *Federalist* are women mentioned, so Hamilton's association of them with "private" and destructive "passions" is significant. The sort of patronage politics practiced by Church could, if unchecked, lead to international warfare.[28]

This, in a larger sense, was the problem of affection in politics: if it were too intense, men would carry their private attachments into the public realm and put them ahead of the needs of the nation, or they might succumb to the blandishments of women who persuaded them to put those private concerns ahead of the public welfare. On the other hand, if affection were too weak because, as in Paris, women went flitting about until "affections" were "thinned to cob-web," then society would be without its cement. Affection was utterly necessary—but only in the right proportion.

The first generation of American political leaders saw danger all around them. The world had not yet seen a democratic government that had stood the test of time. The deep ambivalence of men like Jefferson and Hamilton, Madison and Paine about government and their conviction that it was not an end in itself combined with their fears for the future of democratic government. How could they sustain a government whose purpose was to protect society and all its members? One of the challenges was to make certain that society, in turn, sustained government. That meant making sure that society continued to sustain the bonds of affection that held the nation together. Those bonds of attachment—the love that men and women felt for others near and far—must be strong enough, not cobweb thin, but never too intense, never too passionate. It was passion itself that was the danger, for that was what politics stimulated—"rancorous . . . passions," as Jefferson called them. These were men of the Enlightenment, and their ideal was moderation. Society was the solution to the family feuds and dynastic struggles that had convulsed Europe for centuries. Men like Jefferson and Hamilton imagined a social life whose principal emotions were affection, cheerfulness, and, when the occasion required, sadness—but never despair. Women had an important role to play in social—and, hence, political—life, but that role was carefully scripted. Women must love, but not too much. They were to be the antidote to passion, not its source. By no means would political leaders like Jefferson and Hamilton—the men we often refer to as the founding

28. Alexander Hamilton, "The Federalist No. 6," in Cooke, ed., *Federalist,* 29–30. See Cooke's annotation.

fathers—have segregated women in a separate sphere. Women were at once too necessary—and too potentially disruptive—to the national endeavor to have been left wholly to their own devices.

It remains for historians of American politics and the emotions to determine how much of this formulation has survived into the modern era. To a certain extent, the early national period was a unique moment in American history, a transition between the classical style of the Enlightenment and the romanticism of the Victorian era. Politics was in transition, from a hierarchical system with limits on popular participation to a democratic one that drew in all (white) men, regardless of their wealth or status. Simultaneously, ideas about gender were changing dramatically, as men and women came to believe that sexual difference was a fact of nature.[29] Yet if, as I have tried to suggest, the historians' paradigm of separate spheres has probably exaggerated and delineated too sharply the differences that earlier Americans saw between men's and women's spaces and their natures, it is possible also that we have assumed too readily that they believed that male and female emotions were fundamentally different. Work in the history of the emotions by Carol Zisowitz Stearns and Peter Stearns, C. Dallett Hemphill, and Lucia McMahon suggests that certain nineteenth-century emotional standards—those for anger and love, for example—were the same for middle-class women and men. Affection, too, was the province of both men and women.[30]

Yet for American political thinkers like Hamilton and Jefferson, affection was not simply an emotion, a particular kind of love. It was also a term laden with political and social meaning. Affection was what held men and women together in society and in the nation both. And once a simple human emotion was made a critical term in political thought, it would necessarily have implications for both politics and emotional life, and the way they are held in tension. The twinned notions that public life cannot be emotionally fulfilling and that private life must of necessity be wholly gratifying are the creations of a moment in history, ones that the history of emotions enables us to question.

29. Thomas Laqueur, *Making Sex: Body and Gender from the Greeks to Freud* (Cambridge, Mass., 1990); Nancy F. Cott, "Passionlessness: An Interpretation of Victorian Sexual Ideology, 1790–1850," *Signs: Journal of Women in Culture and Society,* IV (1978), 219–236.

30. Carol Zisowitz Stearns and Peter N. Stearns, *Anger: The Struggle for Emotional Control in America's History* (Chicago, 1986), 46. See also C. Dallett Hemphill, "Class, Gender, and the Regulation of Emotional Expression in Revolutionary-Era Conduct Literature," in Stearns and Jan Lewis, eds., *An Emotional History of the United States* (New York, 1998), 33–51, and Lucia McMahon, "'While Our Souls Together Blend': Narrating a Romantic Readership in the Early Republic," 66–90.

Constitutional *and* Legal History

We the People of the United States, in Order to form a more perfect Union, establish Justice, insure domestic Tranquility, provide for the common defence, promote the general Welfare, and secure the Blessings of Liberty to ourselves and our Posterity, do ordain and establish this Constitution for the United States of America.

Article. I.

Section. 1. All legislative Powers herein granted shall be vested in a Congress of the United States, which shall consist of a Senate and House of Representatives.

FIGURE 4

Constitution of the United States. 1787. Series: The Constitution of the United States, 9/17/1787–9/17/1787. Record Group 11: General Records of the United States Government, 1778–2006. National Archives Identifier, 1667751. Courtesy, National Archives, Washington, D.C.

JAN ELLEN LEWIS'S CONSTITUTION

DAVID WALDSTREICHER

During the 1990s, Jan Lewis branched out from social and cultural, women's, family, and southern history into constitutional history. She did so while remaining in dialogue with scholarship on gender, on slavery, and on race that continued to shape her ongoing work on Jefferson's world. Consequently, she became one of a very few historians of the early Republic to test carefully, in depth, the received wisdom that the men who wrote, debated, revised, and signed the Constitution in 1787 merely inherited and kept silent about, and so did not contribute to, the politics of gender and the politics of slavery and race. She considered constitutions, gender, slavery, and race in relation to each other and, in doing so, helped set an important agenda for the history of the early Republic as a field. She explored how the distinctions of sex and race—worked through slavery—structured U.S. politics in its formative century, with different implications for different groups of people. Women and African Americans did not remain unaffected by, or just eventually benefit from, "the transforming radicalism of the American Revolution," as some historians had presumed and, during Lewis's time, continued to insist. Gender, slavery, and race did not just exist from time immemorial, only to become controversial in the modern world. They were recreated by events that, in the U.S. case, were specifically constitutional and bound up with weighty political matters, such as representation. Lewis established that gender and race were foundational because they were constitutional. Equally so, her work suggests that the Revolution and Constitution succeeded in part because they worked through sex and through slavery.[1]

David Waldstreicher is Distinguished Professor of History at The Graduate Center, City University of New York.

1. For the American Revolution as leading to antislavery, rights consciousness, and modernity—in contrast to what he calls "our present preoccupation with race and gender," which some have foisted on the essentially premodern world of "the Founders," see Gordon S. Wood, *The Radicalism of the American Revolution* (New York, 1991), 7; Wood, *Revolutionary Characters: What Made the Founders Different* (New York, 2006); Wood, *The Purpose of the Past: Reflections on the Uses of History* (New York, 2008); and Wood, *The Idea of America:*

One way of describing her achievement, and to suggest its lasting importance, is to observe that Lewis offered concrete examples from the aftermath of the American Revolution that illustrated the arguments of Joan Wallach Scott and other feminist theorists and historians. They argued for a gendered approach to history in recognition of how gender has been not only good to think with but was also ubiquitous in power relations of all kinds. Her analysis also epitomized — and pushed back in time — more recent appeals to intersectionality that stress the multiple and reciprocal workings of powerful categories of identity. Yet she was not doing history for theory's sake. Her work is equally legible, and will likely be equally appreciated, as a powerful rendering of what some scholars of American political development call "path dependence," by which choices made in the building of institutions and policy constrain later actors in ways that are sometimes as subtle as they are overwhelming.[2]

In this case, decisions made to solve certain key political problems in a constitutional order shaped the place of women and African Americans in the polity in ways that might be called unintended and which might seem to be epiphenomenal. But Lewis shows that these gendered and racializing constitutional moments were not so at all: the woman question and the question of the enslaved proved to be foundational for the democratic Republic. Her first book, *The Pursuit of Happiness: Family and Values in Jefferson's Virginia* (1983), was structured around key themes in social and intellectual and cultural history — family and values — in a way that made women impor-

---

Reflections on the Birth of the United States (New York, 2011), 2, 19, 21 (quotation). Wood's interpretation and his resistance to other historians' accounts of Revolutionary-era backlashes against women, Indigenous peoples, and African Americans had roots in the work of his mentor, Bernard Bailyn; see Bailyn, "General Introduction: The Transforming Radicalism of the American Revolution," *Pamphlets of the American Revolution*, I, *1750–1765* (Cambridge, Mass., 1965), 1–202; Bailyn, *Ideological Origins of the American Revolution* (Cambridge, Mass., 1967); Bailyn, "The Central Themes of the American Revolution: An Interpretation," in Stephen G. Kurtz and James H. Hutson, eds., *Essays on the American Revolution* (Williamsburg, Va., and Chapel Hill, N.C., 1973), 3–31; and Wood, "The Creative Imagination of Bernard Bailyn," in James A. Henretta, Michael Kammen, and Stanley N. Katz, eds., *The Transformation of Early American History* (New York, 1991), 16–50.

2. Joan Wallach Scott, "Gender: A Useful Category of Historical Analysis," in *Gender and the Politics of History*, rev. ed. (New York, 2018), 28–52; Paul Pierson, *Politics in Time: History, Institutions, and Social Analysis* (Princeton, N.J., 2004). For an application of the notion of path dependence to the political history of the early Republic, see Douglas Bradburn, " 'Parties Are Unavoidable': Path Dependence and the Origins of Party Politics in the United States," in Daniel Peart and Adam I. P. Smith, eds., *Practicing Democracy: Popular Politics in the United States from the Constitution to the Civil War* (Charlottesville, Va., 2015), 23–45.

tant subjects. Nevertheless, Lewis afterward declined to sideline political and constitutional history or leading elite men—the most traditional subjects of the study of the early Republic—in pursuit of the female and the enslaved people of the period. Instead, she described and analyzed how questions of sex and race emerged as matters of political thought and political design as well as political economy. Their ambiguous yet all-too-clear role in 1787 and beyond made the seeming accidents of the founding, like the Three-Fifths Clause, into central, shaping facts of U.S. history.[3]

In her article, "'Of Every Age Sex and Condition': The Representation of Women in the Constitution" (1995), Lewis began by going back to the record of the Constitutional Convention and noticing that in the debates about representation in the legislature, Pennsylvania delegate James Wilson proposed that inhabitants "of every age sex and condition" ought to be counted except "Indians not paying taxes" and three-fifths of slaves. Wilson's amendment, stripped of the explicit acknowledgment of "sex," eventually formed the basis of the Three-Fifths Clause and helped resolve the problem of how to count persons for representation and taxation that had plagued the government under the Articles of Confederation.[4]

What made Lewis's account an advance in scholarship was not noticing or bewailing what was not there but rather explicating what was there. Lewis was one of a number of scholars, including Ruth H. Bloch and Rosemarie Zagarri, who were investigating Scottish Enlightenment thought and other strains, apart from or intersecting with the Lockean and civic republican intellectual traditions, to understand both the larger discursive field of the founding and where women and gender fit into it. In this scholarship, Wilson increasingly appeared as an influential figure in the reception of Scottish Enlightenment thought in America. The Scots seemed to think in broader terms about society and its reproduction—about commerce, the stages of civilization, about perception, about feelings (or what they called "sensations" or "sensibility")—in ways that seemed intellectually innovative

3. For an explicit statement, see Jan Lewis, "Women and the American Revolution," *Organization of American Historians Magazine of History*, VIII, no. 4 (Summer 1994), 23. Lewis closed this essay by noting that "the government that was created by the American Revolution clearly excluded women, but whether this outcome was the thwarting or realization of the Revolution's promise is the subject of continuing debate" (26). See also Lewis, "What We Talk about When We Talk about Democracy," *Journal of the Historical Society*, VI (2006), 527–536.

4. Max Farrand, ed., *The Records of the Federal Convention of 1787* (1911; rpt. New Haven, Conn., 1966), I, 201, quoted in Jan Lewis, "'Of Every Age Sex and Condition': The Representation of Women in the Constitution," in this volume.

and politically relevant and yet, in the end, socially conservative. When Wilson made a gesture like this, it probably meant something. Why did Wilson introduce women at all? What was the meaning of this peculiar palimpsest, the writing of sex and erasing of it in the making of such a key provision of the Constitution?[5]

For Wilson, representation, after the politicization of so many people during the American Revolution, had to be democratic. More than that: it had to be liberal. The new regime had to represent inhabitants, the population—not just the stakeholders of the Republic, the propertyowning men, or their property. He reached for the inclusion of women to make just this point. Wilson thus exemplified the transition to the liberal state, in which women become the touchstones, the key reference point, for rights-bearing individuals who have to be protected by the state because they cannot represent themselves. Women became the referent for citizens who were not members of political society.[6]

If Lewis had stopped there, she would have offered a significant modification of widely cited work by feminist scholars like Joan B. Landes and Carole Pateman, who insisted on both republicanism and liberalism's founding and constitutive exclusions of women. She would also have shown, as she put it in a follow-up piece, that the "canonical texts of American politics and political thought are not, as is sometimes thought, irrelevant to women and their history." This much was recognized by her fellow historians, as the essay was widely admired, anthologized, and recapitulated in shorter versions for different audiences.[7]

5. Carroll Smith-Rosenberg in Linda K. Kerber et al., "Beyond Roles, Beyond Spheres: Thinking about Gender in the Early Republic," *William and Mary Quarterly*, 3d Ser., XLVI (1989), 571–572; Rosemarie Zagarri, "Morals, Manners, and the Republican Mother," *American Quarterly*, XLIV (1992), 192–215; Ruth H. Bloch, *Gender and Morality in Anglo-American Culture, 1650–1800* (Berkeley, Calif., 2003). For evaluations of Scottish intellectual influence, see Caroline Winterer, *American Enlightenments: Pursuing Happiness in the Age of Reason* (New Haven, Conn., 2016), 84–90, 121–147, 157–163, 203–207; and Jonathan Israel, *Democratic Enlightenment: Philosophy, Revolution, and Human Rights, 1750–1790* (New York, 2012), 16–17, 209–269, 464.

6. For complementary analyses, see Linda K. Kerber, "The Paradox of Women's Citizenship in the Early Republic: The Case of Martin v. Massachusetts, 1805," *American Historical Review*, XCVII (1992), 349–378; Kerber, *Toward an Intellectual History of Women* (Chapel Hill, N.C., 1997); Kerber, *No Constitutional Right to Be Ladies: Women and the Obligations of Citizenship* (New York, 2006); Bloch, *Gender and Morality;* Rosemarie Zagarri, *Revolutionary Backlash: Women and Politics in the Early American Republic* (Philadelphia, 2007); and Jan Ellen Lewis, "Rethinking Women's Suffrage in New Jersey, 1776–1807," in this volume.

7. Joan B. Landes, *Women and the Public Sphere in the Age of the French Revolution*

But she did not stop there. Quite near the beginning of the 1995 essay, she noted the unplumbed significance of the precise location of this almost-mention of women in the Three-Fifths Clause: "The question of counting women when apportioning representatives was bound up in a matter the framers found much more compelling: the issue of how to count slaves." That women were clearly "members of political society in ways that slaves simply were not" precipitated this new inclusion-by-implication of women as actually being represented—that is, by contrast to slaves who were not represented by white patriarchs in the same way. The enslaved would be represented through the already developed compromise of counting three-fifths of them, instead of deciding whether they should be represented or taxed as persons or as property.[8]

In Wilson's mind, the inclusion of women despite the (partial) exclusion of slaves from representation meshed well with coverture and the idealization of marriage. Wilson, it turned out, had much in common with Lewis's subjects from *Pursuit of Happiness* and her article "The Republican Wife: Virtue and Seduction in the Early Republic" (1987). And far from Virginia, this logic underpinned the subsequent justification of the noncitizenship of free African Americans. As she would put it in her *Common-Place* essay "Women and the Constitution: Why the Constitution Includes Women," "Women (and children) now stood for all those who were represented but who could not represent themselves. The denial of women's right to vote became an instrument for the perpetuation of the power of slaveholders."[9]

In other words, Lewis was one of the first historians of early America, along with Carroll Smith-Rosenberg and Kathleen M. Brown, to trace the mutual construction of gender and race in ways that captured this process as a major political as well as social or cultural development. The reconstruction of gender and race in law and in culture emerged, in both the seven-

---

(Ithaca, N.Y., 1988); Carole Pateman, *The Sexual Contract* (Stanford, Calif., 1988); Kermit L. Hall and Timothy S. Huebner, eds., *Major Problems in American Constitutional History: Documents and Essays,* 2d ed. (Boston, 2010); Jan Lewis, "Representation of Women in the Constitution," in Sibyl A. Schwarzenbach and Patricia Smith, eds., *Women and the United States Constitution: History, Interpretation, and Practice* (New York, 2003), 23–33 (quotation, 24); Lewis, "Women and the Constitution: Why the Constitution Includes Women," *Common-Place: The Journal of Early American Life,* accessed Feb. 18, 2021, http://commonplace.online/article/women-and-the-constitution-why-the-constitution-includes-women/.

8. Lewis, "'Of Every Age Sex and Condition,'" in this volume.

9. Jan Lewis, *The Pursuits of Happiness: Family and Values in Jefferson's Virginia* (New York, 1983); Lewis, "The Republican Wife: Virtue and Seduction in the Early Republic," in this volume; Lewis, "Women and the Constitution," *Common-Place.*

teenth and the eighteenth centuries, as an outcome of crises, as political if not revolutionary acts, rather than a replication or confirmation of what had always been. Not only was gender political: real politics, and the most consequential political thought, had been pursued through gender—and at the same time, inextricably, with slavery—from the colonial era through the early days of the Republic.[10]

But Jan Lewis was not satisfied with that either. Beginning at the Organization of American Historians meeting in 1997, she gave a series of papers about the subsequent fate of the Three-Fifths Clause in which she refined her argument and its longer-term implications. For the lead essay, "The Three-Fifths Clause and the Origins of Sectionalism," in the exceptional Capitol Historical Society symposium volume *Congress and the Emergence of Sectionalism* (2008), Lewis revisited the development of the clause itself and the significance of its emergence out of the desire of large-state delegates to achieve proportional representation—to change the subject, as Madison and Wilson managed to do, from the conflict between large and small states to that between North and South over slavery. In the process, the federal ratio of counting three-fifths of slaves migrated from the problem of taxation that had vexed the Confederation to that of representation that vexed the Constitutional Convention. "In the context of the Federal Convention," she wrote, "democracy and slavery were thus inevitably and inextricably joined."[11]

Moreover, the notion of compromise over slavery through the Three-Fifths Clause as a necessity for federal union, while it spared the delegates from explicitly affirming property in man, made slavery-as-property something else: less itself the law of the land than an under-defined presumption—and an actual structure—of the workings of representation and taxation. It was not property, in law: it was process hardwired into politics in the counting that was necessary to representative government, bound to become more significant the more active, and the more representative, the na-

10. Kathleen M. Brown, *Good Wives, Nasty Wenches, and Anxious Patriarchs: Gender, Race, and Power in Colonial Virginia* (Williamsburg, Va., and Chapel Hill, N.C., 1996); Kirsten Fischer, *Suspect Relations: Sex, Race, and Resistance in Colonial North Carolina* (Ithaca, N.Y., 2002); Carroll Smith-Rosenberg, *This Violent Empire: The Birth of an American National Identity* (Williamsburg, Va., and Chapel Hill, N.C., 2010).

11. Jan Lewis, "The Three-Fifths Clause and the Origins of Sectionalism," in this volume. See also Lewis, "The Problem of Slavery in Southern Political Discourse," in David Thomas Konig, ed., *Devising Liberty: Preserving and Creating Freedom in the New American Republic* (Stanford, Calif., 1995), 265–297; Lewis, "What We Talk about When We Talk about Democracy," *Journal of the Historical Society,* VI (2006), 527–536.

tional government became. Consequently, the major debates about slavery in the Constitutional Convention came after the Three-Fifths Clause was proposed, not before.[12]

The founders compromised not only over slavery: they compromised through slavery. They also sought to cover their tracks in ways that have led to confusion ever since. In a stunning observation, Lewis even suggested that the separate laundry list of congressional powers drafted by Gouverneur Morris—Article I, Section 8—was composed to codify the federal power of taxation in such a way as to make it *not* seem as if slavery was being reintroduced into representation as in the terms of the federal ratio. (Morris and Wilson, she observed, said explicitly that this was the purpose of an enumeration of this power apart from Article 1, Section 2.) For Lewis, the Constitution might have been as antislavery as it was proslavery early on, at that point of the convention—yet only "if we stop the clock" on July 11, before the August compromises that made the dissipation of slavery over time more unlikely.[13]

But most of all, the process of achieving the Three-Fifths Clause and subsequent compromises encouraged the South to make demands on the Convention and to threaten to walk. Sectional politics as it came to be known and practiced was born with heavy doses of oxygen in 1787. Here Lewis built on and contributed to the literature on sectionalism as not merely a reflection of social differences or of divergence over slavery as it spread in the South and constricted in the North after the introduction of the cotton gin, but as constructed in politics, through governance, in a dialectical relationship with social and ideological changes, at the same time or even earlier.[14] The sectional politics of slavery did not simply or only precede the republican experiment or the nation state, or launch an antebellum era after 1800 or 1820; it structured both as a solution to the problems of taxation, representation, and federalism. The nationalists who were willing to make concessions to democracy—especially Madison and Wilson—knew exactly what they were doing. Their compromises gave more to the slave South than its

12. For a contrasting emphasis on property in man and its absence (literally speaking) in the Constitution, see James Oakes, *The Scorpion's Sting: Antislavery and the Coming of the Civil War* (New York, 2014), 51–76; and Sean Wilentz, *No Property in Man: Slavery and Antislavery at the Nation's Founding* (New York, 2018).

13. Lewis, "The Three-Fifths Clause and the Origins of Sectionalism," in this volume.

14. See especially William J. Cooper, Jr., *Liberty and Slavery: Southern Politics to 1860* (New York, 1983); William W. Freehling, *The Road to Disunion: Secessionists at Bay, 1776–1854,* I (New York, 1990); and Robert Pierce Forbes, *The Missouri Compromise and Its Aftermath: Slavery and the Meaning of America* (Chapel Hill, N.C., 2007).

leaders themselves expected and enhanced their ability to wield power in the future. Sectionalism, ironically enough, had to be empowered if nationalism were to triumph. Madison's backpedaling objections to extending the slave trade, as well as his assertion that the Constitution should not mention the word *slavery* so as not to admit of property in men, need to be seen as the very limited damage control that they were.[15]

Having written the clearest exposition of the making of the Three-Fifths Clause and of its larger significance, Lewis brought the emphasis on women and gender of the first essay and the emphasis on slavery in the second together and extended the story to and beyond the Civil War in her 2016 presidential address to the Society for Historians of the Early American Republic, published the following year as "What Happened to the Three-Fifths Clause: The Relationship between Women and Slaves in Constitutional Thought, 1787–1866." She began by explicitly comparing the nonmention of women in the Constitution to the silence around slaves. But she reminds us, immediately, that this ended only after the Thirteenth Amendment mentioned slavery in order to end it—and the next one, the Fourteenth Amendment, enfranchised all males regardless of previous conditions of servitude. Her arguments are still more pointed, focusing and extending her earlier claims. The long story of three score and nineteen years is that "slaves and women are always together" in constitutional thought, and women's "political disabilities [were] used to justify a system of representation that included others—slaves—whose political disabilities were even more severe. . . . Women's assumed political incapacity was used to anchor a system of representation that rested on enslavement."[16]

15. For broadly comparable analyses, see David Brian Robertson, *The Constitution and America's Destiny* (New York, 2005); Robertson, *The Original Compromise: What the Constitution's Framers Were Really Thinking* (New York, 2013); Akhil Reed Amar, *America's Constitution: A Biography* (New York, 2005); David Waldstreicher, *Slavery's Constitution: From Revolution to Ratification* (New York, 2009); Waldstreicher, "The Beardian Legacy, the Madisonian Moment, and the Problem of Slavery," *American Political Thought,* II (2013), 274–282; Waldstreicher, "The Mansfieldian Moment: Slavery, the Constitution, and American Political Traditions," *Rutgers Law Journal,* LXIII (2013), 471–485; George William Van Cleve, *A Slaveholders' Union: Slavery, Politics and the Constitution in the Early American Republic* (Chicago, 2010); Michael J. Klarman, *The Framers' Coup: The Making of the United States Constitution* (New York, 2016). Mary Sarah Bilder's rigorous examination of the manuscripts raises doubts about whether Madison's cavils about slavery, which are generally cited by scholars from his own notes, might have been added later. See Bilder, *Madison's Hand: Revising the Constitutional Convention* (Cambridge, Mass., 2015).

16. Jan Lewis, "What Happened to the Three-Fifths Clause: The Relationship between Women and Slaves in Constitutional Thought, 1787–1866," in this volume.

After summarizing concisely her argument about 1787, Lewis's address establishes 1804 as the moment of the emergence of the critique of the Three-Fifths Clause in Congress and the Missouri Crisis as the moment when the notion of women as citizens first "gave intellectual ballast" publicly to the Three-Fifths Clause, now in future slave states, as not backwards but rather in tune with growing democratic sensibilities. In periodic congressional debates, the exclusion of women from full voting repeatedly justified slave representation. Abolitionists battling each other as well as the slaving class on the implications of the Constitution in the 1840s turned it upside down and inside out, but only to wind up in the same place. "Slaves always came first," and the conversation only reinforced the notion of exceptional, partial citizenship for women.[17]

When Roger Taney drew the line that made the comparison impossible, however—white women being partial citizens, but Africans, slave or free, never citizens at all, the important difference being race—he wittingly or unwittingly, Lewis observed, "revealed the Three-Fifths Clause to be the incoherence that [Gouverneur] Morris had said it was," which Madison had defended in *Federalist* Number 54 as a proper mixing of property and personhood to match the unfortunate mixed reality of slavery. But when the Fourteenth Amendment brought all men in, it clarified and codified female disfranchisement anew even while creating new ambiguities.

> So this is what happened to the Three-Fifths Clause: the Fourteenth Amendment put a nail in its coffin, but the expansive notion of citizenship that had been embedded in it lived on, now made national, near universal, and explicit, along with an even more capacious notion of representation. But the limitations lived on, too, or rather took new forms, authorized by the circumlocutions of the second sentence of the second section. And it is in this space, between expansive and capacious notions of citizenship and the backward pull of history and

17. Ibid. Amy Dru Stanley's scholarship complements Lewis's analyses here. See Stanley, *From Bondage to Contract: Wage Labor, Marriage, and the Market in the Age of Slave Emancipation* (New York, 1998); Stanley, "Instead of Waiting for the Thirteenth Amendment: The War Power, Slave Marriage, and Inviolate Human Rights," *American Historical Review,* CXV (2010), 732–765; Stanley, "Slave Emancipation and the Revolutionizing of Human Rights," in Gregory P. Downs and Kate Masur, eds., *The World the Civil War Made* (Chapel Hill, N.C., 2015), 269–303; and Stanley, "The Sovereign Market and Sex Difference: Human Rights in America," in Sven Beckert and Christine Desan, eds., *American Capitalism: New Histories* (New York, 2018), 140–169.

> custom, written in circumlocutions that mask the operations of power, that American history continues to be made.[18]

This closing paragraph is not only an astonishingly fitting snapshot of current debates about the Constitution as both glorious and oppressive, about constitutional development as at once real and limited, and about politics as a matter of both institutions and rhetoric. It is also an epitome of Lewis's subtle mind at work, reveling in irony and paradox but always, and clearly, counting the costs. Together, these essays, step by logical step, show the historian as intellectual problem solver. As with her increasingly ambitious essays on women and on Jefferson's family, Lewis emerges as a scholar who melds precision with a broad range of vision. We are fortunate that she found subjects like the Constitution and its Three-Fifths Clause too important to be left to historians less attentive to women, to gender, to slavery, and to race.

18. Lewis, "What Happened to the Three-Fifths Clause," in this volume.

"Of Every Age Sex and Condition"

The Representation of Women in the Constitution

It is commonly believed that women are nowhere mentioned in the American Constitution. Although the absence of women from the Constitution has seemed quite clear, scholars have not known what to make of this silence. Some argue that the authors of the Constitution intentionally framed it in gender-neutral language so that women might be encompassed by its provisions, perhaps at some future date, if not just then. It is no accident, such scholars suggest, that the Constitution repeatedly uses such words as "persons," "inhabitants," and "citizens" instead of "men." Other scholars believe that the omission of women, if not intentional, reflected the patriarchal assumptions of the founders and their belief that women had no role to play in government. These debates go to the heart of a larger question, which is the relationship of women to the liberal state that the Constitution created. Is there a place for women within liberalism? Or have they always stood outside it, excluded from its inception?[1]

This essay was originally published as Jan Lewis, "'Of Every Age Sex and Condition': The Representation of Women in the Constitution," *Journal of the Early Republic,* XV (1995), 359–387.

1. For discussions of gender-neutral language in the Constitution, see, for example, Herman Belz, "Liberty and Equality for Whom? How to Think Inclusively about the Constitution and the Bill of Rights," *History Teacher,* XXV (1992), 263–277; Robert A. Goldwin, *Why Blacks, Women, and Jews Are Not Mentioned in the Constitution, and Other Unorthodox Views* (Washington, D.C., 1990). Men, it should be noted, are not mentioned in the Constitution either, except when the male pronoun "he" is used to refer to an officeholder, such as a senator or president. On the patriarchal assumptions of the founders, see, for example, Joan Hoff, *Law, Gender, and Injustice: A Legal History of U.S. Women* (New York, 1991), esp. 117–118. A number of historians have similarly argued that the exclusion of women from the political life and structures of the new nation was intrinsic, rather than incidental. See, for example, Linda K. Kerber, "A Constitutional Right to Be Treated Like American Ladies: Women and the Obligations of Citizenship," in Kerber, Alice Kessler-Harris, and Kathryn Kish Sklar, eds., *U.S. History as Women's History: New Feminist Essays* (Chapel Hill, N.C., 1995), 17–35; Carroll Smith-Rosenberg, "Dis-Covering the Subject of the 'Great Constitutional Discussion,' 1786–1789," *Journal of American History,* LXXIX (1992), 841–873; Smith-Rosenberg, "Subject Female: Authorizing American Identity," *American Literary History,* V (1993), 481–511; Susan Juster, *Disorderly Women: Sexual Politics and Evangelicalism in Revolutionary New England* (Ithaca, N.Y., 1994), esp. 210–211; and Rogers M. Smith, "'One United People': Second-Class Female Citizenship and the American Quest for Community," *Yale Journal of Law and the Humanities,* I (1989), 229–293.

These questions would be easier to answer had the authors of the Constitution been more explicit about the place they envisaged for women in the polity. As Richard B. Morris once remarked, "It would have been helpful" if the framers "had given us a hint" about why they were so vague in their discussion of gender. But, in fact, the framers have left us a hint, in an amendment that James Wilson suggested to the resolutions then being debated in the Philadelphia Convention in the summer of 1787. Curiously, these words have attracted little attention from scholars of the Constitution and, so far as I can tell, none at all from historians of women. Although these words require careful interpretation, once they are placed in the context of contemporary thinking about representation and about women, it becomes evident that the Constitution does include women, although the role it set out for them was different than the one designed for most men.[2]

It was Monday, June 11, and the delegates who had convened in Philadelphia to revise the Articles of Confederation were now into their second week of secret meetings. The issue before the convention was who should vote for each branch of the proposed federal legislature. According to James Madison's notes, Roger Sherman of Connecticut had begun the day's session by proposing that "the proportion of suffrage" in the lower house of the national legislature, which would eventually be known as the House of Representatives, "should be according to the respective numbers of free inhabitants." Two South Carolinians, John Rutledge and Pierce Butler, immediately proposed that representation in the lower house should be based,

2. Richard B. Morris, *The Forging of the Union, 1781–1789* (New York, 1987), 190. Women were, however, noticed on at least several occasions in the nineteenth century. "A Petition for Universal Suffrage" presented to Congress in January 1866 by Elizabeth Cady Stanton and several other feminists noted that "the Constitution classes us as 'free people,' and counts us *whole* persons in the basis of representation." See Stanton et al., "A Petition for Universal Suffrage," Petitions and Memorials, Resolutions of State Legislatures Which Were Presented, Read, or Tabled during the 39th Congress, 1865–1867, 26081744, National Archives and Records Administration, Washington, D.C., copy in E. Cady Stanton, S. B. Anthony, and Lucy Stone, "Appeal by ECS and SBA," Dec. 26, 1865, in Ann D. Gordon, ed., *The Selected Papers of Elizabeth Cady Stanton and Susan B. Anthony,* I, *In the School of Anti-Slavery, 1840 to 1866* (New Brunswick, N.J., 1997), 566–567, esp. 567. See also Senator Samuel Latham Mitchill's 1804 letter to his wife, Catherine: "You must remember . . . that you are one of my constituents, and that I am in some degree responsible to you for my public conduct. In the theory of our Constitution women are calculated as political beings. They are numbered in the census of the inhabitants to make up the amount of population, and the Representatives are apportioned among the people according to their numbers, reckoning the females as well as the males. Though, therefore, women do not vote, they are nevertheless represented in the national government to their full amount" ("Dr. Mitchill's Letters from Washington, 1801–1813," *Harper's New Monthly Magazine* [1879], 748).

not upon the population of free persons, but upon each state's contribution to the national government. As Butler put it, "Money was power." It was in this context, a debate about whether representation should be based upon population or wealth, which would include slaves, that Pennsylvania's Wilson suggested language that would make clear that representation in the lower house would be "in proportion to the whole number of white and other free Citizens and inhabitants of every age sex and condition including those bound to servitude for a term of years and three fifths of all other persons not comprehended in the foregoing description, except Indians not paying taxes, in each State." This wording was voted upon, approved, and incorporated into the resolutions that the group would continue to debate and refine throughout the summer. Wilson's wording, only slightly modified, but with the words of interest to us here—"of every age, sex, and condition"—was included in the resolutions referred to the Committee of Style (chaired by William Samuel Johnson, of Connecticut, and including Alexander Hamilton, Rufus King, James Madison, and Gouverneur Morris) on September 10.[3]

The Committee of Style, reporting back on September 12, compressed Wilson's language into the words that actually appear in the Constitution. The relevant clause—now the third paragraph in Article 1, Section 2—specified that both representatives and direct taxes were to "be apportioned among the several states . . . according to their respective numbers, which shall be determined by adding to the whole number of free persons, including those bound to servitude for a term of years, and excluding Indians not taxed, three fifths of all other persons." This change in the wording seems to have been purely stylistic, rather than a change in meaning. The delegates voted many times over the course of the summer to edit particular wordings, even on August 20 to remove the words "white and other" in the same clause as "superfluous." Later, on September 13, they would replace the word "servitude" for "service," "the former being thought to express the condition of slaves, and the latter the obligations of free persons." Presumably, then, when the Committee of Style dropped the words "of every age, sex, and condition," neither they nor the delegates who accepted the revision thought that the meaning of the clause had been altered.[4]

3. Max Farrand, ed., *The Records of the Federal Convention of 1787* (1911; rpt. New Haven, Conn., 1966), I, 196, 201, 227, 236, II, 547, 553, 554, 571; Adrienne Koch, ed., *Notes of Debates in the Federal Convention of 1787, Reported by James Madison,* Bicentennial Edition (New York, 1987), 149–150.

4. Farrand, ed., *Records of the Federal Convention of 1787,* II, 350, 590, 607.

In fact, if we follow the debate on this clause, we can see that throughout the deliberations the delegates assumed that women, as well as children, were to be included whenever the question came up of who should be counted for purposes of apportionment.[5] Wilson's original wording was part of the resolutions that the convention was considering on June 19, and, as we have seen, most of this wording was still in the resolutions referred to the Committee of Style on September 10. But, over the summer, when the delegates debated the issue of apportionment, they rendered Wilson's words in a kind of shorthand. For example, on July 5, the committee assigned the task of forging a compromise on the issue of representation reported out the following language (and here, of course, we are following the transformation in Wilson's original wording, and not the thorny question the Convention was attempting to address): "that in the 1st. branch of the Legislature each of the States . . . shall be allowed 1 member for every 40,000 inhabitants of the description reported" earlier, on June 19. On July 13, after further debate about the basis for representation, the language was modified again, to "number of inhabitants; according to the provisions hereafter mentioned," leaving aside for the moment the question of how to count slaves.[6]

All subsequent discussion about the question of apportioning representatives would focus on this explosive issue. The term "inhabitants"—later changed to "free persons"—now included women and children. Thus we can see what the Committee of Style probably had in mind when it dropped Wilson's original wording about age and sex. Women, then, certainly were considered by the Constitutional Convention, and, although Wilson's reference to "sex" was ultimately excised, it seems clear that the framers intended that women be included among those who were to be represented by the new government. The Constitution included women.

Because no one objected to Wilson's insertion of the word "sex," and because women seem so readily to have been comprehended by the other delegates in the terms "inhabitants" and "persons," we may be tempted to think that Wilson was simply inserting words that reflected the common practice of the day. Even though no one raised an objection to Wilson's termi-

5. Needless to say, the inclusion of children in the formula for representation had important implications in political thought. A discussion of this issue lies beyond the scope of this article. For a masterful analysis of the place of children in early American political thought and law, see Holly Brewer, "Constructing Consent: How Children's Status in Political Theory Shaped Public Policy in Virginia, Pennsylvania, and Massachusetts before and after the American Revolution" (Ph.D. diss., University of California, Los Angeles, 1994).

6. Farrand, ed., *Records of the Federal Convention*, I, 526, 603.

nology, it seems to have represented a genuine innovation, and, because so few have noticed since, the genuine radicalism of the Constitution's doctrine of representation has been obscured. Although, as J. R. Pole and others have shown, in the Revolutionary period democrats were beginning to insist that persons, not property, were the proper basis for representation, not until the Federal Constitution had any government based representation upon inhabitants rather than taxpayers or adult men. When Massachusetts and Pennsylvania, for example, revised their constitutions, they defined "population" as "ratable polls" or "taxable inhabitants" rather than the total number of inhabitants, whether eligible to vote or not. In fact, none of the new state constitutions enacted at the time of the Revolution numbered women and children as among those who were to be represented.[7] Similarly, the Northwest Ordinance of 1787 specified that representation was to be based upon the number of "free male inhabitants, of full age."[8]

To include female inhabitants when apportioning representatives, then, was a significant extension of democratic trends that were reshaping representation in the states. Wilson took this logic further than others had taken

7. J. R. Pole, *Political Representation in England and the Origins of the American Republic* (1966; rpt. Berkeley, Calif., 1971), 204, 274–275. See also Rosemarie Zagarri, *The Politics of Size: Representation in the United States, 1776–1850* (Ithaca, N.Y., 1987), 39–42, 57–60; and, for a concise overview, Peter S. Onuf, "The Origins and Early Development of State Legislatures," in Joel H. Silbey, ed., *Encyclopedia of the American Legislative System: Studies of the Principal Structures, Processes, and Policies of Congress and the State Legislatures since the Colonial Era,* 3 vols. (New York, 1994), I, 175–194. For the relevant sections in the constitutions of Massachusetts and Pennsylvania, see Francis Newton Thorpe, ed., *The Federal and State Constitutions, Colonial Charters, and Other Organic Laws of the States, Territories, and Colonies Now or Heretofore Forming the United States of America,* 7 vols. (Washington, D.C., 1909), III, 1898, V, 3086. New York's 1777 constitution specified that in years to come, the legislature should be reapportioned on the basis of "the number of electors" in each county (ibid., V, 2629). The following states assigned each county, and in some cases town, a certain number of representatives in the lower house: Delaware (ibid., I, 562); Georgia (ibid., II, 778–779); Maryland (ibid., III, 1691); New Hampshire (ibid., IV, 2452); New Jersey (ibid., V, 2595); New York (ibid., V, 2629); North Carolina (ibid., V, 2790); South Carolina (ibid., VI, 3244–3245); Virginia (ibid., VII, 3815–3816). When the Georgia Constitution was rewritten in 1798, the basis for representation was changed to the "numbers of free white persons, and including three-fifths of all the people of color"; that is, the basis for representation was essentially that of the Federal Constitution, except that race, rather than freedom, was to be used as the principle of inclusion (ibid., II, 791).

8. "Northwest Ordinance, 13 July 1787," in Philip B. Kurland and Ralph Lerner, eds., *The Founders' Constitution,* 5 vols. (Chicago, 1987), I, 27. Each of the states created out of the territory, however, was to be eligible for admission to Congress once it had "sixty thousand free inhabitants" (ibid., 29). But representation was to be based upon the number of free adult males.

it until now and, in fact, further than those who would frame state constitutions in the near future would be willing to go. Kentucky's constitution of 1792 based representation on "an enumeration of the free male inhabitants above twenty-one years of age," and Tennessee's, framed four years later, on "an enumeration of the taxable inhabitants." But, because Wilson's additional language about sex was uncontested, it is not immediately clear what he and the other delegates intended by their innovation.[9]

When we examine Wilson's wording in the context of the convention's debate about the issue of representation, however, we may begin to understand what he and the other authors of the Constitution had in mind. The question of counting women when apportioning representatives was bound up in a matter the framers found much more compelling: the issue of how to count slaves. Although there was no discussion about including women when apportioning representatives, the framers vigorously debated whether and how to count slaves; these discussions are quite revealing about what the delegates thought about the question of representation, in general, and who should be represented, in particular. The slavery issue and one other, balancing the competing claims of the small and large states, were the most difficult ones the convention faced; each threatened to send the delegates home without a plan for a national government. And both of these thorny issues touched upon the overarching question of representation. Any debate about counting slaves or small versus large states soon brought the delegates into discussions not only about very practical considerations, such as which of their states might benefit, but also theoretical views on the nature of representation in a republic. These more abstract discussions yield some clues as to what the delegates had in mind when they simplified Wilson's original language. In fact, if we follow Wilson himself through the debates in the convention, his original intention in adding the language about sex becomes much more clear.

Even before he suggested the wording about "age, sex, and condition," Wilson had developed before the delegates his own theory of representation. Early in the proceedings, on June 9, Wilson "entered elaborately" into a defense of proportional representation. Representation should be based upon population; "as all authority was derived from the people, equal numbers of people ought to have an equal no. of representatives, and different numbers of people different numbers of representatives." It was only two days later that he introduced his amendment to incorporate the additional

9. Thorpe, ed., *Federal and State Constitutions,* III, 1265, VI, 3414.

words, including the terms "of every age sex and condition," as well as the Three-Fifths Clause. In this context, then, it seems evident that Wilson intended women to be included among the people, from whom "all authority was derived." In Wilson's mind, at least, women were included in the "We the People" who authorized the Constitution.[10]

At this particular moment in the deliberations, Wilson was engaged in a debate about whether representation in the lower house should be based upon wealth or population. Hence, Massachusetts's Elbridge Gerry immediately objected to Wilson's amendment, addressing the Three-Fifths Clause and asking, "Why then shd. the blacks, who were property in the South, be in the rule of representation more than the cattle and horses of the North[?]" Gerry did not, however, contest Wilson's suggestion that women should be included among the people who were to be represented.[11]

Nor did any of the other delegates who would argue about the proper basis for representation. Butler of South Carolina would continue to argue "that property was the only just measure of representation. This was the great object of Governt: the great cause of war, the great means of carrying it on." Although conservative nationalists such as New York's Morris agreed "that property was the main object of Society," he was troubled by the South Carolinians' desire to include slaves as part of the population. He thought that the Three-Fifths Compromise was "an incoherence. If Negroes were to be viewed as inhabitants . . . they ought to be added in their entire number, and not in the proportion of 3//5." If, instead, slaves were being counted as a measure of wealth, then the delegates should acknowledge that representation was being based upon population and property both.[12]

Wilson recognized the contradiction that Morris pointed out. He could not "see on what principle the admission of blacks" for purposes of representation "could be explained. Are they admitted as Citizens? Then why are they not admitted on an equality with White Citizens? Are they admitted as property? then why is not other property admitted into the computation?" Earlier, New Jersey's William Paterson had made the same point even more explicitly. "He could regard negroes slaves in no light but as property. They are no free agents, have no personal liberty, no faculty of acquiring property, but on the contrary are themselves property, and like other property entirely at the will of the Master." After neatly distinguishing between slavery and

10. Farrand, ed., *Records of the Federal Convention,* I, 179.

11. Ibid., 179, 201.

12. Ibid., 533, 542, 603–604; see also 562.

freedom, Paterson went on to lay out his theory of representation. "What is the true principle of Representation?" he asked. "It is an expedient by which an assembly of certain individls. chosen by the people is substituted in place of the inconvenient meeting of the people themselves. If such a meeting of the people was actually to take place, would the slaves vote? they would not. Why then shd. they be represented[?]" Although women could vote only in New Jersey, and children were not admitted to the polls anywhere, Paterson made no objection to including them in the basis for representation. In some clear, if unspecified way, women were members of political society in ways that slaves simply were not.[13]

While Wilson recognized the inconsistency of counting slaves, he was willing to compromise on this issue for the sake of the federal union. He would never concede, however, "that property was the sole or the primary object of Govern t. and Society." To the contrary, "the cultivation and improvement of the human mind was the most noble object. With respect to this object, as well as to other *personal* rights, numbers were surely the natural and precise measure of Representation." Now we can see what Wilson had in mind when he added the words "age sex and condition" to the resolutions the delegates were debating. If the purpose of government and society was, not property, but the improvement of the human mind and the protection of other personal rights, then surely women must be included.[14]

Although Wilson's intent seems clear enough, the delegates never commented upon Wilson's wording or the place of women in the government that they were creating. We may infer from their silence a general acceptance of Wilson's reasoning, if not an understanding of its practical application. These delegates were alert to—and spent a long summer debating—the subtlest shifts of meaning; surely, then, someone would have noted and objected to Wilson's formulation had it seemed problematic for the purposes at hand. The implications of Wilson's wording on slavery, in contrast, were very much contested, and there the delegates could achieve no common understanding. The Three-Fifths Compromise, as Wilson suggested, was a compromise both on the place of slavery in the new nation and on the proper basis for representation; in a document that everywhere else insisted that persons, not property, were to be represented, the compromise inserted the principle of the representation of wealth. James Madison would later attempt to wrest a

13. Ibid., 561, 587. For the case of New Jersey, see Judith Apter Klinghoffer and Lois Elkis, "'The Petticoat Electors': Women's Suffrage in New Jersey, 1776–1807," *Journal of the Early Republic,* XII (1992), 159–193. For children, see Brewer, "Constructing Consent."

14. Farrand, ed., *Records of the Federal Convention,* I, 605.

logic out of this "incoherence" by arguing in *The Federalist,* Number 54, that the Constitution intentionally recognized slaves' "mixt character of persons and of property." "This is in fact their true character," Madison asserted. And "if the laws were to restore the rights which have been taken away, the negroes could no longer be refused an equal share of representation with the other inhabitants." By necessary implication, women, who were counted fully, were to be represented fully, as well.[15]

In none of these discussions was it argued that slaves, free blacks, women, or children should vote, although in some states free blacks and in one women were exercising the franchise. Instead, democrats such as Wilson and Madison believed that all free inhabitants were part of the "imagined community" that they called the United States. They drew a distinction between being a member of the nation or community, which they called civil society, and voting. Every state in the new nation restricted the suffrage on the basis not only of age, sex, race, and freedom, but also of wealth.[16] Not even all adult white men could vote. According to the tenets of republicanism, participation in the Republic, and not simply voting, should have been restricted only to those who held enough property to secure a stake in the community and maintain their independence. Nascent liberals such as Wilson and Madison thought of the nation in much more expansive terms. Every free person who inhabited it was, in fact, a citizen, deserving of its protection and entitled to representation in the halls of government. In this context, women, who explicitly were to be represented but who just as explicitly were not permitted to represent themselves, became the touchstone of the modern, liberal state. By construing women as interested citizens incapable of representing themselves, liberalism provided a justification for the state: protecting those who could not protect themselves.[17]

15. James Madison [Alexander Hamilton?], "The Federalist No. 54 [53?]," in Jacob E. Cooke, ed., *The Federalist* (Middletown, Conn., 1961), 368.

16. Benedict Anderson, *Imagined Communities: Reflections on the Origin and Spread of Nationalism,* rev. ed. (London, 1991); Michael Walzer uses the term "political community" in Walzer, *Spheres of Justice: A Defense of Pluralism and Equality* (New York, 1983), 28–30. Of course, the Constitution left the qualifications for suffrage up to the states. For free blacks voting in state elections, see James Oliver Horton, *Free People of Color: Inside the African American Community* (Washington, D.C., 1993), 151. For women, see Klinghoffer and Elkis, '"Petticoat Electors,'" *Journal of the Early Republic,* XII (1992), 159–193. See the useful summary of suffrage restrictions in James Wilson, *Lectures on Law . . . ,* in Robert Green McCloskey, ed., *The Works of James Wilson,* 2 vols. (Cambridge, Mass., 1967), I, 408–411.

17. Here again, the distinction between a republican and liberal understanding of citizenship becomes more clear. For republican thinkers, liberty means the right to self-government, and, because only those who are independent may participate in government,

Wilson set out this theory of representation in his *Lectures on Law.* Over the winters of 1790–1791 and 1791–1792, he delivered two sets of lectures at the College of Philadelphia, but he never completed the entire course, nor had he even completed revisions on the entire set of lectures at the time of his death in 1798. Born in Scotland in 1742, Wilson was not quite fifty years old when he was appointed the first professor of law at the College of Philadelphia, yet he had already played a prominent role in the critical political events of the era. Educated at St. Andrews and the University of Edinburgh, he moved to America in 1765, settling in Philadelphia, where he studied law with John Dickinson. He became active in the Revolutionary movement, serving in a number of important capacities at the state and national level. His "Considerations on the Nature and Extent of the Legislative Authority of the British Parliament" (1774) was one of the models for the Declaration of Independence, and Wilson himself was one of only six men to sign both the Declaration and the Constitution. In 1789, George Washington made him one of the original associate justices of the Supreme Court.[18]

Even in the incomplete form in which Wilson's *Lectures* were published after his death, they constitute one of the most significant—and least explored—documents in political and social thought from this period of American history. If they lack the focus of *The Federalist,* they make up for it with their sweep. And although coherent political and social theories are embedded in the writings of the great thinkers of the age—Thomas Jefferson, Madison, Hamilton, John Adams—none of them set out as systematically to articulate a comprehensive theory of society and politics. In their subject matter, the *Lectures* invite comparison with John Locke's *Two Treatises of Government,* and, as such, they are a key text in the history of liberal thought in America. Moreover, because Wilson was self-consciously a syn-

---

the scope of republican liberty is restricted. That is, even though Republicans distinguished between personal liberty (which included an array of civil rights) and public liberty (the right of a people to govern itself), they thought of freedom fundamentally as the right to participate in government. See Gordon S. Wood, *The Creation of the American Republic, 1776–1787* (Williamsburg, Va., and Chapel Hill, N.C., 1969), 18–28; and Alan Craig Houston, *Algernon Sidney and the Republican Heritage in England and America* (Princeton, N.J., 1991), 118. Liberals such as Wilson shifted the emphasis, or, perhaps more precisely, expanded the compass to include protection of life, liberty, and happiness for the entire society, not simply those who participated directly in government.

18. Robert Green McCloskey, "Introduction," in McCloskey, ed., *Works of Wilson,* I, 28–30. There is no modern biography of Wilson. For brief treatments, see ibid.; and Dumas Malone, ed., *Dictionary of American Biography . . . ,* XX (New York, 1936), s.v. "Wilson, James (Sept. 14, 1742–Aug. 21, 1798)."

thesizer, which is another way of saying that he was not always original, he is an especially useful guide to the assumptions shared by a wide range of political thinkers, particularly those whose thinking ran along liberal lines. Furthermore, because the lectures attempted to discuss systematically the relationship between society and government, they illuminate connections that others left unstated.[19]

All of the dignitaries of the new federal government turned out for Wilson's inaugural lecture as professor of law at the College of Philadelphia. Women also were among the audience—not an unusual occurrence for such events, and, at one point, Wilson addressed them directly. "Methinks I hear one of the female part of my audience exclaim—What is all this to us? We have heard much of societies, of states, of governments, of laws, and of a law education. Is every thing made for your sex? Why should not we have a share? Is our sex less honest, or less virtuous, or less wise than yours?" Women were not, Wilson averred, any less honest, virtuous, or wise than men. Moreover, although he doubted "whether it would be proper" for women to "undertake the management of publick affairs," they had an important role to play in society. He told the women in his audience that "you have, indeed, heard much of publick government and publick law: but these things were not made for themselves: they were made for something better; and of that something better, you form the better part—I mean society—I mean particularly domestick society." Wilson continued with a discussion of the relationship between government and society that recalls Thomas Paine's famous dictum that "society in every state is a blessing, but government even in its best state is but a necessary evil." Wilson noted,

> By some politicians, society has been considered as only the scaffolding of government; very improperly, in my judgment. In the just order of things, government is the scaffolding of society: and if society could be built and kept entire without government, the scaffolding might be thrown down, without the least inconvenience or cause of regret.
>
> Government is, indeed, highly necessary; but it is highly necessary to a fallen state. Had man continued innocent, society, without the

19. Stephen A. Conrad, "Polite Foundation: Citizenship and Common Sense in James Wilson's Republican Theory," in Philip B. Kurland, Gerhard Casper, and Dennis J. Hutchinson, eds., *The Supreme Court Review: 1984* (Chicago, 1985), 359–388, esp. 386–387; Shannon C. Stimson, "'A Jury of the Country': Common Sense Philosophy and the Jurisprudence of James Wilson," in Richard B. Sher and Jeffrey R. Smitten, eds., *Scotland and America in the Age of the Enlightenment* (Princeton, N.J., 1990), 193–208.

> aids of government, would have shed its benign influence even over the bowers of Paradise.

Government was created to serve society, not as an end in itself.[20]

Wilson would return to this point so frequently in his lectures that it is evident that it was not simply a passing thought, intended to placate the women in his audience. Instead, it was one of the central tenets in his political canon. "Government," to put it succinctly, "was instituted for the happiness of society." Like Locke, Wilson believed that government originated in a social compact. As Wilson explained it, in terms reminiscent of Locke, government was created "by a human establishment, to acquire a new security for the possession or the recovery of those rights, to the enjoyment or acquisition of which we were previously entitled by the immediate gift, or by the unerring law, of our all-wise and all-beneficent Creator."[21]

Historians have been at pains to discount the influence of Locke in Revolutionary thought, placing much more emphasis upon its sources in civic humanism, British Opposition party ideas, and the Scottish Enlightenment. As a consequence, it no longer seems possible to make a statement so simple as Carl Becker's comment in 1922 that "Jefferson copied Locke." Still, the influence of Locke on thinkers such as Wilson is so clear that it requires our continued attention; we must ask how he and those who thought like him

20. Wilson, *Lectures on Law,* in McCloskey, ed., *Works of Wilson,* I, 85–86, 86–87; Thomas Paine, *Common Sense* (1776) (New York, 1976), 65. Consider also the philosophy of government embedded in Jefferson's first inaugural address, particularly by reading his encomium to "a wise and frugal Government, which shall restrain men from injuring one another, shall leave them otherwise free to regulate their own pursuits of industry and improvement," in the light of his injunction to his fellow citizens to "restore to social intercourse that harmony and affection without which liberty and even life itself are but dreary things." See "First Inaugural Address," in Merrill D. Peterson, ed., *Thomas Jefferson, Writings: Autobiography, A Summary View of the Rights of British America, Notes on the State of Virginia, Public Papers, Addresses, Messages, and Replies, Miscellany, Letters* (New York, 1984), 493, 494. For the presence of women in similar audiences at this time, see Jan Lewis, "Politics and the Ambivalence of the Private Sphere: Women in Early Washington, D.C.," in Donald R. Kennon, ed., *A Republic for the Ages: The United States Capitol and the Political Culture of the Early Republic* (Charlottesville, Va., 1999), 122–151, also reprinted in this volume.

21. Wilson, *Lectures on Law,* in McCloskey, ed., *Works of Wilson,* I, 239; see similarly ibid., I, 283, 284, II, 585. Near the end of his *Lectures on Law,* Wilson quoted from his Introduction that " 'publick law and publick government were not made for themselves;' but that 'they were made for something better;' that 'I meant society;' that 'I meant particularly domestick society.' " This was no "encomium," he insisted, but a principle "founded in sound politicks and genuine philosophy" (ibid., II, 608). For a different reading, see Smith, " 'One United People,' " *Yale Journal of Law and the Humanities,* I (1989), 245–247.

integrated Lockean ideas with ones they adopted from the British Opposition and the Scottish Enlightenment. We may begin this task by examining how Wilson understood the Lockean social contract and what his interpretation of it meant for women.[22]

Before we proceed with this analysis, we should note that feminist political theorists such as Carole Pateman have argued that women were left out of the social contract that created the liberal state. Applying Pateman's formulation to early America, Linda K. Kerber has written that "men and women have been differently situated in relation to consent theory. . . . Men are imagined as entering the social contract as free agents, but most women enter the social contract already bound by marriage and by antecedent obligations to their husbands." It is undeniable that, as Kerber and others have shown, the common-law doctrine of coverture, which held that upon marriage a woman's legal personality was merged into that of her husband, remained the basis for property and domestic relations law after the Revolution. It is equally true, however, as Kerber herself has demonstrated, that, although some used coverture as a model for women's political position as well, others were beginning to imagine that women could be participants in the social compact, acting independently of their husbands or other male protectors. Wilson was one of those who found a place for women in the social compact.[23]

One of Wilson's earliest statements about the nature of political society succinctly outlined the fundamental beliefs that he would develop at greater length in his *Lectures on Law.* "All men are," Wilson asserted in 1774, recapitulating Locke and anticipating Jefferson,

22. Carl Becker, *The Declaration of Independence: A Study in the History of Political Ideas* (1922; rpt. New York, 1970), 79. For the influence of civic humanism, see, for example, J. G. A. Pocock, *The Machiavellian Moment: Florentine Political Thought and the Atlantic Republican Tradition* (Princeton, N.J., 1975). For British Country thought, see, for example, Wood, *Creation of the American Republic.* For the Scottish Enlightenment, see, for example, Morton White, *The Philosophy of the American Revolution* (New York, 1978); Garry Wills, *Inventing America: Jefferson's Declaration of Independence* (Garden City, N.Y., 1978); and Henry F. May, *The Enlightenment in America* (New York, 1976).

23. Carole Pateman, *The Sexual Contract* (Stanford, Calif., 1988); Kerber, "Constitutional Right," in Kerber, Kessler-Harris, and Kish Sklar, eds., *U.S. History as Women's History,* 17–35, esp. 20; Kerber, "The Paradox of Women's Citizenship in the Early Republic: The Case of Martin vs. Massachusetts, 1805," *American Historical Review,* XCVII (1992), 349–378. For coverture, see Norma Basch, *In the Eyes of the Law: Women, Marriage, and Property in Nineteenth-Century New York* (Ithaca, N.Y., 1982); and Basch, "Equity vs. Equality: Emerging Concepts of Women's Political Status in the Age of Jackson," *Journal of the Early Republic,* III (1983), 297–318.

> by nature, equal and free: no one has a right to any authority over another without his consent: all lawful government is founded on the consent of those who are subject to it: such consent was given with a view to ensure and to increase the happiness of the governed, above what they could enjoy in an independent and unconnected state of nature. The consequence is, that the happiness of the society is the *first* law of every government.

Some of the terms—freedom, equality, the state of nature, the requirement of consent—are familiar from Locke's *Second Treatise.* Other elements betray Wilson's Scottish upbringing and education and his wide reading among ancient and modern authorities both; according to the editor of Wilson's published works, he cited almost two hundred different sources. Moreover, as Morton White has demonstrated, Wilson was something of a plagiarist, sometimes copying a line here or there without citing his source. Perhaps even more important, Wilson was self-consciously a synthesizer who tried to reconcile what seemed to be contradictory points of view.[24]

Wilson's accomplishment was to merge a Scottish Enlightenment sociology and a Lockean politics; accordingly, the happiness of society, a concept that is undeveloped in Locke, becomes the object of government. Although Locke seems to have posited a sphere of civil society, standing between the private realm of family and work and the public domain of government, he did not describe it in any detail or fit it into his social or political theory. In some places, he made it appear as if civil society and government were one and the same. A century later, when civic culture itself was a much more visible feature of public life and such philosophers of the Scottish Enlightenment as Francis Hutcheson and Thomas Reid had helped shift the focus from the individual to society, Wilson could write with much more specificity about both civil society and women's role in it.[25]

24. James Wilson, "Considerations on the Nature and Extent of the Legislative Authority of the British Parliament," in McCloskey, ed., *Works of Wilson,* II, 723, "Bibliographical Glossary," 849–856; John Locke, *Two Treatises of Government,* ed. Peter Laslett (Cambridge, 1960); White, *Philosophy of the American Revolution,* 133; Conrad, "Polite Foundation," in Kurland, Casper, and Hutchinson, eds., *Supreme Court Review: 1984,* 386–387; Stimson, "'A Jury of the Country,'" in Sher and Smitten, eds., *Scotland and America in the Age of the Enlightenment,* 193–208. As Jay Fliegelman has noted, plagiarism was almost an accepted intellectual practice in this period. See Fliegelman, *Declaring Independence: Jefferson, Natural Language, and the Culture of Performance* (Stanford, Calif., 1993), 164–189.

25. Locke observed, "The only way whereby any one divests himself of his Natural Liberty, and *puts on the bonds of Civil Society* is by agreeing with other Men to joyn and unite

Men and women were, by nature, social beings. "We are fitted and intended for society, and . . . society is fitted and intended for us," Wilson asserted in his *Lectures on Law.*

> We have all the emotions, which are necessary in order that society may be formed and maintained: we have tenderness for the fair sex: we have affection for our children, for our parents, and for our other relations: we have attachment to our friends: we have a regard for reputation and esteem: we possess gratitude and compassion: we enjoy pleasure in the happiness of others, especially when we have been instrumental in procuring it: we entertain for our country an animated and vigorous zeal: we feel delight in the agreeable conception of the improvement and happiness of mankind.

Sociability, then, was nurtured in the family, and the bonds of affection that were created there stretched ever outward, from the family, to friends, the community, the nation, and even to humankind itself.[26]

It was for this reason that Wilson would say again and again that government was "instituted for the happiness of society." Although women could play no part in the masculine realm of government without jeopardizing their femininity, they certainly had an important role to play in constituting society.[27] Indeed, marriage was the pattern for all other social relationships

---

into a Community, for their comfortable, safe, and peaceable living one amongst another, in a secure Enjoyment of their Properties. . . . When any number of Men have so *consented to make one Community* or Government, they are thereby presently incorporated, and make *one Body Politick*" (Locke, *Two Treatises of Government,* ed. Laslett, 348–349). On the influence of the Scottish Enlightenment, see White, *Philosophy of the American Revolution;* Wills, *Inventing America;* Conrad, "Polite Foundation," in Kurland, Casper, and Hutchinson, eds., *Supreme Court Review: 1984,* 359–388; and David Daiches, "John Witherspoon, James Wilson, and the Influence of Scottish Rhetoric on America," *Eighteenth-Century Life,* XV (February / May 1991), 163–180.

26. Wilson, *Lectures on Law,* in McCloskey, ed., *Works of Wilson,* I, 233; see also 241–242. So important was this point to Wilson that he would repeat it verbatim in his lecture on "Natural Rights" (ibid., II, 587). See also Thomas Jefferson to Thomas Law ("The Moral Sense: To Thomas Law"), June 13, 1814, in Peterson, ed., *Thomas Jefferson, Writings,* 1335–1339. Consider, as well, James Madison, "Federalist No. 14," in Cooke, ed., *The Federalist,* 88.

27. Wilson, *Lectures on Law,* in McCloskey, ed., *Works of Wilson,* I, 85–88. As Rosemarie Zagarri has pointed out, Wilson followed the lead of Scottish thinkers in advocating social equality for women while insisting upon political inequality. See her "Morals, Manners, and the Republican Mother," *American Quarterly,* XLIV (1992), 207. Wilson's thinking about women, like that of many of his contemporaries, was contradictory. He argued that

and for patriotism itself. Yet, whereas that other influential Scottish émigré, John Witherspoon, could use this logic to assert "the absolute necessity of marriage for the service of the state," Wilson would turn that logic around and insist that government was created for society and for domestic society in particular. Because the purpose of government was to protect and even improve "social life," although women could not participate in the running of government, they had "a most intimate connexion with the effects, of a good system of law and government." Women, in this sense, were the very object of government, and that was precisely why they had to be represented by the new government created by the Constitution.[28]

From our present perspective, perhaps what we confront here is the question of whether the glass of political thought is half empty or half full. It is undeniable that Wilson's philosophy of government justified the exclusion of women from the vote and from officeholding, and that basing this exclusion upon women's feminine nature would ultimately make it difficult for women to enter these political spheres.[29] At the same time, Wilson's liber-

women could not enter politics both because of their status, as unpropertied dependents, and their nature, which he called "female virtue" (Wilson, *Lectures on Law,* in McCloskey, ed., *Works of Wilson,* I, 86–88, 411). Paul A. Rahe has suggested that Wilson's paean to female virtue "was inspired by Jean-Jacques Rousseau's celebration of domesticity as a bulwark against the psychologically debilitating effects of the corrosive individualism at the core of modern life," but there is little evidence that Wilson was particularly concerned by modern individualism or that he shared Rousseau's notorious misogyny. See Rahe, *Republics Ancient and Modern: Classical Republicanism and the American Revolution* (Chapel Hill, N.C., 1992), 564–565. It may be useful to note that the tendency to assign political roles on the basis of status is characteristic of republican approaches to government, while assigning them on the basis of "nature" is more typical of liberal thought. At the same time, it should be remembered that each approach to government offered means both for including and excluding. Because republicanism excluded the poor, the propertyless, and the dependent, it left open the possibility that single, propertied women might vote, which is precisely what happened in New Jersey between 1776 and 1807. See Klinghoffer and Elkis, "'Petticoat Electors,'" *Journal of the Early Republic,* XII (1992), 159–193. As republican approaches to government were replaced by liberal ones, women would be excluded on the basis of their (supposed) nature, including their special virtue. Yet, if post-Revolutionary liberalism restricted women from the suffrage and officeholding, it also, as will be suggested, opened up a space for them as members of civil society.

28. Epaminondas, "To the Publisher of the Pennsylvania Magazine" ["Reflections on Marriage"], *Pennsylvania Magazine; or, American Monthly Museum,* I (September 1775), 409, later published as "Letters on Marriage: Letter I," in John Rodgers, ed., *The Works of the Rev. John Witherspoon,* 2d ed., 4 vols. (Philadelphia, 1802), IV, 161–162, esp. 162; Wilson, *Lectures on Law,* in McCloskey, ed., *Works of Wilson,* I, 88. See also Jan Lewis, "The Republican Wife: Virtue and Seduction in the Early Republic," *William and Mary Quarterly,* 3d Ser., XLIV (1987), 689, 709, also reprinted in this volume.

29. See Rowland Berthoff, "Conventional Mentality: Free Blacks, Women, and Busi-

alism made a place for women not simply in the family but in the large and important sphere of civil society—what Jürgen Habermas has called the "bourgeois public sphere." In fact, although Habermas based his theoretical discussion of society upon European nations, it bears an uncanny resemblance to Wilson's description of the ideal society that he hoped would be sustained by a republican form of government. After expatiating upon the nobility of the individual voter, Wilson reflected, however, that "I am far from insinuating that every citizen should be an enthusiast in politicks, or that the interests of himself, his family, and those who depend on him for their comfortable situation in life, should be absorbed in Quixote speculations about the management or the reformation of the state." As he would frequently note, government was not, after all, the object of society. "There is surely a golden mean in things; and there can be no real incompatibility between the discharge of one's publick and that of his private duty. Let private industry receive the warmest encouragement; for it is the basis of publick happiness." Government, then, was both good and necessary, and so was private enterprise, but neither attracted Wilson's full attention. Instead, Wilson recommended "a little relaxation. . . . It may consist in reading a newspaper, or in conversing with a fellow citizen. May not the newspaper convey some interesting intelligence, or contain some useful essay? . . . May not the conversation take a pleasing and an improving turn?" This, then, was the very stuff of life: the reading of newspapers and conversation among friends. Wilson was describing the bourgeois public sphere, and, at a time when literacy rates for women were increasing, it was a realm that included women.[30]

The public sphere, or civil society, as Wilson described it and Habermas later explained it, is the realm of society that was created when ordinary

ness Corporations as Unequal Persons, 1820–1870," *Journal of American History,* LXXVI (1989), 753–784. Berthoff, however, overemphasizes the persistence of classical republican themes in mid-nineteenth-century justifications for the exclusion of women from politics.

30. Jürgen Habermas, *The Structural Transformation of the Public Sphere: An Inquiry into a Category of Bourgeois Society,* ed. and trans. Thomas Burger (1962; rpt. Cambridge, Mass., 1991); Wilson, "Speech on Choosing the Members of the Senate by Electors: Delivered on 31st December, 1789, in the Convention of Pennsylvania," in McCloskey, ed., *Works of Wilson,* II, 787–788. Wilson liked these ideas so much that he repeated them in his *Lectures on Law.* Stephen A. Conrad notes that "this passage captures the essence of the central argument of Wilson's polite theory of republicanism" in which "the essential opportunities for true republicanism in America . . . can be realized only in the fundamental sphere of the social life of the People 'out of doors'" (Conrad, "Polite Foundation," in Kurland, Casper, and Hutchinson, eds., *Supreme Court Review: 1984,* 384). For women's literacy rates, see Kenneth A. Lockridge, *Literacy in Colonial New England: An Enquiry into the Social Context of Literacy in the Early Modern West* (New York, 1974).

people emerged from their homes to engage in conversation. Habermas defines it as "the sphere of private people com[ing] together as a public," and, although these are not the exact words that Wilson used, they convey his understanding, too, of the relationship between domestic and civil society.[31] As Habermas recognized and subsequent historians have noted, women participated in the public sphere. Much like Wilson, Habermas has suggested that the notion of humanity that was cherished by the rising bourgeoisie of the eighteenth century was born and nourished in the family, which served as a model for all other relationships in society. The family, he wrote, "seemed to be established voluntarily and by free individuals and to be maintained without coercion; it seemed to rest on the lasting community of love on the part of the two spouses; it seemed to permit that non-instrumental development of all faculties that marks [*sic*] the cultivated personality." The family, then, contributed to society precisely the ingredients that defined humanity itself: "voluntariness, community of love, and cultivation."[32]

Little wonder, then, that Wilson would insist that government was created to protect society and domestic society in particular, for it was the source of all that was most valuable in life. Moreover, when any government subverted that end, or even when it failed to protect society, then the people might abolish, alter, or amend their government "at whatever time, and in whatever

31. Habermas, *Structural Transformation of the Public Sphere,* 27; Wilson, *Lectures on Law,* in McCloskey, ed., *Works of Wilson,* I, 238–240. Habermas uses the term "civil society" to encompass the "realm of commodity exchange and social labor" (Habermas, *Structural Transformation of the Public Sphere,* 30). Wilson uses the term "private industry" instead (Wilson, *Lectures on Law,* in McCloskey, ed., *Works of Wilson,* I, 404). As Stephen A. Conrad has pointed out, Wilson used the terms "civil society," "People," and "state" interchangeably. See Conrad, "James Wilson's 'Assimilation of the Common-Law Mind,'" *Northwestern University Law Review,* LXXXIV (1989), 186–219, esp. 213.

32. Habermas, *Structural Transformation of the Public Sphere,* 46–47; and see, in particular, Dena Goodman, "Public Sphere and Private Life: Toward a Synthesis of Current Historiographical Approaches to the Old Regime," *History and Theory,* XXXI (1992), 1–20; Keith Michael Baker, "Defining the Public Sphere in Eighteenth-Century France: Variations on a Theme by Habermas," in Craig Calhoun, ed., *Habermas and the Public Sphere* (Cambridge, Mass., 1992), 198–207. Both Goodman and Baker critique Joan B. Landes's use of Habermas to explain women's supposed exclusion from the public sphere. See Landes, *Women and the Public Sphere in the Age of the French Revolution* (Ithaca, N.Y., 1988), in particular her claim that "the exclusion of women from the bourgeois public was not incidental, but central to its incarnation" (7). See, as well, Goodman, *The Republic of Letters: A Cultural History of the French Enlightenment* (Ithaca, N.Y., 1994), esp. 3–11. For evidence of women in the post-Revolutionary American public and an explanation of why they were there, see Lewis, "Politics and the Ambivalence of the Private Sphere," in Kennon, ed., *Republic for the Ages,* 122–151; and Elizabeth Regine Varon, "'We Mean to Be Counted': White Women and Politics in Antebellum Virginia" (Ph.D. diss., Yale University, 1993).

manner, they shall deem it expedient." Here Wilson synthesized Locke and the radical Whigs into his Scottish Common Sense philosophy. Although government may be necessary to protect society and provide for its security, it is government as well that presents the greatest threat to happiness. Here, once again, Wilson's political thought anticipated that of Habermas, who argues that the bourgeois public sphere defined itself historically in opposition to the authoritarian early modern state. Indeed, political consciousness developed as people began to insist, "in opposition to [the] absolute sovereignty" of a monarch, that the only basis for law was the human values, what Habermas calls "general and abstract laws," that they had learned within the family.[33]

It is for this reason that thinkers such as Wilson did not worry as much about the conflicts between individuals as those between society and the state. In part, they reflected the continuing republican obsession with the threat of governmental tyranny and a difficulty in thinking about the "people" in anything other than corporate terms. In this context, a "right" was a corporate liberty, secured from the state. Yet Wilson's thinking incorporated liberal influences as well, in particular Locke filtered through a Scottish lens. As a consequence, his vision of society and of the rights that might be enjoyed in it was much richer than that of republican thinkers or even Locke. The primary focus always was upon society, for it was only there that individuals could become fully human.[34]

Just as Wilson's larger political and social philosophy synthesized republican and liberal themes, so also did his views on women. Although in other instances Wilson rejected the English jurist Blackstone as an authority, he cribbed Blackstone's description of the common-law principle of coverture: "The most important consequence of marriage is, that the husband and the wife become, in law, only one person: the legal existence of the wife is consolidated into that of the husband." Yet if the common-law doctrine of coverture reflected and perpetuated the dependent social relations of feudal society and helped assure the preservation of property in the male line of descent, Wilson gave that doctrine a sentimental gloss. He rhapsodized it as "sublime and refined." For Wilson, coverture was not so much a legal

33. Wilson, *Lectures on Law,* in McCloskey, ed., *Works of Wilson,* I, 77; Habermas, *Structural Transformation of the Public Sphere,* 54.

34. See, Wood, *Creation of the American Republic,* part 1; and Wilson, *Lectures on Law,* in McCloskey, ed., *Works of Wilson,* I, 227: "Society is the powerful magnet, which, by its unceasing though silent operation, attracts and influences our dispositions, our desires, our passions, and our enjoyments."

fiction or even a mechanism for the transmission of property. Rather, it was the ideal of marriage itself. "By that institution the felicity of Paradise was consummated; and since the unhappy expulsion from thence, to that institution, more than to any other, have mankind been indebted for the share of peace and harmony which has been distributed among them." In other words, if peace and harmony were to be found anywhere, it was in marriage. Hence, the doctrine of marital unity—that two persons would function as one—became the cornerstone of society. Like a number of democrats at the time, Wilson was willing to countenance divorce for marriages that had failed. As he put it, "When . . . the impression of happiness must be obliterated from every succeeding part of the conjugal history, why should any more blackened pages be added to the inauspicious volume?" Wilson's principal concern was not the orderly transmission of property but the happiness of society.[35]

Indeed, by recognizing divorce as the remedy for marriages gone wrong, Wilson was protecting the institution from what he considered more dangerous interventions. Marriage was a civil contract, and, like other civil contracts, it could be dissolved under certain circumstances. But this was the only option available. An aggrieved party could not summon the government to her support, nor could the community routinely call a husband or wife to account.[36] Wilson made the doctrine of marital unity a bulwark to protect the family from the state. In so doing, he transformed a wholly patriarchal vision of the family, in which a father ruled as a king over the dependents in his household, into a liberal one, in which the privacy of the sentimental family must be protected from the interventions of the state. "The rights, the enjoyments, the obligations, and the infelicities of the matrimonial state" all were "removed" from the "protection or redress" of the state. Instead,

35. Wilson, *Lectures on Law,* in McCloskey, ed., *Works of Wilson,* I, 77–79, II, 598, 601, 603; Basch, *In the Eyes of the Law,* 45–54; Basch, "From the Bonds of Empire to the Bonds of Matrimony," in David Thomas Konig, ed., *Devising Liberty: Preserving and Creating Freedom in the New American Republic* (Stanford, Calif., 1995), 217–242. See also Conrad, "James Wilson's 'Assimilation,'" *Northwestern University Law Review,* LXXXIV (1989), 197–215.

36. Contrast Wilson's view to that of Blackstone who, as Norma Basch has explained, dispelled "the notion that marriage is a contract like any other; marriage once contracted is a status" (Basch, *In the Eyes of the Law,* 48). Community intervention had been routine in the Puritan colonies of New England. See, for example, John Demos, *A Little Commonwealth: Family Life in Plymouth Colony* (New York, 1970), 82–106; and Nancy F. Cott, "Eighteenth-Century Family and Social Life Revealed in Massachusetts Divorce Records," *Journal of Social History,* X (1976), 20–43. For changing standards, see Michael Grossberg, *Governing the Hearth: Law and the Family in Nineteenth-Century America* (Chapel Hill, N.C., 1985), 17–21.

the state must stand aside, adopting the stance of "a candid and benevolent neighbour," who must "presume, for she wishes, all to be well." The social order, then, rested upon a sort of wish fulfillment: families that were presumed to be happy.[37]

Yet if Wilson's social and political theory held out little hope for women who were suffering at the hands of their families, it implicitly promised them the full array of civil liberties. To be sure, the doctrine of women's civil rights would come into conflict with the older doctrine of coverture, and, as Linda Kerber has suggested, when it did, the more restrictive interpretation of women's citizenship might prevail. The men who created the new national and state governments after the Revolution barely discussed the question of female citizenship. Hence, even when, as in the case of Wilson, they seemed to expand the sphere of women's civil liberties, the framers offered very little guidance about how those rights should be defined or enforced.[38]

Nonetheless, during the first three-quarters of the nineteenth century, the constitutional foundation for women's citizenship—that is, women's entitlement to civil, but not political, rights—was made increasingly secure.

37. Wilson, *Lectures on Law,* in McCloskey, ed., *Works of Wilson,* II, 602–603. Note also Morton J. Horwitz's observation that "nineteenth-century political, social, and economic thought . . . sought to establish a separate, 'natural' realm of non-coercive and non-political transactions free from the dangers of state interference and redistribution" (Horwitz, *The Transformation of American Law, 1870–1960: The Crisis of Legal Orthodoxy,* 2d ed. [1977; rpt. New York, 1992], 11). I have explored the roots in republican thought of the assumption that marriages must be free of conflict in Lewis, "Republican Wife," *William and Mary Quarterly,* 3d Ser., XLIV (1987), 689–721. If liberals would be more willing than Republicans to confront the reality of conflict in the economy and society—Madison's *Federalist* Number 10 is the key text here—they continued to assume that families were intrinsically free from conflict (Madison, "The Federalist No. 10," in Cooke, ed., *The Federalist,* 56–65).

38. Kerber, "Paradox of Women's Citizenship," *American Historical Review,* XCVII (1992), 349–378. As Kerber has demonstrated in her illuminating analysis of *Martin* v. *Massachusetts,* when the doctrine of coverture came into conflict with the liberal faith in an individual's ability to make her own choices, judges had no clear guide. They might, as did the Supreme Judicial Court of Massachusetts in 1805, decide that the principle of coverture took precedence and that a woman married to a loyalist had effectively no choice but to abandon her country and her property and accompany her husband when he left Massachusetts for England. But, before they made that ruling, they had to consider Attorney General James Sullivan's argument that a married woman could "be an inhabitant in every sense of the word. Who are members of the body politic? are not all the *citizens,* members; infants, idiots, insane, or whatever may be their *relative* situations in society?" (*Martin* v. *Massachusetts,* in Ephraim Williams, *Reports of Cases Argued and Determined in the Supreme Judicial Court of the Commonwealth of Massachusetts,* I [Boston, 1851], 375, also cited ibid., 371). Like Wilson, Sullivan was a liberal who believed that women were members of the original social compact that established government.

Although these conclusions must be offered cautiously, as there is much research to be done on this topic, women's membership in civil society would be defined in relationship to that of free blacks. Just as the issues of race and gender had been joined in Wilson's language on representation offered to the Constitutional Convention, so, too, would they be linked in subsequent discussions in the nineteenth century. In fact, the understanding of women's civil rights emerged most clearly in discussions about attempts to limit the civil rights of free blacks. These discussions suggest that women were considered as members of civil society, entitled to representation and the rights of citizens, even if they could not themselves participate in government.[39]

This understanding emerged as state courts began to define the rights of free blacks. For those states that wished to restrict them from voting, women served a useful purpose as an example of another class of adult citizens who could not vote. In 1838, for example, the North Carolina Supreme Court observed, "Surely the possession of political power is not essential to constitute a citizen. If it be, then women, minors, and persons who have not paid public taxes are not citizens." Yet, at the same time, women could be used to illustrate the sorts of civil rights that had to be extended to all citizens, whether they voted or not. A provision in the proposed Missouri Constitution, which would have prevented free blacks and mulattoes from entering the state, kindled a heated controversy when Congress debated Missouri's admission into the Union in 1820. Opponents argued that, since free blacks were neither aliens nor slaves, they surely were entitled to the privileges of citizens, including the right to move from one state to another. Once again, women served as a point of reference for those who, although not holding political rights, nevertheless enjoyed the protections of citizens. And, in this

39. This conclusion must be advanced cautiously, as most of these statements about women's civil rights were, like Wilson's, abstract and categorical and were advanced to explain why free blacks should or should not have certain rights, not why women should or should not enjoy them. Moreover, although the passing of Married Women's Property Acts in various states, beginning with Mississippi in 1839 followed by New York in 1848, would begin to chip away at the doctrine of coverture, the legal fiction of marital unity continues even today to cast a shadow over women; consider only the reluctance of the police to intervene in so-called "domestic disputes." Nonetheless, the fundamental civil rights of liberalism—freedom of assembly, freedom of religion, freedom of speech, freedom from the oppressions of the state, and perhaps the most fundamental right of all, to own oneself—are far from trivial, and the extension of them to women, even in the abstract, is of considerable significance. For the persistence of coverture, see Kerber, "Constitutional Right," in Kerber, Kessler-Harris, and Sklar, eds., *U.S. History as Women's History*, 34, 355n56. For the concept of self-ownership, see Locke, *Two Treatises of Government*, ed. Laslett, 27.

case, the right under discussion was fundamental to liberalism: the right of a citizen to move freely within the nation.[40]

Women, then, came to play a critical role in the way that democratic liberalism defined itself in practice. They became the referent for citizens who were not members of political society, that is, who could not vote or hold office. In this way, they helped legitimate not so much their own inequality as that of free blacks. In fact, when New Jersey women lost the vote in 1808, so did free blacks. In other words, although the category of female citizenship—as members of civil but not political society—was contested, it was more stable than that of free blacks, and hence could be used in attempts to stabilize the status of free blacks.[41]

Such efforts to stabilize the position of free blacks could not entirely succeed, however, because they rested upon the assumption that all members of society were members of that imagined community known as the nation. Although white men could accept the general principle that women were part of the nation, the notion that blacks were to be included, too, was considerably more problematic. Here it was not so much the specific implications of

40. "*The State v. William Manuel,*" December 1838, in Thomas P. Devereux and William H. Battle, *Reports of Cases at Law, Argued and Determined in the Supreme Court of North Carolina . . . ,* IV (Raleigh, N.C., 1840), quoted in James H. Kettner, *The Development of American Citizenship, 1608–1870* (Williamsburg, Va., and Chapel Hill, N.C., 1978), 312–314, 317. Significantly, the case was about whether free blacks were citizens; the court concluded that they were.

41. Klinghoffer and Elkis, "'Petticoat Electors,'" *Journal of the Early Republic,* XII (1992), 188–189. Before 1820, free blacks also lost the right to vote in Connecticut and Pennsylvania, whereas in New York they had to meet a property requirement no longer demanded of whites. See Horton, *Free People of Color,* 151. On female citizenship, see, for example, Ellen Carol DuBois, *Feminism and Suffrage: The Emergence of an Independent Women's Movement in America, 1848–1869* (Ithaca, N.Y., 1978); and Berthoff, "Conventional Mentality," *Journal of American History,* LXXVI (1989), 753–784. Although Berthoff suggests that state constitutional debates between 1820 and 1870 reveal the persistence of republican notions of the political incapacity of both women and blacks, it is possible to interpret his material in another way. In a more republican political culture, the exclusion of women and blacks from the polity would not have occasioned much debate; after all, women were barely mentioned in the constitutional debates of the Revolutionary period, and it was slavery, not the status of free blacks, that attracted most attention. That there was debate at all suggests the problematic nature of female and black citizenship, leading some to argue for a fuller inclusion for both, and others to justify the status quo or even, in the case of free blacks, to argue for the rescission of those civil rights they already enjoyed. For another argument that American doctrines of female citizenship incorporated a republican assumption of female dependency, see Joan R. Gundersen, "Independence, Citizenship, and the American Revolution," *Signs: Journal of Women in Culture and Society,* XIII (1987), 59–77.

that assumption that proved difficult for whites to accept as the fundamental principle itself. The first federal naturalization act of 1790, although liberal in other regards, offered citizenship to "free white" persons only. When white Americans drew the boundaries between themselves and other nations, their first impulse was to keep dark-skinned people out.[42]

Although Wilson's social theory was not intrinsically racist—and he, himself, was an opponent of slavery—it was ill-equipped to deal with the increasing racism of the new nation. Because Wilson's version of liberalism rested upon the family, it could easily integrate women into its social vision; indeed, they were necessary to it. The same was not true for free blacks. Political pronouncements such as, "We see those persons possess the greatest share of happiness, who have about them many objects of love and endearment," had a certain amount of resonance in a society that was beginning to pay homage to the affectionate family. It was not at all clear, however, that free blacks could as easily be integrated into a political society premised upon the affectionate family and the emotions of love and endearment.[43]

Because of their social unacceptability to whites, free blacks presented a challenge to the liberal notion of social citizenship, that is, the sort of citizenship enjoyed by women. As a number of historians have shown, increasingly public life in the North as well as the South was being segregated. In the North, some public spaces, such as restaurants and hotels, were closed to blacks entirely, whereas others, such as theaters, churches, and various modes of transportation, offered them only segregated spaces. In many places, schools, also, were segregated. In the South, all of these places and more were off-limits for free blacks. Indeed, much of the public sphere—that is, civil society itself—was closed to free blacks. In this context, blacks' civil rights became problematic.[44]

42. Kettner, *Development of American Citizenship,* 236. See also Walzer, *Spheres of Justice.* In this context, the termination of the slave trade may be considered not only an attack upon slavery but as an attempt to prevent the entry of any more Africans into the nation. See James Oakes, "The Rhetoric of Reaction: Justifying a Proslavery Constitution," unpublished paper presented at Symposium of Bondage, Freedom, and the Constitution, Benjamin N. Cardozo School of Law / Yeshiva University, Feb. 20, 1995.

43. Wilson, *Lectures on Law,* in McCloskey, ed., *Works of Wilson,* I, 237; see Lewis, "Republican Wife," *William and Mary Quarterly,* 3d Ser., XLIV (1987), 689–721; and Jay Fliegelman, *Prodigals and Pilgrims: The American Revolution against Patriarchal Authority, 1750–1800* (Cambridge, 1982). For the growth of racism in this period, see Winthrop D. Jordan, *White over Black: American Attitudes toward the Negro, 1550–1812* (Williamsburg, Va., and Chapel Hill, N.C., 1968), 429–569.

44. Ronald T. Takaki, *Iron Cages: Race and Culture in Nineteenth-Century America* (New York, 1979); Leon F. Litwack, *North of Slavery: The Negro in the Free States, 1790–1860* (Chi-

Again and again in the antebellum period, as James H. Kettner has shown, courts in the North and South both would confront the dilemma presented by black citizenship. In general, northern courts would accept the doctrine of free black citizenship, although on occasion begrudgingly. Southern courts until about the second third of the century often were prepared to acknowledge free black citizenship as well, but, as the slave system became more entrenched and challenges to it from outside mounted, southern jurists shifted their approach. Increasingly, they looked for a new way to define free blacks—as more than slaves, but less than citizens. A South Carolina court dubbed free blacks "subjects" instead of "citizens." A Kentucky judge termed them "quasi citizens, or at least denizens." One in Georgia called them "our wards," whereas Mississippi offered the term *"alien strangers,"* and Louisiana suggested "strangers to our Constitution." Other states settled upon "degraded race" or "third class." Understanding full well what citizenship meant, even in the absence of full political rights, southern courts flailed about looking for a category that was different—and less—than that occupied by women.[45]

The worst blow to free blacks came, of course, with the *Dred Scott* decision in 1857. Ruling for the majority, Chief Justice Roger B. Taney argued that blacks, whether slave or free, could not be citizens of the United States.[46] A little over two decades and more than half a million lives later, that decision would be reversed with the Fourteenth Amendment; two years later, free black males were given the right to vote. Then, in another two years, in 1872, Virginia Minor would sue the clerk in her hometown in Missouri who refused to register her to vote. Her case made it to the Supreme Court, which, in denying her the right to vote, confirmed what had become the prevailing wisdom: "There is no doubt that women may be citizens. . . . There cannot be a nation without a people. The very idea of a political community, such as

---

cago, 1961); Ira Berlin, *Slaves without Masters: The Free Negro in the Antebellum South* (New York, 1974), 321–327.

45. This paragraph is drawn from Kettner, *Development of American Citizenship,* 287–324, esp. 319–320.

46. Don E. Fehrenbacher, *The Dred Scott Case: Its Significance in American Law and Politics* (New York, 1978), 335–364. After asserting that, at the time the nation was created, blacks "had no rights which the white man was bound to respect," Taney went on to list some of those rights that the recognition of black citizenship would necessarily confer. It is a veritable catalogue of the civil rights upon which participation in the public sphere depends: "the right to enter every other State whenever they pleased, . . . to go where they pleased at every hour of the day or night without molestation, . . . the full liberty of speech in public and in private upon all subjects upon which . . . citizens might speak; to hold public meetings upon political affairs" (ibid., 347, 355).

a nation is, implies an association of persons for the promotion of their general welfare. Each one of the persons associated becomes a member of the nation formed by the association." Here, finally, was the explicit application of consent theory to women—but for the purpose of denying them the right to vote. The only real question, the court insisted, was "whether all citizens are necessarily voters." The answer, the court held, was no.[47]

Less than a century after the ratification of the Constitution, then, the vision of the public sphere that it had embodied had faded badly. Although it is certainly true, as a number of historians have pointed out, that over the course of this period, the meaning of political participation changed, so also did the context in which it was exercised. As the act of voting became increasingly important—and ever more widely shared—women's exclusion from that privilege of citizenship became all the more glaring. At the same time, free blacks, whose ranks were expanded tenfold by the termination of slavery in the South at the end of the Civil War, were increasingly segregated from those places that constituted the public realm, and that sphere consequently took up less and less space. Wilson's suggestion that persons "of every age sex and condition" should be counted was never, of course, an accurate description of social practices in the new nation. But it was also more than a constitutional mechanism for apportioning representatives in the national government. It was a close enough rendering of the public sphere that had emerged in American society in the eighteenth century to make it the sketch from which a more inclusive social and political vision might be imagined. Departing, as they did, from traditional formulas for representation, Wilson's words made a radical and hopeful statement about what the new nation might be.[48]

47. Minor v. Happersett, 88 U.S. (21 Wall.) 162, 165–166, 170 (1875). For an analysis of this case, see Norma Basch, "Reconstructing Female Citizenship: Minor v. Happersett," in Donald G. Nieman, ed., *The Constitution, Law, and American Life: Critical Aspects of the Nineteenth-Century Experience* (Athens, Ga., 1992), 52–66.

48. Michael E. McGerr, *The Decline of Popular Politics: The American North, 1865–1928* (New York, 1986), 5, 40–41; Morton Keller, *Affairs of State: Public Life in Late Nineteenth Century America* (Cambridge, Mass., 1977), chap. 7. A number of students of Habermas have questioned whether the bourgeois public sphere that he posited could ever have or did include persons other than bourgeois white males. Michael Warner, for example, has argued that the limitations of literacy, which made it disproportionately a privilege of propertied white males, effectively excluded women, racial minorities, and poor white men from the public sphere created by print in the eighteenth century. See Warner, *The Letters of the Republic: Publication and the Public Sphere in Eighteenth-Century America* (Cambridge, Mass., 1990), 15–16, 48–49. He has also argued that the exclusion from the public sphere of those who were not white males was not simply contingent, for the way in which the public

That vision of a broadly inclusive society and a government that worked always on its behalf was not realized then, nor has it been since. From the outset, female citizenship had been defined in relationship, not so much to white male citizenship, but to that of blacks, both slave and free. Originally, women were the paradigmatic citizens of liberalism; that is, they constituted society, enjoyed its rights, and demanded its protection. Increasingly, however, women came to stand for those who were members of society but who did not enjoy full political rights and could not represent themselves. At the same time, free blacks would come to stand for those who enjoyed, nominally at least, complete political rights, but who were excluded from full membership in society. In this manner, the gap between politics and society, which had narrowed considerably in the Revolutionary period as liberal theories of government and society were brought to bear, was forced wider. As gender has been used to construct the political and social practices of race, and race to construct the practices of gender, the fleeting vision of a wide public sphere open to persons of every age, sex, race, and condition has faded, leaving barely a trace.[49]

---

sphere represented the individual presumed a white male body. See Warner, "The Mass Public and the Mass Subject," in Calhoun, ed., *Habermas and the Public Sphere*, 382–383. The presence of women in the public sphere, however, renders Warner's formulation somewhat problematic. See note 32, above.

49. For a different approach to this problem—the growing gap between society and politics—see Wood, *Creation of the American Republic*, 562.

What Happened to the Three-Fifths Clause

The Relationship between Women and Slaves in Constitutional Thought, 1787–1866

Slaves are nowhere mentioned in the Constitution. The founders, as many have noted over the years, went to great lengths to avoid using the word *slave,* alluding to the enslaved in the Three-Fifths Clause, for example, inelegantly and evasively as "all other Persons." Slavery—as an explicit term, rather than an evasion—entered the Constitution only at the moment of its abolition, with the ratification of the Thirteenth Amendment in 1865.[1]

Women are nowhere mentioned in the Constitution. The founders did not, however, have to engage in circumlocutions to avoid discussing them. On the face of it, it would appear that they are absent. The word *male* did not enter the Constitution until three years after the word *slavery,* with the ratification of the next amendment, the Fourteenth, making clear that former slaves were now citizens but that only men were contemplated as potential voters.

Yet, in a government in which representation is based upon population—rather than, for example, property holding or voter status—slaves and women are inescapably present, cemented into the foundation for representation. Nevertheless, because they enter the discussion, not as subjects in themselves, but as means to an end—ways of representing or not representing free men—the discussion of them is almost always oblique, though no less revealing, truth told slant, to paraphrase Emily Dickinson. Moreover,

This essay was originally published as Jan Ellen Lewis, "What Happened to the Three-Fifths Clause: The Relationship between Women and Slaves in Constitutional Thought, 1787–1866," *Journal of the Early Republic,* XXXVII (2017), 1–46.

1. U.S. Constitution, Article 1, Section 2, Clause 3. Subsequent generations noted the omission. In the Missouri debates, Pennsylvania senator Jonathan Roberts asked, "Why is a circumlocution of words used in [the Constitution], to designate such persons, instead of one so appropriate as that of slaves? Either because it was considered as a painful word, or, for the better reason, that it was hoped the Constitution would survive a state of things where the word could be applicable"; see *The Debates and Proceedings in the Congress of the United States . . . Sixteenth Congress—First Session: Comprising the Period from December 6, 1819, to May 15, 1820, Inclusive* (Washington, D.C., 1855), 340.

slaves and women are always together. Any discussion of the Three-Fifths Clause sooner or later leads to a discussion of women, but—once again—never in or of themselves but always in relationship to slaves, or, rather, the institution of slavery, their political disabilities used to justify a system of representation that included others—slaves—whose political disabilities were even more severe. What follows is a story in seven short chapters and a postscript. The subject: the ways in which women's assumed political incapacity was used to anchor a system of representation that rested on enslavement. The chapters: the Constitution itself; John Quincy Adams and the Federalist Critique; the Missouri Compromise; John Quincy Adams's return; the abolitionists' debate; the Dred Scott reversal; the Fourteenth Amendment's resolution; and the modern postscript. The elements in the story: a broad, democratic doctrine of representation; slaves; and women, all bound together—until they were not. And ghosts.

1. THE CONSTITUTION

Slaves entered the Constitution by way of the Three-Fifths Clause, and they brought women with them. At the Constitutional Convention, slaves came up in the discussion about apportionment of representatives in the lower house of Congress. Should it be based upon the "numbers of free inhabitants," as Connecticut's Roger Sherman proposed, or upon "wealth," as South Carolina's John Rutledge and Pierce Butler countered? What has come to be known as the Three-Fifths Compromise took into account each of these principles, by using slaves as a proxy for wealth and adding three-fifths of their number to the total number of free inhabitants. The precise language was that of James Wilson, from Pennsylvania: representation should be "in proportion to the whole number of white and other free Citizens and inhabitants of every age sex and condition including those bound to servitude for a term of years and three fifths of all other persons not comprehended in the foregoing description, except Indians not paying taxes, in each State." The Convention's Committee on Style later edited this language down to the formulation that appears in the Constitution: representation (and direct taxation) were to be "apportioned among the several states which may be included within this Union, according to their respective numbers, which shall be determined by adding to the whole number of free persons, including those bound to servitude for a term of years, and excluding Indians not taxed, three fifths of all other persons." Gender and race—the words *sex* and *white*—ended up on the cutting-room floor, the ghosts of words spoken and unspoken both, which would come back to haunt all the subsequent discussions of this ill-conceived compromise.[2]

The silence on slavery was not accidental. The purpose of the Convention was to frame a government, and, meeting behind closed doors, the delegates worked to persuade one another, not play to a wider audience. Forthright discussions about slavery could only have made compromise more difficult. Most of the delegates believed—or said they believed—that slavery would eventually die out, and no one was prepared to argue that it was either good or necessary. Instead, the delegates made their arguments, for the most part, in terms of interests, and interests are, axiomatically, susceptible to compromise. Only when the issue of slavery returned later in the summer, when the delegates decided to permit reopening the slave trade, did the discussion touch upon the morality of slavery. Maryland's Luther Martin thought such a proposal "inconsistent with the principles of the revolution and dishonorable to the American character." South Carolina's Rutledge effectively conceded the point, asserting that "religion and humanity had nothing to do with this question," pushing the discussion back onto the grounds of interest, and resorting to threats to make his point clear: "Interest alone is the governing principle with Nations—The true question at present is whether the Southn. States shall or shall not be parties to the Union."[3]

The discussion that led to the Three-Fifths Compromise reprised the one in 1783, when the Confederation Congress decided to change the basis for apportioning expenses for the Confederation from land to population. But how to count slaves, who, their owners acknowledged, contributed to wealth, but not as much, they insisted, as free people? Congress settled upon a formula that prefigured the Three-Fifths Compromise both in the ratio of five to three and by substituting the anodyne "other persons" for "slaves." If, in 1783, the slaveowning states had argued for the largest possible discount for their slaves, four years later they hoped to maximize their power—"money was power," as Rutledge put it baldly—by counting as many of their slaves as possible. When Wilson offered his compromise, he was merely importing the one worked out a few years earlier, and now the ratio—and method for

2. Max Farrand, ed., *The Records of the Federal Convention of 1787,* 4 vols. (1911; rpt. New Haven, Conn., 1966), I, 196, 201, II, 590; Jan Lewis, "'Of Every Age Sex and Condition': The Representation of Women in the Constitution," *Journal of the Early Republic,* XV (1995), 359–387, also reprinted in this volume.

3. Farrand, ed., *Records of the Federal Convention,* II, 364. See also Jan Lewis, "The Three-Fifths Clause and the Origins of Sectionalism," in Paul Finkelman and Donald R. Kennon, eds., *Congress and the Emergence of Sectionalism: From the Missouri Compromise to the Age of Jackson* (Athens, Ohio, 2008), 19–46, also reprinted in this volume.

counting slaves—could be used not only for taxation but for representation as well.[4]

But once the topic at hand shifted from taxation to representation, the implications for democratic theory and practice shifted as well. In the Convention, the delegates debated the relative productivity of free and slave labor. Some delegates asked why slaves should be represented at all. Elbridge Gerry, from Massachusetts, asked, "Why then shd. the blacks, who were property in the South, be in the rule of representation more than the cattle and horses of the North?" New York's Gouverneur Morris called the Three-Fifths Compromise "an incoherence." "If Negroes" were to be counted as "inhabitants," then, he thought, all of them should be included. If they were to be used as a proxy for wealth, then why pretend that apportionment was based upon population and not wealth? And, for good measure, he threw Rutledge's threat right back at the South Carolinian: if the price of union was using a fiction to enhance the power of the slave states, then "let us at once take a friendly leave of each other." New Jersey's William Paterson likewise saw an incoherence. Paterson "could regard negroes slaves in no light but as property. They are no free agents, have no personal liberty, no faculty of acquiring property, but on the contrary are themselves property, and like other property entirely at the will of the Master." There it was, slavery in a nutshell. How could slaves be represented? "What is the true principle of Representation?" he asked rhetorically. "It is an expedient by which an assembly of certain individls. chosen by the people is substituted in place of the inconvenient meeting of the people themselves. If such a meeting . . . [were] to take place, would the slaves vote? they would not. Why then shd. they be represented?" But if this were the "true principle of Representation," then what was the basis for including persons of "every age sex and condition" and not just qualified voters? Why include women?[5]

Even Wilson had to acknowledge the doctrinal incoherence of the Three-Fifths Clause a month after he introduced it, saying that he "did not well see

4. Farrand, ed., *Records of the Federal Convention,* I, 196; Lewis, "Three-Fifths Clause," in Finkelman and Kennon, eds., *Congress and the Emergence of Sectionalism,* 23–27.

5. Farrand, ed., *Records of the Federal Convention,* I, 201, 561, 604. Gerry also asked rhetorically, "Are we to enter into a Compact with Slaves?"; see James H. Hutson, ed., *Supplement to Max Farrand's The Records of the Federal Convention* (New Haven, Conn., 1987), 70. As David Waldstreicher points out, James Madison omitted this portion of Gerry's argument in his note; see Waldstreicher, *Slavery's Constitution: From Revolution to Ratification* (New York, 2009), 77. On the significance of Madison's omission of Gerry's argument against the clause—four other notetakers recorded it—see Mary Sarah Bilder, *Madison's Hand: Revising the Constitutional Convention* (Cambridge, Mass., 2015), 81–83.

on what principle the admission of blacks in the proportion of three fifths could be explained. Are they admitted as Citizens? Then why are they not admitted on an equality with White Citizens? Are they admitted as property? then why is not other property admitted into the computation?" These "difficulties," however, were "overruled by the necessity of compromise." But he would never concede that property, rather than persons, was the proper basis for representation. Even with the "difficulties" presented by the Three-Fifths formulation, "if numbers be not a proper rule, why is not some better rule pointed out?" Moreover, "he could not agree that property was the sole or the primary object of Governt. and Society. The cultivation and improvement of the human mind was the most noble object. With respect to this object, as well as to other *personal* rights, numbers were surely the natural and precise measure of Representation." Here was the reason for including women: an expansive notion of representation based upon rights-bearing persons—not voters, not property. In Wilson's mind, the necessary, pragmatic compromise was on including some portion of the enslaved, not women and other free nonvoters, whom government was intended to represent.[6]

It was left to James Madison to wrest a logic out of the Three-Fifths Clause's apparent incoherence on the representation of slaves. He addressed the topic in *The Federalist,* Number 54, observing that "the Fœderal Constitution . . . decides with great propriety on the case of our slaves, when it views them in the mixt character of persons and of property. This is in fact their true character." Moreover, "It is admitted that if the laws were to restore the rights which have been taken away, the negroes could no longer be refused an equal share of representation with the other inhabitants." Madison acknowledged that "the case of the slaves . . . is in truth a peculiar one," but, like his fellow pragmatist Wilson, he fell back upon the necessity of a "compromising expedient" of the Constitution, "which regards them as inhabitants, but as debased by servitude below the equal level of free inhabi-

6. Farrand, ed., *Records of the Federal Convention,* I, 587, 605. My reading of this passage differs from that of George William Van Cleve, *A Slaveholders' Union: Slavery, Politics, and the Constitution in the Early American Republic* (Chicago, 2010), 123–124. Van Cleve does not see an underlying theory of representation; he also believes that the outcome of the debate was close to predetermined (120). For more on Wilson's doctrine of representation and its inclusion of women, see Lewis, "'Of Every Age Sex and Condition,'" *Journal of the Early Republic,* XV (1995), 359–387. For women as rights bearers, see Rosemarie Zagarri, *Revolutionary Backlash: Women and Politics in the Early American Republic* (Philadelphia, 2007), 37–45.

tants, which regards the *slave* as divested of two fifth[s] of the *man*." And what of the objection, which would be raised again by successive generations, that, because the enslaved could not vote, they enhanced the power of those who "represented" them? Here Madison fell back upon the practices of the states, noting that all of them restricted suffrage in one way or another; hence there were always more persons who were represented than actually voted. "The right of choosing this allotted number [of Representatives] in each State is to be exercised by such part of the inhabitants, as the State itself may designate. . . . In every State, a certain proportion of inhabitants are deprived of this right." Here, then, was an expansive view of representation—Jack N. Rakove has rightly, if provocatively, called the Three-Fifths Clause "the closest approximation in the Constitution to the principle of one person, one vote"—coupled with its restriction: the people were to be represented, but not in all cases represent themselves.[7]

This joining of a highly expansive notion of representation with its restriction was highly unstable, not only because, in the case of the representation of slaves, it was almost incoherent but also because the question of where to set the limitation on self-representation was inherently contestable, as Madison surely knew and as the subsequent history of the United States abundantly demonstrates. It is in this context that women were important. They were the exemplary rights-bearing citizens who could not—with the brief exception of propertied unmarried women in New Jersey—vote, the represented who could not represent themselves. After all, women partook of all those qualities that, according to Madison, made a slave a "member of the society": "In being protected . . . in . . . life and in . . . limbs, against the violence of all others, even the master of his labor and his liberty; and in being punishable himself for all violence committed against others; the slave is . . . regarded by the law . . . as a moral person, not as a mere article of property."[8]

7. James Madison, "The Federalist No. 54," in Jacob E. Cooke, ed., *The Federalist*, (Middletown, Conn., 1961), 368–369; Jack N. Rakove, *Original Meanings: Politics and Ideas in the Making of the Constitution* (New York, 1996), 74. See also Bilder, *Madison's Hand*, 188–190. Incidentally, she calls Madison "cagey" (189).

8. Madison, "Federalist No. 54," in Cooke, ed., *Federalist*, 367–368. It should be noted that Madison is talking in idealized terms, not about actual practices for slaves (or by extension, women), who could, of course, be physically beaten with impunity. On New Jersey, see Judith Apter Klinghoffer and Lois Elkis, "'The Petticoat Electors': Women's Suffrage in New Jersey, 1776–1807," *Journal of the Early Republic*, XII (1992), 159–193; and Jan Ellen Lewis, "Rethinking Women's Suffrage in New Jersey, 1776–1807," *Rutgers University Law Review*, LXIII (2011), 1017–1035, also reprinted in this volume. Akhil Reed Amar uses the term *para-*

I want to underscore the significance, indeed the radicalism, of the expansive notion of representation that insists that the purpose of government is to speak for and protect all members of society, without respect to age, sex, or condition. This is the promise of liberal democracy. And a broad, capacious theory of representation was, I believe, the intent of liberals such as Wilson and Madison. It is important to underscore, at the same time, that this notion of representation, embedded in liberal democracy, carried with it, from its inception, its limitation. And, finally, the formulation is inherently and necessarily unstable. This, too, is intrinsic to the history of liberal democracy in the United States.[9]

This instability has three sources. First, the continuing contests over citizenship and voting rights. Second, the incoherence of the Three-Fifths Clause, in particular its linking an expansive notion of representation to human enslavement. Third, growing sectionalism. The instability—and underlying incoherence—of the Three-Fifths Clause became most evident at those times when the United States sought to protect slavery where it existed or to extend its reach by acquiring new slave territory or incorporating it into new slave states. In these instances, antislavery northerners decried the apparent overrepresentation of the slave South because of the clause. Once the subject of the clause had been raised, however, typically in a highly political context about the extension or protection of slavery, rather than a more abstract one about the nature of representation, questions about the underlying theory of representation often arose. Yet the political importance of these discussions in the era before Reconstruction should not be overstated: they had no bearing on outcomes and were rarely more than asides, minor supporting points in arguments whose focus was elsewhere.

---

digmatic, saying that "women and children were paradigmatic citizens"; see Amar, *The Bill of Rights: Creation and Reconstruction* (New Haven, Conn., 1998), 217n.

9. This is what I have argued in Lewis, "'Of Every Age Sex and Condition,'" *Journal of the Early Republic,* XV (1995), 359–387. For a modern statement, see Danielle Allen, *Our Declaration: A Reading of the Declaration of Independence in Defense of Equality* (New York, 2014), 34: "The point of political equality is . . . to engage all members of a community equally in the work of creating and constantly re-creating that community. Political equality is equal political empowerment." For classic statements, see Benedict Anderson, *Imagined Communities: Reflections on the Origin and Spread of Nationalism,* rev. ed. (London, 1991); and Michael Walzer, *Spheres of Justice: A Defense of Pluralism and Equality* (New York, 1983), 28–30. See also Aristide R. Zolberg, *A Nation by Design: Immigration Policy in the Fashioning of America* (Cambridge, Mass., 2006), 17: "The formation of identity always involves a negative aspect as well." Consider also the exchange between James Sullivan and John Adams, May 26, 1776, in Robert J. Taylor, ed., *Papers of John Adams,* IV, *February–August 1776* (Cambridge, Mass., 1979), 208–213, which will be discussed below.

But they do give us an insight into the ways in which American political leaders thought about the doctrine of representation.[10]

2. JOHN QUINCY ADAMS AND THE FEDERALIST CRITIQUE

Opposition to the representation of slaves first appeared in the records of Congress in 1804, fifteen years after the ratification of the Constitution. The clause had always rankled New England Federalists. In a 1794 abolitionist oration, Theodore Dwight had made an oblique reference to its representational injustice. In the South, he observed, slaveowners "force" their slaves "to contribute to the strengthening of the powers, which hold them in bondage. Enjoying no rank in the community, and possessing no voice, either in elections, or legislation, the slaves are bro't into existence, in the Constitution of the United States, merely to afford opportunity for a few more of their masters, to tyrannize over their liberties." A decade later, when Congress voted, by a significant majority, to organize Louisiana as a territory, the Massachusetts legislature instructed its senators to introduce a resolution to amend the Constitution to apportion representatives and direct taxes on the basis of the number of "free inhabitants." Massachusetts warned that the Union could not "harmoniously exist, for a long period" unless "all free citizens" were given "equal political rights and privileges in the Government, so that a minority of free Citizens may not govern a majority, an event, which on the principles of representation now established, has already happened, and may always happen." The resolution, introduced by Timothy Pickering, was never considered, but notice had been given that at least a handful of northerners wanted to eliminate the Three-Fifths Clause. (A similar attempt

10. Historians debate whether or to what extent the Three-Fifths Clause actually enhanced the power of the slave states in the national government, particularly whether it led to Thomas Jefferson's victory over John Adams in 1800. For the case that it did, see Garry Wills, *"Negro President": Jefferson and the Slave Power* (Boston, 2003). For the case that it did not, see Sean Wilentz, "The Details of Greatness: American Historians versus American Founders," *New Republic,* Mar. 29, 2004, 27–35; and Earl M. Maltz, "The Presidency, the Electoral College, and the Three-Fifths Clause," *Rutgers Law Journal,* XLIII (2013), 439–470. For a discussion of the debate, see Van Cleve, *Slaveholders' Union,* 140–141. New Jersey representative Elias Boudinot expressed concern in 1791 about the possible overrepresentation of slave states, while also making it clear that "he would not do any thing which would interfere with the Constitution"; see *The Debates and Proceedings in the Congress of the United States . . . Second Congress: Comprising the Period from October 24, 1791, to March 2, 1793, Inclusive* (Washington, D.C., 1849), 244; see also ibid., 203. For these and other early concerns about the Three-Fifths Clause, see William M. Wiecek, *The Sources of Antislavery Constitutionalism in America, 1760–1848* (Ithaca, N.Y., 1977), 106–108.

was made in 1815.) Massachusetts's other senator, John Quincy Adams, prepared a speech, although there is no evidence that he ever gave it. Instead, he left the speech among his papers and published an expanded version anonymously in the Boston *Repertory*.[11]

A resolution never debated, a speech undelivered, a pamphlet anonymously published: these are hardly earthshaking events. But they mark Adams's emergence as an opponent of slavery, and, for the rest of his career, he would attempt to dismantle the Three-Fifths Clause. In 1804, his argument was a bit incoherent, made on the grounds of morality, expediency, and arithmetic. The ratio of representation was "unjust, immoral, and impolitic." Mixed into the jumble of criticisms, which ranged from enhancing the voting power of slaveholding states and the bad bargain the North had made in trading representation of a portion of the slaves for taxing them too, to the unfairness of excluding northern merchants and shippers from the slave trade while permitting southerners to profit from the internal slave trade, was a critique not simply of the injustice—to nonslaveowners, to the slaves themselves—of the clause but also of fundamental deception. The Constitution "professedly makes *numbers* the measure of representation. But numbers of what? Of free inhabitants? This would undoubtedly be upon the principles of pure republicanism, the only answer to the question, and would to God this were the answer we could make." Instead, in some

11. Theodore Dwight, "An Oration, Spoken before the Connecticut Society, for the Promotion of Freedom and the Relief of Persons Unlawfully Holden in Bondage," 1794, in Charles S. Hyneman and Donald S. Lutz, ed., *American Political Writing during the Founding Era, 1760–1805*, II (Indianapolis, Ind., 1983), 892; "Chapter 39: Resolve for Proposing an Amendment to the Constitution of the United States Respecting an Equal Representation in Congress," in *Acts and Laws of the Commonwealth of Massachusetts* (Boston, 1898), 308–310; *The Debates and Proceedings in the Congress of the United States . . . Eighth Congress—Second Session; Comprising the Period from November 5, 1804, to March 3, 1805, Inclusive* (Washington, D.C., 1852), 21–22; *Journal of the Senate of the United States of America; Being the Third Session of the Thirteenth Congress: Begun and Held at the City of Washington, September 19, 1814, . . .* (Washington, D.C., 1821), 675; John Quincy Adams, "Proposed Amendment to the Constitution on Representation," December 1804, in Worthington Chauncey Ford, ed., *Writings of John Quincy Adams*, III (New York, 1914), 87–100, "Serious Reflections, Addressed to the Citizens of Massachusetts," 46–77. Pickering had given notice three days earlier that it was his intent to introduce such a resolution. For more on Dwight's oration, see Manisha Sinha, *The Slave's Cause: A History of Abolition* (New Haven, Conn., 2016), 108–109. For more on John Quincy Adams's unpublished speech, see Leonard L. Richards, *The Slave Power: The Free North and Southern Domination, 1780–1860* (Baton Rouge, La., 2000), 43; David Waldstreicher, "A Funny Thing Happened on the Way to the Amistad: John Quincy Adams, the Shutdown, and the Restart of Antislavery Politics, 1787–1836," unpublished paper, 11–12. Waldstreicher traces Quincy Adams's development as an opponent of slavery.

of the states, representation was based upon "*numbers* of free inhabitants," while, in others, "numbers of slaves, cut up into fractions and mingled with the numbers of their masters." Adams revealed that "the real meaning" of the Three-Fifths Clause was "expressed in circumlocutions, as if the Constitution was ashamed or afraid to speak in plain terms its own meaning." Language that was seemingly republican effected unrepublican ends. "By making the numbers of slaves a component part of the right to vote," the Three-Fifths Clause "holds out a strong and . . . irresistible temptation to those states which allow slavery, to increase and multiply as much as possible the number of these unhappy beings." Here Adams anticipated Gordon S. Wood's analysis of the "hiatus in American politics between ideology and motives" inaugurated by the use of "the most popular and democratic rhetoric available to explain and justify" a system that was at base "aristocratic." Although Adams would not have used the term *aristocratic,* and neither would I, he recognized the Constitution's sleight of hand in hiding incentives to enslavement in language that on its face was fundamentally democratic. Here was one pole in what would become the debate about the theory of representation underlying the Three-Fifths Clause. According to Adams, it was fundamentally undemocratic, but masked by the language of equality.[12]

The Three-Fifths Clause continued to stick in New England Federalists' craw, the symbol and substance both of slaveowners' overweening power in the nation. They blamed it for Jefferson's victory in 1800, for the odious War of 1812, for their own declining power in the federal government. It was at the top of their list of defects in the government to be remedied by Constitutional amendment when they met at the Hartford Convention in 1814. Presented to the House of Representatives in 1815, the proposed amendments were promptly tabled.[13]

3. THE MISSOURI COMPROMISE

It was not until 1819–1820 that Adams and the critics of the clause would get a response from proslavery Democrats. It came during the debate on the

12. Adams, "Proposed Amendment," December 1804, in Ford, ed., *Writings of John Quincy Adams,* III, 89–90; Gordon S. Wood, *The Creation of the American Republic, 1776–1787* (Williamsburg, Va., and Chapel Hill, N.C., 1969), 562.

13. "Amendments to the Constitution Proposed by the Hartford Convention: 1814," The Avalon Project: Documents in Law, History, and Diplomacy, accessed June 4, 2016, http://avalon.law.yale.edu/19th_century/hartconv.asp; Matthew Mason, *Slavery and Politics in the Early American Republic* (Chapel Hill, N.C., 2006), 60. For a thorough account of Federalists' attempt to aggravate the issue of "slave representation" in this period, see ibid., 51–74.

admission of Missouri into the Union, which necessarily involved Constitutional questions, primarily whether the Constitution authorized Congress to restrict slavery in a new state. This was comfortable ground for southerners. As Alan Taylor has noted, they "claimed to defend the Federal Constitution and the rights of the states, rather than slavery, by opposing restriction." Hence, proslavery congressmen reviewed all of the provisions of the Constitution that appeared to protect slavery, including the Three-Fifths Clause. The piece of the argument about the clause developed slowly, and it was never central to the debate; but, in due course, discussion about it moved from the issues that Adams had raised about the political implications of the compromise to the underlying theory of representation.[14]

John Scott, Missouri's nonvoting representative, introduced the topic of the clause, extrapolating that "this provision was not restricted to the States then formed . . . but to all those States which might be included within this Union," where the same arithmetic of representation would apply. Such arguments drew out antislavery critiques. James Tallmadge, the Democratic-Republican representative from New York who had introduced the amendment restricting slavery in Missouri, insisted that the clause was not applicable to territory across the Mississippi. In the next session of Congress, Pennsylvania's senator Jonathan Roberts, another Democratic-Republican, introduced a resolution from his state likewise declaring that, "when that Constitution was framed, . . . the concession that three-fifths of the slaves in the States then existing should be represented in Congress, could not have been intended to embrace regions at that time held by a foreign Power" (although it had clearly been extended to Louisiana fifteen years earlier). This was an argument ostensibly about the intent of the founders, but, at base, it was about arithmetic. The clause might have been a necessary compromise, but, as Rhode Island Federalist senator James Burrill insisted, "It could not have been in the contemplation of any man, at that time, that the number of such States was ever to be increased by the acquisition of territory. . . . If we now introduce new slaveholding States, we increase the slave representation far beyond the number originally contemplated as possible." The proslavery response? Northerners had agreed to the clause in 1787, and their objections in 1820 reeked of self-interest. Besides, as Kentucky's representative Benjamin Hardin observed, "Their object cannot surely be to

14. Alan Taylor, *The Internal Enemy: Slavery and the War in Virginia, 1772–1832* (New York, 2013), 406.

emancipate; because, in that event, the whole instead of three-fifths, would be represented on this floor."[15]

Back and forth they went, the congressmen who wanted to restrict slavery and those who did not. The debate became, as one historian observed many years ago, "repetitious and boring." Yet, as it unfolded, the underlying theory of representation emerged. It is important to be clear: the ensuing discussions about the representation of women and slaves were far from central to the debate about the admission of Missouri and whether there would be restrictions upon slavery in the growing nation; in fact, it is because they were tangential that they are so revealing. The men who made them expressed what they assumed to be common understandings, marshaling them in the attempt to prove points that were more contentious. John Holmes, the representative from the Maine district of Massachusetts was, unsurprisingly, an antislavery proponent of the admission of Missouri without restrictions upon slavery. He tried to appeal both to other antislavery northerners and opponents of restriction, and he ranged widely in his lengthy speech. Had the Declaration of Independence effectively freed all the slaves? Only, he imagined, if "all relation in society were abolished" by the Revolution and Americans had been thrown back into a state of nature, and "all the people assembled in some vast plain, and there men, women, and children, small and great, black and white" created a new government "purified from the pollution of slavery." But that quite obviously had not happened, and so the laws of enslavement remained in force. This was a bizarre aside, not germane to the argument that Holmes was making, but it does reveal a common understanding among Lockean consent-theory Democrats: everyone—men, women, children, black, white—participated in the original social compact. By this logic, of course, the Constitution includes women—and it includes black people as well among those who are to be represented.[16]

15. *The Debates and Proceedings in the Congress of the United States . . . Fifteenth Congress—Second Session: Comprising the Period from November 16, 1818, to March 3, 1819, Inclusive* (Washington, D.C., 1855), 1198 ("this provision"), 1213; *Debates and Proceedings in the Congress of the United States . . . Sixteenth Congress—First Session,* 70–71 ("when that," 71), 217 ("it could not have been"), 1089 ("Their object").

16. Glover Moore, *The Missouri Controversy, 1819–1821* ([Lexington, Ky.], 1953), 92; *Debates and Proceedings in the Congress of the United States . . . Sixteenth Congress—First Session,* 968–969. It was to John Holmes that Thomas Jefferson addressed his famous "fire bell in the night" letter; see Jefferson to Holmes, Apr. 22, 1820, in Merrill D. Peterson, ed., *Thomas Jefferson, Writings: Autobiography, A Summary View of the Rights of British America, Notes on the State of Virginia, Public Papers, Addresses, Messages, and Replies, Miscellany,*

This point bears underscoring. It has sometimes been claimed that the imaginary social compact that created government was an all-male affair. That is not an accurate characterization of what consent theorists imagined, however: this was a *social* compact, and, because women—and persons of all races and ethnicities—were part of society, they were imagined to have participated in the compact.[17]

Holmes made this assumption even more clear later in his speech while attempting to justify the Three-Fifths Clause. His point, quite simply: "It was a compact, and we are bound by it," whether it was a good bargain or a bad one. But, like Madison before him, he saw an underlying logic in the partial representation of slaves: "Slaves were property, but they were human beings. They had some, but few, political rights secured to them. . . . One side, as a rule of representation, contended for their full enumeration, and the other for their entire exclusion." It should be noted that Holmes made this point, invoking the humanity of the slaves, in service of an argument to authorize the spread of slavery.[18]

Kentucky's Richard Mentor Johnson, a Democratic-Republican, pursued this logic in the Senate the next month, when, near the end of a long speech that touched upon almost all the arguments being offered by slavery's defenders, he came to the Three-Fifths Clause. "In what way," he asked, "is the

---

Letters (New York, 1984), 1433–1435. On Holmes, see Matthew Mason, "The Maine and Missouri Crisis: Competing Priorities and Northern Slavery Politics in the Early Republic," *Journal of the Early Republic,* XXXIII (2013), 675–700. Mason describes him as a "doughface" (683). Holmes had tangled with Federalist opponents on the issue of slave representation several years earlier. See Mason, *Slavery and Politics,* 64–65. For women's natural rights and their place in civil society, see Lewis, "'Of Every Age Sex and Condition,'" *Journal of the Early Republic,* XV (1995), 370–381; and Zagarri, *Revolutionary Backlash,* 173–176.

17. The most important statement is Carole Pateman, *The Sexual Contract* (Stanford, Calif., 1988). For another example, see Jill Lepore, "The Sovereignty of Women," *The New Yorker,* Apr. 18, 2016: "The Lockean idea that men, born equal, create political society, to which women do not belong; women exist only in the family, where they are ruled by men." For a more nuanced version, see Nancy Isenberg, *Sex and Citizenship in Antebellum America* (Chapel Hill, N.C., 1998). Citing Pateman, Isenberg says that women were excluded from the foundational social compact (10, 21–28), but she also notes the contestedness and complexity of this and related concepts. She points, for example, to Paulina Wright Davis's discussion of the "enigma" of women's citizenship, Davis's recognition that women were "'birthright' members of the United States" but also "a politically and legally 'disabled caste'" (xii). For a different view, see Zagarri, *Revolutionary Backlash,* 155, which suggests "the problem is not in the theory of liberalism per se but in the contingent circumstances in which liberal nation-states emerged."

18. *Debates and Proceedings in the Congress of the United States . . . Sixteenth Congress—First Session,* 987.

just principle of representation violated, by taking three-fifths of the slaves into the calculation? The answer is given, because slaves have no political rights." But, Johnson asked rhetorically, "What political rights have the female and the minor?" Here, women—and children, along with unenfranchised men—became the exemplars of citizens, that is, persons to be represented by the government, who could not represent themselves. Johnson's speech is the earliest recognition I have found in congressional debate that women are represented in the Constitution. But here, a capacious understanding of representation is used for decidedly illiberal ends: women serve to reconcile the disparity between a democratic doctrine of representation and the otherwise inexplicable partial representation of slaves. Women are used illiberally, to perpetuate slavery and to justify its overrepresentation, serving, not themselves and certainly not the slaves, but instead the owners of slaves. It should be noted, as well, that when congressmen said "women," they were not imagining actual women; rather, this was an imaginary class of white women who could be summoned to perform a particular piece of political work.[19]

19. Ibid., 356. Johnson argued further that women, slaves, and other nonvoters were included in the basis for apportionment because they were also included in the basis for taxation as well as representation. Other defenders of slavery likewise pointed out that if the slave states gained in representation, they lost in taxation, while opponents of slavery noted that direct taxes had not been levied since and were unlikely to be levied again. See, for example, ibid., 217, 260. I should note that the precise meaning of *citizen* was not fixed in this era. See William J. Novak, "The Legal Transformation of Citizenship in Nineteenth-Century America," in Meg Jacobs, Novak, and Julian E. Zelizer, eds., *The Democratic Experiment: New Directions in American Political History* (Princeton, N.J., 2003), 85–119. The question of children and consent is equally interesting and complicated. For an introduction, see Holly Brewer, *By Birth or Consent: Children, Law, and the Anglo-American Revolution in Authority* (Williamsburg, Va., and Chapel Hill, N.C., 2005); Corinne T. Field, *The Struggle for Equal Adulthood: Gender, Race, Age, and the Fight for Citizenship in Antebellum America* (Chapel Hill, N.C., 2014); and Nicholas L. Syrett, *American Child Bride: A History of Minors and Marriage in the United States* (Chapel Hill, N.C., 2016). Senator Samuel Latham Mitchill was the first congressman to recognize explicitly that women were included in the Constitution, in a private letter to his wife, written in 1804: "You must remember . . . that you are one of my constituents, and that I am in some degree responsible to you for my public conduct. In the theory of our Constitution women are calculated as political beings. They are numbered in the census of the inhabitants to make up the amount of population, and the Representatives are apportioned among the people according to their numbers, reckoning the females as well as the males. Though, therefore, women do not vote, they are nevertheless represented in the national government to their full amount"; see "Dr. Mitchill's Letters from Washington: 1801–1813," *Harper's New Monthly Magazine,* April 1879, 748. Mitchill was a Democratic-Republican. This more expansive notion of representation was much more common among Democratic-Republicans than among Federalists.

Johnson had brought into the open an evolving conception of citizenship that distinguished civil rights from political ones. Maryland senator William Pinkney picked up the thread of Johnson's argument, developing what was becoming a recognizable Democratic-Republican approach and tying it to the clause in the fourth section of Article IV in the Constitution guaranteeing each state a republican form of government. If that meant a government in which "all the men have a share in the public power," then the free states as well as the slave ones failed the test; there were many limitations upon voting, citizenship, age, property, "and they who have not those qualifications are just as much disfranchised . . . as if they were slaves." Such persons, however, had "civil rights . . . (and so have slaves, in a less degree)," for, in a true republic, "rights, political and civil, may be qualified. . . . Minors, resident aliens, who are in a course of naturalization—the other sex, whether maids, or wives, or widows, furnish sufficient practical proof of this." If, Pinkney asked, "it be true that all the men in a republican Government must help to wield its power, and be equal in rights, I beg leave to ask . . . and why not all the *women?*" Pinkney thought that he had taken the logic of pure or "Utopian" republicanism to its extreme, absurd end.[20]

His was the same response that John Adams had given to James Sullivan in 1776 when Sullivan mused that those who were writing the new constitution for Massachusetts would surely "suppose it to be their duty to provide for . . . more equal representation than themselves." Invoking John Locke and Thomas Paine, Sullivan had noted that "Laws and Government are founded on the Consent of the people, and that consent should by each member of Society be given in proportion to his Right. Every member of Society has a Right to give his Consent to the Laws of the Community or he owes no Obedience to them." But how far would this principle be extended? Adams agreed to the general principle: "It is certain in Theory, that the only moral Foundation of Government is the Consent of the People." But surely there were limits. "Shall We Say, that every Individual of the Community, old and young, male and female, as well as rich and poor, must consent, expressly to every Act of Legislation? No, you will Say. This is impossible. How then does the Right arise in the Majority to govern the Minority, against their Will? Whence arises the Right of the Men to govern Women, without their Consent? Whence the Right of the old to bind the Young, without theirs." Adams's real concern was enfranchisement of the property-

20. *Debates and Proceedings in the Congress of the United States . . . Sixteenth Congress—First Session,* 412–413.

less—"Is it not equally true, that Men in general in every Society, who are wholly destitute of Property, are also too little acquainted with public Affairs to form a Right Judgment, and too dependent upon other Men to have a Will of their own?"—but he used women just as Pinkney later would in the case of slaves as a reductio ad absurdum to prove that, even in a republic, the line must be drawn somewhere.[21]

By 1820, when Congress considered the admission of Missouri, the specter of emancipation loomed larger than that of enfranchising the propertyless. Hence, because women's political disability (or to be more precise, their position as exemplary citizens who did not enjoy full political rights) seemed unarguable, it gave intellectual ballast to the more contested propositions in a republic, that some people could be represented without representing themselves. The example of women was particularly useful because it cut two ways. First, women clearly had a claim on the state, because they were under its protection, so of course they should be included in the basis for apportionment. In fact, they probably had a better claim than John Adams would have accorded the propertyless, whom he presumed to be dangerous, or Pinkney would have accorded the enslaved. Second, because women were, as Pinkney put it, "rational creatures" and, as Adams put it, persons with "good Judgment and . . . independent Minds," they had better claims to represent themselves than Adams conceded for the propertyless or Pinkney the enslaved. Thus, if women could be represented but not represent themselves, and this proposition was unarguable, then what was the problem with propertyless men in 1776 or the enslaved in 1820? Women were exemplary because of their greater claims on the state and the seemingly more self-evident disqualification—on the grounds of custom alone—to represent themselves: hence, they had to be represented but could not represent themselves.[22]

21. John Adams to James Sullivan, May 26, 1776, in Taylor, ed., *Papers of John Adams,* IV, 208–213. Sullivan was a Massachusetts jurist who would later align with the Democratic-Republicans, like most Lockean consent theorists. His discussion with Adams prefigured those between Federalists and Whigs, Democratic-Republicans and Democrats.

22. *Debates and Proceedings in the Congress of the United States . . . Sixteenth Congress—First Session,* 413; Adams to Sullivan, May 26, 1776, in Taylor, ed., *Papers of John Adams,* IV, 211. The cases of white men and the enslaved were, to be sure, somewhat different, but both were contentious: What was the basis for excluding some white men from the vote, and what was the basis for including the enslaved among those who could represent themselves? Women proved useful, however, for arguing both cases. By the time of the Missouri debates, the Lockean approach to representation dominated. For an exception, arguing that slaves deserved representation as wealth, see *Debates and Proceedings in the Congress of the United States . . . Sixteenth Congress—First Session,* 995. Sean Wilentz notes that "the democratizing forces unleashed in the northern states, privileging persons over property, also rendered

4. JOHN QUINCY ADAMS'S RETURN

The question of slave representation was never the primary flash point in arguments over slavery; rather, it was slavery itself, not this particular concession made to the slaves' owners in 1787. Still, the question came up when Congress considered the admission of new slave states, which would benefit from including the enslaved when apportioning representatives, as when Congress debated the admission of Texas. Just as it had almost forty years before, when Congress debated admitting Louisiana, Massachusetts instructed its representatives to introduce a resolution to repeal the Three-Fifths Clause. Once again, the honor fell to John Quincy Adams, now returned to Congress as a representative. And, once again, on this specific issue, there was no debate, barely even a debate about whether to have a debate. But, rather than tabling the resolutions, the House instead appointed a select committee, which issued a report—actually five separate reports, collected together—four months later. It would countenance a debate only behind closed doors, with the final report to be printed but not discussed.[23]

The reports are in some respects an odd document—114 pages of argument and counterargument, produced for the record and posterity—but with no hope, or fear, of actually changing the Constitution. Adams argued that "slave representation" was "repugnant to the first and vital principle of republican popular representation," and he set forth his own theory of representation, in the process returning to his father's discussion with Sullivan almost seventy years earlier. Adams asserted that because "there can be no representative without a constituent, and that the constituent can become

---

the Constitution's three-fifths clause ever more an anachronistic, quasi-aristocratic embarrassment"; see Wilentz, *The Rise of American Democracy: Jefferson to Lincoln* (New York, 2005), 226–227. Hence the growing imperative to explain it in democratic terms. As Lucia McMahon shows, women's intellectual capacity was a fraught topic in this era, with women considered intellectually capable at the same time that too much learning—"pedantry"—was considered problematic; see McMahon, *Mere Equals: The Paradox of Educated Women in the Early American Republic* (Ithaca, N.Y., 2012), esp. 6. See also Mary Kelley, *Learning to Stand and Speak: Women, Education, and Public Life in America's Republic* (Williamsburg, Va., and Chapel Hill, N.C., 2006); and Carolyn Eastman, *A Nation of Speechifiers: Making an American Public after the Revolution* (Chicago, 2009).

23. *The Congressional Globe, Containing Sketches of the Debates and Proceedings of the First Session of the Twenty-Eighth Congress,* XIII (Washington, D.C., 1844), 62–64, 65–67, 73, 179–180. Massachusetts senator Isaac Bates introduced the resolutions in the Senate and asked that they be tabled; "Massachusetts Resolutions," H.R. Rep. No. 404-28 (1844). See also Mason, *Slavery and Politics,* 217–219; William W. Freehling, *The Road to Disunion,* I, *Secessionists at Bay, 1776–1854* (New York, 1990), 410–411; and, for Adams's own account, Charles Francis Adams, ed., *Memoirs of John Quincy Adams, Comprising Portions of His Diary from 1795 to 1848,* XI (Philadelphia, 1876), 116, 458, 472–473, 481–482, 499, 511–513.

such only by his own free will and choice; . . . the principle of universal suffrage becomes a fundamental doctrine of *democracy*." To be sure, in a representative democracy, there were restrictions "resulting from the circumstances of age and of intellectual sanity, which affect the freedom of the will, and therefore disable the individual for making a free choice; but *democracy* admits of no such qualification of property, and no such disability for the want of it." The United States, he reiterated, was "'*a government founded on persons, and not on property.*'" Hence, "the representation of slaves . . . *as persons,* conferred not upon them, but upon their owners" was not only "repugnant" but also "doubly deceptive." It bore "on its face the mask of representing *persons,* while, in fact, it is a representation of property. . . . In outward show, it is a representation of persons in bondage; in fact, it is a representation of their masters,—the oppressor representing the oppressed." Just as he had forty years before when he asserted that the clause spoke in "circumlocutions" in order to avoid inserting the term *slave* into the Constitution, Adams once again criticized its sleight of hand, but this time, taking it even further, he argued that it was a misrepresentation of the Constitution itself, for the Constitution itself nowhere recognized "the right of property in persons."[24]

Adams elaborated his theory of representation, adding an unusual affec-

24. "Massachusetts Resolutions," H.R. Rep. No. 404-28, at 2, 4–5 (1844); Adams was quoting New York representative Ely Moore's speech in the House on Apr. 28, 1836, in *Register of Debates in Congress, Comprising the Leading Debates and Incidents of the First Session of the Twenty-Fourth Congress . . . ,* XII (Washington, D.C., 1836), 3430. Adams complained, to his diary, that he was not allowed sufficient time to craft his argument and that it "is consequently feeble and indigested." See Adams, ed., *Memoirs of John Quincy Adams,* XI, 511. Arguing the Amistad case in 1841, Adams also spoke of the Constitution's "circumlocutions": "The words slave and slavery are studiously excluded from the Constitution. Circumlocutions are the fig-leaves under which these parts of the body politic are decently concealed. Slaves, therefore, in the Constitution . . . are recognized only as *persons,* enjoying rights and held to the performance of duties"; see *Argument of John Quincy Adams, before the Supreme Court of the United States, in the Case of the United States, Appellants, vs. Cinque, and Others, Africans, Captured in the Schooner Amistad . . .* (New York, 1841), 39. In both cases, Adams avoided dealing with the three-fifths ratio, what Madison had called the slaves' "mixt character of persons and of property" (Madison, "Federalist No. 54," in Cooke, ed., *Federalist,* 368). In one argument, he said the clause regarded them wholly as property, and, in the other, wholly as persons. His logic in the "Resolutions" is a bit tortured: As James Oakes has pointed out, abolitionists consistently argued that slaves were not "property" under the Constitution, although they might be property under state law. In accusing the clause of facilitating a "representation of property," Adams, however, came perilously close to accepting that the enslaved were (if unjustly) considered as property under the Constitution. See Oakes, *Freedom National: The Destruction of Slavery in the United States, 1861–1865* (New York, 2013), 19–20.

tive element. "On the true principle of democracy," he explained, "the relation between the representative and his constituent . . . is among the most sacred, the most confidential, the most intimate and endearing ties that can bind man to man." Adams encased interest in the language of feeling, thereby making it less narrow, less tawdry. "The representative is but a mirror, reflecting the feelings, the wishes, and, above all, the interests of his constituent. The sympathies between them, as dictates of duty, are tender as those between husband and wife, unswerveable as those between the parent and child: a relation in which the pledge of honor and fidelity as an impulse to action, is but superadded to the ligaments of the heart." How could a representative possibly represent a slave? "The representative is thus constituted, not the friend, agent, and trustee of the person whom he represents, but the most inveterate of his foes." Adams constructed representation in familial terms, using the language of affection and friendship and finding the most apt metaphors in the "tender" relations of husband and wife, parent and child. Such a notion of representation was necessarily gendered; his familial metaphors inescapably incorporated women, as wives and as mothers.[25]

Yet Adams nowhere mentioned women. His omission is doubly odd. Having compared the relationship between representative and represented to that of husband and wife, Adams had already introduced women into the discussion. The only restrictions upon suffrage that he thought he had to explain, however, were the exclusion of minors—"because their will is subject to the control of their fathers or guardians" and because "the immaturity of their reason" made them "incapable of exercising a deliberate choice"—and "the insane, the vicious convicted of crime, the pauper subsisted at the charge of the community." Nevertheless, there was no political leader in the United States at that moment who was more outspoken in his support of women's political participation than Adams. Just a few years earlier, he had presented antislavery petition after petition against the annexation of Texas signed by women—fifty thousand by his own count—and argued for their propriety. When the chair of the Foreign Relations Committee expressed "sorrow" at the women petitioners' "departure from their proper sphere," which he considered "discreditable, not only to their own particular section of the country, but also to the national character," Adams "felt himself

25. "Massachusetts Resolutions," H.R. Rep. No. 404-28, at 5–6 (1844). For a discussion of the affective element in antebellum American politics, see Jan Lewis, "Politics and the Ambivalence of the Private Sphere: Women in Early Washington, D.C.," in Donald R. Kennon, ed., *A Republic for the Ages: The United States Capitol and the Political Culture of the Early Republic* (Charlottesville, Va., 1999), 122–151, also reprinted in this volume.

obliged at once to defend their rights and to vindicate their good name"—and did so in Congress over three mornings. Each of the signers was, he presumed, "a mother, a wife, a daughter, or a sister of some constituent" of his. He asked rhetorically whether "the right of petition itself is to be denied to the female sex? To WOMEN? . . . Are women to have no opinions or action on subjects relating to the general welfare? . . . Does the chairman . . . find . . . that it is 'discreditable' for women to take any interest or any part in political affairs?"[26]

How far was Adams willing to push his egalitarian logic? He agreed that it was women's "duty to attend" to domestic affairs, "to promoting the immediate personal comfort of their husbands, brothers, and sons." But, he argued, women are "not only justified, but exhibit the most exalted virtue when they do depart from the domestic circle, and enter on the concerns of their country, of humanity, and of their God." "Far from being a reproach to her," such action represented "virtue of the highest order." Moreover, in Adams's book, nothing was more "virtuous, pure," or "exalted" than preventing "the perpetuation and spread of slavery through America." And, as if answering a question that had not been posed, Adams mused, "And the right to petition . . . is to be denied to women because they have no right to vote! Is it so clear that they have no such right as this last?" Adams began by defining women as the female kin of his constituents. He concluded by raising the possibility of their enfranchisement, so that they could become constituents themselves.[27]

By 1844, however, Adams seemed to have forgotten that women might

26. "Massachusetts Resolutions," H.R. Rep. No. 404-28, at 2 (1844); *Speech of John Quincy Adams, of Massachusetts, upon the Right of the People, Men and Women, to Petition . . .* (Washington, D.C., 1838), 61, 65–66. For the estimate of fifty thousand signatories, see ibid., 78. This is a pamphlet version of Adams's speeches in the House, June 16–July 7, 1838, that contains some text not included in the *Congressional Globe.*

27. *Speech of John Quincy Adams,* 67–68, 76. For the tension between the belief in women's equality and insistence on their difference, see McMahon, *Mere Equals.* None of Adams's congressional adversaries had posed this question. None, in fact, seemed to pay his arguments much heed. One took exception to his praise of the female exemplars, including Deborah Gannett, "a woman who had usurped the habiliments of the other sex, and, in man's dress, associated with men for years together" (*Speech of John Quincy Adams,* 76). Another, a South Carolinian, took exception to his praise of the Grimke sisters; ibid., 76, 78–79. On Adams and women's right to petition, see Susan Zaeske, *Signatures of Citizenship: Petitioning, Antislavery, and Women's Political Identity* (Chapel Hill, N.C., 2003), 126–144. Zaeske describes these exchanges as "perhaps the first sustained discussion of women's political rights . . . in the history of the U.S. Congress," though Adams's opponents mounted only a token opposition, and that on relatively minor points, not the fundamental one of women's political rights (142).

have any political identity, let alone one that he might forcefully defend on the floor of the House. One cannot help suspecting that his defense of the female petitioners was in some measure opportunistic: they were useful to his antislavery agenda and hence were to be supported in whatever terms he could marshal. Adams's ability to advocate for women's political participation and then forget about it augured poorly for the future.

If Adams had forgotten about women, Virginia representative Thomas Gilmer was happy to remind him. Responding directly to Adams, Gilmer began by asserting the slaves' humanity: "Slaves are persons as well as property. As a part of the human family, whose lives and sustenance are protected by government, they form part of the true basis of representation." Here Gilmer put antislavery northerners in an awkward position, insisting, as Adams had come perilously close to doing, and as Paterson had at the Federal Convention, that slaves were (nothing but) property. "It is true," Gilmer continued, "that the slaves do not vote. Neither do women or minors. Yet these are enumerated in the apportionment of representation. Representation is never confined to that class of population alone who vote." In fact, "the difference in a mere abstract, political point of view, between slaves who have no civil rights whatever, and those citizens who are deprived of a . . . portion of those rights, is evidently one of degree, and not of kind." If women (and children) could be represented, then, surely, so could slaves. But if Adams's argument was doubly odd, so, too, was Gilmer's. In defending a system of representation that enhanced the sway of slaveowners, Gilmer set out a theory of representation that was far more expansive than his antislavery opponent's. He insisted that slaves were "part of the human family" and hence to be represented, and so were women, whom he also explicitly denominated citizens who enjoyed civil rights. But his purpose was, not to represent slaves or women, but to use the latter in service of the subjugation of the former. And, as for Adams, women were a dependent variable, a category to be used in service of an argument about slavery, a topic of much greater interest. Nor were these real women—no one spoke about the precise rights afforded them, or the way that protection might operate—but an imaginary class of persons called upon to illustrate a political principle.[28]

28. "Massachusetts Resolutions," H.R. Rep. No. 404-28, at 39–40 (1844); Farrand, ed., *Records of the Federal Convention,* I, 561. See, for example, New York congressman John Taylor, who opposed the extension of slavery into Missouri, insisting in the Missouri debates that "we also disclaim any wish to alter the basis of compromise on which the Federal Constitution was founded. . . . If the weight and influence of the South be increased by the representation of what they consider a part of their property, we do not wish to diminish them";

This debate was the last challenge to slave representation as such before the Civil War. Once again, it was an odd debate. No one was willing to overturn the Constitutional order, certainly not in the early decades of the American Republic and even less so as the nation matured. Instead, slavery's opponents and defenders engaged in a kind of shadowboxing over the Three-Fifths Clause. Because the discussions of slave representation were often ancillary to the main topic—an "and another things" added in to bolster the main point—the arguments often seem ad hoc and even internally contradictory. The very defenders of slave representation, who insisted that slaves were human beings, could simultaneously suggest that they were property that government ought to represent. And opponents of slavery could invoke the Declaration of Independence and its principle of equality, under which no one could ever be considered property. Such arguments threw proslavery men back on Locke. Like Holmes in the Missouri debates, Virginia political leader R. M. T. Hunter imagined the primordial state of nature, where "all men" were "by nature equally free." Once, however, "men abandon a state of nature, unite in society and resolve to organize a government, the question of representation arises . . . as a political problem, to be determined by a variety of circumstances." He noted that "the friends of what is called universal suffrage, those who talk longest and loudest in favor of natural rights, when they come to apply their principles take care to prohibit females, minors, paupers and convicts from exercising the right of suffrage." Here, once again, the exclusion of women from full voting was used to shore up the representation of slaves. The structure of the argument: of course we believe that in a state of nature all are free and equal and all participate in the social contract, but once government is established, limits of course have to be set, not on who is represented, but on who represents, and it should be obvious on its face that women and minors cannot represent themselves or others. The pillar holding up the whole intellectually shaky enterprise of the Three-Fifths Clause and the representation of the enslaved was the unquestioned exclusion of women from full political participation. They were citizens, rights-bearing persons, who could, it was simply assumed, not fully represent themselves.[29]

---

see *Debates and Proceedings in the Congress of the United States . . . Sixteenth Congress—First Session,* 952. As best I can tell, these reports barely attracted notice. In a letter, Tennessee representative Cave Johnson told President James K. Polk that the "Massachusetts Resolutions," which he called "the Hartford Convention Res[olution]," was in the hands of a committee, which was postponing its report in the hope of doing the least damage; see Johnson to Polk, Jan. 13, 1844, in Wayne Cutler, ed., *Correspondence of James K. Polk,* VII, *January–August 1844* (Nashville, Tenn., 1989), 26.

29. T. H[unter], *Review of the Massachusetts Proposition for Abolishing the Slave Repre-*

5. THE ABOLITIONISTS' DEBATE

As political abolitionism became more powerful, it attacked slavery more directly, and the Three-Fifths Clause came up only as part of discussions about other issues. One discussion was about whether the Constitution recognized slavery, a question that abolitionists had been asking with increasing forcefulness and clarity. The other was the question of citizenship. Both of these issues would be resolved by the Reconstruction Constitutional amendments. Discussions in the 1840s and 1850s provide interesting precursors of the subsequent debates. Yet, even as the locus of the debate shifted, women remained useful precisely because their political exclusion was uninterrogated, even among a wide swath of slavery's opponents. Consider the debate between abolitionist Lysander Spooner and abolitionist Wendell Phillips. In *The Unconstitutionality of Slavery* (1845), Spooner tried to prove by exegesis of canonical political texts that the Constitution did not even recognize slavery, that, for example, the "other persons" of the Three-Fifths Clause meant unnaturalized aliens, not the enslaved. The "we *the* people" of the Constitution's preamble comprised all citizens, "we the *whole* people," and, just because not all of them were allowed to vote on its ratification, it did not mean "they were not made citizens under it; for women and children did not vote on its adoption; yet they are made citizens by it, and are entitled as citizens to its protection." The Constitution "made citizens of all 'the people of the United States.'" From the presumption that those currently enslaved were in fact citizens of the United States proceeded a number of assumptions, including, most importantly, not only that they could not legitimately be enslaved but also that those of them who were natural born and were at least thirty-five years old were eligible to serve as president. This latter inference, however, required a (literal) asterisk in Spooner's text: "*That is, male persons," because the Constitution used male pronouns when talking about the president. Once again, women served as the pillar holding up the edifice, though this time the argument was for universal, or near-universal inclusion, albeit inclusion with an asterisk for gender.[30]

---

sentation (Washington, D.C., 1847), 15–16. The reports on the "Massachusetts Resolutions" continued to resonate, if only faintly. John Adams's vigorous contestation of the bases for enslavement irritated southern defenders of slavery, just as it would, in due course provide, as James Oakes has demonstrated, a Constitutional basis for terminating the institution; see Oakes, *Freedom National,* 34–41. For a concurrence in Adams's argument, see "Letter from Francis Jackson," Boston, July 4, 1844, *Anti-Slavery Examiner* (New York), 1844, 112–119. Hunter's essay was a direct response to Adams's "Massachusetts Resolutions" report; it was originally published in the *Southern Literary Messenger* in 1845.

30. Lysander Spooner, *The Unconstitutionality of Slavery* (Boston, 1845), 88–94, 106–

Spooner's book is a remarkable 156 pages of twisted logic trying to free the Constitution—and the enslaved—from the shackles of slavery. Phillips had no trouble shredding Spooner's logic. Their exchange, to be sure, was part of a larger debate among slavery's opponents about the Constitution and whether it was a proslavery or antislavery document. This argument was resolved only with the ratification of the Thirteenth and Fourteenth Amendments, and it is far more complex and important than this brief discussion can suggest. What is of interest here is those places where women were drawn into the argument, which is what Phillips did in three places in his long response to Spooner. Each of them is instructive. Phillips's main point was that Spooner's method of legal and constitutional analysis was fanciful. Spooner had argued that "no intention in violation of natural justice and natural right . . . can be ascribed to the constitution" and that judges could and should feel free to interpret cloudy passages in the Constitution in favor of justice and right. Phillips pointed out that there were many issues on which honest people disagreed; some thought the government should not impose capital punishment, for example, or "debar women from the right of voting." This was a throwaway line, an offhand example, used to show that what was just and right might not be immediately and obviously clear to all.[31]

Phillips's next invocation of women was more substantive. He attacked

---

107, 111, 117–118. For the evolution of political abolitionism, see Oakes, *Freedom National,* 13–24. See also Sinha, *Slave's Cause,* 475. For a more positive evaluation of Spooner's book, one that explains his method of Constitutional interpretation based on "the indeterminacy of written words," one that "has a very modern ring," see Randy E. Barnett, "Was Slavery Unconstitutional before the Thirteenth Amendment? Lysander Spooner's Theory of Interpretation," in John R. McKivigan, ed., *Abolitionism and American Law* (New York, 1999), 65–102, esp. 66, 69. See also Barnett, "Underlying Principles," *Constitutional Commentary,* XXIV (2007), 405–416. As Barnett notes, Frederick Douglass took up Spooner's argument, suggesting that the "other persons" of the Three-Fifths Clause "might fairly apply to aliens." See "The Constitution of the United States: Is It Pro-Slavery or Anti-Slavery? Speech Delivered in Glasgow, Scotland, March 26, 1860," in Philip S. Foner, ed., *Frederick Douglass: Selected Speeches and Writings* (Chicago, 1950), 383–384. For the evolution of Douglass's thinking on the constitutionality of slavery, see James Oakes, *The Radical and the Republican: Frederick Douglass, Abraham Lincoln, and the Triumph of Antislavery Politics* (New York, 2007), esp. 17–20. For Phillips, see James Brewer Stewart, *Wendell Phillips: Liberty's Hero* (Baton Rouge, La., 1986); Lori D. Ginzberg, *Elizabeth Cady Stanton: An American Life* (New York, 2009); and Isenberg, *Sex and Citizenship.*

31. Spooner, *Unconstitutionality of Slavery,* 70; Wendell Phillips, *Review of Lysander Spooner's Essay on the Unconstitutionality of Slavery . . .* (Boston, 1847), 15. For Phillips's reference to Spooner's argument as fanciful, see ibid., 4. For a starting place on the larger debate, see Oakes, *Freedom National.* For another critique of Spooner, see Charles Stearns, *The Way to Abolish Slavery* (Boston, 1849).

Spooner's reading of the Three-Fifths Clause, showing that the words did not mean what he thought they meant. Spooner insisted that "all other persons" meant unnaturalized aliens and untaxed Indians, not slaves. Phillips reminded him that the Federal Convention had merely adapted the language used by the Confederation Congress for apportioning direct taxes—"in proportion to the whole number of white and other free inhabitants, of every age, sex, and condition, including those bound to servitude for a term of years, and three-fifths of all *other persons,* not comprehended in the foregoing description, *except Indians,* not paying taxes, in each State"—and the language meant what it obviously meant. Phillips's focus was on slaves, aliens, and untaxed Indians. In the process of tracing the textual origins of the Three-Fifths Clause, however, he made it abundantly clear that women were included in the basis for taxation and subsequently in the basis for representation; women were citizens.[32]

Phillips made this point more explicit when he homed in on Spooner's asterisk, his aside that women could not run for president because the Constitution used the masculine pronoun for that office—and meant it. Phillips's real concern was Spooner's method, which he considered absurd. In making their interpretations, Spooner thought judges should look only to the meaning of the words and not to "extraneous or historical evidence." Phillips knew it was common practice for courts to refer "to the institutions of the country . . . to determine . . . the meaning of statutes." Indeed, "any other principle would lead to innumerable absurdities," and he used Spooner's asterisk as a prime example. Let us see how Phillips laid it out: "The Con-

32. Phillips, *Review of Lysander Spooner's Essay,* 45. Had Phillips been able to quote Inigo Montoya, I am sure he would have; see "You Keep Using That Word, I Do Not Think It Means What You Think It Means," Know Your Meme, accessed Aug. 21, 2016, http://knowyourmeme.com/memes/you-keep-using-that-word-i-do-not-think-it-means-what-you-think-it-means. Phillips was not the only male abolitionist to assume that women were represented by and included in the Constitution. Several years later, Gerrit Smith, in one of his speeches railing against slavery, observed, "'We the people of the United States' made [the Constitution]. . . . There is not the least uncertainty in the meaning of the phrase. . . . It necessarily means all and not a part—every kind and not one kind—of the people, who were, at that time, permanent inhabitants of the country. To say, that the phrase means but voters, is to say, that, not only many of the white men, as well as all the black men, were shut out from citizenship, but also all the white women and white children, as well as all the black women and black children." Smith's purpose was to show the unconstitutionality of slavery—from "We the people," he noted, "it follows that, if there were slaves in this country, at the time the Constitution was adopted, that instrument made them all citizens, and, therefore, made them all free." See *Substance of the Speech Made by Gerrit Smith in the Capitol of the State of New York, March 11th and 12th, 1850,* 2nd ed. (Syracuse, N.Y., 1850), 15–16.

stitution makes every 'natural born citizen' eligible to the office of the President. Now, women are citizens." So far, so good. The first two statements seem obvious. And, according to Spooner's method (which says that when there is ambiguity, we choose the "meaning consistent with natural justice"), "women are eligible to the Presidency." But, Phillips continues—and remember, his aim is to catch Spooner in an absurdity—"it is just as plain that this is not law, nor the meaning of the Constitution; and that the Supreme Court would be justified in referring to the history and customs of the country, and of the race and class of nations to which we belong, in so construing this clause." As for Spooner's asterisk, Phillips pointed out the other instances in which the Constitution used masculine pronouns—for example, in the Fifth and Sixth Amendments, which clearly were intended to protect women as well as men. The asterisk did not rescue Spooner from positing an absurdity: "If we construe the Constitution according to [his] rules, women are constitutionally eligible to the Presidency and to Congress; nothing but 'extraneous and historical evidence' shields us from this result."[33]

When Phillips looked for the best example to expose Spooner's method for demonstrating that slavery was unconstitutional, he chose women, and the utterly absurd possibility that they might be eligible to serve as president or members of Congress. In fact, both Phillips and Spooner went out of their way to say that women could not be president. Spooner relied on grammar and an asterisk, Phillips on history and custom. Both saw what the plain language of the Constitution authorized—that women could not only represent themselves, but they could serve in the highest office in the land—and struggled to find ways to deny that is what the Constitution said. Actually, they did not struggle very hard; they just assumed—for Spooner, that it was obvious, for Phillips that it was an absurdity. But Spooner's asterisk took Phillips right back to an assertion of women's citizenship: of course they were protected by the Fifth and Sixth Amendments, just as they were by all of the others. Women were citizens; this was inarguable. But they could not represent themselves. And why not? Because of history and custom.

Yet, here, Phillips snarled himself in his own contradictions. He had argued that in interpreting the relevant passage in the Constitution, the Supreme Court would be "justified in referring to the history and customs of the country, and of the race and class of nations to which we belong," that is not just the history and customs of the United States but also similar nations—for example, Britain. Yet only three paragraphs later, in trying

33. Phillips, *Review of Lysander Spooner's Essay,* 52–54.

to eviscerate Spooner's asterisk, he pointed out that English statutes generally "use only the masculine gender,—'the King,' '*his* Majesty,'—and yet such laws and maxims would be equally binding and valid under a Queen." Clearly, then, a female leader was not an absurdity, as the history of England demonstrated. It is all the more remarkable to have Phillips fasten upon this example to reveal the shakiness of Spooner's method because he himself was one of the leading male supporters of women's rights and would speak in favor of women's right to vote only four years later. In this instance, however, women, and their rights, were a prop, a pillar in the case against slavery, as they had been for John Quincy Adams, a dependent variable, a contingency. In arguments about slavery, slaves came first; this is not surprising. What is noteworthy is the way women were dragged into these arguments, and, in those arguments, too, slaves always came first. You do not need a crystal ball to see how things would turn out later with the Fourteenth and Fifteenth Amendments.[34]

6. THE DRED SCOTT REVERSAL

We are now at a turning point in the history of the Three-Fifths Clause. As we have seen, the clause was a political accommodation without a real basis in underlying theory. It was, as Morris had observed at the Constitutional Convention, "an incoherence," and hence it fell to its supporters to wrest meaning out of it. Beginning in the 1790s, antislavery northerners, primarily Federalists and later Whigs, attacked the clause and sought its removal, arguing that it unfairly disadvantaged nonslaveowners. In defending it, slavery's supporters, for the most part Democratic-Republican and later Democratic southerners, began explaining that slaves were legitimately counted among those to be represented because they were human beings under the protection of the state. Of course people could enjoy civil rights without having political ones: just look at women. They were the exemplary rights-bearing citizens who could not vote, the represented who could not represent themselves. But, so long as these discussions were about the overrepresentation of the slave states, women, slaves, and their status in the American nation came into them slant—in offhand, off-center, underdeveloped assertions about the political status of slaves and women, marshaled in the service of larger arguments about the Constitutional status of slavery itself. Not until the Dred Scott decision in 1857 was the United States called upon to make a clear statement, not simply about slavery, but about slaves'—and free black

34. Ibid., 53.

people's—Constitutional status, one that directly addressed the question of citizenship. And, once again, women were taken along for the ride.

The Dred Scott decision brought questions of citizenship to the fore. Much has been written about this landmark case, and this is not the place to examine the case in its entirety. The focus here is the notion of citizenship as it emerged in discussions of the Three-Fifths Clause. None of the opinions in the case directly addressed that clause, but Chief Justice Roger Taney's majority opinion and Justice Benjamin Curtis's dissent picked up earlier arguments about it. Taney famously insisted that, "when the Constitution was adopted, [free Negroes] were not regarded in any of the States as members of the community which constituted the State, and were not numbered among its 'people or citizens.'" They were consequently not " 'citizens' within the meaning of the Constitution." Moreover, "they had no rights which the white man was bound to respect." Taney listed the multiple ways in which black people's rights had been restricted from the earliest days of colonization, but he also knew that there were others whose rights were encumbered. He acknowledged that some would say that "a person may be a citizen . . . although he does not possess all the rights which may belong to other citizens," for example, the right to vote or hold office. And, here, we come to women. "Undoubtedly," Taney acknowledged, "a person may be a citizen, that is, a member of the community who form the sovereignty, although he exercises no share of the political power and is incapacitated from holding particular offices. Women and minors, who form a part of the political family, cannot vote, and when a property qualification is required to vote or hold a particular office, those who have not the necessary qualification cannot vote or hold the office, yet they are citizens." There it was, a clear statement that women were citizens, but, once again, in the service of propping up slavery and this time with a new twist: to demonstrate that no black people, whether enslaved or free, could ever be citizens or be guaranteed any rights that white people were required to respect.[35]

In another way, however, Taney's statement was a departure. If his predecessors had used women to exemplify those members of the nation—the people to be represented—who could not represent themselves, Taney drew a sharp line between (white) women and black persons; the one group was

35. "Scott v. Sandford," Legal Information Institute, Cornell Law School, accessed Oct. 9, 2016, https://www.law.cornell.edu/supremecourt/text/60/393, 1393, 407, 421–422, 422; Benjamin C. Howard, *Report of the Decision of the Supreme Court of the United States, and the Opinions of the Judges Thereof, in the Case of Dred Scott versus John F. A. Sandford. December Term, 1856* (Washington, D.C., 1857).

clearly made up of citizens, but ones whose rights were limited, while the other had no rights at all. Such an argument revealed the Three-Fifths Clause to be the incoherence that Morris had said it was. In a reversal, Curtis, a Massachusetts Whig, made the argument that proslavery Democrats had made earlier, but this time summoning women to assert the citizenship of free blacks. "In all the States," he pointed out, "numerous persons, though citizens, cannot vote, or cannot hold office, either on account of their age, or sex, or the want of the necessary legal qualifications. The truth is that citizenship, under the Constitution of the United States, is not dependent on the possession of any particular political or even of all civil rights." Curtis proceeded to list some of the variations from state to state, in service of his larger point, with regard to universal citizenship of all native-born Americans, including women: "One may confine the right of suffrage to white male citizens; another may extend it to colored persons and females; one may allow all persons above a prescribed age to convey property and transact business; another may exclude married women. But whether native-born women, or persons under age, or under guardianship because insane or spendthrifts, be excluded from voting or holding office, or allowed to do so, I apprehend that no one will deny that they are citizens of the United States." Both Taney and Curtis agreed that women were citizens, and, astonishingly, Curtis even imagined that in some states women might vote. But they used the same, and, I would argue, truly significant assumption to very different purposes: in one case, to show why free blacks *were* citizens, and, in the other case, the very same premise to show why they were *not.* For both, however, women's citizenship was partial, limited, circumscribed, but citizenship, called just that.[36]

36. "Scott v. Sandford," Legal Information Institute, Cornell Law School, 583. Massachusetts lawyers Horace Gray and John Lowell picked up Curtis's discussion of women's citizenship in their critique of the majority opinion. "The privilege of voting, and the legal capacity for office, are not essential to the character of a citizen, for women are citizens without either"; see *A Legal Review of the Case of Dred Scott, as Decided by the Supreme Court of the United States* (Boston, 1857), 18. The literature on the Dred Scott case is vast, and this is not the place to review it. My understanding of it, however, is shaped by William J. Novak's argument that we should read the history of citizenship forward, from the American Revolution, as it emerged out of the welter of statuses recognized in Common Law, and not backward, from the concept of a national citizenship that developed after the ratification of the Fourteenth Amendment; see Novak, "Legal Transformation of Citizenship in Nineteenth-Century America," in Jacobs, Novak, and Zelizer, eds., *Democratic Experiment,* 85–119. Very few of those who have written about the decision have noted the brief discussions of women's citizenship in the opinions. An exception is Mark A. Graber, who says that "everyone recognized [women] to be citizens," and, in agreement with Taney, that no one

7. THE FOURTEENTH AMENDMENT RESOLUTION

And this is where matters stood on the eve of the Civil War: a consensus that women were citizens—whatever that meant, but a serious disagreement about whether free blacks were citizens, whatever that meant. This is not meant to be flip. Instead, the meaning of citizenship was not at all clear. It was evolving, being crafted in response to challenges such as the ones that have been described, and it would take the Fourteenth Amendment to begin to create clarity. That amendment also voided the Three-Fifths Clause, and it is here that our story comes to an end. How Congress arrived at the particular formulation the amendment took is a complex story, one that has been told many times, and well. It brings together the demise of the Three-Fifths Clause and the beginning of nationally defined citizenship, thus illuminating that the clause had always had embedded in it, inescapably, a theory of citizenship and representation, a notion of the relationship between the represented and the state. But, as I hope has been demonstrated, that connection was never quite clear to those who framed the clause—Madison perhaps being the exception—or argued about it in the subsequent decades. Yet every time the clause came up, those who argued about it sooner or later began talking about women, using them as a point of reference, first for the enslaved, then for free blacks.

---

recognized blacks to be so. He also observes that there were "fundamental differences in the perceived basis of gender and race distinctions" and the situations were not "analogous"; see Graber, *Dred Scott and the Problem of Constitutional Evil* (Cambridge, 2006), 51. But, as I hope the preceding pages show, a number of political leaders before Curtis made just that analogy. See also Henry L. Chambers, Jr., "*Dred Scott:* Tiered Citizenship and Tiered Personhood," *Chicago-Kent Law Review,* LXXXII (2007), 209–232, arguing for a kind of "tiered" citizenship in which women were in the second tier. Looking backward, I believe we can discern tiers of citizenship but that there was no theory of tiered citizenship to explain the existence of such tiers. Hence all the slipperiness and confusion in the discussions I have described above. Nancy F. Cott also notes Taney's discussion of women in her important article, "Marriage and Women's Citizenship in the United States, 1830–1934," *American Historical Review,* CIII (1998), 1440–1474, esp. 1445. I have also found quite useful James H. Kettner's *The Development of American Citizenship, 1608–1870* (Williamsburg, Va., and Chapel Hill N.C., 1978), in particular, his observation that "the Revolution created the status of 'American citizen' and produced an expression of the general principles that ought to govern membership in a free society: republican citizenship ought to rest on consent; . . . it ought to confer equal rights. But if general principles were clear, particular questions about the source, character, and effects of citizenship remained open well into the nineteenth century" (10). For the encumbrances on women's citizenship, see Linda K. Kerber, *No Constitutional Right to Be Ladies: Women and the Obligations of Citizenship* (New York, 1998). Don E. Fehrenbacher's authoritative study, *The Dred Scott Case: Its Significance in American Law and Politics* (New York, 1978), does not mention the brief discussions of women's citizenship in the opinions.

The imperatives of the northern victory in the Civil War brought these questions to the fore. First, slavery was ended, practically by the Union victory and formally by the Thirteenth Amendment, essentially making the Three-Fifths Clause, as Maine representative James G. Blaine put it, "a dead letter." But, as the men of Congress quickly perceived, they would have to make decisions about two pressing matters that also presented them with the opportunity to address two of their greatest complaints about the southern-dominated Constitutional regime: the overrepresentation of slave-owning states in Congress and the Dred Scott decision, which had defined all black people as noncitizens and persons wholly without rights. But addressing these two issues at once proved to be a complicated and consequently drawn-out affair, for the issues did not align perfectly. It seemed quite clear that the formerly enslaved were no longer the "other persons" of the Three-Fifths Clause. But, it followed, then they were to be counted in the basis for representation like everyone else—and that would only increase the South's voting power once the formerly rebellious states were reconstructed and admitted back into the Union. That was simply unacceptable to northern Republicans. "Shall the death of slavery add two fifths to the entire power which slavery had when slavery was living?" New York representative Roscoe Conkling demanded. "This is privilege, class, aristocracy, in its most hateful form," the very system the North had fought to vanquish, come back even stronger. "This will reward traitors with a liberal premium for treason," said Ohio representative William Lawrence.[37]

37. *The Congressional Globe: Containing the Debates and Proceedings of the First Session of the Thirty-Ninth Congress* (Washington, D.C., 1866), 141, 357, 404. As William E. Nelson notes, Republicans "had calculated quite precisely the impact that abrogation of the three-fifths compromise would have." See Nelson, *The Fourteenth Amendment: From Political Principle to Judicial Doctrine* (Cambridge, Mass., 1988), 46. See, for example, Roscoe Conkling's calculations, *Congressional Globe: . . . Session of the Thirty-Ninth Congress,* 357. Nor was such thinking fantastical on the Republicans' part. Southerners anticipated increased representation upon return to the Union. The *Daily Richmond Examiner* explained that "universal assent appears to be given to the proposition that if the States lately rebellious be restored to rights of representation according to the Federal basis, or to the basis of numbers enlarged by the enumeration of all the blacks in the next census, the political power of the country will pass into the hands of the South, aided, as it will be, by Northern alliances"; see "The Political Prospect," Jan. 9, 1866, *Daily Richmond Examiner,* [1], cited in Mark A. Graber, "Constructing Constitutional Politics: Thaddeus Stevens, John Bingham, and the Forgotten Fourteenth Amendment," University of Maryland Francis King Carey School of Law Legal Studies Research Paper, no. 2014-37, 27, accessed Aug. 21, 2016, https://papers.ssrn.com/sol3/papers.cfm?abstract_id=2483355. For fear of a resurgent and strengthened South more generally, see Graber, "Constructing Constitutional Politics," 25–33.

The rough consensus that had emerged before the Civil War suggested that blacks' status was similar to that of women, legitimately counted in the basis for representation because they were, if free, also citizens; or, if enslaved, partially citizens, or persons under the protection of the state; or maybe not citizens at all—the despised Dred Scott decision, which northern Republicans were now in a position to reverse. If there were ambiguity and uncertainty about the precise nature of black persons' citizenship and (white) women's citizenship, that is because there had been few occasions where any precision was required, and one of them—the Dred Scott decision—had inflamed northern public opinion. But now clarity was required. Congress had to rethink the basis for representation in the House. In 1787, this had been a political decision that rested upon underlying notions of representation. So it would be in 1866 as well.[38]

It was not obvious what the solution would be. For half a year, northern Republicans struggled to find the right language. As Mark A. Graber has shown, almost all of the debate over what would become the Fourteenth Amendment focused on what would become the second section of the amendment, which eliminated the Three-Fifths Clause (rather than the first, the privileges and immunities clause). In other words, it proved easier to solve the problem created by the Dred Scott decision than that created by the Three-Fifths Clause. In fact, solving the one actually made the other more difficult. Making free blacks citizens with limitations—like white women, which is what Justice Curtis argued they should be—still would have left a reconstructed South overrepresented. But making free blacks full citizens with full political rights, including voting and holding office, was something only a handful of Republicans were prepared to do in early 1866.[39]

38. For the primacy of politics in the shaping of the Fourteenth Amendment, see Graber, "Constructing Constitutional Politics." The literature on the Fourteenth Amendment is vast. A good starting point is Eric Foner's succinct summary in *Reconstruction: America's Unfinished Revolution 1863–1877* (New York, 1988), 251–261. See also Nelson, *The Fourteenth Amendment;* and Michael Les Benedict, *A Compromise of Principle: Congressional Republicans and Reconstruction, 1863–1869* (New York, 1974).

39. Graber, "Constructing Constitutional Politics," 10. Graber states: "The debate over the first version of Fourteenth Amendment, the version that included only an early draft of Section 2, took more than a month. The debate over the stand-alone version of Section 1 took three days. . . . When both proposals were combined into the omnibus amendment, the first thirteen Republicans who gave lengthy speeches devoted no more than a paragraph or so to the clauses adding new constitutional powers and rights. Most important perhaps, Republicans expressed far more concern with the details of Sections 2 and 3 than with the precise language or meaning of Sections 1 and 5" (42). See also Foner, *Reconstruction,* 251.

By the time Congress began work on the Fourteenth Amendment, there was already widespread agreement among those in a Congress (remember, the states in rebellion had not yet been reconstructed) that black people were citizens, that Dred Scott had been wrongly decided. In 1862, Attorney General Edward Bates had issued an opinion that black people were full citizens of the United States, as were women and children, but he made clear that neither voting nor holding office was "essential to citizenship." The Civil Rights Act of 1866 likewise established blacks' citizenship status nationally. As Missouri representative John Van Horn put it in 1866, "The great struggle now closed has settled the question that the black man has 'rights that the white man is bound to respect.'"[40]

But here was the problem: if representation were to be based upon population, how could the South be prevented from profiting from its treason? But what other basis for representation was there in a republican form of government? The easiest fix, as Eric Foner has noted, would have been to "base representation on the number of qualified voters," but, as he observes, the numbers of women, children, and unnaturalized aliens were distributed unevenly among the states, and, excluding them, it was argued at the time, might have disadvantaged some states. In addition, all states would have been incentivized to enfranchise voters they were currently excluding, something a number of states, particularly in New England, were loathe to do. Moreover, the goal for most Republicans at this point was to diminish southern representation more than to encourage the former slave states to enfranchise their freedmen. Indeed, very few congressmen spoke forcefully for an expanded suffrage. A number of Republicans echoed Bates in asserting that voting was not a natural right. Kentucky senator Garrett Davis said just that: "The right to vote is not a natural, but an artificial right." Even in countries where the franchise was widespread, "It never was allowed to one fourth of the people, the women and minors and many other small classes not being permitted to vote." According to Massachusetts senator Henry Wilson, "Every human being in the country, black or white, man or woman, or little child in the

40. *Opinion of Attorney General Bates on Citizenship* (Washington, D.C., 1862), 7; *Congressional Globe: . . . Session of the Thirty-Ninth Congress,* 284; "An Act to Protect All Persons in the United States in Their Civil Rights, and Furnish the Means of Their Vindication," in George P. Sanger, ed., *The Statutes at Large, Treaties, and Proclamations of the United States of America: From December, 1865, to March, 1867 . . . ,* XIV (Boston, 1868), 27–29. Indeed, Bates went to significant length to explain why voting was not essential to citizenship, using the citizenship status of women, minors, and other nonvoting citizens to prove his point. On Bates's *Opinion,* see Oakes, *Freedom National,* 357–360. On the Civil Rights Act, see Foner, *Reconstruction,* 243–251. Andrew Johnson vetoed the act; Congress overrode the veto.

cradle, has a right to be protected in life, in property, and in liberty; that is, civil liberty. The right to hold an office, the right to vote, the right to take part in the governing power of the country," however, was another matter, wholly under the purview of the states, not the federal government.[41]

This notion of citizenship was shared, in its general contours, even by Democrats such as Maryland's Reverdy Johnson, who had come to terms rhetorically with the effective overturning of Dred Scott. "The right of suffrage" and "the right to be represented" were "altogether distinct." Hence, "the negro who does not vote in Maryland, like the white woman or the infant who does not vote in Iowa, is to be protected. . . . By having representatives from the State." Citing no less an authority than Madison, Johnson invoked the Three-Fifths Clause: "Nobody pretended when the Constitution was formed that the negroes would not be counted independent of the right to vote. . . ." "Minors, women, black or white [this is the only time I believe I have seen black women referenced in these debates], with or without a property qualification," he continued, "have a right to have themselves considered in ascertaining who is to represent that State, numerically," which increases "the security of all the citizens" in the state.[42]

Here was the old argument that southern Democrats had been making since early in the century, but in a radically different context, one where the debate was no longer about the future of slavery—that question had been settled—but about how best to protect the formerly enslaved. The focus had shifted away from defending an apportionment mechanism that protected slavery to devising a Constitutional mechanism to protect freed people. That was the difference between the Republicans who drew a distinction between civil rights and voting and a Democrat like Johnson: the Republicans were intent upon protecting the civil rights of the formerly enslaved, while Johnson was using the old argument to justify full representation of the freed people, regardless of whether it protected blacks' rights or not. Women were still important to Johnson—look, he said, there are lots of groups that do not represent themselves—but beside the point for Republicans. They could say that women were citizens one moment but forget about them the next, and then get tangled up in a contradiction the next.

Consider the case of New York representative Conkling. Like most in

41. Foner, *Reconstruction,* 252; *Congressional Globe: . . . Session of the Thirty-Ninth Congress,* 245, 1255. See also ibid., 219, 117, 1159. Often, when this argument was made, women and minors were used as evidence.

42. *Congressional Globe: . . . Session of the Thirty-Ninth Congress,* 767. Johnson incidentally represented John Sandford, the defendant in the Dred Scott case.

Congress, he believed that women were citizens—and that is why, as much as for other pragmatic reasons, the final version of the Fourteenth Amendment still used total population (excepting Indians) as the basis for apportionment. The first version of what would become the second section of the amendment suggested basing representation on the number of qualified voters. Missouri's John Henderson invoked Madison in asserting that representation should be based on "numbers." Oregon's George Williams was even more direct. Basing representation on voters would "strike out of political existence all the women in the United States and all persons under twenty-one years of age. . . . That violates the fundamental principle adopted by our fathers when they framed the Constitution, and it seems to me that it would be great injustice to adopt such a constitutional provision." Conkling agreed: such a change in the Constitution "would shut out four fifths of the citizens of the country—women and children, who are citizens, who are taxed, and who are, and always have been, represented."[43]

But earlier the same day, women's citizenship had been far from Conkling's thoughts when, in a remarkable speech, he dismantled the logic of the Three-Fifths Clause. New Jersey Democrat Andrew Rogers had goaded him, insisting on "five fifths" representation of the freed people. If, "in the days of the past," the South was allowed partial representation for "a population that was not classed as citizens or a people . . . who had no political *status* . . . who were not entitled even to exercise the right of coming into a court . . . as a plaintiff or defendant," why should it not get to count all the former slaves, who "have gained more by the success of this war than any other class of people in the United States." That was too much for Conkling, who decided to school his colleague. The Three-Fifths Clause, he began,

> owe[d] its existence to the . . . principle. . . . [t]hat political representation does not belong to those who have no political existence.
>
> The government of a free political society belongs to its members, and does not belong to others. . . .
>
> The slaves of the South were not members of that political society which formed the Constitution of the United States. . . .
>
> From this it followed that they were not to be represented as members.

43. Ibid. 3033; *Appendix to the Congressional Globe: Containing Speeches, Important State Papers, and the Laws of the First Session Thirty-Ninth Congress* (Washington, D.C., 1866), 96, *Congressional Globe: . . . Session of the Thirty-Ninth Congress*, 358.

> From this it followed that political power was not to be apportioned by treating them as political persons.

It was only by "a purely arbitrary agreement . . . with nothing to support it but the consent of the parties"—the Three-Fifths Clause—that the "free people" of the states would be counted "and should all have their fair share of power . . . and that then the free people of the slaveholding States should have as much power beside as would be measured by counting every slave as three fifths of a 'person'" in return for including them in the basis for taxation. For Conkling, there were only two categories of people, free persons, "the term employed to describe all who had political rights and standing," and slaves, whom he dubbed "fractional persons." But the Civil War had changed things. "A moral earthquake has turned fractions into units, and units into ciphers. If a black man counts at all now, he counts five fifths of a man." But "this emancipated multitude has no political *status*." Their power, however—their political power—still rested with their former owners. "There is no place logically for this power to go save to the blacks." Moreover, "enfranchisement alone carries with it political rights." This was a powerful and impassioned argument on behalf of enfranchising the former slaves—but, quite obviously, and literally, Conkling had only black men in mind. In this portion of his argument, there was no partial citizenship, no notion of protected classes, no worthy status short of full political rights and enfranchisement. The women—so present a little later in his speech—were missing.[44]

Yet, just as they would later in the day for Conkling, women kept popping up, and, almost every time they did, they were a problem. If, in the decades before the Civil War, women—in Constitutional discourse—served, or, rather were used, primarily to grease the wheels of the machinery of slavery, in 1866 they jammed the gears. The change: the imaginary women had come to life, and congressmen now had to contemplate the possibility of actual women actually voting. Democrats brought them up as an argument against black enfranchisement. Pennsylvania's Benjamin Boyer, for example,

44. *Congressional Globe: . . . Session of the Thirty-Ninth Congress*, 353–356. Predictably, Rogers noted that representation was based on "every man, woman, and child" (353). Conkling recognized that there were exceptions to this general rule of citizenship in the clause: Indians not taxed, "because uncivilized Indians in their tribal state were . . . far beyond the scope" of the Constitution, and "foreigners," who could be naturalized as soon as they were "prepared to assume" their "full political rights" (356). In speaking of partially counted slaves as "fractions," Conkling echoed John Quincy Adams's description of the Three-Fifths Clause's calculus (356). See note 12, above.

observed that reformers were saying, "After the negro will come the women. But I protest against this inverse order of merit; and if both are to vote I claim precedence for the ladies." Kentucky's Aaron Harding was blunt: "I would prefer the white women and . . . young men . . . to the negro. I infinitely prefer giving them the right of suffrage. I am fonder of them than the negro." Neither of these Democrats was serious; this was their way of saying how contemptible they found the idea of black enfranchisement. New York Copperhead Democrat James Brooks used women, too, just to goad his Republican opponents. When Elizabeth Cady Stanton, one of his constituents, sent him a petition for universal suffrage, which Susan B. Anthony had also sent to Thaddeus Stevens, Brooks happily presented it, asking Stevens directly, "Why, in organizing a system of liberality and justice, not recognize in the case of free women as well as free negroes the right of representation?" He proposed changing the language of the bill then being considered "by inserting the words 'or sex' after the word 'color'" so that states would lose representation if they denied not only blacks but also women the vote. Stevens, who was women's strongest ally in Congress—he objected strenuously to the insertion of the word *male* into the Amendment—knew what Brooks was up to and asked him twice if he intended to vote for his amendment. Brooks evaded the question, willing to say only, "I am in favor of my own color in preference to any other color, and I prefer the white women of my country to the negro." The *Congressional Globe* reports that there was "applause on the floor and in the galleries promptly checked by the Speaker." This was the old Democratic move, using women as a prop in the theater of white supremacy.[45]

But, by 1866, much had changed, and the scene played out a bit differently. If previously, women—or the idea of women—had been brought on

45. Ibid., 177 ("after"), 451 ("I would"), 379–380 ("Why," 379, "by inserting," "I am in favor," "applause," 380), 536 ("male"). For an account of this debate, see Faye E. Dudden, *Fighting Chance: The Struggle over Woman Suffrage and Black Suffrage in Reconstruction America* (New York, 2011), 77–78. Stanton and Anthony's petition noted that "the Constitution classes us as 'free people,' and counts us whole persons in the basis of representation, and yet we are governed without our consent, compelled to pay taxes without appeal, and punished for violations of the law without choice of judge or juror" (*Congressional Globe: . . . Session of the Thirty-Ninth Congress,* 380). In a speech well known to historians, Stevens, who preferred that representation be based on population and loss of representation on denial of the vote to black people and that the word *male* be kept out of the Constitution, objected to an amendment that would have apportioned representation on the number of "male citizens of the States. Why has he put in that word 'male?' It was never in the Constitution of the United States before. Why make a crusade against women in the Constitution of the nation?" The *Congressional Globe* reported this question elicited "laughter"; see ibid., 536.

stage to exercise a calming effect, now the entry of women prompted confusion and laughter. And this was in large part because of the women themselves. Brooks brought in Stanton and Anthony's petition—and used it to get laughs, at the expense of women and black men both. Congressmen more sympathetic to women than Brooks introduced petitions from women, but without advocating for them. Two days after Brooks presented the women's petition to the House, Missouri's Republican B. Gratz Brown presented one to the Senate, which was referred to the joint Committee on Reconstruction without any debate. When Kansas's James Lane introduced Stanton and Anthony's petition in the Senate a week later, he was sheepish. "As the petition is very brief and respectfully worded, I ask that a gallant Senate may hear it be read." It, too, was referred to the joint committee. When Henderson presented a similar petition, this one from "Mrs. Gerritt Smith," he tried to make sense of it, trying to reconcile his liberal principles with what Phillips had called history and custom. He began with some ambivalence. "The right to petition is a sacred right, and whatever may be thought of giving the ballot to women, the right to ask it of the Government cannot be denied them." The women deserved "a respectful consideration," but he himself did not know what the response should be. Perhaps coverture explained why married women could not vote, but then, "if the married man be entitled to but one vote, the unmarried man should be satisfied with less than half a vote." This provoked laughter. But Henderson was serious about coverture, and he invoked history and custom; "in almost all Governments" women have been denied the vote "but because it is wholly unnecessary as a means of their protection."[46]

Henderson could have left it there; instead, he launched into a brief lecture on the principles of republican government. "Political power was claimed originally by the people as a means of protecting themselves against the usurpations of those in power, whose interests or caprices might lead to their oppression. But it was never thought the interests or caprices of men could lead to a denial of the civil rights or social supremacy of woman. . . . No civil right can be denied her." In the context of the first section of the Fourteenth Amendment, this was an important statement. Women are citizens. And, if they are citizens, it follows that they should be counted in the basis for representation. But should they vote? Henderson meandered some more, from the terrain of orthodox political theory to that of custom and behavior. Race prejudice was worse than the "prejudice against sex," and "people of one

46. *Congressional Globe: . . . Session of the Thirty-Ninth Congress,* 390, 518–519, 951–952.

race have always been unjust to those of another." So blacks might need the vote to protect themselves, whereas "woman . . . should not descend from her lofty sphere to engage in the angry contests of her creatures."[47]

Perhaps annoyed with Henderson's musings, Illinois's Richard Yates asked him if he was proposing adding the term "sex" to the amendment. No, said Henderson; he'd just presented the petition and did not particularly want to discuss its merits. Charles Sumner piped up to make it clear that he did not "undertake to express any opinion on the great question whether women should vote or not vote. I did venture to say that in my opinion it was not judicious for them at this moment to bring forward their claims so as to compromise in any way the great question of equal rights for an enfranchised race now before Congress." The senators joked among themselves about whether they had presented the petitions in a "creditable way." There was much laughter. The petition was tabled.[48]

47. Ibid., 952.

48. Ibid., 952. In the next session of Congress, after the Fourteenth Amendment had been passed and contemplating women's enfranchisement no longer threatened to derail the amendment, Pennsylvania's John Broomall took Henderson's logic even further, directly confronting the tension between coverture and accepted republican theory:

> What is a republican form of government? If I were to attempt a definition it would be this: it is that form of government in which the rulers are chosen by the suffrages of the people, and in which every citizen may either exercise the right of suffrage himself or have it exercised for him by some one who may be fairly considered as representing his interests by reason of legal, social, or family relations to him. Under this definition, if the right of suffrage be exercised by all the adult males, the women and children may be considered as mediately represented in the government, and hence the form would be republican. But it would meet the requirements of the definition much better if the right of suffrage were extended to all adults without regard to sex; and I am ready to advocate this extension whenever the women of America shall believe themselves unfairly treated by this mediate representation and shall demand the right of suffrage for themselves.

Broomall made these remarks in a debate about Reconstruction. He questioned whether southern states that excluded a majority of men—the freed slaves—from the ballot could be considered "republican." "Who represents [their] interests . . . ?" he asked. "Who represents the interests of their wives and children? Under the slave system there was at least the pretense of mediate representation. . . . Recent events have demonstrated that the slave himself looked upon the matter in a different light. But the slave system has passed away and the farce of mediate representation of the negroes has gone with it." See ibid., 350–351. (Bruce Ackerman cites this passage in *We the People 2: Transformations* [Cambridge, Mass., 1998], 441n. He truncates it before the last sentence, in which Broomall indicated his preference for women's enfranchisement, making it appear as if Broomall believed coverture a sufficient explanation for their disenfranchisement.)

The men really did not want to talk about women's rights. Their focus in 1866 was to solve two specific problems: guaranteeing the freed people basic civil rights and preventing a Reconstructed South from coming back into the Union with more representation than it had when it left, yet to do so without enfranchising black men nationally. The final product, the Fourteenth Amendment, like the infamous clause in the Constitution it replaced, was a compromise, dictated as much by the exigencies of politics as by overarching principle. The first section embraced women. "All persons born or naturalized in the United States, and subject to the jurisdiction thereof, are citizens of the United States and of the State wherein they reside." And the first sentence of the second section expressed the same capacious notion of citizenship: "Representatives shall be apportioned among the several States according to their respective numbers, counting the whole number of persons in each State, excluding Indians not taxed." It undid the harm committed by the Three-Fifths Clause, and, to use Conkling's term, turned fractional persons back into units. But then, in the second sentence, the section took a strange turn, one dictated by political exigency, when it put the word *male* into the Constitution, not once, but three times, by instructing that when any "male inhabitan[t]" was denied the vote, then "the basis of representation therein shall be reduced in the proportion which the number of such male citizens shall bear to the whole number of male citizens twenty-one years of age in such State."[49]

49. For the text of the Fourteenth Amendment, see "U.S. Constitution: Amendments XI–XXVII: XIV—Citizen Rights Not to Be Abridged," The Avalon Project, accessed Aug. 31, 2016, https://avalon.law.yale.edu/18th_century/amend1.asp#14. The Republican committee members who produced the final version of the amendment "eschewed ideology in favor of practicality"; see Benedict, *Compromise of Principle,* 182. Thaddeus Stevens later made clear that the privileges and immunities clause was intended to cover women and that civil and political rights were distinct:

> In making all native born and naturalized persons citizens, this section does not make them voters, for if it did, then would all women and minors have the right of suffrage, since they are just as much persons. . . .
>
> . . . The fact that this section does not give the colored man the right of suffrage constitutes the main reason why the extreme advocates of negro suffrage oppose the amendment.

See "National Citizenship," *North American and United States Gazette* (Philadelphia), Sept. 28, 1866, [2], also cited in Amar, *Bill of Rights,* 217n. There is a significant literature on feminists' anger about the insertion of the word *male* into the amendment and the unwillingness of Congress to advance women's enfranchisement. See Ellen Carol DuBois, *Feminism*

POSTSCRIPT

This sentence gave Congress the ability to punish (southern) states for denying black men the right to vote, but this provision was never implemented. It functioned as a crutch for Republicans until they were reconciled to the necessity of black enfranchisement. Although this was certainly not its primary intent, its chief legacies have been to provide a textual basis for the restriction of women's suffrage—as well as that of felons. That is, rather than working to expand suffrage, the sentence has justified its restriction. In *Minor* v. *Happersett,* a unanimous Supreme Court ruled in 1874 that voting was not one of the "privileges and immunities" of citizenship guaranteed by the Fourteenth Amendment, and neither it nor any other part of the Constitution prohibited its denial to women. As evidence, it cited this very sentence in the second section of the Fourteenth Amendment and interpreted it in the context of the first section: "If suffrage was necessarily one of the absolute rights of citizenship, why confine the operation of the limitation to male inhabitants? Women and children are, as we have seen, 'persons.' They are counted in the enumeration upon which the apportionment is to be made, but if they were necessarily voters because of their citizenship unless clearly excluded, why inflict the penalty for the exclusion of males alone? Clearly, no such form of words would have been selected to express the idea here indicated if suffrage was the absolute right of all citizens." The justices had already made plain that women were citizens, members of the nation, part of the "political community," the "people of the United States." Quite simply, suffrage was not inherent in citizenship. Perhaps the court would have arrived at this decision without having the "male" sentence in the amendment to rely upon—it had abundant evidence to support its ruling that women had always been considered members of the political community and had never been—except briefly in New Jersey—allowed to vote, but, given that the suit was filed on the basis of the Fourteenth Amendment's privileges and immunities guarantee, the "male" provision certainly helped seal the deal.[50]

---

and Suffrage: The Emergence of an Independent Women's Movement in America, 1848–1869 (Ithaca, N.Y., 1978); and Dudden, *Fighting Chance.*

50. Minor v. Happersett, 88 U.S. (21 Wall.) 162, 174–175, 165–166 (1875); Graber, "Constructing Constitutional Politics," 76; Akhil Reed Amar, *America's Constitution: A Biography* (New York, 2005), 395; Benedict, *Compromise of Principle,* 216. For this phase of Reconstruction more generally, see Benedict and Foner, *Reconstruction.* The Supreme Court ruled in *Richardson v. Ramirez* that "the exclusion of felons from the vote has an affirmative sanction in § 2 of the Fourteenth Amendment"; see Richardson v. Ramirez, 418 U.S. 24, 54 (1974). Because disfranchised felons are counted in the basis for apportionment of both congressional and state legislative districts, several rural regions with large prison popula-

That second sentence in the second section, the "male" clause, was just a crutch to help white men craft a solution to the problem of slavery. If, before the Civil War, women had been used to help shore up slavery, in the Fourteenth Amendment, they were used to help dismantle it. But, until the Fourteenth Amendment, they were ghosts, disembodied spirits, and discussions about them had very little practical bearing, one way or the other. Even when they came up in the debates over the Fourteenth Amendment, no one in Congress really wanted to talk about them; they were a distraction. Conservatives used them to goad the Radical Republicans; Radicals feared that they would get in the way of their primary goal, to protect the Union and to protect the freed people. That second sentence is—I would venture to say—as close to a throwaway as any line in the Constitution. But once it was there, it has had an impact, on real women, and their rights.

So this is what happened to the Three-Fifths Clause: the Fourteenth Amendment put a nail in its coffin, but the expansive notion of citizenship that had been embedded in it lived on, now made national, near universal, and explicit, along with an even more capacious notion of representation. But the limitations lived on, too, or rather took new forms, authorized by the circumlocutions of the second sentence of the second section. And it is in this space, between expansive and capacious notions of citizenship and the backward pull of history and custom, written in circumlocutions that mask the operations of power, that American history continues to be made.

---

tions, in Michigan and Pennsylvania, for example, have more representation than they would otherwise have. See Heather Ann Thompson, "How Prisons Change the Balance of Power in America," *The Atlantic*, Oct. 7, 2013, accessed Aug. 31, 2016, http://www.theatlantic.com/national/archive/2013/10/how-prisons-change-the-balance-of-power-in-america/280341/. Thompson discusses the impact of *Richardson v. Ramirez* more generally, citing, for example, one estimate that more than 15 percent of the African American population may be disfranchised. For nineteenth-century views on rights and citizenship, see Cott, "Marriage and Women's Citizenship," 1446.

The Three-Fifths Clause and the Origins of Sectionalism

How early can we find the origins of American sectionalism? Some historians have traced them to the founding of the colonies, created for different purposes by different sorts of people in different regions with different climates. Yet, by definition, there could not be sections until there was a nation, and so, if we want to trace the origins of American sectionalism back to their starting place, we should begin with the Continental Congress. Certainly, by the time the Constitution was written, a little more than a decade later, American leaders had developed a language of sectionalism. James Madison's comments at the Federal Convention of 1787 are well known: "He contended that the States were divided into different interests not by their difference of size, but by other circumstances; the most material of which resulted partly from climate, but principally from [the effect of] their having or not having slaves. These two causes concurred in forming the great division of interests in the U. States. It did not lie between the large and small States: it lay between the Northern and Southern."[1]

Madison's account of sectional difference is so clear and put forth so self-confidently that it is tempting to conclude that he was describing what everyone could see—a simple statement of fact. Hence, sectional difference came into being with the nation, and there never existed a time in the nation's history before there was a profound and obvious difference between the North and South.

Yet, if we place Madison's observation about sectionalism in its context—a high-stakes argument in the Constitutional Convention about the basis for representation in the new nation, which had been preceded by another argument in Congress about the basis for apportioning the costs of the Revolution—we can see that this early formulation of sectionalism was, as much

This essay was originally published as Jan Lewis, "'The Three-Fifths Clause and the Origins of Sectionalism," in Paul Finkelman and Donald R. Kennon, eds., *Congress and the Emergence of Sectionalism: From the Missouri Compromise to the Age of Jackson* (Athens, Ohio, 2008), 19–46.

1. Max Farrand, ed., *The Records of the Federal Convention of 1787*, 4 vols. (1911; rpt. New Haven, Conn., 1966), I, 486. For historians tracing the roots of sectionalism to the founding of the colonies, see, in particular, David Hackett Fischer, *Albion's Seed: Four British Folkways in America* (New York, 1989).

as anything, a political tactic, more a means to an end than a simple statement of fact. To put it another way, the discussions of sectional difference in the Continental Congress and the Federal Convention were not so much descriptions of reality as carefully calculated attempts to achieve particular political ends. This is not to suggest that Madison *created* sectional difference, or even the idea of sectionalism—that would be preposterous—but rather that he used the idea of fundamental sectional difference as a political tool, in the process giving those sectional differences a legitimacy that they would not have otherwise had.

We can see how this process worked if we focus on those moments in the founding—at the Continental Congress, its successor Confederation Congress, and in the Constitutional Convention—when the delegates discussed sections in the kind of terms that Madison used: a "great division of interests" based upon whether they had slaves or not. These are the moments when slavery made its way into the discussion. It should be noted that no one—or almost no one—in Congress or at the convention really wanted to discuss slavery. In each case, the delegates had what seemed to them more pressing questions—declaring independence, fighting and winning the Revolution, and creating a new national government. If any message emerges from the discussions in Congress from 1774 on, it is that the delegates hoped that slavery would go away. In 1774, Congress agreed, without leaving any record of a discussion, to discontinue the slave trade. (This was part of a set of resolutions that cut off imports from Britain.)[2]

2. Worthington C. Ford et al., eds., *Journals of the Continental Congress, 1774–1789*, 34 vols. (Washington, D.C., 1904–1937), I, 77; Donald L. Robinson, *Slavery in the Structure of American Politics, 1765–1820* (New York, 1971), 79. Why the separate paragraph on slaves? The first of the resolutions declared that the signatories would "not import" from Britain "any goods, wares, or merchandise whatsoever." The second resolution specified that neither would they "import nor purchase, any slave imported. . . . We will wholly discontinue the slave trade" (Ford et al., eds., *Journals of the Continental Congress*, I, 76–77). Robinson suggests that, since all trade was to be suspended anyway, why not gain a moral advantage by singling out slaves?: "It would be a mistake to assume that these agreements to suspend the slave trade represent the triumph of moral principle over desire and interest" (*Slavery in the Structure of American Politics*, 79). Yet simply to ask whether slaves were comprehended in the phrase "any goods, wares, or merchandise," as the delegates must have done, was to confront troubling questions about the nature of slavery. By giving slaves their own clause, the delegates recognized, if subtly, the anomalous nature of property in slaves. See also William W. Freehling, "The Founding Fathers and Slavery," *American Historical Review*, LXXVII (1972), 81–93. Although Freehling does not mention this particular action, he argues that the founding fathers engaged in a strategy of "attack[ing] slavery where it was the weakest, thereby driving the institution south and vitiating its capacity to survive" (86). The slave trade represented one of the institution's weakest points.

Two years later, when Thomas Jefferson tried to insert into the Declaration of Independence a paragraph condemning George III for carrying on the slave trade, Congress removed it. Jefferson later explained that the clause was deleted to placate South Carolina and Georgia, "who had never attempted to restrain the importation of slaves, and who in the contrary still wished to continue it." He speculated, too, that "our Northern brethren . . . felt a little tender" on the topic, given their prominent role as slave traders.[3]

Congress, then, was willing to curtail the slave trade but not to condemn it. These are the signs of discomfort, suggestions that the collective hope was simply to keep the problem out of sight. Given this context, it is hard to imagine that Congress—or the Constitutional Convention—would have discussed slavery qua slavery unless it was absolutely necessary. That, in fact, became the case once the issue of apportioning expenses among the states came up—in shorthand, taxation. Congress wrangled with this issue for several years. Each of these discussions was complicated. Not only was this the first time that representatives from all of the states had met together, but most of the delegates were trying out their ideas as they went along. Think of a multiplayer card game, in which each player makes his bids and tries to play his hand without yet knowing the rules of the game. Rather than take you through all the moves—which would be dizzying—we will focus on a few moments, snapshots rather than streaming video.

Our first moment: in Congress, 1775, Benjamin Franklin offers a preliminary draft of articles of confederation to the Continental Congress. He suggests basing both representation and apportionment of expenses upon the "Number of Male Polls between 16 and 60 Years of Age." What might appear an innocuous formula was Franklin's awkward—and ultimately unsuccessful—attempt to forge a compromise between North and South. Representatives from the big states repeatedly argued for proportional representation on democratic and self-serving grounds—and each time went down to defeat, but not before they had had an opportunity to air their democratic theories. As Franklin knew, the small states would never countenance proportional

3. "Notes of Proceedings in the Continental Congress," [7 June–1 August 1776], in Julian P. Boyd et al., eds., *The Papers of Thomas Jefferson,* 43 vols. (Princeton, N.J., 1950–), I, 314–315. Some years later, John Adams partially verified Jefferson's account, telling Timothy Pickering, "I was delighted with [the Declaration's] high tone and the flights of oratory with which it abounded, especially that concerning negro slavery, which, though I knew his Southern brethren would never suffer to pass in Congress, I certainly never would oppose." He described the deleted paragraph as "a vehement philippic against slavery" (Adams to Pickering, Aug. 22, 1822, in Edmund C. Burnett, ed., *Letters of Members of the Continental Congress,* 8 vols. [Washington, D.C., 1921–1936], I, 515n–516).

representation. Hence, the only part of his proposal that stood a chance was the suggestion to apportion assessments on the basis of adult male taxables, not female ones. This formulation actually represented something of a concession to the South. In the colonies, poll taxes were typically levied on adult men, but, in the South, they also were assessed on black women as members of the labor force. In a pattern that would become familiar, an antislavery northerner from a big state, Franklin, offered a concession to the South. This proposal and, indeed, the attempt to forge articles of confederation went nowhere, however; the delegates had more pressing matters at hand.[4]

Our next moment: in 1776, a week after the Declaration of Independence has been signed, John Dickinson presents his draft of articles of confederation, with an array of concessions to the various interests. For the slave states, each state's quota of troops was to be based on the white population only. Congress readily agreed. Yet Dickinson's formulas for representation and allocation of expenses differed from Franklin's. In Dickinson's proposal, each state received one vote, while expenses were allocated on the basis of the total population, including slaves. Samuel Chase, from the slave state of Maryland, objected immediately to the counting of slaves in the basis for taxing the states. His logic was far too convoluted to recapitulate here.[5]

John Adams quickly steered the discussion back on track, in the process laying out what would become the default northern position, which was that "numbers of people"—population—was just an "index of wealth" and that slaves should be counted because, like free laborers, they contribute to the state's wealth. Adams also moved the discussion onto the terrain of political economy, suggesting that slaves were just as productive as free laborers. Hence, when Virginia's Benjamin Harrison offered a compromise—"two slaves should be counted as one freeman"—he justified it by explaining "that slaves did not do as much work as freemen, and doubted if two effected more than one."[6]

4. Ford et al., eds., *Journals of the Continental Congress,* II, 195–197; Robinson, *Slavery in the Structure of American Politics,* 488n.

5. Ford et al., eds., *Journals of the Continental Congress,* V, 546–556; Jonathan Elliot, ed., *The Debates in the Several State Conventions on the Adoption of the Federal Constitution in 1787,* 5 vols. (1888; rpt. New York, 1968), I, 70–71. See also "The Virginia Constitution," [June 1776]," in Boyd, et al., *Papers of Thomas Jefferson,* I, 330–331. The draft articles were presented on July 12, 1776, and Congress began debating them on July 30.

6. Elliot, ed., *Debates in the Several State Conventions,* I, 71–72. Adams wrote in his diary that "Chace [*sic*] is violent and boisterous. . . . He is tedious upon frivolous points" (L. H. Butterfield et al., eds., *Diary and Autobiography of John Adams,* 4 vols. [Cambridge, Mass., 1961], II, 172).

Once Adams shifted the discussion, each section took a position that one may think counterintuitive: northerners insisted that slave and free labor were equally productive, while southerners claimed that slave labor was less productive than free. Self-serving though it was, the southern argument rested on good authority: the world's best political economists also thought that slave labor was comparatively unproductive—and hence on the road to extinction. (James Oakes has recently labeled this the "bourgeois critique of slavery.") Thus, by arguing that slave labor was less productive than free, southern delegates not only justified lower assessments for their states, but they also made themselves appear almost as abolitionists. Slavery, they implied, would be its own undoing. South Carolina's Edward Rutledge, for example, said that he would "be happy to get rid of the idea of slavery. The slaves do not signify property; the old and young cannot work." Similarly, North Carolina's William Hooper insisted, "I wish to see the day that slaves are not necessary." He thought free labor at least four times as valuable as slave.[7]

Let us skip ahead to another moment, 1783, when this question was revisited. In 1777, the delegates had decided that assessments should be based upon the value of land.[8] When it became clear that a new method of levying assessments was needed, nationalists in Congress returned immedi-

7. James Oakes, "The Peculiar Fate of the Bourgeois Critique of Slavery," in Winthrop D. Jordan, ed., *Slavery and the American South* (Jackson, Miss., 2003), 29–48; Ford et al., eds., *Journals of the Continental Congress,* VI, 1080. Oakes notes that, until about 1820, the best minds in the South believed that slave labor was inferior to free and slave labor was on its way to extinction.

8. There were simply too many disagreements among the delegates to make possible a compromise on how to count slaves. Some thought land a better index of wealth. See, for example, Cornelius Harnett to [Richard Caswell], Oct. 10, 1777, in Burnett, ed., *Letters of Members of the Continental Congress,* II, 514, Harnett to William Wilkinson, Nov. 30, 1777, 578; and Richard Henry Lee to Roger Sherman, Nov. 24, 1777, in Paul H. Smith, ed., *Letters of Delegates to Congress, 1774–1789,* 26 vols. (Washington, D.C., 1976–2000), VIII, 320. As a rule, southerners preferred to assess land, and northerners population, but some northern delegates were unwilling at this point to give the South a discount for their slaves. Likewise, some northerners had difficulty comprehending the argument that the South was making about the nature of slavery itself. As Nathaniel Folsom of New Hampshire wrote to the president of that state, "In the first place it appears to me that one third part of the welth [*sic*] of the Southern States which consists in negroes, is entirely left out and no Notice taken of them, in determining their ability to pay taxes, notwithstanding it is by them that they procure their wealth" (Folsom to Meshech Weare, Nov. 21, 1777, ibid., 299). He was objecting to Article VIII, which assessed land, the proxy the delegates had decided upon for wealth, but the same objection could be applied to population: the South had a most peculiar system in which labor was also property, and the instruments of southern wealth were in themselves wealth. Northerners and southerners both struggled for analogies. Were slaves like horses or cattle? Like white dependent laborers? They were neither; slavery was like nothing else.

ately to the idea of taxing population. The question now was how to count slaves. In a letter to Congress, Robert Morris, the superintendent of finance, suggested a one-dollar tax on "all freemen, and all male slaves between 16 and 60," excepting those who were in the army or unfit for service. Like Franklin's proposal in 1775, which it resembled, Morris's plan would have exempted female slaves, normally subject to poll taxes in the South. Connecticut's Oliver Wolcott proposed something similar on the floor of Congress. He thought that the number of inhabitants should be the "rule," but, in a bow to the political economy argument, he "admit[ted] the difference between freemen and blacks; and suggest[ed] a compromise by including in the numeration such blacks only as were within 16 and 60 years." Like Morris, he was offering the South a discount for slaves, implicitly because he agreed that they were less productive than free people or less able to contribute to the general welfare.[9]

The only question was how great the South's discount should be. As Madison explained to Jefferson in early March 1783, "A recommendation is to be included for substituting numbers in place of the value of land as the rule of apportionment. In this all the States are interested if proper deductions be made from the number of Slaves." Congress's *Report on Public Credit* incorporated a variant on Wolcott's proposal, excluding all those "who are bound to servitude for life according to the laws of the State to which they belong, other than such as may be between the ages of [ ]"—and the space was left blank, for Congress to fill in later. Congress had begun to wrestle with the proper formula in 1775, when Harrison suggested counting two slaves for every free person. Now it was struggling with the way to say

9. "Notes on Debates," Jan. 28, 1783, in William T. Hutchinson et al., eds., *The Papers of James Madison,* 17 vols. (Chicago, 1962–1991), VI, 153n, "Notes on Debates," Feb. 11, 1783, 215. In their earliest discussions, the delegates seemed to be looking for a formula that would use age as the basis for providing a discount for slaves. North Carolina's delegates reported home about a recommendation of a "Poll Tax of half a Dollar on all male Slaves from 16 to 60 and all free men from 16 to 21 and a Dollar on all free men from 21 to 60 except those in the foederal army etc." (North Carolina delegates to Alexander Martin, Oct. 22, 1782, in Smith, ed., *Letters of Delegates to Congress,* XIX, 290). Half a year later, North Carolina's delegates reported a new proposal "to exclude all Slaves under 16 Years, which would be rating two slaves for one free men [*sic*]" (North Carolina delegates to Martin, Mar. 24, 1783, ibid., XX, 91). Although there seemed to be a general willingness to give the South some consideration for its supposedly less productive slave population, the basis for the judgment of lower productivity was not entirely clear. Was it that younger and older slaves were less productive than whites of the same age? Or was it that black workers of the same age were less productive than their white counterparts? The discussion implicitly moved from the first proposition to the second.

slave without using the word.[10] Within a few weeks, Congress had found, for the moment, a formula and a more concise way to avoid saying *slave:* assessments should be levied "in proportion to the whole number of free inhabitants and one half of the number of all other inhabitants of every age sex and condition except Indians not paying Taxes in each State."[11]

Now that a formula and terminology—and the need to arrive at some compromise—were on the floor, the debate could begin in earnest. Let us follow the debate, as Madison rendered it in a kind of shorthand. The committee had suggested "that two blacks be rated as one freeman. Mr. Wolcot [Oliver Wolcott, Connecticut] was for rating them as 4 to 3. Mr. Carrol [Charles Carroll, Maryland] was for rating them as 4 to 1." North and South were bickering over the size of the slavery discount. "Mr. Williamson [Hugh Williamson, North Carolina] sd. he was principled agst. slavery; and that he thought slaves an incumbrance to Society instead of increasing its ability to pay taxes." Here, once again, was the South's strategic use of political economy: slavery is less productive than free labor; we hate slavery; we should not have to pay as much because we have slaves. Stephen Higginson, from Massachusetts, responded, not with an argument, but with a return to Wolcott's initial bid—"4 to 3." South Carolina's John Rutledge offered a compromise—"2 to 1, but he sincerely thought 3 to 1 would be a juster proportion." Then Samuel Holten and Samuel Osgood, both from Massachusetts, implicitly rejected it, instead reiterating Wolcott's four to three.[12]

It appeared that the North, having offered the South a small discount, was unwilling to yield any more. Madison then "said that in order to give a proof of the sincerity of his professions of liberality he wd. propose that

10. "Memorandum on a Revenue Plan," [Mar. 6, 1783], in Hutchinson et al., eds., *Papers of James Madison,* VI, 310–311, "Report on Public Credit," [Mar. 6, 1783], 313–314. The text of Congress's *Report on Public Credit* comes from Madison's notes. He had originally written and then crossed out the two words "deemed slaves" and penned in the much more awkward locution, the obvious forerunner of the Three-Fifths Clause's "all other persons" (ibid., 316n).

11. "Amendment to Report on Restoring Public Credit," [Mar. 28, 1783], ibid., VI, 406. Note also that Madison had originally written "free white" and then crossed out "white," reflecting a change made in the debates in Congress (ibid., 407n). It is worth observing that the terms *white* and *free* were generally used interchangeably, as were the terms *slave* and *black,* but that once the discussion moved from debates to formal resolutions, the words *slave, white,* and *black* generally disappeared.

12. "Notes on Debates," Mar. 28, 1783, in Hutchinson et al., eds., *Papers of James Madison,* VI, 407. For the political context of the debate, see Jack N. Rakove, *The Beginnings of National Politics: An Interpretive History of the Continental Congress* (New York, 1979), esp. 297–329.

Slaves should be rated as 5 to 3." John Rutledge, another southerner, immediately seconded this motion, and then Pennsylvania's James Wilson said that he would "sacrifice his opinion to this compromise." The haggling was over; the compromise had been struck—as a measure of wealth, five enslaved black workers were the equivalent of three free white ones.[13]

In 1783, everyone seemed to agree that slave labor was less productive than free labor. As Madison explained in his summary of the debate, even northerners agreed that slaves' "industry and ingenuity were below those of freemen." But northerners also insisted that it cost less to feed and clothe slaves. Moreover, the South had the additional advantage of a better climate. Southerners replied that—and here their debt to the bourgeois critique of slavery is particularly clear—"having no interest in their labor," slaves "did as little as possible, and omitted every exertion of thought requisite to facilitate and expedite it." Northerners and southerners now had agreed that slave labor was less productive than free; the only argument was about how much less. There was no pretense that Congress had accurately assessed the relative value of free and slave labor. As Congress explained to the states when asking them to ratify this amendment to the original articles: "The only material difficulty which attended [the new rule] in the deliberations in Congress, was to fix the proper difference between the labor and industry of free inhabitants, and of all other inhabitants. The ratio ultimately agreed on was the effect of mutual concessions, and if it should be supposed not to correspond precisely with the fact, no doubt ought to be entertained that an equal spirit of accommodation among the several Legislatures, will prevail against little inequalities which may be calculated on one side or on the other."[14]

Although the states never ratified this amendment, Congress had demonstrated that it was able to compromise on the issue of slavery. The delegates agreed that slave labor was less productive than free and hence that the South deserved a discount. The North, it might appear, had won the moral point, and the South the practical one, but the compromise was more complicated than that. By persuading northerners to accept the proposition

13. "Notes on Debates," Mar. 28, 1783, in Hutchinson et al., eds., *Papers of James Madison,* VI, 408.

14. Ibid., 408, "Report on Address to the States by Congress," [Apr. 25, 1783], 492. Madison, Nathaniel Gorham (Massachusetts), and Alexander Hamilton (New York) wrote the report. See also James Madison to Edmund Randolph, Apr. 8, 1783: "The deduction of 2//5 was a compromise between the wide opinions and demands of the Southern and other States" (ibid., 440). Again, see also Oakes, "Peculiar Fate of the Bourgeois Critique of Slavery," in Jordan, ed., *Slavery and the American South,* 29–48.

that slave labor was less productive, southerners conceded that slavery was tainted. In a nation as bourgeois as the new United States, to state that slave labor was inferior, an "incumbrance," was quite a concession.[15]

Even though the South had gained important concessions on troop and tax quotas, the North thought it had struck a fair deal. Not only had the fledgling Union been preserved—always the first priority—but slavery itself also seemed on the road to extinction. Northerners believed that their concessions to the South, accommodating the peculiar institution of slavery, would thus turn out to be temporary expedients, necessary for holding the new nation together. This is why those early concessions that the South made on the slave trade were so important. Not only had the South agreed to discontinue importing slaves, at least for the time being, but also a southern slaveholder had tried to insert into the Declaration of Independence a condemnation of the slave trade so fiery that even northern delegates winced. Now that southerners were telling them that slave labor was so inefficient that two slaves could barely do the labor of one free man, who could fault northerners for believing that slavery would die a quiet death?

Some northerners still thought, in spite of what southern delegates told them, that slavery was an enormously profitable institution. And, of course, they were right. But the southerners sold them a dream, a fantasy that freed them from the contradictions of slavery and freedom and people as property. In the fall of 1783, Rhode Island delegates William Ellery and David Howell reported back to Governor William Greene about the proposed change in Article VIII. They had doubts about its fairness. "If numbers are to be the rule ought not all the blacks in the Southern States to be taken into the census? The nett [*sic*] produce of the labour of a black man in those States is, at least, double to that of a common white labourer in the eastern States." They were still not convinced that slave labor was inferior to free, but, by 1785, Howell had changed his mind. He still thought that all of the slaves should have been counted, but he recognized that some compromise had been necessary. More important, history itself would eventually make the point moot. "An attention to the actual Situation and population of the Southern States where the blacks are most numerous will suggest a probability that in time the proposed rule of apportionment will become less objectionable." He

15. It should be noted that slavery was, in fact, enormously profitable and that the South at the time was the wealthiest section of the new nation. On this point, see Oakes, "Peculiar Fate of the Bourgeois Critique of Slavery," in Jordan, ed., *Slavery and the American South*, 29–48.

then gave his governor a lesson in geography and political economy as he now understood them. "After you leave the Sea co[a]st" of the southern states "and pass on westward . . . , the lands are cultivated by white people, whose method of life and manners are similar to the middle and northern States. . . . So that the number of blacks compared with the whites even in those States will probably diminish in the future. . . . And even the ratio of the States, in which the blacks are numerous . . . will gradually diminish as the tide of population rolls westward and new States arise peopled from Europe where the Slavery of the blacks is unknown, or from the northern States where it is reprobated." Thus, Howell could confidently conclude, "On all these accounts the proposed rule . . . will probably in future approximate to justice." Greatly to their advantage, southerners had persuaded their northern brethren that slavery was a slowly dying institution, for that is what northerners wanted to believe. North and South shared a common fantasy, one that offered them an escape from the dilemma that slavery presented.[16]

Only four years later, many of the same men — Madison, Wilson, and Franklin as well as Alexander Hamilton and Nathaniel Gorham — were in Philadelphia as delegates to the Constitutional Convention. Once again, slavery was an issue, and it came up just as it had in the Continental Congress. The delegates were discussing something else and then, all of a sudden, there it was — slavery. That something else was representation.

On Monday, June 11, the delegates were debating the provision of the Virginia Plan, introduced two weeks earlier, which established the basis for suffrage in the proposed Congress. In fact, the Virginia Plan had dodged this issue, saying that representation in both houses should be proportional — but giving the delegates a choice about how the representatives and senators were to be proportioned: whether by "quotas of contribution, or [by] the number of free inhabitants." Clearly, this formulation was an allusion to the earlier discussions in the Continental Congress, and it would have signaled something specific to the delegates who were familiar with what had transpired there. "Quotas of contribution" was a synonym for wealth that came with its own ready-made formula for measurement: all of the free people (except Indians) and three-fifths of the slaves.[17]

16. Rhode Island delegates to William Greene, Sept. 8, 1783, in Smith, ed., *Letters of Delegates to Congress,* XX, 642, David Howell to William Greene, Aug. 23, 1785, XXII, 587.

17. Farrand, ed., *Records of the Federal Convention,* I, 20.

When the delegates turned to this question, they immediately addressed the two issues that had been combined in this clause of the Virginia Plan: whether representation in both houses should be proportional, and, if the representation in either or both houses was to be proportional, how were those proportions to be determined? These two issues were almost inextricably connected in the minds of the framers, and they raised questions about both state and regional interests as well as underlying political philosophy.

Connecticut's Roger Sherman began the day's discussion by proposing that representatives to the lower house should be apportioned "according to the respective numbers of free inhabitants," while, in the second branch, each state should have one vote. Sherman would have had one house highly undemocratic, just as Congress had been, and the other house seemingly quite democratic but clearly favoring the North by counting only free persons. Sherman offered a representation of states and of persons, with no allowances made for slavery at all. In 1777, when Congress was discussing the apportionment of state quotas, Sherman had told Virginia's Richard Henry Lee that, "as to the Negros, [*sic*] I Should be willing to do what appears equitable," and he suggested a formula for excluding some slaves from the count. A decade later, we see the realpolitik of the convention at work. We should regard Sherman's proposal as an opening bid in what he knew would be a lengthy negotiation. He had established the principle—which he would ultimately gain—of equal representation for the states in the upper house, and he signaled that the South could expect no automatic consideration from the North for its peculiar institution. This was a proposal designed to serve—and balance—the interests of the small states and the large free ones.[18]

South Carolina's John Rutledge and Pierce Butler immediately countered that representatives in the lower house should be apportioned, not on the basis of the number of free inhabitants, but on the basis of quotas of contribution. Sherman had taken up one of the options offered by the Virginia Plan, and the South Carolinians were taking up the other. They knew, even if they did not state so explicitly, that "quotas of contribution" came, courtesy

18. Ibid., I, 196; Lee to Sherman, Nov. 24, 1777, in Smith, ed., *Letters of Delegates to Congress,* VIII, 320–321n. On the point of equal representation for the states, see Jack N. Rakove, *Original Meanings: Politics and Ideas in the Making of the Constitution* (New York, 1996), 61, 68. The equal representation of the states in the Senate is usually regarded as a triumph of the small states. As Rakove notes, however, it also proved a boon to the slave states, which retained control of the Senate long after the North's more rapidly expanding population gave the free states control of the House (93).

of the Congress, with a ready-made formula: all the free people plus three-fifths of the slaves. Still, there is something odd about this provision in the Virginia Plan that the South Carolinians took up. The convention had not yet discussed how or whether the states should be assessed, let alone made any decisions on this subject. And, although everyone in the room knew the congressional formula for calculating "quotas of contribution," the South Carolinians did not mention that it was based upon population, including a proportion of slaves. Instead, Butler explained that "quotas of contribution" were a proxy for wealth. "Money was power," he asserted, and hence, "the States ought to have weight in the Govt.—in proportion to their power." In terms of political theory, this proposal was really quite reactionary. No one in Congress had ever suggested that wealth per se should be represented, and no one had ever suggested previously that slaves be included in the basis for calculating representatives.[19]

To be sure, in both Britain and America suffrage had long been associated with the ownership of property, and it was an axiom of classical political thought that officeholders should be men of property and standing who would give government stability. But those Americans who sought representation for wealth usually focused upon the Senate. Only four days earlier, Dickinson had said that he hoped it would "consist of the most distinguished characters, distinguished for their rank in life and their weight of property, and bearing as strong a likeness to the British House of Lords as possible." Similarly, Madison believed that "the Senate ought to come from, and represent, the Wealth of the nation." But now the South Carolinians were arguing that not only the Senate but the House, too, should represent wealth and that it should do so not by filtering out distinguished characters to hold office or even by restricting suffrage to property holders but by giving the wealthier states more representatives.[20]

In Congress, the question had been whether states were to be represented, or people. Franklin, Wilson, and Adams, representing the populous states of Pennsylvania and Massachusetts, had advocated proportional representation on democratic and nationalist grounds, while representatives from small

19. Farrand, ed., *Records of the Federal Convention,* I, 196.

20. Ibid., I, 150, 158. See also Gordon S. Wood, *The Creation of the American Republic, 1776–1787* (Williamsburg, Va., and Chapel Hill, N.C., 1969), 554–555. For theories of representation at the time, see also J. R. Pole, *Political Representation in England and the Origins of the American Republic* (Berkeley, Calif., 1966); John Phillip Reid, *The Concept of Representation in the Age of the American Revolution* (Chicago, 1989); and Rakove, *Original Meanings.*

states, such as New Jersey's John Witherspoon and Rhode Island's Stephen Hopkins, warned that the confederation would fall apart unless the small states were guaranteed equal representation. The closest anyone came to arguing that representation should be based upon wealth was when Franklin observed sardonically that, "if we vote equally we ought to pay equally: but the smaller states will hardly purchase the privilege at this price." Indeed, Wilson had made clear a distinction that the South Carolinians were now, in 1787, fast eroding: "Taxation should be in proportion to wealth, but that representation should accord with the number of freemen." The point bears repeating: no one in Congress had ever suggested that wealth per se should be represented, and, certainly, no one had ever suggested that slaves be included in the basis for calculating representatives.[21]

With the South Carolinians' proposal, the Constitutional Convention now had before it more theories—and more houses of Congress—than it could deal with at one time. Several members suggested that the discussion focus for the moment only on the House of Representatives, where representation should be "according to some equitable ratio of representation." At this point, some of the northern delegates seemed willing to consider the South Carolinians' suggestion that representation should be based upon wealth. It is worth noting that they seemed to think that they were talking about how much each state would contribute to the national coffers rather than a measure of population that might include slaves. This was too much for Franklin, who began in a conciliatory but disingenuous way by noting that he had originally thought that each state should have the same number of representatives but that he now believed in proportional representation: "The number of Representatives should bear some proportion to the number of the Represented: and that the decisions shd. be by the majority of members, not the majority of States." After all, "The Interest of a State is made up of the interests of its individual members." In fact, Franklin had given much the same speech in 1776, and then, as now, it served two purposes: a statement of democratic principles and a brief for the large states.[22]

It was at just this moment that Pennsylvania's Wilson suggested that representation in the lower house should be based upon an "equitable ratio of representation . . . in proportion to the whole number of white and other free Citizens and inhabitants of every age sex and condition including those

21. Ford et al., eds., *Journals of the Continental Congress,* VI, 1102–1106.

22. Farrand, ed., *Records of the Federal Convention,* I, 196–199, 204–205, 207–208. See also Ford et al., eds., *Journals of the Continental Congress,* VI, 1102–1103.

bound to servitude for a term of years and three fifths of all other persons not comprehended in the foregoing description, except Indians not paying taxes."[23]

Wilson had just proposed what has come to be called the Three-Fifths Compromise; yet a very odd and even incongruous compromise it was. True, it was an attempt to reconcile Sherman's suggestion that representation in the lower house be based upon free population and the South Carolinians' that it be based upon wealth. Wilson was merely inserting the formula for calculating wealth that had been adopted four years earlier by the Continental Congress; conveniently, it happened to be a formula also for counting persons. On the face of it, this was a nice compromise—but compromise usually comes late in the game, when the players are exhausted and everyone knows that something must be surrendered. Why did Wilson's proffer come so early? The delegates had been meeting in earnest for only two weeks, and this part of the discussion—about how to apportion representation in the House—had been going on for less than a day. Thus far, only six other men had spoken.

Why did Wilson give so much away? The seeming compromise was barely a compromise at all. The South Carolinians had asked for "quotas of contribution," and Wilson helpfully offered them the formula by which "quotas of contribution" should be calculated. They could not reasonably have dreamed of more.[24]

And why did Wilson toss slavery, already the new nation's apple of discord, into the gathering? It has sometimes been argued that compromise on the issue of slavery was necessary in order to create the Union—that South Carolina and Georgia would not have joined had they not gained certain concessions. Indeed, later in the summer, the delegates from the Deep South would make their threats. But they had not made them yet, nor had any delegates, at least in public, said the first thing about slavery. The word had not yet even been mentioned. Not only was Wilson giving the South Carolinians just what they had asked for, but he was also signaling to them that they could now, as they had in Congress, make demands on the basis of slavery.[25]

23. Farrand, ed., *Records of the Federal Convention,* I, 201.

24. Indeed, Charles Cotesworth Pinckney later told the South Carolina House of Representatives, "We thus obtained a representation for our property; and I confess I did not expect that we had conceded too much to the Eastern States, when they allowed us a representation for a species of property which they have not among them" (Elliot, ed., *Debates in the Several State Conventions,* IV, 283).

25. See, for example, William W. Freehling, *The Road to Disunion,* I, *Secessionists at Bay, 1776–1854* (New York, 1990), 584n; Freehling, "Founding Fathers and Slavery," *Ameri-*

Wilson, an ardent nationalist and a shrewd politician, was playing a dangerous—but ultimately successful—game. The compromise he laid down was one of those upon which, when all was said and done three months later, the Constitution itself hinged. By throwing slavery into the discussion and by signaling to South Carolina and Georgia that here was a northerner who was willing to make concessions even before they asked for them, he altered the calculus of those discussions. What had, until that moment, been a conflict between the small and the large states now became one also between states that were slave and those that were substantially free. It is in this context that we can come to understand Madison's claim that the principal division was, not between the large states and the small, but between the slave states and the free. In fact, on June 11, when Wilson introduced what would become the Three-Fifths Clause, the fault line ran between the big and small states, not along the Mason-Dixon line; by throwing slavery into the equation, however, he created a new divide, one that Madison was happy almost three weeks later to invoke. Creating a second fault line complicated the politics of the Constitutional Convention and made it easier for big-state nationalists to secure their objectives.

As an opponent of slavery, Wilson did not want to give any encouragement to the institution; but, as a nationalist and a veteran of the Continental and Confederation Congresses, he considered the small states—which had threatened to dissolve the confederation unless they had an equal vote—as a greater menace to the new nation than the slave states. When Sherman had proposed that each state should have one vote in the Senate, he had justified his proposal in terms that must have made Wilson fear that the small states would be just as obstructionist in the new national government as they had been under Congress.[26] Wilson calculated that he could use his pro-

---

can Historical Review, LXXVII (1972), 81–93; Lance Banning, *The Sacred Fire of Liberty: James Madison and the Founding of the Federal Republic* (Ithaca, N.Y., 1995), 459–460n; Don E. Fehrenbacher, *The Dred Scott Case: Its Significance in American Law and Politics* (New York, 1978), 20–27; and Howard A. Ohline, "Republicanism and Slavery: Origins of the Three-Fifths Clause in the United States Constitution," *William and Mary Quarterly,* 3d Ser., XXVIII (1971), 563–584.

26. Farrand, ed., *Records of the Federal Convention,* I, 196. Sherman offered a more elaborate and constitutionally grounded defense of the one-state, one-vote proposition than anyone had offered in Congress, where the threat to dissolve the confederation had been sufficient to win the point. His theory was a modification of British constitutional thought, which held that Parliament embodied the three orders of British society. To justify his proposal that each state should have one vote in the upper house, Sherman compared the states to the English nobility. Like the aristocracy, the "states would remain possessed of certain individual rights," which they ought to be able to protect, without being trampled by the

posal to build a coalition between the large states and the smaller ones of the Deep South. Counting three-fifths of the slave population would give the slave states a bonus, one that would make proportional representation more attractive to them by increasing their weight in Congress.[27] If this strategy were successful, the small states of the North would be isolated. Shortly after making his proposal, Wilson and Alexander Hamilton—another big-state nationalist—suggested that representation in the Senate as well as the House should be proportional to population. This was a clear signal to the small states of the North, just in case they had missed the earlier one, that the large states were on the offensive.[28]

---

larger states. "The House of Lords in England he observed had certain particular rights under the Constitution, and hence they have an equal vote with the House of Commons that they may be able to defend their rights." This was clearly a limited, indeed, an antiliberal notion of "individual rights" that defined them, not as the minority rights of individual citizens, but as the corporate interests of individual states. See ibid. What Sherman gave with one hand—a broad representation of persons, rather than property, in the lower house—he took away with the other—an upper-house check upon majority rule. Jack N. Rakove has argued that Madison's objective was to create an extended republic that would solve the problem that had been presented to national government by self-interested and obstructionist small states. Sherman was proposing the structure that could perpetuate just such obstructionism in the name of "individual rights." See Rakove, "Great Compromise: Ideas, Interest and the Politics of Constitution Making," *William and Mary Quarterly,* 3d Ser., XLIV (1987), 424–457.

27. For evidence that this was Wilson's conscious calculation, see Farrand, ed., *Records of the Federal Convention,* II, 10–11, in which Wilson voiced his fear that "the small States . . . may controul the Govt. as they have done in Congs."

28. Ibid., II, 202. As J. R. Pole has shown, Madison was thinking along similar lines. In April, before the convention had even begun, he explained to Edmund Randolph why he thought that proportional representation would win out: "The Northern States will be reconciled to it by the *actual* superiority of their populousness: the Southern by their *expected* superiority in this point" (James Madison to Edmund Randolph, Apr. 8, 1787, in Hutchinson et al., eds., *Papers of James Madison,* IX, 371, quoted in J. R. Pole, "The Emergence of the Majority Principle in the American Revolution," in Pole, *Paths to the American Past* [New York, 1979], 50). Of course, giving the southern states a bonus for their slave populations would make proportional representation all the more appealing to them. Drew R. McCoy has noted that "the southern delegates to the Philadelphia Convention . . . overwhelmingly [took] the large state position on the matter of proportional representation. That the delegates from Georgia, which actually had a quite small population, and North Carolina, which was middling in demographic size, would join Virginia (a bona fide large state) vividly confirms the power of southern expectations" (McCoy, "James Madison and Visions of American Nationality in the Confederation Period: A Regional Perspective," in Richard Beeman, Stephen Botein, and Edward C. Carter, II, eds., *Beyond Confederation: Origins of the Constitution and American National Identity* [Williamsburg, Va., and Chapel Hill, N.C., 1987], 246n). Garry Wills has suggested that the South's attendant bonus in the Electoral College was responsible for Thomas Jefferson's election in 1800 (Wills, *"Negro President": Jefferson and the Slave Power* [New York, 2003]). As Paul Finkelman has demonstrated,

Wilson justified his proposal not in pragmatic terms, however, but in the democratic ones that he and others had laid out at the Continental Congress more than a decade before and had reiterated in the Federal Convention. When he offered his proposal—I still hesitate to call it a compromise, as there was nothing yet to be compromised between North and South—he was repeating a point he himself had made two days earlier when he argued that representation should be based upon population: "As all authority was derived from the people, equal numbers of people ought to have an equal no. of representatives, and different numbers of people ought to have different numbers of representatives." The South Carolinians had asked for representation of wealth. Wilson was giving them what they asked for, but explaining it as the democratic representation of people.[29]

Wilson had just conflated two discussions that had taken place a few years earlier in the Continental Congress: how representatives should be apportioned and how taxes should be levied. Or, to be more precise, he had taken the ideas developed in one context—a discussion about taxation—and applied them in another—a discussion about representation. The three-fifths ratio was a compromise on taxation, not representation, and there the discussion turned on questions of political economy. The states had always accepted that their quotas of contribution should bear some relation to their wealth. When in 1783 they decided to use population as a proxy for wealth, the only argument had been over the productivity of slave labor. When Wilson proposed using the same formula for representation, he was at once altering the terms of the discussion and muddying them. He himself had trouble making sense out of what he had proposed. And, hence, the big debates about slavery came after the Three-Fifths Clause was proposed, not before.

For all its calculation and cunning, Wilson's proposal was also stunningly radical. With good reason, the Three-Fifths Clause has long been considered

---

when the convention decided that the executive should be chosen by an Electoral College whose composition would be based on each state's representation in Congress, it was consciously choosing to give the South extra representation for its slaves (Finkelman, "The Proslavery Origins of the Electoral College," *Cardozo Law Review,* XXIII [2002], 1145–1157). Yet, by June 11—rather early in the proceedings—Wilson, an important northern antislavery nationalist, had offered the South a significant inducement to agree to proportional representation: a bonus, allowing them to count 60 percent of their slaves. Moreover, by making the offer so early, he signaled a willingness to make other concessions on slavery.

29. Farrand, ed., *Records of the Federal Convention,* I, 179. Rakove notes another dimension to this fundamentally democratic principle: that new states should be brought into the Union on the same terms as the original states (Rakove, *Original Meanings,* 74).

an embarrassment, a blot on the Constitution, a source of national shame.[30] Yet, odious as the clause was, it was also, for the time, a radical statement about the nature of representation. As Jack N. Rakove has suggested, "It was ... the closest approximation in the Constitution to the principle of one person, one vote." Although, as several historians have shown, Revolutionary-era democrats were beginning to insist that persons, not property were the proper basis for representation, not until the Federal Constitution did any government in America base representation upon inhabitants rather than taxpayers or adult men. The nearest any government had come was with the Northwest Ordinance, which linked representation to the number of "free male inhabitants, of full age." Basing representation on population, then, was a significant democratic innovation.[31]

Wilson had grafted a formula for calculating wealth, one that enumerated human beings as property, onto an expansive theory of government—and in the process implied that slaves were at least partial members of the political community. As political theorists Benedict Anderson and Michael Walzer remind us, the political community is both imagined and bounded. Here we see the framers, led by Wilson, imagining the political community to include all white people, all free blacks, and all indentured servants, regardless of age or sex—and setting its boundaries by excluding 40 percent of the slaves and untaxed Indians.[32]

30. See William M. Wiecek, "The Witch at the Christening: Slavery and the Constitution's Origins," in Leonard W. Levy and Dennis J. Mahoney, eds., *The Framing and Ratification of the Constitution* (New York, 1987), 167–184; Paul Finkelman, "Slavery and the Constitutional Convention: Making a Covenant with Death," in Beeman, Botein, and Carter, eds., *Beyond Confederation*, 188–225; and Edward Countryman, *Americans: A Collision of Histories* (New York, 1996), 83–84. See also, for example, John Chester Miller, *The Wolf by the Ears: Thomas Jefferson and Slavery* (New York, 1977), 222–231; and James Oakes, "The Rhetoric of Reaction: Justifying a Proslavery Constitution" (paper presented to symposium on Bondage, Freedom, and the Constitution, Cardozo School of Law and Yeshiva University, New York, Feb. 19–20, 1995).

31. Rakove, *Original Meanings*, 74; "Northwest Ordinance," in Philip B. Kurland and Ralph Lerner, eds., *The Founders' Constitution*, 5 vols. (Chicago, 1987), I, 27; J. R. Pole, *Political Representation in England and the Origins of the American Republic* (1966; rpt. Berkeley, Calif., 1971), 204, 274–275; Rosemarie Zagarri, *The Politics of Size: Representation in the United States, 1776–1850* (Ithaca, N.Y., 1987), 39–42, 57–60; Peter S. Onuf, "The Origins and Early Development of State Legislatures," in Joel H. Silbey, ed., *Encyclopedia of the American Legislative System: Studies of the Principal Structures, Processes, and Policies of Congress and the State Legislatures Since the Colonial Era*, 3 vols. (New York, 1994), I, 175–194.

32. Benedict Anderson, *Imagined Communities: Reflections on the Origin and Spread of Nationalism* (1983; rpt. New York, 1991); Michael Walzer, *Spheres of Justice: A Defense of Pluralism and Equality* (New York, 1983), esp. 28–30.

The delegates to the Constitutional Convention understood immediately that this was the implication, indeed the intellectual underpinning, of Wilson's proposal. It was not Wilson's intent to insist that slaves were members of society or to make an issue out of slavery. Those historians who have argued that slavery was not the primary issue dividing the delegates are substantially right. Slavery was—and this point bears repeating—so divisive an issue that no one who seriously wanted to create a federal union would have brought it up had he been able to avoid it. But Wilson was a democrat who believed that representation should be based upon population, and, if he wanted to win that point, he was going to have to bring up slavery. First, there was the matter of realpolitik. As we have seen, Wilson—and like-minded big-state democrats—needed some way to outflank the small-state delegates who were already clamoring for one state, one vote, and insisting that "individual rights" pertained to states, not to persons. Second, to say that representation should be based upon population was necessarily to raise the issue of whether slaves should be counted as persons. In the context of the Federal Convention, democracy and slavery were thus inevitably and inextricably joined.

But democracy and slavery were also a contradiction, or so it seemed to the northern state delegates especially. No sooner had Wilson made his proposal than Elbridge Gerry of Massachusetts immediately asked, "Why then shd. the blacks, who were property in the South, be in the rule of representation more than the cattle and horses of the North?"[33] New Jersey's William Paterson later made a similar point, in the process offering a succinct definition of freedom: "He could regard negroes slaves in no light but as property. They are no free agents, have no personal liberty, no faculty of acquiring property, but on the contrary are themselves property, and like other property entirely at the will of the Master." The authors of the Constitution understood the theoretical implications of including slaves partially in the basis of representation; it meant that slaves were—in theory at least—to be represented in part by the new federal government. The first impulse of a number of northern delegates was to recoil from the incongruity of grafting a formula for calculating wealth onto an expansive definition of the polity. Ironically—or perhaps it is not so ironic, if one considers the interests that

33. Farrand, ed., *Records of the Federal Convention,* I, 201. For well-informed narratives of the proceedings in the Federal Convention, see Don E. Fehrenbacher, *The Slaveholding Republic: An Account of the United States Government's Relations to Slavery,* completed and edited by Ward M. McAfee (New York, 2001), 28–38; and Rakove, *Original Meanings,* 57–93.

were being advanced—northerners insisted that slaves should not be represented because they were property.[34]

The South Carolinians responded by insisting that it was wealth that was being represented, not persons; hence there was no inconsistency. "Property," John Rutledge said, "was certainly the principal object of Society," and Butler echoed that "property was the only just measure of representation. This was the great object of Governt." Pennsylvania's Gouverneur Morris objected, however, to the "incoherence" of the clause. If representation was to be based upon wealth, then the clause should say just that; and, if representation was to be based upon the number of inhabitants, then all the slaves should be counted. He asked the question in mid-July, and he asked it again in early August: "Upon what principle is it that the slaves shall be computed in the representation? Are they men? Then make them Citizens and let them vote. Are they property? Why then is no other property included?"[35]

Here was the intellectual problem presented by the Three-Fifths Clause, and, try as they might, its supporters could not wrest coherence out of the inconsistency of counting slaves as both inhabitants to be represented and a measure of wealth. Wilson admitted as much. He told the convention that he "did not well see on what principle the admission of blacks in the proportion of three fifths could be explained. Are they admitted as Citizens? Then why are they not admitted on an equality with White Citizens? Are they admitted as property? then why is not other property admitted into the computation?" Madison, reluctant to give up on his dream of proportional representation in both houses, thought he saw a way out of the dilemma: base representation in the lower house on the number of free inhabitants, and in the upper—"which had for one of its primary objects the guardianship of property"—the whole number of persons, including slaves. Under this plan,

34. Farrand, ed., *Records of the Federal Convention,* I, 561. This point was repeatedly made by Antifederalists in the debates over ratification in the press and in the ratifying conventions. See, for example, Luther Martin, "The Genuine Information Delivered to the Legislature of the State of Maryland . . . ," in Herbert J. Storing, ed., *The Complete Antifederalist,* 7 vols. (Chicago, 1981), 2.4.45, "Essays of Brutus," 2.9.39, "A Letter from a Gentleman in a Neighbouring State, to a Gentleman in This City," 4.2.3, "Letters of a Republican Federalist," 4.13.22, "Speeches by Melancton Smith," 6.12.8; as well as "Debate in Massachusetts Ratifying Convention," Jan. 17–19, 1788, reprinted in Kurland and Lerner, eds., *Founders' Constitution,* II, 122. The debate on the Three-Fifths Clause had resumed on July 9, about a month after Wilson's original proposal. For an informed narrative of deliberations in the interim, see Rakove, *Original Meanings,* 60–72.

35. Farrand, ed., *Records of the Federal Convention,* I, 534, 542, 603–604, II, 222.

slaves would have been counted entirely as property and not at all as the represented. Yet, the small states, as many historians have demonstrated, were not willing to agree to any sort of proportional representation in the upper house; instead, the three-fifths formula, which based representation on both wealth and persons, became part of the Constitution.[36]

The compromise was struck, then, just as Wilson had suggested on June 11. After all the threats had been made, the delegates agreed on the need to agree. But the logic of this particular compromise still eluded some of the northern delegates. They could not understand how or why slaves—whom the southerners continued to define as "wealth" or "property" could be represented. Curiously, it was Gouverneur Morris, perhaps the clause's most vehement critic, who suggested a way for the troubled northerners to reconcile themselves to the incoherence. On July 12, he offered a "proviso that taxation shall be in proportion to Representation." In one sense, he was merely reiterating the South Carolinians' suggestion of a month before that representation should be in proportion to "quotas of contribution." Morris was now proposing language that, after editing, became part of Article I, Section 8, of the Constitution: "Representatives and direct taxes shall be apportioned among the several states" by the formula that we have been discussing at such length. Morris's amendment served two purposes. First, it made it appear as if the slave states were going to have to pay, literally, for their bonus: if they got more representatives, they would also have to pay more in taxes. As Morris himself later noted, his proposal was something of a sham. It was almost inconceivable that the federal government would "stretch its hand directly into the pockets of the people scattered over so vast a Country." The sham, however, served as a crutch for hobbled northerners. Wilson caught on immediately, noting that "less umbrage would perhaps be taken agst. an admission of the slaves into the Rule of representation, if it should be so expressed as to make them indirectly only an ingredient in the rule, by saying that they should enter into the rule of taxation: and as representation was to be according to taxation, the end would be equally attained." A few weeks later, Morris suggested removing the clause about direct taxation, as "he had only meant it as a bridge to assist us over a certain gulph" that had now been crossed, but he later reconsidered. He thought the clause still nec-

36. Ibid., I, 587, 562. The convention eventually settled on a compromise by which slaves would be counted at the ratio of five to three for purposes both of representation and taxation. See Finkelman, "Slavery and the Constitutional Convention," in Beeman, Botein, and Carter, eds., *Beyond Confederation*, 188–225.

essary "in consequence of what had passed on this point; in order to exclude the appearance of counting the Negroes in *the Representation*."[37]

In that rhetorical wave of the hand—"in consequence of what had passed on this point"—Morris alluded to the convention's bitter debates over slavery, one of the most fierce of which he himself had provoked with his original proposal to link representation with taxation. No sooner had Morris proposed the clause than South Carolina's Butler, no doubt already recognizing that the taxation part of it was a sham, proposed that representation should be based upon the full number of inhabitants, "including all the blacks." Morris, snapping out of his conciliatory mood, replied that "the people of Pena. will never agree to a representation of Negroes." Charles Pinckney, another South Carolinian, turned Butler's suggestion into a formal motion. Butler and Pinckney had made the same proposal the day before, without causing as much of a stir as it now did. One cannot help surmising that when the South Carolinians brought up the proposal again on the twelfth, their purpose was not to gain the point but to appear as obstinate as possible.[38]

The first time Butler proposed counting all the slaves, he claimed that "the labour of a slave in S. Carola was as productive and valuable as that of a freeman in Massts." In fact, that was the best argument the South Carolinians could come up with. Unfortunately for them, it was directly contrary to what they had argued just a few years before in the Confederation Congress when they were demanding a discount for their supposedly less productive slave labor. The irony of the situation was not lost on North Carolina's Williamson, who observed that when they were arguing about taxation, southerners had said that slave labor was inferior to free and northerners that it was equal. Having earlier insisted—to their advantage—that slave labor was relatively unproductive, the southerners could not effectively mount the opposite argument. They were reduced to simple bullying and a naked assertion of self-interest. As John Rutledge later put it, in another argument about slavery, "Interest alone is the governing principle with Nations—The true question at present is whether the Southn. States shall or shall not be parties to the Union."[39]

37. Farrand, ed., *Records of the Federal Convention,* I, 223, 590–592, 595, II, 106, 607. No one could ever have accused Morris of making a fetish of consistency.

38. Ibid., I, 591–597.

39. Ibid., I, 580–581, II, 364. In this light, Madison's famous speech of July 11, in which he predicted that population in the United States would naturally flow away from the crowded states of the Northeast to the less populated territory, takes on an interesting mean-

On July 12, the argument was so heated that delegates from both the North and South, including Morris himself, threatened to walk out. Now the delegates were having just the sort of argument that normally leads to a difference-splitting compromise such as the one that Wilson had proposed a month earlier. But having offered his compromise a month earlier, Wilson could do nothing more now than to try to make sense out of his own proposal and to reassert the importance of compromise. "If numbers be not a proper rule, why is not some better rule pointed out. . . . In 1783, after elaborate discussion of a measure of wealth all were satisfied then as they are now that the rule of numbers, does not differ much from the combined rule of numbers and wealth." Wilson simply defined the problem away by insisting that this particular formula for including wealth did not materially alter the outcome. Then he reasserted, as if they had not been altered by the compromise, his general principles: that "again he could not agree that property was the sole or the primary object of Governt. and Society" and that "numbers were surely the natural and precise measure of Representation" as they were a close enough approximation of wealth. And then the delegates voted, accepting the Three-Fifths Clause. Not even its own author had been able to render it coherent.[40]

Having settled this point, the delegates would argue seriously about slavery only one more time. The issue then, in late August, was the slave trade. The Committee of Detail, chaired by South Carolina's John Rutledge, reported out a draft of the Constitution that not only explicitly permitted the slave trade but also prohibited taxing either the trade or slaves themselves, which would have made slaves the only import exempt from taxation. This time the opposition was led by delegates from the Upper South; Maryland's Luther Martin thought the proposals "inconsistent with the principles of the revolution and dishonorable to the American character." Once again, the South Carolinians resorted to bullying; Rutledge said that "the true ques-

ing. Asserting the labor theory of value upon which the Confederation's 1783 compromise on taxation rested—and which he had written—Madison stated that "the value of labour, might be considered as the principal criterion of wealth and ability to support taxes; and this would find its level in different places where the intercourse should be easy and free. . . . Wherever labour would yield most, people would resort" (ibid., I, 585). Implicitly, this was a free-soil vision, similar to the one that Howell had shared with his governor: Which free white men would voluntarily migrate to a region where they would have to compete with slaves? In spite of Butler's bluster, and the South Carolinians' and Georgians' insistence that the slave trade remain open until 1808, the convention generally accepted the premises of the bourgeois critique of slavery.

40. Ibid., I, 605–606.

tion at present is whether the Southn. States shall or shall not be parties to the Union."[41]

This time South Carolina and Georgia found allies in the delegation from Connecticut, which urged the rest of the convention to heed the southerners' warnings. Besides, as Sherman put it, "The abolition of slavery seemed to be going on in the U.S. and . . . the good sense of the several States would probably by degrees compleat it." Oliver Ellsworth came up with his own twist on the bourgeois critique of slavery: the climate in South Carolina and Georgia was so deadly to slaves that those two states had to keep importing them. Time, however, would solve even this problem. "As population increases[,] poor laborers will be so plenty as to render slaves useless." Here it was, a sort of Gresham's law of labor in reverse: free labor would drive out slave. "Slavery in time," Ellsworth continued, "will not be a speck in our Country."[42]

Of course, this argument made no sense. There was only one conceivable way in which the continued importation of slavery could not strengthen the institution, and that was if the punishments of the institution killed off more slaves than the Deep South could import. If that is what Ellsworth believed, he was implicitly delivering a more damning indictment of the institution than any of its most outspoken foes. But Ellsworth and his Connecticut colleagues were not trying for consistency. They seemed to think it was enough to point to the eventual demise of the institution. And they urged their colleagues to give in to the Deep South's threats. Sherman "said it was better to let the S. States import slaves than to part with them [for example, South Carolina and Georgia] if they made that a sine qua non." The matter was referred back to another committee, which offered a compromise seemingly much less favorable to the Deep South: the slave trade could not be banned until 1800, and slave imports could be taxed. With very little discussion—and none of South Carolina's blustering or threats—the delegates approved two amendments, moving the date forward to 1808 and setting the tax at no more than ten dollars per slave.[43]

41. Ibid., II, 183, 364.

42. Ibid., II, 364–375. See also Fehrenbacher, *Slaveholding Republic*, 33–37; and Rakove, *Original Meanings*, 85–89. This discussion was part of a larger debate about regulation of trade. In committee, southern delegates were willing to agree to let Congress regulate imports so long as their trade in slaves could be exempted.

43. Farrand, ed., *Records of the Federal Convention*, II, 374, 400, 415–417. It is, of course, an interesting question why the South Carolinians (and the Georgians, their silent junior partners) cut this particular deal with the commercial states of the North, one that brought them into conflict with the Virginians George Mason and Edmund Randolph. True, the

It has been observed that this was a compromise between two extremes—a complete ban on the importation of slavery and no restriction whatsoever, but South Carolina and Georgia got, by far, the better end of the deal. It is hard not to believe that this was the purpose of all of their truculence earlier in the summer. At the moment the compromise was struck, every state except Georgia had either banned or suspended the slave trade or effectively curtailed it with prohibitive duties. The convention had now reversed the tide against the slave trade, guaranteeing any state that wanted to import slaves that right and preventing states—now denied the power to regulate commerce—from blocking the trade with high duties. Just before the delegates approved the clause, Madison commented sardonically that "twenty years will produce all the mischief that can be apprehended from the liberty to import slaves. So long a term will be more dishonorable to the National Character than to say nothing about it in the Constitution." His prediction was correct. In the twenty-one years before a ban on slavery finally was enacted, thousands of African slaves were imported into the United States.[44]

Neither Madison nor Wilson was happy with this compromise. But it was late August, the delegates were tired, the South Carolinians were still raging, and the Constitution was almost finished. They restrained themselves, making only a few brief but bitter comments. Wilson, ever alert to Deep South hypocrisy, "observed that if S.C. and Georgia were themselves disposed to get rid of the importation of slaves in a short time as had been suggested, they would never refuse to Unite because the Importation might be prohibited." Madison struggled to keep any explicit recognition of slavery

---

South had won a ban on export duties, but the two Virginians had also wanted to require a two-thirds majority in Congress for import duties as well. In the end, the South Carolinians agreed to a simple majority for import duties in return for the reopening of the slave trade and the ten-dollar cap on each slave brought into the country. A little more than forty years later, South Carolina would object strenuously to national import duties—the so-called Tariff of Abominations—and develop the novel doctrine of nullification to oppose them. One wonders if, had they been able to see so far ahead, the South Carolinians would have made the bargain they did, trading away an impediment to import duties for keeping the slave trade open another twenty years. The point, however, is that none of the participants in the convention knew how events would turn out—but who ever does? They made a series of calculations based upon their perceptions of their best interests, their expectations about the future, and their understandings of political theory. Sometimes their calculations turned out right, and sometimes they did not.

44. Farrand, ed., *Records of the Federal Convention,* II, 415; Fehrenbacher, *Slaveholding Republic,* 35; Robinson, *Slavery in the Structure of Politics,* 297–299; Oakes, "Rhetoric of Reaction"; Helen Hornbeck Tanner, ed., *The Settling of North America: The Atlas of the Great Migrations into North America from the Ice Age to the Present* (New York, 1995), 51.

out of the Constitution. He "thought it wrong to admit in the Constitution the idea that there could be property in men." Both men sincerely disliked slavery and hoped that it would disappear. They, like many other democrats of the period, thought that it might be on the road to extinction. As many historians have noted, they were probably indulging in fantasy. Even without the thousands and thousands of Africans imported into the South in the next two decades, slavery was far too entrenched and the opposition to it far too weak to make its peaceful elimination a realistic prospect.[45]

Still, there is a certain logic to the words and actions of these nationalist democrats. It is in this context that Jefferson's florid passage condemning the slave trade in the draft of the Declaration makes a certain kind of sense: if the slave trade had been halted, or if it could be curtailed right now, perhaps slavery would die a natural death. The bourgeois critique of slavery suggested that free labor would prevail because it was both morally and economically superior. Cut off the slave trade, encourage white immigration, open the West to settlers, and the rapidly increasing free white population would eventually overshadow the black. This is one reason why Madison and other nationalists were so committed to the opening of the West, so insistent that the new states be brought in on equal terms with the older ones: the West was where slavery would disappear. Later, both Madison and Jefferson consoled themselves with a dream of "diffusion"—the idea that if only the institution of slavery were left alone, it would die out, somewhere in the West. For Jefferson especially, the dream of diffusion became a shibboleth to use against the abolitionists.[46]

It is sometimes observed that creating a national government was so formidable a task that compromise was a fundamental necessity. It is unreasonable of us, with our modern notions of freedom and racial equality, to have expected the founders to have done more than they possibly could do. They gave us a federal government, a Bill of Rights, and a body of ideas that set slavery on the road to extinction.[47] The founders kept the Constitution

45. Farrand, ed., *Records of the Federal Convention,* II, 372, 417.

46. On this point, see Drew R. McCoy, *The Elusive Republic: Political Economy in Jeffersonian America* (Williamsburg, Va., and Chapel Hill, N.C., 1980), 251–252; McCoy, *The Last of the Fathers: James Madison and the Republican Legacy* (New York, 1989), 267–276; and Peter S. Onuf, *Jefferson's Empire: The Language of American Nationhood* (Charlottesville, Va., 2000), 185–187.

47. Most explicitly, see Thomas G. West, *Vindicating the Founders: Race, Sex, Class, and Justice in the Origins of America* (Lanham, Md., 1997), 16. More nuanced versions of this argument can be found in Gordon S. Wood, *The Radicalism of the American Revolution* (New York, 1992), 187; and Fehrenbacher, *Slaveholding Republic,* 47. It is implicit, I think,

as neutral on slavery as they could; it is as much, therefore, an antislavery document as a proslavery one. Such arguments have some truth in them—if we stop the clock in mid-July, just after the Three-Fifths Compromise has finally been agreed to. If one thought, as Wilson did and Madison did, and as Howell did in the Confederation Congress, that slavery was on the road to extinction, then the bonus given to the South for slavery—whether as a discount on the national tax bill or as a little extra representation in the House—would soon be moot: once slavery faded away, the South would lose its temporary advantage.[48]

But, if we move the clock forward, to late August, after the concession on the slave trade (and after an additional one on a fugitive slave clause), then the compromises take on a different cast. The institution of slavery itself has been given encouragement. More slaves can enter the country. The institution will grow. The dream of extinction or diffusion becomes more fantastic by the day. In June and even in July, Wilson's calculation might have appeared shrewd. By September, when an emboldened Deep South had secured even more, we may wonder about its wisdom.

Moreover, not only did the democratic nationalists such as Wilson and Madison enhance the power of the slaveowning states, they authorized—in both senses of the term—sectionalism itself. By anticipating the claims of the Deep South, they encouraged that region to make excessive demands in the Constitutional Convention, which they, in turn, had no choice but to satisfy. And they gave those claims legitimacy, denominating them a legitimate interest and helping a section come into being.

The great abolitionist William Lloyd Garrison once called the Constitution a "covenant with death" and an "agreement with hell." Surely, this is not what antislavery nationalists such as Wilson and Madison intended. But the road to hell, as my father used to say, is paved with good intentions.[49]

---

in Banning, *Sacred Fire of Liberty,* a very fine book that, however, pays too little attention to the issue of slavery.

48. This seems to have been Madison's reasoning, although in the Virginia convention he walked a very fine line, arguing both that Virginians' property in slaves was secure and that allowing the importation of slaves for another twenty years, while distasteful, would do no harm. He believed that the Constitution offered the best hope for securing liberty, and in that context he argued that certain concessions to South Carolina and Georgia were necessary to keep those two states in the Union (Elliot, ed., *Debates in the Several State Conventions,* 453–461).

49. Quoted in Finkelman, "Slavery and the Constitutional Convention," in Beeman, Botein, and Carter, eds., *Beyond Confederation,* 188.

Jefferson Studies

FIGURE 5

View of the West Front of Monticello and Garden. By Jane Braddick Peticolas. 1825. Watercolor on paper. Accession no. 1986-13-30. ©Thomas Jefferson Foundation at Monticello, Charlottesville, Va.

JAN ELLEN LEWIS'S THOMAS JEFFERSON
Domestic Life and Family Values

ANNETTE GORDON-REED & PETER S. ONUF

Jan Lewis did not see herself as a biographer of Thomas Jefferson—or of anyone else. She made her reputation as a student of family life, gender, and emotions but also contributed mightily to the political, legal, and constitutional history of the Revolutionary Republic. Although the essays that follow show her to have produced some of the most astute and elegant writings about Jefferson ever written, he was never the sole point of her work. The four essays collected here approach Jefferson obliquely, keeping faith with her main scholarly preoccupations. She illuminates family, gender relations, and emotions during Jefferson's time by studying his interactions with members of his Jefferson-Randolph family, particularly his daughters and granddaughters.

In the years before Lewis began writing, there was a revival of interest in the history of colonial and Revolutionary Virginia. Edmund S. Morgan's *American Slavery, American Freedom: The Ordeal of Colonial Virginia* (1975) provided a crucial link between the history of settlement and servitude in the seventeenth-century Chesapeake and the history of the peculiar institution in the antebellum South. Morgan showed that racial slavery and republicanism were inextricably and tragically conjoined, strongly suggesting that understanding the history of Revolutionary Virginia would illuminate the new nation's future course. When Morgan wrote, historians were devoting disproportionate attention to colonies and states to the north, with social historians scrutinizing New England town records and historians of political thought elaborating a transatlantic "republican synthesis" that supposedly laid the groundwork for the break with Britain. Lewis and many of her bright

Annette Gordon-Reed is Carl M. Loeb University Professor at Harvard Law School, and Peter S. Onuf is Thomas Jefferson Foundation Professor of History, Emeritus at the University of Virginia and Senior Fellow at Monticello's Robert H. Smith International Center for Jefferson Studies.

young colleagues sensed that the dominant approaches, or paradigms, were beginning to yield diminishing returns. To make the shift southward, these scholars had to exploit new sources and embrace new methodologies. But the rewards would be correspondingly great, as the trajectory of Lewis's career makes clear. Morgan's title is a provocation, conflating "America" and "Virginia"—and "slavery" and "freedom"—in what might be called a synecdoche, the figure of speech in which the part is put in place of the whole. When "Virginia" faded into the historiographical background, it follows, Morgan's fellow historians lost sight of "America" and the much more important story line that culminated in what Gunnar Myrdal called the "American dilemma" of race and the legacies of slavery.[1]

Thomas Jefferson also attracted relatively little scholarly attention in these years. For political theorists he was a negligible figure, famous for his lack of original ideas. Ideological historians also ignored him because of his failure to contribute significantly to the burgeoning "literature of revolution"—and the diminutive reach of the print public sphere in Virginia and the plantation south. Yet again, there was a disconnect between the story Americans told themselves about Jefferson, the iconic democrat, and the story scholars told in which he did not significantly figure. Thanks to Lewis, another story could be told, when she surveyed scholarship on Jefferson in a 1998 essay on the "American Synecdoche" that conflated the Virginian with his country.[2]

Lewis was neither a Virginia historian nor Jeffersonian scholar. She turned to Virginia and to Jefferson as an *American* historian determined to

1. Edmund S. Morgan, *American Slavery, American Freedom: The Ordeal of Colonial Virginia* (New York, 1975); Robert E. Shalhope, "Toward a Republican Synthesis: The Emergence of an Understanding of Republicanism in American Historiography," *William and Mary Quarterly*, 3d Ser., XXIX (1972), 49–80; Gunnar Myrdal, *An American Dilemma: The Negro Problem and Modern Democracy* (New York, 1944); Herbert Sloan and Peter Onuf, "Politics, Culture, and the Revolution in Virginia," *Virginia Magazine of History and Biography*, XCI (1983), 259–284. Outstanding works in the new social history include monographs by Jan Lewis's advisor at the University of Michigan, Kenneth A. Lockridge, *A New England Town: The First Hundred Years, Dedham, Massachusetts, 1636–1736* (New York, 1970); Philip J. Greven, Jr., *Four Generations: Population, Land, and Family in Colonial Andover, Massachusetts* (Ithaca, N.Y., 1970); and John Demos, *A Little Commonwealth: Family Life in Plymouth Colony* (New York, 1970). Landmarks in the history of early American political thought include Bernard Bailyn, *The Ideological Origins of the American Revolution* (Cambridge, Mass., 1967); Bailyn, *The Origins of American Politics* (New York, 1968); and J. G. A. Pocock, *The Machiavellian Moment: Florentine Political Thought and the Atlantic Republican Tradition* (Princeton, N.J., 1975).

2. Bailyn, *Ideological Origins of the American Revolution*, 1; Jan Lewis and Peter S. Onuf, "American Synecdoche: Thomas Jefferson as Image, Icon, Character, and Self," *American Historical Review*, CIII (1998), 125–136 (Lewis suggested the title).

find fresh ways to think about our country's troubled history. Her gifts as a cultural historian enabled her to move beyond the constraints of quantitative social history and of the text-bound study of ideology. Combining the novelist's interest in the character of characters and the intimate history of their relationships with others with the historian's interest in the broad sociocultural changes they experienced, Lewis focused on elite Virginia families in her first book, *The Pursuit of Happiness: Family and Values in Jefferson's Virginia.* At first, she came at Jefferson obliquely, mining his archive to better understand the emotional family dynamics in plantation households. In subsequent work, she followed her subject into public life, offering fresh insights into his political work, while considering the experiences and perspectives of other subjects of his domestic domain.[3]

The title of Lewis's book echoed Jefferson's most famous words, in the Declaration of Independence, underscoring the complex relationships between domesticity and politics and self and society that engaged her so fruitfully throughout her career. Scholars have wondered what the eloquent Virginian meant when he invoked the word "happiness" in a state paper justifying the break with Britain and seeking recognition from the "powers of the earth." American independence is often seen as the culmination of a quarrel within the British imperial family, as liberty-loving sons renounced their filial ties to an imperious mother country. For the Declaration's author, "happiness" was a resonant term with many meanings, public and private, for the people of his country and for the family at home. Jefferson had a genius for binary oppositions, juxtaposing good and evil, friends and enemies, new world and old, black and white. If declaring independence meant drawing a definitive line, the complications of life in the fog of war and political upheaval defied clear-cut distinctions. Lewis's genius was to restore the ambiguity of lived experience and to show how private and public domains were inextricably entangled in Jefferson's world. Jefferson and fellow family members constructed an idealized domesticity that made them "happy," and those family values shaped his public life.[4]

3. Jan Lewis, *The Pursuit of Happiness: Family and Values in Jefferson's Virginia* (New York, 1983).

4. For Lewis's exploration of the meaning of Jefferson's language in the Declaration of Independence, see Jan Lewis, "Happiness," in Jack P. Greene and J. R. Pole, eds., *The Blackwell Encyclopedia of the American Revolution* (Cambridge, Mass., 1991), 641–647. For the American Revolution as a family quarrel writ large, see Edwin G. Burrows and Michael Wallace, "The American Revolution: The Ideology and Psychology of National Liberation," *Perspectives in American History*, VI (1972), 167–306; Winthrop D. Jordan, "Familial Politics: Thomas Paine and the Killing of the King, 1776," *Journal of American History*, LX

What exactly did happiness mean for Jefferson in his own personal life? Lewis looked for answers in his musings on the domestic circumstances that made him happy—or unhappy. Employing her deft analytical skills and taking Jefferson at his word, Lewis discovered the sources of what he meant by "happiness" in the harmonious relationships of a well-regulated plantation family. This is where he and other elite white Virginians in the new republic insisted they had found it (or would or should find it) in its original and most durable form. The Jefferson-Randolphs were the perfect subjects for a close examination of family dynamics and domestic ideology, despite the unusual circumstance of the presence—or, more often, absence—of Jefferson, the world-famous statesman and planter patriarch. Ironically, it was because Jefferson was so often *not* at home—and home is where his heart *was*—that we have such a rich documentary record of him and his family. His commitment to public life took him away from the Mountain and the people whom he loved, and who loved him. Separated by many miles, the usually reticent Jefferson and his family members wrote each other incessantly about the pleasures of their lives together at home with one another. These letters imaginatively constructed their displaced relationships; they emphasized the good and, generally, banished evidence of conflict or discord. They revealed deep feelings, even as they instructed one another about how they were supposed to feel.

All of this was fair game for Lewis, trained as a social historian with a primary interest in the emergence of supposedly modern conceptions of affective family relations. The development of these conceptions was actually part of a protracted moment in the West that resists facile periodization. But the dislocations caused by mobilization and regime change during the Revolutionary period accelerated long-term developments on this front, making Virginia an extraordinarily attractive case study of how ideas about family life evolved. In the end, the American Revolution might not have changed much for most privileged planter families. Yet it did subvert the hierarchical assumptions of the old regime, focusing new attention on what was considered to be the natural organization of society, and of the family of families that constituted the new republic. Virginians talked about themselves, their families, and their commonwealth in new and revealing ways.[5]

(1973), 294–308; and Jay Fliegelman, *Prodigals and Pilgrims: The American Revolution against Patriarchal Authority, 1750–1800* (Cambridge, 1982).

5. Philip Greven, *The Protestant Temperament: Patterns of Child-Rearing, Religious Experience, and the Self in Early America* (New York, 1977).

Lewis focused on how families in an increasingly sentimental age reimagined themselves. What did her Virginians say and not say to each other? What were the often-unarticulated states of mind and feeling that attached individuals to their families? As a social historian taking the "cultural turn," Lewis recognized that the raw demographic data that charted the transformation of family structure did not speak for itself. To recover the lost language of Virginian families, she necessarily focused on the particular voices of elite and highly literate women and men in the newly fashionable genre of the "familiar letter." Lewis thus moved *toward* biography—but never succumbed to its exceptionalist (and for most biographers of the American founders, celebratory) temptations.[6]

Through this lens, a new Jefferson came into view. Lewis defamiliarized an all-too-familiar, even iconic figure, not by lifting him out of his world (as the so-called inventor of America, or the renaissance man for all seasons), but rather by bringing him down to earth, situating him firmly in the provincial Virginian world that shaped his character. Encountering him on his own ground—or, as he imagined himself, in the bosom of his loving family—we can see, thanks to Lewis, how conventional and representative Jefferson was as he adapted to changing times. The eighteenth-century father bore faint resemblance to the nineteenth-century grandfather. Yet if Jefferson's circumstances were anything but typical, they enabled him to fashion a version of himself that conformed to the values of his class and country.

"'The Blessings of Domestic Society': Thomas Jefferson's Family and the Transformation of American Politics" (1993) is Lewis's first great essay in this biographical mode. Family mattered so much to Jefferson because he lost the family he created with his wife, Martha, who died in 1782 at thirty-four after ten years of marriage. Jefferson fled Monticello in the wake of her death, leaving his youngest two daughters, Mary (Maria) and Lucy, with his sister-in-law, while taking his eldest daughter, Martha, with him. Father and eldest daughter were also apart as Congress changed its seat between 1782 and 1784. This established a pattern for the Jefferson household. "Home" was a largely imaginary place, built up over the years of Jefferson's career in public service as a collaborative, familial project. After his return from France, Jefferson redesigned and rebuilt Monticello, his hilltop home

6. Andrew Burstein, "Jefferson and the Familiar Letter," *Journal of the Early Republic,* XIV (1994), 195–220; Burstein, *The Inner Jefferson: Portrait of a Grieving Optimist* (Charlottesville, Va., 1995); Burstein, *Letters from the Head and Heart: Writings of Thomas Jefferson* (Chapel Hill, N.C., 2002).

near Charlottesville. The family that would eventually come together in that home, when he retired from public life in 1809, included daughter Martha Randolph and her children. Maria Jefferson had died in 1804.

For a displaced Jefferson, domesticity stood in stark counterpoint to the "miseries" of public life. At Monticello, he sought refuge from vicious partisan conflict, for it was, as Lewis observed, "the affections nurtured in the family that bound society together." But those affections had to be cultivated, and family values had to be performed. And this is where the patriarch wrote the script and orchestrated the harmonious score, hoping to keep inevitable tensions and conflict at bay. That harmony did not come naturally, or without significant costs. The republican domestic idyll required sacrifices by "legitimate," recognized members of the white family—particularly women—and by the enslaved people at Monticello. Imagining a quasi-familial reciprocity, Jefferson pledged to "watch for the happiness of those who labor for mine." Lewis does not moralize about this state of affairs but instead seeks to explain how Jefferson's need for an idealized family and home reflected broader and deeper changes in his world. The master of Monticello fashioned a domain for himself with the materials at hand. The selves we now cultivate may be much more enlightened, but they are no longer focused on the family, nor can we share Jefferson's faith that family attachments bind "society together."[7]

Jefferson staged a highly artificial, harmonious domesticity at Monticello that contained and suppressed the conflicts that (we would say) naturally erupt in families. He was certainly aware of the risks. In her broader assessment of "Jefferson and Women" (2010), Lewis explains what was at stake in maintaining a stable republican domestic order. Emphasizing the biographical imperative to situate her subject in his proper spatial and temporal contexts, she argues persuasively that his misogynistic outbursts reflect critical moments in his private life and public career. From our contemporary perch, it is too easy to look at Jefferson's actions, read his words, and conclude that he feared and hated women: the low-hanging fruit is there to prove it! The more interesting question is: when and why did Jefferson feel prompted or compelled to express such ubiquitous sentiments. Lewis identifies two misogynistic periods in his life: first, in his adolescence, when he clearly did

7. Jan Lewis, "The Blessings of Domestic Society: Thomas Jefferson's Family and the Transformation of American Politics," in this volume; Thomas Jefferson to [Angelica Schuyler] Church, Nov. 27, 1793, in Merrill D. Peterson, ed., *Thomas Jefferson, Writings: Autobiography, A Summary View of the Rights of British America, Notes on the State of Virginia, Public Papers, Addresses, Messages, and Replies, Miscellany, Letters* (New York, 1984), 1013.

not know what to make of women and bonded with other anxious males; and second, in his years in Paris, when he again found women intimidating and feared their corrupting influence on politics. The latter fixation carried over to the party battles of the 1790s, when the new republic seemed under siege from internal enemies: republican government was, indeed, gendered male. But it does not follow that Jefferson hated women, or exceeded the misogyny of his time. It was instead the unthinkable prospect of female autonomy and power unbounded by the constraints of domesticity that so frightened him, both as an anxious young man and as a republican statesman. For Jefferson, domesticity, individual self-discipline (for men as well as women), and republican self-government were inextricably linked.[8]

We can now say we know that the women at Monticello paid a high price for Jefferson's happiness. But they were by no means merely his victims. If Lewis's oblique approach to biography gives us fresh insights on Jefferson, it also enables us to share the perspectives, hear the voices, and interpret the silences of the great man's supporting cast. Lewis's elegant essay "'A Beautiful Domestic Character': Sarah N. Randolph's *The Domestic Life of Thomas Jefferson*" (2019), shows how the Jefferson-Randolphs reaped returns on their emotional investment in the patriarch's happiness. Randolph, Jefferson's great-granddaughter, wrote a memoir of her family, sharing recollections of Jefferson and life at Monticello. Jefferson appears in these pages as a patient and loving patriarch to his daughters and granddaughters, a "beautiful domestic character." He was even more kind and loving than Randolph's great-grandmother, Martha, whose tart tongue (never directed at her husband) delivered critical comments even to her eldest daughter, also named Martha.[9]

Lewis's essay shows, not only the ways in which family members were complicit in Jefferson's pursuit-of-happiness project, but how they gained great psychological and sentimental benefits from it. Love was the cement of transgenerational family union: perpetuating the story that the great man taught about his and the family's happiness became its religion after his

8. On Jefferson as a misogynist, see Kenneth A. Lockridge, *On the Sources of Patriarchal Rage: The Commonplace Books of William Byrd and Thomas Jefferson and the Gendering of Power in the Eighteenth Century* (New York, 1992).

9. Jan Ellen Lewis, "'A Beautiful Domestic Character': Sarah N. Randolph's *The Domestic Life of Thomas Jefferson,*" in this volume. For views on Jefferson and women, see Jon Kukla, *Mr. Jefferson's Women* (New York, 2007); Virginia Scharff, *The Women Jefferson Loved* (New York, 2010); Cynthia A. Kierner, *Martha Jefferson Randolph, Daughter of Monticello: Her Life and Times* (Chapel Hill, N.C., 2012); and Billy L. Wayson, *Martha Jefferson Randolph: Republican Daughter and Plantation Mistress* (Palmyra, Va., 2013).

death. At the same time, Lewis emphasizes, others in the plantation household were victims: the people the Jeffersons owned and who receded into the dark shadows of "social death" in the midst of a family's celebratory vision of itself. For the Jefferson-Randolphs, Monticello was to be seen as a hallowed place. That it was made physically comfortable by enslaved people was a second-order consideration, if it was any consideration at all.[10]

There was, however, a shadow looming over Randolph's project. As Lewis points out, Randolph had good reasons in 1871, when her book was published, to urgently promote the religion of the total happiness of family life at Monticello. Jefferson's reputation was at a low ebb. This work was, Lewis says, an "act of recovery," an implicit rebuke and refutation of the stories that circulated about a second family at Monticello: the family Jefferson was said to have created with an enslaved woman.[11]

We know now there was something very important missing from Sarah Randolph's paean to the Jefferson-Randolph family life at Monticello. She was telling the story of her own, legal family. There was another part of her family, her biological family, whose story could not be told. As Lewis makes clear, Randolph was constructing an image of *The Domestic Life of Thomas Jefferson,* in part, to counter the rumors about Jefferson's other family, the one he made with Sally Hemings, the half sister of his deceased wife. Lewis's classic essay "The White Jeffersons" (1999) is a counter narrative to Sarah Randolph's vision of life on the Mountain. This essay shows the damage wrought by the Jefferson family religion. Far from harmless, maintaining the facade required systematic efforts to suppress the story of Jefferson's liaison with Hemings. Hemings's life, and those of her children with Jefferson, had to be kept in the shadows, unable to share the love that held the Jefferson-Randolphs together. Why should it matter that Jefferson—like so many of his slaveholding peers—should have had a sexual relationship (which produced a mixed-race shadow family) with someone he owned? Why do we need to remember Hemings? Lewis's essay shows the importance of the truth, and it is the historian's job to get as near the truth as possible.[12]

Jefferson was a wordsmith, famous for the things he said or wrote. Lewis was a close reader of the Jefferson canon, but she was more interested in

10. For the term "social death," see Orlando Patterson, *Slavery and Social Death: A Comparative Study* (Cambridge, Mass., 1982).

11. Lewis, "A Beautiful Domestic Character," in this volume.

12. Sarah N. Randolph, *The Domestic Life of Thomas Jefferson . . .* (1871; rpt. Charlottesville, Va., 1978).

what he did not or could not say, as well as in the unarticulated assumptions and implications of the key words in his lexicon.

Jefferson never explicitly denied the relationship to Hemings, but, Lewis shows, the family's denial is traceable to his silence—and his loving solicitude for his white family's feelings. What might have seemed harmless metastasized across the generations: a family's lie became the nation's history. This is where, in her most beautiful prose, Lewis renders a powerful moral judgment: on our original sin of slavery and the silence surrounding it, on the alliance of family stories with the larger, largely untold story of white supremacy.

For Jefferson, the "blessings" of domesticity required a great deal of hard work. Family members had to embrace their roles, memorize their lines, and look away from what they needed to forget. It all began with Jefferson's tenderness for the feelings of members of his recognized, "legitimate" family, the white children and grandchildren he devoutly loved. And *all* they needed, or so they would claim, was *love.* But what about his other children, Lewis leaves us wondering, and what about his other grandchildren? With great eloquence and compassion, "The White Jeffersons" reveals the untold and enduring cost of perpetuating Jefferson's idealized image of family happiness.

Jefferson and Women

Thomas Jefferson's attitudes about women were remarkably conventional, so conventional, for the most part, that to describe them is essentially to provide an account of the standard views about sexual difference and women's roles held by men of his time, place, and social standing. To be sure, different men (and women, for that matter) had somewhat different ideas: the views and practices of a Jefferson, an Alexander Hamilton, a John Adams, or a Benjamin Franklin are so different, and so well known, that it may be sufficient merely to mention them and a few details of their lives to make the point that not all men of the same class and status share identical views and experiences.

Think only of Hamilton's acknowledgment, in embarrassing detail, of his affair with Maria Reynolds. Or Adams's remarkable partnership with his remarkable wife, Abigail. Or Franklin's common-law marriage to a woman who raised as her own the baby that Franklin had fathered out of wedlock only a short time earlier. Or, finally, Jefferson, who married rather late—at age twenty-nine—but, by all accounts, remarkably happily. After his wife died, from the complications of childbirth, after just ten years of marriage, Jefferson entered into a thirty-eight-year liaison with his slave Sally Hemings, herself the half sister of his deceased wife.

Yet to say that, within a culture, people can behave quite differently does not add a whit to the knowledge that all historians already possess. The varieties of human behavior are infinite. The challenge for anyone who would like to say something significant about Jefferson is that, although the particulars of his personal life are fascinating, his attitudes were almost wholly conventional. It is tempting, then, to provide a biography, to explore in detail Jefferson's experiences with women—not only his marriage and his liaison but his embarrassing assault on Betsey Walker (the wife of his neighbor and friend from childhood, John Walker), his puzzling affair, or nonaffair, with Maria Cosway, his complex attachments to his white daughters and granddaughters. I am going to resist that temptation, however, for several rea-

This essay was originally published as Jan Ellen Lewis, "Jefferson and Women," in John B. Boles and Randal L. Hall, eds., *Seeing Jefferson Anew: In His Time and Ours* (Charlottesville, Va., 2010), 152–171.

sons. First, this Jefferson is already rather well known to us, from the work of Andrew Burstein and others, and he has become even better known in Annette Gordon-Reed's biography of the Hemings family, which tells us a great deal about Jefferson's personal life.[1]

More important, I am reluctant to talk wholly about the private, personal Jefferson. To do so risks accepting without question Jefferson's own belief, forcefully stated, that private life is private and has no bearing upon public matters. On his deathbed, Jefferson told his namesake and favorite grandson that the insults of his political enemies had never really hurt him: "He had not considered them as abusing him; they had never known *him.* They had created an imaginary being clothed with odious attributes, to whom they had given his name." Given the corpus of writings on Jefferson, which considers him in relation to religion, politics, Indians, slaves, ideas, and history, it is not helpful to say that either the private Jefferson or the public one was the real one and the other Jeffersons were, by implication, imaginary or false ones.[2]

I am interested in intersections, the places where the various Jeffersons met, whether imaginary or real—to accept, for a moment, Jefferson's own construction—and especially the places where Jefferson's ideas about women and gender intersected with his ideas about politics and race. But here we come back to the dilemma with which I started: Jefferson's views were so conventional that to describe them is, to a significant extent, to describe the evolution of conventional notions of woman's sphere in the Revolutionary era. So I must beg your indulgence while I retrace a history that has,

1. Andrew Burstein, *Jefferson's Secrets: Death and Desire at Monticello* (New York, 2005); Fawn M. Brodie, *Thomas Jefferson: An Intimate History* (New York, 1974); Annette Gordon-Reed, *The Hemingses of Monticello: An American Family* (New York, 2008). See also Jon Kukla, *Mr. Jefferson's Women* (New York, 2007), although Kukla's interpretation, which emphasizes Jefferson's misogyny and "predatory sexuality," differs from the interpretation I offer here (55). I would like to thank Annette Gordon-Reed for many valuable discussions and several specific suggestions and John Boles and Randal Hall for asking me to write this article.

2. Thomas Jefferson Randolph to Henry S. Randall, n.d., in Sarah N. Randolph, *The Domestic Life of Thomas Jefferson: Compiled from Family Letters and Reminiscences by His Great-Granddaughter* (New York, 1871), 428. I have examined Jefferson's views on the family and the importance of privacy for it in Lewis, "'The Blessings of Domestic Society': Thomas Jefferson's Family and the Transformation of American Politics," in Peter S. Onuf, ed., *Jeffersonian Legacies* (Charlottesville, Va., 1993), 109–146, also reprinted in this volume; and Lewis, "The White Jeffersons," in Jan Ellen Lewis and Onuf, eds., *Sally Hemings and Thomas Jefferson: History, Memory, and Civic Culture* (Charlottesville, Va., 1999), 127–160, also reprinted in this volume.

by now, become quite familiar to all who know the outlines of the Jefferson biography. It becomes interesting, however, when it intersects with Jefferson's thought more generally—but it will take us a few moments to get there.

Let me start, then, with the young Jefferson, the one we meet in the first pages of the first volume of the Julian P. Boyd edition of *The Papers of Thomas Jefferson.* Of course, to meet Jefferson in this way is to confront a puzzle: How does this apparently conventional young member of the Virginia gentry so quickly become the patriot leader? One day, Jefferson is commiserating with his friends about his troubles with the ladies, and, the next, he is writing *A Summary View of the Rights of British America* (1774). I exaggerate only slightly. The text of *A Summary View* begins on page 121 of the first volume of the *Papers,* and, although there are a few documents that touch on politics in the preceding pages, and a few pieces of correspondence from Jefferson's legal practice, most of the documents in the first hundred pages or so of the volume are letters between Jefferson and his male friends. Of these, a significant number concern the women that Jefferson and his friends were courting.

So, how did this conventional young man virtually overnight become—to use one of the clichés that are applied to Jefferson—the apostle of liberty? Phrasing it that way suggests that the mature, political Jefferson bore little or no relationship to the younger, more conventional one, that Jefferson had to emerge from his lovestruck youth before he could become a political leader, like a larva becoming a butterfly. In their youthful letters, however, Jefferson and his friends were defining themselves as men, as the kind of men they would be: this was the work that the correspondence performed. These young members of the gentry were situating themselves in their society and in relationship to one another and defining their society and their place in it. The women, who themselves were never correspondents, were merely incidental, markers of the positions occupied by the men.[3]

Let me try to clarify what I mean by focusing, for a moment, on several of the early letters. The tone of Jefferson's second surviving letter, to his good friend John Page, is jocular. In it, Jefferson compares himself to Job.

3. Eve Kosofsky Sedgwick, *Between Men: English Literature and Male Homosocial Desire* (New York, 1985). Jefferson's first surviving letter from a woman, a Mrs. Drummond, dates from 1771. See Mrs. Drummond to Thomas Jefferson, Mar. 12, 1771, in Boyd et al., eds., *Papers of Thomas Jefferson,* I, 65–66. This, and one other letter, are the only ones to or from a woman in the entire first volume of the Boyd edition of Jefferson's papers. Needless to say, some correspondence might have been lost, and after his wife's death, Jefferson himself destroyed his correspondence with her. See Brodie, *Thomas Jefferson,* 22.

He is "in a house surrounded with enemies"—the mice have chewed up his papers and his silk garters, and the rain, leaking through the roof, has soaked and ruined the silhouette of Rebecca Burwell that he had placed in his pocket watch. The silhouette was a gift from Rebecca, and its destruction has left Jefferson disconsolate, in three languages. Nevertheless, he assures Page that "although the picture be defaced there is so lively an image of her imprinted in my mind that I shall think of her too often I fear for my peace of mind." Note that Jefferson is performing a role—the romantic lover—for his friend Page, not for the female object, or supposed object, of his affection.[4]

Yet Jefferson moved quickly from despair to animation, begging Page for gossip and imploring him to "remember" him "affectionately to all the young ladies of my acquaintance." Now Page must perform Jefferson's heterosexuality for the young women in their acquaintance. Jefferson gave his friend instructions on just which pleasantry to convey to each young woman, a long paragraph of instructions that Jefferson concluded with one further injunction: "Tell—tell—In short tell them all ten thousand things more than either you or I can now or ever shall think of as long as we live." Making an impression on young women, courting them, was entirely performance—telling them whatever they wanted to hear. The content of the words, which would be of critical importance once Jefferson was drafting Revolutionary pamphlets and petitions, was irrelevant.[5]

In the letters Jefferson exchanged with his friends, filled with chatter about young women, he was trying out and trying to make sense of the world of heterosexual relations. Young Jefferson seemed obsessed by women, but, at the same time, almost indifferent to them. Burwell appears in his letters as Miss Burwell, Miss Becca Burwell, R.B., Miss R.B., Belinda, *άδνίλεβ* (that is, Belinda spelled backwards, and the Roman letters turned into Greek), and, most simply, she. In Jefferson's letters, she is everywhere but nowhere—a plenitude of pet names, her chief quality her ability to call forth Jefferson's ability to multiply her names. These secret names and endearments, however, were not for her, a code shared between lovers, but for Jefferson's male friends. The only meaningful discourse was that between men. Women were the language that men shared. They bonded as men engaged in the daunting rituals of courtship, in the process making themselves legible to each other by puzzling over the illegibility of women.

4. Thomas Jefferson to John Page, Dec. 25, 1762, in Julian P. Boyd et al., eds., *The Papers of Thomas Jefferson,* 43 vols. (Princeton, N.J., 1950–), I, 4–5.
5. Ibid., 5–6.

Jefferson's friends seemed possessed by a mania to marry. "You say you are determined to be married as soon as possible: and advise me to do the same," Jefferson wrote one friend. After telling Page that some of their friends were engaged, he asked Page, "Why cannot you and I be married too . . . when and to whom we would chuse? Do you think it would cause any such mighty disorders among the planets? . . . I verily beleive [*sic*] Page that I shall die soon, and yet I can give no other reason for it but that I am tired with living." Here was the problem: Jefferson and his friends were in training to be masters of their universe, not only their plantations but also their local governments, and, in Jefferson's case, also a leader in the Revolutionary movement. Yet they could not, as much as they wanted, marry when and whom they chose. They were at the mercy of the young women they courted. "What do you think of my affair," Jefferson asked Page, "or what would you advise me to do?" Burwell had turned Jefferson into Hamlet: "Had I better stay here and do nothing, or go down and do less"—that is, "receive my sentence, and be no longer in suspence: but, reason says if you go and your attempt proves unsuccessful you will be ten times more wretched than ever." So Jefferson did nothing, and Burwell married Jacquelin Ambler instead. No wonder Jefferson seemed depressed: his future, he thought, was out of his hands.[6]

Jefferson, of course, eventually married. He later described the ten years he and his wife had together before her death as a period of "unchequered happiness." He had found a woman, a young widow, Martha Wayles Skelton, whom he could love deeply and who also brought him a handsome fortune. There is a hint in his letters that the wedding almost did not come off. Nine years after his first letter to Page, Jefferson was still worrying about marrying. He mentioned a friend who was "wishing to take to himself a wife; and nothing obstructs it but the unfeeling temper of a parent who delays, perhaps refuses to approve her daughter's choice." Jefferson found himself in a similar situation, "not from the frowardness of parents, nor perhaps want of feeling in the fair one, but from other causes as unpliable to my wishes as these." The precise impediment is not clear; it is evident, though, that once again, Jefferson found that something stood in the way of his getting what he wanted.[7]

6. Thomas Jefferson to William Fleming, Mar. 20, 1764, ibid., 16, Jefferson to John Page, Jan. 20, 1763, 7–8.

7. Thomas Jefferson, "Autobiography," in Merrill D. Peterson, ed., *Thomas Jefferson, Writings: Autobiography, A Summary View of the Rights of British America, Notes on the State of Virginia, Public Papers, Addresses, Messages, and Replies, Miscellany, Letters* (New York,

It is in this context—a young man's quest to establish himself—that Jefferson's early, gossipy letters should be understood. Courtship was a competitive enterprise, not entirely unlike the political one in which Jefferson would later make such a mark. As Joanne B. Freeman has noted, Jefferson was an avid gossip, and, if the chitchat about who was courting whom did not serve as "conduits for other people's aggression" in the way that political gossip did, it certainly revealed an underlying anxiety about who was getting ahead and who was being left behind. And, as he would later, when insisting that he was sick and tired of politics and wanted nothing more than to retire to his mountaintop, from time to time Jefferson proclaimed himself weary of the whole enterprise of courting the ladies. In one of his more gossipy letters ("You have heard I suppose that J. Page is courting Fanny Burwell. W. Bland, and Betsy Yates are to be married thursday se'nnight"), Jefferson denied not only that he was a gossip ("Who told you that I reported you was courting Miss Dandridge and Miss Dangerfeild?") but that he even planned to marry. "Many and great are the comforts of a single state." True, "St. Paul . . . says that it is better to be married than to burn. Now I presume," Jefferson joked, "that if that apostle had known that providence would at an after day be so kind to any particular set of people as to furnish them with other means of extinguishing their fire than those of matrimony, he would have earnestly recommended them to their practice." Who needed to court young heiresses when more willing women could be had for a considerably lower price? In this gossipy letter, Jefferson's anxieties about the mercenary nature of the relationship between the sexes came through.[8]

Once he married, Jefferson's anxieties about sex and gender abated, and he soon made his stunning entrance on the political scene. By marrying a beautiful and affluent young woman, Jefferson was able to settle down, in several senses of the term. Whatever his earlier anxieties about marrying, he found great joy in domesticity, and it became for him, even after his wife's death, the measure of human happiness. Jefferson moved, then, from a kind of conventional misogyny to a kind of conventional valorization of domesticity. We see this appreciation for the domestic life not only in Jefferson's

---

1984), 46; Thomas Jefferson to James Ogilvie, Feb. 20, 1771, in Boyd et al., eds., *Papers of Thomas Jefferson,* I, 63; Kenneth A. Lockridge, *On the Sources of Patriarchal Rage: The Commonplace Books of William Byrd and Thomas Jefferson and the Gendering of Power in the Eighteenth Century* (New York, 1992).

8. Joanne B. Freeman, *Affairs of Honor: National Politics in the New Republic* (New Haven, Conn., 2001), 74; Jefferson to Fleming, Mar. 20, 1764, in Boyd et al., eds., *Papers of Thomas Jefferson,* I, 16.

reminiscences about his married life but also in his subsequent contrast of the satisfactions of private life and the pure and unabated miseries of the public sphere. Not only was his marriage one of "unchequered happiness," but his wife's death in "a single event wiped away all my plans and left me a blank which I had not the spirits to fill up." Twenty years earlier, the anxieties of courtship had left Jefferson depressed and listless; now it was the death of his beloved wife. Jefferson had grown up.[9]

Jefferson carried this image of happy domestic life with him for the rest of his days; it became a touchstone for him. Jefferson's comparisons of the miseries of public service with the rewards of family life are too well known to require more than a brief mention. "It is in the love of one's family only," he once told his younger daughter, "that heartfelt happiness is known." In government, he found "every thing which can be disgusting," at home with his family, "every thing which is pleasurable to me." His protestations notwithstanding, Jefferson spent most of his adult life in public service; his family—and his idea of family, as those who knew his real self and as his only source of "heartfelt happiness"—anchored him, making his public service possible. I have written about this aspect of Jefferson's life and thought elsewhere. For our purposes we should note only that Jefferson's views about family life were wholly conventional, and also that a happy marriage enabled Jefferson to shed his early misogyny, or at least rub off its sharp edges.[10]

There is, I believe, only one other period in Jefferson's life when his misogyny percolated to the surface. That was when he was in France, between 1784 and 1789, serving as the new nation's minister. Once again, Jefferson was single, engaged in an intense flirtation with the unhappily married artist Maria Cosway and perhaps beginning what would turn out to be a long liaison with his slave Sally Hemings. Whether owing to his own unsettled domestic life, or because he was living in a foreign culture, or some combination of the two, Jefferson had a lot to say about women, in particular about their appropriate roles in society. Some of these comments reveal, if not a streak of misogyny, at least an anxiety about female sexuality and the risks that it posed for both the male body and the body politic.

9. Thomas Jefferson to [François Jean de Beauvoir, marquis de] Chastellux, Nov. 26, 1782, in Peterson, ed., *Thomas Jefferson, Writings,* 780.

10. Thomas Jefferson to Mary Jefferson Eppes, Oct. 26, 1801, in Edwin Morris Betts and James Adam Bear, Jr., eds., *The Family Letters of Thomas Jefferson* (Columbia, Mo., 1966), 210, Jefferson to Martha Jefferson Randolph, May 31, 1798, 164; Lewis, "'Blessings of Domestic Society,'" in Onuf, ed., *Jeffersonian Legacies,* 109–146.

Jefferson made it quite clear to anyone who asked that Europe was no place for a young man. The only question was how old he had to be before he could travel safely. John and Abigail Adams's daughter Nabby (Abigail) remembered Jefferson's saying that "no man was fit to come abroad until 35," while he told Walker Maury that "no American should come to Europe under 30 years of age." He told Charles Thomson that he did not know "one good purpose on earth which can be effected by a young gentleman's coming here." He worried in particular about one of their young friends. "I am in hopes he is discreet and that you need not fear the corruption of his morals." Jefferson worried that such young men might form "a connection, as is the fashion here, which he might be unwilling to shake off when it shall be proper for him to return to his own country [Is that what Jefferson did with Maria Cosway, shake her off?] and which might detain him disadvantageously here." The temptations of Paris, "where beauty is a begging in every street," were often too great. The problem, quite obviously, was women, beautiful women. One sees here a glimmer of the young Jefferson, concerned that men make appropriate marriages in America. A European dalliance—a European woman—might get in the way.[11]

Jefferson warned young men directly and even more explicitly. When John Banister, Jr., asked Jefferson's advice about where to study in Europe, Jefferson told him to go to William and Mary. England, with its "drinking, horse-racing and boxing," was bad enough, but the rest of Europe was even worse. There a young man "is led by the strongest of all the human passions into a spirit for female intrigue destructive of his own and others happiness, or a passion for whores destructive of his health." Moreover, "in both cases," he "learns to consider fidelity to the marriage bed as an ungentlemanly practice and inconsistent with happiness." And, once again, the fundamental threat comes from women, as the young man "recollects the voluptuary dress and arts of the European women and pities and despises the chaste affections and simplicity of those of his own country." Jefferson told Maury that a young man could not come to Europe without threat to his "virtue, . . . health and . . . happiness." One cannot help thinking that Jefferson himself must have been sorely tempted. For our purposes here, what is more impor-

11. *Journal and Correspondence of Miss Adams, Daughter of John Adams, Second President of the United States* . . . (New York, 1841), 49, quoted in Brian Steele, "Thomas Jefferson's Gender Frontier," *Journal of American History,* XCV (2008), 25; Thomas Jefferson to Walker Maury, Aug. 19, 1785, in Boyd et al., eds., *Papers of Thomas Jefferson,* VIII, 409, Thomas Jefferson to Charles Thomson, Nov. 11, 1784, VII, 518–519.

tant is the intensity of Jefferson's feeling that beautiful European temptresses threatened the happiness and health of young American men. The fault was entirely with the women.[12]

To be sure, this sort of misogyny was not unusual. It was, as Hanna Fenichel Pitkin has pointed out, a staple of republican thought. Although Jefferson's political thought was in many ways fundamentally liberal—his belief in the superiority of private life, for example—it also incorporated a misogynist streak, one that he expressed in republican terms. This misogyny, I have tried to suggest, became most pronounced in those periods in his life when he was unattached and either beset by or perhaps was himself besetting women. When he was in France, it became embedded in a republican critique of monarchy. If we return to Jefferson's letter to Banister, we can see how the pieces fit together. When a young American man such as Banister goes to Europe, Jefferson warned, "he is fascinated with the privileges of the European aristocrats, and sees with abhorrence the lovely equality which the poor enjoys with the rich in his own country: he contracts a partiality for aristocracy or monarchy." While acquiring manners that were superficially pleasing, the young man "acquires a fondness for European luxury and dissipation and a contempt for the simplicity of his own country." And, of course, "he is led by the strongest of all the human passions into a spirit for female intrigue . . . or a passion for whores." Hence, aristocracy was seductive and whorish, and seductive women were aristocratic: aristocracy, luxury, dissipation, and women who will destroy a man's health and happiness are all of a piece.[13]

Jefferson's critique of the Old World was deeply gendered, which meant that he could not help depicting America as a gender utopia. In a well-known letter to Anne Willing Bingham, a beautiful young woman who was married to one of the wealthiest men in Philadelphia, he compared the "empty bustle of Paris" with the "tranquil pleasures of America," each of which he embodied as a woman. In Paris, "Madame" was lucky to make it out of bed before noon, perhaps squeezing in a little visiting before having her hair done. Then came more visiting, supper, and, after that, "cards; and after cards bed; to rise at noon the next day, and to tread, like a mill horse, the same trodden circle over again. Thus the days of life are consumed, one by one, without an object beyond the present moment." Jefferson drew a con-

12. Thomas Jefferson to John Banister, Jr., Oct. 15, 1785, in Boyd et al., eds., *Papers of Thomas Jefferson,* VIII, 635–637, Jefferson to Maury, Aug. 19, 1785, 409.

13. Jefferson to Banister, Jr., Oct. 15, 1785, ibid., 636; Hanna Fenichel Pitkin, *Fortune Is a Woman: Gender and Politics in the Thought of Niccolo Machiavelli* (Berkeley, Calif., 1984).

trast with America, where—and remember that he was writing to one of his country's wealthiest women—"the society of your husband, the fond cares for the children, the arrangements of the house, the improvements of the grounds, fill every moment with a healthy and an useful activity." Utility was the measure of a healthy society, and utility consisted in serving the needs of a woman's family and her social circle more generally. Proper gender relations made American society properly bourgeois. "The intervals of leisure are filled by the society of real friends, whose affections are not thinned to cob-web, by being spread over a thousand objects." Here Jefferson set out a vision of the properly functioning society and made women its anchor. "Be you my dear," Jefferson once instructed his elder daughter, not yet twenty years old and just married into a family beset by turmoil, "the link of love, union, and peace for the whole family."[14]

Jefferson was working toward a conventional understanding of sex roles, one that assigned politics to men and domestic life to women. As I have argued elsewhere, this gendered order was deeply important to Jefferson psychologically: he needed his family to sustain him and to provide him with a refuge from the conflicts of politics.[15]

This gendered order was also a cornerstone of Jefferson's politics and his political economy as well. Let us begin with his politics. Jefferson took it as a given that women did not belong in politics. In France, he complained to Bingham in the spring of 1788, "All the world is now politically mad. Men, women, children talk nothing else. . . . The women of this capital, some on foot, some on horses, and some in carriages hunting pleasure in the streets, in routs and assemblies, and forgetting that they have left it behind them in their nurseries." This was pandemonium. The contrast between the Parisian women and American ones, who "have the good sense to value domestic happiness above all other," was "a comparison of Amazons and Angels."[16]

Jefferson's tone with his female friend was lighthearted; he no doubt thought he was being pleasant, perhaps even flirtatious. When he brought up the same subject with George Washington half a year later, however, the tone was serious. Jefferson was troubled by "the influence of women in the

14. Thomas Jefferson to Anne Willing Bingham, Feb. 7, 1787, in Peterson, ed., *Thomas Jefferson, Writings,* 887–888; Jefferson to Martha Jefferson Randolph, July 17, 1790, in Betts and Bear, Jr., eds., *Family Letters,* 60–61.

15. Lewis, "'Blessings of Domestic Society,'" in Onuf, ed., *Jeffersonian Legacies,* 109–146.

16. Thomas Jefferson to Anne Willing Bingham, May 11, 1788, in Peterson, ed., *Thomas Jefferson, Writings,* 922–923.

government." As France moved toward revolution, he worried—and remember that he is writing to the man who will shortly become the first president of the United States—that French attempts at reform would come to naught because of it. "The manners of the nation allow them to visit, alone, all persons in office, to sollicit the affairs of the husband, family, or friends." He had no such worries for his own country, in which, "fortunately for the happiness of the sex itself," female influence "does not endeavor to extend itself in our country beyond the domestic line." In political life as in social, the United States was a gender utopia, a new and improved world, for men, and, Jefferson thought, for women, also.[17]

Let us turn, now, to Jefferson's political economy. His European travels gave him an opportunity to observe society in the countryside as well as the city, and there, too, he saw the baneful effects of Old World despotism. As Jefferson crossed the Rhine from Holland to Germany, he found that the "transition from ease and opulence to extreme poverty is remarkable. . . . The soil and climate are the same; the governments alone differ." Moreover, "With the poverty, the fear also of slaves is visible in the faces of the Prussian subjects." In the villages he visited, "The women do everything. . . . They dig the earth, plough, saw, cut and split wood, row, tow the bateaux, etc." It disturbed Jefferson to see white women engaging in such heavy labor. He saw the same thing in eastern France, and it led him to meditate on the proper roles for men and women. "While one considers" women "as useful and rational companions, one cannot forget that they are also objects of our pleasures; nor can they ever forget it. While employed in dirt and drudgery, some tag of a ribbon, some ring, or bit of bracelet, earbob or necklace, or something of that kind, will show that the desire of pleasing is never suspended in them. It is an honorable circumstance for man, that the first moment he is at his ease, he allots the internal employments to his female partner, and takes the external on himself. And this circumstance, or its reverse, is a pretty good indication that a people are, or are not at their ease." By "ease" Jefferson meant free from the necessity of toil: no proper society would make its women work outdoors, doing backbreaking labor, if it had any real choice in the matter.[18]

Jefferson's ruminations took him back to America and one of his favorite topics, the Native Americans. "Among the Indians, . . . every Indian man

17. Thomas Jefferson to George Washington, Dec. 4, 1788, ibid., 932–933.

18. Thomas Jefferson, "Memorandums on a Tour from Paris to Amsterdam, Strasburg, and Back to Paris," Mar. 3, 1788, ibid., 629–658 (quotations, 634, 640, 651).

is a soldier or warrior, and the whole body of warriors constitute a standing army, always employed in war or hunting. To support that army, there remain no laborers but the women." But "here, then, is so heavy a military establishment, that the civil part of the nation is reduced to women only. But this is a barbarous perversion of the natural destination of the two sexes. Women are formed by nature for attentions, not for hard labor."[19]

When he returned to America, Jefferson tried to get Indians to adopt "natural" gender roles. He hoped that once game became scarce through overhunting, Indian men would willingly take up farming and free their women for work indoors. Once Indians became farmers, everyone would benefit. "When they withdraw themselves to the culture of a small piece of land, they will perceive how useless to them are their extensive forests, and will be willing to pare them off from time to time in exchange for necessaries for their farms and families."[20]

We may be stunned by how self-serving Jefferson's vision was: as Indian men became farmers, they would happily sell parcels of their land in order to purchase American manufactured goods, at the same time tying themselves into global commercial networks and satisfying the land lust of the growing hordes of white settlers. How convenient. Self-serving as this scheme might have been, at least Jefferson understood its inner logic, and, if pressed, he could have justified its underlying premises. After all, he believed that this sort of commerce, based on the family farm, created the conditions for peace and prosperity.

But, where, one wonders, did Jefferson imagine that slavery fit into this scheme? His ideal—and this is commonplace—was the freehold family farm. In his travels through Europe, in his observations about Native Americans, and in his paeans to American self-sufficiency, he seemed to assume that men should work outdoors and women indoors, caring for the home and manufacturing cloth. In this context, the War of 1812 was actually a good thing. "Household manufacture is taking deep root with us," Jefferson told James Ronaldson in 1813. "I have a carding machine, two spinning machines, and looms with the flying shuttle." "Scarcely a family fails to clothe itself," he reported happily to Du Pont de Nemours, and to Philip Mazzei, he wrote, "We are getting the spinning machines into all our farm houses. I have near 100. spindles in operation for clothing our own family." In only the last of these boasts about increased American self-sufficiency is there even

19. Ibid., 651–652.
20. Thomas Jefferson to William H. Harrison, Feb. 27, 1803, ibid., 1118.

a hint that anyone other than the farmwife and her daughters was doing the spinning, and even there the slippage is evident: we are getting spinning machines into all of our farmhouses; I have nearly a hundred spindles in operation to clothe my own family. Which farmhouse can contain a hundred spindles?[21]

Jefferson, however, never directly confronted this contradiction. Instead, he left the impression that industrious farm women were making cloth at home, liberating the United States from foreign dependency. Moreover, as David Waldstreicher has argued, Jefferson made home manufacture of cloth the measure of (white) female virtue, praising, for example, a Mrs. Mason, whose production of homespun during the War of 1812 made her "a more dangerous adversary to our British foes, than all our Generals." "Silence about slavery and its politics undergirds the celebration of a white woman's virtue," Waldstreicher argues.[22]

In this context, Jefferson's 1810 letter to James Madison, in which he set out a scheme for providing every farm in Virginia with merino sheep, is quite extraordinary. Once again, I am touching on a subject—here, Jefferson's merino mania—that is well known. In this particular letter, we see several of Jefferson's characteristic obsessions come together: merino sheep, American economic self-sufficiency, and the breeding of animals (with talk of half bloods, three-quarters bloods, and so on). In this particular scheme, Jefferson set out a plan that would put a merino ram in every county in the state in only seven years, and then, in only a year or two more, a ewe as well. Unless one knew that the state Jefferson was discussing was Virginia, one would think that he was describing a plan to encourage the production of fine wool on family farms. The slippage is stunning.[23]

21. Thomas Jefferson to James Ronaldson, Jan. 12, 1813, in Andrew A. Lipscomb and Albert Ellery Bergh, eds., *The Writings of Thomas Jefferson . . .*, 20 vols. (Washington, D.C., 1903–1904), XIII, 205, Jefferson to E. I. Du Pont de Nemours, Nov. 8, 1812, XVIII, 276; Jefferson to Philip Mazzei, Dec. 29, 1813, in Paul Leicester Ford, ed., *The Works of Thomas Jefferson,* XI (New York, 1905), 366. For Jefferson's views on the freehold family farm, see, for example, Henry Nash Smith, *Virgin Land: The American West as Symbol and Myth* (Cambridge, Mass., 1950).

22. See David Waldstreicher, "Why Thomas Jefferson and African Americans Wore Their Politics on Their Sleeves: Dress and Mobilization between American Revolutions," in Jeffrey L. Pasley, Andrew W. Robertson, and Waldstreicher, eds., *Beyond the Founders: New Approaches to the Political History of the Early American Republic* (Chapel Hill, N.C., 2004), 79–103, esp. 97. For Jefferson's comment about Mrs. Mason, see Thomas Jefferson to John Mason, Aug. 18, 1814, Jefferson Papers, Library of Congress, quoted ibid., 95.

23. Thomas Jefferson to James Madison, May 13, 1810, in Peterson, ed., *Thomas Jefferson, Writings,* 1223–1225.

Or is it? In another of his letters from Paris, this a long one to the South Carolinian William Drayton, Jefferson described his travels through the south of France, which, because its climate was, he thought, similar to that of South Carolina and Georgia, seemed to offer useful lessons. Jefferson closely examined the cultivation of rice, comparing the varieties native to different regions and trying to obtain samples. He was intrigued by accounts of a "dry rice" from Cochin-China, which not only was supposed to have a superior taste and appearance but also could grow on dry land. If it could "supplant" the varieties raised in the Deep South, "it would be a great happiness, as it would enable us to get rid of those ponds of stagnant water, so fatal to human health and life." We know, and Jefferson knew, that in America, rice was a slave crop. How do we know that Jefferson knew? Bear with me for a moment more.[24]

Jefferson continued his descriptions of French agriculture. He recommended against viniculture: "It is a species of gambling." The caper, however, was worth considering. Most of the labor consisted of picking the capers, which had to be done every day from midsummer to mid fall, "but this is the work of women and children." Jefferson considered this fact, the employment of women and children in relatively easy labor, to be an advantage. Thus, he recommended figs and mulberries. "Their culture, too, is by women and children, and, therefore, earnestly to be desired in countries where there are slaves. In these, the women and children are often employed in labors disproportioned to their sex and age. By presenting to the master objects of culture, easier and equally beneficial, all temptation to misemploy them would be removed, and the lot of this tender part of our species be much softened." Here, then, finally, was Jefferson's recognition that in America, slave women—this was the nature of slavery—worked outdoors. And here also is the assertion that slave women, and children, are, like white women, the "tender part of our species" and should be spared backbreaking labor. One of the objects of Jefferson's plans for agricultural reform was to lighten the labor of slave women, to make their condition closer to that of their white sisters.[25]

Of all the plants that Jefferson observed, he was most enthusiastic about the olive tree, with which he hoped to "cover the southern States." If South Carolinians revered those who had introduced rice, "a plant which sows life

24. Thomas Jefferson to William Drayton, July 30, 1787, in Lipscomb and Bergh, eds., *Writings of Thomas Jefferson,* VI, 193–204 (quotations, 197). I thank Professor Annette Gordon-Reed for pointing me toward this important document.

25. Ibid., 198–200.

and death with almost equal hand, what obligations would be due to him who should introduce the olive tree. . . . Were the owner of slaves to view it only as the means of bettering their condition, how much would he better that by planting one of those trees for every slave he possessed!" In earnestly recommending the olive tree to his countrymen in South Carolina and Georgia, Jefferson noted that he himself had been "an eye witness to the blessings which this tree sheds on the poor."[26]

Jefferson's views on slavery are too well known to require analysis here. Suffice it to say that we most often think of him as a man caught on the horns of a dilemma of his own making. On the one hand, he understood—after all, he was one of the authors of the proposition—that human slavery was a violation of the principle of human equality. On the other hand, his racism and his political paralysis made it impossible for him to do anything more than free a handful of his own slaves. As Adam Rothman, Peter Onuf, and others have brilliantly shown, rather than confront this dilemma, Jefferson retreated into fanciful schemes for diffusion and colonization.[27]

It is certainly possible to consider Jefferson's ideas about mulberries and olive trees as equally fanciful. The South Carolina Lowcountry is not Provence. But in his agricultural schemes, we see the desire to improve slaves' working conditions and the recognition that labor in the rice swamps was "fatal to human health and life." We also see Jefferson's unhappy recognition that slavery typically required women to do what he considered men's work. Perhaps, he mused, the mulberry offered a way out.

Jefferson returned from France, then, with several things: a well-developed sense of the superiority of America, with its equality, simplicity, and proper gender relations; a plan for the amelioration of slavery; and one thing more—a slave mistress. It is impossible to know exactly when Jefferson entered into his liaison with Sally Hemings, but, if the memoir of their son Madison Hemings, which has proved accurate in so many particulars, is to be credited, it was while the two of them were in Paris. There is every indication that this was a long-term relationship, lasting perhaps until Jefferson's death in 1826.[28]

And Jefferson left something in France, as well: the extremes of his mi-

26. Ibid., 202–203.

27. Adam Rothman, *Slave Country: American Expansion and the Origins of the Deep South* (Cambridge, Mass., 2005); Peter S. Onuf, *Jefferson's Empire: The Language of American Nationhood* (Charlottesville, Va., 2000).

28. On the reliability of Madison Hemings's memoirs, see Annette Gordon-Reed, *Thomas Jefferson and Sally Hemings: An American Controversy* (Charlottesville, Va., 1997).

sogyny. For the most part, his subsequent writings are free from the invective against political women and prostitutes and the hostility to women more generally that had risen to the surface twice earlier in his life, once when he was courting and then, later, when he was in France and unattached. Perhaps American women really were more chaste, as Jefferson suggested, and, once he was home, he no longer had to deal with women who were more aggressive than he liked.

Or perhaps, once he returned to America with the woman who would turn out to be his lifelong companion, he settled down, and the anxieties that gave rise to his misogyny abated. The evidence for this hypothesis is at best tenuous. It consists almost entirely of a simple correlation: Jefferson's anxieties about women manifested themselves at those times when he was unattached. We do not see the same sort of intense misogyny again after Jefferson's return from France, which is also the time when he entered into his long relationship with Sally Hemings.

It is very difficult to know what their relationship was like. We have very little to go on: their son Madison's brief memoirs, a few comments by others, the details that can be reconstructed about their lives together, the utter absence of any discussion of Sally Hemings in Jefferson's letters. But I cannot help wondering if the relationship functioned in some ways for Jefferson as a marriage. To be sure, the relationship was not a marriage. There was no religious or legal ceremony. Hemings had none of the legal rights of a spouse. The children she bore Jefferson were not legitimate; they were not even acknowledged. There were certainly no public declarations of love or belonging. An outsider, reading only Jefferson's letters, could not have missed Jefferson's devotion to his wife. An outsider, reading Jefferson's letters, could have missed Sally Hemings altogether. This was not a marriage.[29]

But the liaison seems to have provided Jefferson with some measure of psychological peace. Remember that many of Jefferson's paeans to domesticity date from the period after the commencement of his liaison with Sally Hemings. I do not want to go so far as to claim that Jefferson thought of Sally Hemings as "family"; I want to suggest only that the connection to her af-

29. For contrasting views, see the works of Rhys Isaac and Andrew Burstein. Isaac calls the relationship between Jefferson and Sally Hemings "a custom-of-the-place marriage" (Isaac, "Monticello Stories Old and New," in Lewis and Onuf, eds., *Sally Hemings and Thomas Jefferson,* 119). Andrew Burstein, however, is skeptical that Hemings functioned as a "substitute wife." "Jefferson's feelings toward Sally Hemings," Burstein has written, "no matter the duration of their physical intimacy, cannot be analogous to marital affection, first because of the work she did, and second, because Jefferson was not open about the relationship" (Burstein, *Jefferson's Secrets,* 154).

forded him sufficient contentment that he could rhapsodize about domestic happiness rather than rail about the female sex.

In this context, we might revisit Madison Hemings's memoirs. Of his mother, he said, "It was her duty, all her life which I can remember, up to the time of father's death, to take care of his chamber and wardrobe, look after us children and do such light work as sewing, etc." His sister Harriet "learned to spin and to weave in a little factory on the home plantation." Here was the gendered division of labor that Jefferson associated with an ideal American farm society. Of course, there is slippage, as there always seems to be when we are talking about Jefferson and either gender or slavery. This was the sort of work that might be expected of a farmwife; it was certainly not appropriate for the wife of a wealthy planter. But perhaps by giving his Hemings children and Sally Hemings herself the kind of useful but unpunishing work that women and children performed on the freehold farm of his imagination, Jefferson was able to reconcile himself not only to his unorthodox domestic arrangements but also to slavery itself.[30]

30. Madison Hemings, "Life among the Lowly; Number 1," *Pike County Republican* (Waverly, Ohio), Mar. 13, 1873, [4], quoted in Gordon-Reed, *Thomas Jefferson and Sally Hemings,* 248.

"The Blessings of Domestic Society"
Thomas Jefferson's Family and the Transformation of American Politics

Why would Thomas Jefferson's family be interesting to those who are reflecting upon the Jeffersonian legacy? When Jefferson wrote his epitaph, he nowhere mentioned his own family or the families of his fellow Americans: he wanted to be remembered as the "Father of the University of Virginia" as well as the author of the Declaration of Independence and the Virginia Statute for Religious Freedom. He measured his worth in ideas and institutions, not human relationships. Moreover, Jefferson entrusted his legacy, not to his family, but to his compatriot and closest ally, James Madison. A few months before his death, realizing that the end could not be far off, Jefferson told his friend of fifty years that it has "been a great solace to me, to believe that you are engaged in vindicating to posterity the course we have pursued for preserving to them, in all their purity, the blessings of self-government." He asked Madison to "take care of me when dead."[1]

To his immediate posterity, a family that had "blessed me by their affections, and never by their conduct given me a moment's pain," Jefferson bequeathed a debt of more than a hundred thousand dollars and memories that would last them all the days of their lives. Years after her grandfather's death, Ellen Wayles Randolph Coolidge would find herself haunted by the memory of Monticello. "When I dream it is mostly of long past times. Night after night I have been surrounded by the friends of childhood and early youth—my grandfather, mother, brothers, sisters, those whom I dearly loved and who dearly loved me, and who I hope in God's own time to rejoin."[2] So

This essay was originally published as Jan Lewis, "'The Blessings of Domestic Society': Thomas Jefferson's Family and the Transformation of American Politics," in Peter S. Onuf, ed., *Jefferson Legacies* (Charlottesville, Va., 1993), 109–146.

1. Merrill D. Peterson, *Thomas Jefferson and the New Nation: A Biography* (New York, 1970), 988 ("Father"); Thomas Jefferson to James Madison, Feb. 17, 1826, in Peterson, ed., *Thomas Jefferson, Writings: Autobiography, A Summary View of the Rights of British America, Notes on the State of Virginia, Public Papers, Addresses, Messages, and Replies, Miscellany, Letters* (New York, 1984), 1515. See also Dumas Malone, *Jefferson and His Time,* 6 vols. (Boston, 1948–1981), VI, 499.

2. Thomas Jefferson to Thomas Jefferson Randolph, Feb. 8, 1826, in Edwin Morris Betts and James Adam Bear, Jr., eds., *The Family Letters of Thomas Jefferson* (Columbia,

dearly did Jefferson's grandchildren love him that they willingly accepted the huge debt, renouncing in advance the property Jefferson had hoped to be able to leave them and claiming as their only due a lifetime of love.[3]

That Thomas Jefferson's children and grandchildren loved him deeply we cannot doubt, nor could we question his attachment to them. The letters that they wrote each other bespeak a passion that words could barely contain. He closed his letters to his daughters with "unchangeable and tenderest attachment" and "never-ceasing love," and his daughters Martha and Maria (Mary) responded "with the tenderest love and reverence," with "ardent affection," and "with the tenderest love yours."[4] So strong was the love and so inadequate mere words for expressing it that, with almost each letter, the conventional closing would be changed. Even after their marriages and the births of their children, both daughters assured their father that he was the one they loved best. Maria apologized for her "inability to express how much I love and revere you. But you are first and dearest to my heart." Martha used almost the same words, asking her father to "believe your self *first* and unrivaled in the heart of your devoted child," and, as she contemplated his retirement from public office, she assured him that "I make no exception when I say the *first* and most important object with me will be the dear and sacred duty of nursing and chearing your old age."[5]

Jefferson cultivated this love by telling his daughters that his happiness depended upon it. In 1799, he told Maria that the "affectionate expressions" in one of her letters "kindled up all those feelings of love for you and our dear connections which now constitute the only real happiness of my life."

Mo., 1966), 470; Autobiographical fragment, n.d., Correspondence of Ellen Wayles Randolph Coolidge, 1819–1861, Accession No. 9090, 38-584, Albert and Shirley Small Special Collections Library, University of Virginia, Charlottesville, Va.; Malone, *Jefferson and His Time,* VI, 511.

3. See, for example, Ellen Randolph Coolidge to Thomas Jefferson, Aug. 1, 1825, in Betts and Bear, eds., *Family Letters,* 454, Thomas Jefferson Randolph to Jefferson, Feb. 3, [1826], 467, Francis Wayles Eppes to Jefferson, Feb. 23, 1826, 471–472.

4. Thomas Jefferson to Mary [Maria] Jefferson Eppes, Apr. 11, 1801, ibid., 201, Jefferson to Martha Jefferson Randolph, Nov. 7, 1803, 249, Martha Jefferson Randolph to Jefferson, received July 1, 1798, 166, Martha Jefferson Randolph to Jefferson, Nov. 18, 1801, 213, Mary Jefferson Eppes to Jefferson, Nov. 5, [1802], 239. Martha Jefferson was born in 1772 and married Thomas Mann Randolph in 1790; she bore twelve children, of whom eleven survived to adulthood. Maria Jefferson was born in 1778 and married John Wayles Eppes in 1797; only one of her three children, Francis, survived to adulthood. Maria died in 1804, and Martha in 1836.

5. Mary Jefferson Eppes to Thomas Jefferson, Jan. 11, [1803], in Betts and Bear, eds., *Family Letters,* 240, Martha Jefferson Randolph to Jefferson, Apr. 16, 1802, 223, Martha Jefferson Randolph to Jefferson, Mar. 20, 1807, 303.

A year later, he reminded his other daughter "how essential your society is to my happiness." Such expressions became the refrain of his letters from the seat of national government. A year before the end of his second term as president, Jefferson told his only surviving child, Martha (Maria had died in 1804), "I long to be among you where I know nothing but love and delight, and where . . . I would be indulged . . . with the blessings of domestic society." "It is in the love of one's family only," he had once told Maria, "that heartfelt happiness is known."[6]

Jefferson loved his daughters and, in due course, their children, ardently and deeply. Perhaps that is reason enough for us to be interested in Thomas Jefferson's family: he towers so over the landscape of American history, and his legacy is so great, that anything that was of such great importance to him must be important to us, too. Thomas Jefferson adored, not simply his own family, but the very notion of family life. As he explained to Maria just before her marriage to John Wayles Eppes, the event "promises us long years of domestic concord and love, the best ingredient in human happiness." Jefferson believed that true and complete happiness—for him and for everyone—could be found only at home.[7]

These were the sentiments he voiced to his family, but not, as a rule, to the world at large. His views on the family do not form a significant part of his political or social philosophy, yet clearly they were deeply felt beliefs, in some ways an expression of his essential character. Because Jefferson's pronouncement on happiness, which proclaimed its pursuit as one of mankind's unalienable rights, is so central a part of our national heritage, it is perhaps curious that he apparently never discussed the relationship between the happiness he found at home and the public happiness that was a staple of Enlightenment thought. Scholars who have debated what Jefferson meant by "the pursuit of happiness" suggest that it must have been either a social, public happiness, or a more private and individualist pursuit—a euphemism for property. Although it seems clear that Jefferson had in mind a social happiness whose achievement was somehow enhanced by good government, his letters to his family indicate that he believed deeply in a sort of private happiness that was something other than the acquisition of property. His correspondence—indeed, his life—with his family reveals that Thomas

6. Thomas Jefferson to Mary Jefferson Eppes, Feb. 7, 1799, ibid., 173–174, Jefferson to Martha Jefferson Randolph, Feb. 11, 1800, 184, Jefferson to Martha Jefferson Randolph, Nov. 23, 1807, 315, Jefferson to Mary Jefferson Eppes, Oct. 26, 1801, 210.

7. Thomas Jefferson to Mary Jefferson, draft, June 14, 1797, in Betts and Bear, eds., *Family Letters,* 148. See, similarly, Jefferson to Mary Jefferson Eppes, Jan. 1, 1799, ibid., 170.

Jefferson believed in a realm of happiness that his political philosophy did not engage.[8]

It might therefore be argued that Jefferson's family life and the opinions he expressed about it bore no relationship to his public, political writings and actions and that, when he used the term *happiness* in writing to his daughters, the words he had written in the first paragraph of the Declaration of Independence could not have been further from his mind. It is possible that Jefferson segmented his life, drawing a sharp line between the part that was private and the part that was public. But *public* and *private* are always relative rather than absolute terms; they derive their meaning from each other. And, at just this time, the relationship between these two realms was being redefined. In rendering a vision of private life, Thomas Jefferson was necessarily constructing the public world as well.[9]

I

If we want to know what place the family occupied in the Jeffersonian vision of social and political life, we might begin by examining those passages in his letters where he wrote most passionately about the blessings of domestic society. The first time Jefferson said that his happiness derived from his family was in June 1791, when, writing his daughter Maria from Philadelphia, where he was serving as George Washington's secretary of state, he exclaimed, "Would to god I could be with you to partake of your felicities, and to tell you in person how much I love you all, and how necessary it is to my happiness to be with you." It is not clear what, if anything, occasioned this declaration. All of his previous letters to his daughters had been affectionate by any standard, but it was only after he had returned to the United States from Paris, where he had been serving as ambassador, and entered Washington's cabinet, that he began linking his happiness to his family.[10]

8. For a summary of this debate, see Jan Lewis, "Happiness," in Jack P. Greene and J. R. Pole, eds., *The Blackwell Encyclopedia of the American Revolution* (Cambridge, Mass., 1991), 641–647.

9. See Jan Lewis, *The Pursuit of Happiness: Family and Values in Jefferson's Virginia* (New York, 1983). Consider also Ruth H. Bloch, "The Gendered Meanings of Virtue in Revolutionary America," *Signs: Journal of Women in Culture and Society,* XIII (1987), 37–58.

10. Thomas Jefferson to Maria Jefferson, June 26, 1791, in Betts and Bear, eds., *Family Letters,* 86. Jefferson's association of happiness with home was foreshadowed in the letter he wrote François Jean de Beauvoir, marquis de Chastellux, on November 26, 1782. Before the death of his wife, Martha, several months earlier, Jefferson "had folded myself in the arms of retirement, and rested all prospects of future happiness on domestic and literary objects." See Jefferson to Chastellux, Nov. 26, 1782, in Peterson, ed., *Thomas Jefferson, Writings,*

From 1791 on, however, virtually each of Jefferson's explosions of love for his family was so clearly part of an explicit contrast he made with the public world of politics that we might reasonably surmise that his 1791 letter to Maria was occasioned by some disappointment in Philadelphia. In January 1792, for example, he wrote Martha that his "reveries" about the happy times they had spent together "in our wanderings over the world" helped to "alleviate the toils and inquietudes of my present situation, and leave me always impressed with the desire of being at home once more, and of exchanging labour, envy, and malice for ease, domestic occupation, and domestic love and society." Jefferson's biographer, Dumas Malone, reads this letter as Jefferson's first disclosure that he had decided to retire from office. He had grown weary of his conflict with Alexander Hamilton and the rancor of national polities. At the time of his 1791 letter to Maria, Jefferson had become embroiled—not for the last time—in a newspaper controversy about Thomas Paine, and it might well have triggered his longing for the "felicities" of home.[11]

Jefferson, of course, did not resign his office for another two years, and barely two years after that he was back in Philadelphia as vice president. He would not retire from public office until 1809, after two terms as president. Except for several extended visits, his daughters remained in Virginia, where they received their father's ardent letters. Barely had Jefferson returned to government before he was once again telling his daughters, "I feel the desire of never separating from you grow daily stronger, for nothing can compensate me with the want of your society. . . . Continue to love me as I do you." Such expressions, whose effect surely worked to achieve the end that Jefferson explicitly designed—increasing his daughters' attachment to him—continued as long as he held public office.[12]

This construction of public life as a burden and a deprivation had been foreshadowed in a letter Jefferson had written to James Monroe in 1782 when he declined the office of delegate to the Virginia legislature. With his young wife weak after just giving birth and apparently dying in perhaps the same room from which he wrote, Jefferson gave voice to the claims of private life: "I considered that I had been thirteen years engaged in public service,

---

780. Jefferson destroyed the letters he had exchanged with his wife, who died in 1782. See Malone, *Jefferson and His Time,* I, 393–398.

11. Thomas Jefferson to Martha Jefferson Randolph, Jan. 15, 1792, in Betts and Bear, eds., *Family Letters,* 93; Malone, *Jefferson and His Time,* II, 363–366, 431.

12. Thomas Jefferson to Mary Jefferson, May 25, 1797, in Betts and Bear, eds., *Family Letters,* 145.

that during that time I had so totally abandoned all attention to my private affairs as to permit them to run into great disorder and ruin, that I had now a family advanced to years which required my attention and instruction." Here family was, like public service, also an obligation, if a private and inescapably countervailing one. "If we are made in some degree for others, yet in a greater are we made for ourselves. It were contrary to feeling and indeed ridiculous to suppose that a man had less right in himself than one of his neighbors or indeed all of them put together. This would be slavery and not that liberty which the bill of rights has made inviolable and for the preservation of which our government has been charged." Jefferson pitted the claims of society against the rights of the individual; like others at the time, he connected the obligations of family to self-interest, which he believed he had neglected. His conception of the polity, at least for the moment, was individualist.[13]

Jefferson no doubt was disappointed that public life had not been more gratifying. His service as governor had been sharply criticized, and the wounds had not healed. "By a constant sacrifice of time, labour, loss, parental and family duties, I had been so far from gaining the affection of my countrymen, which was the only reward I ever asked or could have felt, that I had even lost the small estimation I before possessed." Jefferson must have anticipated that his public service would bind him to his countrymen by ties of affection; he would willingly have sacrificed his personal interest for this form of love. In its absence, he would return to the pursuit of a private, Lockean sort of happiness. In his letter to Monroe, Jefferson implicitly contrasted a Scottish Enlightenment vision of society, bound together by affection, and a Lockean one, in which "we are made . . . in a greater [degree] for ourselves." In this schema, the family is merely an extension of the self.[14]

13. Thomas Jefferson to James Monroe, May 20, 1782, in Peterson, ed., *Thomas Jefferson, Writings,* 777, 779. Alexander Hamilton thought that "private attachments" to the family could undermine loyalty to the Republic and even lead to oligarchy if a man put the interests of his family ahead of those of the nation (Hamilton, "The Federalist No. 77 [76]," in Jacob E. Cooke, ed., *The Federalist* [Middletown, Conn., 1961], 518–519). George Washington agreed. In fragments of an undelivered first inaugural address, he stated: "The Divine Providence hath not seen fit, that my blood should be transmitted or my name perpetuated by the endearing, though sometimes seducing channel of immediate offspring. I have no child for whom I could wish to make a provision—no family to build in greatness upon my Country's ruins" ("Undelivered First Inaugural Address: Fragments," [Apr. 30, 1789], in W. W. Abbot et al. eds., *The Papers of George Washington,* Presidential Series, II [Charlottesville, Va., 1987], 158–173).

14. Jefferson to Monroe, May 20, 1782, in Peterson, ed., *Thomas Jefferson, Writings,* 777–

In the years to come, Jefferson would return to public service; he would also rework his ideas about the relationship between the self and society. No longer would he expect affection from his fellow citizens; he would plant and nurture it at home. By the 1790s, he had decided that the political world was not simply cold but downright hostile. In 1798, he told Martha, "For you to feel all the happiness of your quiet situation, you should know the rancorous passions which tear every breast here, even of the sex which should be a stranger to them. Politics and party hatreds destroy the happiness of every being here. They seem like salamanders, to consider fire as their element." He longed to be with her, "in the only scene, where, for me, the sweeter affections of life have any exercise." A few weeks later, he would render the contrast almost in a shorthand: the seat of government represented "every thing which can be disgusting," and his "dear family," "every thing which is pleasurable."[15]

The bitterness of political life made Jefferson long for his family. In 1797, he was becoming "more and more disgusted with the jealousies, the hatred and the rancorous and malignant passions of this scene," and added, "[I] lament my having ever again been drawn into public view." In 1798, political life was "a dreary scene where envy, hatred, malice, revenge, and all the worse passions of men are marshalled, to make one another as miserable as possible." In January 1801, writing from Washington where he was waiting to learn if he had been elected president, Jefferson complained that "here . . . there is such a mixture of the bad passions of the heart that one feels themselves in an enemy's country." A month later, he described for Maria "the scene passing here" as a "circle of cabal, intrigue and hatred." By 1807, Jefferson was "tired of a life of contention, and of being the personal object for the hatred of every man, who hates the present state of things."[16]

Jefferson was willing to serve his country, ultimately at great personal

778. See Jay Fliegelman, *Prodigals and Pilgrims: The American Revolution against Patriarchal Authority, 1750–1800* (New York, 1982), esp. 9–29; Daniel W. Howe, "The Political Psychology of *The Federalist*," *William and Mary Quarterly*, 3d Ser., XLIV (1987), 485–509; and Garry Wills, *Inventing America: Jefferson's Declaration of Independence* (Garden City, N.Y., 1978), esp. part 4. Consider also Perry Miller, "The Rhetoric of Sensation," in Miller, *Errand into the Wilderness* (New York, 1956), 167–183.

15. Thomas Jefferson to Martha Jefferson Randolph, May 17, 1798, in Betts and Bear, eds., *Family Letters*, 161–162, Jefferson to Martha Jefferson Randolph, May 31, 1798, 164.

16. Thomas Jefferson to Martha Jefferson Randolph, June 8, 1797, ibid., 146, Jefferson to Martha Jefferson Randolph, Feb. 8, 1798, 155, Jefferson to Martha Jefferson Randolph, Jan. 16, 1801, 191, Jefferson to Mary Jefferson Eppes, Feb. 15, 1801, 196, Jefferson to Martha Jefferson Randolph, Nov. 23, 1807, 315.

cost, but he no longer expected the affection of the public.[17] Public service might yield the satisfaction of duty performed and perhaps even the esteem of his countrymen, but it would never prove emotionally fulfilling. So often and so passionately did Jefferson contrast the love of his family with the enmity of political life that it is evident that, at some level, he had expected that public service would prove more personally gratifying. Moreover, the two terms, *family* and *politics,* were so closely linked in his mind that he could barely mention one without invoking the other.

How easily Jefferson could slide back and forth between descriptions of the pleasures of family and the tribulations of politics is nicely illustrated by the letter he wrote Martha after learning of his other daughter's engagement to John Wayles Eppes, a young man he knew and esteemed. It was a match that not only would ensure Maria's happiness but would also gratify the entire family: "I now see our fireside formed into a groupe, no one member of which has a fibre in their composition which can ever produce any jarring or jealousies among us. No irregular passions, no dangerous bias. . . ." Jefferson shifted smoothly from imagining his daughter's pleasure to fantasizing about his own, and from there it was only one more quick move to railing against the miseries of a life in politics. "When I look to the ineffable pleasures of my family society, I become more and more disgusted with the jealousies, the hatred, and the rancorous and malignant passions of this scene." And from there, another shift to the unrealized emotional expectations of public service: "I have seen enough of political honors to know that they are but splendid torments: and however one might be disposed to render services on which any of their fellow citizens should set a value; yet when as many would deprecate them as a public calamity, one may well entertain a modest doubt of their real importance, and feel the impulse to duty to be very weak. The real difficulty," the then vice president explained, was "that being once delivered into the hands of others, whose feelings are friendly to the individual and warm to the public cause, how to withdraw from them without leaving a dissatisfaction in their mind, and an impression of pusillanimity with the public." No wonder "the impulse to duty" was so weak: the most that the public could offer was friendliness, and, once an individual gave himself over to others, there was no quitting, lest he be thought a coward. Better, perhaps, not even to have entered into public service.[18]

17. See, for example, Thomas Jefferson to Thomas Jefferson Randolph, Feb. 8, 1826, ibid., 469.

18. Thomas Jefferson to Martha Jefferson Randolph, June 8, 1797, ibid., 146. See, similarly, the draft of his letter to Mary Jefferson, June 14, 1797, ibid., 148–149.

When we see how quickly Jefferson could slip from contemplating his daughter's future happiness to reflecting upon his own present misery, we might be tempted to conclude that he was simply an enormously self-centered man. Certainly, his relationship with his daughters was sometimes manipulative; there was the implication, especially in his early letters to these motherless girls, that his love was contingent upon their fulfilling his expectations. "The more you learn the more I love you," he told Martha in 1786, "and I rest the happiness of my life on seeing you beloved by all the world." A year later, spurring her on to industry in her studies, he elaborated upon his hopes not so much for her, but himself: "No body in the world can make me so happy, or so miserable as you. Retirement from public life will ere long become necessary for me. To your sister and yourself I look to render the evening of my life serene and contented. It's [*sic*] morning has been clouded by loss after loss till I have nothing left but you." Patsy and Polly, as the young girls were called, were designated not simply surrogate wives, replacements for their departed mother, but the handmaidens of their father's happiness: their primary function in life was to make him happy. No wonder both would later tell their father that they loved him above all else; that is exactly what he had trained them to do.[19]

But even in his patently manipulative 1787 letter to Martha, Jefferson implied that public life might still offer its own rewards; it would be only after his retirement that he would look to his daughters to make his life "serene and contented." His daughters were supposed to compensate him for losses in the private, not the public realm. So even if we choose to consider Jefferson an emotionally needy man who burdened his daughters throughout their lives with the responsibility for his own happiness, we must also recognize that, over the years, his thinking about the relationship between the private and public realms changed significantly. The variable in this equation is Jefferson's view of public life.

Even with his wife dying and the criticism he had received as governor still ringing in his ears, in 1782 Jefferson's greatest complaint about public service was that he had lost the "estimation" of the public and neglected his family. It was only after he entered Washington's cabinet, beginning a period of government service from which he would not completely retire for two decades, that Jefferson voiced his most passionate complaints about the rancor and malignant passions of political life; it was, not simply that he had

19. Thomas Jefferson to Martha Jefferson, Mar. 6, 1786, ibid., 30, Jefferson to Martha Jefferson, Mar. 28, 1787, 35.

lost the esteem of the public, but that a considerable portion of it seemed to hate him.

II

Like most of the Revolutionary leaders, Jefferson had anticipated that the reward for his disinterested service would be fame. This expectation was an article of the republican faith. Indeed, as Garry Wills has argued, "Fame was . . . a social glue, a structural element, for the republic in its early days." The expectation of fame stimulated leaders to the acts of self-sacrifice that the founding generation called public virtue. As James Wilson had explained it, "The love of honest and well earned fame is deeply rooted in honest and susceptible minds. Can there be a stronger incentive to the operations of this passion, than the hope of becoming the object of well founded and distinguishing applause? Can there be a more complete gratification of this passion, than the satisfaction of knowing that this applause is given—that it is given upon the most honourable principles, and acquired by the most honourable pursuits?"[20] A number of historians have noted that Washington sought this sort of fame, consciously deliberating his actions and contemplating their effect upon his reputation. In this successful effort to secure his reputation, Jefferson encouraged him, giving him pointers along the way.[21] Years later, Jefferson would describe Washington as virtue incarnate: "His integrity was most pure, his justice the most inflexible I have ever known, no motives of interest or consanguinity, of friendship or hatred, being able to bias his decision." This was the standard—and reputation—by which Jefferson would judge himself.[22]

The republican standard of public virtue promised that if one sacrificed one's interest—which included, as Jefferson's 1782 letter to Monroe had suggested, that of one's friends and family as well—one might earn fame,

20. Garry Wills, *Cincinnatus: George Washington and the Enlightenment* (Garden City, N.Y., 1984), 129; James Wilson, *Lectures on Law . . . ,* (1791), in Robert Green McCloskey, ed., *The Works of James Wilson,* 2 vols. (Cambridge, Mass., 1967), I, 405. See also Douglass Adair, "Fame and the Founding Fathers," in Trevor Colbourn, ed., *Fame and the Founding Fathers: Essays by Douglass Adair* (New York, 1974), 3–26; and Jack P. Greene, "Society, Ideology, and Politics: An Analysis of the Political Culture of Mid-Eighteenth-Century Virginia," in Greene, Richard L. Bushman, and Michael Kammen, *Society, Freedom, and Conscience: The American Revolution in Virginia, Massachusetts, and New York,* ed. Richard M. Jellison (New York, 1976), 32–34.

21. See, for example, Wills, *Cincinnatus,* chaps. 7 and 8; and Gordon S. Wood, *The Radicalism of the American Revolution* (New York, 1992), 205–210.

22. Thomas Jefferson to Dr. Walter Jones, Jan. 2, 1814, in Peterson, ed., *Thomas Jefferson, Writings,* 1318–1319.

"the affection of my countrymen." That was the reward for public service that Jefferson asked for and expected. He was confounded when it was not forthcoming. And though the source of his disappointment might in some part have been his own sensitivity to criticism and his emotional neediness, some of it surely must be attributed to the nature of politics in the 1790s.

More than half a century ago, John R. Howe, Jr., described the 1790s as a period of "political violence," one characterized by a "brutality both of expression and behavior." Jefferson, Howe suggests, spoke for many other political leaders when he complained to Edward Rutledge in 1793 that "the passions are too high at present. . . . You and I have formerly seen warm debates and high political passions. But gentlemen of different politics would then speak to each other, and separate the business of the Senate from that of society. It is not so now." Howe attributes the volatility of politics in this era to the republican belief that republican governments were inherently fragile. So great were the risks and so likely the prospect of failure that inevitably "politics was a deadly business, with little room for optimism or leniency, little reason to expect the best rather than suspect the worst of one's political enemies." Political violence, then, was a manifestation of republican ideology.[23]

It was also, of course, an expression of the structure of politics. As Jack N. Rakove has suggested, both the Constitution and the process of ratification brought about a politics that was less stable and more popular than its framers anticipated. Turnover in the first Congresses was high, as members left public service to pursue private interests. Newspapers that published the proceedings of Congress not only helped create a national politics, but public opinion and pressure as well. Anyone who entered service in the federal government expecting to find there a forum for the dispassionate discussion of the issues of the day, isolated from the whims and demands of public opinion, was sure to be disappointed.[24]

And Thomas Jefferson surely was disappointed. He began his service

23. John R. Howe, Jr., "Republican Thought and the Political Violence of the 1790s," *American Quarterly,* XIX (1967), 148–149, 165; Thomas Jefferson to Edward Rutledge, June 24, 1797, in Adrienne Koch and William Peden, eds., *The Life and Selected Writings of Thomas Jefferson* (New York, 1944), 544. Howe excerpts this letter somewhat differently. See also Marshall Smelser, "The Federalist Period as an Age of Passion," *American Quarterly,* X (1958), 391–419.

24. Jack N. Rakove, "The Structure of Politics at the Accession of George Washington," in Richard Beeman, Stephen Botein, and Edward C. Carter, II, eds., *Beyond Confederation: Origins of the Constitution and American National Identity* (Williamsburg, Va., and Chapel Hill, N.C., 1987), 261–294.

in the new national government equipped with republican expectations of fame at a time when politics was becoming increasingly volatile and violent. In theory, fame was supposed to be a manifestation of public esteem, but, in practice, especially at a time when the mechanisms of public opinion were unformed, it was established by a gentleman's peers, not the promiscuous public. Jefferson said he craved only the "affection of my countrymen," but what he effectively meant was the esteem of the relatively small group of men who served with him in the public realm, for how could he possibly know what the mass of men thought?

We have already heard Jefferson complaining to his daughters about the malice and venom of politics. Public approbation, or even a secure sense of the public's esteem, was elusive. In comparison to that vague sense of a public whose feelings were warm to the cause, but merely "friendly to the individual," the "jealousies, the hatred, and the malignant passions" of those whom he encountered daily cut him to the bone. Less than five months from his death, Jefferson had "no complaint against the world which has sufficiently honored me," but it was only his family that had "blessed me by their affections, and never by their conduct given me a moment's pain." Jefferson had won his family's love, not his nation's fame.[25]

It was a bargain that the fierce politics of the first decades of the early republic prepared him to make. That public life at the time was violent was no mere figure of speech; in fact, politics could be decidedly dangerous, as the experience of Jefferson's great rival, Alexander Hamilton, abundantly illustrates. The duel that ended his life was but the last and most lethal of a series of violent encounters that punctuated Hamilton's public life. In 1778 and 1779, while serving as an aide to Washington, he twice came close to dueling.[26] Charles Royster has observed that it was just at this time that dueling, a tradition among European army officers, came into vogue among the young officers of the Continental Army. He explains that dueling "increased because it settled questions of honor in a distinctive, gallant way for men newly self-conscious about their uniqueness and their proper public inviolability." The duel mushroomed in the dank soil of Valley Forge, where anxious and ambitious young men who were strangers to one another were thrown together and compelled to establish their worth and standing in each other's eyes. As Royster notes, the world of the Continental Army officer was

25. Jefferson to Thomas Jefferson Randolph, Feb. 8, 1826, in Betts and Bear, eds., *Family Letters*, 470.

26. Forrest McDonald, *Alexander Hamilton: A Biography* (New York, 1979), 20.

intimate and intense; the duel was a product of the volatile attachments this environment nourished. "The opinion of a circle of friends might decide a man's self-respect or disgrace."[27]

The same held true in the political world of the new nation, where men from a variety of backgrounds, eager for fame and anxious to prove themselves the equal in honor to the most honorable members of the new government, were thrown together on terms of intimacy. Former officers such as Hamilton, who had learned the rituals of the duel in the army, or hotheads such as John Randolph of Roanoke, insecure about their status, might find themselves issuing or provoking challenges throughout their careers. On one Saturday afternoon in July 1795, while Hamilton was out strolling with friends along New York's Wall Street, his group encountered a party of Republican rivals, also out for a walk. Words were exchanged, then insults; Hamilton attempted to intervene, was insulted, and then promptly issued a challenge. The stroll resumed; a few minutes later, Hamilton and his friends met another knot of Republicans, and more arguments, more insults, and another challenge ensued. One dispute was resolved immediately, but it took a week of negotiations to avert a duel in the other case.[28]

When men such as Hamilton believed that their standing with the public, and, hence, their capacity to win fame by serving it, rested upon their honor, "the potential for violence hovered around every public dispute." Robert H. Wiebe has noted that, in order to prevent politics from becoming a virtual bloodbath, gentleman politicians began to devise rules and customs that could channel aggressions yet still protect reputations. One tack was to attempt to identify and isolate a private realm, off-limits to both insult and the necessity of defending one's honor. Nonetheless, "anything that could be justified on grounds of republican principle, no matter how vicious or destructive to an individual's reputation, fell within a public realm and lent itself only to political or legal redress." And, conversely, any attack on a public man's character might be construed as sedition. As St. George Tucker would explain, "The right of character is a sacred and invaluable right, and is not forfeited by accepting a public employment. Whoever knowingly departs from any of these maxims is guilty of a crime against the community, as well as the person injured." Until the line between public and private could be sharply drawn—effectively narrowing the perimeters of public virtue and re-

27. Charles Royster, *A Revolutionary People at War: The Continental Army and American Character, 1775–1783* (Williamsburg, Va., and Chapel Hill, N.C., 1979), 209–211.
28. McDonald, *Alexander Hamilton,* 308–309.

working the assumptions of republicanism—any word or deed that seemed to call into question a man's public honor could lead to political violence.[29]

Wiebe has suggested that the wars of words waged by pamphleteers and newspaper editors in this period were nothing less than sublimated duels, contests of honor by proxy. Jefferson, for example, who had no taste for physical and life-threatening encounter, did not hesitate to spur polemicists on. "A free press," Wiebe explains, "served deep emotional as well as broad public needs." But as long as politics itself remained intimate and emotionally intense, it would retain its capacity for violence, and even pamphlets or articles could provide the stimulus to duels. It was a pamphlet that led Hamilton to challenge James Monroe.[30]

The "Reynolds affair" is of particular interest to us for what it tells us about the way in which private affairs could become matters of public interest. The story began in November 1792, when the comptroller of the Treasury sued James Reynolds and Jacob Clingman for attempting to defraud the government by filing false claims. Charges were dropped when the pair agreed to make restitution and supply certain information, but, while in jail and after his release, Reynolds hinted darkly that he was in possession of certain information that reflected very badly upon the secretary of the Treasury. Eventually this information found its way to Frederick Muhlenberg, a Pennsylvania Republican and Speaker of the House in the first Congress; he then brought it to the attention of two Virginia Republicans, Senator James Monroe and Representative Abraham Venable, who then sought confirmation from Reynolds. In mid-December, the Republican delegation went to visit Hamilton; he denied Reynolds's allegations and claimed that Reynolds was blackmailing him for having carried on an adulterous affair with Reynolds's wife, Maria. "The result," Hamilton would write later, after the whole sordid affair had become public knowledge, "was a full and unequivocal acknowlegement on the part of the three gentlemen of perfect satisfaction with the explanation and expressions of regret at the trouble and embarrassment which had been occasioned to me." He thought the matter had been laid to rest.[31]

29. Robert H. Wiebe, *The Opening of American Society: From the Adoption of the Constitution to the Eve of Disunion* (New York, 1984), 100; St. George Tucker, *Blackstone's Commentaries . . .*, I, part 2 (Philadelphia, 1803), Appendix, note G, 29–30, cited in Leonard W. Levy, *Emergence of a Free Press* (New York, 1985), 327.

30. Wiebe, *Opening of American Society,* 103.

31. Alexander Hamilton, "Printed Version of 'The Reynolds Pamphlet,'" August 1797, in Harold C. Syrett et al., eds., *The Papers of Alexander Hamilton,* 27 vols. (New York, 1961–

Rumors, however, circulated, and, in the summer of 1797, pamphleteer James Thomson Callender made them public. If Hamilton had sought to deflect the accusation of public impropriety—specifically, speculating in public funds—by admitting to the private vice of adultery, Callender would recognize no such distinction. Although Callender believed that Hamilton fabricated the story of an affair with Maria Reynolds to cover up his unseemly financial activities with her husband, the pamphleteer was happy to have it both ways, faulting Hamilton both for defrauding the government and committing adultery. Callender would later spell out his rationale for examining what some suggested were purely private matters: "The world has no business with that part of a public character, unless . . . it shall be connected with some interesting political truth." In Hamilton's case, the relevant issue seemed to be his hypocrisy; "We shall presently see this great master of morality," Callender told his readers, "though himself the father of a family, confessing that he had an illicit correspondence with another man's wife." Hamilton was driven to publish an extended and passionate defense, which would call forth another of Callender's tracts. Hamilton, he charged, "has published ninety-three pages to prove, that he was guilty of conjugal infidelity. . . . This is the man, who, at the same moment, has the hardiness to announce 'a conspiracy of vice against virtue.' Mr. Hamilton should speak with reserve as to the faults of others."[32]

It is worth examining Hamilton's defense in some detail so that we may be able to compare it with the response Jefferson would make when, five years later, Callender turned his acid pen against him. In his defense, Hamilton worked hard to erect a barrier between his private and public lives. The stakes, he argued, were high. The attack upon him was a manifestation of the "spirit of jacobinism. . . . Incessantly busied in undermining all the props of

---

1987), XXI, 258. The Reynolds affair is detailed in "Introductory Note: From Oliver Wolcott, Junior, [July 3, 1797]," ibid., 121–144, as well as in McDonald, *Alexander Hamilton,* 227–230; and Broadus Mitchell, *Alexander Hamilton: The National Adventure, 1788–1804* (New York, 1962), 399–422. My account of this episode relies upon these works.

32. [James Thomson Callender], *The Prospect before Us,* I (Richmond, Va., 1800), 145, quoted in Michael Durey, *"With the Hammer of Truth": James Thomson Callender and America's Early National Heroes* (Charlottesville, Va., 1990), 94; [James Thomson Callender], *The History of the United States for 1796 . . .* (Philadelphia, 1797), 205; Callender, *Sketches of the History of America* (Philadelphia, 1798), 91. Callender made his original charges in a series of pamphlets that have not survived; he later published them in book form as *The History of the United States for 1796.* Hence, it is from the book, rather than the original publications, that subsequent histories have been written. See "Introductory Note," Syrett et al., *Papers of Hamilton,* XXI, 121–122.

public security and private happiness, it seems to threaten the political and moral world with a complete overthrow." Hamilton assumed that his effectiveness as a political figure—that is, his power—rested on his character. His enemies were attempting to destroy "the influence of men of upright principles." They were engaged in a conspiracy "against honest fame," and their strategy was to "wear away the reputations which they could not directly subvert." One of their tactics was to "stab the private felicity" of the person under assault. "With such men, nothing is sacred. Even the peace of an unoffending and amiable wife is a welcome repast to their insatiate fury against the husband." Invading Hamilton's privacy and upsetting his wife is the final and lowest blow.[33]

Although Hamilton argued that his private life was "sacred," and that his enemies should honor its inviolability, his defense reveals that his primary concern was his "public character" and his fame. His focus was upon the public sphere, and it is clear from the argument he would make several years later in the Croswell case that he believed the press ought to be given wide latitude in discussing the character and behavior of not only public figures but even "private persons." "If this be not to be done, then in vain will the voice of the people be raised against the inroads of tyranny." Republican principles legitimated "fair and honest exposure." Anything that was true might be published—except if it were "for the purpose of disturbing the peace of families."[34]

Hamilton recognized a small private sphere whose sanctity should be inviolable, not because it contributed something to the public realm, but, instead, because so clearly it did not. The private realm is without political meaning. It becomes relevant only when it affects the composure and happiness of the public man. In other words, Hamilton depicted his wife and his family as merely extensions of his self. It is as if Hamilton had said to Callender and his other enemies, "Let there be something of mine that you cannot use to hurt me." His concern for his wife was merely a reflection of his interest in his own "private felicity." Had her happiness been a central preoccupation, he would not so coolly have confessed (or invented, if one follows the alternate interpretation) the details of his adultery with Mrs. Reynolds:

33. Hamilton, "Printed Version of the 'Reynolds Pamphlet,'" August 1797, in Syrett et al., eds., *Papers of Alexander Hamilton,* XXI, 238–239.

34. Ibid., 239; People *v.* Harry Croswell, New York Supreme Court, 1803–1804, in Julius Goebel, Jr., et al., eds., *The Law Practice of Alexander Hamilton: Documents and Commentary,* 5 vols. (New York, 1964–1981), I, 809, 810, 820.

"After this, I had frequent meetings with her, most of them at my own house; Mrs. Hamilton with her children being absent on a visit to her father." When all is said and done, "There is nothing worse in the affair than an irregular and indelicate amour." If, in the schemes of things, Hamilton's adultery was such a trifle, then it was not so much his "indelicate amour" that must be upsetting to his wife as public discussion of it, which merely ate at *her* peace but threatened him with eternal shame. Mrs. Hamilton was merely an auxiliary to her husband's happiness; in his mind, he apparently has very little bearing on hers. Hamilton would protect himself by sectioning off a private realm, but, in comparison to the wide public arena in which his fame would be won, it was a very small space indeed.[35]

And it was in the public arena that Hamilton attempted to defend his honor. Not only did he publish this extraordinary pamphlet, but he challenged James Monroe to a duel. Once Callender published his pamphlets, Hamilton anxiously sought affirmation from Muhlenberg, Venable, and Monroe that they had been satisfied with his defense five years earlier. Muhlenberg's and Venable's responses were adequately reassuring; Monroe's, however, was not. There was an interview and an extended correspondence. Hamilton issued a challenge; Monroe accepted it; Hamilton backed off. More letters ensued. Finally, Monroe enlisted Aaron Burr and John Dawson to help him either make arrangements for a duel or resolve the matter. Although a duel once again seemed imminent, it somehow—and the record is unclear on this point—was averted.[36]

Less than four years later, Hamilton's son Philip would be killed in a duel. Philip and a friend had been challenged when they loudly mocked a speech critical of the Federalists. Philip accepted the challenge and took a bullet in

35. Hamilton, "Printed Version of the 'Reynolds Pamphlet,'" August 1797, in Syrett et al., eds., *Papers of Alexander Hamilton,* XXI, 239, 251, 267. Hamilton charged that "jacobin news-papers" and "pamphlets" were "artfully calculated to hold up the opponents of the FACTION to the jealousy and distrust of the present generation and if possible, to transmit their names with dishonor to posterity" (239). Hamilton places most of the blame for his affair on the seductive Mrs. Reynolds. In order to entice him, she presented herself as appealingly weak: affecting an "air of affliction," she had "appl[ied]" to his "humanity" with a tale of abuse and abandonment (250). But once the affair had commenced, Mrs. Reynolds became dangerously strong: "Her conduct, made it extremely difficult to disentangle myself. All the appearances of violent attachment, and of agonizing distress at the idea of a relinquishment, were played off with a most imposing art" (252).

36. For a thorough account, see "Introductory Note," in Syrett et al., *Papers of Hamilton,* XXI, 133–138, and James Monroe to Alexander Hamilton, Dec. 2, 1797, 316–320; for the relevant correspondence, see ibid.,146–346.

his side. His mother's grief, an observer at the young man's deathbed said, "beggars . . . description." Just over two years after that, Hamilton himself would engage in his fatal duel with Burr.[37]

Robert Wiebe has suggested that the first political parties functioned, much like the newspapers, as vessels for containing political violence by making a ritual of it.[38] That assessment is no doubt true for the long run, but, for at least the first few years of the First Party System, factional conflict could just as easily stimulate as sublimate violence. Burr had apparently been nursing a grudge against Hamilton for the role he played in denying him the presidency in 1800 and the governorship of New York in 1804, but it was not until the summer of 1804 that Burr thought he had grounds for a duel. Finally Hamilton said something—exactly what is unknown—that "could . . . be taken hold of." Burr issued the challenge; Hamilton accepted, and, like his son, he took a bullet in his side. He had left a letter for his wife, to be delivered only in the event of his death. "If it had been possible for me to have avoided the interview, my love for you and my precious children would have been alone a decisive motive. But it was not possible, without sacrifices which would have rendered me unworthy of your esteem." His honor took precedence over her happiness; or rather, Hamilton believed his honor, his reputation, and his fame were, even more than his love, his essential contribution to her happiness.[39]

III

There is little evidence of Thomas Jefferson's reaction to the death of one of his rivals at the hands of another. It is rather evident, however, that he

37. Mitchell, *Alexander Hamilton,* 496–499 (quotation, 496).

38. Wiebe, *Opening of American Society,* 101.

39. For a thorough description of the duel and the supporting documents, see Syrett et al., *Papers of Hamilton,* XXVI, 235–349. Burr is quoted in "Introductory Note: The Duel Between Aaron Burr and Alexander Hamilton," [June 18–Oct. 23, 1804], ibid., 240. For Hamilton's letter to Elizabeth Hamilton, [July 4, 1804], see ibid., 293. See also Hamilton's "Statement on Impending Duel with Aaron Burr," [June 28–July 10, 1804], ibid., 278–280. Among the reasons not to duel were: "My wife and Children are extremely dear to me, and my life is of the utmost importance to them, in various views." Nonetheless, he had to accept Burr's challenge. "To those, who with me abhorring the practice of Duelling may think that I ought on no account to have added to the number of bad examples—I answer that my *relative* situation, as well in public as in private aspects, enforcing all the considerations which constitute what men of the world denominate honor, impressed on me . . . a peculiar necessity not to decline the call. The ability to be in future useful, whether in resisting mischief or effecting good, in those crises of our public affairs, which seem likely to happen, would probably be inseparable from a conformity with public prejudice in this particular."

must have followed Hamilton's discomfiture in the Reynolds affair with some glee. James Monroe had kept him informed, and, as early as December 1792, Jefferson made note, albeit cryptically, of "the affair of Reynolds and his wife."[40] A number of years later, though, when Jefferson reflected on Alexander Hamilton and his character, he was able—in a way that Hamilton himself never had been—to separate the public from the private man: "Hamilton was indeed a singular character. Of acute understanding, disinterested, honest, and honorable in all private transactions, amiable in society, and duly valuing virtue in private life, yet so bewitched and perverted by the British example, as to be under thoro' conviction that corruption was essential to the government of a nation." In retrospect, Hamilton's flaws were all in his public and political actions.[41]

Perhaps it was his own experience at Callender's hand that made Jefferson not only more charitable but also more careful in distinguishing between public and private virtue. By 1802, for reasons that need not detain us here, Callender had moved to Virginia, begun editing the Richmond *Recorder,* and turned against Jefferson and the Republicans.[42] In September of that year, he began publication of a series of articles attacking Jefferson's reputation. "It is well known," the first of these articles began, "that the man, *whom it delighteth the people to honor,* keeps, and for many years past has kept, as his concubine, one of his own slaves. Her name is SALLY." The story that Jefferson maintained a sexual relationship with his slave Sally Hemings and fathered a number of her children has been in circulation ever since, never

40. Thomas Jefferson, "Notes on the Reynolds Affair," Dec. 17, 1792, in Julian P. Boyd et al., eds., *The Papers of Thomas Jefferson,* 43 vols. (Princeton, N.J., 1950–), XXIV, 751. See also "Introductory Note," Syrett et al., *Papers of Hamilton,* XXI, 136. Michael Durey has suggested that it might have been Jefferson who gave Callender the documents that he primed in his exposé of Hamilton. After he, Venable, and Muhlenberg had interviewed Hamilton in December 1792, Monroe had kept the originals, which he later claimed to have sent to a friend, whom Durey claims was Jefferson (Durey, *"Hammer of Truth,"* 98–101). The evidence is circumstantial and inconclusive. Most historians have believed that Callender probably got the documents from John Beckley, the Republican clerk of the House, to whom Monroe had passed on the originals for subscribing. Whether or not Jefferson saw the documents before Callender published them, it is evident that copies of them, at least, and reports of their contents were well known in Republican circles.

41. Thomas Jefferson, "The Anas," Feb. 4, 1818, in Jefferson, Peterson, ed., *Thomas Jefferson, Writings,* 671. My interpretation follows that of Malone, *Jefferson and His Time,* IV, 431.

42. For an account of Callender's career, see Durey, *"Hammer of Truth,"* esp. chaps. 6 and 7; and Fawn M. Brodie, *Thomas Jefferson: An Intimate History* (New York, 1974), chap. 23.

effectively proved or disproved. The veracity of the charges is not what concerns us. Instead, it is the manner in which Callender framed the accusation and the way in which Jefferson and his friends responded to it.[43]

In the Reynolds affair, Callender's ostensible rationale for discussing Hamilton's relationship with Mrs. Reynolds had been Hamilton's hypocrisy. Maria Reynolds's connection to the allegation that Hamilton had speculated in government securities should have been reason enough for examining her relationship with the secretary of the Treasury. Callender, however, was incensed that a "great master of morality, though himself the father of a family," would commit adultery and confess that he had "an illicit correspondence with another man's wife." Similarly, he accused Jefferson of violating the sanctity of the family. His original charge—later amended—was that Jefferson had brought Sally over to France along with his two daughters. "What a sublime pattern for an American ambassador to place before the eyes of two young ladies!" Other Federalist newspapers would pick up and republish Callenders's allegations, elaborating on that theme. The *Lynchburg Weekly Gazette,* for example, judged Jefferson a failed father. "Those daughters, who should have been the principal objects of his domestic concern, have had the mortification to see illegitimate, mulatto sisters, and brothers, enjoying the same privileges of parental affection with themselves." A good father protected his daughters and gave them all of his affection.[44]

In focusing on the character of Jefferson's fatherhood, Callender and his followers shifted the ground on which the discussion of character took place. No attempt was made to suggest that Jefferson's relationship with Sally Hemings or his daughters directly affected his capacity for governance or had immediate bearing upon his public virtue. It was simply, as Callender put it, that "the public have a right to be acquainted with the real characters of persons who are the possessors or the candidates for office." Hamilton's *New-York Post* would elaborate (somewhat disingenuously, perhaps, considering Hamilton's own experience): "We feel for the honour of our country—And when her Chief Magistrate labours under the imputation of the most abandoned profligacy of private life, we do most honestly and sincerely wish

43. "The President Again," *Recorder; or, Lady's and Gentleman's Miscellany* (Richmond, Va.), Sept. 1, 1802, [2], quoted in Durey, *"Hammer of Truth,"* 158.

44. Callender, *History of the United States for 1796,* 205; "The President Again," *Recorder; or, Lady's and Gentleman's Miscellany,* Sept. 1, 1802, [2], quoted in Durey, *"Hammer of Truth,"* 158; "From the Lynchburg Gazette," *Recorder* (Richmond, Va.), Nov. 3, 1802, [4], cited in Brodie, *Thomas Jefferson,* 353.

to see the stain upon the nation wiped away." Honor, then, was a reward for private, as much as public, virtue.[45]

Several years later, when these and other charges became the subject of debate in the Massachusetts legislature, the committee charged with considering them reported that "the preservation of our Republican Constitutions, and the impartial and faithful administration of laws enacted in conformity to them, depend alone on the knowledge which the people may have of the *conduct, integrity* and *talents* of those of their fellow citizens, who have been, or who may be called to offices of trust and honour." What hitherto might have been defined as private virtue was of public interest. As Callender asked rhetorically, in defense of his revelations, "What virtuous character has been destroyed by this paper? If seduction, and hypocrisy, if the grossest breach of personal friendship, and of domestic confidence, form a department in the new code of morality," then, and only then, would the newspaper he published have been in the wrong. The personal had been rendered political.[46]

Everything in a man's life was relevant, and the Federalist press, in its attempt to discredit the president, cast a wide net. Most of the charges originated with Callender, and they eventually included allegations of both a clearly public and just as clearly a private nature: Jefferson's behavior during the Revolution was cowardly; he had paid back a debt in depreciated currency; he had attempted an affair with Betsey Walker, the wife of his neighbor and friend; he had paid Callender to slander Washington; he was destroying the navy; he did not believe in God; the Louisiana purchase was unwise.[47] This promiscuous mingling of political and personal accusations served to break down the precarious wall that had separated the public and private realms. In the fall of 1802, as the Federalist papers were filled with allegations, and the Republican press attempted a defense, everyone's char-

45. "From Callender's Recorder," *Boston Gazette; Commercial and Political,* Nov. 11, 1802, [1]; "From the Boston Gazette," *New-York Evening Post,* Dec. 8, 1802, [2].

46. *The Defence of Young and Minns, Printers to the State, before the Committee of the House of Representatives* (Boston, 1805), preface; "Answer to That Part of the Speech of George Hay, Which Was Inserted in Last Wednesday's Recorder," *Recorder,* Feb. 2, 1803, [4], quoted in Durey, *"Hammer of Truth,"* 163.

47. In 1805, the *New-England Palladium* (Boston) pulled these charges together in an article entitled "The Monarchy of Federalism" (Jan. 18, 1805). The focus of the article was Jefferson's public character (he was described as "a patriot regardless of his country's welfare, and entirely devoted to raise himself and his partizans upon the nation's ruin," [1]); the editors assumed without explaining the relevance of the Sally Hemings and Betsey Walker stories. For a summary, see Malone, *Jefferson and His Time,* IV, 206–235.

acter became fair game. The Richmond *Examiner* devoted more space to defaming Jefferson's enemies than to defending the president. It recirculated the tale of the Hamilton-Reynolds affair and insinuated that John Marshall, whom it suspected of supplying information to Callender, kept a slave mistress. It alleged that Callender was consorting with a black prostitute. It even raised questions about the manhood of Charles Cotesworth Pinckney, a potential Federalist candidate for the presidency, dubbing him "Miss *Charlotte* Cotesworth PINCKNEY" and referring to him repeatedly as "she." In the heated political climate, the sexual behavior of any partisan was grist for the mill.[48]

At the same time that the Republican press was tarring Jefferson's enemies with the brush that had been used on him, it began to frame a different sort of defense, one that would attempt to make impregnable the wall between public and private. To be sure, the press was working at contradictory and self-defeating purposes. While one column was defending the sanctity of Jefferson's personal life, another was violating Hamilton's or Marshall's, without even a pretense to consistency. Yet out of this unstable combination of approaches to the question of a public man's sexual behavior, a new understanding of the relationship between the family and the public world would emerge.

The first element in this new configuration was the assertion that the family ought to be protected from political scrutiny. The Richmond *Examiner* charged, in language reminiscent of that which Hamilton had used in his "Reynolds Pamphlet," that because the opponents of Republicanism could find no fault with its policies or its leaders, "they are driven into the sacred recesses of privacy, to hunt up malicious falsehood and obloquy at

48. "The Examiner," *Examiner* (Richmond, Va.), Sept. 22, 1802, [3], "The Examiner," Oct. 2, 1802, [3], "The Examiner," Nov. 6, 1802, [3]. Republican suspicions about Marshall are discussed in Durey, *"Hammer of Truth,"* 161. For the allegations against Callender, see "The Examiner," *Examiner,* Sept. 22, 1802, [2–3], "The Examiner," Oct. 2, 1802, [3]; and Durey, *"Hammer of Truth,"* 161–162. The basis for this slur against Pinckney is not entirely clear. Since 1799, allegations had been circulating that, while serving as emissaries to France, he and Marshall had been intimate with a French woman, who bore the already-married Pinckney a child and followed him back to South Carolina, where either Pinckney and Marshall were supporting her or she had been cast off. It is not clear how this story might have been construed as a reflection upon Pinckney's masculinity, unless the mere association with France and South Carolina (where he enjoyed "the Asiatic luxuries of a southern climate") somehow feminized him ("The Examiner," *Examiner,* Sept. 22, 1802, [3]). The insinuation might have been that, as Hamilton's puppet, Pinckney was, like a woman, weak. For the allegations against Pinckney, see Marvin R. Zahniser, *Charles Cotesworth Pinckney: Founding Father* (Williamsburg, Va., and Chapel Hill, N.C., 1967), 175–176, 208–209, 239–241.

the hazard of family repose." In response, the Federalist press repeated the standard republican defense that anything that had bearing on a man's public actions was relevant. Hence, a contributor to the *Boston Gazette* would recoil in horror at "the new principles recently advanced . . . that it is unfair to expose the private vices of a public man" and confess himself "unable to discover upon what basis of morals, or of policy, the axiom can be supported, that the most detestable crimes of which a human being can be guilty, must be overlooked and concealed, if committed by a public man, unless they were committed in his *official capacity.*" As in the Reynolds affair, the arguments circled each other warily, like equally matched opponents, neither one capable of winning the round.[49]

IV

As long as the political press saw the family as nothing more than an extension of the man who was its head, there could be no effective defense of its privacy. The harm that came from disrupting a family's repose, after all, was imagined to fall most heavily upon the public man, who was distracted from his important endeavors. Moreover, the lines of influence led entirely in one direction, from a man and his family, through society to the nation. That the nation—as distinct from a tyrant who perverted its will—might harm the family was a novel thought. When the Jeffersonian press asserted the sanctity of the private recesses of the family and began to describe the family in ways that would make the preservation of its privacy a positive and necessary good, it was redefining both the family and its relation to the political world. In fact, the political press was not the only or the most important sector of society that was rethinking the family; as a number of historians have shown, at just this time, educators, essayists, and novelists (both male and female), ministers, and political theorists, as well as middle-class and elite men and women on both sides of the Atlantic, were beginning to think in new ways about the nature of family and its relationship to the wider public. Indeed, because the redefinition of the family was hardly their central occupation, it seems more likely that the political newspapers were reflecting, and in the process, politically legitimating, changes that were taking place in both society and thought as they attempted to craft a defense for their slandered leaders.[50]

49. "The Examiner," *Examiner,* Sept. 25, 1802, [3]; "Miscellany; Elegant Extracts," *Boston Gazette,* Dec. 2, 1802, [1].

50. The literature on this topic is vast. One might begin with Fliegelman, *Prodigals and Pilgrims;* Melvin Yazawa, *From Colonies to Commonwealth: Familial Ideology and the Begin-*

And so it was that defenders of Thomas Jefferson began to offer his character as a family man as an argument in his defense. If Callender accused Jefferson of carrying on a sexual relationship with a slave woman "before the eyes of his two daughters," the Richmond *Examiner* would respond that the presence of Jefferson's daughters rendered such behavior unthinkable. Moreover, that Hemings, "who [was] daily engaged in the ordinary vocations of the family, . . . should have a mulatto child" was not possible. "Mr. Jefferson has been a Bachelor for more than twenty years. During this period," the paper explained, "he reared with parental attention, two unblemished, accomplished and amiable women, who are married to two estimable citizens. In the education of his daughters, this same Thomas Jefferson, supplied the place of a *mother*—his tenderness and delicacy were proverbial—not a spot tarnished his widowed character" until Callender starred spreading his lies.[51] "The ordinary vocations of the family" precluded the sort of behavior of which Jefferson was accused. The unblemished daughters served as proof of their father's virtue. Family life implicitly was virtuous, and, if anything, required protection from the contamination of politics. One Massachusetts legislator was disgusted by the newspapers' discussions of Thomas Jefferson's character. "He asked, whether any gentleman, who had a family, and whose females, or daughters, were in the habit of reading the public papers, would permit a paper containing such matter to come into his house." It was the public—not the tender father—that threatened the sanctity of the family.[52]

---

nings of the American Republic (Baltimore, Md., 1985); Jan Lewis, "The Republican Wife: Virtue and Seduction in the Early Republic," *William and Mary Quarterly,* XLIV (1987), 689–721, also reprinted in this volume; and Lewis, *Pursuit of Happiness.* Changes in the American family are summarized in Steven Mintz and Susan Kellogg, *Domestic Revolutions: A Social History of American Family Life* (New York, 1988), chaps. 2 and 3.

51. "After We Thought That the Public Had Enough," *Recorder; or, Lady's and Gentleman's Miscellany,* Sept. 29, 1802, [4], quoted in Brodie, *Thomas Jefferson,* 352; "The Examiner," *Examiner,* Sept. 25, 1802, [3]. This vision of Thomas Jefferson's family life was not entirely a creation of the political press; it was the way that his family saw it, too. Half a century later, Jefferson's granddaughter would also use it to rebut Callender's charges: "Some of the children earnestly reported to be Mr. Jefferson's were about the age of his own grandchildren. Of course he must have been carrying on his intrigues in the midst of his own grandchildren. . . . His apartment had no private entrance not perfectly accessible and visible to all the household. . . . But I put it to any fair mind to decide if a man so admirable in his domestic character as Mr Jefferson . . . would be likely to rear a race of half-breeds under their eyes and carry on his low amours in the circle of his family" (Ellen Wayles Coolidge to Joseph Coolidge, Jr., Oct. 24, 1858, Correspondence of Ellen Wayles Randolph Coolidge).

52. *Defence of Young and Minns,* 50–51.

And it was at home, and on the basis of his fatherhood, that Jefferson was willing to be judged. Hamilton accepted Burr's challenge because, in the end, he had no other choice. He could not go home because his wife, or so he imagined, would consider him dishonored. Jefferson's passionate letters to his daughters should be understood in this context. It was no exaggeration to say that political life was filled with cabal, hatred, and intrigue. When he told Maria that "it is in the love of one's family only that heartfelt happiness is known," he spoke from both experience and desire. Yet the family is not naturally or necessarily happy or warm, nor is it the opposite of political life. Jefferson, the tender and delicate parent, made it—or at least saw it—as he needed it to be.[53]

And because he fell back upon the happiness of home, Jefferson offered no public response to the charges of his enemies. They were astounded, taking Jefferson's silence as proof of their charges. Some expected a public denial, perhaps his own version of Hamilton's "Reynolds Pamphlet." The *Boston Gazette* "waited in expectation either that Mr. Jefferson himself would deem it not beneath his dignity, to meet the accusation of a crime so deeply infamous, at least with a pointed denial, or that some of his numerous friends and admirers would have taken the task upon themselves." In 1805, a Massachusetts legislator would accept the charges as true, for, after all, they "had been made and repeated for more than four years. . . . They had been published and republished again and again, at the seat of government; avowedly and before the face of Mr. JEFFERSON. . . . Yet, during this whole time, these charges had not been contradicted, either by Mr. JEFFERSON or his friends.—This . . . in his mind, amounted to at least a tacit confession." Others speculated about possible duels. The Richmond *Examiner* published a report, later retracted, that Light-Horse Harry Lee had carried a challenge from John Walker to the president. Some sort of response was expected.[54]

Jefferson, however, remained almost completely silent. In 1805, he confessed to his secretary of the navy that "when young and single I offered love" to Mrs. Walker. "It is the only one founded in truth among all their alle-

53. Thomas Jefferson to Mary Jefferson Eppes, Oct. 26, 1801, in Betts and Bear, eds., *Family Letters,* 210.

54. "Elegant Extracts," *Boston Gazette,* Oct. 21, 1802, [1]; *Defence of Young and Minns,* 53, 61; "Examiner," *Examiner,* June 25, 1803, [3], "We Have Never Noticed the Ribaldry," July 2, 1803, [3]. For Lee's role in the Walker affair, see Charles Royster, *Light-Horse Harry Lee and the Legacy of the American Revolution* (New York, 1981), 208–209. See, similarly, "From the Boston Gazette," *New-York Evening Post,* Dec. 8, 1802, [2].

gations against me." In 1803, he wrote out his religious creed, explaining to Martha, "I have thought it just that my family, by possessing this, should be enabled to estimate the libels published against me on this, as on every other possible subject."[55] The allegations troubled him, of course, as did the general tenor of the Federalist press. He gave both direct and indirect encouragement to the states to prosecute for libel, telling Pennsylvania's governor Thomas McKean that he had "long thought that a few prosecutions of the most prominent offenders would have a wholesome effect in restoring the integrity of the presses." Although, as Leonard Levy has pointed out, Jefferson's willingness to use not only the state but the federal courts to prosecute seditious libel marked a retreat from the more libertarian theories of freedom of the press developed by Republicans in response to the Sedition Act of 1798, Jefferson himself did not seem willing to pursue his policy vigorously or publicly.[56] He wanted McKean to keep "entirely confidential" his recommendation for intimidating the press in Pennsylvania, and he ordered a halt to the prosecution of a Connecticut minister when he learned that a trial would require a public discussion of the Walker affair. Jefferson's later explanation for terminating the prosecution—"I had laid it down as a law to myself, to take no notice of the thousand calumnies issued against me, but to trust my character to my own conduct, and the good sense and candor of my fellow citizens"—surely casts his motive in the most favorable possible light; undoubtedly he must also have wanted to avoid the embarrassment that a public airing of the allegation that four decades earlier he had attempted to seduce his friend's wife was sure to bring. If we consider Jefferson's prosecutions as yet another means of displacing political violence, it is striking that even in this sublimated version of the duel, Jefferson would try to hold his fire.[57]

55. Thomas Jefferson to Robert Smith, July 5, 1805, in Brodie, *Thomas Jefferson,* 375; Jefferson to Martha Jefferson Randolph, Apr. 23, 1803, in Betts and Bear, eds., *Family Letters,* 243–244.

56. Thomas Jefferson to Thomas McKean, Feb. 19, 1803, in Paul Leicester Ford, ed., *The Works of Thomas Jefferson,* 12 vols. (New York, 1904–1905), IX, 451–452; Levy, *Emergence of a Free Press,* 309–349. For Jefferson's views on freedom of the press, see also Frank L. Mott, *Jefferson and the Press* (Baton Rouge, La., 1943); and Leonard W. Levy, *Jefferson and Civil Liberties: The Darker Side* (New York, 1973), chap. 3. For freedom of the press in Virginia, see Steven H. Hochman, "On the Liberty of the Press in Virginia: From Essay to Bludgeon, 1798–1803," *Virginia Magazine of History and Biography,* LXXXIV (1976), 431–445.

57. Jefferson to McKean, Feb. 19, 1803, in Ford, ed., *Works of Thomas Jefferson,* IX, 451, Jefferson to Wilson Cary Nicholas, June 13, 1809, XI, 109.

V

Certainly, Jefferson's attitudes were shaped by his personality. He was by nature sensitive to criticism and averse to direct conflict. Yet, as was his nature, he transformed his inclinations into maxims, and, when they were applied to public affairs, they became part of an emergent political culture. We have already seen how smoothly Jefferson would change subjects in letters to his daughters; evocations of the pleasures of family life would quickly and almost inevitably be transformed into diatribes about the miseries of political life. The object of these letters, in fact, was to shape family life so that it would continue to be an effective counter to the ravages of politics. He would tell his daughters both explicitly and indirectly how to behave in a way that would foster peace and family love. In the letters he addressed to their husbands and sons, Jefferson also would discuss family and political life in tandem, but here his objective was to instruct them how to behave in public so that they would live to enjoy the pleasures of family life.

In 1808, as he was nearing the end of his last term of office, Jefferson wrote his grandson and namesake, Thomas Jefferson Randolph, then studying medicine in Philadelphia, a long and, as Dumas Malone put it, "excessively didactic" letter. Clearly he was worried that his young charge, away from home for the first time in his life, would fall in with a bad crowd. The ostensible purpose of the letter was to inculcate in young Jeff, as the president's grandson was known, the personal habits that would enable him to resist the usual temptations of youth—gambling, drinking, and so forth. But, along with injunctions about what not to do, Jefferson also told his grandson exactly how to behave. This advice constitutes Jefferson's political sociology, his doctrine about the way men in public ought to act. Thomas Jefferson wrote his grandson a primer on how to avoid the duel.[58]

First of all, a man had to develop the proper frame of mind. Jefferson counseled "good humor as one of the preservatives of our peace and tranquillity." If he could not summon it naturally, he could always feign it: "In truth, politeness is artificial good humor, it covers natural want of it, and

58. Malone, *Jefferson and His Time,* V, 624; Thomas Jefferson to Thomas Jefferson Randolph, Nov. 24, 1808, in Betts and Bear, eds., *Family Letters,* 362–365. See, similarly, Jefferson's letter to his other grandson, Francis Wayles Eppes, (May 21, 1816, ibid., 415): "Above all things, and at all times, practice yourself in good humor. This, of all human qualities, is the most amiable and endearing to society." See, similarly, Jefferson to Thomas Jefferson Randolph, Dec. 7, 1808, ibid., 369; and Jefferson to Charles L. Bankhead, Nov. 26, 1808, in Andrew A. Lipscomb and Albert Ellery Bergh, eds., *The Writings of Thomas Jefferson . . . ,* 20 vols. (Washington, D.C., 1903–1904), XVIII, 253–254.

ends by rendering habitual a substitute nearly equivalent to the real virtue." Politeness, in Jefferson's view, was a scaled-down version of public virtue—self-sacrifice for the common good, not so much of the nation as the society in which a man happened at the moment to be. "It is the practice of sacrificing to those whom we meet in society all the little conveniences and preferences which will gratify them, and deprive us of nothing worth a moment's consideration; it is the giving a pleasing and flattering turn to our expressions which will conciliate others, and make them pleased with us as well as themselves." It might well be true, as Jefferson would observe at another time, that "the Creator would indeed have been a bungling artist, had he intended man for a social animal, without planting in him social dispositions," but those dispositions required cultivation and even conscious calculation.[59]

In the context of his wider social philosophy, Jefferson seems to have considered anger and political disputation as variants on self-love, the "antagonist of virtue." The self-sacrifice and self-control required to walk away from an argument, then, constituted virtue. And it was just this form of virtue that Jefferson passionately enjoined upon his grandson. He told him quite directly never to enter "into dispute or argument with another." To make his point, he attempted a number of tacks: He invoked the example of the revered Benjamin Franklin, "the most amiable of men in society," whose rule was "never to contradict any body." He told Jeff that argument was always in vain anyway: "I never yet saw an instance of one of two disputants convincing the other by argument"; if anything, such disagreements only made matters worse. He resorted to philosophy, sharing with his grandson the secret of his own success: "When I hear another express an opinion, which is not mine, I say to myself, He has a right to his opinion, as I to mine; why should I question it. His error does me no injury, and shall I become a Don Quixot to bring all men by force of argument, to one opinion?" And he tried simple scare tactics. He had seen too many antagonists "getting warm, becoming rude, and shooting one another." Disputation, Jefferson warned, could lead to death.[60]

Perhaps Jefferson had in mind the sad example of Philip Hamilton when he told young Jeff not to worry about defending his grandfather's reputation

59. Thomas Jefferson to Thomas Jefferson Randolph, Nov. 24, 1808, in Betts and Bear, eds., *Family Letters,* 363; Thomas Jefferson to Thomas Law, June 13, 1814, in Peterson, ed., *Thomas Jefferson, Writings,* 1337.

60. Jefferson to Law, June 13, 1814, in Peterson, ed., *Thomas Jefferson, Writings,* 1336; Thomas Jefferson to Thomas Jefferson Randolph, Nov. 24, 1808, in Betts and Bear, eds., *Family Letters,* 364.

from the "puppies in politics" he was sure to encounter. Jefferson assured his grandson that his character was "in the hands of my fellow citizens at large, and will be consigned to honor or infamy by the verdict of the republican mass of our country, according to what themselves will have seen, not what their enemies and mine shall have said." A public man's reputation rested not on his willingness to defend it by force or even on what a small circle of gentlemen in Washington or Philadelphia conceived it to be. Jefferson's character was a matter of public opinion, not the debating or dueling skills of his kin.[61]

When Jefferson instructed his grandson how to avoid political violence, it is even more probable that he had in mind the duel that Jeff's father had narrowly avoided only two years earlier. In 1806, much to his chagrin, Thomas Jefferson's son-in-law almost entered into a duel with his even more volatile cousin, John Randolph of Roanoke. This was not the first time that there had been trouble between John Randolph and the Jefferson sons-in-law, two congressmen whom the Speaker of the House seemed to regard as tools of the president. After one minor altercation, Jefferson attempted to mollify the Speaker. He explained that there were "no men on earth . . . more independent in their sentiments" than his sons-in-law; nor would Jefferson even consider talking politics with them. In fact, Jefferson would barely risk political dispute with anyone, even members of his own party, "experience having long taught me the reasonableness of mutual sacrifices of opinion among those who are to act together for any common object." Jefferson had little interest in establishing a political dynasty, let alone a family one, or so he led Randolph to believe.[62]

Such reassurances, however, could not cool tempers that were inclined to inflame, and, in 1806, Thomas Mann Randolph and John Randolph came close to a duel. The dispute began, as it so often did, over a trifle—a debate in the House about repealing a duty on salt. The proponents were accused of trying to embarrass the administration; their heated response elicited a counter-response from Jefferson's supporters, including Thomas Mann Randolph, who objected to an opponent's tone. John Randolph, then chairman of the House Ways and Means Committee and increasingly hostile to Jefferson and his policies, took the floor, making one of his typical speeches, nasty yet somehow vague. Jefferson's son-in-law thought it was aimed at

61. Thomas Jefferson to Thomas Jefferson Randolph, Nov. 24, 1808, in Betts and Bear, eds., *Family Letters,* 365.

62. Thomas Jefferson to John Randolph, Dec. 1, 1803, in Ford, ed., *Works of Thomas Jefferson,* X, 53–54.

him; he took offense and rose in his own defense, effectively challenging the chairman to a duel. The chairman sent a second, the son-in-law chose a second and then backed down, issuing an apology for his insults from the House floor. Yet other congressmen assailed the chairman's leadership, and the newspapers transformed this undoubtedly merited criticism into a conspiracy to ruin John Randolph. Thomas Mann Randolph's character was called into question, and it appeared as if the duel might once again be on.[63]

Jefferson was beside himself with anxiety. He was afraid to write his son-in-law at home, where he had gone after Congress had recessed, for fear his daughter would read the letter and learn of the impending duel. He entrusted his letter to a mutual friend, to whom he complained that the newspapers were encouraging the duel. Jefferson decried the custom of resolving disputes by duels. They were especially inappropriate for men with families, and he was certain that "the mass of mankind . . . would condemn . . . a husband and father of a numerous family" who engaged in dueling. He underscored the point to Randolph himself in a letter written several weeks later when the threat of a duel, mercifully, seemed to have passed. "The young ones indeed would have got over it; but to two persons at least it would have ended but with life. This period might have been long with one; with the other short, but unceasingly bitter. A sincere affection for you personally, a reliance on you for succeeding to cares which age is unfitting me for, sympathies with a beloved survivor, and tender anxieties for those who would have had to embark in the world without guide or protection, would have filled with gloom my remaining time." In this light, fighting a duel would be an act of supreme selfishness, unforgivable for a man with a family.[64]

The family, then, and not honor, was a man's primary obligation. As Jefferson explained it to his son-in-law, "unnecessary risk . . . indeed is the falsest of honour . . . a mere compound of crime and folly." Hamilton had had it all wrong. It was attention to his familial responsibilities that made even a public man worthy of his family's esteem. And it was in the family that a man could find the certain and unchanging love that the public world denied him. In counseling complacency and coolness in public, Jefferson was

63. Malone, *Jefferson and His Time,* V, 127–132; Peterson, *Thomas Jefferson and the New Nation,* 839–840. For a different interpretation, see William Cabell Bruce, *John Randolph of Roanoke, 1773–1833 . . . ,* 2 vols. (New York, 1922), I, 261–265. See also Henry S. Randall, *The Life of Thomas Jefferson,* 3 vols. (New York, 1858), III, 164–167.

64. Thomas Jefferson to James Ogilvie, June 23, 1806, in Lipscomb and Bergh, eds., *Writings of Thomas Jefferson,* XVIII, 247–248; Jefferson to Thomas Mann Randolph, July 13, 1806, in Ford, ed., *Works of Thomas Jefferson,* X, 274–275.

attempting to alter the tenor of public life; he was struggling to make politics less personal and emotionally intense. Don't argue, he said; don't fight; do as I do, and think of home. Only by constructing the family as the sole realm where heartfelt happiness might be found could Jefferson divest politics of the passions that threatened always to push it over the edge into violence. Not only was political passion in this age displaced, as Robert Wiebe has suggested, into newspapers, political parties, and similar ritualized and less lethal forms of dispute, but it was also transmuted into the love that was experienced at home. Family life would become more intense as political life became cooler.[65]

VI

This process was just beginning as Thomas Jefferson achieved his long-proclaimed desire to retire from politics, but its effects would be profound. Indeed, it might be argued that a viable, relatively modern politics would not be possible until it became less emotionally intense, that is, less personal. It would be a number of years, of course, before the code of the duel would be replaced entirely by less dangerous means of resolving political dispute, but, after the War of 1812, the duel—like other forms of violence—became increasingly confined to certain regions and classes.[66] An effective politics would not be possible until a man could argue a position without risking its being construed as a reflection on another man's honor. By the same token, an orderly politics would have to offer men other sources for constituting their identities. A man accepted a challenge in order to maintain his reputation among a small circle of political intimates; these were the men who validated his identity. Jefferson sought to ground reputation in an even wider sphere, "the republican mass of our country." But this wider public could not be the guarantor of a man's fame until mechanisms of communication were developed for registering public opinion. The newspapers and party organizations that were coming into being while Jefferson served in government and that at first seemed only to exacerbate conflict would even-

65. Jefferson to Thomas Mann Randolph, July 13, 1806, in Ford, ed., *Works of Thomas Jefferson*, X, 275.

66. Wiebe, *Opening of American Society*, 327–332. Until that time, however, any dispute between gentlemen risked becoming the occasion for a duel. Although the absolute number of duels fought might have remained relatively small, the number of challenges must have been much greater, and the presence in politics of volatile men such as John Randolph of Roanoke ensured that any debate could easily be interpreted as a slur upon one's personal honor. See ibid., 186. Consider also the accounts of duels printed in the Richmond *Examiner* during the fall of 1803.

tually bring into political being the sort of mass public to which Jefferson attempted to appeal.

Jefferson knew, however, that, although this public might esteem him, it could never bathe him in the sort of affection that as a young man he had seemed to crave.[67] For that he would have to turn to his family. They would provide him with the emotional sustenance that would make his continued participation in public affairs possible, and he in turn would serve his family, first and foremost, by not getting himself killed. He would also endeavor to keep the violence that seemed endemic in politics from spilling over into the home. The wall separating the home from politics could be built higher and stronger, now that there was something to protect. This process, which would define the home and what took place in it as sacred and private would not be accomplished until a number of years later after the newspapers and pamphleteers had examined Andrew Jackson's marriage in the minutest detail, insinuating that his most intimate relationship had profound public implications. Although politics would periodically—especially in the nineteenth century—attempt to scale the wall that was supposed to separate it from the private realm, it turned out that the republican mass of the people in whom Jefferson placed his faith would accept the notion that the public and private spheres were separate and distinct. In the long run, they would demonstrate that they cared relatively little about what their leaders did in "the sacred recesses of privacy."[68]

The connection between public and private virtue was in the process of being severed. It was not so much that the meaning of virtue was feminized as that different standards of behavior for politics and the home developed. The notion of public virtue would still have a specific, if less encompassing content; the specter of corruption, for example, a central republican fear, would continue to haunt American politics in the decades to come.[69] New

67. Jefferson to Thomas Jefferson Randolph, Feb. 8, 1826, in Betts and Bear, eds., *Family Letters,* 470.

68. Norma Basch, "Marriage, Morals, and Politics in the Election of 1828," paper presented to the American Studies Association, Costa Mesa, California, November 1992, later published as Basch, "Marriage, Morals, and Politics in the Election of 1828," *Journal of American History,* LXXX (1993), 890–918. I am indebted to Professor Basch for letting me see the expanded version of her paper and for her invaluable insights into the ways in which gender figured in early American politics.

69. Bloch, "Gendered Meanings," *Signs,* XIII (1987), 37–58; Richard L. McCormick, "Scandal and Reform: A Framework for the Study of Political Corruption in the Nineteenth-Century United States and a Case Study of the 1820s," paper presented to the Shelby Cullom Davis Center for Historical Studies, Princeton University, 1982; Robert V. Remini, *Andrew Jackson and the Course of American Freedom, 1822–1832* (New York, 1981), esp. chap. 2;

standards of personal conduct, particularly for the genteel, would be applied to both men and women concerning their behavior at home. Jefferson, after all, would instruct both his sons-in-law and his daughters, his granddaughters as well as his grandsons, to avoid conflict and disputation at all cost. "Honesty, disinterestedness, and good nature are indispensable to procure the esteem and confidence of those with whom we live, and on whose esteem our happiness depends," Jefferson instructed one grandson. He could easily have given that advice to a granddaughter as well. Personal integrity and unfailing good humor were qualities that knew no gender.[70]

That is not to say that the new political and familial order that Jefferson worked to achieve would affect men and women in the same way, or even that Jefferson had identical expectations for his male and female kin. If a man's primary responsibility was to provide for his family and to return to it in one piece, a woman's was to create the environment that would sustain masculine identity. The sort of behavior Jefferson enjoined upon women and men was similar: avoid conflict at all cost. But because the primary focus of their endeavors was different, so, also, would be the meaning of their actions.[71]

Jefferson counted on women to make family life agreeable, just as he expected men of good sense to keep political life calm. In his expectations of family life, Jefferson shared one of the contradictions of republican thinking; it assumed at one and the same time that family life was inherently conflict free and that it was only the self-effacement of women that made it so. Like republican theorists of the family, Jefferson believed that a peaceful society was founded in a harmonious marriage, and a harmonious marriage required a deferential wife.[72] When his daughter Martha married Thomas Mann Randolph, her father warned her, "Your new condition will call for

---

Rubil Morales, "The Cloudy Medium of Language: John Quincy Adams, Andrew Jackson, and the Uses of Republican Language in the 1820s" (M.A. thesis, Rutgers University, 1993).

70. Thomas Jefferson to Francis Wayles Eppes, May 21, 1816, in Betts and Bear, eds., *Family Letters,* 415. For similar letters to female kin, see Jefferson to Mary Jefferson, Apr. 11, 1790, ibid., 52, and Jefferson to Ellen Wayles Randolph, Nov. 27, 1801, 214.

71. For Jefferson's view on proper gender roles, see Thomas Jefferson to William H. Harrison, Feb. 27, 1803, in Peterson, ed., *Thomas Jefferson, Writings,* 1117–1119, "To the Brothers of the Choctaw Nation," Dec. 17, 1803, 559–560, and "Memorandums on a Tour from Paris to Amsterdam, Strasburg, and Back to Paris," 1788, 651–652.

72. Lewis, "Republican Wife," *William and Mary Quarterly,* XLIV (1987), 689–721. This is not to say, however, that all of Jefferson's attitudes about women and marriage were republican. Jefferson retained a streak of misogyny that was characteristic of an earlier age. See Kenneth A. Lockridge, *On the Sources of Patriarchal Rage: The Commonplace Books of William Byrd and Thomas Jefferson and the Gendering of Power in the Eighteenth Century* (New York, 1992).

abundance of little sacrifices but they will be greatly overpaid by the measure of affection they will secure to you. The happiness of your life depends now on the continuing to please a single person." Several years later, he would offer similar words of advice to Maria. "Harmony in the marriage state is the very first object to be aimed at. Nothing can preserve affections uninterrupted but a firm resolution never to differ in will and a determination in each to consider the love of the other as of more value than any object whatever on which a wish has been fixed." Married people should never argue or criticize, especially in public, no matter what the provocation. "Much better therefore," he advised, "if our companion views a thing in a light different from what we do to leave him in quiet possession of his view."[73]

Although the words were strikingly similar to those he would address to his grandson several years later, it must be remembered that Jeff Randolph was instructed on how to avoid disputes in public, not at home. It is clear from his letters to his daughters that Jefferson expected husbands to be almost naturally disputatious and that he placed almost the entire burden of family happiness on women alone. Nor was it just the peace of their immediate families with which women were entrusted; women were responsible for the harmony of all domestic society, that is, of all the homes in which men and women mixed and met. Again and again, Jefferson would tell his daughters to suppress their own feelings and spread the balm of affection wherever they went. When her sister-in-law was caught in a scandal of incest and infanticide, Jefferson advised Martha to be charitable. "Never throw off the best affections of nature in the moment when they become most precious to their object; nor fear to extend your hand to save another, lest you should sink yourself." Jefferson offered this advice in 1793, well before he himself became embroiled in lesser scandals, yet it suggests how he thought a family ought to respond to a scandal that touched one of its members.[74]

73. Thomas Jefferson to Martha Jefferson Randolph, Apr. 4, 1790, in Betts and Bear, eds., *Family Letters,* 51, Thomas Jefferson to Mary Jefferson Eppes, Jan. 7, 1798, 151–152. Jefferson also instructed Martha that she must now put her husband ahead even of him; this advice she was not able to follow.

74. Thomas Jefferson to Martha Jefferson Randolph, Apr. 28, 1793, in Betts and Bear, eds., *Family Letters,* 115–116. Thomas Mann Randolph's unmarried sister, Nancy, had been accused of bearing her brother-in-law Richard Randolph's baby; Richard Randolph was tried and acquitted of the murder of the baby, whose body had never been found, although slaves had reported seeing both it and blood stains at the house where Richard and his wife, Judith, and her sister Nancy had been staying. Richard Randolph was the brother of John Randolph of Roanoke, and it is possible that his animosity to Nancy and her family exacerbated the political tensions that would grow between him and Jefferson. For a full account of the "scandal at Bizarre," see Bruce, *John Randolph,* I, 107–123, II, 273–277.

Martha's response would show that she grasped her father's intent: to display affection, even in the face of error, in the interest of maintaining harmony. Several years earlier, not long after Martha's marriage, her widowed father-in-law remarried a much younger woman and gave signs that he would begin a new family, threatening his older children's expectations for inheritance. Jefferson told Martha not to contest the marriage settlement but instead to conciliate not only her father-in-law and his bride but the bride's mother as well. He gave his daughter detailed instructions in how to manipulate her in-laws. "Be you my dear," Jefferson advised, "the link of love, union, and peace for the whole family." Not only the peace of the family but her material well-being depended upon it. When women maintained domestic order, they were doing nothing less than securing the basis for their society's economic and political stability.[75]

Martha learned her lesson well. If we read between the lines of her response to her father's letter recommending charity toward Nancy Randolph, we can see how she absorbed her father's philosophy and transmitted it to her husband. Martha told her father that, under the pressure of the scandal, the "divisions" in her husband's family were increasing daily, but that her husband was succeeding in healing them. Her husband's "conduct," she reported, "has been such as to conciliate the affections of the whole family. He is the Link by which so many discordant parts join. . . . There is not one individual but what looks up to him as one, and the only one who has been uniform in his affection." Under her tutelage, her husband, radiating affection, had become the center of his family. And that was the way it was supposed to be: by "sacrifices and suppressions of feeling," a woman would cultivate the affections of the family, flattering even its most difficult members like a master politician, but it was always to install a man at its head.[76]

Here was the difference, finally, between the home and the world of politics. The methods for achieving harmony in each were similar: they required forbearance, deference to the wishes of others, flattery even, and the suppression of the will. Yet the rewards for men and for women were necessarily different. Jefferson told both of his daughters that the compensation for their self-effacement would be gratifying, but indirect. He promised Martha that "your own happiness will be the greater as you perceive that you promote that of others," and a decade later he renewed the pledge to Maria: "Go on

75. Thomas Jefferson to Martha Jefferson Randolph, July 17, 1790, in Betts and Bear, eds., *Family Letters,* 60.

76. Martha Jefferson Randolph to Thomas Jefferson, May 16, 1793, ibid., 118, Jefferson to Martha Jefferson Randolph, June 22, 1792, ibid., 102.

then, my dear, as you have done in deserving the love of every body; you will reap the rich reward of their esteem, and will find that we are working for ourselves while we do good to others." A woman's work was to promote others' happiness, thereby ensuring her own.[77]

Women, in other words, had to earn love; it was the return for love freely given. For men, it was their due. When Jefferson rhapsodized about the happiness of home, he assumed that his daughters would always love him; he never had to worry about earning their love. He could speak with confidence about the blessings of domestic society because he believed its love was eternal. As he told Maria, "The circle of our nearest connections is the only one in which a faithful and lasting affection can be found, one which will adhere to us under all changes and chances." For women, however, love was contingent; it had to be earned. "Be good and be industrious," he told Martha when she was fifteen, "and you will be what I shall most love in this world."[78]

The letters that Jefferson wrote later, when he was in Philadelphia or New York or Washington, attending to his nation's affairs, with their affectionate closings and their protestations of never-ceasing love more than implied that his daughters had met his expectations. It should not be surprising that they took him at his word when he said that he despised the rancor of politics and longed for the harmony of home. That was another way of saying that he loved them best. How painful it must have been for Martha, then, in the summer of 1800, when her father returned to Monticello for one of his long-anticipated visits and she could barely spend "one sociable minute" with him for the crowds of people who came in his pursuit. So distressed was Martha that it took her a full two months before she could write. She complained that her father was "allways in a crowd, taken from every useful and pleasing duty to be worried with a multiplicity of disagreeable ones which the entertaining of such crowds of company subjects one to in the country." It was worse for her than if he had been in Philadelphia, "for then at least I should have enjoyed in anticipation those pleasures which we were deprived of by the concourse of strangers which continually crowded

77. Thomas Jefferson to Martha Jefferson Randolph, July 17, 1790, ibid., 61, Jefferson to Mary Jefferson Eppes, Feb. 12, 1800, 186. See, similarly, Jefferson to Mary Jefferson, May 30, 1791, ibid., 84: "To see you in short place your felicity in acquiring the love of those among whom you live, and without which no body can ever be happy."

78. Thomas Jefferson to Mary Jefferson Eppes, Jan. 1, 1799, ibid., 170, Jefferson to Martha Jefferson, May 21, 1787, 41–42. See, similarly, Jefferson to Martha Jefferson, Nov. 28, 1783, ibid., 20, and Jefferson to Mary Jefferson, Sept. 20, 1785, 29.

the house when you were with us." If, as her father told her, it was only the duties of home that were useful and pleasing, why was he entertaining this disagreeable crowd?[79]

Jefferson answered the letter immediately. He assured Martha, "Nobody can ever have felt so severely as myself the prostration of family society from the circumstance you mention." It was more painful for him than it could have been for her. "Worn down here with pursuits in which I take no delight, surrounded by enemies and spies, catching and perverting every word which falls from my lips or flows from my pen, and inventing where facts fail them, I pant for that society where all is peace and harmony, where we love and are loved by every object we see." No, she had not misunderstood him; yes, he would prefer to be at home. "But there is no remedy." As a public figure, he had to bring at least part of the public home. Yet customs were changing, and, before long, perhaps, the public might intrude only during the day, leaving the family "to tranquility in the evening." Jefferson concluded by asking his daughter to look on the brighter side and "to consider that these visits are evidences of the general esteem which we have been able [*sic*] all our lives trying to merit." But it was, of course, Jefferson, and not his daughter, that these crowds of strangers were coming to see, just as it was Jefferson who was the object of their esteem.[80]

Jefferson was, after all, a public man, and his aspiration was to serve the public in a way that would win him, if not fame, at least esteem. That is the hidden text of all of his letters. The complaints about enemies and spies notwithstanding, Jefferson was not about to leave public life. Even when he retired from government service, the crowds would still come to his home. And he enjoyed the public, but he wanted it on his own terms. When he became president, he implored his daughters to come visit. Maria was reluctant; she had lived in the country so long that she was fearful of the capital's more sophisticated milieu. Her father empathized. Between his retirement from Washington's cabinet and his election as vice president, he, too, had "remained closely at home, saw none but those who came there, and at length became very sensible of the ill effect it had upon my own mind, and of it's direct and irresistible tendency to render me unfit for society, and uneasy

79. Martha Jefferson Randolph to Thomas Jefferson, Jan. 31, 1801, ibid., 192–193.

80. Thomas Jefferson to Martha Jefferson Randolph, Feb. 5, 1801, ibid., 195. As long as he lived, strangers would feel free to visit Jefferson at home; Martha never reconciled herself to this situation. See Martha Jefferson Randolph to Ellen W. Coolidge, Sept. 18, 1825, Correspondence of Ellen Wayles Randolph Coolidge.

when necessarily engaged in it." He had learned his lesson, and she should, too. Society was good.[81]

In most of his letters home, Jefferson drew a stark contrast between the world of politics and home, but there was really a third realm, one that he always assumed but rarely discussed. "Domestic society" was but a smaller, more affectionate distillation of society at large, differing from it more in degree than kind. Indeed, contemporary political thought conceived the family as the smallest of the concentric circles of social organization to which a man belonged. As a man moved from his immediate family, through various degrees of his kin, he entered his neighborhood, and then society, and after that, the nation or government, beyond which extended the universe of mankind at large. Scottish moral philosophers such as Adam Smith believed that man was by nature affectionate and sympathetic; the sort of love that bound him to his family also knit him to everyone else. This is what Jefferson also meant when he said that man was a social animal. Yet political life confounded Jefferson's expectations, or at least hopes, of a universalizing sympathy. It was out of this frustration that he turned back to his family, as well as to his friends. As much as he relied upon his friends, however, Jefferson never developed a vision of friendship that could compare to the one he crafted of the family. His hopes dashed at the political end of the social spectrum, he fell back upon the smallest and most comforting unit he knew, making the family his model for social relations. Jefferson described the family so passionately that it is little wonder that his daughters thought their father considered it the only place where he could be happy.[82]

81. Martha Jefferson Randolph to Ellen W. Coolidge, Sept. 18, 1825, Correspondence of Ellen Wayles Randolph Coolidge; Ellen W. Coolidge to [Henry] Randall, 185[6], in Sarah N. Randolph, *The Domestic Life of Thomas Jefferson . . .* (1871; rpt. Charlottesville, Va., 1978), 344–345; Thomas Jefferson to Mary Jefferson Eppes, Mar. 3, 1802, in Betts and Bear, eds., *Family Letters,* 218–219.

82. See Note 14 above; see also Adam Smith, *The Theory of Moral Sentiments,* ed. D. D. Raphael and A. L. Macfie (Indianapolis, Ind., 1982). In his *Notes on Virginia,* Jefferson repeated the Comte de Buffon's charge that because Native Americans did not love their women, they did not love their fellow men: "Il ne faut pas aller chercher plus loin la cause de la vie dispersée des sauvages et de leur éloignement pour la société: la plus précieuse étincelle du feu de la nature leur a été refusée; ils manquent d'ardeur pour leur femelle, et par consequent d'amour pour leur semblables." In defending Native Americans, Jefferson implicitly accepted the comte's sociology: "He is affectionate to his children. . . . His affections comprehend his other connections, weakening, as with us, from circle to circle, as they recede from the center." See Thomas Jefferson, "Notes on the State of Virginia," in Peterson, ed., *Thomas Jefferson, Writings,* 183–185. See also Rhys Isaac, "The First Monticello," in Peter S. Onuf, ed., *Jeffersonian Legacies* (Charlottesville, Va., 1993), 100.

Jefferson was no hypocrite; he loved his daughters dearly, and surely it was their love that sustained him in his darkest days. But he also shaped his family—and indeed, the idea of the family—to meet his needs. It was the family that made a modern politics possible, by divesting it of the emotional intensity that led all too often to violence and by giving men alternate sources of identity. On his deathbed, according to Jeff Randolph, his grandfather was still thinking about the rancor of politics. "In speaking of the calumnies which his enemies had uttered against his public and private character with such unmitigated and untiring bitterness, he said that he had not considered them as abusing him; they had never known *him*. They had created an imaginary being clothed with odious attributes, to whom they had given his name." It was a man's family, not those he encountered in public life, who knew who he really was.[83]

VII

We have suggested that the requirements of modern politics would define and erect a wall between itself and the family, but that is not to imply that the family occupied a small or inconsequential space. The family, instead, was the prototype of society, the vast domain where men and women met and mingled and behaved with virtue, good humor, and self-restraint. For the wall that protected the family encompassed society as well; it was the world of politics—and perhaps that of business—that was isolated by this fictive wall. Anywhere that women went, affection might prevail. Responding to a female friend who had congratulated him on his election to the presidency, Jefferson replied, "The post is not enviable, as it affords little exercise for the social affections. There is something within us which makes us wish to have things conducted in our own way and which we generally fancy to be in patriotism. This ambition is gratified by such a position. But the heart would be happier enjoying the affections of a family fireside." Jefferson had reinterpreted public virtue—patriotism—as ambition and will; it was the affections nurtured in the family that bound society together. These were the best affections of our nature, the fulfillment of the disposition that the Creator had implanted in mankind's breast.[84]

Politics and governance were separate and distinct. But this was the arena

83. Thomas Jefferson Randolph to Henry S. Randall, n.d., in Randolph, *Domestic Life,* 428.

84. Thomas Jefferson to Catherine Church, Mar. 27, 1801, in Lipscomb and Bergh, eds., *Writings of Thomas Jefferson,* XVIII, 240–241.

in which Jefferson had made his mark, and this was where his legacy, he hoped, would be. He asked Madison to help preserve the blessings of self-government, not those of domestic society. The latter he entrusted to his family. And the wall between the two realms had been built so strong that it could not be breached; it was the wall, finally, that separated women from men. Half a year before his death, Jefferson commiserated with his granddaughter Ellen. She had married a Bostonian and moved north. The ship that was carrying her baggage had been lost, taking with it all of her letters and books. "And your life cut in two, as it were, and a new one to begin, without any records of the former." Moreover, a beautiful writing desk made by the talented slave carpenter John Hemings was also gone. It could never be replaced. Jefferson, however, offered a substitute, "not claiming the same value from it's [*sic*] decorations, but from the part it has *borne* in our history": the lap desk upon which he had written the Declaration of Independence. He surmised that such objects were beginning to "acquire a superstitious value because of their connection with particular persons" and events and that, in years to come, the desk might have a place in celebrations of the Fourth of July. With that purpose in mind, Jefferson entrusted his desk, not to his granddaughter, but to her husband. "Mr. Coolidge must do for me the favor of accepting this. Its imaginary value will increase with the years, and if he lives to my age, or another half century, he may yet see it carried in the procession of our nation's birthday, as the relics of the saints are in those of the church." Near death, Jefferson imagined himself a saint in his own religion. It was a faith that his female kin, too, had helped him create, but from whose rituals they were excluded.[85]

85. Thomas Jefferson to Ellen Randolph Coolidge, Nov. 14, 1825, in Betts and Bear, eds., *Family Letters,* 461–462.

The White Jeffersons

This is what we now know. A man and a woman have children. The woman is the half sister of his now-departed wife; she is the aunt, then, of his two grown daughters. She is also his slave. By law, their children are his slaves as well. The children grow up on his plantation, and, like their mother, they work there, but their work is always light. They all seem to know that one day they will be free. Then, in the year 1802, a newspaper publishes a story that says this man is the father of this woman's children. He does not deny this story explicitly; instead, he says his enemies have spread a number of untruths. Everyone, including his family, takes the evasion as a denial, a refusal to honor an ugly story with a direct comment.

A man and a woman have children. He already has children. This woman is those children's aunt, the half sister of the man's now-deceased wife. The man has two families: a first family and a second. Because the mother of his second family is his slave, their children are also slaves. His first family does not know about his second family, even though they all live together on a plantation at the top of a mountain in Virginia. Or perhaps they know, in the way that children and grandchildren know these things but cannot acknowledge.

Four children are born on a plantation at the top of a mountain in Virginia. Their mother is the half sister of their father's wife, a woman who died ten years before the youngest of them was born. They have two older half sisters, the children of the aunt they never knew, the woman their mother has replaced. And they have nieces and nephews, their sisters' children; they grow up with these children, on top of the mountain, but their nieces and nephews do not seem to know that they are all related, that the man some of them call Grandpapa, the others know is their father.

This essay was originally published as Jan Ellen Lewis, "The White Jeffersons," in Lewis and Peter S. Onuf, eds., *Sally Hemings and Thomas Jefferson: History, Memory, and Civic Culture* (Charlottesville, Va., 1999), 127–160.

Two daughters are born on a plantation at the top of a mountain in Virginia. Their mother dies when they are quite young. Their father becomes mother and father both to them. Sometime later, when they, themselves, are young mothers, a newspaper prints a story saying that their father has kept one of his slaves as a mistress, that together they have had children, and that one of the children looks just like him. What do these daughters say? What do they tell their children? What do their children say? They love their father more than anything.

Thomas Jefferson was the third president of the United States. After bearing him six children in ten years, his wife died, leaving him only two surviving daughters, Martha and Mary, whom he called Patsy and Polly. Twenty years after her death, in the second year of his first term as president, a newspaper published a story accusing him of fathering children by a slave mistress. He never honored the rumor with a direct response, but he implied that it was a lie, fomented by his political enemies. To his dying day, Jefferson was troubled by the scurrilous stories that his political rivals spread; they bothered the daughter who outlived him, and they bothered her children, too. Abolitionists kept the rumor about the slave mistress and slave children alive, and, after the Civil War, one of those children published an interview in which he claimed to be the son of Thomas Jefferson. For almost two centuries, most historians discredited the rumor, seeing in it only scandal and in the ex-slave's story only a longing to belong to something greater than himself. Still, the rumor stayed alive, and people continued to debate its merits. Then, in 1997, a scientist decided to perform a DNA test that might help resolve the dispute.

These are the stories of families, of parents and children, of a white family and a black family, of a national family of blacks and whites. These are the stories of Thomas Jefferson and Sally Hemings, of white Jeffersons and black, of Americans black and white. They are the stories of a family and of a nation.

All families have secrets. The family itself rests upon the terrible secret that mothers and fathers share: their children were conceived in passion in the dark of night. This is a truth that the child is at once driven to discover and terrified to behold. And this truth, its hiddenness, its compulsion to be discovered, is a metaphor for family life itself. The child perceives her parents as through a veil; there are always mysteries she cannot fathom, even in the happiest of families, even in those that are seemingly the most banal.

The white Jeffersons thought of themselves as, and told each other that they were, a happy family. Less than half a year before he died, Thomas Jefferson counted his blessings, and they were many, but, "above all, a family which has blessed me by their affections, and never by their conduct given me a moment's pain." Families are not, by their nature, happy. Making a family happy requires work, and sometimes it is work of imagination pure and plain: we imagine ourselves to be a happy family; we tell ourselves that we are; we suppress those murmuring suspicions that we are not. As a young widower in the 1780s, Thomas Jefferson worked very hard to make his small family—two surviving daughters and, later, their children—into a model of happiness. When they were young, he wrote his daughters deeply affectionate—and patently manipulative—letters. "I have placed my happiness on seeing you good and accomplished, and no distress which this world can now bring on me could equal that of your disappointing my hopes," he wrote Patsy when she was only twelve, placing a huge burden upon the motherless girl, but one that she happily shouldered. In years to come, she would entertain her friends by showing them her father's letters, the ones in which he told her how well she had succeeded in making him happy.[1]

In August 1809—a little more than a year after Sally Hemings's last child, Eston, was born—Margaret Bayard Smith visited Jefferson and his family at Monticello. One morning, Patsy, by now a married woman with eight children of her own, was indisposed. Mrs. Smith visited her in her room, where "the conversation turned chiefly on her father." Patsy showed her friend some of her father's letters. Mrs. Smith copied certain passages into her journal, ones that contrasted the pleasures of family life with the miseries of politics. "When I look to the ineffable pleasures of my family society," Jefferson had written his daughter, "I become more and more disgusted with the jealousies, the hatred, the rancorous and malignant passions of this scene, and lament my having ever again been drawn into public view." Mrs. Smith copied another passage in which Jefferson contrasted the miseries of govern-

1. Thomas Jefferson to Thomas Jefferson Randolph, Feb. 8, 1826, in Edwin Morris Betts and James Adam Bear, eds., *The Family Letters of Thomas Jefferson* (Columbia, Mo., 1966), 470, Jefferson to Martha Jefferson, Nov. 28, 1783, 20.

mental service to family life: "Worn down here with pursuits in which I take no delight, surrounded by enemies and spies, catching and perverting every word which falls from my lips, or flows from my pen, and inventing where facts fail them, I pant for that society, where all is peace and harmony, where we love and are beloved by every object we see. . . . These are the only times existence is of any value to me."[2]

As everyone who has read Jefferson's *Family Letters* knows, during the 1790s, when Jefferson served in the Washington administration and then as John Adams's vice president, he wrote both his daughters a number of letters in which he contrasted the realm of politics and the realm of the family. So familiar have these opposing ways of describing politics and the family become that they are what literary scholars call tropes, rhetorical devices in which words are used to convey something other than their literal meaning. Politicians seemed like "salamanders, to consider fire as their element." Family was "the only soil on which it is worth while to bestow much culture."[3]

These tropes have become familiar to us. Many of us would agree, instinctively, with Jefferson's characterization of the nation's capital as representing "every thing which can be disgusting" and the family as "every thing which is pleasurable to me in this world." But when Jefferson spoke in these terms, they were novel. Only recently had men and women begun to sentimentalize the family, to think of it in almost religious terms as a sanctuary or haven. We need think only of Shakespeare's families—the warring Montagues and Capulets, the conflict-ridden Lears, the scheming Macbeths—to realize

2. Gaillard Hunt, ed., *The First Forty Years of Washington Society: Portrayed by the Family Letters of Mrs. Samuel Harrison Smith (Margaret Bayard) from the Collection of Her Grandson J. Henley Smith* (New York, 1906), 74–77. These letters are reprinted in full in Betts and Bear, eds., *Family Letters.* See Thomas Jefferson to Martha Jefferson Randolph, June 8, 1797, ibid., 146, and Jefferson to Martha Jefferson Randolph, Feb. 5, 1801, 195–196. Smith's transcriptions were generally accurate, although one error, in copying a passage from the Feb. 5, 1801, letter is telling. In the original, Jefferson concluded with a variant of his usual, loving closing: "My personal affections would fix me for ever with you. Present me affectionately to Mr. Randolph, kiss the dear little objects of our natural love, and be assured of the constancy and tenderness of mine to you" (ibid., 196). In Smith's transcription, the passage reads this way: " 'My personal affections would fix me forever with you. Kiss the dear little objects of our mutual love,' etc. etc." (Hunt, ed., *First Forty Years of Washington Society,* 78). Here, not only has Patsy's husband, Thomas Mann Randolph, been excised, but her children have incestuously become those of her father as well. At the time, husbands and wives often called their children "pledges of our mutual love," or, as Smith rendered the phrase, "objects of our mutual love."

3. Thomas Jefferson to Martha Jefferson Randolph, May 17, 1798, in Betts and Bear, eds., *Family Letters,* 162, Jefferson to Mary Jefferson Eppes, Jan. 1, 1799, 170.

how remarkable, how revolutionary was the notion that a family might be a source of any pleasure at all, let alone the source of everything pleasurable.[4]

Likewise, Jefferson's depiction of the world of politics in such starkly negative terms was also an innovation. Only a few years before, American Revolutionaries had thought of public service as the highest of callings; to give oneself over to the public, to sacrifice personal interest for the public good was the measure of greatness. For complex reasons involving changing political thought and practices both, Americans began to question the moral worth of government itself. Thomas Paine had said that "government even in its best state is but a necessary evil," and many Americans came to agree. Private life, social life, all life that was outside of government was what was valuable, and the purpose of government was to protect that life, primarily from government itself. From time to time, good men would have to take their turn in public service, but the public had no right to demand this sort of sacrifice. As Jefferson wrote in a particularly bitter moment, shortly after his wife had died and his friends were trying to draw him back into government, "If we are made in some degree for others, yet in a greater are we made for ourselves. It were contrary to feeling and indeed ridiculous to suppose that a man had less right in himself than one of his neighbors or indeed all of them put together."[5]

When Jefferson wrote to his daughters, telling them how he hated his life in government and how he longed to be with them, he was weaving together the strands of liberal political thought, which held that the purpose of government was to protect private life. Patsy and Polly and their children were the fleshly embodiment of the abstract reason that Jefferson worked for the public good. Moreover, once Jefferson and other liberal political practitioners disparaged the political life, they could no longer draw from it the sense of fulfillment and worth that was available to men like George Washington who thought of public service as a noble calling. Jefferson turned to his family for the appreciation, the love—the validation, we would say today—that he could not get from an increasingly boisterous and democratic citizenry. By telling his daughters and their children how much they meant to

4. Thomas Jefferson to Martha Jefferson Randolph, May 31, 1798, ibid., 164. For the changing estimation of the family, see Jan Lewis, *The Pursuit of Happiness: Family and Values in Jefferson's Virginia* (New York, 1983).

5. Thomas Paine, *Common Sense* (1776) (New York, 1976), 65; Thomas Jefferson to James Monroe, May 20, 1782, in Merrill D. Peterson, ed., *Thomas Jefferson, Writings: Autobiography, A Summary View of the Rights of British America, Notes on the State of Virginia, Public Papers, Addresses, Messages, and Replies, Miscellany, Letters* (New York, 1984), 777–780.

him, how much he needed them, he trained them to give him the love that he needed for personal and political reasons both.[6]

As we read Jefferson's letters, we can infer his intent. It is somewhat more difficult to imagine what might have been the effect of receiving such missives. As historians and amateur psychologists, we read the letters of the dead, and we wonder. What did it mean to Jefferson's daughters to be told, in letter after letter, that their love was "the best solace remaining to me in this world"; that "my only object in life is to see yourself and your sister, and those deservedly dear to you, not only happy, but in no danger of becoming unhappy"; that they ought "to love me as I do you"? What might it have meant to see every letter closed in a slightly different way—"with constant love," "in all the warmth of my love," "everlasting love," "tender and unmingled effusions of my love," "tender and unceasing love," "unspeakable tenderness," "constant and unbounded love," "unalterable and tenderest love," "tenderest and unalterable love," and "tenderness without bounds"?[7]

In the case of Martha Jefferson Randolph—Patsy—we need not speculate much at all. She showed the letters to her friend Margaret Bayard Smith. Years later, when they renewed acquaintance, when Martha Randolph was an aging widow and her father had died, she was still showing her old friend her father's letters and displaying the artifacts of family love. One day, when Martha was not feeling well, Mrs. Smith sat with her in her room. They talked about Jefferson, and Martha took "up the down cover-lit, which was over her," and explained that it "'was the one he used for 40 yrs. and this bed was his.'—The one, I imagine, on which his last hours were past, for she stopped, choked by emotion and could not restrain her tears, tho' she concealed them by drawing the bedclothes over her face." Another day, Martha showed Mrs. Smith "the last lines he ever wrote." She told the story of how

6. Jan Lewis, "'The Blessings of Domestic Society': Thomas Jefferson's Family and the Transformation of American Politics," in Peter S. Onuf, ed., *Jeffersonian Legacies* (Charlottesville, Va., 1993), 109–146, also reprinted in this volume.

7. Thomas Jefferson to Martha Jefferson Randolph, Mar. 10, 1793, in Betts and Bear, eds., *Family Letters,* 114, Jefferson to Mary Jefferson Eppes, Jan. 7, 1798, 153, Jefferson to Mary Jefferson, May 25, 1797, 145, Jefferson to Martha Jefferson Randolph, June 10, 1793, 120, Jefferson to Mary Jefferson, draft of letter on June 14, 1797, 149, Jefferson to Mary Jefferson Eppes, Apr. 1, 1798, 159, Jefferson to Martha Jefferson Randolph, Jan. 23, 1799, 172, Jefferson to Martha Jefferson Randolph, Jan. 21, 1800, 182, Jefferson to Mary Jefferson Eppes, Apr. 6, 1800, 187, Jefferson to Martha Jefferson Randolph, Apr. 22, 1800, 188, Jefferson to Martha Jefferson Randolph, Jan. 16, 1801, 192, Jefferson to Martha Jefferson Randolph, Dec. 3, 1804, 265, Jefferson to Martha Jefferson Randolph, May 6, 1805, 270.

her father wrote these lines during his final illness, how he gave them to her the day before he died, how she did not read them until after he was gone. He had written her a poem, telling her not to cry for him, "that his last pang would be in parting from her, but that he would carry her love and memory to the two happy spirits (her mother and sister) who were waiting to receive him."[8]

Every family constructs a narrative. It tells itself a story about itself. Jefferson's family told themselves they were a happy family, and so deeply did they believe their family narrative that the story engraved itself on the unconscious. As a grown woman, living in Boston, Jefferson's granddaughter Ellen Wayles Randolph Coolidge found herself haunted by the ghosts of her happy childhood. "When I dream it is mostly of long past times. Night after night I have been surrounded by the friends of childhood and early youth—my grandfather, mother, brothers, sisters, those whom I dearly loved and who dearly loved me, and who I hope in God's own time to rejoin."[9]

To be able to drive away the demons that haunt us in the night, to suppress the memories of family conflicts, of loss, of terror—this is an extraordinary accomplishment. No family, of course, is without its share of anguish and grief. In the case of the Jeffersons, they had more than their share, with not only the early death of Jefferson's wife and four of their babies but also the loss of Monticello to satisfy Jefferson's debts, a calamity that befell his descendants. The white Jeffersons proved themselves more than able to add to that sum of misery that life entails upon us all.

Perhaps it is a false distinction, to differentiate between natural catastrophes and the misery we make ourselves. The premature death of a loved one, the sudden collapse of the economy—these disasters hit Jefferson and hit him hard. He can hardly be faulted. Yet a biographer has suggested that Jefferson should have understood that his wife was frail and that repeated pregnancies—six births in ten years of marriage—put her life at risk.[10] With perhaps more justification, others have remarked that Jefferson's expensive tastes and poor judgment were more to blame for his late-life insolvency than inherited debts and the collapse of Virginia's economy. Curiously, there is no consensus about the role Jefferson's slaveholding played in

8. Hunt, ed., *First Forty Years,* 309, 316.

9. Autobiographical fragment, n.d., Correspondence of Ellen Wayles Randolph Coolidge Correspondence, 1819–1861, Accession No. 9090, 38–584, Albert Shirley Small Special Collections Library, University of Virginia, Charlottesville, Va.

10. Jack McLaughlin, *Jefferson and Monticello: The Biography of a Builder* (New York, 1988), 196.

his financial demise. Some have argued that Jefferson's taste for expensive wine and rich brocade made it impossible for him to live as he wished without relying upon the labors of slaves. Others have seen his refusal to liquidate his slaves to pay off his debts as a sign of his softheartedness, a tenderness at odds with the requirements of a heartless economy.[11]

How deeply is the individual implicated in those vast impersonal forces of life, death, and profit that give shape to his life? This is a hard question, one with no easy answers. Most of us are inclined to cut the individual a little slack, whether out of too much appreciation for life's complexities or too little comprehension of those forces we cannot direct. When it comes to choices that seem purely personal, however, we are often more ready to judge. And if we are so inclined, then we might note that the Jefferson women had a tendency to marry badly. Both Patsy Jefferson and her oldest daughter, Anne, married young, even for their time and place, and their marriages, in their family's eyes, were unhappy. Each was seventeen, and each married a man from the neighborhood who had Jefferson's hearty approval. He had known Patsy's young husband, her first cousin, Thomas Mann Randolph, all his life. Four years earlier, when only seventeen himself, young Randolph had asked Jefferson for his advice about his studies, and the older man gladly complied, with a letter so long and so full of sage advice that he finally cut himself off, worrying that "by this time . . . you will think I have sermonized enough." Perhaps that is, indeed, what Randolph thought; it does not appear that he ever answered his future father-in-law's letter. Whatever his early promise, Randolph turned out to be a man of unstable temperament who ended his unhappy life estranged from his family. His eldest son once described him as "more ferocious than the woulf [*sic*] and more fell than the hyena."[12]

Patsy's daughter fared even worse. Like her mother, she had been free to choose her own mate, and, like her mother, she selected someone who appeared at first as if he might be one of Jefferson's protégés. Shortly after his marriage to Jefferson's granddaughter, Charles Bankhead returned to Monticello with his young bride so that he might read law with the family

11. For example, see Paul Finkelman, "Jefferson and Slavery: 'Treason against the Hopes of the World,'" in Onuf, ed., *Jeffersonian Legacies,* 181–221; and Garry Wills, "The Aesthete," *New York Review of Books,* Aug. 12, 1993, 6–10.

12. Thomas Jefferson to Thomas Mann Randolph, Jr., Aug. 27, 1786, in Peterson, ed., *Thomas Jefferson, Writings,* 860–864; Dumas Malone, *Jefferson and His Time,* 6 vols. (Boston, 1948–1981), II, 250–251; Thomas Jefferson Randolph to Dabney S. Carr, July 11, 1826, Carr-Cary Family Papers, box 2, Albert Shirley Small Special Collections Library.

patriarch, who had just retired from the presidency. Jefferson welcomed his granddaughter and her husband, inviting them to stay at Monticello as long as they wished. "I hope . . . that you will both ever consider yourselves as a part of our family until you shall feel the desire of separate establishment insuperable." At the time, Sally Hemings's last child, Eston, was an infant, having been born the previous spring. Whatever Bankhead's early promise, within a few years' time, he had become an alcoholic who beat his wife and had bankrupted himself and his own small family. Just as the family—that is, the members who thought of themselves as the family—worried about how to cope with the erratic Thomas Mann Randolph, so they struggled with the problem presented by Charles Bankhead. Anne's brother Thomas Jefferson Randolph (Jeff), the oldest of Jefferson's grandsons and the one who seemed to take upon himself the role of family protector, once got into a violent fight with Charles in Charlottesville's courthouse square. When it was over, Jeff had been stabbed in the hip and Charles smacked in the face with the butt of Jeff's horsewhip. Still Anne refused to leave her husband and return to the sanctuary of Monticello. In the last letter he ever wrote Jeff, Thomas Jefferson reported the sad news that Anne had died, at her home, at the age of thirty-five. Only then was she brought home to Monticello, where her bones still rest in the family graveyard.[13]

One cannot help wondering how far into the future a seventeen-year-old girl might have seen. Is character fixed at so early an age? Might a girl have observed the signs of her husband's later erratic behavior? Might a young man have anticipated his life's trajectory as a member of a great and greatly loved man's household? Thomas Mann Randolph later described himself as a duck, "the proverbially silly bird . . . in the company of the Swans." Presumably, no one chooses to be the duck, but one day he realizes that the duck he has become.[14]

Every family is two families. First, there are those who are born into it, marry into it, and give birth to its children. These are the figures on the family

13. Thomas Jefferson to Anne Randolph Bankhead, Nov. 8, 1808, in Betts and Bear, eds., *Family Letters,* 357. For accounts of Charles Bankhead's drunkenness, the fight, and Anne's death, see Malone, *Jefferson and His Time,* VI, 159–160, 299–300, 476–477; Martha Jefferson Randolph to Thomas Jefferson, Nov. 20, 1816, in Betts and Bear, eds., *Family Letters,* 417, Martha Jefferson Randolph to Jefferson, Aug. 7, 1819, 430, and Jefferson to Thomas Jefferson Randolph, Feb. 11, 1826, 470.

14. Thomas Mann Randolph to Thomas Jefferson, Oct. 29, [1802], in Julian P. Boyd et al., eds., *The Papers of Thomas Jefferson,* 43 vols. (Princeton, N.J., 1950–), XXXVIII, 601–602, also cited in William H. Gaines, Jr., *Thomas Mann Randolph, Jefferson's Son-in-Law* (Baton Rouge, La., 1966), 48.

tree, their place on it signified by the facts of the demographic record, members in name, but sometimes name only. Then there are those who think of themselves as the real family—those who write its family story. Chief among those who considered themselves the real Jeffersons, of course, was Thomas Jefferson himself, the man who created the original idea of the family as "every thing which is pleasurable" and worked all his life to make his white family conform to that ideal. And then there was his oldest surviving daughter and her children, chief among them her first son, Jeff, and her second daughter, Ellen. But there were others who were members in name only. Two of them we have already met: the estranged son-in-law, Thomas Mann Randolph, and the knife-wielding drunkard, Charles Bankhead. But there was also Jefferson's second surviving daughter, Polly, the one who was left with her aunt in Virginia while her father went off with Patsy to represent the new nation in France. At the age of nine, against her desperate pleas, Polly was put on a ship, accompanied only by the fourteen-year-old slave Sally Hemings, to join her father in Europe. Ten years later, she married her cousin John, the son of the beloved aunt from whom she had been torn. Polly received, as best we can tell, the same expressions of her father's tender love, the same entreaties to love him well. But she did not always answer his letters. "I did not write to you, my dear Poll, the last week, because I was really angry at receiving no letter. . . . I ascribed it at first to indolence, but the affection must be weak which is so long overruled by that," her father scolded. And he closed his letter with a simple "Adieu." It had been nine weeks since he had heard from her; she was twelve. Once she married, she rarely returned home.[15]

So this was the Jefferson family constellation—an inner circle, committed to and writing with its every breath the story of a happy family and returning to Monticello even in its dreams, and an outer circle, so estranged, so remote, that a son could describe his father as more lethal than the earth's wildest beast. And yet there was another family still, one that grew up alongside the white Jeffersons: Sally Hemings and her children—the unacknowledged children of Thomas Jefferson.

Everyone said that Sally Hemings's children looked like Thomas Jefferson. That had been one of the chief items in James Callender's 1802 newspaper article, the first public assertion that Jefferson was their father. The fourth line of that scurrilous piece of journalism had pointed out that Sally's

15. Thomas Jefferson to Mary Jefferson, Jan. 5, 1790 [1791], in Betts and Bear, eds., *Family Letters*, 67.

son's "features are said to bear a striking although sable resemblance to those of the president himself."[16]

The family resemblances must have been quite remarkable, indeed, for even Jeff Randolph acknowledged them. Jeff said "the resemblance" between his grandfather and one of the Hemings children was "so close, that at some distance or in the dusk the slave, dressed in the same way, might be mistaken for Mr. Jefferson." He also said that one day "a gentleman dining with Mr. Jefferson, looked so startled as he raised his eyes from the latter to the servant behind him, that his discovery of the resemblance was perfectly obvious to all." That, at least, is what Henry S. Randall, an early Jefferson biographer, told the historian James Parton in 1868. The letter that Randall sent Parton, describing his conversation with Jeff Randolph about ten years earlier, constitutes part of what Fawn M. Brodie once termed "the family denial." Thirty and more years later, after Jefferson's death, his oldest surviving grandchildren, Jeff Randolph and Ellen Coolidge, each offered a semiofficial refutation of the allegation that their grandfather had been the father of Sally Hemings's children. Ellen set out her answer to the questions in a letter to her husband, written in 1858, when she was visiting Jeff and his family in Virginia. A little while earlier, Jeff had told Randall his version of the family story, which Randall recounted in a letter to Parton. Then, in late 1873 or early 1874, Jeff wrote, but apparently never sent, a letter to the editor of the *Pike County Republican,* which had published autobiographical essays by Sally Hemings's third son, Madison, and Israel Jefferson, a former Monticello slave. Jeff's letter was a direct response to Israel's essay; its main purpose seems to have been to cast doubt upon Israel's credibility and thereby to refute his contention that Madison Hemings was speaking the truth when he claimed Thomas Jefferson as his father.[17]

16. "The President Again," *Recorder; or, Lady's and Gentleman's Miscellany* (Richmond, Va.), Sept. 1, 1802, [2]. This son, Tom, has been supposed, but not proven, to be Thomas Woodson. The DNA tests on his descendants, however, seem to have ruled out Jefferson as the father. See Appendix K in Monticello's online "Report of the Research Committee on Thomas Jefferson and Sally Hemings," https://www.monticello.org/thomas-jefferson/jefferson-slavery/thomas-jefferson-and-sally-hemings-a-brief-account/research-report-on-jefferson-and-hemings.

17. Henry S. Randall to James Parton, June 1, 1868, reprinted in Annette Gordon-Reed, *Thomas Jefferson and Sally Hemings: An American Controversy* (Charlottesville, Va., 1997), 254; [Thomas Jefferson Randolph] to Sir, [1873 or 1874], copy, courtesy of Lucia Stanton, Robert H. Smith International Center for Jefferson Studies, Charlottesville, Va. The texts of all the other documents—Randall's letter to Parton, Ellen Randolph Coolidge's letter to her husband, and the memoirs of Israel Jefferson and Madison Jefferson as well, can be found in

None of these accounts entered the public record immediately. Parton described Randall's letter in his biography of Jefferson, published in 1874, but the letter itself was not published until 1951, in a biography of Parton. Ellen Coolidge's letter remained in the hands of her descendants, although a copy is in the collection of her papers at the Albert and Shirley Small Special Collections Library of the University of Virginia. As late as the summer of 1976, two years after Fawn M. Brodie argued that Jefferson was the father of Sally Hemings's children and eight years after Winthrop D. Jordan had suggested the same thing, the librarians' notation at the top of the letter said, *"RESTRICTED absolutely."* Copies—either in xerox or in one's own hand—were forbidden; publication in whole or in part was banned. The restrictions placed upon Coolidge's letter only enhanced its credibility, making it seem, like a whispered family secret, more true than the published record. The family story seemed true precisely because it was secret.[18]

Similarly, Randall's letter to Parton, which has the form of a private communication of confidential information, did not become fully public until 1951. Jeff Randolph's response to Israel Jefferson still has not been published, although it has been available to researchers. If the family had an alternate explanation for the family resemblance of Sally Hemings's children, and an answer to Callender's never-forgotten charge, they never offered it publicly or in any private communications that have made their way into the historical record. Indeed, the family kept its denial almost entirely to itself, sharing it only with a trusted biographer, whom Randolph forbade to publish it. In their penchant for privacy, Jefferson's white family followed his example. During his lifetime, Jefferson had refused to answer the accusation directly. In 1805, he acknowledged to his secretary of the navy that "when young and single I offered love to a handsome lady"—Betsey Walker, the wife of a good friend. "I acknolege [*sic*] its incorrectness. It is the only one founded in truth among all their allegations against me." Implicitly, the allegation about Sally Hemings was false.[19]

So far as we know, that is the closest Jefferson ever came to addressing di-

---

Gordon-Reed, *Jefferson and Hemings,* 245–260. See also Fawn M. Brodie, *Thomas Jefferson: An Intimate History* (New York, 1974), 471–482, 493–498.

18. Malone, *Jefferson and His Time,* IV, 493–498, esp. 497; Winthrop D. Jordan, *White over Black: American Attitudes toward the Negro, 1550–1812* (Williamsburg, Va., and Chapel Hill, N.C., 1968); Ellen Wayles Coolidge to Joseph Coolidge, Oct. 24, 1858, in Ellen Wayles Coolidge Letterbook, Coolidge Correspondence, box 3.

19. Thomas Jefferson to Robert Smith, July 5, 1805, quoted in Brodie, *Thomas Jefferson,* 375.

rectly the Sally Hemings allegation, in either public or private. We have no record of his having denied the charges to his family, although he certainly led them to believe that the allegations were untrue. In 1806, William Burwell, Jefferson's former secretary, showed Patsy a scurrilous poem written about her father by a young Irishman, Thomas Moore. He pointed out the most offensive passages, ones that intimated the president "dreams of freedom in his bondmaid's arms." According to Randall, the "indignant pair" showed Jefferson the poem, and "Mr Jefferson broke into a hearty, clear laugh." From this distance, we might say that the laugh was on Patsy and Burwell, and through them and Randall, on posterity, although Randall interpreted Jefferson's laugh as a clear denial. "There was more than argument—there was conviction in that laugh." As was his habit, Jefferson had implied the denial, and for those who wanted to believe him, the implication was as good as his word.[20]

When children confront their parents, they do not necessarily want to be told the truth. Sometimes they want only for order to be restored to their world, their suspicions laid to rest. When Patsy and the ever-loyal Burwell burst in upon Jefferson, waving Moore's scurrilous poem, they wanted a denial, not a tear-filled confession. So, also, when Patsy and Polly asked their father why they no longer visited John Walker's, "knowing [how] intimate they were before he went to F[rance]." There was, in fact, a very good reason: in 1768, when he was unmarried, Jefferson made some improper advances to his friend's wife, Betsey, when her husband was away from home for several months. As John Walker later told the story, after its outlines had been revealed in 1805 by the partisan press, Jefferson continued pushing himself on Betsey for more than a decade, long after he had married, once stuffing a sort of love letter up the sleeve of her dress and several times accosting her when one or the other of them was in a state of partial undress. Most Jefferson biographers have been willing to concede only what Jefferson himself conceded: that he had propositioned Betsey Walker only once, when he was young and unmarried. Dumas Malone concluded that "our knowledge of Jefferson's temperament and personality" make it hard to believe Jefferson would have approached Betsey repeatedly and grossly, as her hus-

20. Thomas Moore, "To Thomas Hume, Esq. M.D. from the City of Washington," (1807), quoted in Werner Sollors, "Presidents, Race, and Sex," in Jan Ellen Lewis and Peter S. Onuf, eds., *Sally Hemings and Thomas Jefferson: History, Memory, and Civic Culture* (Charlottesville, Va., 1999), 199; Henry S. Randall, *The Life of Thomas Jefferson,* III (New York, 1858), 118–119, esp. 119.

band charged. But since these are the same historians who rejected the Sally Hemings story because of their supposed knowledge of Jefferson's temperament and personality, perhaps we should not be so quick to accept Jefferson's account and reject John Walker's.[21]

According to Walker, his wife did not tell him about Jefferson's unwanted attentions until Jefferson left the country in 1784. Whether that is exactly what happened or not, when Jefferson returned to Virginia, he was no longer welcome at his old friend's house. His children seemed to sense that something was wrong. Rather than telling them just what that something was, "to quiet them [Jefferson] said some difference had arisen about money matters." This account, by the way, comes from William Burwell, who seems to have been present during the only two recorded times that Jefferson's daughters confronted him with questions about his private affairs. In this instance, his daughters had guessed right: there had been a rupture with the Walkers. Although it was about love, Jefferson told them it was about money.[22]

It is not clear why Jefferson thought this lie about his break with Walker would quiet his daughters. He had told them, after all, that one of his oldest and dearest friends had—and this was the way Burwell put it—tried "to defraud him in some money transactions." Someone their father had loved and trusted had tried to cheat him, and he was too honorable, too decent, to denounce his old friend; no one would have known had not his daughters pressed him. It should not be surprising that Patsy and Polly talked; if their father would not denounce Walker, they would. And, in this way, Jefferson's lie about his old friend made its way out into the public, as family secrets will.[23]

Jefferson's daughters told David Meade Randolph, whose brother-in-law was Patsy's husband, Thomas Mann Randolph. It was still a family lie—an extended family lie, we might say. As sometimes happens, however, families have fallings-out. Jefferson sued David Meade Randolph in a complex lawsuit over Jefferson's father-in-law's estate. A few years later, Jefferson fired Randolph from his post as United States marshal; shortly after that, Randolph was telling people that Jefferson had slurred John Walker's reputation.

21. Malone, *Jefferson and His Time,* I, 447–451; Brodie, *Thomas Jefferson,* 73–79. Once again, Brodie is the exception among Jefferson biographers. She thought it possible that Jefferson and Betsey Walker had an affair—that is, not only had Jefferson persisted in his advances, but Betsey Walker might have reciprocated.

22. Gerald W. Gawalt, "Strict Truth: The Narrative of William A. Burwell," *Virginia Magazine of History and Biography,* CI (1993), 119–120, esp. 120.

23. Ibid., 120; Malone, *Jefferson and His Time,* I, 153–155, 447–451.

The newspapers had gotten hold of the Betsey Walker story at just the time that Callender was publishing his allegations about the Sally Hemings liaison, so Randolph was able to contribute his own mite: not only had Jefferson attempted to seduce Walker's wife, but he had also "fabricated a falsehood to explain the cause of their rupture." Burwell, ever the Jefferson loyalist, was scandalized by Randolph's behavior. Jefferson had meant no harm, but once his daughters "incautiously" told their kinsman, "an explanation intended to preserve the happiness and tranquility of his daughters, and *never* given elsewhere was made the basis of that charge against him and handled and attributed to the iniquity of his heart."[24]

The lie Jefferson told his daughters to protect his good name, by this logic, was less wicked than that same lie repeated in public. Perhaps that is the way Jefferson saw it as well. He tried to erect a wall between his family and the wider world, but that wall—even at its strongest—was but a thin membrane, the skin of a bubble, shimmering in the light. The story he made up to "quiet" his daughters made its way out into the public, just as his confession to a single act of "incorrectness" must have made its way back into his family. We do not know what Patsy and Polly thought if they read in the newspapers the story about their father and Betsey Walker. Perhaps they believed just what most historians have believed ever since: Jefferson had an embarrassing lapse when he was young, and his embarrassment and subsequent efforts to hide it from his family are proof of his character.

Parents, as a rule, do not confess their sins to their children, although they vary in the means they use to protect their children—that is, to protect themselves. In Jefferson's case, when his daughters confronted him about some embarrassing matter, he either evaded the question (the "hearty laugh" when shown Moore's poem) or lied (blaming the rupture with John Walker on his old friend). As for the accusations made by his enemies, so far as we know, Jefferson never acknowledged to his family that any of them were truthful. Instead, he told his family that his enemies had lied about him and that the lies hurt. He was always the person done to, never the one doing. His chief defense within the family was to point out that he was the victim of vicious attacks. In 1803, for example, he wrote out his religious creed so that "my family, by possessing this, should be enabled to estimate the libels published against me on this, as on every other possible subject"—as if proving that he was not an infidel would answer also the charges about fathering

24. Gawalt, "Strict Truth," *Virginia Magazine of History and Biography,* CI (1993), 119–120; Brodie, *Thomas Jefferson,* 350–356; Gordon-Reed, *Jefferson and Hemings,* 74.

Sally Hemings's children. Even on his deathbed, Jefferson was still brooding about these allegations. "In speaking of the calumnies which his enemies had uttered against his public and private character with such unmitigated and untiring bitterness," Jeff Randolph reported that his grandfather said "that he had not considered them as abusing him; they had never known *him*. They had created an imaginary being clothed with odious attributes, to whom they had given his name." Jefferson's family knew the real him—and that person could not have engaged in a liaison with Sally Hemings. The proof against the accusation was Jefferson's character as a family man, that is, the kind of person he was in his family.[25]

Of course, these, too, are familiar tropes: the outer self that the world sees and the better, purer inner self—the self as it "really" is. In this sense, Jefferson was one of the first moderns, feeling himself misunderstood by and at odds with the world. And, as we now know, Jefferson was almost certainly lying about his relationship with Sally Hemings—to his political allies, to his daughter, and to her son. And the form his lie took was particularly insidious, for it gave as its proof, not a fact or something that had the appearance of a fact, but, instead, a seductive and contingent offer of love. To believe Jefferson innocent of the slurs against him was to know the real him; to accept the slanders was not, he said, to know him at all. No child could resist this invitation into her father's naked heart. The thrill of the invitation, the relief at the sight. It is as if Ham had lifted the flap of his father's tent—only to find him fully clothed and sleeping like a lamb.

When Jefferson implied that he was innocent of the Sally Hemings charges, perhaps he believed that he was telling the truth, or, at least, that he was not lying. Perhaps he thought some part of Callender's charge was untrue, and he could implicitly deny the whole thing. Perhaps he did not think of Sally Hemings as his "concubine." He might have thought of her as something more: a true love, a second wife. Or he might have thought of her as something less: an occasional sexual partner, at best. Or perhaps he knew that the slave known as Tom and reputed to be his son by Sally Hemings was some other man's child. The DNA evidence strongly suggests that Jefferson was not this slave's father.[26]

But whatever Jefferson thought, we now know, almost for a certainty,

25. Thomas Jefferson to Martha Jefferson Randolph, Apr. 23, 1803, in Betts and Bear, eds., *Family Letters,* 210; Thomas Jefferson Randolph to Henry S. Randall, n.d., in Sarah N. Randolph, *The Domestic Life of Thomas Jefferson . . .* (1871; rpt. Charlottesville, Va., 1978), 428.

26. "The President Again," *Recorder; or, Lady's and Gentleman's Miscellany,* Sept. 1, 1802, [2], quoted in Brodie, *Thomas Jefferson,* 349.

that he was the father of Sally Hemings's son Eston, and probably Beverley, Harriet, and Madison as well. And, unless he was delusional—and whatever has been said about Jefferson, no one has ever made this charge—he must have known why the Hemings children looked like him. He must have known that all the defenses put up by his political friends and allies were in part or in whole untrue. So far as we know—and when we have only a written record and not a spoken one, that phrase covers much uncertainty—Jefferson's defenders were the first to mount what might be called a derivative family defense. That is, they said the stories could not be true because Jefferson was a good family man; they derived the defense from Jefferson's status and character rather than from (asserted) personal knowledge about life within his family. The Richmond *Examiner,* for example, noted that, in the twenty years since the death of his wife, Jefferson had "reared with parental attention, two unblemished, accomplished and amiable women, who are married to two estimable citizens. In the education of his daughters, this same Thomas Jefferson, supplied the place of a *mother*—his tenderness and delicacy were proverbial—not a spot tarnished his widowed character."[27]

The charge against Jefferson, then, was a moral one, about his character as a family man and a father. His family and his defenders asked the rhetorical question, How could the man who signed his letters to his daughters with every possible permutation and combination of tenderness and affection have fathered another family by one of his slaves? "There are such things," his granddaughter Ellen Coolidge later told her husband, "as moral impossibilities."[28]

Yet to say that it was morally impossible for a tender father to betray his children by fathering another set of children was to define the issue in wholly private terms; such behavior would have been a crime against the family—the white family, that is. From our vantage point, more than two hundred years later, it may be difficult for us to see it as any crime at all. Of course, we can only speculate about the nature of Jefferson's relationship with Sally Hemings. Some assume that it was necessarily coerced. Others guess that it might have been consensual. We have two reports—one from Jefferson's overseer Edmund Bacon and the other from Israel Jefferson, a former slave on the plantation—that Jefferson promised his wife on her deathbed that

27. "The Examiner," *Examiner* (Richmond, Va.), Sept. 25, 1802, [3]. This claim was made only three weeks after Callender's original charge.

28. Ellen Randolph Coolidge to Joseph Coolidge, Oct. 24, 1858, reprinted in Gordon-Reed, *Jefferson and Hemings,* 259.

he would not remarry and bring in a stepmother "over" her children. If that was the case, then Jefferson's liaison with Sally Hemings might be seen—and perhaps Jefferson himself saw it this way—as a fulfillment of his commitment to his departed wife and their daughters rather than a betrayal. It is also possible, considering the length of Jefferson's relationship with Sally Hemings and his apparent honoring of a commitment to her to free their children, that their relationship might have had elements of love. If we were so inclined, we might even say that, within the constraints imposed by the mores of his time and its peculiar institution of slavery, Jefferson behaved rather honorably, fulfilling his promises to his wife, his children, and his mistress. Our problem, as historians, is that we cannot know, with the evidence available to us today. We can tell you what the normal pattern was—the institution of slavery placed enormous power in the hands of masters—but we cannot tell you whether Jefferson was the exception or the rule.[29]

Even to engage the issue in this way, however, as if it were only and wholly a family matter, is to accept the way it was framed by Callender and his opponents: as one about individual character. Individual character was measured by private behavior, within the family. At the time, the issue was only secondarily one of race—the added outrage of fathering children by a mulatto woman—and even less one of slavery. If the charges had been true—and let us not forget that, indeed, they were—then the affront would have been to Jefferson's family, and not to society, much less its members who were black or enslaved.

Of course, we cannot help wondering whether his allies' responses to Callender's charge made Jefferson feel guilty or only more secretive. It is hard to imagine he had not considered that his liaison with Sally Hemings would be perceived as an affront to his white family, but he certainly could not help knowing it once it had become a topic of public discussion. As soon as he entered into the relationship, Jefferson had no real alternatives, however, than to keep the relationship secret. It is unthinkable that he would have acknowledged Sally Hemings and her children, but then again, that is not the issue here; the question is the anatomy of the lie and its consequent costs.

To say simply that those were different times—the slavery, the racism, his inability to acknowledge the affair—is, finally, too simple. Those excuses obscure the other facts: that slavery itself, at least in a land that extols freedom, is a lie, for it denies that one person is another's equal; and racism is

29. Brodie, *Thomas Jefferson,* 167; "Memoirs of Israel Jefferson," in Gordon-Reed, *Jefferson and Hemings,* 252.

another lie, the kind that follows in the first lie's train by attempting to explain and legitimate that inequality. Neither slavery nor racism is a natural fact; both are contingent historical conditions, created by human beings to serve particular ends. To say that Thomas Jefferson could not have acknowledged his relationship with Sally Hemings, whatever it was, because of race and slavery is only to say that lies beget other lies, something we would do well to remember.

The derivative family defense, then, set the terms for the actual family defense, which was mounted decades later. Its primary element was Jefferson's status as a family man. Its primary mechanism (or methodology) was the privileged information about Jefferson's character vouchsafed to his children. Who, after all, would dare argue with the child who claimed to have lifted the flap of her father's tent? And its primary problem was to explain the uncanny resemblance of the Hemings children to Thomas Jefferson, master of Monticello.

If not Jefferson, then who? Given the striking familial resemblance, the family defense of necessity had to be a family accusation. Jeff Randolph accused his mother's cousin—Jefferson's nephew—Peter Carr. In fact, Jeff Randolph told Henry Randall that Carr had confessed to him. At about the same time, Jeff's sister Ellen was placing the blame on Peter Carr's brother Sam. This is the story that Jeff told Randall: One day, a visitor to Monticello just happened to drop a newspaper that contained an article with "some very insulting remarks about Mr. Jefferson's Mulatto Children." Jeff was so "provoked" that he confronted the Carr brothers, who just happened to be at Monticello that day, lazing beneath a tree. When shown the article, Peter and Sam both burst into tears, and "Peter exclaimed, 'arnt you and I a couple of —— pretty fellows to bring this disgrace on poor old uncle who has always fed us! We ought to be —— by ——!'" Jeff told Randall that Sally Hemings was Peter's mistress and her sister, Sam's. Ellen told a similar, but not identical, story. She said Jeff had told her that he and a Mr. Southall had heard Peter Carr "say with a laugh, that 'the old gentleman had to bear the blame of his and Sam's . . . misdeeds.'" There was "a general impression" that Sally Hemings's four children were "*all* the children of [Sam] Carr, the most notorious goodnatured Turk that ever was master of a black seraglio kept at other men's expense."[30]

Of course, if we were inclined to believe these stories, we would point to

30. Randall to Parton, June 1, 1868, in Gordon-Reed, *Jefferson and Hemings*, 254–257, and Coolidge to Coolidge, Oct. 24, 1858, 258–260.

their inconsistencies as proof of their authenticity. It could have been Peter; it could have been Sam. They were emotional, so they could have laughed, or they could have cried. Both were of bad character, and did it really make any difference which was consorting with Sally and which with her sister? Both had repaid Ellen and Jeff's grandfather's generosity by bringing a scandal upon his name. But now we know that these stories were lies. If the DNA evidence proves anything, it is that Eston Hemings was not a Carr; he was not the son of Sam, and he was not the son of Peter, either. When Ellen said that the "general impression" was that all four of Sally Hemings's children were Sam's, she was putting forth a falsehood. Jeff might have told her that, and she might simply have been repeating it. Maybe it even was a general impression, but, if so, everyone was generally wrong. Maybe Jefferson was made to bear the blame for some number of Sam's and Peter's misdeeds, but fathering Sally Hemings's children was not one of them.

Jeff, too, had Peter confessing, even more explicitly, and perhaps more sympathetically. Now that we know that neither Jeff's nor Ellen's story was true, that Peter neither confessed himself nor pinned the blame on Sam, the details of their fictions become rather intriguing. Ellen had Peter laughing, while Jeff had him crying in shame, which may tell us something about Ellen and Jeff and how they thought a man who had fathered children by a slave might feel. Curiously, it was Jeff, the male, who imagined remorse. The operative word, however, is *imagine,* for we must remember that no one, not Sam or Peter and certainly not Thomas Jefferson, acknowledged fathering Sally Hemings's children, hence his grandchildren's stories, fascinating as they are, were fabrications. Lies may be simple, or they may be elaborate, and, in this case, with the details that Ellen and Jeff added in—Jeff's Edenic scene with the Carr brothers lounging beneath a tree and Ellen's more sinister one, with Peter cast as a sort of devil—the lies are elaborate.

In our attempts to plumb their complex depths, we should not forget that, as lies, they are also stunning. We cannot help sympathizing with the child who wishes her father an innocent, the grandchild who wants to protect the family name. But to shift the blame to a relative, to put words into his mouth: this is a shocking thing. One imagines that Jeff Randolph knew blaming his cousin was wrong. In his apparently unsent letter to the *Pike County Republican,* the only one of the three documents in the family denial addressed to the public, he claimed, "To my own knowledge and that of others 60 years ago the paternity of these parties were admitted by others." Here, Jeff Randolph was not willing to name names. To put it another way, for most of a century, the family denial was virtually a within-the-family denial. Jeff Randolph told Henry Randall about the Carrs; Ellen Coolidge told her husband but instructed him that this part of her letter was "in confidence." Randall told Parton, but when Parton published his biography, he did not mention the Carrs. One would have to imagine that Jeff, Ellen, her husband, Randall, and Parton told a few others, but whatever the whispers might have been, these documents did not enter the public record until the middle of the twentieth century. It would appear that the chief audience for the lie about the Carrs was the white Jeffersons themselves.[31]

All they were willing to tell the public was that Jefferson was too good a family man, that the rumors were just part of the partisan political fights of the age, and one other story, which may not have been a lie but only a misrepresentation. According to what Jeff Randolph told Randall, his mother "took the Dusky Sally stories much to heart." And let us note, in passing, that the woman Jeff dubbed "Dusky Sally" was almost certainly his grandmother's half sister, his mother's aunt. The story among the slaves—and we should also note that the oral testimony among the slaves is turning out to be rather accurate—was that Sally Hemings was the child of John Wayles, Martha Wayles Jefferson's father, and his mulatto slave Betty Hemings. There is no evidence, however, that Martha Jefferson ever acknowledged this blood tie. On her deathbed, legend has it, she gave Sally a small bell, but that is as close as we get. As for her daughter Patsy, according to Jeff, "She never spoke to her sons but once on the subject. Not long before her death"—in 1836, a decade after Jefferson's death—she took Jeff and his brother George Wythe aside. She asked Jeff if he could remember when " 'Henings (the slave who most resembled Mr. Jefferson) was born.' " Jeff said he would look it up in one of Jefferson's farm books; he confirmed that this one of the Hemings family ("the slave") was born just when his mother had supposed. Then she told her sons that her father and Sally Hemings had not been near each other for fifteen months before that Hemings child's birth. "She bade her sons remember this fact, and always to defend the character of their grandfather." In repeating the story that Jeff had told him, Randall added that sometime later he, himself, was looking at one of Jefferson's account books when "I came *pop* on the original entry of this slaves birth: and I was then able from well known circumstances to prove the fifteen months separation." We now know, from the careful work of Winthrop Jordan and others, that Jeff, his mother, and Randall were all wrong; Thomas Jefferson and Sally

31. [Randolph] to Sir, [1873 or 1874]; Randall to Parton, June 1, 1868, in Gordon-Reed, *Jefferson and Hemings*, 255, Coolidge to Coolidge, Oct. 24, 1858, 259.

Hemings were both at Monticello nine months before the birth of each of her children.[32]

Sometimes we lie to others; sometimes we lie to ourselves. Sometimes we wish something to be true so badly that we can convince ourselves. If Jeff Randolph was telling the truth, and his mother was deeply troubled about the stories of her father and Sally Hemings, then surely Patsy would have wanted to know that they were impossible. She could have asked her father, but perhaps she knew from experience what his response would be—either the hearty laugh that made her feel foolish or the denial that later turned out to be false. Perhaps it was more reassuring to look among her father's papers and perform some calculations, searching desperately for the exculpatory evidence. And so badly might she have wanted that evidence that she might accidentally have miscalculated. Or perhaps Jeff Randolph made the story up, just as he made up the one about his cousins the Carrs. But then there is the question of Randall and his research methods. Like Patsy and Jeff, so badly did he want to believe Jefferson innocent that he misread the account book, or perhaps he was just lying when he told Parton about coming *"pop"* on the entry that proved Jefferson could not have been the father of that particular Hemings child. He equivocated a bit to Parton, telling him the details had "faded from my memory," but he had "no doubt I could recover them . . . did Mr. Jefferson's vindication in the least depend upon them." But one wonders why he told Parton in the first place about Jeff's account of the exculpatory evidence and his own subsequent encounter with that strangely popping account book had he not thought that Jefferson's vindication in some measure depended upon it. The train of misreadings, misrememberings, or lies seems too significant, too much trouble, whether conscious or unconscious, were the information it transmitted not important.[33]

Now that one looks at it closely, one can see also that there are too many fortuitous occurrences in Randall's account of Jeff's defense of his grandfather. Someone happened to drop a newspaper article on the grounds at Monticello. The story circulated first in 1802, when Jeff was all of ten years old, and then, after a few years, so far as we know, fell out of circulation for the next several decades, until abolitionists fastened on it again. And at that moment when the newspaper fell to the ground at Monticello, the Carr

32. Susan R. Stein, *The Worlds of Thomas Jefferson at Monticello* (New York, 1993), 16; Randall to Parton, June 1, 1868, in Gordon-Reed, *Jefferson and Hemings,* 255; Brodie, *Thomas Jefferson,* 296; Lucia Stanton, "'Those Who Labor for My Happiness': Thomas Jefferson and His Slaves," in Onuf, ed., *Jeffersonian Legacies,* 173–174n. 20.

33. Randall to Parton, June 1, 1868, in Gordon-Reed, *Jefferson and Hemings,* 255.

brothers happened to be lounging under a tree. And, as if these were not coincidences enough, one day Randall came *"pop"* upon the entry in Jefferson's account book that proved Jeff's account right.[34]

When James Parton published his biography of Thomas Jefferson in 1874, he included Henry Randall's account of Jeff Randolph's account of his mother's telling him that the timing was all wrong. He omitted the part about the Carr brothers. The part of the family defense that was a family accusation stayed within the family, leaving us with something of a puzzle. It is not clear why Jeff and Ellen confined their defamation of their mother's cousins almost entirely to the family. Part of the explanation must be the unseemliness of the matter: it would have been a violation of contemporary mores to discuss matters of sexuality and reproduction publicly, let alone accuse your second cousin of being the "master of a black seraglio." In the part of her letter to her husband that she authorized him to share, Ellen allowed that "'dusky Sally' was pretty notoriously the mistress of a married man, a near relation of Mr. Jefferson's, and there can be small question that her children were his." It was only in the portion of the letter marked "confidential" that she named Sam Carr as the culprit. How curious, incidentally, that both Ellen and Jeff called their aunt "Dusky Sally" in their accounts. It suggests either that they were cooking up their stories in concert or that they felt themselves, or wanted to place themselves, so far distant from their aunt that they called her by the name used in the newspapers.[35]

There is another reason why the white Jeffersons would not have wanted to publish their accusation against their cousins: the possibility that it would be refuted. Peter's and Sam's kin could have done just what Jeff did—or said he did—and gone to the old account books to prove that Peter and Sam were not in the vicinity nine months before each of Sally Hemings's children was born. But all we have explained is why Ellen and Jeff would not have bruited the Carr name in public; we have not explained why they would have spoken it among themselves.

The need to demonstrate to themselves that their beloved grandfather was not the father of Sally Hemings's children must have been intense. Her children were about their ages. They all grew up at Monticello, more or less

34. Robert M. S. MacDonald, "Race, Sex, and Reputation: Thomas Jefferson and the Sally Hemings Story," *Southern Cultures,* IV, no. 2 (Summer 1998), 46–63; Sidney P. Moss and Carolyn Moss, "The Jefferson Miscegenation Legend in British Travel Books," *Journal of the Early Republic,* VII (1978), 253–274.

35. Coolidge to Coolidge, Oct. 24, 1858, in Gordon-Reed, *Jefferson and Hemings,* 259; Gordon-Reed, *Jefferson and Hemings,* 96.

together. Perhaps one or more of those Hemings children—who were, almost certainly, their own half aunt and half uncles, their mother's half sister and half brothers, just as Sally Hemings had been their mother's half aunt—looked more like Thomas Jefferson than they did. How desperately they would have wanted an explanation other than the most obvious one.

Then there is the question of the rivalry among brothers and sisters, common enough in conventional families, something else again when a father has two sets of children, by two different women. Perhaps it seems absurd to suggest that the white Jeffersons might have thought of the Hemings children as rivals for Thomas Jefferson's affection. They were, after all, black, the children of a slave. Yet, if Jefferson took Sally Hemings as his concubine in order to fulfill a promise to his dying wife, then it was precisely to make certain no other woman assumed the position in Jefferson's household that a white wife would have, and no other children exercised a legitimate claim upon his affections or material resources. This is how race worked its powerful magic, for it was only the color of the Hemings children's skin and their status as Jefferson's property that assured they could not become their white siblings' rivals. They were the children of Jefferson's wife's half sister and the children of Jefferson himself; yet, because of their race, they were denied what their white sisters claimed as right. There is the true absurdity.

But inheritance in Virginia was a serious business, complicating matters of love with those of money. Jefferson's falling-out with David Meade Randolph, after all, had been over the terms of a family inheritance. In a time and place where grown children depended upon their parents to set them up with a plantation and slaves or some other means of making a living, every additional child was a potential rival for the family inheritance; a second set of children, by a second wife, threatened to displace the first set altogether. That is what happened to Patsy and Thomas Mann Randolph when her widowed father-in-law remarried a much younger woman who began bearing him children. All of a sudden, the elder Randolph raised the price of the family farm that he had been planning to let Jefferson purchase as a marriage settlement for the young couple. Perhaps this is when Patsy's husband began to feel like a duck among the swans, his new father-in-law taxed to pay the freight of a young stepmother and her growing number of little Randolphs.[36]

The white Jeffersons never acknowledged that they had black Jefferson

36. Malone, *Jefferson and His Time,* II, 320; Thomas Jefferson to Martha Jefferson Randolph, July 17, 1790, in Betts and Bear, eds., *Family Letters,* 60–61.

kin. The Hemings children, however, knew that they were the disfavored children of a loving and powerful man. Madison Hemings remembered that Jefferson was "not in the habit of showing partiality or fatherly affection to us children. . . . He was affectionate toward his white grandchildren, of whom he had fourteen, twelve of whom lived to manhood and womanhood." And Madison Hemings named each one of those children, his nieces and nephews, by name: "Ann, Thomas Jefferson, Ellen. . . ." Madison Hemings, incidentally, named his youngest daughter Ellen Wales, after his white niece. When Jeff Randolph wrote of his aunt and uncles, they were "these parties," or—according to Randall—"these slaves." For his sister Ellen, they were "the 'yellow children.'" They could not even be allowed their names.[37]

How painful it must be to be the discarded children, to know that somewhere, perhaps in your own neighborhood, are sister and brother, or niece and nephew, whom you cannot claim. Perhaps you honor those who have abandoned you, nonetheless. If you are Madison Hemings, you may remember each of your thirteen nephews and nieces by name, and you may note proudly that one was "Chairman of the Democratic National Convention in Baltimore last spring" and that another was "Jeff. Davis' first Secretary of War in the late 'unpleasantness.'" Madison Hemings's son, Thomas Eston, named after his brother, lost his life in that "unpleasantness," dying at Andersonville prison. Until just a few years ago, it was possible for intelligent and reputable historians to assert that Madison Hemings, or perhaps his mother, Sally, was making up stories. Madison Hemings invented a Jefferson family connection, it was surmised, because he felt "cheated by life" and "entitled to the respect and consideration that had hitherto been denied him," or "to provide an otherwise undistinguished biracial carpenter a measure of social respect," or because of "the Negroes' pathetic wish for a little pride"—as if, in reminiscing about his father and bragging about his nieces and nephews, Madison Hemings was attempting a bit of genetic social climbing. Now we know that Madison Hemings was, almost certainly, telling the truth, whereas it was his niece and nephew who were making up stories. And we must wonder about people who would sooner accuse their cousins of something they believed to be unspeakable—"the thing will not bear telling," Ellen Coolidge had said—than acknowledge their beloved grandfather's other children.[38]

37. "Memoirs of Madison Hemings," in Gordon-Reed, *Jefferson and Hemings,* 247; [Randolph] to Sir, [1873 or 1874]; Randall to Parton, June 1, 1868, in Gordon-Reed, *Jefferson and Hemings,* 255, Coolidge to Coolidge, Oct. 24, 1858, 258.

38. "Memoirs of Madison Hemings," in Gordon-Reed, *Jefferson and Hemings,* 247,

Perhaps when one has called one's own father "more fell than the hyena," it is not such a leap to invent a confession for one's mother's cousin. Perhaps that judgment is too harsh. It is possible that Peter Carr really had confessed to something terrible and that, if Jeff Randolph's report was not the literal truth, it was not really a lie. It is unbecoming to us to be absolutists, to wash away the gray that shades the black into white and back again. As historians, we are uncomfortable making such judgments. But here we are confronted with the DNA evidence, which, although not incontrovertible, surely demonstrates—beyond the kind of certainty that most historians ever have about the evidence they are called upon to interpret—that the Carrs did not father all four of Sally Hemings's children.

We have to wonder why Jeff picked his cousins the Carrs. By the time he told his story to Randall, they were dead—but there were other dead Jefferson males as well, including Jefferson's brother Randolph, who, at the time of the DNA study, suddenly emerged as the prime suspect for die-hard Jefferson purity defenders.[39] Perhaps that is only to say that people will go to great lengths to protect the reputation of a man like Jefferson, who has come to function as a sort of virgin father for some portion of the nation. It might only have been convenience that made Jeff and Ellen turn to the Carr brothers. Perhaps the primary qualification for suspicion was being a male Jefferson who was not Thomas Jefferson himself. Or it might have been some quality that the brothers shared. Both Jeff and Ellen considered Sam Carr, in particular, licentious, and they seemed to think of both cousins as moochers. As we saw above, Ellen, who had a real way with words, called her cousin Sam "the most notorious good-natured Turk that ever was master of a black seraglio kept at other men's expense." Jeff had Peter confessing his shame at disgracing the man "who has always fed us!"

It is not unusual for the members of families to think they are playing a zero-sum game for the finite emotional and material resources the family has at its disposal. Jeff's outburst against his father had been prompted by the fear that he was going to make a claim upon Thomas Jefferson's estate. We know that the material resources of the Jefferson family were severely depleted by the time of Jefferson's death. Anyone who has read the *Family Letters* knows how anxious the white Jeffersons were about their declining fortunes. Perhaps the white Jeffersons also felt that there was not enough

---

Coolidge to Coolidge, Oct. 24, 1858, ibid., 259; Gordon-Reed, *Jefferson and Hemings,* 17–18, 19–20, 82.

39. For example, Dennis Cauchon, "Group Flags Other Jefferson as Father," *USA Today,* Jan. 7, 1999.

love to go around, although that is, at best, an educated guess; no one complained directly about not getting enough love, while there were complaints aplenty about the family's plummeting fortunes.

Then, too, there was the matter of reputation. Perhaps the Carrs' reputations were already sullied in some way, at least within the family, and adding another item to the bill of particulars against them might have seemed a small price to pay in order to secure the reputation of the family founder. Whatever scorn we now may have for the false accusation against the Carrs, we have to assume that Ellen and Jeff at least knew how to pick likely suspects. In this context, the current slurring of Jefferson's brother Randolph seems a bit bizarre, as if today's Jefferson defenders might be better situated to find an alternate candidate for the father of Sally Hemings's children than those of Jefferson's kin, who had a far greater interest in pointing a convincing finger. Or perhaps one of these defenders came pop on incriminating information while perusing the Jefferson family tree.

But, once again, we wander from our point. In order to protect the reputation of the family patriarch, some of the white Jeffersons blamed some of the other white Jeffersons for fathering Sally Hemings's children. These things happen in families; for some members, the assigned role is to be the bearer of blame. But, blame for what? For, as Jeff Randolph had his cousin Peter Carr say, bringing "this disgrace on poor old uncle." For letting people think that Thomas Jefferson might have been the sort of man who would insult "the sanctity of the home by his profligacy." For letting people imagine that Thomas Jefferson might have "selected the female attendant of his own pure children to become his paramour."[40]

Perhaps it makes little difference whether Thomas Jefferson was the father of Sally Hemings's children or whether it was one of his nephews. In either case, Jefferson kept on his plantation as slaves persons who were his kin. To be sure, their tasks were light, and all of them, as Annette Gordon-Reed has shown, were permitted their freedom at about the time they turned twenty-one. But they were all disinherited. Does it make Jefferson a substantially better man if those children were his nephew's, rather than his own? Is he significantly less implicated in the institution of slavery?

Perhaps these are not even questions we should be addressing, either as citizens or historians. As historians, we are always concerned with the matter of truth. We argue about what is knowable, about what standards should

40. Coolidge to Coolidge, Oct. 24, 1858, in Gordon-Reed, *Jefferson and Hemings,* 258–259.

apply. Some of us may be uncomfortable with categorical statements about what is and is not true, but we know that some things are more true than others. We know that we are not allowed to make things up. We would all agree that the Holocaust, for example, happened, or the Civil War, and to deny them is to lie. We sometimes make the occasional categorical statement, risking our reputations on a claim, but it may have more to do with the significance of the question than the certainty of the evidence. Surely the details of Thomas Jefferson's private life would not compare to either of these examples—that is, something that it is morally important to assert as fact or something so incontrovertible that no one would consider denying. Historians have written some foolish things about Jefferson, no doubt thinking that the questions they addressed required some sort of answer. Like Jefferson himself, they have considered his reputation of such great importance that a strict attention to questions of veracity and verifiability was not necessary.

It is not clear, however, why questions about Jefferson's private behavior should be of concern to us, as either historians or citizens. Nor is it clear why the evidence from the DNA tests should be of any interest to us. Until November 1998, we had at our disposal a great deal of what lawyers call circumstantial evidence that argued powerfully, if not conclusively, that Jefferson was the father of Sally Hemings's children. Now we have a small piece of DNA evidence that, although far from conclusive in itself, when added to the circumstantial evidence, makes it very close to certain. Of course, there are always other possibilities. But the DNA evidence invalidates what, until 1998, had been the only coherent alternate story. We should now be certain, beyond any reasonable doubt, that Jefferson was the father of Eston and probably Beverley, Harriet, and Madison as well. Whether this sort of evidence would hold up in a court of law is beside the point. This is not a court of law. It is the court of history, and the standards may be somewhat different.

As historians, we might begin by asking, What is the significance of knowing whether Thomas Jefferson fathered Sally Hemings's children? To some extent, we are inquiring into the most personal and intimate aspects of one man and one woman's lives. We can say, with relative certainty, that loving relationships between powerful white men and their female black slaves were atypical. The historical record leaves us few examples. Moreover, many of us would recoil at the notion that love can arise in a relationship so unequal, although that is a matter of interpretation more than of fact. Yet delineating the norm tells us very little about Sally Hemings and Thomas Jefferson as individuals. Is it possible that Thomas Jefferson and Sally Hemings had a loving relationship? History is very bad at answering metaphysical questions. History cannot answer with any certainty.

But let us, for the sake of argument, or imagination, assume that Thomas Jefferson and Sally Hemings made the best out of the possibilities offered under the institution of slavery, and that, even if they did not love each other, they honored their commitments to each other and their children. Sally Hemings and all her children ended their days in freedom, and very few women who began their lives as slaves could claim as much. To put it another way, let us say that they behaved as well as they could, given the circumstances, and therefore we should not judge Jefferson harshly for evading questions, denying implicitly, and complaining about his political enemies. Jefferson believed fervently in the right to privacy, and of course he deserved privacy himself. Perhaps we should conclude that whatever took place between Thomas Jefferson and Sally Hemings was private and historically atypical — a poignant story, but nothing more.

Does it make a difference if Jefferson lied? This, finally, is the question we confront: the meaning of a lie or lies told in private, by one member of a family to another, about a private matter. Jefferson certainly threw his allies and his family off the track. It also seems that he conducted his relationship with Sally Hemings with sufficient discretion that his family either did not know about it or, more likely, could avoid confronting its reality. If Jefferson did not lie about Sally Hemings, he misled; and, if he misled, he did it to protect himself (that is, his reputation) — and his family (that is, their reputation) — as well as their notions of themselves as a family near-perfect in its happiness.

Because Jefferson's denial was not complete or coherent enough — there was that troubling matter of the family resemblance, after all — his white family had to elaborate his little lie. His daughter Patsy tried to document it, making her sons cross-check some dates. His grandson told a historian about this account-book evidence, and the historian, thinking that secondhand "documentary" record somehow inadequate, asserted that he had double-checked it, using an account book that conveniently went pop, as if opened by the hand of God. Patsy could have been mistaken, but probably not Jeff Randolph, and certainly not the historian Randall. We are now into the realm of demonstrable falsehood, a falsehood that became part of the historical record when Randall told it to Parton in the middle of the nineteenth century. Once that falsehood entered the historical record, the defense of Jefferson then seemed to rest upon something more empirical than notions of his character: secondhand testimony about a verifiable documentary record. Jeff Randolph's motive was understandable; he wanted to preserve his grandfather's reputation, and he was, after all, talking to a historian. He must have known, however, that the account book could not have demonstrated his grandfather's innocence. He lied for history and to history. And then history told us that Jefferson could not have been the father of Sally Hemings's children.

Yet these were not the only lies the white Jeffersons told history. When Jeff Randolph and his sister Ellen Coolidge implicated their cousins Carr, they were lying only among themselves. But it was a stunning lie, all the more stunning because they told it primarily for the other white Jeffersons. Perhaps it offered the assurance they needed in order to be able to hold their heads high when defending their beloved grandfather in more general terms. Perhaps it assuaged old wounds, determining for once and for all who was in the family and who was out. But these lies, even if told first and foremost to and for the family, made their way into the historical record. They have become part of history.

Let us assume that the relationship between Thomas Jefferson and Sally Hemings was founded and maintained, or one or the other, in love, or commitment, or a sense of responsibility—in other words, somewhere along the spectrum of what we would consider responsible behavior. Let us assume, also, that the relationship was kept a secret from Jefferson's daughters and their children, although Sally Hemings might well have told her children while they were still living at Monticello. "We were free from the dread of having to be slaves all our lives long," her son Madison remembered, "and were measurably happy." Is it possible that the black Jeffersons knew who their father was, and the white Jeffersons did not?[41]

When we look at this story, or imagine it, from the perspective of Sally Hemings or Thomas Jefferson, it is one thing. When we try to see it from the point of view of the children, it is quite another. This is always the case in families. If Sigmund Freud was right in the slightest, then the relationship between parent and child always embodies at least an element of conflict, of disappointment, of unrequited love. The secrets that look so understandable, so necessary for Thomas Jefferson, look quite another thing to his two families. How could you do this to us? his white family must have asked. Or, rather, If we wish to confine ourselves to what we know, he could not have done this to us, they said. There are such things as moral impossibilities, which is another way of saying that our lives cannot make sense if

41. "Memoirs of Madison Hemings," ibid., 245–248.

such a thing is possible. If you were a white Jefferson and your world was ordered by the knowledge that your father or grandfather loved you above all else, that you were entrusted with the knowledge of the real him, and if these things were more real to you than the features on the faces of your Hemings kin, then perhaps you would have lied, too.

And perhaps if you were Beverley Hemings or his sister Harriet, you would have gone to Washington, taking the freedom your mother had made your father give you as his only legacy, other than a face so like his that in the moonlight strangers could not tell you apart. And if you were Beverley or Harriet, you would have married whites, seizing for your children the privilege of fair skin, promised in the moonlight of a Monticello night. And you would have turned your backs on your father's family and your mother's, as well, perhaps concluding that family was a bad business, in the process trading the truth of who you knew you were—the child of Thomas Jefferson, the child of a slave—for the lie of who you now claimed to be. And perhaps if you were Madison Hemings or his brother Eston, you would care for your mother until she died, marry a black woman, raise a family, and tell your children who they were—that is, who their parents were, and their parents before them, and who you wanted them to be. And they would tell their children and their children's children after them, and even though white people would scoff and say that you were just trying to make yourself into something you were not, one day a scientist would come asking for a sample of your DNA. And it would confirm the story your mother had told you and your father had never acknowledged, except by the ambiguous act of letting you go free.

Let us imagine a man. Let us call him Thomas Jefferson. Let us imagine that he evades the truth, or tells a lie, perhaps to save face, perhaps to spare the ones he loves. It is probably both, for the two are, in some measure, inextricable. He needs his family to love him, and they cannot, he fears, if he appears to them as less than the devoted father he has claimed to be. And in the moment he evades the truth or tells the lie, if not before, he has made a decision about whose love matters most, about who will receive his tenderest love. And those white children, and their children after, are bound by his lie, or his evasion, and they have to prop it up. It will not stand of itself. There are, at the very least, the family resemblances of their Hemings kin, and who knows how many half-caught glances and troubling sounds, not to mention the newspapers that just happen to fall to the ground. And there may be the nagging fears that all children have: the uncertainties about the certainty of a father's love. So the white family imagines or invents a documentary record, fortuitously confirmed in account books that go pop. They imagine or invent a family confession, the convenient Carrs. And, in protecting the reputation of one kinsman, they tar another's.

A century later, that lie, like the ones before, becomes part of the public record. White cousins whose names otherwise would have been lost to history are now known as scoundrels. Black children are written out of their family, their claim upon it dismissed by history as "the Negroes' pathetic wish for a little pride." The lie begun in the family becomes part of the national lie of race, which is itself a kind of truth, a fiction that orders the national life much as the moral impossibility of Jefferson's interracial liaison ordered that of his white kin.

How are we to reckon the costs entailed upon the Hemings family, first by their father's silence and then by his white family's lies? Perhaps we just add them to the unpaid bill of race, the interest still compounding, year after year, day after day.

And how are we to reckon the costs to the nation of an evasion compounded and elaborated until it became a thing in itself, a cornerstone of our civic culture?

Monticello sits atop a mountain; its slopes are slippery, indeed. A public man enters into a private relationship. He attempts to keep it private, even from his family, even, in fact, from the family that the relationship begets. He gives his white family his love, his black family their freedom. Which legacy is the greater? The white part of his family uses its legacy—the love, the knowledge of him that this love provides—to disinherit their black kin, to dismiss their black family's claim as moral impossibility. Theirs is a lie founded in love. Half the black family uses its freedom to escape the grasp of history altogether. The other half uses it to claim its rightful inheritance, which is to say, a heritage, a connection to history itself. Subsequent generations take sides. A family quarrel becomes a national one as well. These are the things we do for love.

"A Beautiful Domestic Character"
Sarah N. Randolph's The Domestic Life of Thomas Jefferson

Sarah N. Randolph's biography of her great-grandfather Thomas Jefferson, *The Domestic Life of Thomas Jefferson: Compiled from Family Letters and Reminiscences by His Great-Granddaughter,* is not really a biography. Instead, it is a collection of letters, many never previously published, interspersed with brief introductory remarks and the occasional anecdote. Of course, as Bernard Mayo would later demonstrate, it is eminently possible to construct a readable, coherent biography of Jefferson out of his own writings, but Randolph's compilation coheres into a narrative only with some effort by the reader. Without headnotes or other editorial interventions, it is often impossible for those not already familiar with Jefferson's life to understand the context for the letters or all the references within them. The book is organized chronologically for the most part, which means that even in a book whose focus is Jefferson's domestic life, there are awkward jumps from one topic or correspondent to the next. A letter to the Reverend Isaac Story about whether there is an afterlife is followed immediately by one to John Dickinson about "the delights of domestic . . . tranquillity." Likewise, Randolph moves immediately from an excerpt from Jefferson's first inaugural address to the observation that "the house at Monticello was still unfinished when Mr. Jefferson returned there on a visit early in April."[1]

The result of Randolph's seemingly artless method is to force the reader to focus on what she identifies as the subject of her work: "a faithful picture of him as he was in private life—to show that he was, as I have been taught

This essay was originally published as Jan Ellen Lewis, "'A Beautiful Domestic Character': Sarah N. Randolph's *The Domestic Life of Thomas Jefferson,*" in Robert M. S. McDonald, ed., *Thomas Jefferson's Lives: Biographers and the Battle for History* (Charlottesville, Va., 2019), 83–105.

1. Sarah N. Randolph, *The Domestic Life of Thomas Jefferson: Compiled from Family Letters and Reminiscences by His Great-Granddaughter* (New York, 1871), 277, Thomas Jefferson to Isaac Story, [Dec. 5, 1801], 283, Jefferson to John Dickinson, [Dec. 19, 1801], 283; Bernard Mayo, ed., *Jefferson Himself: The Personal Narrative of a Many-Sided American* (Boston, 1942). J. Jefferson Looney makes the same point about Mayo's work in his essay "'Merely Personal or Private, with Which We Have Nothing to Do': Thomas Jefferson's Autobiographical Writings," in Robert M. S. McDonald, ed., *Thomas Jefferson's Lives: Biographers and the Battle for History* (Charlottesville, Va., 2019), 25–46.

to think of him by those who knew and loved him best, a beautiful domestic character." Randolph brings us back to Monticello and Jefferson's white family, returning him to his domestic setting. Events important to national politics and Jefferson's public life serve as grace notes, ornaments that decorate Randolph's account of her great-grandfather.[2]

Let us look more closely, for example, at the positioning of the excerpt from the first inaugural. Randolph describes succinctly the complications of the election of 1800, culminating in Jefferson's selection as president by the House of Representatives in its thirty-sixth ballot on February 17, 1801. Immediately thereafter, she excerpts a letter to Thomas Mann Randolph in which Jefferson explains to his son-in-law that he hopes he "may be able to leave this place by the middle of March." Next follows Randolph's description of Jefferson's "unostentatious" inauguration and the characterization of the address, "whose chaste and simple beauty" was widely familiar but whose "eloquent close" she could not resist reprinting. Thence Randolph returns her great-grandfather directly to Monticello for a "visit early in April," without explaining what business might have detained him in the capital longer than his predicted departure, in mid-March. She is interested only in the beauty of the inaugural address, as an illustration of her grandfather's character. The content concerns her not at all.[3]

In the way that it addresses Jefferson's public life, Randolph's biography is in some ways the obverse of Henry S. Randall's *The Life of Thomas Jefferson.* Together they are the opposite faces of the same coin. Both Randolph and Randall prefer to let Jefferson speak for himself. As Randall puts it, he prefers "in all cases to give Mr. Jefferson's words . . . instead of attempting to convey the substance in any briefer synopsis." Both, then, are largely the books Jefferson might have written about himself. Randall, however, tends to segregate Jefferson's family life by placing a group of letters to his daughters at the back of the first of his three volumes, explaining that "we . . . prefer it to scattering them in chronological order, amidst a recital of events with which they have so little connection as with politics and general history." In

2. Randolph, *Domestic Life of Thomas Jefferson,* vii. Sarah N. Randolph acknowledges the existence of the Hemings family in only the most oblique ways—for example, by stating in her preface that "no man's private character has been more foully assailed than Jefferson's" (viii). It is important to note that at Monticello, Jefferson had two families, one white and one black, a subject I have explored in "The White Jeffersons," in Jan Ellen Lewis and Peter S. Onuf, eds., *Sally Hemings and Thomas Jefferson: History, Memory, and Civic Culture* (Charlottesville, Va., 1999), 127–160, also reprinted in this volume.

3. Randolph, *Domestic Life of Thomas Jefferson,* 275–277, Thomas Jefferson to Thomas Mann Randolph, [Feb. 19, 1801], 75.

the subsequent volumes, Randall frequently places family letters, in particular those to and from Jefferson's daughters and granddaughters, at the end of chapters and in several of the appendixes at the end of the final volume. Here, domestic life provides the grace notes. Randolph herself considered her book a complement to Randall's rather than a replacement. "I am well aware," she wrote, "that the tale of Jefferson's life, both public and private, has been well told by the most faithful of biographers in 'Randall's Life of Jefferson,' and that much of what is contained in these pages will be found in that admirable work, which, from the author's zealous devotion to truth, and his indefatigable industry in collecting his materials, must ever stand chief among the most valuable contributions to American history."[4]

Yet, with a subject so amorphous as "domestic character," and with neither the signposts of political events nor an active authorial hand shaping the material, Randolph's biography can seem unshaped as well. Still, certain themes emerge. *The Domestic Life of Thomas Jefferson* is an act of recovery. Randolph brackets her account with descriptions of ruin. Her book concludes with a description of the monument that Jefferson instructed be placed upon his grave. It was to be made of "coarse stone . . . that no one might be tempted hereafter to destroy it for the value of the materials." But his plans were for naught, Randolph explains. The gates enclosing the family graveyard "have been again and again broken open, the grave-yard entered, and the tombs desecrated. The edges of the granite obelisk over Jefferson's grave have been chipped away until it now stands a misshapen column. Of the slabs placed over the graves of Mrs. Jefferson and Mrs. Eppes not a vestige remains, while of the one over Mrs. Randolph only fragments are left." The vandals have destroyed not only Jefferson's grave but those of his wife and two daughters. The memory of the women in the family has been desecrated as well.[5]

The last lines of the preface strike a similar note as Randolph describes three illustrations in the book. First are a portrait of Jefferson by Gilbert Stuart and one of his daughter Martha Jefferson Randolph by Thomas Sully. Finally, "the view of Monticello represents the home of Jefferson as it existed during his lifetime, and not as it now is—a ruin." The physical deterioration of the gravesite and the home symbolizes the destruction of Jefferson's repu-

4. Henry S. Randall, *The Life of Thomas Jefferson,* 3 vols. (New York, 1858), I, viii, 622; Randolph, *Domestic Life of Thomas Jefferson,* vii. For Randall, see Andrew Burstein, "'Dexterity and Delicacy of Manipulation': Biographers Henry S. Randall and James Parton," in McDonald, ed., *Thomas Jefferson's Lives,* 62–82.

5. Randolph, *Domestic Life of Thomas Jefferson,* 431, 432.

tation by his enemies: "No man's private character has been more foully assailed than Jefferson's." Randolph's task is to impart "to my readers a tithe of that esteem and veneration which I have been taught to feel for him" by her father, Jefferson's grandson and namesake, Thomas Jefferson Randolph, "the person with whom he was most intimate during life."[6]

Judging by the review of her book in the *New York Times,* Randolph succeeded at her task. "We think [The Domestic Life of Thomas Jefferson] will forever set at rest all the aspersions upon the private character of the author of the Declaration of Independence, and prove him not only to have been a great statesman, but a good man." The review, however, is not so much an account of Randolph's book as a short biography of Jefferson compiled from Randolph's book and the author's own knowledge. For example, the *Times* review describes briefly how Jefferson was chosen as one of Virginia's delegates to the Continental Congress and his role in drafting the Declaration of Independence. Randolph tells us only that "in the year 1775 Jefferson went to Philadelphia as a member of the first Congress" and that his mother died on March 31 the next year and "thus . . . did not live to see the great day with whose glory her son's name is indissolubly connected." Her only explicit mention of the Declaration of Independence comes in an anecdote at the bottom of the page, taken from an appendix to Randall's biography: According to a "gentleman who had been a frequent visitor at Monticello during Mr. Jefferson's life"—identified by Randall as General J. Spear Smith—because Congress met near a livery stable, the delegates were pestered by flies that they continuously had to swat away with handkerchiefs. "So very vexatious was this annoyance, and to so great an impatience did it arouse the sufferers, that it hastened, if it did not aid, in inducing them to promptly affix their signatures to the great document which gave birth to an empire republic."[7]

Both the *Times* reviewer and Randall set out the standard political narrative. Randolph undercuts it. As J. Jefferson Looney's essay in *Thomas Jefferson's Lives* makes clear, Randolph's biography is not the one that Jefferson would have written himself or had written for him. Both the short and long lists of accomplishments and milestones that Jefferson recorded for biographers as well as the more extensive notes that he compiled concerned politics and public affairs almost exclusively. He declined to provide one biographer all the information he requested, saying that "many of the objects

6. Ibid., viii.

7. "Thomas Jefferson," *New York Times,* Aug. 3, 1871, 2; Randolph, *Domestic Life of Thomas Jefferson,* 49–50; Randall, *Life of Thomas Jefferson,* III, 680–681.

of your enquiry are too minute for public notice. the number, names, and ages of my children, grandchildren, great grandchildren Etc would produce fatigue and disgust to your readers."[8]

These are the objects out of which Randolph constructs her biography. She intends her book to complement Randall's political biography, but her work cannot help being a commentary on the political narrative as well. She recognizes that her great-grandfather is remembered for the Declaration of Independence, but she can do no more than allude to the "glory" of the "great day" and imagine the pride it would have inspired in Jefferson's mother. She cannot even utter the words "Declaration of Independence" in this portion of the text, relegating them to a footnote. Moreover, the anecdote recounted there suggests that, more than anything, Jefferson and his colleagues were eager to conclude their business in Philadelphia so that they could escape the fly-infested meeting room.[9]

In Randolph's recounting of her great-grandfather's life, the political arena is always one from which to flee. Modern readers, of course, are familiar with Jefferson's frequent descriptions to his daughters of the tortures of public life. While holding office, he characterized the nation's capital as a "circle of cabal, intrigue and hatred" and "a dreary scene where envy, hatred, malice, revenge, and all the worse passions of men are marshalled to make one another as miserable as possible." He was "disgusted with the jealousies, the hatred, and the rancorous and malignant passions of this scene." Political honors were but "splendid torments." In 1871, when Randolph published her book, however, it was not common knowledge that Jefferson had disparaged public life in this way.[10]

Although Jefferson's family had given Randall access to the family letters, and he used them liberally, he did not quote all the passages that deprecated politics. When he did, he relegated them, for the most part, to the

8. Thomas Jefferson to Joseph Delaplaine, Apr. 12, 1817, in J. Jefferson Looney, et al., ed., *The Papers of Thomas Jefferson: Retirement Series,* 15 vols. (Princeton, N.J., 2004—), XI, 252, cited in Looney, "'Merely Personal or Private,'" in McDonald, ed., *Thomas Jefferson's Lives,* 27.

9. Randolph, *Domestic Life of Thomas Jefferson,* 50.

10. Thomas Jefferson to Mary Jefferson Eppes, Feb. 15, 1801, in Edwin Morris Betts and James Adam Bear, Jr., eds., *The Family Letters of Thomas Jefferson* (Columbia, Mo., 1966), 196, Jefferson to Martha Jefferson Randolph, Feb. 8, 1798, 155, Jefferson to Martha Jefferson Randolph, June 8, 1797, 146; all three letters are also quoted in Jan Lewis, "'The Blessings of Domestic Society': Thomas Jefferson's Family and the Transformation of American Politics," in Peter S. Onuf, ed., *Jeffersonian Legacies* (Charlottesville, Va., 1993), 114–115, also reprinted in this volume. These letters have been cited by many authors.

chapter ends. The exception is the letter Jefferson wrote to his daughter Mary Jefferson, known to the family as Polly, on February 17, 1801, as the House continued balloting to select a president. Jefferson told her that a resolution was expected the following day but that "the scene passing here makes me pant to be away from it—to fly from the circle of cabal, intrigue, and hatred, to one where all is love and peace." Randolph does not know what to make of such a letter, "in which we find strangely blended politics and fatherly love—a longing for retirement and a lurking desire to leave to his children the honor of his having filled the highest office in his country's gift." Randall, though, reprints the letter in context, the balloting in the House, and thereby shows that Jefferson's complaint about "cabal" and "intrigue"—at the moment when rumors circulated of Aaron Burr's agents busily at work in Albany, others prepared to sell themselves to the highest bidder, and Jefferson's followers talked about the possibility of taking up arms to thwart a Federalist usurpation—was not mere literary fancy. Randolph glides over the balloting with phrasing that foretells the happy outcome—a "storm, which for a week convulsed the country with excitement, and shook the young Government to its centre."[11]

With her focus almost wholly on Jefferson's domestic life and no interest in politics, not even as context for that life, Randolph leaves the reader with the impression that Jefferson entered politics only out of "a lurking desire to leave to his children the honor." When Jefferson retired from office after his second term as president, "his whole demeanor betokened the feelings of one who had been relieved of a heavy and wearisome burden." Government service was merely burdensome. It kept Jefferson from those he loved best. Randolph includes the encomiums to family love that have become so familiar over the years. In 1798, for example, Jefferson tells his older daughter of his impatience to leave Philadelphia "and every thing which can be disgusting, for Monticello and my dear family, comprising every thing which is pleasurable to me in this world." A year earlier, upon learning that Polly was engaged to her cousin John Wayles Eppes, he wrote her rapturously, imagining the future. He wrote her sister, Martha, "I now see our fireside

11. Randolph, *Domestic Life of Thomas Jefferson,* 271, 274, Thomas Jefferson to Mary Jefferson Eppes, Feb. 15, 1801, 274; Randall, *Life of Thomas Jefferson,* II, 594–602 (esp. Feb. 15, 1801, 599–600). Although he named her Mary at birth, Jefferson later addressed his younger surviving (white) daughter by her nickname Polly, and that is how I identify her as well. For the historical context, including predictions of constitutional and paramilitary turmoil, see the essays in James Horn, Jan Ellen Lewis, and Peter S. Onuf, eds., *The Revolution of 1800: Democracy, Race, and the New Republic* (Charlottesville, Va., 2002).

formed into a group, no one member of which has a fibre in their composition which can ever produce any jarring or jealousies among us. No irregular passions, no dangerous bias, which may render problematical the future fortunes and happiness of our descendants." Family was the antidote to the poison of political life.[12]

And politics became the explanation for the family's lack of fortune. Repeatedly, Randolph tells us that Jefferson's public service cost his family dearly. Upon returning to Monticello at the end of his presidency, "it required but a brief sojourn at home, and a thorough investigation of his affairs, for Jefferson to see that his long-continued absence had told fearfully on the value of his farms; that his long enlistment in the service of his country had been his pecuniary ruin." Although Randolph generally lets Jefferson's correspondence speak for itself (even when clarification of transitions might be helpful), when it comes to what she calls her great-grandfather's "pecuniary embarrassments," she thinks it necessary not only to fill in missing information but to tie it in to an explanation. Jefferson, she notes, was "in public life almost continuously from 1774 to 1809"; no matter how "beneficial to the public his services to his country had been, on himself they were allowed to entail bankruptcy and ruin." She takes the reader through Jefferson's career and a succession of financial reverses. Although Jefferson had added to a handsome inheritance and owned five thousand acres by 1774, he had also acquired the debt that came along with his wife's dower. Randolph implies, incorrectly, that Jefferson had discharged the dower debt relatively early in his career, but, as Herbert Sloan has explained in his authoritative study, the effort to settle these debts "would drag on for decades."[13]

It is necessary for Randolph, however, that public service, rather than anything to do with the family itself, be the cause of the family's ruin. "When Jefferson resigned as Secretary of State in 1794," she explains, "he hoped he had turned his back forever on public life, and proposed to devote the residue of his days to the restoration of his shattered fortunes." Her great-grandfather returned to public service, but only because he was "besieged by deputations of the most distinguished men of the day—old associates of the Revolution, who pressed his country's claim on him with an earnestness

12. Randolph, *Domestic Life of Thomas Jefferson,* 274, 329, Thomas Jefferson to Martha Jefferson Randolph, May 31, [17]98, 250, Jefferson to Martha Jefferson Randolph, June 8, 1797, 245; Jefferson to Mary Jefferson, draft, June 14, 1797, in Betts and Bear, eds., *Family Letters,* 148–149.

13. Randolph, *Domestic Life of Thomas Jefferson,* 329, 397, 399, 408; Herbert E. Sloan, *Principle and Interest: Thomas Jefferson and the Problem of Debt* (New York, 1995), 22.

and pertinacity not to be resisted, and which finally recalled him to public life." Jefferson's "shattered fortunes" were everyone else's fault rather than his own. When he returned to Monticello in 1809, it was "with hands, as he himself said, as clean as they were empty"—penniless, yet of impeccable character.[14]

Jefferson held the members of his family to the same high but impoverishing standard. Twice, his great-granddaughter tells us in introducing separate letters, he refused to secure government positions for family members. Both times, she contrasts Jefferson's practices favorably with those of her own day. The first letter is one from March 1801 in which Jefferson turned down a request from his cousin (and business agent) for a position for his brother, explaining, "The public will never be made to believe that an appointment of a relative is made on the ground of merit alone, uninfluenced by family views; nor can they ever see with approbation offices, the disposal of which they intrust to their Presidents for public purposes, divided out as family property." Here, Jefferson intended to follow George Washington's example, not that of John Adams, who had "degraded himself infinitely by his conduct on this subject." Jefferson knew that his course "places the relations of the President in a worse situation than if he were a stranger, but the public good, which can not be effected if its confidence be lost, requires this sacrifice." The only consolation to the leader's family was "sharing in the public esteem," which, Randolph added, "in an age when nepotism is so rife, may, from its principles, seem now rather out of date." Randolph repeats the point later in her book—which is significant since her own editorial interventions are so infrequent. In introducing a passage from Jefferson's 1824 letter to Joseph Cabell in which he discussed faculty appointments to the University of Virginia, Randolph says it "sounds strangely now in an age in which nepotism is so rife." In that letter, Jefferson boasted, "I can say with truth, and with unspeakable comfort, that I never did appoint a relation to office." But here, the explanation was not only principle but also "because I never saw the case in which some one did not offer, or occur, better qualified."[15]

14. Randolph, *Domestic Life of Thomas Jefferson,* 400.

15. Thomas Jefferson to George Jefferson, [Mar. 27, 1801], ibid., 277, Jefferson to J[oseph] C[arrington] Cabell, [Feb. 3, 1824], 388–389. This passage illustrates Randolph's method. In introducing the letter, she mentions only that George Jefferson was a "kinsman" and that her own ancestor rejected nepotism (277). George Jefferson had written Thomas Jefferson several weeks earlier to forward, abashedly, a letter from his brother pleading for a government position. George Jefferson came close to begging Jefferson *not* to find an office for his brother, knowing both that Jefferson's Federalist enemies would "censure" him for it and that his brother's qualifications for any office would probably not, as he delicately put it,

If she read her great-grandfather's letters closely, Randolph might have found them cutting. True, they show Jefferson to be highly principled—precisely the point Randolph wanted to make—and a model contemporary politicians might well emulate. But Jefferson also told his correspondents that his own kin were undeserving and that, anyway, the family that he impoverished would have to subsist off his "public esteem," which is exactly what his descendants tried to do. Jefferson bequeathed his papers to his eldest grandson and namesake, Thomas Jefferson Randolph (Sarah Randolph's father), "as of his own property." To "relieve the massive debts that were," as Francis D. Cogliano puts it, "another of Jefferson's legacies," Thomas Jefferson Randolph tried to turn the papers into cash. He published four volumes of the papers as the *Memoir, Correspondence, and Miscellanies from the Papers of Thomas Jefferson* (1829). Preparing the papers for publication was a kind of cottage industry for Jefferson's grandson, his mother, and his sisters. The women spent five to eight hours each day transcribing the documents, which in some cases were already so deteriorated that they had to place a magnifying glass behind the pages in the full light of the noonday sun in order to detect the impression of the pen and ink. "A few lines will sometimes cost as many days," Martha Jefferson Randolph explained.[16]

The family treated the papers as a legacy with a monetary value. In 1848, Thomas Jefferson Randolph sold his grandfather's papers to the United States for twenty thousand dollars. The family had wanted to withhold three boxes of "private family letters," but Secretary of State James Buchanan insisted that they be deposited with the government. These papers were not returned to the family until late 1870 or early 1871. Whether by accident or design, the family kept some of the private correspondence. As Andrew Burstein tells us, in 1851 the family just happened to find "in a dark and entirely forgotten receptacle" a cache of papers including more than three hundred letters between Jefferson and his daughters, which they turned over to the biographer Randall. Randall claimed to have the entirety of Jefferson's "family correspondence," including every letter that Jefferson had ever sent

---

"stand the test of investigation." George Jefferson's request was a very easy one for Thomas Jefferson to turn down. See George Jefferson to Thomas Jefferson, Mar. 4, 1801, in Julian P. Boyd et al., eds., *The Papers of Thomas Jefferson,* 43 vols. (Princeton, N.J., 1950–), 158–160.

16. Paul G. Sifton, "The Provenance of the Thomas Jefferson Papers," *American Archivist,* XL (1977), 18 ("as of his own property"); Francis D. Cogliano, *Thomas Jefferson: Reputation and Legacy* (Charlottesville, Va., 2006), 81, Martha Jefferson Randolph to Joseph Coolidge, May 12, 1829, Jefferson Papers, Massachusetts Historical Society, quoted ibid., 82 ("a few lines"). Cogliano notes that, not surprisingly, the family made a number of errors, which were repeated in subsequent editions of Jefferson's writings.

his daughter Polly, "not one" of which "has ever been published," along with the account Jefferson's doctor, Robley Dunglison, wrote about Jefferson's final illness and death.[17] When Sarah Randolph published her *Domestic Life* in 1871, she said that her work had been made possible by the government's return of the "family letters and private papers" so that she was "enabled to give in these pages many interesting letters never before published." She claimed the fact that the reader could now see truly private papers "never before published" enhanced the value of the book.[18]

Randolph's *Domestic Life* is manifestly about love—Jefferson's love for family and the love they returned to him. Chief among the "outstanding traits of the 'beautiful domestic character' created" in her book, according to Merrill D. Peterson, was Jefferson's "enormous capacity for love." Yet the letters themselves and Randolph's own insertions suggest that this love was not wholly unconflicted. It might be observed that family love never is. As we have already seen, Randolph described politics as an unwelcome intrusion into Jefferson's life. In her view, a late-life letter demonstrates "what little interest he took in politics," and there is almost no indication in the letters Randolph includes that even at the peak of his career Jefferson considered public service anything more than an unpleasant and heavy burden.[19]

But the letters also suggest that Jefferson could be both indulgent and withholding. He refused on principle to appoint relatives to public office. His hectoring letters to his young daughters suggest that his love, though

17. Sifton, "Provenance of the Thomas Jefferson Papers," *American Archivist,* XL (1977), 20–24, T. J. Randolph to H. A. Washington, Aug. 6, 1850, quoted ibid., 21; Burstein, "Dexterity and Delicacy of Manipulation," in McDonald, ed., *Thomas Jefferson's Lives,* 64. Burstein is quoting from an article published in the *New York Commercial Advertiser,* as reprinted in "From the New York Commercial Advertiser; The Life of Thomas Jefferson," *Georgia Telegraph* (Macon, Ga.), May 12, 1857, [1], that profiled Randall just before the publication of his biography. A copy of this article can also be found as "Literary Intelligence," *American Publishers' Circular and Literary Gazette,* July 25, 1857, 469–470. The family told Randall that the papers had been found "amongst the old, cast-aside account books and other trumpery of a closet connected with Mr. Jefferson's bedroom"—the one "above the alcove, with its two eye-like holes opening into the bedroom"—and then moved to Edgehill, where they remained forgotten for several decades (470).

18. Randolph, *Domestic Life of Thomas Jefferson,* viii. It is not clear what happened to the cache of papers that the family turned over to Randall and exactly which letters had been held by the government between 1848 and 1870–1871. Merrill D. Peterson concluded that "much" that Sarah Randolph "published was taken from Randall's *Life,* for the New Yorker had drawn from the same bundles of family papers and the same wells of family remembrance." See Peterson, *The Jefferson Image in the American Mind* (Charlottesville, Va., 1998), 232. I thank Jeff Looney for sharing his insights with me.

19. Peterson, *Jefferson Image,* 232; Randolph, *Domestic Life of Thomas Jefferson,* 388.

abundant, was also contingent. In the first extant letter Jefferson wrote his daughter Martha, he lectured her: "The conviction that you would be more improved in the situation I have placed you than if still with me, has solaced me on my parting with you, which my love for you has rendered a difficult thing. The acquirements which I hope you will make under the tutors I have provided for you will render you more worthy of my love; and if they can not increase it, they will prevent its diminution." And, finally, at the end of the letter, in case the message had not been fully clear, Jefferson added a "P.S.—Keep my letters and read them at times, that you may always have present in your mind those things which will endear you to me." Jefferson had left his eleven-year-old daughter in Philadelphia to be educated while he attended Congress in Annapolis. Her mother had died the year before. Her younger sisters remained with their aunt in Virginia. Here was Jefferson's parental style distilled into two sentences: the sacrifices were all his. He was the only one who needed solace; he was the one, implicitly, who was undertaking an expense, all for his daughter's good. She owed him compensation, and, if she did not improve—in her studies, in her acquirements, in her love—he would love her less. Her father's love always had to be earned.[20]

We do not know how this motherless girl reacted to her father's letter at the time, but, a quarter century later, Martha invited a good friend into her bedroom at Monticello, where she showed the friend her father's letters. The friend copied down some of those passages in which Jefferson spoke most strongly about the importance of family love as the antidote to the poison of politics. We know the reaction of Martha's younger sister Polly, the one who was left in the care of her aunt and uncle while her father served his nation, first in the capital and then in Paris. In her first letter to her father, then in Paris, Polly, then five or six, told him, "I want to know what day you are going to come and see me." A few months later, her baby sister died and, Randolph notes, "the death of this child was felt keenly by Jefferson." Once settled in Paris, "he became impatient to have" Polly sent to him. She remained in Virginia, however, until 1787, in part because, as Randolph puts it, "the child herself could not bear the thought of being torn from the kind uncle and aunt, whom she had learned to love so devotedly, to go to a strange land."[21]

20. Thomas Jefferson to Martha Jefferson, Nov. 28, 1783, in Randolph, *Domestic Life of Thomas Jefferson,* 69–70; Cynthia A. Kierner, *Martha Jefferson Randolph, Daughter of Monticello: Her Life and Times* (Chapel Hill, N.C., 2012), 42–43.

21. Gaillard Hunt, ed., *The First Forty Years of Washington Society: Portrayed by Family Letters of Mrs. Samuel Harrison Smith (Margaret Bayard) from the Collection of Her Grand-*

Randolph introduces the first of Jefferson's letters to his younger daughter by observing that "it is touching to see how gently her father tries to reconcile her . . . to her separation from her good uncle and aunt, and how he attempts to lure her to France with the promise that she shall have in Paris 'as many dolls and playthings' as she wants." But Polly resisted. Her aunt had to use, as she told Jefferson, "every stratagem to prevail on her to consent to visit you." Randolph tells us about the ploy that finally got Polly aboard ship, bound across the Atlantic: her cousins boarded with her and played with her "until she had become somewhat at home and acquainted with those around her. Then, while the child was one day asleep, they were all taken away, and before she awoke the vessel had cut loose from her moorings, and was fairly launched on the tedious voyage before her." Randolph does not mention that Polly was not entirely alone; she was accompanied by another girl also torn from her family, her father's fourteen-year-old slave, Sally Hemings.[22]

Whether we view Jefferson's efforts to draw his daughter to Paris as "touching" or not will, no doubt, depend on how each of us understands relationships within families and how we read the transcripts of family love. Abigail Adams, into whose care Polly and Sally Hemings were deposited when their ship arrived in London, observed Polly's distress and described it to Jefferson. Just as she had been tricked into boarding the ship, Polly had to be "decoyed" off it. Once in London, she became so attached to Adams that she would not leave her side. As Adams explained, "she has been so often deceived that she will not quit me a moment least she should be carried away." Moreover, Polly was puzzled that her father had not come to London himself to pick her up but instead sent a French-speaking servant. She told Adams "that as she had left all her Friends in virginia to come over the ocean

son J. Henley Smith (New York, 1906), 74–77; Mary Jefferson to Thomas Jefferson, Apr. [1], 1784, in Randolph, *Domestic Life of Thomas Jefferson,* 102. I have discussed Smith's transcription of Jefferson's letters to Martha in Lewis, "White Jeffersons," in Lewis and Onuf, eds., *Sally Hemings and Thomas Jefferson,* 130, 158n. Both Henry S. Randall and Sarah Randolph include one of these letters, that of June 8, 1797, in their books (Randall, *Life of Thomas Jefferson,* II, 358; Randolph, *Domestic Life of Thomas Jefferson,* 245). Neither, however, includes Jefferson's letter to her of February 5, 1801, and it is not clear whether Randall or Randolph had it available. This letter is reproduced in full in Betts and Bear, eds., *Family Letters of Thomas Jefferson,* 194–196; and in Boyd et al., eds., *Papers of Thomas Jefferson,* XXXII, 556–557.

22. Randolph, *Domestic Life of Thomas Jefferson,* 103, 125, [Elizabeth Wayles] Eppes to Thomas Jefferson, [Mar. 31, 1787], 124; Annette Gordon-Reed, *The Hemingses of Monticello: An American Family* (New York, 2008), 193–195. See also Fawn M. Brodie, *Thomas Jefferson: An Intimate History* (New York, 1974), 216–219.

to see you, she did think you would have taken the pains to have come here for her" and not have sent a man "whom she cannot understand."[23]

Randolph does not include the letters Adams wrote Jefferson about his daughter, but she does reproduce a letter that Adams wrote her own sister just after Polly's departure. The little girl spent two weeks with Adams, during which "she would sit, sometimes, and describe to me the parting with her aunt, who brought her up, the obligation she was under to her, and the love she had for her little cousins, till the tears would stream down her cheeks. . . . Her papa would break her heart by making her go again." Many years later, Polly would marry one of those cousins, the son of the aunt who had brought her up.[24]

In his first letter to Polly, when he was trying to attract her to Paris, Jefferson had held out various enticements, not only "as many dolls and playthings" as she wanted but also instruction in how "to play on the harpsichord, to draw, to dance, to read and talk French, and such other things as will make you more worthy of the love of your friends." Just as in Jefferson's first letter to Polly's older sister, a father's love was contingent. "If you always practice these lessons we shall continue to love you as we do now, and it is impossible to love you any more." There is the hint, too, that a daughter's love could be bought—with toys and dolls and expensive lessons. In her first letter to her father, Polly had thanked him for the sashes he had sent her. Such items were the stuff of love. When the women in Jefferson's family reflected upon his perfect love, they often associated it with specific items. Sometimes these were the letters themselves, which, as we have seen, Martha Jefferson Randolph shared with her friend. After her father's death, she kept and used not only his bed but his "down cover-lit" as well. When, late in life, she told a friend who had come to visit her in her sickbed where these objects had come from, "she stopped, choked by emotion and could not restrain her tears, tho' she concealed them by drawing the bedclothes over her face."[25]

Like his daughters, Jefferson's granddaughters associated him with objects, gifts of particular value. As Ellen Randolph Coolidge reminisced to

23. Abigail Adams to Thomas Jefferson, July 6, 1787, in Boyd et al, eds., *Papers of Thomas Jefferson,* XI, 551.

24. Abigail Adams to [Mary Smith Cranch], [July 16, 1787], in Randolph, *Domestic Life of Thomas Jefferson,* 126. Randall also includes this letter. See Randall, *Life of Thomas Jefferson,* I, 480.

25. Randolph, *Domestic Life of Thomas Jefferson,* 102, Thomas Jefferson to Mary Jefferson, Sept. 20, 1785, 103–104; Hunt, ed., *First Forty Years of Washington Society,* 309.

Randall, in a letter that Randolph includes in *The Domestic Life,* "When about fifteen years old, I began to think of a watch, but knew the state of my father's finances promised no such indulgence." This would have been around 1811, after Jefferson had retired to Monticello where his daughter Martha and her children took up residence with him while Martha's husband, Thomas Mann Randolph, struggled to turn a profit at his own plantation. "One afternoon the letter-bag was brought in," Coolidge continued. "Among the letters was a small packet addressed to my grandfather. It had the Philadelphia mark upon it. I looked at it with indifferent, incurious eye. Three hours after, an elegant lady's watch, with chain and seals, was in my hand, which trembled for very joy. My Bible came from him, my Shakspeare [*sic*], my first writing-table, my first handsome writing-desk, my first Leghorn hat, my first silk dress. What, in short, of all my small treasures did not come from him?" What, indeed, did not come from Thomas Jefferson? Nor was Coolidge the only granddaughter who was favored. "My sisters, according to their wants and tastes, were equally thought of, equally provided for. Our grandfather seemed to read our hearts, to see our invisible wishes, to be our good genius, to wave the fairy wand, to brighten our young lives by his goodness and his gifts."[26]

Ellen Coolidge's sister Virginia Randolph Trist had similar memories. "Often," she reminisced to her husband, Nicholas, their grandfather "discovered, we knew not how, some cherished object of our desires, and the first intimation we had of his knowing the wish was its unexpected gratification." Among his granddaughters, Jefferson functioned as a cross between an all-seeing god and a wish-granting genie: "Sister Anne gave a silk dress to sister Ellen. Cornelia (then eight or ten years old), going up stairs, involuntarily expressed aloud some feelings which possessed her bosom on the occasion, by saying, 'I never had a silk dress in my life.' The next day a silk dress came from Charlottesville to Cornelia, and (to make the rest of us equally happy) also a pair of pretty dresses for Mary and myself." Another time, after Virginia tore her own dress, Jefferson "himself selected"—and paid for—"another beautiful dress." Every wish became her grandfather's command. She had long coveted a guitar. A neighborhood woman offered to sell her one, but for "so high a price that I never in my dreams aspired to its possession." Yet one morning, when Virginia came down to breakfast, there

26. Ellen W. Coolidge to Henry S. Randall, n.d., in Randolph, *Domestic Life of Thomas Jefferson,* 345; Randall, *Life of Thomas Jefferson,* III, 347–349; Kierner, *Martha Jefferson Randolph,* 142–156.

the guitar was, a gift from her grandfather if only "I would promise to learn to play on it." The memory and the emotions they evoked were vivid more than twenty years later. "I never shall forget my ecstasies. I was but fourteen years old, and the first wish of my heart was unexpectedly gratified."[27]

These gifts came at a price. The extent to which a silk dress here or a guitar there contributed significantly to Jefferson's mountain of debt is hard to gauge. We know that he was not one to deny either himself or his loved ones indulgences such as these. Many years later, his daughter and her children would have to abandon Monticello and the enslaved people who lived at it because they could no longer afford to keep them. Randolph believed that somehow her grandfather's generosity to others was responsible for the calamity of the loss of Monticello. He had given selflessly of his time to his nation, and, after his retirement, he offered hospitality without regard to the expense to "the crowds of visitors which his reputation drew to his house." Randolph insists that Jefferson "was in no wise responsible for having incurred" his debts, and the "pecuniary embarrassments" were the product of "circumstances beyond his control."[28]

In surveying Randolph's *Domestic Life,* Merrill D. Peterson has observed that the Jefferson she describes "knew no happiness outside the bosom of his family." That is certainly the impression her book conveys. As I have suggested elsewhere, that also is what Jefferson wanted his family to believe. His happiness required many sacrifices on their part; at least they could be assured—for he so assured them—that they were the source of his only true happiness. It should be noted that most of these assurances were delivered to the women in Jefferson's family. Indeed, his closest family relationships were almost all with women. Although Randolph is at pains to depict Jefferson as "manly," Peterson believes that "her narrative suggested, nevertheless, there was something to be said for the other view." He catalogs the qualities that Randolph describes—Jefferson's "unfailing joy in household cares, the raising of children, the arrangements of the house, the cuisine and the garden . . . [and] most of all, the sweetness of his temper, seldom ruffled and almost never broken by anger—these traits would commonly be counted more effeminate than masculine." Peterson is not the

27. Virginia J. Trist to Henry S. Randall, May 26, 1839, in Randolph, *Domestic Life of Thomas Jefferson,* 347–348; Randall, *Life of Thomas Jefferson,* III, 349–351.

28. Randolph, *Domestic Life of Thomas Jefferson,* 397, 404, 406; Paul Finkelman, "Jefferson and Slavery: 'Treason against the Hopes of the World,'" in Onuf, ed., *Jeffersonian Legacies,* 181–221, makes the case for Jefferson's profligacy. Sloan, *Principle and Interest,* describes Jefferson's finances more generally.

only historian before or since to consider Jefferson "effeminate," but, as the historian Joseph J. Ellis discovered, such inferences from the documentary record about a historical figure's gender identity can be dangerous. Extrapolating from Henry Adams's observation that "Jefferson's temperament was 'almost feminine,'" Ellis concluded that "for most of his adult life" Jefferson "lacked the capacity for the direct and physical expression of his sexual energies" and hence could not have fathered Sally Hemings's children. Yet we now know—as Ellis has acknowledged—that Jefferson was indeed their father and that Jefferson was fully capable both of picking out dresses for his granddaughters and expressing directly his sexual energies.[29]

What may mislead historians is that, perhaps more than any of the other political leaders of his generation—or many generations—Jefferson had many close attachments to women, from which hundreds of letters survive. By accident of nature, his two surviving white children were both women, and the older of these had six surviving daughters. Perhaps by no accident, Jefferson's bonds to their husbands were not especially strong. In the family circle, there were no men to rival Jefferson for dominance. This family configuration was unusual for the time. Moreover, the bonds between Jefferson and his female relatives were especially close. Yet, if these bonds—and his discussions about women's clothing and household arrangements—may make him seem "effeminate," at the same time Jefferson fostered a kind of intellectual development for the women in his family that was less gendered than one might well have expected—particularly of a man like Jefferson, who could betray streaks of misogyny.[30]

Jefferson, to be sure, was not only aware of sexual difference but in fact constructed it. His early letter to Martha, then eleven, in which he lectured her on proper female grooming, is well known. Randolph includes the key passage in *The Domestic Life:* "Be you, from the moment you rise till you

29. Peterson, *Jefferson Image,* 232–333; Lewis, "'Blessings of Domestic Society,'" in Onuf, ed., *Jeffersonian Legacies,* 109–146; Joseph J. Ellis, *American Sphinx: The Character of Thomas Jefferson* (New York, 1997), 305; Ellis, "Jefferson: Post-DNA," *William and Mary Quarterly,* 3d Ser., LVII (2000), 125–138.

30. I have explored this topic in Jan Lewis, "Jefferson, the Family, and Civic Education," in James Gilreath, ed., *Thomas Jefferson and the Education of a Citizen* (Washington, D.C., 1999), 63–75; and Lewis, "Jefferson and Women," in John B. Boles and Randal L. Hall, eds., *Seeing Jefferson Anew: In His Time and Ours* (Charlottesville, Va., 2010), 152–171, also reprinted in this volume. See also Brian Steele, "Thomas Jefferson's Gender Frontier," *Journal of American History,* XCV (2008), 17–42; and Steele, *Thomas Jefferson and American Nationhood* (New York, 2012), 53–90. For ideas about women's intellectual capacity in this period more generally, see Lucia McMahon, *Mere Equals: The Paradox of Educated Women in the Early American Republic* (Ithaca, N.Y., 2012).

go to bed, as cleanly and properly dressed as at the hours of dinner or tea. A lady who has been seen as a sloven or a slut in the morning, will never efface the impression she has made, with all the dress and pageantry she can afterwards involve herself in. Nothing is so disgusting to our sex as a want of cleanliness and delicacy in yours." This from a man who was known to "gree[t] guests in slovenly clothes," "linnen [that] was much soiled," and worn-out slippers. Different standards applied to women and to men, and women were supposed to work to make themselves attractive to men.[31]

At the same time, Jefferson could instruct his daughters just as he might have a son. When his daughter Martha, then about fifteen, complained about studying Livy, her father encouraged her to redouble her efforts: "We are always equal to what we undertake with resolution." She must remember that she was an American and that "it is a part of the American character to consider nothing as desperate; to surmount every difficulty by resolution and contrivance." In Europe, one could walk into a shop and purchase everything that was ever needed, but, in America, we have "to find the means within ourselves, and not to lean on others. Consider, therefore, the conquering of your Livy as an exercise in the habit of surmounting difficulties; a habit which will be necessary to you in the country where you are to live, and without which you will be thought a very helpless animal, and less esteemed." Here was Jefferson, enjoining upon his daughter that most American of traits, self-reliance, to be acquired by the assiduous study of Livy. Two decades later, he praised Martha's young daughter Cornelia on learning to write, because, he explained, it is to writing that "we are indebted for all our reading," "for the Iliad, the Aeneid," and other works.[32]

Jefferson could cross the gender line in both directions; it was not so much that he was "effeminate" as that he could identify with both women and men. When he worried that his daughter Polly, now married, was too inclined to "withdraw from society"—her husband had told Jefferson that they would not be spending the summer at Monticello—he lectured her

31. Thomas Jefferson to Martha Jefferson, Dec. 22, 1783, in Randolph, *Domestic Life of Thomas Jefferson,* 71; Louis-André Pichon to Ministère des Affaires étrangères, 26 Pluviôse an 10, *Correspondence Politique,* vol. 54, Les Archives Diplomatiques, quoted in Jon Meacham, *Thomas Jefferson: The Art of Power* (New York, 2012), 363 ("gree[t] guests"); *William Plumer's Memorandum of Proceedings in the United States Senate, 1803–1807,* ed. Everett S. Brown (New York, 1923), 193, quoted in Dumas Malone, *Jefferson the President: First Term, 1801–1805* (Boston, 1970), 371 ("linnen"); R. B. Bernstein, *Thomas Jefferson* (New York, 2003), 140.

32. Thomas Jefferson to Martha Jefferson, Mar. 28, 1787, in Randolph, *Domestic Life of Thomas Jefferson,* 115–116, Jefferson to Cornelia Randolph, Dec. 26, 1808, 320.

from his own experience: "I am convinced our own happiness requires that we should continue to mix with the world . . . and that every person who retires from free communication with it is severely punished afterwards by the state of mind into which he gets." Jefferson was not using "he" generically: he had himself in mind. "From 1793 to 1797," he confessed to his daughter, "I remained closely at home, saw none but those who came there, and at length became very sensible of the ill effect it had on my own mind, and of its direct and irresistible tendency to render me unfit for society." Jefferson was referring to the period when he returned home after his resignation as secretary of state—as Randolph had put it, turning "his back forever on public life"—in order to "devote the residue of his days to the restoration of his shattered fortunes." This was the only extended period of time that Jefferson spent at Monticello between 1774 and 1809.[33]

Because Jefferson could identify with the women in his family, it is no surprise that they could identify with him and devote their lives to protecting his reputation. That reputation, as we have seen, became their living. Not only did Randolph publish *The Domestic Life,* but, after her father died and he left the family papers to her, she proposed a new edition of Jefferson's writings to the Library of Congress. A new edition was necessary she testified to Congress, both to correct numerous errors in the nine-volume Henry Augustine Washington edition and, by including the family letters in her possession, to "throw much light upon the private and public life of the great statesman, and present him in many phases of life, heretofore unknown." In 1888, a congressional committee recommended paying Randolph $2,500 a year to prepare a new edition of the Jefferson papers, but then, the subsequent year, it considered buying the family papers outright. While Congress debated, Randolph died, and the papers passed to her sister Carolina.[34]

Randolph believed that the family correspondence provided the key to Jefferson's character. Jefferson himself had taught his family that he had two selves, an "imaginary" one constructed by the public and his real one, known only to them. Twice in *The Domestic Life,* we see Jefferson using this defense mechanism to deflect the criticism that stung him so badly. In both cases, the reports come from family members, and, in fact, an Internet search of the

33. Randolph, *Domestic Life of Thomas Jefferson,* 400, Thomas Jefferson to Mary Jefferson Eppes, Mar. 3, 1802, 284.

34. Sifton, "Provenance of the Thomas Jefferson Papers," *American Archivist,* XL (1977), 25. Carolina sold some of the papers to a male cousin and left the rest to female relatives. Some of the family papers were lost in a fire, but the remainder were eventually deposited by family members in a series of repositories. See ibid., 27–29.

Jefferson papers at the Library of Congress does not provide any instance of Jefferson using this wording in his correspondence. There is no reason, however, to doubt his family's memory of this distinctive phrase. One comes from the pen of Thomas Jefferson Randolph, who remembered his grandfather's final days for Randall. As Jefferson lay on his deathbed, he called in the members of his family for a "parting interview." He spoke fondly of his long friendship with James Madison but also talked about his enemies. "In speaking of the calumnies which his enemies had uttered against his public and private character with such unmitigated and untiring bitterness, he said that he had not considered them as abusing him; they had never known *him*. They had created an imaginary being clothed with odious attributes, to whom they had given his name; and it was against that creature of their imaginations they had levelled their anathemas."[35]

The other instance comes from an anecdote, told "from the most authentic source," that Sarah Randolph recounted about her great-grandfather. Randolph situates the story during Jefferson's first term as president. As he was out riding one day, she tells us, he came upon a pedestrian and struck up a conversation with the man who, not recognizing him, immediately started discussing politics, "as was the habit of the day—and began to abuse the President, alluding even to some of the infamous calumnies against his private life." Jefferson asked the stranger, a Kentuckian, if he actually knew the president. No, he did not, but he would "never shrink from meeting Mr. Jefferson should he ever come in my way." Jefferson promised him an introduction if he would meet him at the Executive Mansion the next day. The abashed Kentuckian appeared before Jefferson at the appointed time, saying, "I have called, Mr. Jefferson, to apologize for having said to a stranger—" Before the man could finish, Jefferson disarmed him by making clear that he took no offense at "hard things [said] of an imaginary being who is no relation of mine." He then invited the Kentuckian to stay for dinner.[36]

Two themes from this anecdote recur in *The Domestic Life*. So often, it seems, did Jefferson go unrecognized in public that one might be forgiven for wondering if some of the stories might be apocryphal. At the very least, tales of the unknown Jefferson struck a chord with Sarah Randolph. One of the stories sounds almost like a folk tale. Jefferson stopped one evening at a country inn, where he entered into conversation with a stranger who did not

35. Thomas Jefferson Randolph to Henry S. Randall, n.d., in Randolph, *Domestic Life of Thomas Jefferson*, 425, 427–428. The letter is also reproduced in Randall, *Life of Thomas Jefferson*, III, 544.

36. Randolph, *Domestic Life of Thomas Jefferson*, 289–290.

recognize "this plainly-dressed and unassuming traveller." They talked about every topic imaginable—law, medicine, theology—on all of which Jefferson seemed "perfectly acquainted." When the stranger later asked the innkeeper who this astonishing man was, there came the reply, "Oh . . . why I thought you knew the Squire." All the stories about the unrecognized Jefferson speak to his modesty and good nature. In a story told by Thomas Jefferson Randolph, Jefferson once again encountered a stranger when out riding. This time, the president and several companions were returning home to Virginia on horseback, and the stranger asked Jefferson's assistance alone in fording a stream, judging him a good man from his appearance.[37]

Two other anecdotes suggest that in some circumstances Jefferson wanted to be recognized and his authority acknowledged. Sarah Randolph tells us that she knows of only two occasions when Jefferson lost his temper. In one instance, Jefferson and his daughter Martha were crossing a stream by ferry. The two ferrymen began an argument on shore and continued it on the ferry, coming almost to blows. Jefferson "remonstrated with them," but still they raged. Finally, "with his eyes flashing," Jefferson "snatched up an oar" and shouted to the ferrymen to "Row for your lives" or be knocked overboard. The other instance involved Jefferson's "favorite coachman," Jupiter. Jefferson had ordered another slave, a boy, to take one of the horses and go on an errand for his master, but Jupiter considered these horses as his and would not let the boy use one. When the boy told Jefferson about Jupiter's countermand, Jefferson thought the coachman was playing a joke on the boy, so he sent the boy back again, with the same order. Jupiter once again refused. Then, in "an excited tone," Jefferson directed that Jupiter himself appear, whereupon he "received the order and a rebuke from his master in tones and with a look which neither he nor the terrified bystanders ever forgot." This may be the only account we have of Jefferson terrifying anyone; it cannot be an accident that the object of Jefferson's anger was enslaved, nor that the objects of his oar-wielding threat of physical violence were two lower-class men. Jefferson rarely expressed anger, but, when he did, it was at those far beneath him in status who had failed to oblige him.[38]

Slaves haunt the pages of *The Domestic Life* like ghosts. They are presences

37. Ibid., 38, 337.

38. Ibid., 321–322. Annette Gordon-Reed informs us that Jupiter's last name was Evans and that he had been Jefferson's boyhood companion and served as his attendant until, at the age of thirty-one, he was replaced by Robert Hemings and moved to the position of custodian of the stables and sometime coachman. See Gordon-Reed, *Hemingses of Monticello,* 95, 124–125.

who do not speak, yet appear from time to time, at the edge of the stage. Randolph nowhere discusses the institution of slavery. The closest she comes is when she reproduces a portion of Duc de la Rochefoucauld-Liancourt's description of his visit to Monticello in 1796. Jefferson's "negroes," we are told, "are nourished, clothed, and treated as well as white servants could be. . . . He animates them by rewards and distinctions; in fine, his superior mind directs the management of his domestic concerns with the same abilities, activity, and regularity which he evinced in the conduct of public affairs." Slavery at Monticello, like its master, is orderly and wholly benign. Randolph mentions also that Jefferson owned 154 slaves, "a very small number in proportion to his landed estate."[39]

Of course there is the now-familiar story about the slaves welcoming Jefferson and his daughters home from Paris, with the slave men unhitching the horses from the carriage and drawing it up the mountain with their "strong black arms up to the foot of the lawn in front of the door at Monticello." Randolph recounts another family story, this one about Polly, who had come to visit her father so sick and weak that she was "carried to Monticello in a litter borne by men." Surely these nameless men were enslaved. Although sometimes Jefferson mentioned particular slaves by name—not just Jupiter, but Critta, Remus, Phill, Davy, Melinda, John, and James—more often the slaves are ghosts. "The house, its contents, and appendages and servants, are as freely subjected to you as to myself," Jefferson offered Polly in an attempt to lure the gravely ill woman back to Monticello. Three years earlier, a similar offer: "I insist that you command and use every thing as if I were with you, and shall be very uneasy if you do not." A few months earlier: "The servants will be here under your commands."[40]

The most haunting ghost, of course, is Sally Hemings, nowhere mentioned but always a presence, the rationale, even, for the book. "No man's private character has been more foully assailed than Jefferson's," Randolph had written on the first pages of her book. Of the "calumnies" that Jefferson's "enemies had uttered against his public and private character," surely none had been more troubling to Jefferson's family than the allegations that

39. Randolph, *Domestic Life of Thomas Jefferson,* 229, 238. Immediately after enumerating the slaves on Jefferson's plantations, Randolph moves on to list the number of horses, mules, cattle, hogs, and sheep.

40. Ibid., 153, 300, Thomas Jefferson to Mary Jefferson, May 25, 1797, 244, Jefferson to Mary Jefferson Eppes, Apr. 11, 1801, 278, Jefferson to Mary Jefferson Eppes, July 16, 1801, 279, Jefferson to Mary Jefferson Eppes, July 2, 1802, 286, Jefferson to John W. Eppes, Mar. 15, 1804, 298, Jefferson to John W. Eppes, Aug. 7, 1804, 308–309, Jefferson to Cornelia Randolph, Dec. 26, 1808, 320.

he had fathered Sally Hemings's children. When the Kentuckian Jefferson had met while out riding one day had launched into his diatribe against the president, he had alluded "even to some of the infamous calumnies against his private life." Randolph nowhere mentions what these calumnies were, nor does she attempt to refute them with any specificity. Instead, she offers as a rebuttal the entire book, a portrait of "a beautiful domestic character," as if this were the only defense her great-grandfather could ever need.[41]

Here, then, is the importance of the stories about the multiple strangers who, when meeting Jefferson, "did not know who he was," and the invocation of the "imaginary being" created by those who did not know *him.* If Randolph's book is to be accepted as a true portrait of Jefferson, then it must rest on the claim that she and her father and grandmother and her aunts and uncles and the rest of her white kin knew the real man. That is the book's burden.[42]

But did they?

Randolph reproduces her father's description of his father's death. The scene is deeply moving as we see the old man slipping away. At four in the morning of July 4, as his end approached, Jefferson "called the servants in attendance with a strong and clear voice, perfectly conscious of his wants. He did not speak again." Jefferson's last words, then, were to his slaves, a summoning of them to meet his final needs. Here they are again, the ghosts. At ten in the morning, according to Thomas Jefferson Randolph, his grandfather "fixed his eyes intently upon me, indicating some want, which, most painfully, I could not understand, until his attached servant, Burwell, observed that his head was not so much elevated as he usually desired it." "Upon restoring it to its usual position," Thomas Jefferson Randolph continued, "he seemed satisfied." There, with the end only a few hours away, and, with his grandfather staring intently at him, Thomas Jefferson Randolph could not read his grandfather, and it caused him pain. Only Burwell could tell what the dying man needed to make himself comfortable.[43]

41. Ibid., vii, viii, 289, Thomas Jefferson Randolph to Henry S. Randall, n.d., 428.

42. Ibid., 38, 289–290.

43. Thomas Jefferson Randolph to Henry S. Randall, n.d., ibid., 428. Gordon-Reed notes the presence of the slaves at Jefferson's deathbed. She surmises that among them were not only his personal servant Burwell Colbert but also Sally Hemings. See Gordon-Reed, *Hemingses of Monticello,* 650–651.

ACKNOWLEDGMENTS

BARRY BIENSTOCK

Nothing made Jan happier than spending time at the University of Virginia (UVA) and at Monticello. Jan first did research at UVA in the 1970s while working on her doctoral dissertation and then later, in the late 1970s and early 1980s, while turning her dissertation into her first book *The Pursuit of Happiness: Family and Values in Jefferson's Virginia* (1983). As Jan's professional career took off, she made many trips to UVA and Monticello without me, participating in board meetings, seminars, and conferences. In 2003, she spent a semester as a Gilder Lehrman Fellow at the Robert H. Smith International Center for Jefferson Studies at Monticello.

Jan made Peter Onuf's acquaintance in 1991, while she and Peter were fellows at Washington University in St. Louis. They were among a group of scholars charged with contributing to a volume on the history of freedom in the early American Republic. During their time as fellows, I heard many stories of Peter's passion for strong coffee, which Jan thereafter would refer to as "Onuf coffee." In their meeting, a splendid partnership was born. That, of course, meant more visits to Charlottesville and UVA, where Peter was the Thomas Jefferson Foundation Professor. Later in the decade, Jan and Peter would go on to coauthor an essay "American Synecdoche: Thomas Jefferson as Image, Icon, Character, and Self" that was published in the *American Historical Review* (1998).

Two conferences stand out among the many professional collaborations that brought Jan and Peter together in Charlottesville. The year 1992 marked the 250th anniversary of the birth of Thomas Jefferson. That October, Peter convened a six-day conference on "Jeffersonian Legacies" at UVA, bringing scholars together to discuss Jefferson's ideas on rights, education, the democratic tradition, and race and their impact on present-day concerns. Jan's contribution, "'The Blessings of Domestic Society': Thomas Jefferson's Family and the Transformation of American Politics," to the conference volume, *Jeffersonian Legacies,* edited by Peter, appears in this collection.

Barry Bienstock teaches history at Horace Mann School, Bronx, New York.

In March 1999, Jan and Peter teamed up to organize a conference held at Monticello and UVA that would result in the publication of *Sally Hemings and Thomas Jefferson: History, Memory, and Civic Culture,* a volume that Jan coedited with Peter. Conference participants assessed the implications of recent DNA testing that confirmed Jefferson's long-term sexual relationship with Hemings, the enslaved woman he claimed to own. Jan's extraordinary essay on "The White Jeffersons," also included in this book, set the tone for an outstanding collection. Jan and Peter would subsequently coedit a series for the UVA Press on Jeffersonian America.

The depth and warmth of Jan and Peter's personal and professional friendship is on full display in an August 1997 C-SPAN interview at Monticello. That morning brought Jan and Peter up to the Mountaintop at daybreak. Their task: to conduct a newspaper roundtable, with a twist. They had to comb the morning's newspapers for stories they felt might have attracted Jefferson's attention. In the midst of their banter on articles ranging from "Wine Talk" to "Fighting for Fido: Lawyers Defend Pet Causes in Court," the C-SPAN anchor, observing their rapport, could not help but interject as to whether Jan and Peter had ever met before and whether they always debated with such vigor. After replying in the affirmative to the first question, Jan's response to the second was instantaneous. "Of course," she said, "Historians have fun!" "Right" Peter agreed, though "the dirty secret of th[e] broadcast," in Peter's view, was that "we are trying to argue about things, but the fact is, we see things quite the same way." Despite a rather sleepless night after discovering Jan was allergic to cats while she and I were staying as guests with Peter and his wife, Kristin, whatever difficulties Jan experienced overnight disappeared in the joy of watching the sun come up over Monticello and trading playful jibes over Thomas Jefferson with a dear friend and colleague.

Jan's friendship with Annette Gordon-Reed also started in the 1990s. Annette, then a law professor, had written a manuscript that would later be published as *Thomas Jefferson and Sally Hemings: An American Controversy* (1997). Annette called Jan and asked if she would read the manuscript. Much to Jan's chagrin, the manuscript sat on her desk, unread, until prompted by another phone call from Annette, requesting that she take a look at a revised version. As Jan recalled in a talk at Georgia State University in 2010, she knew that "this time" she "*had* to read" it.

Jan and Annette first met in person in 1995, when they were both invited to attend a production of what I can only describe as a madcap musical called *Sally and Tom (The American Way)* by Fred Newman with music by

Annie Roboff at the Castillo Theater in New York City. Jan and Annette were asked to participate in a post-performance discussion. Let's just say that the bond that emerged had far more staying power than the musical. What followed was an intense friendship, lots of email, frequent trips, lunches, and dinners. Jan helped Annette transition to the historical profession and even hired her to teach at Rutgers-Newark. Jan also invited Annette to participate at her first historical conference, the annual meeting for the Society for Historians of the Early American Republic (SHEAR) in 1997 held at Penn State University. Jan was program chair for the conference, and Peter was the SHEAR president that year.

A Board of Trustees meeting brought Jan back to Monticello in October 2010. For Jan, the highlight of the weekend, and one that I got to participate in, was a black-tie dinner inside Jefferson's house. Peter and Annette were among the many historians who had the opportunity to roam through the house with us and to explore Monticello free of tourists. Tables were set up in several rooms, and we dined, much as Jefferson would have, by candlelight. Toasts were made to Jefferson's memory. Life could not get better than that, Jan thought.

Jan's professional duties brought her into frequent contact with Annette and Peter. Jan served on the Advisory Board of the Papers of Thomas Jefferson and the Advisory Board of the International Center for Jefferson Studies (ICJS), which holds conferences around the world. I was able to accompany Jan on a three-city ICJS conference on "Ireland, America, and Empire in the Age of Jefferson" in May 2017. Once again, Peter and Annette participated in the conference and took turns sitting with Jan on the bus from Galway to Connemara to Dublin. Jan and I flew into Dublin early, explored the city, and were delighted to discover Hodges Figgis, one of the world's great bookstores. This was the last trip that we took together.

It was during Jan's funeral that Peter, Annette, and I talked about the need to bring out a collection of Jan's essays. Her publications were scattered in many books and journals, and some of them were unknown to even her closest friends, not to mention her reviews of novels that appeared in Phi Beta Kappa's *Key Reporter.* In many ways, Jan's essays opened up new ways of exploring the past, from introducing the history of emotions to reconsidering how women and slaves fit into the Constitution, making it important to bring out her most lasting contributions. In addition to Jan's pathbreaking work in studies of Jefferson; women, slavery, and the Constitution; gender; and the history of emotions, there was another reason for publishing such a book. The thing that Jan found most distressing about her terminal illness was that our granddaughters, Beatrice and Ida, would grow up not remembering her. Anyone who was friends with Jan knew how central they were to her existence. Nothing pleased Jan more than being a grandmother. In fact, Beatrice attended Jan's SHEAR presidential conference in New Haven in the summer of 2016, when she was four and Ida was not yet born. This volume takes on a personal mission to ensure that Beatrice and Ida will one day get to know the grandmother that loved them deeply and left them much too soon.

Putting *Family, Slavery, and Love in the Early American Republic: The Essays of Jan Ellen Lewis* together has been a bittersweet experience. Reviewing Jan's scholarly output over a nearly forty-year career was, at times, emotionally challenging. Fortunately, Peter and Annette were there every step of the way. Sometimes, it meant tracking down source material, and that meant reviewing files and reading Jan's meticulous notes. No less essential to this enterprise was Cathy Kelly. I can't imagine working with a more caring, capable editor (now friend).

In the summer of 2019, at the SHEAR conference in Cambridge, Massachusetts, where Annette would give a presidential address, I had a conversation with Karin Wulf about my desire to bring out a collection of Jan's essays. Karin reported that to Cathy, who registered a deep desire to publish such a collection. "It will be a labor of love," Cathy said, and I never doubted her. I knew, instantly, that Jan's essays had found a home, and no one else but Cathy could have brought such humanity and editorial skill to the project. She also put up with my demands about how the book would look. When COVID-19 hit, Cathy persevered, as did her remarkably talented team at the Omohundro Institute. Let me extend my supersized thank you's to Kaylan Stevenson for her copyediting, to Emily Suth, and to Virginia Chew. What a talented group of people! Despite a pandemic, Cathy, Kaylan, Virginia, and Emily continued to advance the project. They have all become Marvel Super Heroes to me. I am forever grateful for the professional and emotional support that they brought to this volume. I have nothing but admiration and respect for Kim Bryant at the University of North Carolina Press. There is not a better book designer. I would also like to extend my deep appreciation to Cynthia Ingham who brought her professional skill to indexing the book.

I heard from a great many people in the days, weeks, and months after Jan's passing. Jan's professional reach spread far beyond Rutgers-Newark, where she spent her academic career. I learned about the countless ways that she touched peoples' lives. I wondered, at times, if Jan understood the impact that she had on so many people. I'd like to thank Mary Kelley for organizing an "Honoring Jan Lewis" session at the annual meeting of the Organization of American Historians in Philadelphia in April 2019. Many thanks to the panelists: Ann Fabian, James Goodman, Annette-Gordon Reed, Lucia McMahon, Nicholas Syrett, Serena Zabin, and, of course, the indispensable Mary Kelley. Three months later, Serena Zabin organized a roundtable on "The Scholarship of Jan Lewis" at SHEAR's annual meeting in July 2019 in Cambridge, Massachusetts. This volume took shape from that session. The session was chaired by Diane Sommerville, and papers were delivered by Carolyn Eastman, Nicole Eustace, Peter Onuf, and David Waldstreicher. Many audience members, including Mary Bilder, suggested that Jan's scholarship deserved a wider audience, and I could happily report that the Omohundro Institute was interested in publishing such a book.

Some months earlier, Rutgers-Newark hosted a celebration of Jan Ellen Lewis. I'd like to thank the participants: Nancy Cantor (the Chancellor of the Newark Campus), Karen Caplan, Ronald Chen, Carolyn Eastman, Ann Fabian, Matthew Guterl, Danielle McGuire, Scott Sandage (who read from a large packet of email that he printed up), and Salamishah Tillet. James Goodman moderated the memorial service. Christina Strasburger brought her enormous love and commitment to the celebration.

Jan's professional career started at the University of Michigan. Ken Lockridge served as her dissertation director and became a close friend until her death. Ken introduced Jan to Rhys Isaac, who influenced how Jan thought about historical analysis and suggested *Pursuit of Happiness* as the title of Jan's first book. Jan also developed a friendship with Frank Smith, her editor at Cambridge University Press. Jan would often talk about her influential teachers at Michigan, Leslie Owens, John Shy, and J. Mills Thornton.

Rutgers-Newark (and Jan always insisted on appending Newark to Rutgers) became Jan's academic home for more than forty years. She began her career there as a member of the History Department, becoming the first woman tenured in that department. Later, she was the first woman to serve as department chair. Still later, she became the first woman to serve as Dean of the College of Arts and Sciences. Thanks go to many people at Rutgers-Newark. Let me acknowledge Sherri-Ann Butterfield, Nancy Cantor, Ronald Chen, Sallie Kasper, Mirela Ngela (who taught Jan the joys of forensic bookkeeping), Betsy Rowe, Beryl Satter, and Deborah Williams. Jan's mornings began with a call to James Goodman as she drove to campus. Her evenings ended with a phone call to Betsy Rowe. Jim and Betsy were Jan's indispensable people. Thanks also go to Karen Caplan, Kornel Chang, Melissa Cooper, Ruth Feldstein, Eva Giloi, Mark Krasovic, Brian Murphy, Mary

Rizzo, Rob Snyder, Whit Strub, and Laura Troiano. Jan had a deep commitment to the arts at Rutgers-Newark, and thanks go to Alice Dark, Rachel Hadas, Tayari Jones, John Keene, Jayne Anne Phillips, Brenda Shaughnessy, and Kimi Takesue. When Jan went on what she thought would be a short leave of absence, she left the college in the hands of Denis Pare. One of her last hires was Jack Tchen. She was looking forward to the wonderful things that Jack would do at the Price Institute. Thanks also to Fran Bartkowski, Marge Derrick, Steven Diner, Belinda Edmondson, Mary Sue Sweeney Price, Kehinde Togun, and Phil Yeagle. Jan always enjoyed her encounters with Barbara Lee, Barry Qualls, and Karen Stubaus. Let me also extend my personal thanks to Cami Townsend. Jan's early years at Rutgers-Newark were spent in the company of Norma Basch and Clement Price. It's impossible to think that all three are no longer with us.

Jan's professional career was sustained by friendships with Jeanne Boydston, Paul Gilje, Mary Kelley, David Konig, Martha King, Michael McGerr, James Oakes, Barbara Oberg, Robert Parkinson, Bethel Saler (who displayed her cinematography skills at the 2019 SHEAR roundtable, which is available on YouTube), Alan Taylor, and Serena Zabin. Apologies to the many people that I have left out.

Thanks also go to Jan's Monticello family: Leslie Greene Bowman (President of the Thomas Jefferson Foundation), Andrew J. O'Shaughnessy (Vice President and Saunders Director of the ICJS), Susan Stein (the Richard Gilder Senior Curator and Vice President of Museum Programs at Monticello), and Lucia (Cinder) Stanton (Shannon Senior Historian Emeritus at the Thomas Jefferson Foundation).

On a personal level, I want to acknowledge friends that have sustained me for years, and the last few especially. Thanks go to Nafie Selimaj. It's hard to imagine a better, more loyal friend. Also in that essential category, James Goodman, Jenny McFeely, Peter Sheehy, Janice Min, Ellen Adler, Deb Bohr, James Oakes, Curtis Darbasie, Anna Rabinova, and Leah and David Gomberg. Some former students have become good friends. Thank you Meg Jacobs (who brought Julian Zelizer into my world of friends), David Leonhardt, Marc Lerner, Emily Straus (who is now my colleague), Anna Taruschio, and Sarah Zeng. Beth Kobliner deserves a mention, as does Dr. Manjit Bains (who only saved my life), and Dr. Ash Tewari, as good a person as he is a surgeon. Bob Caro and Ina Caro are valued friends. I feel better whenever I am in their company. At Horace Mann, Tom Kelly has been generous and supportive. Also, thanks to Jessica Levenstein, Dan Link, and Elisa Milkes as well as former colleagues and friends Susan Cahn and

Barbara Berg. Thanks also to my friends in publishing, Kathy Hourigan, Steve Forman, and Max Rudin.

Finally, let me thank my brother Martin as well as Emily, Charlie, Gregg, Gena, and Gayla. Jan's sister Beth and her husband, Don, were always there for us and remain there for me. My stepson James Grimmelmann has been with me pretty much forever. He was two-and-a-half when he came into my life. For six years, he slept in the passenger seat as we made our way to Horace Mann, except when I had to wake him so he could become a human GPS. James brought Aislinn into our family, and James and Aislinn brought Beatrice and Ida into our world, the greatest gift of all. Ever since August 28, 2018, I've been thinking of the words of Toni Morrison. "We die. That may be the meaning of life. But we *do* language. That may be the measure of our lives." This book is Grandma Jan's gift to you, Beatrice and Ida, that you may be able to one day come to understand the "measure" of Grandma Jan's life.

INDEX